The Routledge Companion to Auditing

Auditing has been a subject of some controversy, and there have been repeated attempts at reforming its practice globally.

This comprehensive companion surveys the state of the discipline, including emerging and cutting-edge trends. It covers the most important and controversial issues, including auditing ethics, auditor independence, social and environmental accounting as well as the future of the field.

This handbook is vital reading for students and researchers involved with auditing and accounting. The collection will also prove an ideal starting place for researchers from other fields looking to break into this vital subject.

David Hay is Professor of Auditing at the University of Auckland, New Zealand.

W. Robert Knechel is Frederick E. Fisher Eminent Scholar Chair and Professor of Accounting and Auditing at the University of Florida, USA.

Marleen Willekens is Professor of Accounting and Auditing at KU Leuven, Belgium and BI Norwegian Business School.

Contributors: Henri Akono, Urton Anderson, Stephen Kwaku Asare, Ashley A. Austin, Jean Bédard, Jean C. Bedard, Robert L. Braun, Steven F. Cahan, Tina D. Carpenter, Elizabeth Carson, Margaret Christ, Tiphaine Compernolle, Paul Coram, Emer Curtis, Dain Donelson, Marshall Geiger, Lynford Graham, David Hay, D. Kip Holderness Jr., Christopher Humphrey, Debra Jeter, Kathryn Kadous, W. Robert Knechel, John Christian Langli, Justin Leiby, Clive Lennox, Anne Loft, John McInnis, Roger Meuwissen, Mona Offermanns, Brenda Porter, Anna Samsonova-Taddei, Divesh S. Sharma, Michael K. Shaub, Lori B. Shefchik, Roger Simnett, Dan A. Simunic, Mike Stein, Tobias Svanström, Ken Trotman, Stuart Turley, Ann Vanstraelen, Marleen Willekens.

Routledge Companions in Business, Management and Accounting

Routledge Companions in Business, Management and Accounting are prestige reference works providing an overview of a whole subject area or sub-discipline. These books survey the state of the discipline including emerging and cutting-edge areas. Providing a comprehensive, up to date, definitive work of reference, Routledge Companions can be cited as an authoritative source on the subject.

A key aspect of these Routledge Companions is their international scope and relevance. Edited by an array of highly regarded scholars, these volumes also benefit from teams of contributors, reflecting an international range of perspectives.

Individually, Routledge Companions in Business, Management and Accounting provide an impactful one-stop-shop resource for each theme covered. Collectively, they represent a comprehensive learning and research resource for researchers, postgraduate students and practitioners.

Published titles in this series include:

The Routledge Companion to Fair Value and Financial Reporting
Edited by Peter Walton

The Routledge Companion to Nonprofit Marketing
Edited by Adrian Sargeant and Walter Wymer Jr

The Routledge Companion to Accounting History
Edited by John Richard Edwards and Stephen P. Walker

The Routledge Companion to Creativity
Edited by Tudor Rickards, Mark A. Runco and Susan Moger

The Routledge Companion to Strategic Human Resource Management
Edited by John Storey, Patrick M. Wright and David Ulrich

The Routledge Companion to International Business Coaching
Edited by Michel Moral and Geoffrey Abbott

The Routledge Companion to Organizational Change
Edited by David M. Boje, Bernard Burnes and John Hassard

The Routledge Companion to Cost Management
Edited by Falconer Mitchell, Hanne Nørreklit and Morten Jakobsen

The Routledge Companion to Digital Consumption
Edited by Russell W. Belk and Rosa Llamas

The Routledge Companion to Identity and Consumption
Edited by Ayalla A. Ruvio and Russell W. Belk

The Routledge Companion to Public-Private Partnerships
Edited by Piet de Vries and Etienne B. Yehoue

The Routledge Companion to Accounting, Reporting and Regulation
Edited by Carien van Mourik and Peter Walton

The Routledge Companion to International Management Education
Edited by Denise Tsang, Hamid H. Kazeroony and Guy Ellis

The Routledge Companion to Accounting Communication
Edited by Lisa Jack, Jane Davison and Russell Craig

The Routledge Companion to Visual Organization
Edited by Emma Bell, Jonathan Schroeder and Samantha Warren

The Routledge Companion to Arts Marketing
Edited by Daragh O'Reilly, Ruth Rentschler and Theresa Kirchner

The Routledge Companion to Alternative Organization
Edited by Martin Parker, George Cheney, Valerie Fournier and Chris Land

The Routledge Companion to the Future of Marketing
Edited by Luiz Moutinho, Enrique Bigne and Ajay K. Manrai

The Routledge Companion to Accounting Education
Edited by Richard M. S. Wilson

The Routledge Companion to Business in Africa
Edited by Sonny Nwankwo and Kevin Ibeh

The Routledge Companion to Human Resource Development
Edited by Rob F. Poell, Tonette S. Rocco and Gene L. Roth

The Routledge Companion to Auditing
Edited by David Hay, W. Robert Knechel and Marleen Willekens

The Routledge Companion to Auditing

Edited by
David Hay, W. Robert Knechel and Marleen Willekens

Routledge
Taylor & Francis Group
LONDON AND NEW YORK

First published 2014
by Routledge
2 Park Square, Milton Park, Abingdon, Oxon OX14 4RN

and by Routledge
711 Third Avenue, New York, NY 10017

Routledge is an imprint of the Taylor & Francis Group, an informa business

British Library Cataloguing in Publication Data
A catalogue record for this book is available from the British Library

Library of Congress Cataloging in Publication Data
The Routledge companion to auditing / edited by David Hay, W. Robert Knechel and Marleen Willekens.
pages cm. – (Routledge companions in business, management and accounting)
Includes bibliographical references and index.
1. Auditing. I. Hay, David, 1955. II. Knechel, W. Robert. III. Willekens, Marleen.
HF5667.R774 2014
657'.45 – dc23
2014006834

ISBN: 978-0-415-63363-5 (hbk)
ISBN: 978-0-203-09492-1 (ebk)

Typeset in Bembo
by Taylor & Francis Books

Printed and bound in the United States of America by Publishers Graphics, LLC on sustainably sourced paper.

Contents

List of figures

List of tables

Notes on contributors

Henri Akono is a PhD candidate at the University of Texas at San Antonio, USA.

Urton Anderson, CIA, is the Director of the Von Allmen School of Accountancy at the Gatton College of Business and Economics, University of Kentucky, USA. Professor Anderson has been a member and Chair of the Institute of Internal Auditor's Board of Regents and twice Chair of the Internal Auditing Standards Board (2002–3 and 2007–10). He currently serves as Chair of the IIA's Committee of Research and Education Advisors and is on the Board of Trustees for the IIA Research Foundation. Urton is also active in the Auditing Section of the American Accounting Association and served as its President for 2009–10.

Stephen Kwaku Asare is the KPMG Term Professor of Accounting at the University of Florida, USA. He is a Certified Fraud Examiner and a member of the Florida Bar. His scholarly articles have appeared in accounting, psychology and law journals and have been presented at various workshops and conferences. He has received research funding from the American Institute of Certified Public Accountants, International Accounting and Auditing Standards Board, KPMG Research Foundation and Center for Audit Quality. Dr Asare has participated in management education programmes for PricewaterhouseCoopers (PwC) and has been a guest lecturer at many schools, including Boston College, Aarhus School of Business (Denmark), Norwegian School of Business, Sogang University (Korea) and GIMPA (Ghana). He is a recipient of several teaching awards.

Ashley A. Austin is an accounting doctoral student at the University of Georgia, USA. Her research interests focus on the study of auditors' decision making, using psychology theory and experimental methods.

Jean Bédard PhD, FCPA auditor, FCA, is a Professor at Laval University, Canada, and holds the Chair in Corporate Governance. He is the author of several articles on auditing and corporate governance and audit committees. He is a member of the editorial board of various accounting journals and is currently an editor at *Auditing*. He has been a member of the Auditing and Assurance Standards Board of the Canadian Institute of Chartered Accountants.

Jean C. Bedard is Timothy B. Harbert Professor of Accountancy at Bentley University, USA. She is also a Professorial Visiting Fellow at the University of New South Wales, and an Extra-mural Fellow at Maastricht University. Professor Bedard has published extensively on topics such as analytical procedures, risk assessment, audit planning, internal control assessment, audit client portfolio management, and the effects of using information technology in the audit process. She was Vice-President (Publications) of the American Accounting Association (AAA) in 2009–11, and has also served the AAA's Auditing Section as President, Secretary and Historian.

Robert L. Braun is Professor of Accounting at Southeastern Louisiana University,USA, where he teaches accounting ethics, auditing and principles of accounting. His contributions to research have been published in various journals including *Accounting Organizations and Society*, *Issues in Accounting Education*, and the *Journal of Accountancy*. He serves on the editorial board of *Issues in Accounting Education*. Research interests include the examination and advancement of ethics in the accounting profession, pedagogical inquiry, and auditing judgment and decision making.

Steven F. Cahan is Professor of Financial Accounting at the University of Auckland Business School, New Zealand. He is currently the editor of *Accounting & Finance*, the journal of the Accounting and Finance Association of Australia and New Zealand (AFAANZ). His research interests are in the areas of auditing and financial reporting, and his published work has appeared in journals such as *The Accounting Review*, *Contemporary Accounting Research*, *Auditing*, and *Accounting Horizons*. His PhD is from the University of Colorado Boulder. Steven is a Chartered Accountant and is a Fellow of the New Zealand Institute of Chartered Accountants. He has also been active in the International Federation of Accountants. He was a member of the Business and Economics Peer Review Panel for the New Zealand government's Performance Based Research Funding (PBRF) exercise in 2006 and 2012. Steven is a past President of AFAANZ and was named a Life Member of AFAANZ in 2010. At the University of Auckland, he was the inaugural PhD Director for the Business School from 2006–9 and received the Business School's Research Excellence Award for Sustained Research in 2005 and in 2010.

Tina D. Carpenter is associate professor in the J. M. Tull School of Accounting at the University of Georgia, USA. Her research focuses on fraudulent financial reporting using theories from psychology to guide investigations of the decision making of auditors, investors and managers. Her teaching responsibilities include forensic accounting and fraud examination, auditing and financial accounting. She has published in several journals including *The Accounting Review*, *Auditing: A Journal of Practice & Theory*, *Journal of Business Ethics*, *Current Issues in Auditing*, *Issues in Accounting Education*, and *Journal of Accountancy*.

Elizabeth Carson is a professor at the Australian School of Business in Sydney. She received her Masters and PhD in Accounting from the University of New South Wales (UNSW). Prior to joining UNSW, she worked with PricewaterhouseCoopers (PwC) and is qualified as a Chartered Accountant. Her research interests include economics of global and national audit markets, industry specialization by auditors and audit reporting. She has published in leading academic journals including *The Accounting Review*, *Auditing: A Journal of Practice & Theory* and *Accounting and Finance*.

Margaret Christ, CIA, is an assistant professor in the J. M. Tull School of Accounting at the University of Georgia, USA. Her research focuses on the effects of control systems on employees, management and organizations and has been published in *The Accounting Review*, *Contemporary Accounting Research*, *Accounting Horizons* and the *Internal Auditor*. Prior to her PhD, Margaret worked as an internal auditor with a public accounting firm, providing assurance and insights to a variety of clients in the energy services, manufacturing and financial industries.

Tiphaine Compernolle, PhD, is a professor at Laval University, Canada. Her research interests are auditing, corporate governance and audit committees, which are the subject of her PhD thesis. She has written several articles in these areas.

Paul Coram is a professor at the University of Adelaide, Australia. His research has focused on audit quality and audit reporting and he has presented and published his research widely. Paul's research has predominantly used experimental and survey methods to complement or address issues that cannot be directly observed by archival research. He was part of an international team of researchers that performed research on the value of expanded auditor's reports for the International Auditing and Assurance Standards Board (IAASB) and the American Institute of Certified Public Accountants (AICPA). More recently, he was on an American Accounting Association Auditing Section PCAOB research synthesis team that produced a report on research into the auditor's reporting model. As well as audit research, he is a co-author of a leading auditing text in Australia. Paul originally worked as an auditor at a Big-4 firm and qualified as a Chartered Accountant.

Emer Curtis is a lecturer in Accounting at the National University of Ireland, Galway. She is a fellow of the Institute of Chartered Accountants in Ireland and prior to joining NUI Galway Dr Curtis worked as an audit manager with one of the large international firms. She completed her PhD on business risk auditing at the University of Manchester. Dr Curtis's research and publications relate to innovation in audit methodology and also include work on the use of control systems to manage creativity and innovation in industrial settings.

Dain Donelson is an assistant professor at the McCombs School of Business at the University of Texas at Austin, USA. His research focuses primarily on securities litigation and financial accounting. He has taught courses involving the legal liability and regulation of accountants, financial accounting and business law. Dain's research has been published in numerous accounting and law journals, including *The Accounting Review, Review of Accounting Studies, Contemporary Accounting Research, Journal of Empirical Legal Studies,* and *North Carolina Law Review.*

Marshall Geiger is a former Academic Fellow in Accounting at the US Securities and Exchange Commission and is a past holder of the Joseph A. Jennings Chair in Business at the University of Richmond, Richmond, VA and has held the position of Honorary Professor of the Faculty of Business and Law, Deakin University in Melbourne, Australia. He earned his PhD from the Pennsylvania State University in 1988. He has published over 80 articles and monographs on auditing, financial reporting and accounting education in journals such as *The Accounting Review, Review of Accounting Studies, Auditing: A Journal of Practice & Theory, Contemporary Accounting Research, Issues in Accounting Education, Journal of Accounting, Auditing and Finance, Journal of Accounting and Public Policy*, and the *Journal of Accounting Education*. He currently serves as editor for *Auditing: A Journal of Practice & Theory*.

Lynford Graham is a Certified Public Accountant with more than 30 years of public accounting experience in auditing and policy development. He is a Visiting Professor of Accountancy at Bentley University, USA, and a past member of the AICPA's Auditing Standards Board. Dr Graham was responsible for BDO's implementation of audits of internal control under PCAOB AS2, and participated with professional groups in developing industry-wide guidance.

David Hay is Professor of Auditing at the University of Auckland, New Zealand. He is a Fellow of the New Zealand Institute of Chartered Accountants and a Fellow of CPA Australia. He recently completed a term as Head of the Department of Accounting and Finance at the University of Auckland, which is ranked twentieth best Accounting and Finance Department in the world by QS World University Rankings. He is an editor of *Auditing: A Journal of Practice & Theory* and editor-in-chief of the *International Journal of Auditing*. His research interests include auditor independence, corporate governance and meta-analysis. He teaches auditing at undergraduate and postgraduate levels.

D. Kip Holderness Jr, PhD, CPA, CFE, is an assistant professor at West Virginia University, USA. Kip's research focuses primarily on the impact of fraud and employee deviance on individuals and organizations as well as improving detection methods.

Christopher Humphrey is Professor of Accounting at Manchester Business School, University of Manchester, UK. His main current research interests include international auditing regulation and standard setting, the developing regional and global strategies of professional accountancy bodies, international audit quality and the scope for innovation in audit practice, the rise of the International Integrated Reporting Council (IIRC) and the sustainability of accounting academia. He is a qualified Chartered Accountant and has served as a co-opted academic member of the governing Council of the Institute of Chartered Accountants in England and Wales (ICAEW). He is currently Vice-Chair of the UK's Conference of Professors of Accounting and Finance (CPAF), having been its Chair for the previous three years.

Debra Jeter is Associate Professor of Management in the Owen Graduate School of Management at Vanderbilt University, USA, where she received her PhD in accounting. She has co-authored two textbooks, *Advanced Accounting* (Wiley & Sons) and *Managerial Cost Accounting: Planning and Control*. She also serves as a Visiting Research Professor at the University of Auckland. Jeter is an editor of *Auditing: A Journal of Practice & Theory* and a past associate editor of *Issues in Accounting Education*. She currently serves on several editorial boards including *The Accounting Review*. She has published in *The Accounting Review*, the *Journal of Accounting and Economics*, *Auditing: A Journal of Practice & Theory*, *Contemporary Accounting Research* and *Accounting Horizons*, as well as in popular magazines including *Working Woman* and *Savvy*. She writes fiction in her spare time.

Kathryn Kadous is Professor of Accounting at the Goizueta Business School at Emory University, USA. Her research considers judgment and decision-making issues in auditing and accounting, and is focused in three areas: using psychology judgment and decision-making theory to improve auditor decision making; identifying determinants of litigation judgments against auditors; and identifying how investors' motivations influence their decision making. Kathryn's research has been published in *The Accounting Review*, *Contemporary Accounting*

Research, Organizational Behavior and Human Decision Processes, the *Journal of Behavioral Finance* and *Auditing: A Journal of Practice & Theory*. She has served as an editor of *The Accounting Review* and *Auditing: A Journal of Practice & Theory*.

W. Robert Knechel, PhD, CPA, is Frederick E. Fisher Eminent Scholar Chair and Professor of Accounting at the University of Florida, USA. He is currently the Director of the International Center for Research in Accounting and Auditing (ICRAA) located within the Fisher School of Accounting. He is also a Professor of Accounting Research at the University of Auckland. His prior research has been published in *The Accounting Review*, the *Journal of Accounting Research*, *Contemporary Accounting Research*, *Accounting, Organizations and Society* and *Auditing: A Journal of Practice & Theory*.

John Christian Langli is Professor of Business Economics at BI Norwegian Business School. His areas of interest are accounting and auditing. He has published papers in national and international journals including *Accounting, Organizations and Society*, *The Accounting Review*, the *European Accounting Review* and the *International Journal of Accounting*.

Justin Leiby is an assistant professor in the Fisher School of Accounting at the University of Florida, USA. His research has been published in *The Accounting Review,* and focuses on judgment and decision making in auditing. He earned a PhD in Accountancy at the University of Illinois at Urbana-Champaign, and Bachelor's degrees in Accounting and German from the University of Pittsburgh.

Clive Lennox is a professor at Nanyang Business School in Singapore. He received his Masters and PhD in Economics from the University of Oxford. Before joining Nanyang Business School in 2009, he taught at the University of Bristol from 1998–2001 and the Hong Kong University of Science and Technology from 2001–9. His research interests include auditing, disclosure, fraud, bankruptcy and empirical methods. He has published twenty-seven articles, including seventeen in five of the leading accounting journals: *Journal of Accounting and Economics*, *Journal of Accounting Research*, *The Accounting Review*, *Contemporary Accounting Research*, and *Review of Accounting Studies*.

Anne Loft is Professor of Accounting at Lund University, Sweden. Gaining a PhD from the London Business School in 1986, she moved to Denmark, becoming Professor of Auditing there in 1997, moving to Lund University in 2005. She was one of the founder editors of the *European Accounting Review* (1992–2000), and is currently an editor of the *International Journal of Auditing*. She was the Vice-President for Education for the International Association for Accounting Education and Research (IAAER), 2010–13. Her main research interests are in the accounting profession and in auditing regulation – from both historical and contemporary perspectives, including a particular focus on the historical development of the International Federation of Accountants (IFAC).

John McInnis is assistant professor at the McCombs School of Business at the University of Texas at Austin, USA. His research interests include securities litigation, earnings management, standard setting and the effect of accounting information on stock prices. He teaches financial accounting at the undergraduate level. Professor McInnis has published articles in top scholarly journals such as *The Accounting Review*, *Journal of Finance*, *Management Science*, *Journal of Accounting & Economics* and *Contemporary Accounting Research*.

Roger Meuwissen is Professor of Control and Auditing at Maastricht University, the Netherlands. He earned his graduate degree in business administration at Maastricht University in 1992 and received his PhD from Maastricht University in 1999. Furthermore, in 1994 he finished the postgraduate auditing programme at Maastricht University to become a Registered Accountant. He was formerly a researcher at the Maastricht Accounting and Auditing Research and Education Center, where he was involved in commissioned research in the field of accounting and auditing. He is author of several articles in academic journals such as *Contemporary Accounting Research*, the *European Accounting Review* and *Accounting Education*. Currently, he is also a member of the editorial board of *Accounting Education*.

Mona Offermanns has completed her PhD at the Department of Accounting and Information Management at Maastricht University, the Netherlands. She has been Visiting Researcher at the University of Auckland and the University of Florida. Her research is focused on auditing and capital markets and has been presented at numerous international conferences. She is currently working at the Department of Corporate Planning & Controlling at Metro AG in Düsseldorf.

Brenda Porter is a Visiting Professor teaching auditing at Exeter University, UK, in the spring Semester, and at Chulalongkorn University, Bangkok, during the fall Semester. She recently retired as Professor and Head of the School of Accounting and Commercial Law at Victoria University, New Zealand. She is a Chartered Accountant and holds a PhD from Massey University, New Zealand. Her main research interests are the role of external auditors in society, the audit expectation gap and the role of the tripartite audit function (external and internal auditors and audit committees) in securing responsible corporate governance. She has published widely in academic, business and professional journals and is the primary author of *Principles of External Auditing*.

Anna Samsonova-Taddei is Lecturer in Accounting at Manchester Business School, University of Manchester, UK. Anna's research covers a range of topics, including audit reforms in the context of a transitional economy, various aspects of accounting and audit regulation, trans-national policy processes and networks, and others. Anna has recently published work on international auditing developments, in such academic journals as *Critical Perspectives on Accounting* and *Abacus*. Anna is a member of the European Auditing Research Network.

Divesh S. Sharma is Associate Professor and Coordinator of the doctoral program at Kennesaw State University, USA. He holds a PhD from Griffith University (Australia) and is a Fellow of the Institute of Chartered Accountants in Australia. Divesh has taught in Australia, Canada, New Zealand, Singapore and the USA. He serves on the Pathways Commission Task Force on Non-traditional doctoral education. He applies both empirical archival and behavioural/experimental methods to his research. Some of his research has been published in *The Accounting Review, Auditing: A Journal of Practice & Theory, Behavioral Research in Accounting, Journal of Business Finance & Accounting, Journal of Accounting & Public Policy, Accounting and Business Research, Management Accounting Research*, the *International Journal of Accounting*, the *British Accounting Review, Accounting & Finance* and the *Australian Accounting Review*. He serves on the editorial boards of *Auditing: A Journal of Practice & Theory, International Journal of Accounting, Canadian Journal of Administrative Science* and *Accounting Research Journal*, and served on the board of *Accounting Education*.

Michael K. Shaub is Clinical Professor and Accounting PhD program Administrative Director in Mays Business School at Texas A&M University, USA, where he teaches auditing and accounting ethics in the Professional Program in Accounting. His research encompasses accounting ethics issues, including professional scepticism in auditor–client relationships and wisdom in professional decision making. His articles have been published in a wide variety of journals including *Behavioral Research in Accounting*, *Accounting Horizons*, and *Journal of Business Ethics*. An editorial board member and reviewer for numerous accounting journals, he just completed his term as the book review editor for *Issues in Accounting Education*.

Lori B. Shefchik is a PhD candidate in the Scheller College of Business at the Georgia Institute of Technology, USA. Prior to pursuing her PhD in accounting, she worked for Deloitte as an auditor for four years. Her research focuses primarily on judgment and decision making in auditing, aimed at better understanding auditor behaviour and improving audit quality. She has published in *Auditing: A Journal of Practice & Theory* and *Accounting Horizons*. She has been an ad hoc reviewer for *Contemporary Accounting Research*, *Managerial Auditing Journal*, and *Auditing: A Journal of Practice & Theory*. She teaches auditing, and was the recipient of the 2013 Ashford Watson Stalnaker Memorial Award for student excellence in the PhD program at the Georgia Institute of Technology.

Roger Simnett is currently a Scientia Professor of Accounting at the Australian School of Business, University of New South Wales, Australia. Roger's research covers both auditor decision making and the economics of auditing, and has appeared in leading academic and professional journals, including *The Accounting Review*, *Accounting, Organizations and Society*, *Auditing: A Journal of Practice & Theory* and *Contemporary Accounting Research*. Roger is heavily involved in standard setting, including in his roles as a member of the Australian Auditing and Assurance Standards Board and the International Auditing and Assurance Standards Board (IAASB). He was the Co-Chair of the IAASB task force which recently produced an assurance standard on greenhouse gas disclosures, and is currently a member of the International Integrated Reporting Committee technical task force.

Dan A. Simunic is the Certified General Accountants' Professor at the Sauder School of Business, University of British Columbia, Canada. He has also served as Visiting Professor at various universities around the world. Dan's research interests are in the economics of auditing and in international auditing. He has published research papers in numerous scholarly journals, including the *Journal of Accounting Research*, *Journal of Accounting & Economics*, *The Accounting Review*, *Contemporary Accounting Research*, and *Auditing: A Journal of Practice & Theory*. Dan obtained a PhD in accounting and economics from the Graduate School of Business, University of Chicago, in 1979. He worked in the Chicago office of Ernst & Ernst (now Ernst & Young) and served for ten years as a technical advisor from Canada to the International Auditing Practices Committee (now the International Auditing & Assurance Standards Board [IAASB]) of the International Federation of Accountants. Dan is a US CPA (State of Illinois) and an FCGA (British Columbia). Dan served as co-editor of *Contemporary Accounting Research* from 1997 to 2000, and as the editor of *Auditing: A Journal of Practice & Theory* from 2005–8 and is currently a co-editor of the *Journal of Contemporary Accounting & Economics*.

Mike Stein is Professor of Accounting at Old Dominion University – Norfolk, VA, USA.

Tobias Svanström is a Postdoctoral Research Fellow at BI Norwegian Business School. His area of interest is auditing. He has published papers in national and international journals including *Contemporary Accounting Research, European Accounting Review, Accounting and Business Research* and *International Journal of Auditing.*

Ken Trotman is a Scientia Professor and was Head of the School of Accounting at the University of New South Wales from 1991 to February 2000. He has held visiting appointments at a range of overseas institutions including Cornell University, University of Michigan and the University of Illinois at Urbana-Champaign. His main current research interests are concerned with judgment and decision making in accounting. He is a Fellow of the Institute of Chartered Accountants in Australia and a Fellow of CPA Australia. Ken was the 1993/94 President of the Accounting and Finance Association of Australia and New Zealand (AFAANZ). In 1998 he received the AFAANZ Outstanding Contribution to the Accounting Literature award and was later awarded life membership of AFAANZ. In 1998 he was elected as a Fellow of the Academy of Social Sciences. He received the 2000/01 Outstanding Auditing Educator Award from the Audit Section of the American Accounting Association. He received the 2008 Notable Contribution to the Auditing Literature Award from the Auditing Section of the American Accounting Association and the 2009 Notable (Lifetime) Contribution Award in Behavioral Accounting Literature from the American Accounting Association. He received ARC Professorial Fellow Grant 2011–15 and was inducted into the Australian Accounting Hall of Fame in 2011.

Stuart Turley is Professor of Accounting at Manchester Business School, University of Manchester, UK. He is a past editor of the *British Accounting Review* and the *International Journal of Auditing* and between 2003 and 2012 he was also a member of the Auditing Practices Board, which had responsibility for setting practice and ethical standards for auditors in the United Kingdom. Professor Turley's research and publications cover a range of issues in auditing and financial reporting regulation, including topics such as audit methodology, audit quality, auditor independence and the audit expectations gap.

Ann Vanstraelen is Professor of Accounting and Assurance services at Maastricht University, the Netherlands. She is currently also the scientific director of Maastricht University Graduate School of Business and Economics. Her research is situated in the broad field of governance, financial reporting and auditing. She has been involved in several commissioned research projects such as for the EC, IFAC and ACCA. Her research has been published in international journals including *The Accounting Review, Auditing: A Journal of Practice & Theory, Accounting and Business Research, European Accounting Review* and *Journal of Accounting, Auditing and Finance.* She is associate editor of the *European Accounting Review* and serves on the editorial board of *Accounting Horizons* and *Auditing: A Journal of Practice & Theory.*

Marleen Willekens is Professor of Accounting and Auditing at KU Leuven (Belgium) and BI Norwegian Business School (Norway). She is an editor of *Auditing: A Journal of Practice and Theory.* Her research has been published in *Journal of Accounting and Economics, Accounting Organizations and Society, Journal of Business Finance and Accounting, Auditing: A Journal of Practice and Theory, The European Accounting Review, Corporate Governance: An International Review*, and many others.

Preface

When compiling this book was suggested to us, we were very pleased, because it meets a clear need in several areas. The first is in the area of policy and the ongoing changes to the regulation of auditing around the world. Auditing research has now developed to a point where it can make a useful contribution to many policy issues. There was very little research available on auditing issues prior to 1980; and while research developed over the following decades, research had little impact on the reforms to auditing introduced in the early twenty-first century. The body of audit research literature has grown dramatically in the past decade and current research is sometimes discussed in leading media outlets. Further, there is a greater prospect that relevant research will be used to inform future developments in international auditing standard setting and regulation. This book provides concise summaries of many of the important areas of auditing where further professional and regulatory changes may occur. We hope that it will help legislators, regulators, professionals and other interested parties to consider the current state of audit research-based knowledge as they make decisions affecting the future of the audit profession.

Second, we feel that this collection of research reviews will be valuable for informed observers of the business scene such as reporters and commentators. Even the most well-informed media experts are unlikely to be able to keep up with current research in auditing. We hope that this reference source will meet a need for background information on a large number of issues that are covered in the business media from time to time.

Third, practitioners of auditing, and related professionals such as chief financial officers and financial analysts, often have limited opportunities to keep up with research. The findings of research may nevertheless be very important to their understanding of issues such as audit quality or corporate governance. We hope that this book will be of value to these stakeholders as well.

In addition, this should be a valuable resource for doctorial and masters students. The extent of auditing research is now such that few postgraduate students are able to cover all areas of research by reading all of the key research articles. This book may provide a guide that will help them to focus on the most relevant studies in an area in which they are interested.

We hope that this book is useful to all of the people mentioned, and that it helps to contribute to an environment in which auditing research is more widely known and used.

Acknowledgements

We are grateful to the world in which this book can be produced and, we hope, appreciated. This book is dedicated to the people who take part in the world of auditing, including everyone involved in notorious cases of fraud, earnings management or audit failure; and, even more, to all of the auditors, managers and accountants who were never involved in anything notorious. We would also like to recognize the standard setters and regulators who helped contribute to the environment where auditing events, bad and good, were possible; and most of all, the auditing researchers who wrote about them and who are responsible for our knowledge of auditing.

We give especial thanks to all of the chapter authors, and to many other colleagues in the auditing community who have helped us by discussing auditing issues and ideas.

1

Introduction

The function of auditing

David Hay, W. Robert Knechel and Marleen Willekens

Overview of the topic and its importance

Auditing is important because financial reporting misstatements are dangerous. Auditing has economic benefits, some of which are not always immediately obvious, for both individual companies and the national (or global) economy as a whole. It helps in understanding auditing to be aware of those benefits and the explanations for its existence.

Auditing is an assurance service which improves the quality of information or its context. Financial reporting information is 'better' – more credible, more reliable – because an audit firm has examined evidence about the assertions making up the financial statements and convinced management to make changes that improve the accuracy and informativeness of financial statements. This allows financial statement users to better rely on the information because it has been vetted by an auditor whose conclusions are stated in the audit report.

A simple explanation of the benefits of auditing is provided by Willekens (2007), using the market for used cars as a parallel. Buying a used car is risky. Most car buyers are not experts, and cannot judge whether assertions made by the car salesman are reasonable. In the same way, shareholders and other stakeholders in a company are not able to find out whether assertions made by the directors are also reliable. In the case of the company, the assertions might be about how much profit the company is making or how liquid is its financial position. Assertions are made through the financial statements.

The used car buyer has the choice of not buying the car and taking the bus to work instead; or (s)he could get an expert to investigate and give an opinion on the assertions made by the seller. To help the deal to go through, the seller might even pay for a trustworthy expert to provide a report (e.g., CARFAX in the USA). In much the same way, potential investors have the option of not buying shares if they are uncertain about the reliability of the accounts. Or they can rely on an auditor, as the expert on financial statement assertions, to give them a report on management-provided information. It might be in management's interests to engage a respected auditor if that helps investors to decide to commit their funds to the company. The auditor does not give an opinion of the worth of the company or whether it is a wise investment. Rather, the audit report provides assurance that what management says is reliable.

The used car example is helpful up to a point. But auditing of financial statements takes place in a setting of much greater complexity. It is more complex than buying a used car because of the number of people involved and the ambiguity of financial information. If there are many shareholders and other stakeholders, it is not feasible to allow them all to examine the company's records in detail. There is also a wide range of parties involved in running the company – directors, audit committee members, management, all with their own self-interest, as well as their own views of what are the company's best interests. In addition, there is a well-known expectation gap, whereby many users have a different idea of what the auditor can do compared to what the auditor intends. In addition, the amounts involved may be very large, and the underlying financial and accounting issues can be very complex. In many cases, there are operations and stakeholders in a variety of different international jurisdictions. And finally, auditing is usually controlled by regulation and professional standards.

There are a number of economic explanations for auditing similar to the used car example discussed above, and these explanations overlap. They all provide reasonable explanations as to why managers might find it to be in their interests to submit to an audit, which they do implicitly when taking a job in a large company. In addition, in many cases auditing is required by law. The regulation of auditing can be explained by the legislators looking after the interests of stakeholders who may not be able to influence the decisions of a company directly but have their own interests in the behaviour and performance of a company. The next section discusses fundamental theories underlying the benefits of auditing.

Summary of current state of research findings

Explanations for companies to choose auditing

Auditing can be seen as having an information role; an agency role; an insurance role; an organizational control role; a confirmation role; and a risk management role. These are the economic explanations for auditing. In all of these, managers might voluntarily submit to being audited because it is in their own interests. In addition, in many settings auditing is compulsory – but the economic explanations for why auditing is desirable still apply, and companies may engage an auditor for something more than the absolute minimum level of audit effort required by standards. The reasons why auditing is often compulsory are also important in understanding the function of auditing, and explanations for compulsory auditing are discussed in the next subsection.

The information (or signalling) explanation

Better information leads to better, more informed decisions, by both managers and outsiders. Auditing can be a way both to improve information, and to show that it is better. Company managers have better information about the value and quality of the business that they run than do outside investors or stakeholders. This imbalance in knowledge about a business is called 'information asymmetry'. But if managers make statements in the financial report that claim that their business is a better investment than others, their claims may not be believed. One way of overcoming this information asymmetry is for them to engage an auditor to provide assurance about their statements. Appointing an auditor is then a signal to investors that they can place more credibility on the company's financial statements. Where auditing is compulsory, then managers can provide a signal of higher quality by appointing an auditor of higher quality – perhaps a large international firm or a firm that is considered a specialist in the client's industry.

This can be a means of signalling insiders' knowledge of superior performance and reduced measurement error (Wallace, 1987).

The agency (or monitoring) explanation

Shareholders are aware that managers may act in their own interest, and could report misleading information as a result. If so, the shareholders might discount the information they receive, and pay a lower price for shares than the financial fundamentals would justify if the financial reports could be trusted (if they can be persuaded to invest at all). It becomes worthwhile from a manager's point of view to provide auditing as a form of bonding of the manager, or monitoring on behalf of the shareholders. A similar explanation might apply when the managers are asking for a loan – they can expect a better response, and perhaps a lower interest rate, if they have audited financial statements. Where auditing is compulsory, they can reduce agency costs by providing auditing of more than the minimum standard required. Monitoring, bonding and other contracting explanations are supported by previous studies that provide evidence that auditing (or similar assurance services) is associated with high agency costs, indicated by greater size, higher debt leverage or lower managerial ownership (Chow, 1982). In 1994, a senior partner in the US firm of KPMG wrote that 'auditing adds tremendous value' (Elliott, 1994). Elliott estimates that audits reduce the cost of capital by 1 per cent to 3 per cent.

The insurance (or 'deep pockets') explanation

Chow *et al.* (1988) suggest that providers of external financing and custodians of others' funds may demand audits as a way of increasing the chance of recovering certain types of losses. For example, an audit provides a 'target' that they might be able to sue to recover their investment losses. They can sue those directly involved, including directors and management, but these people may not have the resources to make up the losses of investors. Auditors are seen as the 'deep pockets' defendant (who will have greater funds available after the company has failed than most managers or directors individually) and, as a result, auditors can face costly litigation even when they have little or no responsibility for the losses. This view treats the audit almost like a put option against future bad behaviour or misleading reporting.

The organizational control explanation

Organizational control for the benefit of internal management is another explanation for auditing, especially in smaller companies that may be family-owned or have less complex financial structures. In a small organization, the owner or manager controls operations by direct supervision and personal observation. As an organization grows larger, control becomes more difficult. Delegation becomes necessary, and there is a risk of moral hazard and opportunism. Abdel-Khalik (1993) proposes that owners seek voluntary audits as a compensatory control system for organizational loss of control in hierarchical organizations. He finds evidence to support this explanation because there are significant relationships between audit fees and number of layers of hierarchy and size.

The confirmation hypothesis

A further explanation is provided by the 'confirmation' hypothesis. The confirmation hypothesis examined by Ball *et al.* (2012) states that audited financial reporting and the disclosure of managers' private information are complementary. An early study, Ball and Brown (1968), showed that earnings announcements have little impact on share prices. That paper, and others like it, appeared to leave little room for auditing to be of value to the financial markets – audited financial information arrives too late for it to be useful. The confirmation hypothesis suggests that it is still necessary for announcements to be independently verified at a later stage. Firms that commit to higher audit fees (a measure of greater financial statement verification) are regarded as more credible. Ball *et al.* (2012) provide evidence to support the confirmation hypothesis by showing that firms which make more frequent and more specific management forecasts also commit to greater financial statement verification by independent auditors, and these firms also have larger market reactions associated with their management forecasts. Ball *et al.* (2012) argue that committing to higher audit fees is associated with management forecasts that are more frequent, specific, timely, accurate and informative to investors.[1]

Risk management

It is also useful to see auditing as a critical element in an organization's risk management strategy. Auditing can be useful for organizations whose stakeholders are subject to higher risk. Other mechanisms are also used to reduce risk, such as internal audits and processes, audit committees and independent directors. The interaction of these various mechanisms can sometimes have complex results, because the audit committee members and external directors become stakeholders themselves, and also seek to minimize risk. Knechel and Willekens (2006) show that demand for external auditing, illustrated by audit fees, increases in situations where there are multiple stakeholders. Because individual decisions about control processes and procedures may shift benefits and costs across groups of stakeholders, the net investment in auditing may increase when multiple stakeholders become involved in corporate governance decisions. Each stakeholder benefits from a greater level of control, while being able to shift a share of the costs to the other stakeholders. Knechel and Willekens (2006) found evidence that audit fees are higher when a company has an audit committee, discloses a relatively high level of financial risk management, and has a larger proportion of independent board members. Audit fees are lower when a company discloses a relatively high level of compliance risk management. These results are consistent with other studies.

Evidence

Evidence for or against these explanations is not easy to come by, since auditing is highly regulated in most settings. Nevertheless, even when auditing is mandatory, firms are free to choose which auditors they hire. There are many arguments suggesting that larger audit firms are of higher quality, especially the Big 4 international auditing firms (Deloitte, Ernst & Young, KPMG and PwC). These firms have more incentive to maintain high quality to protect their brand name, and more to lose if there is an audit failure. They also charge higher fees, which also suggests that they are more highly valued. More recent studies have also considered whether audit firms specializing in a particular industry provide higher quality audits.

Research studies have shown that there are associations between companies choosing higher quality auditors and the incentives of the companies under the information and agency explanations. For example, companies choosing larger (higher quality) auditors have less initial public offering (IPO) under-pricing, and higher earnings response coefficients[2] (Beatty, 1989; Teoh and Wong, 1993). A study using historical data from a period before auditing was compulsory found that debt contracts were associated with engaging an independent auditor (Chow, 1982).

These explanations, as they have developed over recent decades, have also had a practical effect on how judges in lawsuits against auditors view the role of the auditor. Pacini *et al.* (2002) review the trend in auditors' liability in the United Kingdom, Canada, Australia and New Zealand. They show that in the second half of the twentieth century, judges in cases involving auditors initially showed a trend towards an insurance explanation for auditing, and tended to increase the responsibility and liability placed on auditors, and allowed stakeholders with a relatively distant relationship with auditors to claim for losses. Later judgments moved more towards contracts-based monitoring views of auditing, and restricted liability to those contracting for the audit and to a very limited class of third parties.

The economic explanations for the value of auditing are relevant to understanding current issues because they portray auditing as something that is beneficial in itself, not a necessary evil that must be imposed by regulation. In the issues discussed in later chapters, such as whether auditors should be required to report on internal control, or whether auditor rotation is beneficial, it is helpful to recall that auditing is fundamentally in the interests of a company and its managers and directors.

Each of these explanations also tends to imply that demand for auditing arises naturally, since there are many reasons why companies would of their own accord choose auditors of a suitable quality. In addition, however, there are elements of auditing related to a 'public good' that suggest that auditing should be regulated. In practice, auditing is usually regulated, and there has been a tendency for it to become more and more regulated. The question is not whether regulation is needed but, rather, how much is needed. This includes standard setting. The economic explanations for auditing help to explain why auditing has been a long-established part of doing business, and its strong position has not been weakened by decades of auditing scandals and audit failures.

Explanations for the regulation of auditing

The explanations discussed so far are very helpful in showing why auditing is provided on a voluntary basis. It offers many advantages to investors and other stakeholders, as well as to managers. But in most cases where auditing is important, it is required by some form of regulation. To understand the function of auditing, we need to consider why in many settings auditing is compulsory, especially for listed companies.

Part of the answer is that auditing is a form of public good. That is, once an audit is produced, many stakeholders can benefit, even if they are not a party to hiring and compensating the auditor. Economic theory suggests that public goods will be produced at a less than ideal level unless some form of regulation is introduced. Since most stakeholders have little direct control over a company, there is a concern that too little auditing may be produced in spite of the natural demand of auditing as a risk management tool. Small shareholders, potential investors and many other groups are perceived to benefit from an audit, but they cannot impose it on a company. For that reason, legislators impose auditing requirements for the benefit of the community (however, there are also arguments in opposition to this view of regulation, which we discuss in the paragraph after next).

A second (and overlapping) explanation is that auditing is beneficial to a country's economy. A vice-president of the World Bank has described auditing as: 'an agent of transparency in development of an economy' (Muis, 1999).[3] Similarly, studies of economic development include better auditing and accounting among measures of the investor protection environment and have shown that they are associated with better economic performance. For example, Rajan and Zingales (2001: 480) provide evidence that countries with better accounting have greater investment and more economic growth, and write: 'a country intent on economic development should fix its financial plumbing first.' Evidence about the value of an auditing profession is provided by the differing impact of an economic crisis, for example the Asian economic crisis of the 1990s. Those countries that had better established auditing professions were able to shake off the effects of the Asian economic crisis more quickly (according to Muis, 1999). These two explanations show that mandatory auditing is imposed because it is in the public interest.

An alternative set of views about regulation consider the incentives of those who can impose regulated auditing, either elected representatives or bureaucrats appointed by them, or independent standard setters. These explanations are more in line with public choice economics, and take into account the self-interest of regulators. If an audit failure is controversial, especially if it causes harm to voters, there will be an incentive for these powerful groups to impose further regulation. Ball (2009: 289) argues that such groups have an incentive to regulate in order to avoid perceived responsibility for investor losses, and that any legislative action is a political attempt to escape blame. Similar arguments are made by Watts and Zimmerman (1986). Ball (2009) sees the Sarbanes-Oxley Act as a 'rushed' attempt by Congress and President Bush to avoid being held responsible for the audit failures of the early twenty-first century. In auditing, there appears to be a continuing cycle of increases in regulation in response to any problems that are seen as relating to auditing, and auditing has become much more highly regulated over the last 100 years. This lends credibility to the public choice explanation.

Historical development

Historical evidence about auditing is consistent with the explanations set out in this chapter. As long ago as 1494, Pacioli in his treatise on double-entry bookkeeping recommended the appraisal of accounts by an independent person (Willekens, 2007: 4). Watts and Zimmerman (1986: 312) describe how voluntary auditing existed for 600 years in circumstances where there was a need for stewardship, as 'part of the efficient technology for organising firms'. Auditors changed with the coming of the industrial revolution from amateur shareholder representatives to professional firms.

Maltby (2009) indicates how the explanation by Watts and Zimmerman (1983) that auditing was desirable as it reduced the risks inherent in agency relationships is also helpful in explaining why auditors are still valued, even when auditing failures are evident. While auditing is regulated in most large-organization settings, it shows 'extraordinary resilience' considering the failures associated with it (Maltby, 2009: 240). And auditors have been described as 'invulnerable to their own failure' (Power, 1994). This speaks to the overall benefit of auditing even when delivered at a level that is less than perfect. This can be partially explained by the difficulty in observing the outcome of an audit and recognition that the entire model of auditing is built on an assumption of residual risk, i.e., no matter how good the audit, there is always some remaining risk that material misstatements can exist in a set of financial statements that have been examined by an auditor. This potential is specifically reflected in the audit risk model that guides much of what an auditor does. The fact that auditors cannot reduce residual risk to zero is partially the cause of the so-called expectations gap between what an auditor can realistically accomplish and what the general public expects, especially when using hindsight after an audit failure has been revealed by circumstances.[4]

Unresolved issues requiring future research

Audit failures of the twenty-first century have led some to believe that auditing is in a state of crisis, and further radical reforms are required. Many of the chapters in this book provide information relevant to current proposals or potential proposals for change to auditing. In considering such proposals, it is helpful to be aware of the theoretical background to auditing, as far as it is known from current research. Is it necessary to impose more compulsory requirements upon auditors? On the one hand, there are ample economic reasons for directors and managers to choose auditing, because it is in their interests or in the interests of the company. There is also evidence from research studies to support the economic reasons for auditing; but the evidence is still relatively sparse, and more research into the function of auditing will be valuable. In particular, while the research discussed in this chapter suggests that more auditing is often in the interests of directors and managers, it is much more common in practice to find that directors and managers regard auditing as a cost to be minimized as far as possible while still meeting their statutory requirements. More examination of this issue will be worthwhile.

At a time when more regulation of various kinds is heavily on the agenda, it would be helpful to know a lot more about the settings and circumstances in which voluntary auditing works best, and the situations in which regulation is needed. One possible explanation for the perceived conflict between unregulated auditing and regulated auditing is that it is not always clear what aspect of auditing is being considered in the debate about regulation.

There are at least four aspects that should be separated to some extent in the discussion of audit regulation. First, there is the demand for auditing, which is well established by literature and economic theory. There are very few organizations or situations where auditors are not already operating where imposition of an audit requirement would add value to the economy. Second, there is the issue of who should conduct audits and under what conditions. These issues are often discussed under the general framework of competence and independence, that is, what is the best way to ensure that an auditor possesses adequate expertise to conduct an audit and to remain professionally sceptical about a client so as to not yield to pressure from various parties to reach specific conclusions. Regulations related to the education, training and licensing of auditors are aimed at this problem, as are regulations that constrain the economic and personal links between a client and the auditor. Third, there is the manner in which auditing is actually delivered. Do auditors do enough work? Can their procedures be improved? It is here where some regulation and standard setting may be beneficial, since neither clients nor stakeholders are in a position to evaluate whether an auditor's work is appropriate and comprehensive. Finally, there is a strong concern about how to evaluate audit quality after the audit is completed. Regulations related to peer review and inspections are directed to this challenge.

Conclusion

Auditing reduces the risk of a financial report being materially misstated. Auditing does not directly prevent financial losses, but it can ensure that information is more reliable, and that decisions are less likely to be made based on misleading information. Thus auditing can be valuable to the users of financial reports, and therefore of value to a company, its directors and managers, and outsiders such as investors and creditors.

More detailed explanations of the value of an audit to the company reporting are based on economic models: auditing as a way of signalling better quality financial reporting; auditing as a way to provide voluntary monitoring and bonding; auditing as a means of insurance for losses; auditing as a way to help managers to provide organizational control; auditing as a means of confirming the information in earlier announcements; and auditing as part of an overall risk management strategy.

Auditing is often compulsory. There are competing explanations for why legislators require auditing. Public interest models see compulsory auditing as a way to protect the interests of those stakeholders who cannot otherwise obtain auditing. Public choice models emphasize the interests of the legislators themselves, perhaps in showing that they have taken some action during a crisis, and to deflect blame.

This chapter shows that auditing is complicated. Many of the explanations for auditing are counter-intuitive: it is in the manager's interest to arrange for auditing, so that it ceases to be necessary for it to be imposed by shareholders or regulators. Regulation may be for the benefit of the economy and for stakeholders who cannot impose their own controls on the company – but it may also be for the benefit of the regulators. It may be helpful when reading the subsequent chapters of this book to consider the function of auditing and the models that explain the need for it and its regulation.

Notes

1 Although there may be other explanations for the higher audit fees, e.g., more public information released that is financial (even if not directly related to the financial statements) may also suggest greater risk and greater audit effort.
2 Defined as a larger stock market reaction to unexpected earnings announcements.
3 In making recommendations, the World Bank frequently makes improving the auditing standards within a country part of its priorities, e.g., in Argentina (World Bank, 2007).
4 There is also an argument that the adoption of voluntary auditing took place partly as a means for companies to avoid other kinds of regulation, specifically, to avoid having to disclose financial reports (Maltby, 2009: 230). Maltby suggests that later adoption of voluntary auditing mechanisms may also have been intended to pre-empt regulation being imposed.

References

Abdel-Khalik, A.R. 1993. 'Why Do Private Companies Demand Auditing? A Case for Organizational Loss of Control', *Journal of Accounting, Auditing and Finance* 8(Winter): 31–52.

Ball, R. 2009. 'Market and Political/Regulatory Perspectives on the Recent Accounting Scandals', *Journal of Accounting Research* 47(2): 277–323.

Ball, R. and Brown, P. 1968. 'An Empirical Evaluation of Accounting Income Numbers', *Journal of Accounting Research* 6(2): 159–78.

Ball, R., Jayaraman, L. and Shivakumar, S. 2012. 'Audited Financial Reporting and Voluntary Disclosure as Complements: A Test of the Confirmation Hypothesis', *Journal of Accounting and Economics* 53: 136–66.

Beatty, R. 1989. 'Auditor Reputation and the Pricing of Initial Public Offerings', *Accounting Review* 64(October): 693–709.

Chow, C.W. 1982. 'The Demand for External Auditing: Size, Debt and Ownership Influences', *Accounting Review* 57(April): 272–91.

Chow, C.W., Kramer, L. and Wallace, W. A. 1988. 'The Environment of Auditing', in A. R. Abdel-Khalik and I. Solomon (eds) *Research Opportunities in Auditing: The Second Decade*. Sarasota, FL: American Accounting Association.

Elliott, R.K. 1994. 'The Future of Audits', *Journal of Accountancy* 178(3): 74–82.

Knechel, W. and Willekens, M. 2006. 'The Role of Risk Management and Governance in Determining Audit Demand', *Journal of Business Finance & Accounting* 33(9/10): 1344–67.

Maltby, J. 2009. 'Auditing', in Edwards, J.R. and Walker, S.P. (eds) *Routledge Companion to Accounting History*. Abingdon: Routledge.

Muis, J. 1999. *Accounting and Transparency*, paper presented by the Vice President and Controller, World Bank, Asia-Pacific Conference on International Accounting Issues, Melbourne, 20–3 November.

Pacini, C., Hillison, W., Alagiah, R. and Gunz, S. 2002. 'Commonwealth Convergence Toward a Narrower Scope of Auditor Liability to Third Parties for Negligent Misstatements', *Abacus* 38(3): 425–64.

Power, M. 1994. *The Audit Explosion*. London: Demos.

Rajan, R.G. and Zingales, L. 2001. 'Financial Systems, Industrial Structure, and Growth', *Oxford Review of Economic Policy* 17(4): 467–82.

Teoh, S.H. and Wong, T.J. 1993. 'Perceived Audit Quality and the Earnings Response Coefficient', Accounting Review 68(2): 346–66.

Wallace, W.A. 1987. 'The Economic Role of the Audit in Free and Regulated Markets: A Review', *Research in Accounting Regulation* 1: 7–34.

Watts, R. L. and Zimmerman, J. L. 1983. 'Agency Problems, Auditing, and the Theory of the Firm: Some Evidence', *Journal of Law and Economics* 26(3): 613–33.

Watts, R.L. and Zimmerman, J.L. 1986. *Positive Accounting Theory*. Englewood Cliffs, NJ: Prentice-Hall.

Willekens, M. 2007. 'To Audit or not to Audit? On the Use of Auditing in a Continental European Setting', Inaugural lecture at Tilburg University, the Netherlands, 17 October.

World Bank. 2007. 'Argentina – *Report on the Observance of Standards and Codes (ROSC): Accounting and Auditing*'. Washington, DC: World Bank. Available online at https://openknowledge.worldbank.org/handle/10986/7907 (accessed 13 May 2014).

Part I

The social environment of auditing

2
The auditing profession

Roger Meuwissen

Origin of the auditing profession

The term 'audit' comes from the Latin verb 'audire', which means 'to hear'. In the ancient civilizations of Egypt, Greece and Rome, checking activities were performed to make sure that public revenues and expenditures were properly accounted for. The regimes were worried about corrupt officers committing fraud and incompetent officers making book keeping errors. Checking clerks were therefore appointed to check the public accounts, by hearing verbal explanations from those responsible for keeping the books, judging their explanations and after an examination announcing the results of their audit. Hence, in ancient days, auditing existed primarily as a method to maintain and check public or government accounts.

Modern day auditing originated from the Industrial Revolution in the United Kingdom. Businesses expanded during this period, and the ongoing development of the separation of ownership and control led to the passing of the Joint Stock Companies Act by the British parliament in 1844. This Act required directors of joint stock companies to provide balance sheet accounts to their shareholders and stipulated the appointment of auditors to check these accounts. At that time, however, auditors were not required to be independent from the company or licensed in any way. A couple of scandals at the end of the nineteenth century (Afrikaanse handelsvereeniging, 1879; City of Glasgow Bank, 1883; Kingston Cotton Mill, 1896) changed this situation. In 1900, a new Companies Act required companies to appoint an independent auditor. This reinforced that the main objective of the audit was the detection by an independent individual of errors and fraud, and actually led to the start of modern day auditing.

In these early days of modern day auditing, the first professional bodies and accounting firms were also established. In 1854, the Royal Charter of the Society of Accountants in Edinburgh – the predecessor of the current Institute of Chartered Accountants of Scotland – became the first officially recognized association of accountants. At the same time, several accountants established themselves in London and opened accountancy offices which form the origins of some of the global Big 4 audit firms that we know nowadays (e.g. Samuel Lowell Price in 1849, William

Deloitte in 1845, William Cooper in 1854, and William Barclay Peat in 1870). With the inception of the Society of Accountants, Scotland also formally recognizes the title of 'chartered accountant'. In 1880, the title 'chartered accountant' was also adopted by the newly formed Institute of Chartered Accountants in England and Wales. This institute was formed by a merger of five associations (the Incorporated Society of Liverpool Accountants, the Institute of Accountants in London, the Manchester Institute of Accountants, the Society of Accountants in England, and the Sheffield Institute of Accountants), which were founded between 1870 and 1877.

Also outside the UK, the auditing profession was developing rapidly by the end of the nineteenth century. In the Netherlands, the first independent audit was carried out in 1879 (at the Nieuwe Afrikaansche Handelsch Vereeniging in Rotterdam; see Metzemaekers and van Maastrigt, 1983: 53). The first Dutch professional body auditors, the Nederlandsch Instituut van Accountants, was founded in 1895. Outside Europe, professional bodies of auditors were established, predominantly in commonwealth countries, according to the British model: the Institute of Accountants of New Zealand was incorporated in 1894; the first professional body of auditors in South Africa was the Institute of Accountants and Auditors, formed in Johannesburg in 1894; while the Canadian Institute of Chartered Accountants was established in 1902.

Simultaneously, large amounts of British capital were flowing to the rapidly growing economy of the United States. Scottish and British accountants travelled to the United States to audit these investments, a number of whom stayed on and set up practice. Several existing international and national audit firms can trace their origins to one or more of these visiting Scottish or British chartered accountants. The Scottish-born Arthur Young, for example, immigrated to the United States in 1890 and formed several accounting firms, starting with Stuart & Young in 1894 and Arthur Young & Company in 1906. The New York based James Marwick founded the accounting firm Marwick, Mitchell & Co. with Roger Mitchell in New York City in 1897; and Alwin Ernst formed the Cleveland accounting firm Ernst & Ernst with his brother Theodore in 1903. In 1887, the first professional accounting body was formed, the American Association of Public Accountants, predecessor to the American Institute of Certified Public Accountants.

The growth of the stock market in the following years led to widespread development of the accounting profession in the United States. It was nevertheless only after the stock market crash of 1929 that audits became mandatory in the United States. In particular, the Securities and Exchange Act of 1934 created the Securities and Exchange Commission (SEC). Among other responsibilities, the SEC was entitled to issue accounting standards and to enforce that publicly traded companies should submit audited financial statements. The principal role of auditors was to ensure that these reports were created in accordance with generally accepted accounting principles. The further growth of the US economy in subsequent years caused a shift of auditing development from the UK – where modern day auditing started – to the United States.

To provide an overview of the start of the audit profession in some audit markets, Table 2.1 shows the first professional body of accountants for ten audit markets (the current name of the professional body) and year of inception.

In the following three sections, we will discuss current issues in the auditing profession and the major research findings in these areas. The first section will expand on the development of the auditing profession, including the professional bodies of accountants and their regulatory roles. The following section, 'The supply of auditing', will provide an overview of the supply of audit services. The final section will present the conclusions.[1]

Table 2.1 The year of establishment of the audit profession in ten developed audit markets

Country	*First (current name) professional body of accountants*	*Year*
Scotland	Society of Accountants in Edinburgh (Institute of Chartered Accountants of Scotland)	1854
UK	Incorporated Society of Liverpool Accountants (Institute of Chartered Accountants in England and Wales)	1870
Australia	Incorporated Institute of Accountants (CPA Australia)	1886
US	American Association of Public Accountants (American Institute of Certified Public Accountants)	1887
New Zealand	Institute of Accountants of New Zealand (New Zealand Institute of Chartered Accountants)	1894
South Africa	Institute of Accountants and Auditors (South African Institute of Chartered Accountants)	1894
Netherlands	Nederlandsch Instituut van Accountants (Nederlandse Beroepsassociatie van Accountants)	1895
Germany	Verband Deutscher Bucherrevisoren (Institut der Wirtschaftsprüfer)	1896
Sweden	Svenska Revisorsamfundet (Föreningen auktoriserade revisorer – 2006)	1899
Canada	Dominion Association of Chartered Accountants (Canadian Institute of Chartered Accountants)	1902

The development of the auditing profession

The auditing profession has undergone constant changes between its inception in the late 1900s and the present. These changes were a response either to major business events such as corporate failures or fraud cases, or to changes in the demand for auditing services (for example the growth and globalization of clients). As a result, the objectives of the audit, the regulatory environment, and the audit approach were constantly changing.

Regulation and audit objectives

In most auditing environments, the authority to regulate the auditing profession is with government or a government agency (e.g. the SEC in the US, the Financial Reporting Council in the UK). From the start of the auditing profession, the authority to set rules and regulations was delegated to the profession itself (see for example Garner *et al.*, 2007). Professional bodies of accountants issued ethical standards, auditing standards and independence guidelines. Refinements of these standards and rules generally resulted from regulatory actions in response to significant negative business events. For example, audit tasks such as physical inspection of inventories and confirmation of receivables were optional until fraudulent activities were uncovered at the McKesson & Robbins Company in 1939 in the United States. The McKesson & Robbins Company was given a clean audit opinion and an investigation by the SEC revealed that the auditor performed the audit according to the applicable standards. However, as investors considered this unacceptable, the American Institute of Certified Public Accountants adjusted the auditing standards. As a result, Statement on Auditing Procedure (SAP) No. 1 was issued requiring auditors to inspect inventories and confirm receivables. Another example was the case of the Royal Mail in 1931 in the UK. This highlighted the need for audit of the profit and loss statements, as they had been falsified but were not subject of the audit. Accordingly, the audit of the profit and loss account became mandatory with the enactment of the Companies Act in 1948 in the UK and the SEC Act in 1934 in the United States.

After a relatively stable period of self-regulation, the auditing profession has witnessed substantial change since the 1990s, because of the accelerating growth of the world economy. The growth of consulting services especially, which eventually exceeded auditing revenues at all the large global audit firms, raised doubt with both regulators and investors as to whether audit firms could remain independent on audit issues when the firms were so dependent on consulting revenues. After a series of business failures and fraudulent reporting scandals, the quality of audits was being placed under scrutiny. The collapse of such companies as Enron, Sunbeam, Adelphia, and WorldCom, brought about a confidence crisis in the work of auditors. Although most accounting firms split their consulting arms into separate companies and made announcements on their more stringent measures to ensure better independence and audit quality, governments stepped in and ended the era of self-regulation by creating government bodies that were given the authority to regulate the auditing profession. In the US, the Public Company Accounting Oversight Board (PCAOB) was created following the Sarbanes-Oxley Act of 2001, while in Europe the amended Eight Directive of the European Union promulgated the creation of oversight bodies in each EU member state. This ended the period of self-regulation of the auditing profession.

The financial scandals and government intervention also brought about more stringent regulation to the auditing profession. The Sarbanes-Oxley Act extended the duties of auditors to inspect the adequacy of internal controls over financial reporting. This is in view of the fact that internal control is regarded as an important mechanism to prevent financial misstatements. Research in this area indeed shows that companies that report material internal control weaknesses tend to have lower earnings quality (Doyle *et al.*, 2007; Chan *et al.*, 2008); exhibit lower conservatism (Goh and Li, 2011); and have larger management forecast errors (Feng *et al.*, 2009). A recent study by Costello and Wittenberg-Moerman (2011) furthermore shows that lenders decrease their use of accounting numbers for contractual terms following the disclosure of a material internal control weakness. A more extensive overview of research in this area will be presented in Chapter 25, Reporting on Internal Control.

In Europe, a similar development took place. In the light of the financial scandals and crises, the European Commission (EC) was concerned about the structure of the audit market and potential threats to audit quality. Specifically, the EC stated that the societal role of auditors in offering an opinion on the true and fair presentation of financial statements of audited entities should be robust and contribute to financial stability (EC, 2010). Although the EC did not introduce reporting on internal control, they lined up with the PCAOB to prohibit the provision of some important non-audit services to audit clients (e.g. tax services and some other advisory services), based on the idea that the simultaneous provision of audit and non-audit services to clients may endanger auditor independence. Research in this area nevertheless shows mixed results. Studies have tested the effect of non-audit services on qualified or going concern opinions (see e.g. DeFond *et al.*, 2002; Basioudis *et al.*, 2008; Lim and Tan, 2008); on the degree of earnings management (see e.g. Frankel *et al.*, 2002; Ashbaugh *et al.*, 2003; Huang *et al.*, 2007); or on restatements (see e.g. Kinney *et al.*, 2004). Although some studies found a negative effect (e.g. Frankel *et al.*, 2002; Basioudis *et al.*, 2008), most studies did not find that provision of non-audit services had any effect on auditor independence.

A further regulatory measure that impacts the auditing profession is the proposed mandatory rotation of audit firms. Several countries, such as Brazil and Italy, have introduced mandatory rotation in the past, while, for example, Spain has abolished such regulation. Proponents of mandatory rotation claim that an increase in the auditor–client relationship could result in auditors being more lenient towards management on critical reporting issues, while opponents argue that the loss of client-specific knowledge outweighs the benefits. A vast amount of empirical research has been conducted on the impact of auditor rotation on earnings quality (see e.g. Myers *et al.*, 2003); on going-concern opinions (see e.g. Knechel and Vanstraelen, 2007); and on audit failures (see e.g. Stice, 1991). The studies on earnings quality indicate that audit quality increases with tenure in the early years of an engagement, while in later years some studies see a decrease in audit quality (see e.g. Davis *et al.*, 2009). The studies on going-concern opinions suggest a decrease in audit quality with tenure, whereas the studies on audit failures show that failures are more likely to occur on the early years of an engagement. Overall, the results on the effect of mandatory rotation are mixed.

Audit approach

Audits in the 1930s were mainly concerned with ensuring the correctness of financial accounts and detecting frauds and errors. In order to keep up with the growth and internationalization of clients, involving voluminous transactions and an increase in audit locations, the concept of materiality and sampling techniques (see e.g. Brown, 1962) were introduced in auditing. As it was no longer practicable for auditors to verify all the transactions, sampling and the development of judgment of materiality were essential.

Corresponding to the use of sampling techniques, auditors also needed to rely on internal accounting controls of the company to facilitate the use of sampling. Consequently, the audit approach changed in the 1950s from verifying transactions in the books of accounts to relying on the accounting and control system. Such a change was required because of the increase in the number of transactions resulting from the continued growth in size and the complexity of clients.

In the early 1980s there was a readjustment in auditors' approaches where the assessment of internal control systems was found to be an expensive process. Hence, auditors began to cut back their systems work and made greater use of analytical procedures. A further extension of audit analytics was the development during the mid-1980s of risk-based auditing (Turley and Cooper, 1991). As a result, more audit focus went to risky areas and less audit focus to less risky areas. Bell *et al.*, (1997) provide an overview of the key differences between the traditional audit approach and business risk auditing methodologies.

Simultaneously, most of the clients introduced computer systems to process and monitor their financial data. This resulted in the development of audits of the Electronic Data Processing system (EDP-audit), but also to the greater use of computer audit tools by audit firms to facilitate their audit procedures.

Another development in the auditing profession is the provision of non-audit services. In addition to auditing the financial statements, auditors started in the 1970s and culminating in the 1990s and the early 2000s to provide advisory services to audit clients. Since then, the role of auditors has always been highly associated with such advisory services, and according to Robson *et al.* (2007) the provision of advisory services emerged as a secondary audit objective.

There has been extensive research conducted on the concept of materiality, audit sampling, internal control reliance, the use of analytical procedures, risk assessment, EDP-audit, computer-aided audit analyses, and the effects of the provision of non-audit services to audit clients. These topics are discussed more extensively in later chapters of this volume.

The supply of auditing

Audit firms have developed into global accounting firms which provide a wide array of services including assurance, tax, and consulting services. The global Big 4 firms currently have revenues in excess of US$100 billion and employ over 700,000 people in total. In this section we will discuss some contemporary issues with respect to the supply of audit services: the organization of audit firms, the size of audit firms, the reputation of audit firms, industry specialization by audit firms, and the provision of non-audit services by audit firms.

Organization of audit firms

The global organization of the international Big 4 accounting firms differs substantially from how multinational corporations are organized. Whereas multinationals usually have a board from which all operations are managed, none of the Big 4 accounting firms is similarly structured. Instead, they are networks of firms, owned and managed at national level, which have entered into agreements with other member firms in the network to share a common name, brand, and quality standards. Each network has established an entity to coordinate the activities of the group. In one case (KPMG), the coordinating entity is Swiss, and the other three Big 4 accounting firms have a UK limited company as coordinating entity. Similar to law firm networks, these entities do not own and control the network. Research on the existence of this phenomenon is as yet non-existent.

Gradually, firms feel pressure to be organized as integrated global firms that can act as one entity and deliver uniform services worldwide. Some of the large firms have already moved towards complete globalization by merging member firms in certain regional areas. In 2007, KPMG announced a merger of four member firms (from the United Kingdom, Germany, Switzerland, and Liechtenstein) into a single firm. Ernst & Young also introduced separate legal entities which manage three of the four areas: Americas, EMEIA (Europe, Middle East, India and Africa) and Asia-Pacific. In other firms, similar developments are taking place.

Although limited liability partnerships in the UK and US limit the liabilities of non-negligent partners, the negligent partners' personal wealth is still at risk. Negligent partners in such a limited liability partnership therefore have a liability exposure similar to those in a general – unlimited – partnership. In some countries, this is however not the case. For example, the limited liability structure in China limits the liabilities of both the negligent partners and non-negligent partners.

The organizational form of audit firms is an interesting, but still fairly underdeveloped, research topic. The liability exposure in unlimited partnerships encourages auditors to be independent and induces mutual monitoring by the partners, because each partner is liable for the other partners' actions. Dye (1995) nevertheless shows that auditors – when possible – try to choose an organizational form that limits their liability.

Size

In the green paper *Audit Policy: Lessons from the Crisis* (EC, 2010), the EC is worried about the structure of the audit market. The Commission indicates that the market is dominated by four large international firms, and that the potential collapse of one of these firms could not only disrupt the availability of audits, but would also damage investor trust and confidence. A further consideration for the EC is whether any single audit firm should be allowed to become so large. It is important to discuss these concerns by the EC and we therefore first present an overview of the largest global audit firms to establish how dominant are these large firms; and second, we discuss the relevant research regarding sizes of firms and economies of scale.

Table 2.2 Top 20 international audit firms, 2011 global revenues

Rank	*Audit firm*	*Country (headquarters)*	*2011 Revenues (in US$b)*	*Employees (headcount)*
1	PricewaterhouseCoopers	UK	29.2	169,000
2	Deloitte	US	28.2	182,000
3	Ernst & Young	UK	22.9	152,000
4	KPMG	Netherlands	22.7	145,000
5	BDO	Belgium	5.7	44,000
6	Geneva Group International	Switzerland	4.3	24,000
7	RSM International	UK	4.0	29,000
8	Grant Thornton	UK	3.8	28,000
9	Praxity AISBL	UK	3.7	27,000
10	Baker Tilly	UK	3.2	22,000
11	Crowe Horwath International	US	2.9	25,000
12	The Appleton Alliance Group	US	2.9	15,000
13	PKF International	UK	2.6	20,000
14	Leading Edge Alliance	US	2.6	21,000
15	Nexia International	UK	2.3	17,000
16	Moore Stephens International	UK	2.3	19,000
17	IGAF Polaris	US	2.0	17,000
18	HLB International	UK	1.8	15,000
19	Kreston International	UK	1.8	22,000
20	AGN International	UK	1.5	12,000

Source: Annual reports and websites of the firms and networks

Table 2.2 contains the top 20 global accounting firms, based on the 2011 revenues in US$b. Total revenues of these 20 firms are US$150.4 billion. The sum of US$103 billion is from the Big 4 firms, indicating a market share of almost 70 per cent. Another observation is the gap between number 4 (KPMG) and number 5 (BDO) in terms of revenues (22.7 *vs* 5.7 US$b). The conclusion must be that the global Big 4 accounting firms do dominate the market. The issue however is whether these firms misuse the power of this oligopoly. Numan and Willekens (2012), for example, show that there is still competitive pressure on pricing within the Big 4 oligopoly.

The existence of large audit firms can partly be explained by economies of scale. If large audit firms benefit from economies of scale, they will show superior audit efficiency leading to lower audit fees or higher profits. To test for economies of scale, studies either focus on audit fees and audit effort or on industry specialization. Overall, the audit fee studies conclude that large audit firms obtain cost advantages through economies of scale, but also receive fee premiums probably owing to product differentiation (Craswell *et al.*, 1995) or industry specialization (Fung *et al.*, 2012; Numan and Willekens, 2012). One must also look at the rivalry between the Big 4 firms. Dynamic analyses of market structure do indicate that in some markets there is a high level of competition between the large firms (see Buijink *et al.*, 1998). Such effects offset the high levels of concentration.

Reputation

Given the notion that auditing is a so-called 'credence good' (see Causholli and Knechel, 2012), the quality of audits is costly to evaluate. Therefore, clients need to rely on the auditor's reputation. From an economics perspective, reputation will increase the demand for the audit service as well as the audit fee. Previous studies have found that auditors with a high quality reputation are regarded as more capable and more independent (see e.g. Teoh and Wong, 1993); that companies having a Big 4 auditor are able to obtain more equity financing (Chang *et al.*, 2009); and that companies with a Big 4 auditor have a lower cost of equity and a lower cost of debt (Pittman and Fortin, 2004). Furthermore, earlier studies indicate that fee premiums are associated with auditor reputation (see, e.g. Craswell *et al.*, 1995).

Industry specialization

Research on industry specialization examines whether specialized knowledge results in economies of scale for audit services provided in particular industries or market segments. The early studies generally conclude that audit firms obtain economies of scale in regulated industries, in large client segments of other industries, and in the market for IPOs. In the last couple of years, research focus has shifted from the entire market and/or firm to office-level effects (see e.g. Reichelt and Wang, 2010). The premise is that the pricing of auditor industry expertise is based on office-level industry leadership instead of national industry leadership. A paper by Francis and Yu (2009), however, indicates that the size of the office is the important driver of the effect. Large offices have more in-house expertise and thus greater capacity to deliver high audit quality.

Provision of non-audit services

The Big 4 accounting firms deliver a wide array of services, ranging from the traditional audit to risk assurance services, tax services, and consulting services, including systems design and implementation, and human resource consulting. The increased demand for non-audit services and the need to differentiate services have led in the last decade to a few recent developments. The term 'assurance' services has become an umbrella for audit activities and other services historically provided by the audit staff, such as assistance in mergers and acquisitions, and risk assurance. Furthermore, the specialized assurance services (e.g., due diligence) are more and more performed by experts in those fields instead of by the traditional auditors. Also, to compete with the traditional consulting firm, the consulting services portfolio has been enlarged.

When auditors supply non-audit services to audit clients, one can expect knowledge spillovers between audit services and non-audit services. On the other hand, one can expect that auditor independence may be compromised when clients pay high non-audit fees as compared to audit fees. As previously mentioned, the results of empirical studies on this issue do not provide consistent evidence of knowledge spillovers or impaired independence. Nevertheless, are the audit firms forced to cut back on non-audit services, given that the combination of audit and non-audit services for the same client has recently been restricted by the regulators.

Conclusion

This chapter provides an overview of the auditing profession. Hereto, the origins and history of the profession are discussed, followed by a discussion of the most important topics regarding the supply of audit services within the auditing profession.

The historic overview of the profession indicates that changes came to the profession through major business events, such as corporate failures and fraud cases, or through developments initiated by clients (globalization, need for advisory services). Over time, the regulatory environment has changed drastically from a pattern of self-regulation to that of external regulation of audit firms.

Several current developments in the auditing profession have been discussed, from mandatory rotation of audit firms, and the prohibition of non-audit services, to the audit of internal controls over financial reporting, as well as from the organizational structure of audit firms to industry specialization.

In the last few years, much research on the auditing profession has focused on the consequences of regulatory changes; more and more studies indicate that such regulatory interventions will benefit the quality of the audit. And although clients nowadays call for an extended role of (independent) business partner, the recent regulatory changes will probably take the profession back to its core activity: audit.

Note

1 An overview of the demand for audit services is already provided in Chapter 1.

References

Ashbaugh, H., LaFond, R. and Mayhew, B.W. (2003). 'Do Non-audit Services Compromise Auditor Independence? Further evidence', *The Accounting Review* 78: 611–39.

Basioudis, I.G., Papakonstantinou, E. and Geiger, M.A. (2008). 'Audit Fees, Non-audit Fees and Auditor Going-Concern Reporting Decisions in the United Kingdom', *ABACUS* 44(3): 284–309.

Bell, T.B., Marrs, F.O., Solomon, I. and Thomas, I. (1997). *Auditing Organizations through a Strategic Systems Lens*. Montvale, NJ: KPMG LLP.

Brown, R. (1962). 'Changing Audit Objectives and Techniques', *The Accounting Review* 37(4): 696–703.

Buijink, W.F.J., Maijoor, S.J. and Meuwissen, R.H.G. (1998). 'Competition in Auditing: Evidence from entry, exit and market share mobility in Germany and the Netherlands', *Contemporary Accounting Research* 15(3): 385–404.

Causholli, M. and Knechel, W.R. (2012). 'An Examination of the Credence Attributes of an Audit', *Accounting Horizons* 26(4, December): 631–56.

Chan, K., Farrell, B. and Lee, P. (2008). 'Earnings Management of Firms Reporting Material Internal Control Weaknesses under Section 404 of the Sarbanes-Oxley Act', *Auditing, A Journal of Practice and Theory* 27(2): 161–79.

Chang, X., Dasgupta, S. and Hillary, G. (2009). 'The Effect of Auditor Quality on Financing Decisions', *The Accounting Review* 84(4): 1085–117.

Costello, A. and Wittenberg-Moerman, R. (2011). 'The Impact of Financial Reporting Quality on Debt Contracting: Evidence from internal control weakness reports', *Journal of Accounting Research* 49(1): 97–136.

Craswell, A.T., Francis, J.R. and Taylor, S.L. (1995). 'Auditor Brand Name Reputations and Industry Specializations', *Journal of Accounting and Economics* 20(3): 297–322.

Davis, L.R., Soo, B.S. and Trompeter, G.M. (2009). 'Auditor Tenure and the Ability to Meet or Beat Earnings Forecasts', *Contemporary Accounting Research* 26: 517–48.

DeFond, M.L., Raghunandan, K. and Subramanyam, K.R. (2002). 'Do Non-audit Service Fees Impair Auditor Independence? Evidence from going concern audit opinions', *Journal of Accounting Research* 40: 1247–74.

Doyle, J., Ge, W. and McVay, S. (2007). 'Determinants of Weaknesses in Internal Control over Financial Reporting', *Journal of Accounting and Economics* 44(1–2): 193–223.

Dye, R.A. (1995). 'Incorporation and the Audit Market', *Journal of Accounting and Economics* 20(1): 75–114.

European Commission (EC). (2010). 'Green paper – *Audit Policy: Lessons from the crisis*', October. Brussels: European Commission.

Feng, M., Li, C. and McVay, S. (2009). 'Internal Control and Management Guidance', *Journal of Accounting & Economics* 48(2–3): 190–209.

Francis, J.R. and Yu, M. (2009). 'The Effect of Big 4 Office Size on Audit Quality', *The Accounting Review* 84(5): 1521–52.

Frankel, R.M., Johnson, M.F. and Nelson, K.K. (2002). 'The Relation between Auditors' Fees for Nonaudit Services and Earnings Management', *The Accounting Review* 77(4): 71–105.
Fung, S., Gul, F. and Krishnan, J. (2012). 'City-level Auditor Industry Specialization, Economies of Scale, and Audit Pricing', *The Accounting Review* 87(4): 1281–307.
Garner, D., McKee, D. and McKee, Y. (2007). *Accounting and the Global Economy after Sarbanes-Oxley*. New York: M.E. Sharpe.
Goh, B.W. and Li, D. (2011). 'Internal Controls and Conditional Conservatism', *The Accounting Review* 86(3): 975–1005.
Huang, H.W., Mishra, S. and Raghunandan, K. (2007). 'Types of Nonaudit Fees and Financial Reporting Quality', *Auditing: A Journal of Practice & Theory* 26(1): 133–45.
Kinney, W.R., Palmrose, Z.-V. and Scholz, S. (2004). 'Auditor Independence, Non-Audit Services, and Restatements: Was the U.S. Government right?', *Journal of Accounting Research* 42: 561–88.
Knechel, W.R. and Vanstraelen, A. (2007). 'The Relationship between Auditor Tenure and Audit Quality Implied by Going-Concern Opinions', *Auditing: A Journal of Practice and Theory* 26: 113–31.
Lim, C-Y. and Tan, H-T (2008). 'Non-audit Services and Audit Quality: The impact of auditor specialisation', *Journal of Accounting Research* 46: 199–246.
Metzemaekers, L. and van Maastrigt, A. (1983). *Een eeuw in balans: De wordingsgeschiedenis van Moret & Limperg (1883–1983).* Rotterdam: Moret & Limperg.
Myers, J., Myers, L.A. and Omer, T.C. (2003). 'Exploring the Term of Auditor–Client Relationship and the Quality of Earnings: A case for mandatory auditor rotation?', *The Accounting Review* 78: 779–99.
Numan, W. and Willekens, M. (2012). 'An Empirical Test of Spatial Competition in the Audit Market', *Journal of Accounting & Economics* 53(1–2): 450–65.
Pittman, J. and Fortin, S. (2004). 'The Impact of Auditor's Reputation on the Cost of Financing', *Journal of Accounting & Economics* 37(1): 113–36.
Reichelt, J.K. and Wang, D. (2010) 'National and Office-specific Measures of Auditor Industry Expertise and Effect on Audit Quality', *Journal of Accounting Research* 48(3): 647–86.
Robson, K., Humphrey, C., Khalifa, R. and Jones, J. (2007). 'Transforming Audit Technologies: Business Risk Audit Methodologies and the Audit Field', *Accounting, Organization and Society* 32(4-5): 409–38.
Stice, J. D. (1991). 'Using Financial and Market Information to Identify Pre-engagement Factors Associated with Lawsuits against Auditors', *The Accounting Review* 66(3): 516–33.
Teoh, S.H. and Wong, J.J. (1993). 'Perceived Auditor Quality and the Earnings Response Coefficient', *The Accounting Review* 68(2): 346–66.
Turley, S. and Cooper, M. (1991). *Auditing in the United Kingdom: A Study of Development in the Audit Methodologies of Large Accounting Firms*. London: Prentice-Hall/Institute of Chartered Accountants in England and Wales (ICAEW).

3
Globalization of auditing

Elizabeth Carson

Introduction

Global expansion by large providers of audit and accounting services began before the 1980s and continued steadily through the 1990s and into the twenty-first century, driven by factors such as national deregulation, privatisation of industries, integration of regional economies, liberalisation of world trade (including multilateral and bilateral agreements), the formation of the European common market, the shift from planned to market economies and privatisation of government assets. These factors have created additional demand for services provided by audit firms across a broader range of countries, cultures and languages. As product markets and financial markets become increasingly internationally integrated and the use of international accounting standards has become more widespread, the demand for related professional services on a global scale has also risen which has accelerated the globalization of the audit industry. At the same time, decreases in cost and an increase in the availability of technology, telecommunications and travel have enabled providers of professional services to more readily overcome traditional barriers of time and location.

The audit industry underwent significant change over the period of the late 1980s and 1990s. Consolidation, resulting from overcapacity, saw the largest eight providers reduce to six by 1989 (Sullivan, 2002). Increasingly, audit services were viewed as undifferentiated commodities lacking value to purchasers, putting pressure on stock exchanges and corporate regulators to review the mandatory nature of financial statement audits. Increased price competition resulted between the audit firms (Carson *et al.*, 2012) and additional services were included with the audit product in order to increase the perceived value of the audit. Costs were reduced by the introduction of technology, increases in partner/staff leverage and older partners being encouraged to retire early. Litigation and insurance costs increased during this period in many countries due to corporate collapses which were attributed to poor quality auditing (for example, the Savings and Loans crisis in the United States). During this time, there was a focus on increased audit quality through a reduction of risk (improved audit methodologies and more extensive client screening) and the provision of value-added services. This period was marked by internal firm tension between the consultants (high margin, high growth) and the audit partners (low margin and stable or declining revenues).

During the 1990s, significant consolidation also occurred within client industries, and the enhanced requirements of multinational clients dictated that audit firms also needed to consolidate to provide sufficient scale to service their largest clients. Relatively stagnant audit fee revenues during this period put pressure on firms to enhance profitability by increasing audit efficiency, or by increasing revenue through expansion and sale of other services (GAO, 2003). Restructuring of audit firms along industry lines facilitated increased overall efficiency as, once the initial investment was made in developing industry specialisations, audits were performed more efficiently and a more targeted approach to the design and sale of other services emerged. At the same time, audit methodologies evolved based on a broader understanding of industry risks, norms and practices stemming from the use of industry-based experts (Bell *et al.*, 2005). In the early 2000s, a number of financial reporting and auditing failures (including Enron and the demise of Arthur Andersen) caused a collapse in confidence in financial reporting and in the integrity of the financial markets. In response, the Sarbanes-Oxley Act was passed in the United States in July 2002 creating a new audit regulator, PCAOB (Public Company Accounting Oversight Board), having substantial powers with the aim of restoring confidence in financial reporting and to improve the independence and quality of audits, with considerable changes in regulation impacting auditors adopted in other countries (J-SOX in Japan, Korea-SOX in South Korea, CLERP 9 in Australia, among others).

The recent financial crisis and its impact in varying degrees throughout the rest of the world demonstrated the interconnectedness of the global economy, particularly in relation to the tightness of credit markets. Investigations into the cause of the financial crisis and the role of auditors in providing early warning as to financial markets have been conducted in Europe (EC, 2010), the UK (House of Lords Economic Affairs Committee, 2011) among others and into the collapse of Lehmann Group in the United States (Jenner and Block, 2010). While government policy, investment banks and credit rating agencies have all been considered to have key roles in the root causes of the financial crisis, the role of auditors has also come under scrutiny. As a result, it seems likely that regulatory change will be demanded in a number of key economies, particularly in relation to audit firm tenure and the structure and content of the audit report. In a globalised profession, it would be likely that these changes would be seen to be adopted successively by other countries.

This chapter proceeds as follows, first describing the structure of the global audit market and the large audit firms that dominate the provision of audit services globally. The organisational form adopted by audit firms operating in multiple countries is discussed in detail, together with the research undertaken to address global issues in auditing, as well as opportunities for future research.

Global audit market structure

The audit industry is commonly described as having a tiered structure. The top tier (also referred to as 'brand name auditors') comprises the largest audit firms, which are structured as global firm networks. These global firm networks employ tens of thousands of employees worldwide to service their clients in a broad range of accounting, audit and other services. Until 1989, this group of brand name auditors was collectively referred to as the 'Big 8'. During 1989, Arthur Young and Ernst & Whinney merged to form Ernst & Young, while Deloitte Haskins & Sells merged with Touche Ross to form Deloitte Touche Tohmatsu, forming the Big 6. In 1997, Price Waterhouse and Coopers & Lybrand merged, leaving a group of five large firms. The firm of Arthur Andersen, which collapsed in 2002, was the fifth member of the so-called Big 5. This collapse resulted from the firm's involvement as auditors and consultants to Enron Corporation which was found to have misstated profits over an extended period of time. The current global Big 4 firm networks are Deloitte, Ernst & Young, KPMG and PricewaterhouseCoopers. Despite the important role played by these audit firm networks in enhancing the credibility of financial information, little is known about the structure and economics of these networks; however, regulators are making attempts for there to be greater disclosure of these issues. For example the European Union Eighth Directive (2006) requires large audit firms to issue transparency reports, although Deumes *et al.* (2012) do not find an association between disclosures in such reports and proxies for audit quality.

The second tier comprises a more diverse group of firms. Commonly referred to as national firms, these often have relationships with firms in other countries. Examples of these second tier firms are BDO, Grant Thornton, Horwarth, RSM and Moores Rowland. Some second tier firms, for example, BDO and Grant Thornton, have established more extensive firm networks on a global scale compared to other second tier firms. Clients of these firms tend to be smaller than those of the Big 4. These firms offer a comprehensive, but narrower, range of accounting, auditing and taxation services to their clients. Particularly in countries outside the United States, these firms provide a significant portion of assurance services to small to medium-sized companies, as well as accounting and taxation services. The remainder of the global audit market is made up of smaller, primarily local single-office firms. These firms generally service one geographic locality, offering a niche speciality or a 'one stop shop'. Clients of these firms tend to be small businesses and individuals. This group of firms is numerically large but the firms are not significant when examining the global audit market. Accordingly the remainder of this chapter will focus on the global audit firm networks and their role in the globalization of auditing.

Global audit firm networks

Global audit firm networks comprise individual audit firms operating together under the same brand name, sharing knowledge and resources on a global scale. They dominate the provision of audit services to publicly listed corporations globally and in key economies such as the United States and Europe. The network mode of organization permits audit firms operating multinationally to access the efficiency benefits of markets and integrated multinational corporations simultaneously while maintaining individual legal structures (Lenz and James, 2007). In a network, authority and control are not tightly centralised, and in theory, the network is not dependent on any single member for its viability or survival. This is not to suggest that the global firm networks are necessarily homogeneous. For example, the Arthur Andersen 'one-firm' network structure was considered to be tighter than other global firm networks, which may provide an explanation for the dissolution of the firm globally rather than just the US firm. One of the advantages of a network structure is the ability to externalise risks throughout the network rather than internalising such risks within a hierarchical structure. This risk diversification strategy is important in a high litigation environment such as auditing and provides one explanation for this choice of operating structure by the key participants in the global audit market.

Firms in a global network have the dual advantage of being both global and local. Other strategic advantages arising from the use of network structures may include economies of scale, learning and access to knowledge, and better management of risk. Additionally, less capital is required by original network members to fund expansion into new environments. This is particularly relevant for audit firms which are generally structured as partnerships and are unable to access equity markets for financing. The existence of a global network enables choices as to how future expansion of economic activities will occur. For example, will the entire network or specific network members sponsor expansion into a new market? The choice of a network structure allows members to access the disciplinary benefits of markets in that there is a credible threat that a network member could utilise the services of audit firms outside the network, as network members are encouraged, but not necessarily compelled, to use network partners. Costs of participating in a network structure include costs of coordination with network partners, potential erosion of competitive position by other members of the network, and creation of an adverse bargaining situation within the network (if leaving the network is not a credible threat).

There are benefits from the use of these network structures enabling this group of firms to expand efficiently in the global audit market. This results in raised barriers to entry for other firms. This has important implications for the competitiveness of the global audit market and for the regulation of audit providers. Global firm networks are found to have increased their concentration in the global audit market to levels which generally concern regulators, particularly if there were to be any future reduction in the current number of large audit providers whether by merger or collapse. The market share of the four largest firms based on audit fees of publicly listed companies in many countries is over 80 per cent, suggesting a highly concentrated market (Carson, 2009).

However, some of the benefits from a network structure are eroded when global audit network firms fail to maintain consistent quality control across the network, which has been implicated in recent corporate collapses such as Parmalat in Italy, Ahold in the Netherlands and Satyam in India. This has fuelled concerns by regulators as to the consistency of quality of audit services provided in multiple locations by networked audit firms, for example Goelzer of the PCAOB said in 2011: 'We know from our inspections that firm quality varies from country to country, even when the firms in question have the same name and are part of the same global network' (PCAOB, 2011b).

Regulators in national financial markets have responded to shareholder demands for greater regulation and accountability by corporations by imposing higher standards of transparency on global audit firms. Outside the United States, the European Commission (EC) also had concerns that there may have been a discrepancy between the image of global firm networks and the real level of control exercised over individual member firms (EC, 2003). The European Union (EU) also has noted the risk of an expectation gap arising from the belief that a brand name implies a universally high level of audit quality for all audits undertaken by that brand throughout the world. As a result of these concerns the EU initiated requirements for audit firm networks to be more transparent about individual member firms, their networks and their relationship to the network, requiring disclosure of information about internal quality assurance systems designed to ensure an equivalent audit quality across the member firms. Specifically, 'the Commission views transparency as a natural requirement for audit firms which fundamentally operate to ensure the transparent financial reporting by companies' (EC, 2003: 13). Accordingly, the EU requires that global firm networks provide assurance that quality control policies and procedures are complied with throughout the network. These may include periodic inter-firm reviews, tests of operating policies and procedures and review of workpapers of selected audits. Other controls may include common policies on recruitment, training, advancement, audit methodology and audit independence.

Multinational audit clients

The benefits of purchasing audit services from global firm networks are most apparent for multinational companies that require delivery of audit services on a multi-country basis.

Motivation for purchasing global audit services from a single networked provider, rather than multiple providers, arises from an efficiency perspective. It is costly to contract with multiple providers in different countries that are using different methodologies and different standards. By purchasing from one network provider, the multinational client outsources the coordination of the audit to one firm in the network that will then set deadlines and work programmes for the other audit firms. Network theory would suggest that an audit firm would utilise and coordinate with other firms in their own network to aid in the completion of the multi-country audit rather than using firms outside the network, as it is more efficient to use firms with similar quality and implementation standards (Lenz and James, 2007). However, overseas subsidiaries may appoint their own auditors who are not members of the network of the parent company auditor. Given the tight deadlines for completion of multi-country audits, the network firm is likely to be more efficient and consistent relative to an unknown firm. Multi-country audits necessitate the provision of higher quality audit expertise. These audits often are extremely complex, involving multiple sets of national accounting and taxation regulations. Barrett *et al.* (2005) provide a perspective on this issue using a field study of a multinational audit which provides an example of a research methodology that could be employed in examining these issues.

Currently 20 per cent of the companies listed on the New York Stock Exchange (NYSE) are foreign, as are 50 of the 100 largest companies listed on the NYSE. To date, there has been little research into the purchase of audit services by multinational clients. While the national-level and to some extent, city-level offices have been the subject of much research, there are relatively few examples of research examining the global audit market, regulation of auditing globally or the global networks themselves. This is despite concerns expressed by regulators (for example, UK House of Lords, 2011) and market participants about the market power of global firm networks, the consistency of audit quality provided by these networks and the transparency of their network structures. The current research in this area is discussed in the following section.

Research findings regarding global audit markets

Changes in the number of suppliers from Big 8 to Big 4 would have an impact on any analysis of the global audit market, however, most research examining changes in the capacity of the audit market is focused at a national level. Despite the importance of the non-Big 4 global networks there is little research investigating these smaller audit firm networks. In relation to audit fees, there have been few attempts to model these on a global basis or to compare fees across a limited range of countries (see Hay *et al.*, 2006 for a summary of country coverage of audit fee studies). The finding of higher fees being paid to large auditors is a relatively consistent one at a national level (Hay *et al.,* 2006 in their meta-analysis of audit fee studies find consistent evidence of a fee premium for large firms). With respect to fee premiums for specialists, Carson (2009) using large samples from 62 countries in 2000 and 2004 finds that in both periods, audit fee premiums are consistently associated with global specialist auditors, irrespective of whether those audit firms are or are not national specialists. Verleyen and De Beelde (2011) provide further evidence of network industry specialisation within a broad group of European countries.

Research examining global audit firms focuses on the structure of these organisations. Prior research associates larger audit firms with higher audit quality as they have greater investments in brand names, their reputation and their professional staff (DeAngelo, 1981). Higher quality auditors are considered more likely to detect questionable accounting practices and report material errors as they have the expertise, resources and incentives to enhance the credibility and informativeness of financial information. A major mechanism by which audit firms have acted to ensure competence (and accordingly, audit quality) in a globalised environment is by the formation of global firm networks, with its resultant network-level quality controls including standardisation of delivery of audit services and extensive office and engagement level quality control processes.

Few studies have been undertaken regarding the quality of global audits or comparing audit quality by audit firm networks across countries (Francis, 2011). Francis and Wang (2008) find that Big 4 audit firms are associated with higher quality audits in countries where legal systems are strong, but do not find any difference between types of audit firms in countries with less strict legal regimes. Michas (2011) compares the extent of development of the audit profession across countries and finds more conservative accounting is associated with better developed auditing professions but only when audits are conducted by Big 4 auditors. Within countries there is a large literature where most of these studies confirm the expectation that hiring a large audit firm is associated with higher audit quality. Various proxies and constructs have been used to represent this higher audit quality attributed to large audit firm networks. Examples of such proxies of higher audit quality include higher audit fees and lower discretionary accruals.

Regulation of globalized auditing

In the context of increasing globalization of business in general, and the audit market in particular, the global regulators of the audit profession have become increasingly active and important. In particular, the International Federation of Accountants (IFAC) and its related board, the International Auditing and Assurance Standards Board (IAASB) have responsibility for the development of a high quality global audit profession. The role of the IAASB is to develop internationally consistent auditing standards by a board that asserts to represent the public interest. As discussed by Humphrey, Loft and Samsonova-Taddei in Chapter 13 of this volume, the role of IFAC is to provide guidance and funding to support the IAASB, including the development of a Code of Ethics for professional accountants. IFAC is overseen by a Public Interest Oversight Board, members of which include International Organization of Securities Commissions (IOSCO), the World Bank, the Financial Stability Board and representatives of international banking, financial and insurance regulators. Of particular importance to both IFAC and the IAASB are the global firm networks that hold the main responsibility for implementation of the standards developed as well as the moral guidance and leadership of the audit profession, especially in countries where the quality of audit practice has been regarded as sub-optimal.

The concern commonly expressed by regulators and users of financial statements is whether high quality auditing can be achieved at a consistent level globally. Regulators recognize that the global firm networks are of critical importance in developing confidence in the integrity of financial statements throughout the world. The global audit firm networks have organized themselves through the Forum of Firms and Transnational Auditors Committee of IFAC as well as through the Global Policy Symposium as a means of jointly influencing regulators at the international and national levels. At the same time, the membership bodies of the accounting profession have themselves become more globally focused. Greater reciprocal recognition of qualifications gained in other countries is happening between professional bodies as part of groups such as the Global Accounting Alliance (GAA) which represents 11 leading professional accounting institutes with over 785,000 members, including the American Institute of Certified Public Accountants, the Institute of Chartered Accountants in England and Wales and Canadian Institute of Chartered Accountants, as well as Japan, Hong Kong, Germany, South Africa,

Australia and New Zealand. Global accounting bodies such as Chartered Institute of Management Accountants and Association of Chartered Certified Accountants have seen increased membership numbers with qualification programmes being offered in multiple countries. Currently the Institute of Chartered Accountants in Australia is merging with the New Zealand Institute of Chartered Accountants to create a larger organisation and further mergers of professional bodies particularly at the regional level seem likely to occur.

Currently the US Securities Exchange Commission (SEC) has not endorsed International Standards on Auditing (ISAs) for use in the audit of companies listed in the United States, as standards for auditing are set by the PCAOB (which has observer status at the IAASB). The PCAOB was set up under the Sarbanes-Oxley Act, as a legislative response to concerns regarding the quality of audits as a result of the collapse of Arthur Andersen associated with Enron's demise. In a global economy, national regulation can also have an impact on the global audit market. For example, the Sarbanes-Oxley Act has extraterritorial implications for audit firms and clients outside the United States requiring registration and inspection of audit firms located outside the United States by the PCAOB. This impact is particularly evident in relation to audit firms' abilities to offer specific services to subsidiaries of US listed multinationals operating in other countries and for auditors of other firms with cross-listings on US stock exchanges.

While global firm networks are an important mechanism in maintaining audit quality throughout the world, they demonstrate a regulatory concern in that the structure of regulation of the audit profession is at a national level, and there is no effective regulation or enforcement at a global level. The current system of regulation and enforcement of audit firm networks, which predominately occurs at a national level, is likely to be inadequate when audit firm networks and their clients span multiple jurisdictions. Accordingly, cross-border issues may essentially be unregulated. As a result, the IAASB, as a standard setting body without enforcement powers, runs the risk of being ineffective in the current environment. While standards for auditing practice are set at the international level (by the IAASB), they are adopted at a national level and accordingly enforcement is conducted entirely at this level. It has been difficult for regulators to enforce standards in a similarly integrated fashion across countries, however the formation of the International Forum of Independent Audit Regulators (IFIAR) is one step towards exchange of information between regulators across countries. One area where national regulators are connected but yet have taken different paths is in inspections of registered public audit firms and in particular the nature of disclosure regarding the results of the inspections. The PCAOB has the ability to conduct inspections of over 900 non-US audit firms involved in the conduct of audits of firms listed on US stock exchanges in 85 countries where local regulations permit them to do so. In some cases, inspections are conducted jointly with local regulators. Chairman Doty of the PCAOB (2011a) highlighted a key difficulty that the

> ... PCAOB is unable to inspect audits of firms that have registered with the PCAOB in order to be able to conduct or participate in audits of U.S. public companies but that are located in certain jurisdictions that have resisted inspections. This means enormous components of the audits of multi-national companies escape review, even when the firm that signed the audit report is a large U.S. accounting firm.

The jurisdictions referred to are China and parts of Europe. While in May 2013 a memorandum of understanding was signed with Chinese authorities, to date, the PCAOB has yet to gain access to working papers located in China to conduct audit firm inspections.

When foreign companies list in the US they earn a cross-listing premium for subjecting themselves to US institutions and US compliance activities which better protect minority investors. Bonding to a stricter investor protection regime rewards companies located in markets with less strict investor protection regimes, including lower costs of capital (Doidge *et al.*, 2009). Part of these heightened regulatory requirements includes the role played by the PCAOB in relation to inspections of foreign audit firms that issue audit opinions or provide substantial audit services to US listed companies. There are currently 900 non-US audit firms located in 84 countries registered with the PCAOB (as at December 2012). While there are several studies that have examined national inspection reports for audit firms in the U.S., there is now research emerging regarding PCAOB inspection reports of non-US audit firms. Bishop *et al.* (2012), using 175 first-time and 56 second-time inspection reports as at 4 February 2012, find that Big 4 affiliates are less likely to have deficiencies than non-Big 4 firms. They also find that the inspection deficiencies are not impacted by whether the PCAOB acts alone or cooperates with a local regulator in conducting the inspection, or whether or not these are based on the home country's legal tradition (common law versus other). Carcello *et al.* (2011) highlight the importance that investors place on PCAOB inspections of international audit firms. Their finding is based on identification of negative stock price reactions to international audit firms registered with the PCAOB which were not inspected due to prohibition by their respective countries. As noted by Loft *et al.* (2006) and Humphrey *et al.* (2009), there is a need for research into the international governance structures that underpin globalised auditing, in particular IFAC and its audit standard setter the IAASB and committees such as the Forum of Firms, in light of the changes occurring in governance structures at IFAC.

Challenges in researching globalization of auditing

Until recently, high quality databases containing accounting and auditing information at a global level were not available. Accordingly, prior studies of the global audit market suffer from a lack of data, especially in relation to audit fees paid by individual clients or relatively small sample sizes, often based on surveys or voluntary disclosures. While in the late 1990s and early 2000s there was a greater availability of quality data available to researchers from global data providers, most recently researchers have noted the deficiencies in previously high quality databases which, until resolved, are likely to inhibit future large sample research using auditor identity (Francis *et al.*, 2013). Metrics used to compare institutional factors across countries (for example, La Porta *et al.*, 1998 and Wingate, 1997) are now outmoded and to be useful to researchers require updating. In terms of data regarding the audit firm networks themselves, the availability and content of audit firm inspection reports varies between jurisdictions. As the audit firm networks are not listed companies, publicly available information regarding the individual member firms of networks and of the network in total is still fairly limited despite the emerging availability of information presented in transparency reports as mandated in some jurisdictions. Using a range of methodological approaches there are many opportunities for research (Maijoor and Vanstraelen, 2012).

Conclusions and recommendations

Globalization is a significant factor in any understanding of audit firms, markets and clients shaping regulation and enforcement of regulation. Future research could address the internal operations of these global firm networks, including transfer pricing, to better understand the differences between networks. Like their global clients, there is little global regulatory oversight of the activities of global firm networks despite the existence of the IAASB. These issues are of greatest concern in countries where legal enforcement of quality financial reporting practices is weak (Choi and Wong, 2007). A key way in which to improve regulation of audit firms is to increase the transparency of disclosure of membership of global firm networks. In many cases, it is difficult to assess dates and the extent to which national firms are members of a particular global firm network and the nature of the relationship (e.g. full membership, an affiliate or correspondent relationship) from firms' websites. Clearly defining the boundaries of the network and providing information on the quality control practices maintained across the network are important for both network members and users of financial statements audited by global firm networks.

Regulatory intervention by the EC (a regional regulator) is likely to be more successful than the currently unenforceable global regulatory requirements and could represent a ready-made *de facto* standard for national standard setters. In addition, IOSCO and individual national security regulators coordinated through organizations such as IFIAR could play a greater role in improving transparency by requiring additional disclosures by audit firm networks under stock exchange listing rules. The current PCAOB proposals regarding transparency around who is conducting the audit, the partner responsible and other firms involved in conducting parts of the audit, as well as extending audit firm inspections into jurisdictions such as China and parts of Europe, are also positive steps towards providing investors with information which will assist in assessing the quality of the audit and will also aid researchers investigating these issues.

References

Barrett, M., Cooper, D. and Jamal, K. 2005. 'Globalization and the Coordinating of Work in Multinational Audits', *Accounting Organizations and Society* 30(1): 1–24.

Bell, T., Peecher, M. and Solomon, I. 2005. *The 21st Century Public-Company Audit: Conceptual Elements of KPMG's Global Audit Methodology*. Montvale, NJ: KPMG.

Bishop, C.C., Hermanson, D.R. and Houston, R.W. 2012. 'PCAOB Inspections of International Audit Firms: Initial Evidence', *International Journal of Auditing* 17(1): 1–18.

Carcello, J., Carver, B. and Neal, T. 2011. 'Market Reaction to the PCAOB's Inability to Conduct Foreign Inspections', SSRN. Available at http://ssrn.com/abstract=1911388 (accessed 19 July 2013).

Carson, E. 2009. 'Industry Specialization by Global Audit Firm Networks', *The Accounting Review* 84(2): 355–82.

Carson, E., Simnett, R., Soo, B.S. and Wright, A.M. 2012. 'Changes in Audit Market Competition and the Big N Premium', *Auditing: A Journal of Practice & Theory* 31(3): 47–73.

Choi, J.H. and Wong, T.J. 2007. 'Auditors' Governance Functions and Legal Environments: An International Investigation', *Contemporary Accounting Research* 24(1): 13–46.

DeAngelo, L.E. 1981. 'Auditor Size and Audit Quality', *Journal of Accounting and Economics* 3(3): 183–99.

Deumes, R., Schelleman, C., Vander Bauwhede, H. and Vanstraelen, A. 2012. 'Audit Firm Governance: Do Transparency Reports Reveal Audit Quality?', *Auditing: A Journal of Theory and Practice* 31(4): 193–214.

Doidge, C., Karolyi, G.A. and Stulz, R.M. 2009. 'Has New York Become less Competitive than London in Global Markets: Evaluating Foreign Listing Choices over Time', *Journal of Financial Economics* 92: 253–77.

European Commission (EC). 2003. *Communication from the Commission to the Council and the European Parliament: Reinforcing the Statutory Audit in the EU*. Luxembourg: Office for Official Publications of the European Communities.

European Commission (EC). 2010. *Audit Policy: Lessons from the Crisis*. Available online at http://europa.eu/rapid/pressReleasesAction.do?reference=IP/10/1325&format=HTML&aged=0&language=EN&guiLanguage=en (accessed 19 July 2013).

Francis, J.R. 2011. 'Auditing without Borders', *Accounting, Organizations and Society* 36(4–5): 318–23.

Francis, J.R. and Wang, D. 2008. 'The Joint Effect of Investor Protection and Big 4 Audits on Earnings Quality around the World', *Contemporary Accounting Research* 25(1): 157–91.

Francis, J.R., Michas, P.N. and Seavey, S. 2013. 'Does Audit Market Concentration Harm the Quality of Audited Earnings? Evidence from Audit Markets in 42 Countries', *Contemporary Accounting Research* 30(1): 325–55.

General Accounting Office (GAO). 2003. *Public Accounting Firms: Mandated study on consolidation and competition*. GAO-03-864. Washington, DC: General Accounting Office.

Hay, D.C., Knechel, W.R. and Wong, N. 2006. 'Audit Fees: A Meta-analysis of the Effect of Supply and Demand Attributes', *Contemporary Accounting Research* 23(1): 141–91.

House of Lords Economic Affairs Committee. 2011. *Auditors: Market Concentration and their Role*. Available online at www.parliament.uk/business/committees/committees-a-z/lords-select/economic-affairs-committee/publications/ (accessed 19 July 2013).

Humphrey, C., Loft, A. and Woods, M. 2009. 'The Global Audit Profession and the International Financial Architecture: Understanding regulatory relationships at a time of financial crisis', *Accounting, Organizations and Society* 34(6–7): 810–25.

Jenner and Block. 2010. *Lehman Brothers Holdings Inc.* 'Chapter 11 Proceedings Examiner Report'. Available online at http://jenner.com/lehman/ (accessed 19 July 2013).

LaPorta, R., Lopez-de-Silanes, F., Shleifer, A. and Vishny, R. 1998. 'Law and Finance', *Journal of Political Economy* 106(6): 1113–55.

Lenz, H. and James, M. 2007. 'International Audit Firms as Strategic Networks – The Evolution of Global Professional Service Firms', *Economics and Management of Networks*: 367–92.

Loft, A., Humphrey, C. and Turley, S. 2006. 'In Pursuit of Global Regulation: Changing Governance and Accountability Structures at the International Federation of Accountants (IFAC)', *Accounting, Auditing & Accountability Journal* 19(3): 428–51.

Maijoor, S. and Vanstraelen, A. 2012. 'Research Opportunities in Auditing in the EU Revisited', *Auditing: A Journal of Practice and Theory* 31(1): 115–26.

Michas, P.N. 2011. 'The Importance of Audit Profession Development in Emerging Market Countries', *The Accounting Review* 86(5): 1731–64.

Public Company Accounting Oversight Board (PCAOB). 2011a. *PCAOB Investor Advisory Group Meeting – Opening remarks by James Doty*. Washington, DC: PCAOB. Available online at http://pcaobus.org/News/Speech/Pages/03162011_DotyOpeningRemarks.aspx (accessed 29 November 2012).

Public Company Accounting Oversight Board (PCAOB) 2011b. 'Association of Audit Committee Members Annual Meeting', speech by Daniel L. Goelzer. Washington, DC: PCAOB. Available online at http://pcaobus.org/News/Speech/Pages/10042011_GoelzerAACMMeeting.aspx (accessed 19 July 2013).

Sullivan, M.W. 2002. 'The Effect of the Big Eight Accounting Firm Mergers on the Market for Audit Services', *Journal of Law and Economics* 45(2): 375–99.

Verleyen, I., and De Beelde, I. 2011. 'International Consistency of Auditor Specialization', *International Journal of Auditing* 15(3): 275–87.

Wingate, M. (1997) 'An Examination of Cultural Influence in Audit Environments', *Research in Accounting Regulation* 11(Supplement 1): 129–48.

4

The market for audit services

Dan A. Simunic

Overview

The study of the economic incentives and relations surrounding the independent audit of client financial statements emerged as a topic for academic research about 40 years ago (see Simunic and Stein, 1995). Prior to the mid-1970s, auditing was viewed as a purely practical activity, governed by technical rules largely set by the profession itself. But of course, auditing is a professional *business* practised by public accounting firms in the wider economy. As such, auditors (audit firms) are subject to economic incentives and the discipline of the markets in which they operate. Moreover, the incentives facing auditors are unusually complex. An independent audit largely benefits both existing and potential shareholders and creditors who do not contract directly with the auditor. Rather, an auditor usually transacts with a legal entity (the company) and interacts extensively with the entity's management whose assertions in the financial statements are being verified. The terms of the transaction between the auditor and the client – that is, the price, quantity, quality and other features of the service performed – are obviously important, and will be influenced by the market in which the audit firm operates.

Research in the economics of audit markets has both theoretical and empirical streams. Much of the theoretical work is concerned with the microeconomics of the demand for audit services. For example, the theory of agency relationships has been extensively used to analyze the demand for verified reports of a firm's economic performance prepared by management, whose productive actions are unobservable. Other theoretical work has modelled how audit firms may interact strategically when the market is less than perfectly competitive. The empirical research, on the other hand, has tended to focus more on the supply side or production of audit services, particularly the characteristics of market transactions between auditors and their clients. In this chapter, I discuss some of the principal issues and important research findings in this large and quite complex research area.

Competition among audit firms

Major stimuli for academic research into auditing markets were the several investigations undertaken in the 1970s by government agencies, particularly in the United States, into the competitiveness of markets for various professional services, including public accounting. Certain provisions in professional codes of ethics which were commonplace at the time – such as restrictions on fee bidding, advertising, and direct solicitation of clients – were seen by regulators as hindering competition and therefore harmful to consumers. Pressures from US regulatory bodies, including the Antitrust Division of the US Department of Justice and the US Federal Trade Commission, eventually caused the American Institute of Certified Public Accountants to eliminate virtually all such economic restrictions from its ethical code. The professional accounting bodies in other countries generally followed suit.

At the same time, regulators noted that the market for audit services was (and is) quite highly concentrated. That is, a few major public accounting firms dominate the market in virtually all (particularly the economically developed) countries, and the number of dominant firms has been decreasing over time. This observed concentration led the staff of the US Senate's Subcommittee on Reports, Accounting and Management (1977: 46) to conclude that:

> The information … clearly shows an excessively high concentration of auditing influence among the Big Eight firms. The degree of concentration in providing independent auditing services to major corporations is so great that it constitutes evidence of a serious lack of competition.

In making this allegation, the Senate staff embraced the *structure-conduct-performance* paradigm of research in industrial organization. That is, if an industry's structure (few suppliers) makes collusion possible, then it is reasonable to assume that collusion among suppliers, and its negative consequences for consumers, will actually occur.

When studying the organization of an industry, economists classify markets into the three categories: (1) perfect competition (competitive markets); (2) monopolistic competition; and (3) monopoly/oligopoly. The latter two market structures are often termed imperfectly competitive markets. Competitive markets are characterized by large numbers of individual suppliers (auditors) and consumers (clients) who transact impersonally. Each market participant is a price-taker in the sense that each believes that his or her individual supply or demand for that good will not affect the market price. Competitive markets in equilibrium have several desirable properties: (1) they efficiently allocate resources; (2) the market outcomes are Pareto optimal – the economic property that no participant in an economy can be made better off without making another participant worse off; and (3) the market provides suppliers with a normal return on their investment.

In contrast, an imperfectly competitive market is characterized by the existence of a market participant who singly (a monopolist), or with the cooperation of others (oligopolists), possesses the ability to affect the price at which transactions occur. Collusion among oligopolists in order to affect price can be either explicit (for example when OPEC ministers get together to set oil production quotas) or tacit (for example the restrictions on competitive bidding formerly found in accountants' codes of ethics). If a supplier or group of suppliers (a cartel) possesses this ability to affect prices, then transactions under such imperfect competition will be less numerous and priced higher than under competition, will lack Pareto optimality, and will result in above normal returns on investment to the seller. All of these effects transfer wealth from consumers (clients) to producers (auditors). More importantly, an artificially high price for audit services will motivate client companies to under-invest in auditing, either by curtailing the voluntary demand for audits by privately owned companies or by decreasing the demand for costly audit quality by listed companies which are required by law to purchase an audit. In both situations, the quality of client financial reporting can be expected to decline.

The allegation that the Big 8 firms in the US priced their services as a cartel in the 1970s was investigated (Simunic, 1980). I observed that while the Big 8 audited about 90 per cent of US publicly held companies whose sales exceeded US$100 million in 1976, these dominant firms only audited about 65 per cent of smaller companies. Thus I assumed that the market segment for small audits was competitive (because of the large number of non-Big 8 suppliers) and tested the hypothesis that the Big 8 colluded to increase the price (per unit) of large company audits. To perform the test, I surveyed a stratified random sample of US companies and obtained data on audit fees paid and a variety of other client characteristics from 397 companies, about evenly divided between large and small firms. Of course, a direct comparison of audit fees paid by different sized clients with different characteristics is not meaningful. To extract the effect of auditor behaviour on the market price, I developed an empirical model in which audit fees are a nonlinear function of client size and complexity, riskiness of client operations, and the identity of the auditor. I found no evidence of monopoly pricing by the Big 8. In fact, there was some (weak) evidence that Big 8 firms enjoyed economies of scale which were passed through in the form of lower prices to all of their audit clients, irrespective of size. Subsequent research on this issue using data from many different countries (see Hay *et al.*, 2006) has also failed to find evidence of cartel pricing.

Product differentiation among audit firms

There is a type of market structure, monopolistic competition, which has interesting potential implications for auditor behaviour as well as how we think about the audit service itself. Monopolistic competition can occur if products are quality differentiated; that is, vary along some dimension of value to clients. For example, audits may differ in the audit risk (assurance level) which financial statement users attach to an audit report, depending upon which audit firm performs the work. Or audit firms may be perceived as providing differing amounts of 'insurance' (differing 'depth of pockets') in the event a business fails and a substandard audit has been performed.

Quality differentiation in auditing is a controversial subject. Many auditors and their professional associations argue that 'an audit is an audit is an audit'. Proponents of this view argue that generally accepted accounting principles (GAAP) and generally accepted auditing standards (GAAS) are invariant with respect to the individual or firm performing the audit, and since all auditors are professionally certified, all audits must have the same expected quality.

However there are counter-arguments. For example, the 'one size fits all' notion is not so reasonable when the audit is viewed from the client's perspective. Clients vary in their characteristics (e.g. financial leverage, nature of ownership) and therefore, perhaps, the level of audit assurance they require and are willing to purchase. Moreover, auditors have an economic incentive to differentiate themselves from their peers. Product differentiation creates the possibility of earning above normal returns from a market niche where competition is less than perfect. The desire of businesses to differentiate themselves and their products from those of their competitors in order to create less competitive and more profitable market niches is often argued to be one of the main functions of advertising and seems to be pervasive in the business world.

The possibility of quality differentiation complicates the conclusions drawn from the existence of imperfectly competitive markets. Imperfectly competitive markets are inefficient, not Pareto optimal, and result in consumers paying higher prices than they would in competitive markets. With differentiated products, consumers willingly pay higher prices because they obtain more preferred products, and producers may earn abnormal returns, if market demand in a particular niche is not sufficiently large to attract a large number of suppliers. Therefore, monopolistic competition may not warrant government intervention since both consumers and suppliers may be better off (a Pareto improvement) with imperfect competition and a differentiated product than with perfect competition and a uniform product.

My 1980 study provided the first bit of evidence that audit quality was not uniform across audit firms. I found that prices paid by clients of the firm of Price Waterhouse (PW) were significantly higher than those paid to the other Big 8 firms, across the entire market – that is, irrespective of client size. This was consistent with an article appearing in *Fortune* magazine about that time (Bernstein, 1978) which described PW as 'the premier accounting firm'. However, subsequent research using different samples and methods for different time periods in different countries has not confirmed this 'PW effect' nor demonstrated that audit quality is otherwise significantly differentiated *within* the set of Big (8, 6, 5 or 4 and hereafter simply Big) international audit firms.

Rather, most research in this area has hypothesized that the Big accounting firms deliver a higher average level of audit assurance than the non-Big audit firms, and then tested for various economic effects that would follow if this hypothesis were true. This research falls into four categories: tests for differentially higher audit prices for the Big firms; tests of stock market price reactions to auditor changes and audited financial statements; examination of the determinants of auditor choice; and studies of the relative incidence of litigation across public accounting firms.

Audit pricing studies

The general approach developed by Simunic has been refined by subsequent researchers and used to test for evidence of higher prices (per unit) paid to Big audit firms. The basic argument is that if smaller companies, which can potentially be served efficiently by both large and small public accounting firms, are voluntarily willing to pay a higher price for an audit by a Big firm, then this constitutes evidence of a quality differentiated service from the Big firm(s). Much of the research is summarized in the meta-analysis conducted by Hay *et al.* (2006), who find that there is overwhelming support for the hypothesis that the Big firms charge differentially higher (unit) prices.

Studies of stock market price reactions

The pricing evidence indicates that clients of Big firms voluntarily purchase something different – for which they pay a higher price. However, researchers further hypothesize that Big firms deliver a higher average level of audit quality than non-Big firms, where audit quality is the assurance level (1 – audit risk) associated with a particular audit firm's attestation. The basic argument is that compliance with GAAS defines a minimum acceptable level of assurance, while specific audit firms are free to develop a reputation for delivering assurance above the GAAS floor. Thus, one can think of the non-Big firms as delivering a GAAS audit, while the Big firms, on average, deliver a 'better than GAAS' audit.

If this hypothesis is correct, and the incremental cost of a Big firm audit is not too high, then the stock market should react positively (negatively) when a publicly held company switches to (from) a Big firm. The first test for this effect was performed by Nichols and Smith (1983) using a sample of auditor changes in the 1970s among US companies listed on the New York or American stock exchanges. They found that while Big firm to non-Big firm changes elicited a negative market reaction around the announcement date, and non-Big to Big firm changes elicited a positive market reaction, the net difference was not statistically significant. Using a larger sample of US auditor change data from the early 1980s, Johnson and Lys (1990) reported similar results – no significant market reaction when the auditor change is formally announced through the filing of a form 8-K with the US Securities & Exchange Commission. However, in that study, clients that shifted to larger (smaller) audit firms exhibited significant share price increases (declines) over the 60-day trading period before the auditor change was publicly announced. This suggests that the auditor change itself may be motivated by and predictable from underlying changes in client characteristics.

A different type of market reaction test to Big vs non-Big firm audits was performed by Teoh and Wong (1993). If client earnings audited by a Big firm are viewed by the market as being more believable (credible) than earnings verified by a non-Big audit firm, then the magnitude of the stock market price reaction to an earnings 'surprise' (unexpected earnings) should be greater if a Big audit firm is involved. This is true because market participants should be motivated to discount (ignore) unusually high or low earnings which are seen as having a greater likelihood of being materially misstated. In the study, the authors compared market reactions for a large sample of earnings announcements by US companies in the 1980s, where each company using a Big auditor was matched with a company in the same industry using a non-Big auditor. In addition, the market reaction to the earnings announcements of a sample of companies switching auditors from a Big to non-Big firm and *vice versa* in the 1980s was also analysed. The same results were obtained from the two independent tests: the magnitude of market price response to unexpected earnings (the earnings response coefficient) was significantly greater for Big firm clients, than for the clients of non-Big firms. In short, the clients of Big firms get more 'stock market bang for their reported earnings buck' than do non-Big clients.

Determinants of auditor choice

Obviously, not every company is motivated to purchase, at a higher price, the quality differentiated service supplied by Big firm auditors. Smaller public accounting firms are viable competitors in the auditing market. Thus the identification of specific client characteristics that motivate the purchase of audit services from a Big firm is an interesting research issue.

One of the first studies of this type was performed by Simunic and Stein (1987), who examined the determinants of auditor choice for a sample of 397 US companies which made initial public offerings (IPOs) of common shares in 1981. The economic theory of agency predicts that potential agency costs – arising from the difference between actions of the agent which maximize the welfare of the agent vs actions that would maximize the welfare of the principal – are greatest when management owns a small proportion of shares in the company and/or when financial leverage is high. In the first case, management is not highly motivated to maximize the value of the firm, while in the second case management is motivated to take actions which are not in the best interests of creditors. Both situations increase the value of the higher quality of auditing (i.e. an audit by one of the Big firms) to monitor managements' behaviour. The purpose of the study was to test these agency hypotheses, along with other plausible determinants of auditor choice, such as the nature of the IPO contract ('best efforts' vs 'firm commitment'), and the size and other operating characteristics of the client.

One interesting finding was that non-Big auditors were extensively involved with the 1981 IPOs – about half the companies in the sample used a non-Big audit firm. Not surprisingly, the companies using Big firms tended to be larger, more complex, and have a greater geographic dispersion of operations. However, contrary to the predictions of agency theory, the percentage shares held by management had no effect on auditor choice, while the degree of financial leverage had a significant effect *opposite* to that predicted – higher leverage decreased the likelihood of using a Big firm as the auditor. Given this unexpected result with respect to leverage, which is often used as a measure of the risk of bankruptcy, we extended the study by analysing the detail disclosures included in the offering prospectus to obtain a measure of the degree of each issuer's cash flow risk. We found that the operating riskiness of the client was a major determinant of auditor choice, as the companies using non-Big auditors tended to be smaller, more risky and more simple enterprises whose security offerings were usually made on a 'best efforts' basis by underwriters with lower quality reputations. Further, we conjectured that higher cash flow risk probably significantly increased the potential supply price which would be charged by a Big firm with 'deep pockets'. These firms would have the most to lose in any subsequent litigation that occurred if a new issuer suffered a severe decline in stock-market value or went bankrupt. Thus a Big firm audit would tend to be prohibitively expensive for very risky issuers.

The conjecture that a company's cash flow risk has a major impact on the supply price of audits by Big firms was later tested by Clarkson and Simunic (1994). They contrasted auditor choices in an IPO context in the US vs Canada. The authors argued that the supply side effect of issuer risk would be stronger in the very litigious US environment than in Canada. Comparing the 1981 US IPOs analysed by Simunic and Stein with a sample of 174 Canadian IPOs that began trading on the Toronto Stock Exchange in the years 1984–7, the authors found that high client cash flow risk had the opposite effect in Canada to that of the US. That is, while the Big firms serviced few high risk US IPO clients, a high risk Canadian company involved in an IPO was much more likely to use a Big rather than a non-Big audit firm. This result was consistent across a variety of plausible measures of cash flow risk. This difference is consistent with client cash flow risk having a relatively small effect on the supply price of Canadian audits, presumably because of the relatively benign legal environment in that country relative to the US.

Finally, an interesting study by Francis and Wilson (1988) continued the research on auditor choice by examining client characteristics and changes in characteristics associated with companies' decisions to change auditors. They examined 129 US publicly held companies that changed to a different size audit firm in the early 1980s and found that the likelihood of changing to a larger audit firm increased when companies adopted new incentive compensation plans (based on reported income) for management, and when companies experienced significant growth in the size of their operations. However, the overall explanatory power of the authors' model was quite low, and I think it is fair to say that the factors motivating companies to change their auditors are still not well understood.

Auditor litigation studies

If the average level of assurance provided by a Big audit is higher than the assurance provided by non-Big firms, then the incidence of successful lawsuits against Big auditors should be relatively lower, other things remaining constant. If the Big firms' target level of assurance is higher than that implicitly required by GAAS, then the Big firms should experience lower rates of audit failure (i.e. failure to detect material misstatements in financial statements) and be less likely to be found in violation of GAAS by a court, in the event of subsequent lawsuit.

The first, and in some ways still the best, evidence consistent with this prediction was developed by Palmrose (1988). She studied 472 legal cases filed against US audit firms during the period 1960–85, and found that 3 per cent of the publicly held clients of Big firms were involved in litigation, while 5.1 per cent of the publicly held clients of non-Big firms were involved in auditor lawsuits. Note that if all cases of audit failure lead to subsequent litigation, then Big auditors provide, on average, about a 97 per cent level of assurance, while non-Big 6 auditors provide about 95 per cent assurance. Interestingly, the audit manual of at least one of the Big firms mandates 97 per cent as the target assurance level for all of that firm's audit engagements.

Litigation risk and the market for audits

Beginning with Simunic (1980), auditor litigation risk has been considered to play a very important role in understanding the market for audits. Auditors are viewed as facing a two-part cost function when performing an audit engagement. As an audit firm does more work (expends more 'effort') the out-of-pocket and opportunity costs of audit resources utilized increase, while the expected losses (penalties) from a failure to detect and/or truthfully report material misstatements in the client's financial statements decrease. The basic trade-off between auditor effort costs and the possible penalties from litigation associated with audit failure is a powerful idea that can be used to analyse numerous problems, including audit service production, audit quality, and auditor responses to and the setting of auditing standards (Dye, 1993; Willekens *et al.*, 1996; Ye and Simunic, 2013).

The empirical studies by Clarkson and Simunic, Palmrose, and many others highlight the importance of litigation risk in understanding the real-world behaviour of auditors and the structure of the market for audit services. It is usual to characterize the Big firms as having differentially higher wealth levels at risk when they perform audits, relative to the more limited wealth of non-Big firms. Thus the loss function of a Big audit firm will differ from the loss function of a non-Big firm for a given audit engagement.

Combining the assumption of different wealth levels of Big vs non-Big firms with differences in litigation risk across countries motivated the study by Choi *et al.* (2008). The authors first developed an analytical model in which national legal environments play a crucial role in determining auditor effort and audit fees. The model predicts that (a) audit fees for Big and non-Big audit firms increase monotonically with the strength of a country's legal liability regime; (b) given a legal regime, Big firms exert more effort and charge higher audit fees than non-Big firms; and (c) the Big firm fee (and effort) premium is lower in countries with strong legal regimes than in countries with weaker legal regimes. Using a large sample of audit clients from 15 countries with different legal regimes where audit fees are publicly disclosed, along with a more limited sample of audit hours data from four countries, the authors' test results are consistent with each of these predictions. Among other things, this study demonstrates that audit quality is very much a local phenomenon. Even though the dominant Big firms operate 'around the world', their audit quality levels are essentially country-specific.

Impact of fixed investments on the audit services market

In the absence of any evidence of cartel pricing by the Big firms, it is usual to assume that the market for audits is therefore competitive. While there is much evidence of product differentiation *between* the Big and non-Big audit firms, there is, to my knowledge, no empirical evidence of systematic product differentiation *within* these categories. Thus, it is usual to assume that perfect competition prevails among the Big firms as well as among the non-Big firms. Furthermore, in the two-part auditor cost function discussed at the beginning of the earlier section titled 'Litigation risk and the market for audits', it is also reasonable to assume that all costs are essentially variable, since performing the audit is a very labour intensive activity. Finally, the difference in behaviour between the Big and non-Big firms can be explained by differences in their exogenously determined wealth levels.

I believe that this description captures the way audit markets are usually conceptualized by auditing researchers. The picture becomes strained when small markets – such as city specific markets, or client-industry markets – are examined. For example, it is difficult to argue that one or two client-industry specialists who produce a quality differentiated service will behave as perfect competitors. The development of industry expertise will likely require some form of fixed investment. But this implies that the specialists may earn quasi-rents associated with their investments and possibly monopoly rents, if the fixed investments deter adequate entry to the market niche occupied by the industry specialist(s).

The role of fixed investments in the market for audits was analysed by Sirois and Simunic (2011). In their paper, the authors investigate how audit quality is related to auditor size and the structure of the auditing industry. They discuss a model of audit firm competition based on the work of Sutton (1991) where both audit quality and audit firm size are endogenous. They examine how certain market characteristics, namely market size and investor protection regime, affect the structure of the auditing industry, differences between Big firm and non-Big firm audit quality and audit fees. In the model, audit technology plays a central role in determining the level of audit quality and fees, and the authors argue that Big firms and non-Big firms fundamentally differ with respect to their investment strategies in technology. Specifically, Big firms compete on audit value (i.e. quality and price) through fixed investments in technology, the level of which is increasing in both market size and the level of investor protection. The model offers a coherent explanation for the well documented 'Big /non-Big firm dichotomy' and dual structure of the industry.

Among other things, the model predicts that the average level of audit quality and the difference in audit value between Big and non-Big auditors increases as the size of the market increases, and/or as the level of investor protection in a market increases. The analysis also provides insights as to how audit firms compete and how the industry evolves, and suggests that despite high levels of market concentration, the market for audit services remains competitive and innovative. This is consistent with an absence of evidence to suggest that the high degree of Big firm market concentration in certain markets has impaired audit quality and/or led to an abusive increase in fees.

Finally, fixed investments also play an important role in the spatial model of oligopolistic completion among Big firms developed by Chan *et al.* (2004). The authors assume that clients vary in characteristics that are relevant to audit production (e.g. size, complexity, risk, industry, etc.). Each characteristic can be thought of as a dimension in an n-dimensional space. Also, there is a set of non-colluding audit firms that simultaneously choose production specializations (each firm can have more than one specialty) which correspond to a location in the n-dimensional space. A key feature of the model is that operating at any location requires a fixed, irreversible investment, and the relevant cost of performing an audit is an increasing function of the 'distance' between the characteristics of clients and the location of the auditor.

Solving the resulting auditor location and pricing game yields some interesting results. Equilibrium audit fees in this model are such that, given a set of client and auditor locations, the lowest cost audit firm is hired by the client but the fee charged by that firm is equal to the cost incurred by the second lowest cost firm. That is, there will be quasi-rents to fixed investments and possible monopoly rents, in equilibrium, if the magnitude of fixed investments required to operate at a 'location' serves as a barrier to entry. The market is not perfectly competitive and is characterized by price discrimination – some clients will pay more and others less, depending upon the 'closeness' of the incumbent audit firm's nearest competitor. In a recent paper, Numan and Willekens (2012) report audit pricing evidence consistent with this spatial oligopoly model.

Conclusion

The study of the market for audit services began with a test of the hypothesis that the Big public accounting firms which dominate the market engage in cartel-like pricing behaviour in the US, increasing the price and reducing the quantity demanded of audit services, and thereby adversely affecting the quality of financial reporting. However, to my knowledge, no evidence of cartel pricing by the Big firms has ever been found. As a result, the market for audit services is normally characterized as being perfectly competitive. However, it is also well documented that the Big public accounting firms are different from the non-Big accounting firms in several attributes, including the average quality of their service. In addition, it is now common for researchers to examine various local sub-markets, such as cities and client industries, where the assumption of perfect competition among the auditors who operate in a local market is difficult to sustain, a priori. This raises the potential importance of fixed investments and their attendant costs. The result is a characterization, at least of the dominant Big audit firms, as unlikely to behave as perfect competitors but rather to perform as non-colluding, price-discriminating strategic players in an oligopolistic market. I believe that further research along these lines is likely to improve our understanding of the economics of the market for audit services.

References

Bernstein, P. 'Competition Comes to Accounting', *Fortune* July 17, 1978: 89–96.

Chan, D., A. Ferguson, D. A. Simunic and D. Stokes. 'A Spatial Analysis and Test of Oligopolistic Competition in the Market for Audit Services', unpublished working paper. Vancouver, BC: University of British Columbia, 2004.

Choi, J.H, J-B Kim, X. Liu and D.A. Simunic. 'Audit Pricing, Legal Liability Regimes, and Big 4 Premiums: Theory and Cross-Country Evidence', *Contemporary Accounting Research* 25(1) Spring 2008: 55–99.

Clarkson, P.M. and D. A. Simunic. 'The Association between Audit Quality, Retained Ownership, and Firm-Specific Risk in US vs Canadian IPO Markets', *Journal of Accounting and Economics* 17 1994: 207–28.

Dye, R. 'Auditing Standards, Legal Liability, and Auditor Wealth', *Journal of Political Economy* 101(5) 1993: 887–914.

Francis, J.R. and E. R. Wilson. 'Auditor Changes: A Joint Test of Theories Relating to Agency Costs and Auditor Differentiation', *The Accounting Review* 63(4) October 1988: 663–82.

Hay, D.C., W. R. Knechel and N. Wong. 'Audit Fees: A Meta-Analysis of the Effect of Supply and Demand Attributes', *Contemporary Accounting Research* 23(1) Spring 2006: 141–91.

Johnson, W.B. and T. Lys. 'The Market for Audit Services: Evidence from Voluntary Auditor Changes', *Journal of Accounting and Economics* 12 1990: 281–308.

Nichols, D.R. and D. B. Smith. 'Auditor Credibility and Auditor Changes', *Journal of Accounting Research* 21(2) Autumn 1983: 534–44.

Numan, W. and M. Willekens. 'An Empirical Test of Spatial Competition in the Audit Market', *Journal of Accounting and Economics*, 2012: 450–65.

Palmrose, Z. 'An Analysis of Auditor Litigation and Audit Service Quality', *The Accounting Review* 63(1) January 1988: 55–73.

Simunic, D.A. 'The Pricing of Audit Services: Theory and Evidence', *Journal of Accounting Research* 18(1) Spring 1980: 161–90.

Simunic, D.A. and M. T. Stein. *Product Differentiation in Auditing: Auditor Choice in the Market for Unseasoned New Issues*. Research Monograph No.13. Vancouver, BC: Canadian Certified General Accountants' Research Foundation, 1987.

Simunic, D.A. and M. T. Stein. 'The Auditing Marketplace: Exploring the Economics of Auditing Services in the Real World', *CA Magazine* Education section, January/February 1995: 53–8.

Sirois, L-P. and D. A. Simunic. 'Auditor Size and Audit Quality Revisited: The Importance of Audit Technology', unpublished working paper. Vancouver, BC: University of British Columbia, 2011.

Subcommittee on Reports, Accounting and Management of the Committee and Government Operations: United States Senate. *The Accounting Establishment: A Staff Study*. Washington, DC: US Government Printing Office, 1977.

Sutton, J. *Sunk Costs and Market Structure: Price Competition, Advertising and the Evolution of Concentration*. Cambridge, MA: MIT Press, 1991.

Teoh, S.H. and T. J. Wong. 'Perceived Auditor Quality and the Earnings Response Coefficient', *The Accounting Review* 68(2) April 1993: 346–66.

Willekens, M., A. Steele and D. Miltz. 'Audit Standards and Auditor Liability: A Theoretical Model', *Accounting and Business Research* 26 1996: 249–64.

Ye, M. and D. A. Simunic. 'The Economics of Setting Auditing Standards', *Contemporary Accounting Research* 30(3) Fall 2013: 1191–215.

5

The audit expectation gap

A persistent but changing phenomenon

Brenda Porter

Introduction

When corporate debacles occur, such as those of Enron, WorldCom and Lehman Brothers in the United States of America (USA), Barings Bank and Equitable Life in the United Kingdom (UK), Parmalat in Italy, HIH in Australia and Satyam in India, those who suffer loss (investors, employees, creditors, suppliers, customers and others), as well as politicians and society in general, ask: Where were the auditors? Such questions reflect the failure of the auditors in question to deliver the services expected of them – a failure which results not only in criticism of, and often litigation against, the auditors concerned but also in criticism of the auditing profession as a whole and a loss of confidence in its work.

Some 80 years ago, Limperg (1932) asserted:

> The [audit] function is rooted in the confidence that society places in the effectiveness of the audit and in the opinion of the accountant [i.e., auditor] … [I]f the confidence is betrayed, the function, too, is destroyed, since it becomes useless.
>
> *(as reproduced in Limperg Instituut, 1985: 16)*

He went on to explain that auditors have a dual responsibility: not to arouse 'in the sensible layman' greater expectations than can be fulfilled by the work done, and to carry out the work in a manner that does not betray the expectations evoked (1985: 18). In other words, auditors have a responsibility to ensure that society does not have unreasonable expectations of them and for satisfying its reasonably held expectations. However, widespread criticism of, and litigation against, auditors signify that they do not fulfil this dual responsibility – that there is a gap between what society expects from auditors and what it perceives they deliver.

Definitions and studies

The term 'expectation gap' was first applied in the context of auditing by Liggio (1974), who defined it as the difference in the level of expected performance 'as envisioned by both the user of financial statements and the independent accountant' (1974: 27). This definition was extended in the terms of reference of the Commission on Auditors' Responsibilities (CAR, 1978)

(Cohen Commission) from 'users of financial statements' to 'the public', and from 'expected performance' to 'what auditors can and should reasonably expect to accomplish'. The Commission was required to consider 'whether a gap may exist between what the public expects or needs and what auditors can and should reasonably expect to accomplish' (CAR, 1978: xi). Porter (1993) contended that even this definition is too narrow to encapsulate the gap which results in criticism of auditors and loss of confidence in their work as it fails to recognize that auditors may not accomplish what they 'can and reasonably should'. Accordingly, she suggested the gap (more appropriately termed the 'audit expectation-performance gap')[1] should be defined as the gap between society's expectations of auditors and its perception of auditors' (deficient) performance. Following from this definition, Porter (1993) proposed that the gap has two major components:

(i) a reasonableness gap – the gap between the responsibilities society expects auditors to perform and those it is reasonable to expect of them;
(ii) a performance gap – the gap between the responsibilities society reasonably expects of auditors and those it perceives they deliver (or, more precisely, those it perceives they perform deficiently). This component comprises:
   (a) a deficient standards gap – the gap between the responsibilities reasonably expected of auditors and those that auditors are required to perform by statute or case law, regulations or professional promulgations (and are performed to the expected standard);
   (b) a deficient performance gap – the gap between the standard of performance of auditors' existing responsibilities which is expected, and perceived to be delivered, by society.

This structure of the audit expectation-performance gap is shown in Figure 5.1.

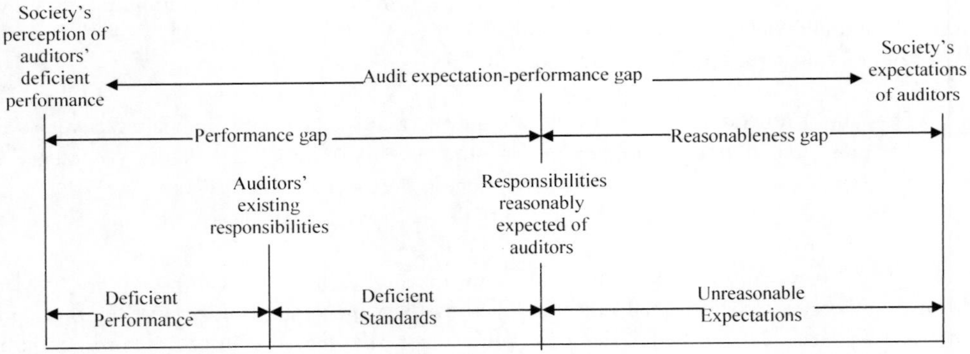

Figure 5.1 Structure of the audit expectation-performance gap

The audit expectation gap is neither new nor is it limited geographically; it has existed for more than 100 years (Chandler and Edwards, 1996) and during the past four decades it has been studied in a wide range of countries – for example, in Australia, Canada, China, Finland, Lebanon, New Zealand (NZ), Saudi Arabia, Singapore, South Africa, Spain, the UK and the USA.[2] Most of these studies were designed to ascertain whether an audit expectation gap exists in the country where the research was conducted and to identify its contributing factors. They universally found that financial statement users (in some cases, a broad range of interest groups) have little understanding of the role and responsibilities of external auditors and, in general, expect far more of auditors than is feasible for them to provide. Other studies have sought to determine whether institutional and/or cultural factors affect society's expectations of auditors and/or auditors' performance of their responsibilities. Lin and Chen (2004), for example, found that in China institutional factors are influential in these regards and Haniffa and Hudaih (2007) reached a similar conclusion in respect of cultural factors in Saudi Arabia.

The profession's response

Until the 1990s, the auditing profession focused on addressing society's (or, more specifically, financial statement users') unreasonable expectations of auditors. Largely swayed by the conclusions of the Cohen Commission (CAR, 1978), it sought to achieve this by developing the standard auditor's report into an educational tool. While noting, *inter alia*, that 'users are unaware of the limitations of the audit function and are confused about the distinction between the responsibilities of management and those of the auditor', the Cohen Commission observed: 'the auditor's standard [short form] report[3] is almost the only formal means used to educate and inform users of financial statements concerning the audit function' (1978: 71). In 1988, adopting the Cohen Commission's recommendations, the American Institute of Certified Public Accountants (AICPA) issued Statement on Auditing Standards No. 58: *Reports on Audited Financial Statements*.[4] This introduced a 'long form' standard audit report which included an explanation of the responsibilities of the auditee's management (or directors) and auditor for the financial statements, a brief description of the audit process, and a statement of the level of assurance provided by the audit opinion. The AICPA's lead was soon followed by professional bodies around the world and by the early 1990s the long form audit report was the norm.

Since the early 1990s (and, more particularly, during the twenty-first century), in addition to seeking to narrow the audit expectation gap by increasing the educational content of the auditor's report, the auditing profession has taken steps to: (i) develop auditing standards which better align auditors' responsibilities with society's reasonable expectations of them, and (ii) monitor auditors' performance so as to reduce (if not eliminate) sub-standard performance.

The effect of the profession's efforts can be assessed from studies of the audit expectation gap, and changes therein, by Porter (1993), Porter and Gowthorpe (2004), Porter *et al.* (2012) in, respectively, NZ in 1989, and NZ and the UK in 1999 and 2008. The studies were conducted by means of mail surveys of randomly selected members of four broad interest groups – auditors, auditees and audit beneficiaries from both the financial and non-financial community. A list of suggested responsibilities of auditors was provided in the survey instrument and respondents were asked to indicate those they believed to be existing responsibilities of auditors and how well these are performed, and those they expected auditors to perform.[5]

Changes in the audit expectation-performance gap in NZ and the UK 1989–2008

The structure and extent of the audit expectation-performance gap in NZ in 1989, and in NZ and the UK in 1999 and 2008, and changes in the gap, are summarized in Figure 5.2. In this figure, the extent of the audit expectation-performance gap and each of its components is shown in 'units of society's unfulfilled expectations of auditors' – expectations not fulfilled as a result of auditors failing to perform expected responsibilities (for the reasonableness and deficient standards gaps) or from not performing responsibilities to the expected standard (for the deficient performance gap).

United Kingdom

Year	Responsibilities performed OK	Deficient performance gap	Existing responsibilities	Deficient standards gap	Reasonably expected responsibilities	Reasonableness gap	Responsibilities expected by society	Responsibilities in survey instrument
	No. of constituent responsibilities							
1989	-	-	-	-	-	-	-	
1999	6	8	14	9	23	24	47	51
2008	13	6	19	9	28	21	49	55
		Contribution of components to the audit expectation-performance gap						
1989		-		-		-		
1999		9%		39%		52%		
2008		4%		41%		55%		
		Measure of unfulfilled expectations[1]						
1989		-		-		-		
1999		144 units		591 units		804 units		
2008		41 units		415 units		557 units		
		Total extent of audit expectation gap[2]						
1989		-						
1999		1.539 units						
2008		1.013 units						

New Zealand

Year	Responsibilities performed OK	Deficient performance gap	Existing responsibilities	Deficient standards gap	Reasonably expected responsibilities	Reasonableness gap	Responsibilities expected by society	Responsibilities in survey instrument
		No. of constituent responsibilities						
1989	3	5	8	10	18	9	27	30
1999	4	5	9	14	23	23	46	49
2008	7	7	14	11	25	28	53	53
		Contribution of components to the audit expectation-performance gap						
1989		11%		58%		31%		
1999		6%		51%		43%		
2008		7%		43%		50%		
		Measure of unfulfilled expectations[1]						
1989		125 units		667 units		348 units		
1999		94 units		832 units		713 units		
2008		116 units		725 units		834 units		
		Total extent of audit expectation gap[2]						
1989		1.140 units						
1999		1.639 units						
2008		1.675 units						

1 'Units' are determined by totalling the proportion of the society group whose expectations are not being fulfilled for the responsibilities constituting each gap. The number of responsibilities totalled for each gap is shown in the figure 'No. of constituent responsibilities'. The 'society group' comprises the three non-auditor interest groups (auditees, and financial and non-financial audit beneficiaries). In order to avoid bias resulting from differential sample sizes, the opinion of 'the society group' was derived from the average of the opinions expressed by respondents in each of the non-auditor interest groups.

2 Determined by totalling the measures of unfulfilled expectations attaching to each of the three constituent gaps.

Figure 5.2 Changes in the audit expectation-performance gap in the UK 1989–2008 and in NZ 1989–2008

Although no survey equivalent to that conducted in NZ was undertaken in the UK in 1989, the findings of a study by Humphrey *et al.* (1993) suggest that, in 1990, the structure of the audit expectation gap in the UK was similar to that in NZ in 1989 and that changes in the gap in the UK between 1989 and 1999 are similar to those that occurred in NZ over the decade.

A review of Figure 5.2 reveals that four changes in the audit expectation-performance gap between 1989 and 2008 are particularly notable, namely:

(i) the significant increase in the number of responsibilities constituting (a) society's expectations of auditors, and (b) the reasonableness gap between 1989 and 1999;
(ii) the marked increase in the number of auditors' actual responsibilities between 1999 and 2008;
(iii) the sharp narrowing of the deficient performance gap in NZ between 1989 and 1999 and, more particularly, in the UK between 1999 and 2008;
(iv) the similarity in the extent of the audit expectation-performance gap in NZ and in the UK in 1999 and its marked difference in 2008.

Each of these changes is discussed below.

As shown in Figure 5.2, in NZ between 1989 and 1999, the number of responsibilities constituting society's expectations of auditors and the reasonableness gap increased from 27 to 46, and nine to 23, respectively. Similarly, the contribution of the reasonableness gap to the audit expectation-performance gap jumped from 31 per cent to 43 per cent, and the level of NZ society's unfilled expectations resulting from auditors not performing these (unreasonably) expected responsibilities increased from 348 to 713 units[6] (an increase of 105 per cent). (As noted above, it is conjectured that similar changes occurred in the UK.) These changes can be traced to significant developments in auditing's external environment over the decade – in particular, to growth in the size and incidence of corporate fraud; the development of corporate governance requirements (especially in the UK[7]); increasing societal concern about the environmental and social impact of major companies, expansion in the quantity and range of information in companies' annual reports, and the emergence of the internet as an effective means of communication.

Between 1999 and 2008, the developments in auditing's external environment which characterized the previous decade continued but at a slower pace. Additionally, stimulated by well-publicized corporate failures around the turn of the twenty-first century and the global financial crisis which commenced in early 2008, there was more public discussion than previously about corporate and financial matters and related auditing issues. Such discussion and debate were particularly evident in the UK where it was stimulated by frequent publications on relevant topics by the Financial Reporting Council (FRC); (for example, FRC, 2006b, 2007, 2008b) and the Auditing Practices Board (APB) (for example, APB, 2007) and by regular updates of the *Combined Code of Corporate Governance* (FRC, 2003, 2006a, 2008a). In NZ, although the NZX (the New Zealand Stock Exchange) and the New Zealand Securities Commission (NZSC) produced corporate governance guidelines (NZX, 2003; NZSC, 2004), unlike in the UK, listed companies are encouraged, rather than required, to comply with them. Further, compared with the UK, there was little to stimulate public discussion and debate about corporate and financial affairs and related auditing issues aside from the infamous corporate failures and global financial crisis. It seems likely that the greater public discourse in the UK compared with NZ largely explains the differential changes in the reasonableness gap in the two countries between 1999 and 2008. While in NZ the number of responsibilities constituting this gap increased from 23 to 28, in the UK it decreased from 24 to 21. Similarly, the level of society's unfulfilled expectations resulting from auditors not performing these (unreasonably) expected responsibilities rose in NZ from 713 to 834 units (an increase of 17 per cent) but fell in the UK from 804 to 557 units (a decline of nearly 31 per cent).

Between 1999 and 2008, as many of the environmental developments of the 1989–99 period became more commonplace or further advanced and there was greater public discussion about relevant issues, it seems that NZ and UK society gained some appreciation of both the limits of the audit function and the benefits to be derived from auditors performing some extended responsibilities. This is reflected in some of the responsibilities which contributed to the reasonableness gap in 1999 failing to feature in 'society's expectations of auditors' in 2008 (for example, examining and reporting on auditees' policies and procedures relating to equal employment opportunities and product safety) and others (such as reporting on auditees' risk management processes) meeting the cost–benefit criterion to be reasonably expected of auditors and, thus, featuring in the deficient standards gap in 2008.

Analysis of the responsibilities comprising the reasonableness gap reveals that they fall into two broad groups:

(a) those that are not economically feasible for auditors to perform – for example, *guaranteeing* the accuracy of the auditee's financial statements and/or its solvency; detecting and reporting minor theft of auditee assets; and detecting illegal acts by the company's directors/senior managers that only indirectly impact on the financial statements. Notwithstanding the educational efforts of the long form audit report, society's unreasonable expectation that auditors will perform these responsibilities persists and these responsibilities featured in the reasonableness gap in both NZ and the UK throughout the two decades covered by the surveys;

(b) those relating to relatively 'new' issues in the corporate arena – for example, examining and reporting (in the audit report) on (i) the effectiveness of the auditee's internal non-financial controls; and (ii) the reliability of all of the information in its annual report, including information about its equal employment opportunities, product safety, and occupational health and safety. It is in respect of this group of responsibilities (which constituted the major portion of the reasonableness gap in both NZ and the UK in 1999 and 2008) that society seems to gain some appreciation of the limits and benefits of auditors performing them.

Although changes in the responsibilities constituting society's expectations of auditors and the reasonableness gap between 1989 and 2008 can largely be explained by reference to developments in auditors' external environment, changes in its internal environment (especially changes in auditing and accounting standards and the introduction of monitoring of auditors' performance) largely account for the increase in auditors' actual responsibilities and the sharp narrowing of the deficient performance gap which were particularly evident in the 1999–2008 period.

As might be expected, the increase in auditors' actual responsibilities between 1999 and 2008 helped to narrow the deficient standards component of the audit expectation-performance gap (as responsibilities changed from being reasonably expected to required of auditors). However, as a result of the developments in auditing's external environment, and some responsibilities changing from being unreasonably to reasonably expected of auditors, a small number of responsibilities also served to extend the deficient standards gap in both NZ and the UK between 1999 and 2008.

As shown in Figure 5.2, between 1999 and 2008 the number of auditors' actual responsibilities increased from nine to 14 in NZ and from 14 to 19 in the UK.[8] This increase resulted primarily from the International Auditing and Assurance Standards Board's (IAASB) 'clarity project' (undertaken between 2004 and 2009). This involved a review of all of the International Standards on Auditing (ISAs) and produced, *inter alia*: 'One new standard … [and] 16 standards containing new and revised requirements … ' (IAASB, 2010). However, in NZ, one of auditors' 'new' actual responsibilities ('to report, in the audit report, on the reliability of information in the auditee's annual report on director's remuneration') was the outcome of a change in 2004 in the NZ version of International Accounting Standard 24: *Related Party Disclosures* (this responsibility was an actual responsibility of UK auditors in both 1999 and 2008).

Like the responsibilities comprising the reasonableness gap, those constituting the deficient standards gap tend to fall into two broad groups:

a) those that involve disclosing in the audit report and/or to an appropriate authority, matters of concern that are uncovered during an audit. These include reporting theft of a material amount of the auditee's assets; illegal acts by the company's directors/senior managers which directly impact on the financial statements; and doubts about the entity's continued existence.[9] Given that the information is already within the auditor's knowledge, it does not seem too great a step to convert these 'reasonably expected' responsibilities into actual responsibilities of auditors – a notion to which, in some cases, the standard setters gave practical effect between 1999 and 2008;
b) those that relate to corporate governance issues; for example, examining and reporting (in the audit report) on the effectiveness of the auditee's internal financial controls and the adequacy of its procedures for identifying financial risks.[10]

The third significant change in the audit expectation-performance gap reflected in Figure 5.2 is the sharp reduction in NZ and UK society's perception of deficient performance by auditors. In 1989, NZ society adjudged auditors' performance of five of their responsibilities to be sub-standard. A decade later, auditors' performance of these same five responsibilities (which included, for example, detecting theft of a material amount[11] of the auditee's assets by (a) non-managerial employees and (b) the directors/senior executives) was similarly perceived but the measure of society's unfulfilled expectations attaching to these responsibilities decreased from 125 to 94 units (a reduction of nearly 25 per cent) and the contribution of the deficient performance component to the audit expectation gap declined from 11 per cent to six per cent.

Between 1999 and 2008, as indicated above, five additional responsibilities became actual responsibilities of auditors in both NZ and the UK and, as a consequence, a widening of the deficient performance gap might be expected. In NZ this did occur; the number of responsibilities comprising this gap increased from five to seven and the level of unfulfilled expectations resulting from society's perception of their deficient performance increased from 94 to 116 units (an increase of 23 per cent). However, in the UK, the number of responsibilities constituting the deficient performance gap dropped from eight to six and the level of society's unfulfilled expectations attaching to these responsibilities declined from 144 to 41 units (a decrease of 72 per cent).[12]

It seems likely that the introduction of monitoring of auditors' performance is primarily responsible for the perceived improvement in auditors' performance in NZ between 1989 and 1999 and in the UK between 1999 and 2008. Practice Review was introduced in NZ by the NZ Institute of Chartered Accountants (NZICA) in 1990. It involved a Practice Review Panel (appointed by NZICA) reviewing the performance of all NZICA members holding a Public Practice Certificate, which includes all company auditors. In the UK, monitoring of auditors' performance was introduced in 1991 as an element of a governmental regulatory system that focuses exclusively on company auditors and audits.

Monitoring of auditors' performance may have resulted in auditees observing improved performance by their auditors and/or in society perceiving improved performance as a consequence of becoming aware of the monitoring through reference to it in the financial press or by other means. However, in NZ, Practice Review remained virtually unchanged from 1990 until 2012 when the Auditor Regulation Act 2011 became effective and introduced a regulatory regime similar to that pertaining in the UK. Further, no reports on the process or outcomes of Practice Review were placed in the public domain and little publicity was given to disciplinary action taken against errant auditors. The reason for NZ society's perception of a decline in the standard of auditors' performance between 1999 and 2008 may lie in the absence of new developments in, and publicity about, the monitoring of NZ auditors' performance, combined with extensive media coverage of corporate debacles and apparent audit failures in a number of countries during the 2000s.

In the UK, in 1991, the Recognised Supervisory Bodies (RSBs) (with which UK company auditors are required to be registered) became responsible, *inter alia*, for monitoring the performance of their registrant auditors.[13] Since that time, the rigour of the monitoring process has gradually increased. Additionally, since 2004, monitoring by the RSBs has been supplemented by inspections of the audits of public interest entities by the Audit Inspection Unit (AIU).[14] Further, information on the monitoring/inspection process and its outcomes is placed in the public domain and, when disciplinary action is taken against an errant auditor, the matter is publicized in the financial press. It seems likely that these factors contributed to UK society's perception of a marked improvement in UK auditors' performance between 1999 and 2008.

The remaining significant change in the audit expectation-performance gap in NZ and the UK between 1989 and 2008 concerns the relative extent of the gap in the two countries. Figure 5.2 reveals that, in 1999, the extent of the gap in NZ and the UK was remarkably similar (it differed by just six per cent). However, between 1999 and 2008, while the gap in NZ widened from 1,639 to 1,675 units of society's unfulfilled expectations (an increase of two per cent, a result which is not statistically significant), in the UK, it narrowed from 1,539 to 1,013 units (a decrease of 34 per cent). In 2008, as a consequence of these changes, the extent of the gap in the two countries differed by nearly 40 per cent. Notwithstanding this difference, it may be discerned from Figure 5.2 that the structure of the gap in the two countries was not dissimilar. The key difference is that auditors in the UK leave society with less unfulfilled expectations than do their NZ counterparts.

The differential changes between 1989 and 2008 in the audit expectation gap in NZ and the UK – and, more especially, the reasons therefor (in particular, the more widespread societal discussion of corporate and financial matters and related auditing issues in the UK together with more rigorous monitoring of auditors' performance and the provision of information about the monitoring process and outcomes) – may point the way to how the gap may be narrowed in other countries in the world where it has been found to exist.

Conclusion: A process identified

By reflecting on the changes in the audit expectation-performance gap between 1989 and 2008 in NZ and the UK a process may be discerned. It seems that, when significant changes occur in the corporate arena, society expects auditors to accept a range of new responsibilities to help constrain corporate managements from exploiting the changes to their, rather than society's, benefit. Initially, society appears to give little thought to the costs of auditors performing these responsibilities and most contribute to the reasonableness component of the audit expectation gap. However, as the 'emerging issues' become more commonplace, society begins to recognize that the potential costs of auditors performing some of the 'newly expected' responsibilities outweigh the potential benefits to be derived therefrom, and these responsibilities are discarded from society's expectations of auditors and, thus, from the audit expectation gap. At the same time, the potential benefits to be derived from auditors performing other emerging issues-related responsibilities are gradually appreciated. This changes the cost–benefit equation, and the responsibilities concerned change from being unreasonably, to reasonably, expected of auditors and move from the reasonableness to the deficient standards component of the audit expectation gap.

As society's familiarity with the developments in auditing's external environment evolves, recognition of the benefits to be obtained from auditors performing responsibilities that are reasonably expected (but not required) of them increases until, through a change in legislation, regulations or auditing standards, they become actual responsibilities of auditors. Most often this change follows a major crisis (such as the 1987 Stockmarket crash, the 2001 collapse of Enron, or the 2008 global financial crisis) which prompts a review by politicians, regulators and the auditing profession of the part played by auditors in – or, more frequently, not played by them in preventing – the crisis, and in regulatory reform designed to correct the perceived deficiency. This process can be seen, for example, in enactment of the Sarbanes-Oxley Act of 2002 in the USA following the Enron and WorldCom debacles, and the UK's House of Lords Economic Affairs Committee's enquiry into the role of auditors following the 2008 financial crisis (House of Lords, 2011). As politicians become involved in the profession's affairs, the profession's standard setting bodies review – and in many cases revise – their auditing standards (as occurred as an outcome of the IAASB's 'clarity project').

As the number of auditors' actual responsibilities increases or become more demanding (particularly if the changes are prompted by a major crisis), society's perception of their performance may, at least initially, deteriorate. Nevertheless, history suggests that legislative and regulatory changes like those mentioned above usually include enhanced requirements for auditors' competence and/or performance. For instance, following the 1987 Stockmarket crash, the UK Companies Act 1989 introduced a requirement for company auditors to be registered with an RSB which was responsible, *inter alia*, for monitoring its registrants' competency and performance. Along similar lines, during the House of Lords' enquiry into the role of auditors, following publication of critical reports by the AIU of auditors' performance in the UK in 2010, it was mooted that the auditors of public listed companies be specially licensed or required to meet new competency requirements (Christodoulou, 2010).

The findings of research conducted in NZ and the UK since 1989 indicate that auditors' performance (or society's perception thereof) has improved markedly during the past two decades – particularly in the UK. The apparent improvement may result from auditing standards becoming more demanding or specifying auditors' responsibilities more clearly, and/or from auditors becoming more familiar with the requirements. However, it seems likely that increased scrutiny of auditors' performance has been a particularly influential factor.

Some eight decades ago Limperg (1932) asserted that auditors have a dual responsibility: not to arouse in the 'sensible layman' (1932: 18) greater expectations than can be fulfilled by the work done, and to carry out the work in a manner that does not betray the expectations evoked. This suggests that it is incumbent on auditors to restrain society's expectations of them to those that it is cost-beneficial for them to perform, to accept responsibilities which meet the cost–benefit criterion as rightfully theirs, and to perform these responsibilities to the high standard society expects. If the auditing profession takes the initiative and implements measures designed to meet these goals, society's perception of the services auditors deliver will be better aligned with its expectations. As a consequence, the criticism faced by auditors should abate and confidence in the profession and its work should gradually be restored.

Notes

1 Traditionally, the gap has been termed the 'audit expectation(s) gap' and defined as the gap between the responsibilities society expects auditors to perform and those auditors acknowledge to be theirs. While recognizing that this ignores the contribution of auditors' sub-standard performance to their failure to meet society's expectations, in this chapter the terms 'audit expectation gap' and audit expectation-performance gap' are used interchangeably.

2 Details of these studies are reported in Porter *et al.* (2012: part 1).

3 The standard short form report in use in 1978 did little more than identify the financial statements which had been audited and express the auditor's opinion thereon.

4 This was issued as one of nine 'expectation gap standards'; i.e., auditing standards designed to narrow the gap between 'what the public or financial statement users expect from accountants and auditors, and what accountants and auditors believe they are responsible for' (Guy and O'Neil, 1986).

5 'Society's' opinions were derived from the responses of the non-auditor interest groups (auditees and financial and non-financial community audit beneficiaries).

6 Calculation of society's unfulfilled expectations of auditors is explained in Porter (1993).

7 In 1992 the Committee on the Financial Aspects of Corporate Governance (CFACG, 1992) (the Cadbury Committee) produced a Code of Best Practice with which companies listed on the London Stock Exchange were required to comply or explain their non-compliance. A series of other corporate governance reports followed with consequential increases in the corporate governance requirements of UK listed companies.

8 The difference in the number of auditors' actual responsibilities in NZ and the UK results from the requirement in the UK for auditors to report certain matters of concern discovered during an audit to a 'proper authority' when it is in the public interest to do so. In NZ, auditors' duty of confidentiality prohibits such reporting.

9 In 2008 auditors (especially in the UK) had an existing duty to report any particular 'matter of concern' discovered during the audit *either* in the audit report *or* to an appropriate authority. The

aspect that was not an actual responsibility of auditors met the criterion to be reasonably expected of them.

10 Since 2006, the UK Listing Authority's rules have required auditors in the UK to review their listed company auditees' compliance statement with respect to nine provisions of *The Combined Code on Corporate Governance* (and its successor, *The UK Code on Corporate Governance*).

11 A 'material amount' was defined as greater than five per cent of the auditee's turnover or assets.

12 The difference in the number of auditors' actual responsibilities and those constituting the deficient performance gap are responsibilities that society considers auditors perform satisfactorily.

13 The RSBs are the Institutes of Chartered Accountants in England and Wales, of Scotland, and in Ireland, and the Associations of Certified Chartered Accountants and Authorised Public Accountants.

14 Until the Financial Reporting Council (FRC) was restructured in July 2012, the Audit Inspection Unit (AIU) was an element of the FRC's Professional Oversight Board. In July 2012, the AIU was replaced by the Audit Quality Review team and this became an element of the FRC's Monitoring Committee.

References

Auditing Practices Board (APB). (2007). *The Auditor's Report: A Time for Change?* London: Financial Reporting Council.

Chandler, R. and Edwards, J. R. (1996). 'Recurring Issues in Auditing: Back to the Future?', *Accounting, Auditing & Accountability Journal* 9(2): 4–29.

Christodoulou, M. (2010, 7 October). 'Small Firms Threatened with Licence Reform', *Accountancy Age*. Available online at www.accountancyage.com/aa/analysis/1808542/small-firms-threaten-licence-reform (accessed 25 November 2012).

Commission on Auditors' Responsibilities (CAR) (Cohen Commission). (1978). *Report, Conclusions and Recommendations*. New York: American Institute of Certified Public Accountants.

Committee on the Financial Aspects of Corporate Governance (CFACG) (Cadbury Committee). (1992). *Report of the Committee on the Financial Aspects of Corporate Governance*. London: Gee and Co.

Financial Reporting Council (FRC). (2003, 2006a, 2008a). *The Combined Code on Corporate Governance*. London: FRC.

Financial Reporting Council (FRC). (2006b, 2007). *A Report on the Main Findings of the Review of the Combined Code on Corporate Governance*. London: FRC.

Financial Reporting Council (FRC). (2008b). *Consultation Paper: Going Concern and Financial Reporting*. London: FRC.

Guy, D. M. and O'Neil, M. L. (1986). 'The Auditing Standards Board Responds to Public Expectations', *CPA Journal* 56(7): 76–8.

Haniffa, R. and Hudaih, M. (2007). 'Locating Audit Expectation Gap within a Cultural Context: The Case of Saudi Arabia', *Journal of International Accounting, Auditing and Taxation* 16: 179–206.

House of Lords. (2011, March). *House of Lords Select Committee on Economic Affairs 2nd Report of Session 2010–2011, Auditors: Market Concentration and Their Role, Vol. 1: Report*. London: Stationery Office.

Humphrey, C. G., Moizer, P. and Turley, S. (1993). 'The Audit Expectations Gap in Britain: An Empirical Investigation', *Accounting and Business Research* 23(91A): 395–411.

International Auditing and Assurance Board (IAASB). (2010). *IAASB Clarity Center: The Clarified Standards*. Available online at web.ifac.org/clarity-center/the-clarified-standards (accessed 24 November 2012).

Liggio, C. D. (1974). 'The Expectation Gap: The Accountant's Legal Waterloo', *Journal of Contemporary Business* 3: 27–44.

Limperg, T. (1932). *The Social Responsibility of the Auditor*, reproduced in Limperg Instituut, (1985). The Netherlands: Limperg Institute.

Lin, Z. J. and Chen, F. (2004). 'An Empirical Study of Audit "expectation gap" in the People's Republic of China', *International Journal of Auditing* 8: 92–115.

New Zealand Securities Commission (NZSC). (2004). *Corporate Governance in New Zealand Principles and Guidelines*. Wellington: NZSC.

New Zealand Stock Exchange (NZX). (2003). *NZX Corporate Governance Best Practice Code*. Wellington: NZX.

Porter, B. A. (1993). 'An Empirical Study of the Audit Expectation-Performance Gap', *Accounting and Business Research* 24(93): 49–68.

Porter, B. A. and Gowthorpe, C. (2004). *Audit Expectation-Performance Gap in the United Kingdom in 1999 and Comparison with the Gap in New Zealand in 1989 and 1999:* Edinburgh: Institute of Chartered Accountants of Scotland.

Porter, B. A., Ó'hÓgartaigh, C. and Baskerville, R. (2012). 'Audit Expectation-Performance Gap in New Zealand and the United Kingdom and Changes to the Gap in New Zealand 1989–2008 and the United Kingdom 1999–2008', *International Journal of Auditing* (16)2: 101–29; (16)3: 215–47.

6

Research on litigation against auditors[1]

Dain Donelson, Kathryn Kadous and John McInnis

Introduction

Auditors attest to whether a firm's financial statements fairly present its financial position, results of operations, and cash flows in accordance with generally accepted accounting principles. In the United States, auditors' liability to third parties generally arises when they provide an unqualified audit opinion on financial statements that are subsequently alleged to have been misstated due to negligence or fraud. For our discussion, we generally confine our focus to auditor liability under US law because most prior research on auditor liability has focused on the US legal system.

Litigation against audit firms involves both state and federal law. Federal securities laws allow for class action suits, but they typically require the plaintiff to demonstrate fraud under Rule 10b-5, which calls for scienter (knowledge or recklessness). That is, to successfully sue the auditor, plaintiffs must demonstrate that the auditor participated in or knowingly disregarded the risk of deception of financial statement users. This is a difficult standard for plaintiffs to meet, particularly in light of the pleading standard under the Private Securities Litigation Reform Act of 1995 (PSLRA), which requires that plaintiffs allege facts that provide a strong inference of scienter prior to being allowed discovery. In contrast, cases filed under state law against auditors do not involve class actions, but do allow plaintiffs to allege either fraud or negligence. These cases are typically filed under a more plaintiff-friendly negligence theory. Federal cases involving securities issuance are also subject to a negligence standard for the auditor under Section 11 of the Securities Act of 1933.

Securities class action cases involve a large number of investors who must be informed of the case's resolution. Data regarding these cases is thus publicly available. Only a handful of securities class actions have ever gone to trial, likely due to defendants' fear of a jury making a large damage assessment (e.g., CAQ 2008). In contrast, state negligence cases generally involve two private parties and thus settlements (and other information) need not be disclosed. These cases have been tried somewhat more frequently (see Palmrose 1991).

The majority of studies examining litigation against auditors under federal rules employ archival methods, taking advantage of available data. They consider factors associated with the incidence of litigation against auditors, the extent to which the legal merits of the case influence incidence and outcomes of those cases, and the impact of legal reform on litigation against auditors. A small set of studies in the experimental economics tradition examines the impacts of various liability regimes (that is, combinations of rules for determining negligence and for apportioning liability) on auditor decisions and general market outcomes. In contrast, although some studies of state law cases make use of archival data, most of these studies use psychology-based experiments to examine how jurors assess blame against auditors. Additionally, a few experimental studies examine the decisions and decision processes of judges and potential plaintiffs. We first discuss the literature based on federal law, and then we turn to the literature examining state negligence cases. We also briefly discuss how the legal environment affects the auditor–client relationship. We conclude with a discussion of open questions.

Federal litigation against auditors

Litigation involving auditors under federal law involves securities class actions and government enforcement through the Securities Exchange Commission (SEC). In both of these areas, trials are extremely rare, and the outcomes of the cases are typically settlements or dismissals. While many studies examine the incidence of litigation, relatively less research examines the merits of cases. Importantly, federal securities law was significantly reformed in the mid-1990s, leading to research on the effects of these reforms as well as opportunities for future research.

Incidence of litigation

The largest body of work with respect to audit litigation examines factors associated with lawsuits against auditors (St. Pierre and Anderson 1984; Stice 1991; Lys and Watts 1994). These studies find that variables tied to potential damages (client size and stock performance), difficulty in performing the audit (working capital as opposed to fixed asset levels), and the probability that the client may not be able to pay its share of damages (client financial distress or bankruptcy) increase the incidence of auditor litigation, presumably because these factors make it easier to allege wrongdoing and increase plaintiffs' recoveries from the auditor. However, no factor is determinative. For example, although bankruptcy increases the incidence of auditor litigation, the majority of client bankruptcies involve no litigation against auditors (Carcello and Palmrose 1994).

Due to the relatively higher incidence of auditor litigation for bankrupt clients, numerous studies examine whether going concern opinions deter litigation. Kaplan and Williams (2013) examine this issue through a simultaneous equations approach and find that going concern opinions deter litigation.

Other recent work on litigation incidence focuses on topics related to regulator concerns, such as the increase in earnings management in the 1990s and the focus on non-audit services in the wake of the Enron scandal. Using abnormal accruals as a proxy, Heninger (2001) confirms that earnings management is related to audit litigation. Schmidt (2012) finds that restatements for firms with abnormally high non-audit service fees are more likely to result in litigation. Finally, Donelson *et al.* (2012) examine all accounting-related securities class actions (rather than simply auditor litigation) and find that accounting standards significantly influence the filing of litigation. Specifically, they find that plaintiffs tend to allege violations of principles-based accounting standards, consistent with rules-based accounting standards shielding firms and auditors from litigation.

Legal reform and the merits of cases

Legal reform

In the early 1990s, many scholars and legislators began to question whether federal securities class action settlements reflected the merits of the case (Alexander 1991). The large audit firms claimed that they were often forced to settle regardless of the merits of the case, primarily because the doctrine of joint and several liability made the potential costs of losing a case too high (Cook *et al.* 1992). Under a joint and several liability regime, each defendant is responsible for the full amount of assessed damages, regardless of degree of fault. Audit firms lobbied strongly for reforms, especially a change to proportionate liability, under which the firm would pay only assessed damages according to its assessed share of responsibility. Interestingly, despite the firms' claims, Palmrose (1991) found that audit firms took a higher percentage of cases to trial than other types of defendants. This finding indicates that, at the time at least, auditors had a viable trial option. An update of this study is needed – the audit firms now argue that the trial option has disappeared due to the potential for large verdicts that would force the firms to liquidate (CAQ 2008).

Legal changes relevant to auditors began with the Supreme Court's ruling in *Central Bank of Denver v. First Interstate Bank of Denver*, 511 U.S. 164 (1994). *Central Bank of Denver* eliminated aiding and abetting liability under federal securities laws. Shortly thereafter, Congress passed the PSLRA, which provided much of the relief the audit firms sought under federal law. Particularly relevant to auditors, the PSLRA increases the burden on the plaintiff by requiring specific facts to support allegations of fraud (thus making it more likely that allegations are meritorious) and eliminates in most cases joint and several liability for auditors. In addition, the PSLRA reduces the cost of litigation by preventing discovery in non-meritorious cases (those that do not survive the defendant's motion to dismiss).

As a result of the significant changes in the legal landscape for auditors, several studies have examined what factors explain when an auditor is named in a securities class action subsequent to the legal reforms. Fuerman (2000), for instance, finds that the presence of an accounting and auditing enforcement release (AAER) by the SEC, the client's bankruptcy, the length of the class period, and the presence of an annual restatement make it more likely the auditor will be named, while large auditors (the Big 6 at the time) were less likely to be named. Also of interest, Fuerman (2000) finds that auditors were named as defendants in only 83 of 468 cases examined, or 17.7 percent of the time. Similarly, Palmrose and Scholz (2004) find that auditors are named 35 percent of the time in cases involving restatements, and that restatements involving revenue are particularly likely to generate litigation for auditors. It appears from this work that the factors that lead to litigation against auditors are very similar in the pre-PSLRA and post-PSLRA periods; however, a direct comparison of pre-PSLRA versus post-PSLRA data to determine whether plaintiffs' filing decisions have systematically changed would be a valuable addition to the literature.

The PSLRA largely eliminated joint and several liability for secondary actors such as auditors, switching to a proportional liability system. This was a key reform for which the audit firms had lobbied (Cook *et al.* 1992). Despite these reforms to federal law, the issue is still important as many states still utilize joint and several liability schemes. Archival research could exploit the exogenous shock from the PSLRA to proportional liability to learn about the impact of this change. However, this may be difficult because several reforms took effect simultaneously. Thus, the best current evidence regarding joint and several versus proportional liability arises from analytical and experimental economics studies.

Dopuch *et al.* (1994) utilized an experimental market to investigate the effect of three liability systems, utilizing a verifier (auditor), seller (client), and buyer (a third party who relies on the audit report). They find that proportional liability is the most efficient liability system, resulting in the greatest economy-wide wealth. The disadvantage of a joint and several liability system is that auditors cannot pass the full cost of liability to the client through fees. The disadvantage of a proportional system in which the client cannot also pay (e.g., because of bankruptcy) is that buyers reduce prices they are willing to pay for a company. In a related study, Burton *et al.* (2011) find that a deterministic penalty system (e.g., a penalty to the auditor based on a fixed percentage of the client's market value of equity), rather than a skewed penalty system (i.e., the current environment with damages that are difficult to predict), increases effort by auditors and inhibits fraudulent reporting more effectively.

Choice of a liability rule is problematic in that auditors may reduce effort if joint and several liability were to be eliminated, while higher risk clients may be unable to obtain audit service if it were retained because they expose the auditor to high potential litigation costs. Gramling *et al.* (1998) investigate these issues in an experimental market and find some evidence that auditors reduce effort under proportionate liability, as compared with joint and several liability, for clients of moderate risk. They also find some reduced audit service availability to high-risk clients under joint and several liability. Overall, these results are consistent with both auditor effort and audit availability for high-risk clients being influenced by auditor liability.

Yu (2001) utilizes an experimental market to examine the relation between the level of auditor liability and firm investment. He finds that auditor liability that is either too low or too high produces lower firm investment in new projects than a medium liability system, indicating the importance to society of identifying an appropriate level of auditor liability. Future research could focus on developing new regimes or mechanisms that maintain audit quality and availability of service at high levels.

The merits of cases

Given that auditors are not usually named even when their client is sued for accounting fraud (Fuerman 2000), it seems likely the merits make at least some difference in audit litigation. However, there is relatively little direct evidence on the extent to which the merits of cases affect outcomes. In the pre-reform period, Palmrose (1988) finds that Big 8 auditors had lower litigation activity than other audit firms, consistent with their stronger reputations and with the merits of cases being considered. Also in the pre-reform period, Bonner *et al.* (1998), drawing their sample from a set of AAERs, find that auditors are more likely to be named as defendants in cases involving fictitious transactions or commonly occurring frauds as compared to other types of cases. These results are also consistent with the merits of the case being considered in the filing decision. Schmidt (2012) is a rare recent study that examines outcomes of auditor litigation, finding that cases are more likely to settle, and that they settle for larger amounts, when allegations of fee dependence are included in the suit. In particular, she finds that non-audit service fees appear to generate stronger cases for plaintiffs.

There is no systematic examination in the audit literature of the changes in the extent to which the merits of cases influence incidence and outcomes of cases from the pre-reform environment to the post-reform environment. This is in contrast to the law literature, in which the importance of merits has been the subject of significant research (Johnson *et al.* 2007). Such studies could be particularly interesting, considering that scholars such as Coffee (2006: 1550) state that auditors now have "virtual immunity" under federal securities laws, while the audit firms contend that they are exposed to excessive liability under the same laws (CAQ 2008). The reality appears to lie somewhere between these two views, given that auditors are still sued on a regular basis, but are not named in the majority of cases where their clients are accused of accounting fraud.

State litigation against auditors

Litigation against auditors filed in state courts usually alleges negligence, which is easier to prove than fraud. The details of negligence laws vary by jurisdiction; however, they typically hold auditors responsible for providing the level of care and competence that a reasonable auditor would provide in the circumstances. Thus, the standard of care is vague and is dependent on the circumstances surrounding the audit, and the jury plays an important role in assessing whether the standard is met. Further, as noted above, state cases are more likely to go to jury trial than are federal cases. Jury judgments are particularly important in these cases, and research in this area tends to focus on explaining the psychological processes that lead to jurors' judgments and decisions. Most research in this area uses psychology-based experiments and can be characterized as examining jurors' (lay) assessments of blame, though a few studies examine judgments of judges and other third parties in addition to or instead of juror judgments. This research provides insight into questions such as when and why will the merits of the case matter, what legally irrelevant factors will influence jury decisions, what role do specific audit procedures, auditor relationships with clients, and auditing and accounting standards play in determining auditor blame, and what legal strategies can auditors employ to reduce blame assigned to them.

Juror assessments of auditor blame

The process of assessing blame

Early studies of jurors' assessments of auditor blame relied on theory about hindsight and outcome effects. These studies were largely concerned with (1) demonstrating that jurors' assessments were unfair to auditors, because learning about an audit failure biases verdicts against auditors; and (2) identifying strategies to reduce this bias (debiasers). Studies consistently found that higher assessments of blame and liability arose from auditors being evaluated in the presence (versus absence) of information about an audit failure. However, debiasers designed to reduce the apparent foreseeability of the audit failure yielded inconsistent results. For example, Lowe and Reckers (1994) found that asking jurors to consider potential alternative outcomes that could have occurred decreased liability assessments, but Anderson *et al.* (1997) found a similar manipulation to be ineffective with judges. Clarkson *et al.* (2002) found that a weak warning not to use outcome information did not influence jurors' liability assessments, but stronger warnings that included telling jurors use of such information is inappropriate and/or illegal reduced liability assessments.

More recent research of juror assessments of blame tends to make more explicit use of the theoretical background provided by attribution theory. Attribution theory explains how people (jurors and others) assess responsibility and blame for events (Fincham and Jaspars 1980). Culpable control theory (Alicke 2000; Alicke *et al.* 2008) builds on attribution theory. Those theories assert that learning about harmful events, such as audit failures and the resulting plaintiff's losses, provokes attributional activity. That is, people seek explanation for harmful events. They tend to do so by using counterfactual reasoning to search for possible alternative outcomes and to determine how the negative event could have been avoided (Roese 1997). For example, a would-be vacationer who missed her flight would engage in counterfactual thinking to determine how she could have been on time for the flight. Likewise, a juror who is deciding a case in which a costly audit failure occurred would engage in counterfactual thinking to determine how the failure could have been avoided. In considering possible alternative outcomes, unusual or unexpected circumstances stand out as potential causal factors (Kahneman and Miller 1986). These theories can explain some of the results found in experimental and archival studies, and they have also led to new findings.

The initial search for counterfactuals appears to be caused by the negative feelings that are aroused by the negative event (Roese 1997). Consistent with this idea, jurors report a higher need to "figure out who was to blame" when more severe consequences are described following an audit failure, and they assess a higher standard of care for auditors in this case (Kadous 2000). Thus, although the legal system contemplates that jurors assess standards of care and auditor behavior separately, and then compare the two in forming their verdicts, they do not appear to do so. In Kadous's (2000) study, jurors took the auditors' work (audit quality) into consideration when consequences of audit failure were described as less severe, but not when they were described as severe. This implies that jurors' high motivation to lay blame is sufficient to override the merits of the case, at least in some situations. This phenomenon could explain why auditors are reluctant to engage in litigation even when they have performed an audit of high quality.

More direct evidence of the importance of jurors' negative feelings, or affect, in driving a search for blame was obtained by Kadous (2001). In that study, a simple manipulation to discredit affect as a valid predictor of blame eliminates the impact of reporting severely negative outcomes on jurors' verdicts against auditors and restores the predictive ability of audit quality for those verdicts. This key role for affect in determining liability implies that features of the setting or situation that increase jurors' negative affect will increase auditor liability. For example, Brandon and Mueller (2006) found that liability assessments and verdicts against auditors are higher when the client is more financially important to the auditor. This apparently occurs because jurors view the auditor's motives as being more self-serving when the client is important, increasing negative affect (though this result could also reflect juror focus on merit, if auditors' decisions are of lower quality for more important clients). Archival studies could validate the importance of affect by testing whether cases with features more likely to arouse negative affect in jurors are more likely to settle or settle for higher amounts.

The key role for jurors' affect in determining blame assessments also implies that reducing jurors' negative affect may reduce verdicts against auditors. Cornell *et al.* (2009) found that having the defendant auditor issue an apology for the plaintiff's loss reduced jurors' need to assign blame and reduced the likelihood of verdicts against auditors. However, Grenier *et al.* (2012) show that remedial tactics that can reduce liability when client importance is low can backfire when client importance is high, presumably because jurors' negative affect is aroused by the lack of credibility of remedial tactics in light of auditors' presumed self-serving motives. More research is needed on means of counteracting the impact of jurors' negative affect on verdicts against auditors.

Recent research delves deeper into how counterfactual reasoning influences jurors' verdicts. Based on the ideas that (1) the extent to which observers engage in counterfactual reasoning depends on how easy it is to imagine that a different outcome could have occurred (Kahneman and Miller 1986); and (2) it is easier to imagine more positive outcomes arising from prior events when positive outcomes were missed by a narrow margin rather than by a wide margin (Kahneman and Miller 1986), Reffett (2010) hypothesized and found that evaluators have more intense thoughts about what auditors could have done differently to detect a fraud when their working papers describe them investigating for fraud (and not finding it) than when they do not. More intense counterfactual thoughts are associated with higher assessments of auditor liability. Similarly, Backof (2012) shows that auditors' documentation of their consideration of alternative accounting treatments can increase the likelihood that jurors find auditors negligent by increasing jurors' views of the foreseeability of the misstatement. These findings are important because they indicate situations in which performing and documenting more audit work can lead to higher likelihood of a negligence finding against the firm. In other words, the merits matter, but in the wrong direction!

Culpable control theory provides a specific process by which counterfactuals, negative affect, and blame are related (Alicke 2000; Alicke *et al.* 2008). The theory asserts that while knowledge that a harmful outcome could have been avoided causes negative affect in observers, whether this negative affect results in blame depends on whether an actor has exercised control in a way that allows observers to blame him. That is, if the actor has taken all reasonable precautions and the harmful event occurs regardless, increased blame will not result. Thus, auditors can reduce their liability by following the recommendations of a highly reliable decision aid (Lowe *et al.* 2002), by following audit standards set by a government body, rather than by the profession (Buckless and Peace 1993), and by requiring one's client to adhere to precise accounting standards, or, in the absence of precise standards, reporting norms, so that jurors can readily establish compliance (Kadous and Mercer 2012).

Attribution theory and culpable control theory have proven fruitful in generating new and important insights into how jurors and others evaluate and assign blame to auditors. There remain many open questions that would benefit from careful application of theory. Many of the early debiasing studies, for example, were conducted in the belief that the process that resulted in outcome effects was "purely cognitive" and "data driven", and so the design of potential debiasers was generally not informed by theories about counterfactuals and attribution. This could account for the mixed results of those studies. More recent work provides a detailed accounting of how hindsight and outcome effects are linked with counterfactuals (Roese and Vohs 2012) and links important elements of counterfactuals with blame (Alicke 2000; Alicke *et al.* 2008), providing a richer knowledge base from which to reexamine and generate new debiasers. Future theory-based experiments can also provide ex ante evidence about how proposed changes in regulation (e.g., about auditor rotation) or firm policies (e.g., out-sourcing parts of the audit work, documentation policies) will influence auditor liability. They may also provide additional insight into when auditors are likely to be punished for higher audit quality and how these effects can be avoided.

Methodological issues

A common criticism of experimental research on juror assessments of auditor blame is that undergraduate students are frequently used as research participants. Students tend to be younger and better educated than the general adult population, and thus may make different judgments. However, use of students as jurors in experiments generally is not problematic for experiments that are designed to test theoretical relationships. As long as the predicted relationship relates to a general human judgment process and it is very unlikely that students would show a different relationship than the broader adult population, an accurate picture can be obtained by using the more accessible student population. Research verifies that across a wide variety of experimental cases, undergraduate students acting as mock jurors tend to come to verdicts that are indistinguishable from those of sitting jurors and other groups of older adults, and population does not significantly interact with manipulated variables (Bornstein 1999).

This conclusion does not imply that any undergraduate student population is acceptable for any study of juror decision making. Researchers must reason through whether their chosen participant population is appropriate for their study, given their manipulated variables. In general, advanced accounting or business students constitute a poor participant pool for auditor studies in which case facts are manipulated. Student knowledge of accounting and auditing could interact with manipulated variables (e.g., they should be more responsive to audit quality cues than the general public) and their presumed affinity for auditors could cause them to interpret case facts in a way that favors auditors. For example, they may be more forgiving of an auditor's mistake than the general public would be. The most appropriate student subject pools for auditor liability studies are thus diverse populations such as those that take general electives.

A second common criticism of experimental studies is that they rarely allow jury deliberation. That is, although auditor liability is ultimately determined by juries, rather than by individual jurors, researchers tend to draw conclusions from the judgments and decisions of individual mock jurors, working alone. This design choice is typically justified by the fact that prior research using criminal cases finds that the jury's ultimate verdict matches that of the majority of jurors on the first ballot over 90 percent of the time (Kalven and Zeisel 1966; Sandys and Dillehay 1995). Recent research in audit litigation verifies that jury verdicts in the audit litigation context are also determined by the pre-deliberation verdicts of a majority of individuals assigned to the jury (Kadous and Mercer 2012). A caveat is that, in this study, jurors knew they would be deliberating when they made their initial decisions. It is possible that these participants thought more carefully about their verdicts than participants acting as jurors in studies without this feature. This is an open issue for future research. A preliminary conclusion is that, despite the intuitive appeal of the deliberation, it appears to have very little impact on jury decisions.

Differences in blame assessments of jurors and other parties

Studies on the "expectations gap" in auditing tend to find that jurors, judges, and other third parties believe that auditors can and should do more to prevent plaintiff losses than auditors believe they can and should do. However, few studies examine whether these groups employ different processes in assessing blame, or even whether they rely on similar factors to make their decisions. This is important in light of the fact that potential jurors with knowledge or experience in auditing are unlikely to be selected for a trial of an auditor, and so jurors tend to be relatively uninformed. Because uninformed jurors do not have firmly established ideas about what auditors can and should do, they are more swayed by the facts of the case before them, and this may at least partially explain why they rely on legally irrelevant information such as the severity of the loss (Kadous 2000). Thus, it is reasonable to wonder whether more informed evaluators, such as a panel of auditors, would use a more defensible process and therefore come to higher quality verdicts (e.g., Palmrose 2006). Reffett *et al.* (2012) provide initial evidence that jurors and auditors rely on different legally irrelevant inputs in assessing auditor negligence. While there is some evidence that experts rely more than jurors on legally relevant inputs, such as audit quality, this evidence is weak, and additional evidence indicates that experts base their verdicts primarily on affective considerations. This indicates that replacing jurors with expert panels is not a panacea for unfair jury decisions.

Auditor–client relationship

Numerous studies examine how the auditor–client relationship impacts and is impacted by litigation. The two most prominent areas for research involve audit fees and auditor resignations. Starting with Simunic (1980), a vast literature examines the relation between audit fees and litigation risk. This literature generally finds a strong, positive relation between proxies for litigation risk, such as the client's financial condition, and audit fees (e.g., Simunic 1980; Pratt and Stice 1994). More recent work utilizes finer distinctions, such as variation in auditor liability standards associated with initial public stock offerings, to confirm the relation between audit fees and litigation risk (Venkataraman *et al.* 2008). Simunic and Stein (1996) provide a survey of the relevant work in this field.

Several studies find that litigation risk affects client retention. Auditors are more likely to resign from clients that impose high litigation risk (e.g., Krishnan and Krishnan 1997; Shu 2000). In addition, Choi *et al.* (2004) find that audit firms adjusted the risk of their client portfolios in response to shifts in the legal environment from 1985 to 1999. A related literature in auditor judgment and decision making demonstrates that auditors are less willing to allow high-risk clients to take aggressive reporting positions (e.g., Hackenbrack and Nelson 1996).

Overall, the audit fee, auditor resignation, and auditor decision-making literature supports the view that auditors are well attuned to litigation risk and consider it closely in their practice. However, audit firms also contend that they cannot fully price risk in their engagements (Bell *et al.* 2001). Thus, future research might consider not simply whether there is a relation between audit fees and risk, but also how accurately auditors are able to price litigation risk, for instance by comparing future litigation costs to abnormal fees.

Some remaining questions

Here, we summarize several of the open research issues in the area of litigation against auditors that we consider most pressing.

Liability standards

We noted above that the liability standard (e.g., negligence versus intent/scienter) is a key determinant of auditor liability. Other liability standards are also possible. For example, under strict liability, the auditor would be held responsible for losses due to financial statement misstatements, regardless of auditor fault or negligence. Several analytical and experimental economics studies have examined the effect of liability standards on social welfare. Dopuch and King (1992) examine the effect of three liability standards (no liability, strict liability, and negligence) on seller decisions to hire verifiers and resulting decisions of buyers. They find that the negligence standard produces outcomes at least as economically efficient as the other two standards. Radhakrishnan (1999) also finds higher investor welfare under a negligence standard than a strict liability standard.

While these studies provide important results, they do not directly compare the liability standards of most interest to auditors today. Future market-based experiments could compare the impact on social welfare of a negligence standard to that of a higher *intent* standard (e.g., reckless or knowing), which generally decreases auditor liability because proving auditor recklessness or knowledge of misstatement is often difficult. Such a comparison would be of immediate relevance to the current debate regarding liability (e.g., ACAP 2008; CAQ 2008), which has focused on decreasing auditor liability, as audit firms contend that even the negligence standard could produce catastrophic results for their business models. Because there is variation in existing law regarding the legal standard for liability (e.g., securities class actions involving Rule 10b-5 claims versus Section 11 claims), it may also be possible to investigate this area with archival data. Finally, as most studies of juror decision making rely on a negligence standard, it is unclear whether and how a higher intent standard would influence jurors' assessments of auditor blame for losses associated with financial statement misstatements. Future research could investigate this issue.

Settlement model

While prior research generally focuses on the decisions of jury members, relatively few cases involving audit litigation ever go to jury trial. Rather, these cases nearly always settle out of court (e.g., CAQ 2008). The focus on juror decisions is justified by the idea that settlement decisions depend on the parties' expectations of a jury resolution. However, it is unclear how third parties anticipate jurors' decisions and how accurate these expectations are. Because humans tend to view themselves as relatively unbiased and others as biased (e.g., Pronin *et al.* 2004; Pronin 2007), it is likely that both plaintiffs and the defendant audit firm perceive juror bias to be higher than the actual bias. Research on this issue could potentially help auditors revise their settlement decision rules.

Damage awards

Because so few cases go to trial, archival data about damage awards is sparse. Experimental work, relying on and building rich theory in blame assessment, has proven very useful in predicting verdicts. However, research has not provided much insight into damage awards, perhaps because theory in this area is not as well developed. Developing and testing such theory is an important goal for future research.

Merits of the case

An issue of critical importance is identifying conditions under which the merits of the case are more and less likely to impact the incidence and resolution of litigation. Some of the research cited above addresses this issue, but there is still much to learn. This is an area in which archival and experimental research complement each other and we encourage researchers to make use of both literatures to increase our understanding. The development of deeper theory about the role of counterfactual thinking in lay assessments of blame has provided some compelling insights that can be leveraged. For example, this theory predicts that auditors would be blamed more for easier to identify and more common frauds, because it is easier for jurors to imagine a different outcome from auditors' investigations in these cases (e.g., Bonner *et al.* 1998). In this case, the merits of the case and the effect of counterfactuals are predicted to have similar impacts on verdicts. However, in other cases, counterfactual theory predicts that auditors will be more likely to be found negligent when they conduct higher quality audits (e.g., Reffett 2010). Researchers may be able to leverage this theory, as well as theory about the role of affect in blame assessment to make new predictions that can be tested with archival data. Such research could better identify conditions under which verdicts rely on legally irrelevant factors, improving predictability of verdicts for auditors. Follow-up research could attempt to determine how to eliminate the impact of these legally irrelevant factors to improve the fairness of verdicts and the efficiency of the legal system from a social welfare perspective.

Note

1 We thank Bob Mocadlo for research assistance, and Jon Grenier, Molly Mercer, Robert Prentice, Drew Reffett, Jamie Schmidt, and Dan Zhou for helpful comments on previous drafts of the chapter.

References

Advisory Committee on the Auditing Profession (ACAP). 2008. "Final Report of the Advisory Committee on the Auditing Profession to the US Department of the Treasury". Available online at www.treasury.gov/about/organizational-structure/offices/Documents/final-report.pdf (accessed 14 April 2014).

Alexander, J. C. 1991. "Do the Merits Matter? A Study of Settlements in Securities Class Actions", *Stanford Law Review* 43: 497–598.

Alicke, M. D. 2000. "Culpable Control and the Psychology of Blame", *Psychological Bulletin* 126(4): 556–74.

Alicke, M. D., J. Buckingham, E. Zell, and T. Davis. 2008. "Culpable Control and Counterfactual Reasoning in the Psychology of Blame", *Personality and Social Psychology Bulletin* 34(10): 1371–81.

Anderson, J. C., M. M. Jennings, D. J. Lowe, and P. M. J. Reckers. 1997. "The Mitigation of Hindsight Bias in Judges' Evaluation of Auditor Decisions", *Auditing: A Journal of Practice and Theory* 16(2): 20–39.

Backof, A. G. 2012. *The Impact of Audit Evidence Documentation on Jurors' Negligence Verdicts and Damage Awards*, working paper. Charlottesville, VA: University of Virginia.

Bell, T. B., W. R. Landsman, and D. A. Shackelford. 2001. "Auditors' Perceived Business Risk and Audit Fees: Analysis and Evidence", *Journal of Accounting Research* 39: 35–43.

Bonner, S. E., Z.-V. Palmrose, and S. M. Young. 1998. "Fraud Type and Auditor Litigation: An Analysis of SEC Accounting and Auditing Enforcement Releases", *The Accounting Review* 73: 503–32.

Bornstein, B. H. 1999. "The Ecological Validity of Jury Simulations: Is the Jury Still Out?", *Law and Human Behavior* 23(1): 75–91.

Brandon, D. M. and J. M. Mueller. 2006. "The Influence of Client Importance on Juror Evaluations of Auditor Liability", *Behavioral Research in Accounting* 18(1): 1–18.

Buckless, F. and R. Peace. 1993. "The Influence of the Source of Professional Standards on Juror Decision Making", *The Accounting Review* 68(1): 164–75.

Burton, F. G., T. J. Wilks, and M. F. Zimbelman. 2011. "The Impact of Audit Penalty Distributions on the Detection and Frequency of Fraudulent Reporting", *Review of Accounting Studies* 16: 843–65.

Carcello, J. V. and Z.-V. Palmrose. 1994. "Auditor Litigation and Modified Reporting on Bankrupt Clients", *Journal of Accounting Research* 32: 1–30.

Center for Audit Quality (CAQ). 2008. Report of the Major Public Company Audit Firms to the Department of the Treasury Advisory Committee on the Auditing Profession. Washington, D.C.: CAQ.

Choi, J.-H., R. K. Doogar, and A. R. Ganguly. 2004. "The Riskiness of Large Audit Firm Client Portfolios and Changes in Audit Liability Regimes: Evidence from the US Audit Market", *Contemporary Accounting Research* 21: 747–85.

Clarkson, P. M., C. Emby, and V. W. S. Watt. 2002. "Debiasing the Outcome Effect: The Role of Instructions in an Audit Litigation Setting", *Auditing: A Journal of Practice & Theory* 21(2): 7–20.

Coffee, J. C. 2006. "Reforming the Securities Class Action: An Essay on Deterrence and its Implementation", *Columbia Law Review* 106: 1534–86.

Cook, J. M., E. M. Freedman, R. J. Groves, J. C. Madonna, S. F. O'Malley, and L. A. Weinbach. 1992. "The Liability Crisis in the United States: Impact on the Accounting Profession", *Journal of Accountancy* 174: 19–23.

Cornell, R. M., R. C. Warne, and M. M. Eining. 2009. "The Use of Remedial Tactics in Negligence Litigation", *Contemporary Accounting Research* 26: 767–87.

Donelson, D. C., J. McInnis and R. D. Mergenthaler. 2012. "Rules-based Accounting Standards and Litigation", *The Accounting Review* 87(4): 1247–79.

Dopuch, N. and R. R. King. 1992. "Negligence Versus Strict Liability Regimes in Auditing: An Experimental Investigation", *The Accounting Review* 67(1): 97–120.

Dopuch, N., R. R. King, and J. W. Schatzberg. 1994. "An Experimental Investigation of Alternative Damage-sharing Liability Regimes with an Auditing Perspective", *Journal of Accounting Research* 32(Supp): 103–30.

Fincham, F. D. and J. M. Jaspars. 1980. "Attribution of Responsibility: From Man the Scientist to Man as Lawyer", *Advances in Experimental Social Psychology* 13: 80–138.

Fuerman, R. D. 2000. "Auditors and the Post-Litigation Reform Act Environment", *Research in Accounting Regulation* 14: 199–218.

Gramling, A. A., J. W. Schatzberg, A. D. Bailey, and H. Zhang. 1998. "The Impact of Legal Liability Regimes and Differential Client Risk on Client Acceptance, Audit Pricing, and Audit Effort Decisions", *Journal of Accounting, Auditing and Finance* 13(4): 437–60.

Grenier, J. H., B. Pomeroy, and A. B. Reffett. 2012. "Speak up or Shut up? The Moderating Role of Credibility on Auditor Remedial Defense Tactics", *Auditing: A Journal of Practice and Theory* 31(4): 65–83.

Hackenbrack, K. and M. W. Nelson. 1996. "Auditors' Incentives and their Application of Financial Accounting Standards", *The Accounting Review* 71(1): 43–59.

Heninger, W. G. 2001. "The Association between Auditor Litigation and Abnormal Accruals", *The Accounting Review* 76: 111–26.

Johnson, M. F., K. K. Nelson, and A. C. Pritchard. 2007. "Do the Merits Matter More? The Impact of the Private Securities Litigation Reform Act", *Journal of Law, Economics & Organization* 23: 627–52.

Kadous, K. 2000. "The Effect of Audit Quality and Consequence Severity on Juror Evaluations of Auditor Responsibility for Plaintiff Losses", *The Accounting Review* 75: 327–41.

Kadous, K. 2001. "Improving Jurors' Evaluations of Auditors in Negligence Cases", *Contemporary Accounting Research* 18: 425–44.

Kadous, K. and M. Mercer. 2012. "Can Reporting Norms Create a Safe Harbor? Jury Verdicts against Auditors under Precise and Imprecise Accounting Standards", *The Accounting Review* 87: 565–87.

Kahneman, D. and D. T. Miller. 1986. "Norm Theory: Comparing Reality to its Alternatives", *Psychological Review* 93: 136–53.

Kalven, H. Jr and H. Zeisel. 1966. *The American Jury*. Boston, MA: Little, Brown.

Kaplan, S. E. and D. D. Williams. 2013. "Do Going Concern Audit Reports Protect Auditors from Litigation? A Simultaneous Equations Approach", *The Accounting Review* 88(1): 199–232.

Krishnan, J. and J. Krishnan. 1997. "Litigation Risk and Auditor Resignations", *The Accounting Review* 72: 539–60.

Lowe, D. J. and P. M. J. Reckers. 1994. "The Effects of Hindsight Bias on Jurors' Evaluations of Auditor Decisions", *Decision Sciences* 25(3): 401–26.

Lowe, D. J., P. M. J. Reckers, and S. M. Whitecotton. 2002. "The Effects of Decision-aid use and Reliability on Jurors' Evaluations of Auditor Liability", *The Accounting Review* 77: 185–202.

Lys, T. and R. L. Watts. 1994. "Lawsuits against Auditors", *Journal of Accounting Research* 32: 65–93.

Palmrose, Z.-V. 1988. "An Analysis of Auditor Litigation and Audit Service Quality", *The Accounting Review* 63: 55–73.

Palmrose, Z.-V. 1991. "Trials of Legal Disputes Involving Independent Auditors: Some Empirical Evidence", *Journal of Accounting Research* 29: 149–85.

Palmrose, Z.-V. 2006. "Maintaining the Value and Viability of Independent Auditors as Gatekeepers under SOX: An Auditing Masters Proposal", in Y. Fuchita and R. Litan (eds) *Financial Gatekeepers: Can They Protect Investors?*, pp. 103–35. Washington, D.C.: Brookings Institute Press.

Palmrose, Z.-V. and S. Scholz. 2004. "The Circumstances and Legal Consequences of Non-GAAP Reporting: Evidence from Restatements", *Contemporary Accounting Research* 21: 139–80.

Pratt, J. and J. D. Stice. 1994. "The Effects of Client Characteristics on Auditor Litigation Risk Judgments, Required Audit Evidence, and Recommended Audit Fees", *The Accounting Review* 69: 639–56.

Pronin, E. 2007. "Perception and Misperception of Bias in Human Judgment", *TRENDS in Cognitive Sciences* 11: 37–43.

Pronin, E., T. Gilovich and L. Ross. 2004. "Objectivity in the Eye of the Beholder: Divergent Perceptions of Bias in Self versus Others", *Psychological Review* 111: 781–99.

Radhakrishnan, S. 1999. "Investors' Recovery Friction and Auditor Liability Rules", *The Accounting Review* 74(2): 225–40.

Reffett, A. B. 2010. "Can Identifying and Investigating Fraud Risks Increase Auditors' Liability?" *The Accounting Review* 85(6): 2145–67.

Reffett, A., B. E. Brewster and B. Ballou. 2012. "Comparing Auditor versus Non-auditor Assessments of Auditor Liability: An Experimental Investigation of Experts' versus Lay Evaluators' Judgments", *Auditing: A Journal of Practice & Theory* 31(3): 125–48.

Roese, N. J. 1997. "Counterfactual Thinking", *Psychological Review* 121: 133–48.

Roese, N. J. and K. D. Vohs. 2012. "Hindsight Bias", *Perspectives in Psychological Science* 7(5): 411–26.

Sandys, M. and R. C. Dillehay. 1995. "First-ballot Votes, Predeliberation Dispositions, and Final Verdicts in Jury Trials", *Law and Human Behavior* 19(2): 175–95.

Schmidt, J. 2012. "Perceived Auditor Independence and Audit Litigation: The Role of Nonaudit Services Fees", *The Accounting Review* 87(3): 1033–65.

Shu, S. Z. 2000. "Auditor Resignations: Clientele Effects and Legal Liability", *Journal of Accounting and Economics* 29: 173–205.

Simunic, D. 1980. "The Pricing of Audit Services: Theory and Evidence", *Journal of Accounting Research* 18: 161–90.

Simunic, D. and M. T. Stein. 1996. "The Impact of Litigation Risk on Audit Pricing: A Review of the Economics and the Evidence", *Auditing: A Journal of Practice & Theory* 15: 119–34.

St. Pierre, K. and J. Anderson. 1984. "An Analysis of the Factors Associated with Lawsuits against Public Accountants", *The Accounting Review* 59: 242–83.

Stice, J. D. 1991. "Using Financial and Market Information to Identify Pre-engagement Factors Associated with Lawsuits against Auditors", *The Accounting Review* 66: 516–33.

Venkataraman, R., J. P. Weber and M. Willenborg. 2008. "Litigation Risk, Audit Quality, and Audit Fees: Evidence from Initial Public Offerings", *The Accounting Review* 83: 1315–45.

Yu, H. 2001. "Experimental Evidence of the Impact of Increasing Auditors' Legal Liability on Firms' New Investments", *Contemporary Accounting Research* 18(3): 495–528.

7

Non-audit services and auditor independence

Divesh S. Sharma

Introduction

The contrasting views about auditors providing non-audit services are illustrated by these statements: "(The) performance of (non-audit) and auditing for the same client by the same accountant (is) a combination of incompatible services" (Mautz and Sharaf 1961: 223); and: "Synergies ... exist when a firm provides a broad array of auditing and nonauditing services to its clients" (Melancon 2000: 3). Ever since the external financial statement auditor's firm (hereafter auditor) provided consulting or non-audit services (NAS) to audit clients, concerns about the auditor's independence have been paramount. NAS became a significant concern following deregulation of the audit market in the 1970s. The intent of deregulating the audit market was to create competition and increase audit quality. However, competition and active advertising including pursuit of clients by audit firms resulted in discounted audit fees and paring of margins. To compensate, audit firms entered the consulting market which rapidly became very lucrative. The audit was a loss-leader commodity as firms low-balled to secure new clients. Some commentators argue that deregulation of the audit market brought unintended consequences such as revenue and profit focus through NAS resulting in recurring audit failures (Hay and Knechel 2010).

As audit firms expanded the breadth and depth of NAS, it became clearer that such services placed auditors in positions where they act in a management role, review their own work, trade-off audit quality for lucrative consulting fees, or are hostage to the economic bargaining power held by management. Thus, regulators around the world continue to be concerned about the negative impact of auditors jointly providing audit and NAS. The historical and unprecedented Sarbanes-Oxley Act of 2002 (hereafter SOX) (SOX 2002) initiated regulations on NAS following the string of financial scandals unveiled at Enron and WorldCom. SOX banned most NAS in the US; mandated that audit committees be responsible for appointing, remunerating, and terminating the auditor; pre-approving NAS; and asserting that approved NAS do not threaten auditor independence. The SOX also mandated separate disclosure of audit fees and types of non-audit fees paid to the auditor.[1]

The accounting profession and corporate executives were critical of the SOX ban on NAS primarily on grounds of lack of persuasive and pervasive evidence. They argued that regulators failed to provide sufficient, necessary, and conclusive evidence that unequivocally demonstrated auditor-provided NAS impaired an auditor's independence. The accounting profession also argued that the joint provision of audit and NAS provides many benefits, most notably, knowledge spillovers and audit efficiencies (Knechel and Sharma 2012).

Despite these contentions, regulators around the world also reacted to SOX by proposing, adopting, or modifying governance of NAS purchases from the external auditor. Australia, Belgium, Brazil, Germany, Hong Kong, Malaysia, New Zealand, Singapore, Spain, and the UK are some of the many countries that modified their regulations on NAS, with these ranging from detailed disclosure of fees paid to audit firms for audit and NAS to audit committee pre-approval of NAS and limitations on certain types of NAS.[2] Although France and Italy adopted a prohibitive approach, French and Italian auditors have been known to provide NAS because their regulations are ambiguous (Ianniello 2012).

The 2010 European Union (EC 2010) green paper proposed a complete ban on auditor-provided NAS by recommending the establishment of "audit-only" firms. Rather than limit the scope of NAS and require audit committee pre-approval as in the US under SOX, the EU model would completely eliminate NAS from the portfolio of services that audit firms can provide. This idea is receiving intense attention and scrutiny from the profession both in Europe and elsewhere. If the EU proposal is implemented, public accounting firms will experience significant economic consequences and regulators elsewhere could mimic such reforms. It could also have serious ramifications for the audits of multinational companies where different portions of the audit are conducted by different branches of a Big 4 firm but operating under different independence rules. However, the EU proposal is not scientifically supported because of the lack of research evidence in Europe concerning potential auditor independence problems.[3] It is also not known if a zero NAS audit provider will be more independent because independence problems can also stem from dependence on audit fees.

In this chapter, I review the literature published since the turn of the century in a selection of journals that publish a good quantity of archival audit research from authors around the world.[4] The review is not exhaustive but illustrative; the idea is to provide a flavor of the developments so as to inform future regulatory developments, provide feedback on what works and does not, and shape the evolution of policy formulation and academic research.

Overview of NAS research

Auditors are required to maintain independence by exercising objectivity in their judgments and decision making. Since auditors' independence is a state of mind that cannot be observed, their watchdog role on behalf of shareholders brings into play the perception dimension of auditor independence. Therefore, auditors' independence is evaluated with reference to auditor behavior and situations that may raise doubts about their objectivity. Consequently, researchers have investigated how NAS can potentially threaten auditor independence by investigating the association between NAS and various proxies to capture the quality of the audit (e.g., going concern modification, restatements, and earnings management). As originally noted by DeAngelo (1981), to provide high quality audits, auditors must be competent (i.e., capable of detecting misstatements) and have market-based incentives to exercise independent judgment (i.e., willing to report misstatements that are discovered). The central premise in the literature on NAS is that an adverse association between NAS fees and audit quality or proxies for investor attitudes (e.g., cost of equity, bond ratings, perceptions of the quality of earnings) is indicative of the undermining of auditor independence. Given the regulatory impact on NAS, the focus of this chapter is on studies examining *reported* NAS fees paid to the auditor as the variable of interest.[5]

Table 7.1 chronologically summarizes the prior research examining independence in fact (Panels A to E) followed by the limited prior research examining independence in appearance

Table 7.1 Published literature on NAS and auditor independence

Study	*Dependent Variable*	*Independent Variables*	*Sample*	*Main Findings*
		PANEL A: AUDITOR OPINION STUDIES		
Sharma and Sidhu (2001) Australia JBFA	Going concern modification (GCM)	NAS fees to total fees (hereafter FEERATIO)	49 involuntary bankrupt Australian companies between 1989 and 1996	Significant negative association between FEERATIO and CGM
DeFond *et al.* (2002) USA JAR	GCM	FEERATIO, natural log of audit, NAS, and total fees (hereafter audit, NAS, and total fees)	1,158 US distressed firms including 96 with first-time GCM in fiscal year 2000	No significant association between any of the fee variables and GCM
Geiger and Rama (2003) USA AJPT	GCM	NAS and audit fees	66 distressed GCM and matched 66 distressed non-GCM manufacturing firms with proxy filings between Sept 30, 2000 and Feb 28, 2001	No significant association between NAS fees and GCM. Audit fees significantly positively associated with GCM.
Hay *et al.* (2006) NZ JBFA	Qualified or GCM	FEERATIO	644 New Zealand firm-years from 1999–2001	No significant association between fees and audit opinion
Basioudis *et al.* (2008) UK Abacus	GCM	NAS and audit fees	58 UK distressed companies from 2003	Significant negative association between NAS fees and GCM
Fargher and Jiang (2008) Australia AJPT	GCM	Client importance at audit firm level measured using total fees NAS fees	5,113 Australian listed company firm-years of which 1,309 are financially distressed for 1998, 1999, and 2003–5	Significant negative association between client importance and GCM across all samples but authors do not discuss auditor independence
Robinson (2008) USA AJPT	GCM	Audit, NAS, and Tax NAS fees	209 bankrupt US firms between 2001 and 2004	Significant positive association between GCM and tax NAS fees
Li (2009) USA CAR	GCM	Client importance at office level measured using audit, NAS, and total fees	Financially stressed companies comprising 1,681 in 2001 and 1,780 in 2003	No significant association between any of the three client importance measures and GCM in 2001 but significant positive association between audit and total fee based measures

Table 7.1 (continued)

Study	*Dependent Variable*	*Independent Variables*	*Sample*	*Main Findings*
Hope and Langli (2010) Norway TAR	GCM	Unexpected, levels and changes in audit, NAS, and total fees	42,296 private limited liability companies in Norway from 1997–2002	No evidence of a negative association between fee variables and GCM
Callaghan *et al.* (2011) USA AJPT	GCM	Audit, NAS, and total fees, and FEERATIO	92 companies filing Chapter 11 bankruptcy between Jan 1, 2001 and March 16, 2005. 42 GCM companies.	No significant association between any of the fee variables and GCM
Ye *et al.* (2011) Australia AJPT	GCM	FEERATIO	626 financially distressed Australian firms in 2000	Significant negative association between FEERATIO and GCM. Result is more pronounced for clients with audit firm alumni serving on the board.
Blay and Geiger (2012) USA CAR	GCM	Current FEERATIO, NAS, and total fees, and future total fees (subsequent two years)	1,479 distressed firms comprising 180 first time going GCM in fiscal years 2004–6	Clients with higher current FEERATIO and NAS fees, and higher future total fees, are less likely to receive a GCM
Ianniello (2012) Italy IJA	Qualified opinion	Various NAS ratios	239 Italian listed companies for fiscal year ended Dec 31, 2007	Some significant positive associations between NAS and a qualified opinion
		PANEL B: RESTATEMENT STUDIES		
Raghunandan *et al.* (2003) USA AH	Financial restatements	Actual and unexpected NAS fees, FEERATIO, and total fees	110 restatement and 3,481 non-restatement companies for fiscal years 2000 and 2001	Univariate median tests show no evidence that restatement and non-restatement firms differ on fees paid to auditors
Kinney *et al.* (2004) USA JAR	Financial restatements	Six types of fees paid to auditors: audit, audit-related, FISDI, internal audit, tax, and unspecified. Fee data obtained from surveys sent to audit firms.	Sample size varies from 180 matched-pairs of first-time restating and non-restating companies to 432 restatement and 512 non-restatement companies for restatements announced between Jan 1, 1995 and Dec 31, 2000	No significant association between fees paid for FISDI or internal audit services and restatements. Significant positive association between unspecified services and restatements, and significant negative association between tax NAS fees and restatements.

Table 7.1 (continued)

Study	*Dependent Variable*	*Independent Variables*	*Sample*	*Main Findings*
Bloomfield and Shackman (2008) USA MAJ	Financial restatements	FEERATIO, NAS fees and client importance at audit firm level measured using NAS fees	250 restatement and 250 randomly selected firms for 2000–02	Mixed results; some significant positive associations between client importance and restatements, some non-significant results
Paterson and Valencia (2011) USA CAR	Financial restatements	Recurring and non-recurring types of NAS fees (audit-related, tax, and other). Fees recur if they are consecutively paid for two years to the same auditor.	3,232 restatement and 15,087 non-restatement firm-years between 2003 and 2006	Recurring (non-recurring) tax NAS fees are negatively (positively) associated and both recurring and non-recurring audit-related and other NAS fees are positively associated with restatements
Ferguson *et al.* (2004) UK CAR	Criticism of firms' accounting practices by media and regulators Financial restatements Discretionary working capital accruals estimated using the modified-Jones model	FEERATIO, NAS fees, and client importance measured as decile rank of relative size of average NAS fees paid by client to audit office	542 to 610 UK firms for FYE 1996–8	All NAS fee variables are positive and significantly associated with lower quality financial reporting
		PANEL C: EARNINGS QUALITY STUDIES		
Frankel *et al.* (2002) USA TAR	Absolute discretionary accruals (ABSDACC) using cross sectional modified Jones (1991) model (CMJM).	FEERATIO Audit, NAS, and total fees	3,074 firms with proxy statements between Feb 5, 2001 and June 15, 2001	Significant positive association between fees and ABSDACC and SURPRISE. Significant negative association between NAS and CAR.

Table 7.1 (continued)

Study	*Dependent Variable*	*Independent Variables*	*Sample*	*Main Findings*
	Meet or beat analysts' forecasts by $0.01 (SURPRISE). Small earnings increase between 0 and 2% (INCREASE). Cumulative abnormal returns (CAR)			
Ashbaugh *et al.* (2003) USA TAR	Portfolio performance adjusted discretionary current accruals (PADCA) and ROA augmented discretionary current accruals (REDCA). SURPRISE INCREASE CAR	FEERATIO Audit, NAS, and total fees	3,170 US firms with proxy statements during Nov and Dec 2001	FEERATIO is positively (negatively) related to absolute (negative) values of PADCA and REDCA, and NAS fee is positively (negatively) related to absolute (negative) values of PADCA. FEERATIO and NAS fees are positive but insignificant in their association with positive values of PADCA and REDCA. No significant findings are observed for fee variables in the INCREASE, SURPRISE, or CAR tests.
Chung and Kallapur (2003) USA TAR	CMJM	Client importance at audit firm and office levels measured using total and NAS fees	1,871 clients of Big-5 audit firms at the audit firm level and 1,778 firms at office level for year 2000	No significant association between any client importance measure and abnormal accruals
Reynolds *et al.* (2004) USA AJPT	CMJM	FEERATIO and total fees	2,507 US listed companies with proxy filings between Feb 5, 2001 and May 25, 2001	Results of Frankel *et al.* (2002) are replicated but hold for smaller firms only. No significant association between fee variables and discretionary accruals when high firm growth is controlled for.

Table 7.1 (continued)

Study	*Dependent Variable*	*Independent Variables*	*Sample*	*Main Findings*
Gul *et al.* (2007) USA AJPT	REDCA	Audit, NAS, and total fees, and FEERATIO Auditor tenure	4,720 firm-years for 2000 and 2001	NAS fee is positively associated with discretionary accruals for smaller clients with short auditor tenure (≤ 3 years)
Huang *et al.* (2007) USA AJPT	PADCA REDCA SURPRISE. INCREASE.	Types of NAS fees	Sample ranges between 2,969 and 6,722 firm-years for fiscal years 2003 and 2004	No strong association between types of NAS fees and accruals but some evidence that audit-related fees are positively related to accruals
Hunt and Lulseged (2007) USA JAPP	Discretionary and total accruals estimated using the Jones model augmented by ROA (Kothari *et al.* 2005) GCM	Client importance at the audit firm level measured using total fees, NAS fees, and FEERATIO. Client importance also measured using sales.	1,680 firm-years for accruals test and 996 firm-years for GCM test across 2001–3 for non-Big 5 auditors	Sales based measure of client importance shows clients of non-Big 5 auditors report lower accruals. No such evidence using fee based measure of client importance. GCM results are mixed; FEERATIO client importance measure is negatively, while sales and total fee based measures are positively, related to GCM.
Mitra (2007) USA JAAF	CMJM	FEERATIO, NAS fees to audit fees, total fees, and client importance measured using NAS fees and total fees at audit firm level	71 oil and gas companies with proxy filings between Feb 5, 2001 and June 30, 2001 relating to fiscal year 2000	No significant association between any fee variables and accruals
Srinidhi and Gul (2007) USA CAR	Accrual quality estimated using the modified Dechow-Dichev 2002 model (Francis *et al.* 2005)	Audit, NAS, and total fees, and NAS to audit fee ratio	1,709 and 2,573 listed US firms in 2000 and 2001, respectively	Higher NAS fees associated with lower accruals quality
Cahan *et al.* (2008) NZ AF	CMJM	Growth in NAS fees Client importance measured as NAS fees relative to total NAS fees and total fees of audit firm	237 New Zealand firms over 1995–2001	Results are mixed; some evidence to suggest firms paying higher fees report greater discretionary accruals

Table 7.1 (continued)

Study	*Dependent Variable*	*Independent Variables*	*Sample*	*Main Findings*
Lim and Tan (2008) USA JAR	SURPRISE REDCA GCM CAR to test for ERC	NAS and total fees Percentile rank of client importance at firm level	1,692 to 4,493 US firm-years for FYE 2000 and 2001	NAS positively related to SURPRISE for clients with non-industry specialist auditors. GCM and NAS positively related only for specialist auditors. Positive ERC when NAS is high but only for firms with specialist auditors.
Krishnan *et al.* (2011) USA AJPT	Industry portfolio performance adjusted discretionary accruals estimated using the CMJM	Percentile rank of NAS fee declines from pre-SOX to post-SOX period. Higher ranks reflect greater declines in NAS	1,768 unique firms with fee data for 2000, 2001, 2004, and 2005.	Firms with larger declines in NAS from pre- to post-SOX had higher absolute discretionary accruals in the pre-SOX period. Positive association between income-decreasing accruals in pre-SOX period and subsequent declines in NAS. Such effects weakened in post-SOX period.
Koh *et al.* (2012) USA RAST	CMJM INCREASE CAR to test for ERC	Lagged NAS fees to audit fees Lagged information system fees (ISFEE) to audit fees	1,344 S&P 500 firm-years for 1978–80	NAS fees are not related to accruals but ISFEE is negatively related to accruals. Both NAS and ISFEE negatively related to INCREASE and both fee variables have positive ERC.
		PANEL D: ROLE OF GOOD GOVERNANCE		
Larcker and Richardson (2004) USA JAR	Absolute and signed values of abnormal accruals estimated using the modified-Jones (1991) model augmented by book to market ratio and cash from operations	FEERATIO, client importance at audit firm level measured using NAS fees and total fees. Abnormal total and NAS fees (residuals from fee models).	5,103 firm-years for fiscal years 2000 and 2001	Smaller firms with weak governance (low institutional holdings, high insider ownership, and fewer external board members) exhibit a significant positive association between fees and abnormal accruals.

Table 7.1 (continued)

Study	*Dependent Variable*	*Independent Variables*	*Sample*	*Main Findings*
Sharma *et al.* (2011) NZ AJPT	CMJM discretionary accruals augmented by ROA (TACC) REDCA	Client importance measured at audit firm and office levels using NAS fees. Audit committee best practice is a composite score of four audit committee characteristics.	224 firm-years of listed companies in New Zealand for 2004 and 2005	Economically important clients report significantly higher TACC and REDCA. However, an audit committee meeting best practices moderates this effect.
		PANEL E: COSTS AND BENEFITS OF JOINT PROVISION		
Knechel *et al.* (2009) USA TAR	Audit efficiency = measured using data envelopment analysis where output is disaggregated audit hours across 8 activities and input is audit staff costs	MAS = 1 if auditor provides consulting services, 0 otherwise. TAX = 1 if auditor provides tax services, 0 otherwise.	226 audit client data from a single audit firm for fiscal year ended 1991	MAS is not related but TAX is negatively related to audit efficiency
Knechel and Sharma (2012) USA AJPT	CMJM discretionary accruals augmented by ROA, financial restatements. Audit efficiency = difference in days between the financial year end date and audit report date.	HINAS = 1 if NAS fees greater than median, 0 otherwise. NAS fee. SHORTLAG = 1 if audit lag is less than median, 0 otherwise.	5,004 firm-years of listed US companies for fiscal years 2000–03	HINAS not related to accruals or restatements. Restatements less likely when NAS is high in conjunction with short audit lag. Audit lag is negatively related to NAS in the pre-SOX but not in post-SOX period.

Table 7.1 (continued)

Study	*Dependent Variable*	*Independent Variables*	*Sample*	*Main Findings*
Knechel *et al.* (2012) NZ JBFA	CMJM discretionary accruals augmented by ROA. Audit efficiency = difference in days between the financial year end date and audit report date.	HIGHNAS = 1 if NAS fees greater than median, 0 otherwise. SHORTLAG = 1 if audit lag is less than median, 0 otherwise. FEERATIO and NAS fees at firm and city office levels.	230 firm-years of listed companies in New Zealand for 2004 and 2005	HIGHNAS is not associated with discretionary accruals. HIGHNAS and SHORTLAG in conjunction are not related to discretionary accruals. HIGHNAS, FEERATIO, and NAS fees are negatively related to audit lag but more pronounced at the city office level.
		PANEL F: INVESTOR PERCEPTION STUDIES		
Chaney and Philipich (2002) USA JAR	CAR	NAS fees scaled by total assets	257 Andersen clients	No significant association between NAS fees and CAR
Brandon *et al.* (2004) USA AJPT	Moody's bond rating	FEERATIO, NAS fees, total fees, and audit fees	333 unsecured bond issues between Feb 2001 and Dec 2002	FEERATIO, NAS fees, and total fees are negatively associated with bond ratings
Krishnan *et al.* (2005) USA AJPT	CAR to test for ERC	FEERATIO, NAS fees, total fees, and their respective unexpected fees	1,581 to 2,816 firms filing proxies in 2001	ERC is negative and significant for firms with higher NAS
Francis and Ke (2006) USA RAST	CAR to test for ERC	NAS fees above or below median	3,133 unique firms with initial fee disclosures for fiscal quarters ending 1999–2002	ERC is lower for firms with higher NAS fees in the post-fee disclosure period
Higgs and Skantz (2006) USA AJPT	CAR to test for ERC	Unexpected NAS fees to proxy client profitability	1,313 firms with proxy filings between Jan 1, 2001 and Feb 4, 2002	Limited evidence that ERC is negative for firms with abnormally high NAS fees

Table 7.1 (continued)

Study	*Dependent Variable*	*Independent Variables*	*Sample*	*Main Findings*
Krishnamurthy *et al.* (2006) USA CAR	CAR	Audit fee ratio, NAS fees, and total fees	812 firms that dismissed Andersen with fee data in calendar year 2001	NAS and total fees negatively associated with CAR
Zhang (2007) USA JAE	CAR	NAS fees less tax fees scaled by market value of equity	1,224 firms in 2001	NAS fee measure is negatively related to CAR
Khurana and Raman (2006) USA CAR	Cost of equity capital	Client importance at audit firm and office levels measured using NAS and total fees	2,163 clients of Big 5 from 2000 and 2001	All measures of client importance are positively related to the cost of equity capital
Dhaliwal *et al.* (2008) USA JAAF	Cost of debt (bond issue)	NAS and total fees, and FEERATIO	560 first bond issues during Feb 5, 2001 to Dec 31, 2003	Cost of debt is positively related to NAS and total fees, and FEERATIO but only for investment grade firms

(Panel F).[6] Details about the study such as authors, journal and year of publication, country, measures of the dependent and independent variables, description of the sample and main findings are provided in Table 7.1. The ensuing discussion of prior research mirrors the structure of Table 7.1 beginning with research on the association between NAS and the auditor's opinion (Panel A),[7] followed by studies that employ proxies of earnings quality to capture audit quality (Panels B and C), studies that examine NAS and auditor independence within the corporate governance framework (Panel D), and studies that examine simultaneously the costs and benefits of NAS (Panel E). Market-based research on perceptions of auditor independence is discussed next (Panel F). Implications from the literature for various stakeholders are presented prior to the conclusion of the chapter.

NAS and audit opinions

Table 7.1 shows that NAS and auditor reporting studies span five countries (Australia, Italy, New Zealand, UK, and the US) and most are based on US data. Sharma and Sidhu (2001) is one of the first studies to examine how publicly disclosed NAS fees paid by clients to their auditors are associated with an auditor's propensity to issue a going-concern modification (GCM). Sharma and Sidhu (2001) illustrate that an effective test of threats to auditor independence requires a design where the correctness of the auditor's opinion can be evaluated. Accordingly, they are the first to examine NAS and GCM for clients experiencing severe financial distress.[8] They also consider how a GCM may be influenced by non-financial mitigating factors such as reconstruction and refinancing plans. Sharma and Sidhu (2001) theorize that if certain conditions suggest a GCM is more than likely warranted, then after controlling for factors that mitigate a GCM, a negative association between the proportion of NAS fees to total fees (FEERATIO hereafter) and GCM could be indicative of the auditor compromising independence. Using Australian fee data one year prior to involuntary bankruptcy, Sharma and Sidhu (2001) find that clients with relatively higher FEERATIO are less likely to receive a GCM. Subsequent Australian studies (Fargher and Jiang 2008; Ye *et al.* 2011) echo the results of Sharma and Sidhu (2001) over different time periods.[9] Moreover, Ye *et al.* (2011) find that the adverse impact of NAS on GCM is more pronounced when a director on a client's board is an audit firm alumnus.

DeFond *et al.* (2002) is the first US study to examine how NAS are related to GCM for clients in financial distress. They use actual fee data reported in proxy statements following the Securities Exchange Commission (SEC) (2000) rules on fee disclosure. Financial distress is defined as either negative earnings or cash from operations in the current fiscal year. Since they find no significant association between various fee variables (FEERATIO, NAS fees, audit fees, and total fees) and GCM, DeFond *et al.* (2002) conclude there is no evidence that NAS impair auditor independence. This study makes other several important contributions to the literature as they perform additional analyses to examine the relationship between NAS and the correctness of the auditor's opinion and the impact of unexpected NAS fees.

Most other US studies reported in Table 7.1 also find no significant association between NAS and GCM, and conclude that NAS do not threaten auditor independence because of high litigation risk, whereas those in the UK (Basioudis *et al.* 2008) and Italy (Ianniello 2012), countries that are less litigious than the US (and similar to Australia), find a significant negative association.[10] For non-Big 5 auditors, Hunt and Lulseged (2007) find that FEERATIO is negatively related to GCM in the US. A unique and interesting study is that of Hope and Langli (2010); they examine private limited liability companies in Norway. Private companies are not traded in the market, are closely held, and pose low reputational risk for auditors. In addition, Norway is a less litigious society. Hence, Hope and Langli (2010) argue that if auditor independence problems are present, their setting provides a good chance of detection. Their results do not yield any significant association between NAS and GCM.

Another reason for the lack of finding of an adverse association between NAS and GCM in the US is that studies include data from a tumultuous period, i.e., 2000 to 2002 was signified by the SEC rules on fee disclosure, Enron-led scandals, SOX-initiated reforms, and significant regulatory, market, and media scrutiny of auditors which would have sensitized auditors to exercise abnormal levels of due care. Consequently, Blay and Gieger (2012) re-examine US auditors' propensity to issue a GCM to distressed manufacturing clients (both negative earnings and cash from operations) in fiscal years 2004 to 2006, at least two years after the tumultuous period. They find that clients with higher current NAS fees and future total fees are less likely to receive a GCM. A unique feature of Blay and Geiger (2012) is the use of future fees, and their results imply auditors evaluate the costs and benefits of qualifying the accounts of a lucrative client in terms of future revenues. I now turn to studies examining NAS and proxies of audit quality, beginning with financial restatements followed by proxies for earnings management.[11]

NAS and audit quality proxies

Financial restatements

Surprisingly, only a few studies focus on NAS and financial restatements, of which one is UK based. Financial restatements provide a relatively suitable context because restatements made to correct prior audited financial statements suggest the auditor may have failed to detect and/or report the misstatement. Studies in this paradigm distinguish intentional from unintentional misstatements and assume that the auditor detected but failed to report the intentional misstatement committed by management. An important issue to address is to determine restatements that are less ambiguous representations of the auditor's failure to detect and/or report a misstatement so that a clear link can be established.[12] The four US studies provide mixed results. Raghunandan *et al.* (2003) report no univariate differences in unexpected NAS fees between firms with and without a restatement. Kinney *et al.* (2004) find unspecified NAS fees are positively related while tax fees are negatively related to restatements. Bloomfield and Shackman (2008) report mixed results, while Paterson and Valencia (2011) conclude that some types of recurring and non-recurring NAS fees undermine auditor independence.[13] Ferguson *et al.* (2004) report that in the UK NAS is positively related to financial restatements.

Discretionary accruals and earnings surprises

Table 7.1 identifies numerous studies using some form of discretionary accruals and a small number using earnings surprises to capture earnings management, and hence, the quality of the audit. Chapters 10 and 11 examine earnings management and audit quality in more detail. The assumption in this stream of the literature is that auditors permit management to engage in opportunistic earnings management, which leads to biased financial reporting. Studies implicitly assume the auditor is competent and almost never question this ability. Accordingly, researchers interpret a positive association between NAS and discretionary accruals or earnings surprises indicative of breach of the auditor's independence.[14]

Frankel *et al.* (2002) is the first published study to examine the relationship between NAS and earnings management. Their results show two proxies for earnings management – discretionary accruals and meet or beat analysts' forecasts – are positively associated with FEERATIO and rank measure of NAS fees. An interesting finding in Frankel *et al.* (2002) that is often overlooked in the literature is that there were no significant results for any of the NAS fee variables for the now defunct audit firm Arthur Andersen; but their significant results were driven by three firms, EY, KPMG and PwC. Ashbaugh *et al.* (2003) posit that the results in Frankel *et al.* (2002) are potentially due to design issues, particularly how discretionary accruals and economic bonding between the auditor and client are estimated. Upon replicating Frankel *et al.* (2002), Ashbaugh *et al.* (2003) show mixed results: there are some positive and significant results, some negative and significant, and some insignificant results. The significance of the results depends on how the empirical models are specified.[15] The battery of tests in Ashbaugh *et al.* (2003) illustrate that results can be sensitive to the design of a study, how variables are measured, and how the empirical models are specified.

Although this paradigm often concludes that NAS do not threaten auditor independence, the literature remains unclear. Research subsequent to Frankel *et al.* (2002) and Ashbaugh *et al.* (2003), such as Srinidhi and Gul (2007), use a different estimate of earnings management (Dechow-Dichev 2002 model)[16] (Dechow and Dichev 2002) and find that NAS are positively associated with lower quality accruals. Huang *et al.* (2007)[17] report that audit-related fees, a specific type of NAS, are positively related to discretionary accruals; Krishnan *et al.* (2011)[18] report that firms with most declines in NAS from pre- to post-SOX exhibited higher discretionary accruals in the pre-SOX period; and the results in Reynolds *et al.* (2004) and Gul *et al.* (2007) suggest that threats to auditor independence from NAS is confined to smaller audit firms.

Another approach in the literature is to estimate the degree of economic bonding as the relative importance of the client in the auditor's client portfolio rather than as the magnitude or ratio of NAS fees. Chung and Kallapur (2003) posit that if regulators are concerned about the economic bonding effects between a client and the auditor then auditors will give preference to clients that are economically more important. As such, they argue that examining the magnitude of fees may not adequately capture how economically important a client is in the auditor's portfolio of clients. Therefore, they derive client importance measures by taking a client's fee (NAS or total fees) divided by the total fee revenue of the auditor at both the office and firm levels. Their results show no significant associations between this new measure of economic bonding and earnings management. Mitra (2007) finds similar results for client importance in the oil and gas industry.

Given the differences in results due to variations in research design (e.g., variables studied, different measures for audit quality, etc.), Lim and Tan (2008) employ both the magnitude of fees and audit firm level client importance measures, and multiple proxies for audit quality (discretionary accruals, meet or beat analysts' forecasts, and GCM). They also examine how auditor specialization plays into the NAS–independence issue. Their results suggest that NAS may pose independence problems for clients with non-specialist auditors.[19]

There are two striking observations about the NAS-earnings management literature. First, almost all studies examine US firms even though regulators in other countries that currently do not ban NAS are calling for more stringent regulations on NAS. An exception is Cahan *et al.* (2008), who examine discretionary accruals, growth in NAS fees, and audit firm level client importance in New Zealand. New Zealand does not impose bans on NAS but encourages auditors to consider how NAS could threaten their independence. Because Cahan *et al.* (2008) find mixed results, no conclusions about auditor independence can be made. Such results are probably due to their small sample, which explains why researchers tend to situate their studies in larger markets such as the US. The second striking observation about the NAS-earnings management or even NAS-audit quality literature is that research has largely ignored the role of corporate governance. I now turn to the two studies examining the relationship between NAS and auditor independence within a governance framework.

The role of good governance

One of the reasons for the mixed results in the prior literature discussed above could be explained by the governance framework within which the auditor and the client operate. Boards of directors and/or audit committees have typically been charged with overseeing the performance of the audit, purchase of NAS from the auditor, and the quality of financial reporting. Auditors and management are now under greater scrutiny from the audit committee and the board, with auditors in the US required to report directly to the audit committee under SOX. Similar governance guidelines have been developed in other countries such as Australia, UK, and Singapore. Prior to SOX in the US, audit committees were not required by law to oversee the work of the auditor.

From a research design perspective, studies examining NAS and auditor independence issues may suffer from a significant bias if they do not include corporate governance variables relating to the board and/or audit committee. Prior research shows that good governance is related to auditor reporting decisions (e.g., Carcello and Neal 2003); earnings management (e.g., Dhaliwal *et al.* 2010); and NAS purchases from the auditor (e.g., Naiker *et al.* 2013). Specifically, Naiker *et al.* (2013) examine the presence of audit firm alumni on the audit committee and NAS purchases, and how this dynamic influences audit quality. They find that firms appointing audit firm alumni to their audit committees procure fewer NAS from their alma mater, and the presence of audit firm alumni do not harm the quality of the audit. Since SOX in the US, as well as SOX-style reforms in other countries, bestow responsibilities on the audit committee (or board of directors) to oversee the financial reporting and audit processes (including the purchase of permissible NAS), it is important for research to recognize the role of the audit committee. Two studies to date have recognized this issue, Larcker and Richardson (2004) and Sharma *et al.* (2011). Both these studies amplify the importance of examining NAS and auditor independence within the framework of corporate governance.

Larcker and Richardson (2004) examine whether NAS are related to discretionary accruals and pose a threat to auditor independence when management has a controlling ownership in the firm, institutional ownership is low, and there are fewer outside directors on the board. They find that NAS do pose a threat when these conditions are met but only for smaller companies. Larcker and Richardson (2004) do not examine the role of audit committees. Sharma *et al.* (2011) are the first to examine how the audit committee mitigates threats to auditor independence emanating from NAS. First, they find a positive association between client importance at the city and national levels and discretionary accruals in New Zealand. Second, they posit that clients with stronger audit committees would mitigate potential threats to auditor independence and protect the quality of financial reporting. When Sharma *et al.* (2011) introduce a measure of audit committee best practices they find that the positive association between NAS and discretionary accruals is significant for clients with weak audit committees only.

Costs and benefits of NAS

While prior studies examine the impact of NAS on audit quality, they have not focused on the non-financial reporting benefits (or costs) that may arise from the joint provision of audit and NAS. One of the arguments against proposals to ban NAS in the US was that a ban on all or most NAS would eliminate the synergistic benefits audit firms derive from joint provision.

More specifically, audit firms and the AICPA argued that a substantial ban on NAS would reduce or eliminate knowledge spillovers between the audit and consulting functions, and potentially affect the performance and quality of the audit. Despite these arguments against the ban and in favor of NAS, there are only three studies that consider such issues.

First, Knechel and Sharma (2012) contend that if NAS provide knowledge spillover benefits then one way to capture this effect is by examining how audit efficiency is influenced by NAS. However, they argue that any audit efficiency benefits stemming from NAS would only make sense if audit quality is not adversely affected. In other words, NAS derived knowledge spillovers leading to a timelier audit only makes sense if the auditor does not weaken the quality of the audit. They test this idea using pre- and post-SOX data and find that high NAS fees in conjunction with a timely audit (short audit lag) does not undermine the quality of the audit. In support of the audit firms, they find that higher NAS are related to more efficient performance of the audit but this effect disappears after SOX banned most NAS. They conclude that the SOX ban on NAS has had the unintended consequence of eroding synergies in the production of the audit.

Second, Knechel *et al.* (2012) examine the same general issue as Knechel and Sharma (2012) but at both the audit firm and city office levels. Knechel *et al.* (2012) argue that knowledge spillovers are more likely to occur at the office performing the audit and not necessarily so at the audit firm level. They find results consistent with this view. Another important finding in Knechel *et al.* (2012) is that knowledge spillover benefits do not occur in a linear fashion as assumed in prior research. Rather, they find that knowledge spillover benefits begin to occur after a moderate level of NAS has been provided to the audit client.

Knechel and Sharma (2012) and Knechel *et al.* (2012) utilize publicly available data such as audit lag to proxy for audit efficiency. Knechel *et al.* (2009) develop a measure of audit efficiency using data envelopment analysis and audit data from a single audit firm for the financial year ended 1991. They regress their measure of audit efficiency on dichotomous variables capturing whether the auditor provides management advisory services (MAS) and tax services (TAX), and audit lag. Their results suggest there are no efficiency gains when the auditor provides MAS and TAX. In fact, they find that TAX is negatively related to audit efficiency implying increased risk or complexity reduces overall audit efficiency. They also find that audit lag is not a strong proxy for overall audit efficiency. However, Knechel *et al.* (2009) caution generalizing their results from 1991 to current periods due to changes in audit technologies, regulations, and governance of audit and NAS.

Investor perceptions of NAS

Panel F of Table 7.1 lists a number of studies focusing on market perceptions of auditor independence. These studies predicate their hypotheses on the notion that if investors perceive NAS threaten auditor independence, then the quality of reported financial information will be affected. Consequently, investors will react adversely to higher NAS which can have an economic impact on the company in the form of a negative earnings response coefficient (ERC), negative cumulative or abnormal returns (CAR),[20] higher cost of debt or equity capital, or lower bond ratings. The majority of studies (Frankel *et al.* 2002; Brandon *et al.* 2004; Krishnan *et al.* 2005; Francis and Ke 2006; Higgs and Skantz 2006; Khurana and Raman 2006; Krishnamurthy *et al.* 2006; Zhang 2007; Dhaliwal *et al.* 2008; Lim and Tan 2008) conclude that investors perceive NAS are a problem while a few find no adverse perceptions (Chaney and Philipich 2002; Ashbaugh *et al.* 2003; Koh *et al.* 2012).

Comparing the results of the independence in fact (Panels A–E of Table 7.1) and independence in appearance (Panel F) studies reveals some interesting observations. First and foremost, on balance, investor perception studies suggest investors believe NAS pose a threat to auditor independence, and clients purchasing both audit and NAS suffer economic consequences. While the audit quality studies suggest auditors may be upholding their independence even if their audit firm provides NAS, it appears that perceptions of market participants are of more economic significance. Second, the two governance studies (Panel D) suggest appropriate governance may mitigate potential threats of NAS on auditor independence. Deductively, one would expect investors to perceive NAS less of a threat to independence in the presence of good governance. However, this issue has yet to be empirically investigated and provides an opportunity for future research to inform policy makers as to whether governance reforms to address NAS threats on auditor independence are working.

Implications from the literature

Several milestones in the NAS–auditor independence literature have been achieved. Researchers have developed and refined various proxies of economic dependence such as FEERATIO, unexpected or abnormal fees, growth in fees, future and recurring/non-recurring fees, and client importance. Researchers have examined aggregate and specific types of NAS fees, various clienteles (listed, private, large and small firms) across different countries and time periods. Implications of the evolution of this literature are discussed in relation to future research, practice, and policy making.

Intense debates between policy makers and the profession in various countries concern new bans or expanding the bans to currently permissible NAS. To protect investors, regulators are pushing for bans (e.g., EC 2010; Public Company Accounting Oversight Board (PCAOB) 2005) on NAS even though research evidence on NAS impairing the auditor's independence remains unclear. Moreover, bans on NAS may not be necessary because research evidence suggests governance mechanisms such as audit committees can provide sufficient oversight of NAS and audit quality, thus mitigating NAS threats to auditor independence.

A major conundrum in the auditor independence policy making process has been the lack of supporting evidence from the accounting profession and hasty regulatory actions. The profession has long argued that auditor-provided NAS generate synergies and hence knowledge spillovers but has provided limited evidence. Likewise, policy makers resorted to anecdotes and hastily crafted regulations with unintended consequences. Policy makers and regulators (e.g., PCAOB) need to heed the evidence in research and support further academic research so that more informed policy making can take place, and the costs and benefits of NAS can be better understood. The profession's role here is also critical because while audit firms argue NAS provide benefits and do not harm auditor independence, they cite client confidentiality and are less willing to cooperate by sharing much needed audit and non-audit data with researchers.[21] Policy makers and regulators specialize in rules and regulations, audit firms specialize in accounting, audit, and other consulting; neither specialize nor have the expertise in research. Therefore, policy makers, audit firms, and academicians need to work in concert if we as a profession are to develop sound regulations on NAS and auditor independence. We know that the SOX bans brought unintended consequences which may not have occurred if both policy makers and CPA firms jointly engaged in robust research with academics.

A clear observation from this literature review is that variations in measures of NAS and audit quality and different model specifications have led to different conclusions. A way forward is to employ multiple measures and model specifications in a single study.[22] Since the audit engagement partner makes and is ultimately responsible for all audit judgments, from client acceptance to issuing the audit report, and for managing the client, partner level analysis is important and would be of interest to policy makers.[23] Such analysis would provide evidence on partner rotation policies and potentially on the dynamics of intra-firm partner relationships. Several other emerging trends and issues that deserve greater attention from policy makers, regulators, the profession, and researchers include:

- the role of corporate governance (e.g., Larcker and Richardson 2004; Sharma *et al.* 2011) because audit contracting takes place in this broader context. In particular, the role of the audit committee should be given more focus because the audit committee is responsible for hiring, firing, setting the scope and fees for audit and NAS, overseeing the quality of the audit and independence of the auditor;
- the simultaneous examination of audit effectiveness and audit efficiency in relation to NAS because the arguments from both sides, regulators versus the profession, encompass joint provision effects on effectiveness and efficiency (e.g., Knechel and Sharma 2012; Knechel *et al.* 2012);
- the turning point at which NAS yield synergies and potentially harm audit quality so that regulators, auditors, management, and audit committees can make more informed NAS policy decisions (Knechel *et al.* 2012);
- developing a better understanding of why clients still purchase NAS in an environment where regulators are limiting NAS and implementing stricter governance regulations over NAS and the audit. For example, investors – the very people regulators are protecting from potential harm from NAS – will benefit from understanding how NAS are related to firm value and future earnings, and thus, make more informed NAS ratification decisions;
- examining how types of NAS affect audit quality because the results of prior research are not conclusive and researchers have yet to investigate how investors perceive different types of NAS. Such research is important to inform policy makers because blanket bans on all NAS as proposed by the EU may not be necessary;[24]
- determining a clear set of conditions that define an audit failure. Using the type of audit report issued is arguably one of the most direct measures of the auditor's decision making. However, an appropriate context that permits researchers to make inferences that the audit opinion was the correct one is critical (Sharma and Sidhu 2001). Perhaps more productive measures of audit quality can be based on internal audit firm metrics of audit quality because "catching" and addressing audit quality defects before an opinion is issued is preventative rather than damage control. Such analyses would also be of value to audit firm regulators such as the PCAOB. However, access to proprietary data is paramount for such an approach;
- As regulators move toward restricting NAS, audit markets will become more concentrated and highly competitive. In such markets, auditors may face more pressure to comply with client requests yet effectively manage the audit budget. Banning all NAS will simply shift the source of auditor–client economic bonding to the audit fee basket. Moreover, as seen historically, audit firms' entrepreneurial creativity will likely produce innovative NAS not currently subject to regulatory bans (e.g., consulting on corporate social responsibility activities, audit of environmental activities not part of a financial statement audit, etc.).

Conclusion

It is critical to reiterate that research examining how NAS are related to auditor independence is unable to provide direct or causal evidence on auditor behavior because an auditor's independence is a state of mind that is unobservable. Furthermore, NAS are not a proxy for auditor independence as claimed by some; they are a potential source of economic bonding between an auditor and client which may influence an auditor's independence. Regulators and policy makers need to demonstrate that NAS actually cause auditors to impair their independence and this has been lacking. Likewise, the profession needs to provide compelling evidence that NAS do not harm but enhance audit quality and efficiencies. Neither side has provided conclusive proof.

The academic community attempted to inform debates on NAS and auditor independence by examining the association between NAS fees and proxies for audit quality and auditor reporting decisions. Such research provides circumstantial evidence from which inferences about auditor independence have been made. Some researchers attempt to provide causation-type analysis through change specifications or difference-in-difference tests (e.g., Hope and Langli 2010; Krishnan *et al.* 2011; Knechel and Sharma 2012). While experimental methods are well suited to examine causation, the sensitivity of the issue and internal validity threats (e.g., demand threats) are likely to preclude finding results from auditor studies supporting breach of independence.[25] Future researchers can consider designing both archival and experimental studies that can provide more compelling evidence on whether NAS (and audit and total fees) "cause[s]" auditors to impair their independence. Schmidt (2012) is an example of a context – litigation against auditors for an audit failure defined as financial restatements when NAS fees are higher – that provides relatively compelling evidence of "causation."

In closing, while the research evidence on NAS and their impact on auditor independence is far from conclusive, many advances have been made in the literature and many more are to come. Researchers have resorted to developing measures of audit output constructs such as audit quality using publicly available data that are not error free and audit inputs are typically fee data. Some useful proprietary audit input, process, and output data that can help researchers provide new and clearer insight include data on budgeted and actual audit and NAS hours, mix of staff allocated to the audit, various risk and materiality judgments, errors detected and extent of adjustments made, internal audit firm quality measures, revisions to fees, and audit tendering processes. In addition, linking client data to characteristics of audit engagement, review and other firm and office partners, and audit team members, partner compensation schemes, etc., can help significantly advance knowledge and understanding of auditor independence. Although audit client information is confidential, there certainly are ways for audit firms to provide the data so that the research community can produce more reliable and less controversial results for guiding policy formulation. Similarly, data gathered by the PCAOB through its inspections can be utilized to provide more insight. We as a profession should not place ourselves in a Catch-22 situation and hide behind the veil of client confidentiality if our objective is to genuinely address if, why, and how NAS are related to auditor independence. A creative profession like ours can certainly innovate avenues for dealing with client confidentiality for altruistic reasons.

Notes

1 Between 1978 and 1982, US listed companies were required to disclose the ratio of NAS to audit fees under ASR 250 (SEC 1978), which the SEC withdrew in 1982. Subsequently, in 2000, the SEC issued auditor independence rules that required disclosure of fees paid to auditors for the audit and various types of NAS. These disclosure rules were further amended by SOX.

2 For example, see Sharma *et al.* (2009) for comparisons on audit committee governance regulations in the US, UK, Australia, New Zealand, Singapore, Spain and China. The Belgium Company Law prohibited many NAS but permitted bookkeeping and accounting services on an ad hoc and non-recurring basis, which was prohibited following the Royal decree of 4 April 2003 (Vanstraelen and Willekens 2008).

3 To test the EU proposal, the research design should include companies that do not purchase any NAS from their auditor and companies that do. Most extant research excludes firms with zero NAS fees from their sample.

4 I used the following keywords or its variants "nonaudit, non-audit, fee, auditor independence, independence, independent", etc., and searched the following 16 journals: *The Accounting Review (TAR), Journal of Accounting Research (JAR), Journal of Accounting & Economics (JAE), Contemporary Accounting Research (CAR), Auditing: A Journal of Practice & Theory (AJPT), Review of Accounting Studies (RAST), Journal of Accounting, Auditing and Finance (JAAF), Journal of Accounting & Public Policy (JAPP), Accounting Horizons (AH), Journal of Business Finance & Accounting (JBFA), Abacus, Accounting and Finance (AF), International Journal of Auditing (IJA), and Managerial Auditing Journal (MAJ).* Searches of *Accounting and Business Research* and *European Accounting Review* yielded no relevant studies in the twenty-first century.

5 Experimental, survey, or field studies on auditor independence are beyond the scope of this chapter.

6 Since sufficient citation information (authors, year of publication and journal name) on each study is provided, to save space they are not listed in the references. Journal abbreviations can be found in note 4.

7 Hunt and Lulseged (2007) and Lim and Tan (2008) examine multiple proxies for audit quality (e.g., earnings management and going concern reporting) and are categorized under earnings management because all studies in the going concern reporting category examine only the auditor's opinion decision. Similarly, Ferguson *et al.* (2004) is categorized under financial restatements because two of their three proxies for audit quality focus on violations of GAAP and restatements.

8 They use a sample of involuntary bankrupt firms because firms entering voluntary bankruptcy may do so for strategic or political reasons and the auditor's failure to issue a GCM may be justified. For example, in the US firms can voluntarily enter into a Chapter 11 bankruptcy to protect themselves from creditors or avoid government regulations and labor union actions.

9 Interestingly, neither of these two studies cites Sharma and Sidhu (2001). Also, Fargher and Jiang (2008) do not discuss auditor independence issues.

10 An epistemological/philosophical issue is the extent to which non-significant results can be supportive of a null hypothesis or refute an alternative hypothesis without an evaluation of the power of the tests. See Burgstahler (1987) for details.

11 While financially distressed or bankrupt companies provide an appropriate context to examine threats to auditor independence due to NAS, a common limitation of going concern studies is that sample sizes are relatively smaller. Studies using proxies for audit quality have fewer sample size constraints and thus typically comprise a much larger sample. The trade-off is the extent to which proxies for audit quality actually capture the quality of the auditor's work and judgments.

12 For example, restatements that subsequently are subject to litigation and the audit firm is charged or settles the case provides a relatively less ambiguous indicator of the auditor undermining independence.

13 Paterson and Valencia (2011) conclude that non-recurring tax and audit-related fees pose threats to auditor independence. However, they provide no explanation as to why non-recurring fees would incentivize an auditor to compromise independence.

14 I use the term discretionary accruals to represent the array of estimates of accruals (total, current, working capital, etc.). Researchers define earnings surprises as when a company just misses, meets, or just beats analysts' consensus forecasted earnings by up to ±$0.02 or when there is a small increase in earnings of up to two percent.

15 Ashbaugh *et al.* (2003) use the term "biased financial reporting" when referring to the magnitude of discretionary accruals, which is common in the literature. An issue worth considering is whether income-decreasing discretionary accruals constitute biased financial reporting. Ashbaugh *et al.* (2003) find significant negative associations between the fee variables and negative values of performance adjusted discretionary current accruals (PADCA) and ROA augmented discretionary current accruals (REDCA). Since the data are from a tumultuous period, clients may have sought the auditor's help to report lower current income and perhaps shift them to future periods.

16 The Dechow-Dichev (D-D) (Dechow and Dichev 2002) approach measures the quality of current accruals rather than separating total accruals into its discretionary and non-discretionary components. The main advantage of the D-D approach is that it is a more direct measure of managerial opportunism and private information that is not clearly discernible from discretionary accruals measures (Srinidhi and Gul 2007).

17 In replicating Ashbaugh *et al.* (2003), Huang *et al.* (2007) exclude institutional ownership from their models although Ashbaugh *et al.* (2003) find this variable to be highly significant.

18 Results in Krishnan *et al.* (2011) also suggest that, if one considers larger income-decreasing accruals as more conservative earnings, NAS have a beneficial effect on financial reporting quality. Alternatively, the results suggest auditors permit large NAS clients to engage in earnings management for "cookie jar" reserve purposes (i.e., increase future income).

19 However, in an earlier version and confirmed with the first author, Koh *et al.* (2012) report results contrary to Lim and Tan (2008) by documenting lower earnings management when NAS and information systems fees are high for clients of non-industry specialist auditors only. They find no significant results for specialist auditors.

20 ERC captures investors' perceptions of the quality of earnings, given the level of NAS provided by the auditor based on a regression of CAR (cumulative abnormal returns) on earnings, NAS and interaction of earnings and NAS. The coefficient on the interaction term is the ERC. CAR is the cumulative abnormal stock return over a given period.

21 There certainly are ways to deal with the issue of client confidentiality so the failure of audit firms to cooperate raises doubts about their claims that NAS do not harm audit quality or auditor independence.

22 With a few exceptions (e.g., Sharma and Sidhu 2001), researchers have also tended not to report effect size or power analysis that could enable drawing a relatively more uniform conclusion across studies.

23 Very few countries require disclosure of the audit report signing partner and fees. Australia is one such country but hand-collection of the relevant data is a major hurdle. Taiwan requires audit partner disclosure but not fee data.

24 An emerging stream of the literature examines tax NAS fees and tax reporting behavior (e.g., Gleason and Mills 2011; Seetharaman *et al.* 2011).

25 Prior experimental/survey studies of auditor subjects show no breach of independence but third-party subjects such as lenders and investors tend to perceive NAS cause independence problems.

References

Burgstahler, D. 1987. "Inference from Empirical Research", *The Accounting Review* 62(1): 203–14.

Carcello, J. V. and T. L. Neal. 2003. "Audit Committee Characteristics and Auditor Dismissals Following 'new' Going-concern Reports", *The Accounting Review* 78(1): 95–117.

DeAngelo, L. E. 1981. "Auditor Size and Audit Quality", *Journal of Accounting and Economics* 3(August): 183–99.

Dechow, P. and I. Dichev. 2002. "The Quality of Accruals and Earnings: The Role of Accrual Estimation Errors", *The Accounting Review* 77(Supplement): 35–59.

Dhaliwal, D. S., V. Naiker, and F. Navissi. 2010. "The Association between Accruals Quality and the Characteristics of Accounting Experts and Mix of Expertise on Audit Committees", *Contemporary Accounting Research* 27(3): 787–827.

European Commission. 2010. *Green Paper on Audit Policy: Lessons from the Crisis.* Brussels: EC.

Gleason, C. and L. F. Mills. 2011. "Do Auditor-provided Tax Services Improve the Estimate of Tax Expense?" *Contemporary Accounting Research* 28(5): 1484–1509.

Hay, D. and W. R. Knechel. 2010. "The Effects of Advertising and Solicitation on Audit Fees", *Journal of Accounting and Public Policy* 29: 60–81.

Mautz, R. K. and H. A. Sharaf. 1961. *The Philosophy of Auditing.* Sarasota, FL: American Accounting Association.

Melancon, B. 2000. "The Proposed SEC Rule on Auditor Independence and its Consequences", *Journal of Accountancy* 190(4): 26–8.

Naiker, V., D. S. Sharma, and V. D. Sharma. 2013. "Do Former Audit Firm Partners on Audit Committees Procure Greater Non-audit Services from the Auditor?" *The Accounting Review* 88(1): 297–326.

Public Company Accounting Oversight Board (PCAOB). 2005. "Ethics and Independence Rules Concerning Independence, Tax Services, and Contingent Fees." PCAOB Release No. 2005–14, PCAOB Rulemaking Docket Matter No. 017, July 26, 2005.

Sarbanes, P. and M. Oxley. 2002. *The Sarbanes-Oxley Act of 2002.* Washington D.C.: U.S. Congress.

Schmidt, J. M. 2012. "Perceived Auditor Independence and Audit Litigation: The Role of Nonaudit Services Fees", *The Accounting Review* 87(3): 1033–65.

Securities Exchange Commission (SEC). 1978. *Accounting Series Release No. 250: Disclosure of Relationships with Independent Public Accounts.* Washington D.C.: Government Printing Office.

Securities Exchange Commission (SEC). 2000. *Revision of the Commission's Auditor Independence Requirements*. November 21, 2000. Release Nos. 33–7919; 34–43602; 35–27279; IC-24744; IA-1911; FR-56; File No. S7-13-00. Washington D.C.: Government Printing Office.

Seetharaman, A., Y. Sun, and W. Wang. 2011. "Tax-related Financial Statements Restatements and Auditor-provided Tax Services", *Journal of Accounting, Auditing and Finance* 26(4): 677–98.

Sharma, V. D., V. Naiker, and B. Lee. 2009. "Determinants of Audit Committee Meeting Frequency: Evidence from a Voluntary Governance System", *Accounting Horizons* 23(3): 245–63.

Vanstraelen, A. and M. Willekens. 2008. "Audit Regulation in Belgium: Overregulation in a Limited Capital Market Oriented Country?" in *Auditing, Trust and Governance: Developing Regulation in Europe*, Edited by R. Quick, S. Turley and M. Willekens (Routledge: London).

8
Auditor tenure and rotation

Clive Lennox

Importance of the topic

There has been a long-standing debate as to the relative merits of mandatory auditor rotation. In the United States (US), Section 203 of the Sarbanes-Oxley Act (2002) (SOX) requires rotation of the lead engagement partner and the concurring review partner at least once every five years. Section 207 also requires a study on the potential effects of mandatory audit firm rotation. After conducting the study, the General Accounting Office (GAO, 2003: 2) concluded that:

> mandatory audit firm rotation may not be the most efficient way to enhance auditor independence and audit quality, considering the costs of changing the auditor of record and the loss of auditor knowledge that is not carried forward to the new auditor.

However, the GAO (2003: 2) also stated that

> it will take at least several years for the SEC [Securities Exchange Commission] and the PCAOB [Public Company Accounting Oversight Board] to gain sufficient experience with the effectiveness of the act in order to adequately evaluate whether further enhancements or revisions, including mandatory audit firm rotation, may be needed to further protect the public interest and to restore investor confidence.

The debate has gathered pace recently. In late 2010, the European Commission (EC) issued a Green Paper which stated (2010: 11):

> Situations where a company has appointed the same audit firm for decades seem incompatible with desirable standards of independence. Even when 'key audit partners' are regularly rotated as currently mandated by the Directive, the threat of familiarity persists. In this context, the mandatory rotation of audit firms – not just of audit partners – should be considered. The Commission acknowledges arguments relating to a loss of knowledge as a result of rotation. It would nevertheless like to examine the pros and cons of such rotation, especially with a view to instilling and maintaining objectivity and dynamism in the audit

> market. To prevent partners from changing firms to "take along" certain clients with them, rotation rules, if adopted, should ensure that not only firms, but partners are also rotated.

In August 2011, the PCAOB issued a call for public comments on the desirability of mandatory audit firm rotation. It is therefore an opportune time to consider the contribution that the academic literature can make to this debate.

The next section, "Experiences of different countries", reviews the rules on mandatory audit firm rotation and mandatory partner rotation across different countries. I then outline the arguments for and against mandatory rotation before briefly reviewing the academic evidence. Finally, I conclude with a personal perspective on how academic research can be made more useful as an input to policy making.

Experiences of different countries

The rules on audit firm rotation and audit partner rotation are summarized in Table 8.1. Mandatory audit firm rotation is required for all types of publicly traded companies in the following countries: Bangladesh, Bolivia, Bosnia Herzegovina, Costa Rica, Indonesia, Italy, Mongolia, Oman, Paraguay, Serbia, Tunisia, and Uzbekistan. In most countries that require audit firm rotation, the maximum permissible length of audit firm tenure is set at around five years. Audit firm rotation is not required in most developed economies, including Australia, Canada, most of Europe, and the US. Among the countries that do not impose mandatory audit firm rotation, most require rotation of the audit partners.

Table 8.1 finds that many countries require audit firm rotation for specific types of listed entity: typically banks, insurance companies, and government entities. Presumably, audit quality is deemed to be particularly important for financial institutions and government companies which is why these types of entities are singled out for special treatment. However, Brazil and Saudi Arabia are two exceptions, as they require audit firm rotation for all listed entities *except* banks.

Interestingly, Table 8.1 finds that several countries introduced some form of mandatory audit firm rotation policy, only to withdraw it later. For example, in Austria, mandatory audit firm rotation was introduced in 2001 but abandoned in 2004. Canada dropped its audit firm rotation requirement for banks in 1991. Similarly, Singapore has suspended its policy of mandatory audit firm rotation for local banks in 2008, having earlier introduced the policy in 2002. Spain introduced mandatory audit firm rotation every nine years starting in 1988, but this policy was abandoned seven years later, in 1995.

These policy reversals seem to indicate some uncertainty by policy makers as to the desirability of mandatory rotation. Moreover, the reasons put forward for the policy reversals seem unpersuasive. For example, Singapore officials stated that the mandatory audit firm rotation requirement for local banks was introduced in 2002 in order to:

> (1) safeguard against public accounting firms having an excessive focus on maintaining long-term commercial relationships with the banks they audit (2) maintain the professionalism of audit firms – where with long-term relationships, audit firms run the risk of compromising their objectivity by identifying too closely with the banks' practices and cultures, and (3) bring a fresh perspective to the audit process.
>
> *(GAO, 2003: 13)*

Table 8.1 Rules on mandatory audit firm rotation and mandatory audit partner rotation for listed entities

Country	*Mandatory audit firm rotation?*		*Mandatory audit partner rotation?*	
Albania	Partial	Every two years for insurance companies and every three years for banks.	n.a.	
Argentina	No		Yes	Every five years.
Australia	No		Yes	Every five years.
Austria	No	A policy of rotation every six years was enacted in 2001 and abandoned in 2004.	No	
Bahrain	No		Yes	Every five years for financial institutions.
Bangladesh	Yes	Every three years.	n.a.	
Belarus	Partial	Every three years for banks.	n.a.	
Belgium	No		Yes	Every six years.
Bolivia	Yes	Every six years (except three years for insurance companies and pension funds).	No	
Bosnia Herzegovina	Yes	Every five years (but rotation can be postponed for two years if a new engagement partner is appointed).	No	
Brazil	Partial	Every five years (except banks).	No	
Canada	No	A policy of rotation every two years for banks was abandoned in 1991.	Yes	
Chile	No		n.a.	
China	Partial	Every five years for government entities meeting certain criteria.	Yes	Every five years.
Costa Rica	Yes	Required in 2005, repealed in 2006, re-implemented in 2010.	No	
Croatia	Partial	Every seven years for banks and every four years for insurance companies.	No	
Cyprus	No		Yes	Every seven years.
Czech Republic	No	Adopted between 1992 and 1995, then abandoned.	Yes	Every seven years.
Denmark	No		Yes	Every seven years.
Ecuador	Partial	Every five years for banks and every six years for insurance companies.	No	
El Salvador	No		Partial	Every five years for banks and insurance companies.

Table 8.1 (continued)

Country	*Mandatory audit firm rotation?*		*Mandatory audit partner rotation?*	
Estonia	No		Partial	Every five years for banks and investment companies.
Finland	No		Yes	Every seven years.
France	No		Yes	Every six years.
Germany	No		Yes	A maximum of six audits can be performed during a ten year period.
Ghana	No		No	
Greece	No		Yes	Every seven years.
Honduras	No		Yes	Every five years.
Hong Kong	No		Yes	Every five years.
Hungary	No		Yes	Every five years.
Iceland	Partial	Every five years for financial institutions and insurance companies.	No	
India	Partial	Every four years for banks, insurance companies, and government entities.	Partial	Every four years for banks, insurance companies, and government entities.
Indonesia	Yes	Every six years.	n.a.	
Israel	Partial	Every three years for government entities, but not strictly enforced.	No	
Italy	Yes	Every nine years.	No	
Japan	No		n.a.	
Latvia	No	Required for banks in 1998, 1999, and 2000, but repealed in 2002.	Yes	Every five or seven years.
Lithuania	No		Yes	Every five years.
Luxembourg	No		Yes	Every seven years.
Macedonia	Partial	Every five years for banks and insurance companies.	n.a.	
Malaysia	No		n.a.	
Malta	No		Yes	Every seven years.
Mexico	No		Yes	Every five years.
Mongolia	Yes	Every three years	n.a.	
Montenegro	No		Yes	Every seven years.
Nepal	No		No	

Table 8.1 (continued)

Country	*Mandatory audit firm rotation?*		*Mandatory audit partner rotation?*	
Netherlands	No		Yes	Every five years.
New Zealand	No		Yes	Every seven years.
Nicaragua	No		Partial	Every three years for banks.
Nigeria	Partial	Every ten years for banks and every five years for insurance companies.	n.a.	
Norway	No		Yes	Every seven years.
Oman	Yes	Every four years.	n.a.	
Pakistan	Partial	Every five years for financial institutions and insurance companies. A policy of rotation every five years for other listed entities was dropped in 2002.	n.a.	
Panama	No		Yes	Every three years.
Paraguay	Yes	Every three years.	n.a.	
Peru	Partial	Every two years for government entities.	n.a.	
Poland	Partial	Every five years for insurance companies.	Yes	Every five years.
Portugal	No	Every eight to nine years is recommended on a 'comply or explain' basis.	Yes	Every seven years.
Qatar	Partial	Every five years for banks.	n.a.	
Romania	No		Yes	Every seven years.
Russia	No		Yes	Every seven years.
Saudi Arabia	Partial	Every five years except for banks.	Partial	Upon request from the central bank, banks are allowed to request partner rotation instead of audit firm rotation.
Serbia	Yes	Every five years for banks. For other companies, rotation is required every ten years instead of every five years when combined with partner rotation.	n.a.	
Singapore	Partial	Every five years for local banks ('temporarily' suspended in 2008 but the suspension had not been lifted as of 2012).	Yes	Every five years.
Slovakia	No	Mandatory rotation for banks was dropped in 2000.	n.a.	
Slovenia	Partial	Every five years for insurance and investment management companies.	Yes	Every seven years.

Table 8.1 (continued)

Country	*Mandatory audit firm rotation?*		*Mandatory audit partner rotation?*	
South Africa	No		No	
South Korea	No	Rotation every seven years was enacted in 2003, became effective in 2006, but dropped in 2009.	Yes	Every six years.
Spain	No	Rotation every nine years was enacted in 1988 and dropped in 1995.	Yes	Every seven years.
Sri Lanka	No		Yes	Every five years.
Sweden	No		Yes	Every seven years.
Taiwan	No		Yes	Every five years.
Tajikistan	No		No	
Thailand	No		Yes	Every five years.
Tunisia	Yes	Every three to five years (the rotation period depends on certain criteria of the company and audit firm).	n.a.	
Turkey	No	A policy of rotation every five to eight years (depending on certain criteria) was abandoned in 2011.	Yes	
Ukraine	Partial	Every seven years for banks.	Yes	
Ukbekistan	Yes	Every six years.	No	
United Kingdom	No		Yes	Every five years.
United States	No		Yes	Every five years.
Venezuela	Partial	A policy of rotation every three years for banks is scheduled for 2014.	No	

The following information sources were used to compile this table: Cameran *et al.* (2005); GAO (2003); Siregar *et al.* (2012); Ewelt-Knauer *et al.* (2012); www.worldbank.org/ifa/rosc.html; http://pcaobus.org/Rules/Rulemaking/Docket037/163_Deloitte_Touche_LLP.pdf. These information sources revealed inconsistent information for a handful of countries and those countries are not included in this table. I am also grateful to the following academics who told me about the applicable rules in their countries: Carlos Alves (Portugal), Costas Caramanis (Greece), John Christian Langli (Norway), David Hay (New Zealand), Lasse Niemi (Finland), Galina Preobrazhenskaya (Russia), Stefan Sundgren (Sweden), Steven Taylor (Australia), Frank Thinggaard (Denmark), Marleen Willekens (Belgium), Xi Wu (China). Overall, the information presented is based on a best-effort research initiative and I provide no guarantee as to its accuracy.

Singapore's suspension of mandatory rotation in 2008 occurred because it was felt that auditor changes would be excessively costly during the global financial crisis. However, it was not explained why the original justification for the policy – i.e., maintaining high audit quality – had become less important during the crisis. It is somewhat strange that the financial crisis was cited as a reason for suspending the policy given that most audit failures are revealed when companies fail. Moreover, as of 2012, the 'temporary' suspension of 2008 had not yet been lifted, casting further doubt as to whether the financial crisis was the real reason for dropping mandatory rotation.

In Canada, the policy of mandatory audit firm rotation for banks was abandoned in 1991. Two reasons were given: (1) it was felt that the costs of mandatory rotation exceeded the benefits; and (2) Canada was largely alone among the developed countries in imposing mandatory audit firm rotation (GAO, 2003). With respect to the first argument, this article will argue that there is little persuasive evidence as to whether mandatory rotation is beneficial or harmful. As to the second argument, the decision to follow other developed countries suggests that policy makers were unsure in their own minds as to whether the costs of mandatory rotation really did exceed the benefits.

In Spain, the policy of mandatory audit firm rotation was dropped in 1995. According to a director of the Comision Nacional del Mercaso de Valores (CNMV) – the agency in charge of supervising and inspecting the Spanish stock markets – the policy was dropped because:

> The main objective of increased competition among audit firms had been achieved and because of listed companies' increased training costs incurred with a complete new team of auditors from a new public accounting firm.
>
> *(GAO, 2003: 84)*

No mention was made as to the potential consequences for audit quality and it is unknown whether audit quality considerations influenced the decision to drop mandatory rotation in Spain.

In summary, there is a wide divergence of policies around the globe. Some countries have mandatory audit firm rotation alone, some have both mandatory audit firm rotation and mandatory audit partner rotation, while other countries have mandatory audit partner rotation alone. Further, some countries have introduced mandatory audit firm rotation before abandoning it later; in Spain the policy was dropped without mandatory rotation ever having taken effect. These policy reversals suggest a high degree of uncertainty as to whether mandatory rotation is desirable. This motivates the next part of my article where I discuss the arguments for and against mandatory rotation and the evidence to date.

Arguments in favor of mandatory rotation

A reduced threat of economic dependence

By reducing the expected length of auditor–client tenure, it is argued that mandatory rotation can strengthen an auditor's economic incentives to remain independent of the client. For example, suppose that – in the absence of mandatory rotation – the expected length of future tenure is ten years. If the auditor expects to earn a profit of $10 in each year, the auditor's expected profits are $100 (= 10 x 10). If instead, the audit firm has to be rotated in, say, five years' time, the auditor's expected profits from the client are halved. This means that the auditor has less incentive to curry favor with the client's management in order to retain the business.

A "fresh eyes" benefit

Proponents of mandatory rotation argue that a change of auditor can improve audit quality by bringing a fresh perspective to the audit. The American Institute of Certified Public Accountants (AICPA) introduced mandatory partner rotation "for the specific purpose of periodically bringing a fresh perspective to each audit" (AICPA 1992: 4). A fresh perspective can reveal problems that were not apparent to the previous partner. Rotation of either the audit firm or the audit partner can yield a fresh eyes effect but the effect is likely to be bigger when the entire audit team is rotated rather than just the partner.

Avoidance of close personal relationships and misplaced trust

When an auditor audits the same client for many years, the auditor may become overly trusting of the management or complacent in conducting the audit. While mandatory partner rotation may be sufficient to prevent such problems at the partner level, much of the audit work is carried out by juniors, seniors, and audit managers. Thus, mandatory audit firm rotation may be necessary to prevent close personal relationships and misplaced trust at all levels of the audit team.

Greater competition

Mandatory audit firm rotation would increase the frequency of auditor–client terminations and therefore lead to more situations in which audit firms submit bids for new clients. The EC is keen to increase the intensity of competition in the audit market and believes that mandatory audit firm rotation is an important means to achieve this objective. However, it is unclear whether a more dynamic and competitive audit market is conducive to high audit quality. An increase in the frequency of tendering could lead to cut-throat competition, with audit firms offering lower audit fees in an attempt to increase their market shares. Numan and Willekens (2011) find that greater competition results in downward pressure on audit fees and may motivate audit firms to reduce the extent of testing. Therefore, it is not obvious that an increase in competition would in fact result in higher quality audits as the EC has claimed.

Arguments against mandatory rotation

Diminished incentives to acquire client-specific knowledge

Auditing standards require an auditor to have a detailed understanding of the auditee. Some of the knowledge gained from auditing one client can be transferred to the audits of similar clients. However, no two companies are exactly alike. Much of the time and effort that an auditor invests in getting to know a client's business cannot easily be transferred to a different engagement. Mandatory rotation reduces the auditor's expected period of incumbency and therefore reduces the time horizon over which an auditor can recoup the benefits from acquiring client-specific knowledge. Therefore, mandatory rotation can reduce the auditor's incentive to gain client-specific knowledge.

A loss of knowledge at the time of rotation

Because of learning-by-doing, a newly appointed auditor starts off with less client-specific knowledge and is therefore less able to determine whether the company's accounting and reporting choices are proper. In contrast, an auditor who has audited the same company for an extended period is better placed to judge the appropriateness of the company's accounting choices. By instigating a change of auditor, mandatory rotation increases the risk that the new auditor will know less about the client than the former auditor.

Costly auditor switching

A chief argument against mandatory rotation is that it is costly for companies to change auditor. This is one reason that voluntary auditor changes occur infrequently. Although the EC appears to be in favor of mandatory audit firm rotation, it acknowledges that many companies would find it costly to change auditors on a frequent basis.

A "lame duck" effect during the final year of tenure prior to mandatory rotation

Mandatory rotation may have perverse effects on audit quality as the scheduled date for rotation approaches. Because mandatory rotation makes the termination date completely predictable, the audit team knows that they will cease to audit the company beyond the final year of tenure. This may mean that the audit team has less incentive to exert effort during the final year. Moreover, mandatory rotation could result in audit firms re-allocating their most knowledgeable and experienced staff as the end of tenure approaches in order to attract or retain other clients where the expected period of incumbency is longer. On the other hand, there may be a beneficial final year effect if the departing auditor works harder during his/her final year of tenure because s/he knows that his/her work will be scrutinized by a new incoming auditor. Therefore, it is unclear *ex ante* whether audit quality will be lower or higher in the auditor's final year prior to mandatory rotation.

The evidence

As there are arguments both for and against mandatory rotation, it is an open empirical question as to whether it is in fact desirable. This section reviews the major findings from four areas of the literature:

- audit firm tenure
- audit partner tenure
- mandatory audit firm rotation
- mandatory audit partner rotation.

Of these, the first two categories account for the vast majority of published articles. I shall provide relatively more discussion of studies in categories 3 and 4, as these are more relevant for assessing the potential consequences of *mandatory* rotation.

Audit firm tenure

Proponents of mandatory rotation argue that long tenure can erode auditor independence because of economic bonding and/or the development of close personal relationships between the auditor and client. However, the weight of evidence offers little support for these arguments.

Many studies use earnings quality metrics in an attempt to isolate the impact on audit firm tenure on audit quality (e.g., Johnson *et al.*, 2002; Myers *et al.*, 2003; Davis *et al.*, 2009).

Johnson *et al.* (2002) measure audit quality using absolute discretionary accruals and the mapping of current accruals to future earnings. Using dummy variables for short audit firm tenure (< four years) and long audit firm tenure (> nine years), they find that short tenure is associated with lower earnings quality relative to medium periods of tenure (between five and eight years), while tenure exceeding nine years is not associated with lower earnings quality. Myers *et al.* (2003) revisit the relation between auditor tenure and earnings quality using the dispersion and sign of absolute abnormal accruals and absolute current accruals. They find that both accruals measures are declining in longer audit firm tenure. Moreover, longer tenure is associated with smaller income-increasing and smaller income-decreasing accruals.

By examining accruals unconditionally, these studies implicitly assume that if discretionary accruals are large (small), earnings management is more (less) prevalent. Davis *et al.* (2009) remedy this by examining whether discretionary accruals are used to meet or beat the consensus analyst earnings forecast. They find a nonlinear U-shaped relation between audit firm tenure and the use of positive discretionary accruals to meet or beat analysts' forecasts during the pre-SOX period. However, this relation disappears during the post-SOX period.

Another stream of literature uses fraudulent financial reporting and financial restatements to measure audit quality (Carcello and Nagy, 2004; Myers *et al.*, 2005). Carcello and Nagy (2004) examine the relation between audit firm tenure and fraudulent financial reporting, which is identified using SEC Accounting and Auditing Enforcement Releases (AAERs). Comparing AAER firms with a matched sample of non-fraud firms and the population of non-fraud firms, they find that fraudulent reporting is more likely to occur during the first three years of audit firm tenure. They find no significant relationship between fraudulent reporting and audit firm tenure exceeding nine years. Similarly, Myers *et al.* (2005) find an insignificant relationship between audit firm tenure and restatements of the audited financial statements.

A third stream of literature examines the relationship between audit firm tenure and the market's perception of earnings quality (Mansi *et al.*, 2004; Ghosh and Moon, 2005). Mansi *et al.* (2004) find a significant negative association between audit firm tenure and the required returns of bondholders, suggesting that bondholders value longer tenure. Using the earnings response coefficient (ERC) as a proxy for shareholders' perceptions of earnings quality, Ghosh and Moon (2005) document a positive relation with audit firm tenure. They also examine the perceptions of credit ratings agencies. They find a stronger link between credit ratings and earnings when audit firm tenure is longer. They also find a stronger association between reported earnings and one-year-ahead analyst earnings forecasts when audit firm tenure is longer, suggesting that analysts perceive earnings as being more informative when tenure is longer.

Overall then, except for Davis *et al.* (2009), most studies find no evidence of a decline in earnings quality as audit firm tenure increases.

Audit partner tenure

Compared with the literature on audit firm tenure, there are relatively few studies on audit partner tenure. This is probably because most countries do not require partners' names to be disclosed and so academic researchers are generally unable to identify when a change of partner occurs. Two studies have been published using data from Australia and Taiwan where partners' names are publicly disclosed.

Carey and Simnett (2006) investigate the association between audit partner tenure and audit quality in Australia. Three measures of audit quality are examined: the auditor's propensity to issue a going-concern opinion to a distressed company; the sign and magnitude of abnormal working capital accruals; and the incidence of just beating (or missing) various earnings benchmarks. In their long tenure sample (where partner tenure exceeds seven years), Carey and Simnett (2006) find that auditors are less likely to issue going-concern opinions and companies are more likely to just beat earnings benchmarks. They conclude that this is consistent with audit quality deteriorating when partner tenure exceeds seven years. However, they find an insignificant association between audit partner tenure and abnormal working capital accruals.

As noted by Chen *et al.* (2008), a limitation of the Carey and Simnett (2006) study is that it does not distinguish between audit firm tenure and audit partner tenure. Chen *et al.* (2008) remedy this by examining both audit firm tenure and audit partner tenure using a sample of companies from Taiwan. They find that the absolute and positive values of discretionary accruals decrease significantly with audit partner tenure. After controlling for partner tenure, they also find that absolute discretionary accruals decrease significantly with audit firm tenure. This suggests an incrementally positive association between audit firm tenure and earnings quality, above and beyond the positive association between audit partner tenure and earnings quality.

Limitations of the literature on auditor–client tenure

This section discusses three limitations of the literature on audit firm tenure and audit partner tenure.

First, it is very difficult to determine the direction of causality between earnings quality and tenure. The causality issue arises because audit firm tenure is determined by voluntary rotation decisions rather than by a mandatory rotation rule. For example, the literature has generally found that short audit firm tenure is associated with low earnings quality. The problem is how to interpret this relation. One possibility is that short audit firm tenure causes low earnings quality (e.g., due to the new auditor having less or little client-specific knowledge). An alternative possibility is that the auditor–client relationship is more likely to be terminated when earnings quality is relatively low. The second explanation cannot be easily refuted. For example, companies are more likely to voluntarily change audit firms when they manage earnings and when they are shopping for clean audit opinions (DeFond and Subramanyam, 1998; Lennox, 2000). These companies with low quality reporting tend to have short audit firm tenure because they have a higher propensity to dismiss their auditors. There is also an endogeneity problem arising from auditors' resignation decisions because audit firms are more prone to resign from clients that have poor quality financial reporting (Johnstone and Bedard, 2004).

Second, most studies use abnormal accruals metrics but it is questionable whether abnormal accruals are even suitable for measuring earnings quality, never mind audit quality. Abnormal accruals may reflect opportunistic earnings management or they may instead capture fundamental performance due to poorly specified models of normal accruals (Dechow *et al.*, 2010). Even if abnormal accruals are suitable for measuring earnings quality, it is doubtful whether they reliably capture audit quality, because earnings quality is a function of *both* the manager's reporting choices *and* the quality of the audit. Earnings quality can be high even when audit quality is low as long as the manager prepares a high quality report. Further, there can be an inverse relationship between the quality of the manager's financial reporting and the effort exerted by an auditor due to the strategic nature of the interaction between the manager and auditor (Melumad and Thoman, 1990). If an auditor suspects that the manager cannot be trusted to prepare high quality reports, then the auditor has an incentive to work harder and undertake more testing. Conversely, if the manager can be trusted to report fairly, there is less need for abnormally high audit effort.

Third, most studies on audit firm tenure have been conducted in the US. While this setting has the advantage that the SEC is considering introducing mandatory audit firm rotation, an important limitation is that it is impossible to control for the tenure of audit partners because the names of individual partners are not disclosed. This means that researchers are unable to assess whether mandatory audit partner rotation alone is sufficient or needs to be supplemented with mandatory audit firm rotation. This is an important question because many countries with mandatory partner rotation are considering whether to also introduce mandatory audit firm rotation. Except for Chen *et al.* (2008), I am unaware of any study that examines both audit firm tenure and audit partner tenure jointly.

Mandatory audit firm rotation

As discussed in the previous section, "Limitations of the literature on audit–client tenure", identifying causality is a major issue for the literature on auditor tenure. Moreover, the potential consequences of mandatory rotation are difficult to replicate in a voluntary setting. For example, the introduction of mandatory rotation might reduce an auditor's incentives to acquire client-specific knowledge. Mandatory rotation may also result in a "lame duck" situation whereby the departing auditor has little incentive to provide a high quality audit during his final year of tenure. Therefore, it is useful to consider the emerging evidence on mandatory audit firm rotation.

Ruiz-Barbadillo *et al.* (2009) examine the case of Spain, which introduced mandatory audit firm rotation in 1988 before dropping the policy in 1995. They measure audit quality by examining the issuance of going-concern opinions to financially distressed companies. Their sample period covers a period of mandatory audit firm rotation (1991–4) and a subsequent period in which audit firm rotation period is no longer required (1995–2000). Comparing the frequency of going-concern opinions in these two periods, Ruiz-Barbadillo *et al.* (2009) find no evidence that the abandonment of mandatory rotation affected audit reporting.

Kwon *et al.* (2011) examine the case of South Korea, where mandatory audit firm rotation became effective for listed entities in 2006 before the policy was abandoned in 2009. They use a remarkable dataset on audit hours and audit fees for 12,463 firm-year observations over the period 2000 to 2007. They find a significant increase in audit hours and audit fees during the first year of tenure following the introduction of mandatory rotation. However, their models of audit fees and audit hours apparently do not control for year fixed effects. Thus, it is unclear whether their findings are driven by mandatory rotation or because audit hours and fees are higher in 2006–7 than in 2001–5. Kwon *et al.* (2011) also examine various measures of audit quality and obtain mixed findings. Consistent with a negative impact on audit quality, they find larger income-increasing accruals during the initial year of tenure following mandatory rotation. However, they find insignificant results when alternative metrics for audit quality are employed. In particular, there is no change in the issuance of going-concern opinions to financially distressed companies and there is no change in the likelihood of just meeting or beating the zero earnings benchmark.

Cameran *et al.* (2014) examine the case of Italy, which introduced mandatory audit firm rotation in 1975. Like Kwon *et al.* (2011), they use a proprietary database of audit hours and audit fees. Because Italy has a much longer history of mandatory rotation than South Korea, Cameran *et al.* (2014) focus on a period during which mandatory rotation is already in effect (i.e., 2006–9) rather than a before-versus-after analysis. A nice feature of the Cameran *et al.* (2014) research design is that they are able to control for year fixed effects because the mandatory rotation events in their sample occur at different points in time. Similar to Kwon *et al.* (2011),

Cameran *et al.* (2014) find that audit hours are significantly higher during the first year of tenure. Differing from Kwon *et al.* (2011), Cameran *et al.* (2014) find that audit fees are not higher during the first year of tenure. They also examine earnings quality using abnormal working capital accruals. They find some evidence of lower earnings quality during the first three years following rotation relative to later years of the audit firm's tenure.

In a unique cross-country study, Harris and Whisenant (2012) examine the experiences of Brazil, South Korea, and Italy. They first investigate whether earnings quality improves following the adoption of mandatory audit firm rotation rules. Because Italy has had the rules in place for several decades, this first analysis is conducted on just Brazil and South Korea.[1] After pooling the companies from Brazil and South Korea into a single sample, Harris and Whisenant (2012) find an improvement in earnings quality following the introduction of mandatory rotation. Their second analysis investigates whether audit quality is different in the years before and after a mandatory change of audit firm compared with the other years of audit firm tenure. They find lower earnings quality in the years before and after mandatory rotation, compared with other years of the tenure period. They conclude that the introduction of audit firm rotation rules improved earnings quality due to an improvement in auditor independence, whereas mandatory audit firm changes caused lower earnings quality due to a loss of knowledge effect.

Mandatory audit partner rotation

Two studies examine the consequences of mandatory partner rotation. Chi *et al.* (2009) capitalize on the fact that in Taiwan, audit partners are identified in audit reports, and in 2004 the two leading Taiwanese stock exchanges effectively mandated audit partner rotation. Chi *et al.* (2009) find that abnormal accruals during the replacement partner's first year following a mandatory partner change are not significantly different from abnormal accruals in a no rotation sample. Moreover, the ERC during the incoming partner's first year is not significantly different from the ERC in the no rotation sample. Chi *et al.* (2009) also compare the first year following mandatory rotation with the first year following voluntary rotation. They find that the ERC is significantly larger in the mandatory rotation sample than in the voluntary rotation sample. However, abnormal accruals are not significantly different in the first year following mandatory rotation compared with the first year following voluntary rotation.

Overall, then, most of the results in the Chi *et al.* (2009) study are statistically insignificant. In their discussion of that article, Bamber and Bamber (2009) point out that it is difficult to interpret a "no-results" study. On the one hand, it could be that the study's tests lack power because the abnormal accruals and ERC measures are noisy proxies for audit quality. On the other hand, it could be that mandatory partner rotation has only a small impact on audit quality relative to the impact of mandatory audit firm rotation. Thus, any effect of mandatory partner rotation may be too small to be discerned using traditional measures of audit quality.

Lennox *et al.* (2014) address the audit quality measurement issue using a proprietary database of audit adjustments obtained from the Ministry of Finance in China. They argue that mandatory partner rotation can improve audit quality in both the departing partner's final year of tenure and in the first year of the incoming partner's year of tenure. Audit quality is improved during the partner's final year of tenure because the departing partner has a strong incentive to detect and correct any accounting misstatements before the engagement is handed over to the new partner. In addition, audit quality is improved during the first year under the new partner because the incoming partner brings a fresh approach to the audit and is therefore more likely to find financial reporting problems that were missed by the departing partner. Consistent with these arguments, Lennox *et al.* (2014) find a higher frequency of audit adjustments during the departing partner's final year of tenure prior to mandatory partner rotation and during the incoming partner's first year of tenure following mandatory partner rotation.

Limitations of the literature on mandatory rotation

Mandatory rotation settings have the advantage that audit firm changes and audit partner changes are determined exogenously by the regulatory requirements. This is important because it helps to identify the *causal* effects of rotation. As noted previously, it is difficult to identify causality under voluntary rotation settings. That said, the mandatory rotation literature also has its limitations.

One limitation that is specific to the literature on mandatory audit firm rotation is that the experiences of Italy, South Korea, and Spain may not generalize to the rest of the world due to the unique institutional features of these countries. For example, Italy imposes a policy of mandatory audit firm *retention* in addition to its policy of mandatory audit firm rotation. The way this works is that an audit firm in Italy receives a three-year contract which can be renewed a maximum of three times. The audit firm then has to be rotated off the engagement at the end of the third contract, i.e., the ninth year of tenure. Similarly, South Korea introduced a three-year audit firm retention requirement in its External Audit Act of 1996. These special arrangements are quite different from most countries where regulatory agencies are considering whether to introduce mandatory audit firm rotation *without* the dual requirement of mandatory audit firm retention.

Spain is another unique setting because although mandatory rotation was introduced in 1988 the policy was never actually enforced. The tenure clock of each auditor–client relationship was reset at zero in 1988, meaning that the first round of mandatory rotation events was scheduled for nine years later, in 1997. However, Spain dropped its mandatory rotation requirement in 1995, two years short of when the first rotation events were scheduled to occur. This means that some of the potential consequences of mandatory rotation were never experienced in Spain. For example, there was no loss of client-specific knowledge around the time of rotation because no mandatory rotation events ever occurred. This needs to be considered in light of Ruiz-Barbadillo *et al.*'s (2009) conclusion that audit quality did not change after Spain's mandatory audit firm rotation policy was dropped.

Another limitation is that the commonly used proxies for audit quality may lack construct validity. Except for Ruiz-Barbadillo *et al.* (2009) and Lennox *et al.* (2014), all of the mandatory rotation studies rely on earnings quality proxies. The Lennox *et al.* (2014) study is a novel attempt to measure audit quality more directly using proprietary data on the incidence of audit adjustments to reported earnings. Since 2006, the Ministry of Finance in China has required audit firms to report to it the pre-audit annual earnings of all of their publicly traded audit clients. Using this data, Lennox *et al.* (2014) identify an audit adjustment as occurring when pre-audit profits are different from post-audit profits. They point out that an audit adjustment occurs when two conditions are met: (1) the client's pre-audit profits are misstated; and (2) the auditor detects the misstatement and requires the client to correct the misstatement through an adjusting entry. The key to their identification strategy is that mandatory rotation can affect condition (2) (i.e., rotation can affect audit quality) but there is no reason to believe that mandatory rotation would directly affect condition (1). In other words, *holding audit quality constant*, mandatory rotation is unlikely to affect the quality of the client's pre-audit financial statements. Accordingly, any association between mandatory rotation and audit adjustments is through condition (2) (audit quality).

A final limitation that is specific to the literature on mandatory audit partner rotation is that most regulatory agencies are interested in the consequences of audit *firm* rotation rather than partner rotation. Bamber and Bamber (2009) point out that the consequences of partner rotation may not transfer to the audit firm rotation setting because partner rotation and audit firm rotation involve different cost and benefits. For example, audit firm rotation generally involves a change of all the staff assigned to an audit. In contrast, when a partner is rotated but the client's audit firm remains the same, other members of the audit team may not be rotated. Further, when partners are rotated but the audit firm remains unchanged, the incoming partner retains access to the audit firm's internal working papers.

Unresolved issues and challenges

There are at least two major issues that remain unresolved. First, we still do not have a clear idea as to whether mandatory audit firm rotation would make audit quality better or worse. Many studies have examined the length of audit firm tenure, but they have done so in regimes where audit firm changes are voluntary rather than mandatory. This makes it difficult to interpret the direction of causality. Is it the case that shorter audit firm tenure causes lower audit quality? Or do the factors associated with low financial reporting quality (e.g., poor management integrity) cause audit firm tenure to be relatively short? The causality issue is further complicated by the fact that most studies use measures of *earnings* quality to evaluate *audit* quality. Second, we have little idea whether mandatory audit partner rotation is an effective substitute for mandatory audit firm rotation. This is the key policy question in many western countries where partners are already subject to mandatory rotation. What policy makers need to know is whether audit firms *also* should be periodically changed.

Clearly these are major challenges for researchers to tackle. To address the causality issue, a researcher would ideally examine mandatory rotation events rather than voluntary rotation events. The problem, however, is that relatively few countries have experimented with mandatory audit firm rotation and the countries that have experimented with this policy tend to have few publicly traded companies for analysis.[2] Another limitation is that some of the countries that rely on mandatory audit firm rotation have other regulatory requirements that impinge on auditor selection. For example, Italy and South Korea have rules on mandatory audit firm retention as well as mandatory rotation.

A second challenge is that – when a country introduces mandatory audit firm rotation – the new rule tends to be introduced for *all* publicly traded companies at the same point in time. For example, Italy introduced mandatory audit firm rotation for all of its listed entities in 1975; likewise the rule in South Korea became effective for all of its listed entities in 2006. In such settings, researchers lack an effective control sample to assess what would have happened to companies in the absence of the rule change. For example, there is no control sample of Italian companies that were *not* affected by the rule change in 1975. Therefore, it is difficult to determine whether audit quality is affected by the introduction of mandatory rotation or by other factors that changed around the same time. These other factors can be controlled for if the researcher has a control group of companies that are not subject to the new rule.

A third challenge is that most countries do not require public disclosure of audit partners' names. Accordingly, it is difficult for researchers to examine whether audit firm rotation has incremental consequences above and beyond the consequences of mandatory audit partner rotation.

In the Conclusion, I discuss two ways in which policy makers and academic researchers can work together to overcome these major challenges.

Conclusion: A way forward

Academic research has been unable to provide clear answers about the consequences of mandatory audit firm rotation, but the absence of clear answers is not the fault of academics. Rather, there are major external challenges that prevent us from doing research that would be truly informative for policy makers. I have two suggestions to help resolve this impasse.

1. If mandatory audit firm rotation is to be introduced then do so on a partial basis

Given the PCAOB's recent comments and the EC Green Paper, there is a distinct possibility that some form of mandatory audit firm rotation will be introduced in the US and/or Europe. If it is introduced, then policy makers will presumably want to assess the consequences. My concern is that if a new rule is introduced for *all* publicly traded entities, it will be difficult to assess the impact because researchers and policy makers will lack a control sample of companies that are not affected by the new rule. From an experimental design perspective, the best way to assess the impact of a new policy is to introduce it for some companies but not for others. There is a clear precedent for this in Section 404 of SOX, which requires auditor attestation of internal control reports for accelerated filers but *not* for non-accelerated filers. This quasi-natural experiment has allowed academic researchers to provide compelling evidence on the causal impact of S404 (e.g., see Doogar *et al.*, 2010; Iliev, 2010; Kinney and Shepardson, 2011). I am not trying to claim that SOX made a distinction between accelerated and non-accelerated filers in order to facilitate academic research. Rather my point is that academics have been able to provide fairly compelling evidence because the rule was applied to some but not all companies. Policy makers were then able to draw upon this evidence when they decided that internal control audits should not be extended to non-accelerated filers. *If mandatory audit firm rotation is to be introduced*, I would argue that the same prudent approach can be used. That is, regulators can consider initially introducing mandatory rotation to a subset of publicly traded companies rather than all publicly traded companies. This would allow for a careful assessment of the consequences before regulators decide whether the policy should be extended to all publicly traded entities or the policy should be abandoned.

2. Disclose partners' names

The United Kingdom has recently required audit partners' names to be disclosed in audit reports. The PCAOB is considering introducing the same requirement in the US. I see little downside from requiring audit partners' names to be disclosed. A potential upside is that researchers would then be able to control for audit partner rotation when assessing whether mandatory audit firm rotation has an *incremental* effect on audit quality. This would be useful from the perspective of policy making.

Notes

1 Their treatment of South Korea is different from that of Kwon *et al.* (2011) because Harris and Whisenant (2012) use the year in which the mandatory rules were first *enacted* (i.e., 2003) whereas Kwon *et al.* (2011) use the year in which the rules first became *effective* (i.e., 2006).

2 Several countries impose audit firm rotation for special types of entity, e.g., banks. However, the problem remains that few reporting entities are affected by these rules. For example, Singapore has

imposed mandatory audit firm rotation on its six local banks, which is too few for a meaningful statistical analysis.

References

American Institute of Certified Public Accountants (AICPA). (1992) *Statement of Position Regarding Mandatory Rotation of Audit Firms of Publicly Held Companies*. New York: AICPA (SEC Practice Section).

Bamber, E. M. and Bamber, L. S. (2009) "Mandatory Audit Partner Rotation, Audit Quality, and Market Perception: Evidence from Taiwan", *Contemporary Accounting Research* 26(2): 393–402.

Cameran, M., Merlotti, E., and Di Vincenzo, D. (2005) "The Audit Firm Rotation Rule: A Review of the Literature", research paper. Milan: SDA Bocconi.

Cameran, M., Francis, J. R., Marra, A., and Pettinicchio A. (2014) "Are there Adverse Consequences of Mandatory Auditor Rotation? Evidence from the Italian Experience", *Auditing: A Journal of Practice & Theory*.

Carcello, J. V. and Nagy, A. L. (2004) "Audit Firm Tenure and Fraudulent Financial Reporting", *Auditing: A Journal of Practice & Theory* 23(2): 55–69.

Carey, P. and Simnett, R. (2006) "Audit Partner Tenure and Audit Quality", *Accounting Review* 81(3): 653–76.

Chen, C. Y., Lin, C. J., and Lin, Y. C. (2008) "Audit Partner Tenure, Audit Firm Tenure, and Discretionary Accruals: Does Long Auditor Tenure Impair Earnings Quality?", *Contemporary Accounting Research* 25(2): 415–45.

Chi, W., Huang, H., Liao, Y., and H. Xie (2009) "Mandatory Audit Partner Rotation, Audit Quality, and Market Perception: Evidence from Taiwan", *Contemporary Accounting Research* 26(2): 359–91.

Davis, L. R., Soo, B. S., and Trompeter, G. M. (2009) "Auditor Tenure and the Ability to Meet or Beat Earnings Forecasts", *Contemporary Accounting Research* 26(2): 517–48.

Dechow, P., Ge, W., and Schrand, C. (2010) "Understanding Earnings Quality: A Review of the Proxies, their Determinants and their Consequences", *Journal of Accounting and Economics* 50(2–3): 344–401.

DeFond, M. L. and Subramanyam, K. R. (1998) "Auditor Changes and Discretionary Accruals", *Journal of Accounting and Economics* 25(1): 35–67.

Doogar, R., Sivadasan, P., and Soloman, I. (2010) "The Regulation of Public Company Auditing: Evidence from the Transition to AS5", *Journal of Accounting Research* 48(4): 795–814.

European Commission (EC) (2010) *Green Paper. Audit policy: Lessons from the Crisis,* Commission Staff working paper, COM(2010) 561 final (October 13, 2010). Brussels: EC.

Ewelt-Knauer, C., Gold, A., and Pott, C. (2012) *What do we Know about Mandatory Audit Firm Rotation?*, research report. Edinburgh: Institute of Chartered Accountants of Scotland (ICAS).

General Accounting Office (GAO) (2003) *Public Accounting Firms: Required Study on the Potential Effects of Mandatory Audit Firm Rotation*. Washington, DC: United States General Accounting Office.

Ghosh, A. and Moon, D. (2005) "Auditor Tenure and Perceptions of Audit Quality", *Accounting Review* 80(2): 585–612.

Harris, K. and Whisenant, S. (2012) "Mandatory Audit Rotation: An International Investigation", working paper. Houston, TX: Bauer College of Business, University of Houston.

Iliev, P. (2010) "The Effect of SOX Section 404: Costs, Earnings Quality, and Stock Prices", *Journal of Finance* 65(3): 1163–96.

Johnson, E., Khurana, I. K., and Reynolds, J. K. (2002) "Audit-Firm Tenure and the Quality of Financial Reports", *Contemporary Accounting Research* 19(4): 637–60.

Johnstone, K. M. and Bedard, J. C. (2004) "Audit Firm Portfolio Management Decisions", *Journal of Accounting Research* 42: 659–90.

Kinney, W. R. and Shepardson, M. L. (2011) "Do Control Effectiveness Disclosures Require SOX 404(b) Internal Control Audits? A Natural Experiment with Small U.S. Public Companies", *Journal of Accounting Research* 49(2): 413–48.

Kwon, S. Y., Lim, Y., and Simnett, R. (2011) "Mandatory Audit Firm Rotation and Audit Quality: Evidence from the Korean Audit Market", working paper. Kensington, NSW: University of New South Wales.

Lennox, C., (2000) "Do Companies Successfully Engage in Opinion-shopping? The UK Experience", *Journal of Accounting and Economics* 29(3): 321–37.

Lennox, C., Wu, X., and Zhang, T. (2014) "Does Mandatory Rotation of Audit Partners Improve Audit Quality?", *Accounting Review*.

Mansi, S. A., Maxwell, W. F., and Milller, D. (2004) "Does Auditor Quality and Tenure Matter to Investors? Evidence from the Bond Market", *Journal of Accounting Research* 42(4): 755–93.

Melumad, N. and L. Thoman (1990) "An Equilibrium Analysis of Optimal Audit Contracts", *Contemporary Accounting Research* 7(1): 22–55.

Myers, J., Myers, L. A., and Omer, T. C. (2003) "Exploring the Term of the Auditor-client Relationship and the Quality of Earnings: A Case for Mandatory Auditor Rotation?", *Accounting Review* 78(3): 779–99.

Myers, J., Myers, L., Palmrose, Z. V., and Scholz, S. (2005) "Mandatory Auditor Rotation: Evidence from Restatements", working paper. Urbana, IL: University of Illinois at Urbana-Champaign.

Numan, W. and Willekens, M. (2011) "Competitive Pressure, Audit Quality and Industry Specialization Strategies", working paper. Leuven: Katholieke Universiteit.

Ruiz-Barbadillo, E., Go´mez-Aguilar, N., and Carrera, N. (2009) "Does Mandatory Audit Firm Rotation Enhance Auditor Independence? Evidence from Spain", *Auditing: A Journal of Practice & Theory* 28(1): 113–35.

Siregar, S. V., Amarullah, F., Wibowo, A., and Anggraita, V. (2012) "Audit Tenure, Auditor Rotation, and Audit Quality: The Case of Indonesia", *Asian Journal of Business and Accounting* 5(1): 55–74.

9

Fraud and auditors' responsibility

Tina D. Carpenter and Ashley A. Austin

Introduction

Imagine someone tells you that the risk of contracting a certain rare disease this year is less than one percent. Unless you happen to know someone with the disease, you are not likely to be concerned about the possibility of such an unlikely event. This is what it is like to be an auditor looking for fraudulent financial reporting.[1] Unfortunately, the public does not fully understand auditors' responsibility for fraud or the rarity of its occurrence, creating an expectation gap between the audit profession and the public. It is also difficult for auditors to detect fraud because the perpetrators of fraud are often highly sophisticated executives who collude with their staff to deceive the auditors. Another difficulty is that unlike law enforcement and forensic accountants who investigate crimes after detection of a fraud, auditors do not have the benefit of hindsight. Auditors must consider fraud on every audit, although there is a less than one percent likelihood that a given client experiences fraud.

When fraud does occur, it is often very expensive and receives significant media attention. In a recent study of frauds investigated by the Securities and Exchange Commission (SEC), Beasley *et al.* (2010) reported that the median size of misstatements due to fraud tripled over the last decade resulting in a total misstatement of $120 billion for the 300 examined cases.[2] As stated by former SEC Chairman Mary Schapiro, "fighting financial fraud is an especially urgent task," one that will require that the SEC "work collaboratively with other organizations, agencies, academics, and activists to protect investors. The fight against fraud will take a serious effort from us all" (Schapiro 2011).

We believe that improving auditors' fraud detection skills is a significant challenge for the accounting profession and will remain a priority for many years. As such, the objective of this chapter is to provide a deeper understanding of auditors' responsibility for fraud that will be useful to members of both the academic and practice communities. Accordingly, we expect this chapter to contribute to the literature by providing conclusions and insights that should be informative to academics, students, auditors, media, standard setters, and policy makers.

Current issues in auditors' responsibility for fraud

Auditors face several important issues with respect to fraud. First, after over a century of self-regulation, auditors now have a quasi-public agency scrutinizing their work. Following the discovery of major accounting scandals such as Enron and WorldCom, Congress enacted the Sarbanes-Oxley Act (SOX) in July 2002, creating the Public Company Accounting Oversight Board (PCAOB) to oversee, regulate, inspect, and discipline audit firms. A few months later in October 2002, the issuance of Statement on Auditing Standards (SAS) No. 99 (AU Section 316) dramatically expanded the procedures that auditors must perform related to their consideration of fraud, including requiring a brainstorming session by the audit team, greater inquiry with client personnel, and identification of fraud risk factors using the fraud triangle. Auditors have had difficulty implementing SAS No. 99 to the PCAOB's expectations. In 2007, the PCAOB reported that inspection teams observed cases where auditors failed to demonstrate that they held brainstorming sessions, failed to document performance of required fraud inquiries, and failed to expand audit procedures after identifying fraud risk factors (PCAOB 2007). In August 2012, the PCAOB reported that audit firms did not perform sufficient procedures to identify, assess, and respond to fraud risks in 13 out of 23 broker–dealer audit inspections (PCAOB 2012a). Thus, auditors continue to struggle with meeting the regulatory demands related to fraud.

A second important issue related to fraud is the expectation gap between auditors' actual responsibility for detecting fraud and the public's understanding of that responsibility. While the public generally believes that auditors are responsible for detecting all fraud at a company, the audit report provides only reasonable (not absolute) assurance that the financial statements are free of material misstatement, whether due to fraud or error. The expectation gap often reveals itself after massive frauds like the Madoff scandal in 2008, when the public makes comments about auditors, such as "They were supposed to be the watchdogs. Why did they sign off on these funds' books?" (Gandel 2008). To help close the expectation gap, the Center for Audit Quality (CAQ) tries to educate the public by publishing resources that provide non-auditors with an overview of the auditing process, including an explanation of the auditor's responsibility for fraud (CAQ 2011). Additionally, the PCAOB is considering modifying the audit report language to explain more clearly auditors' role and limitations in finding fraud (PCAOB 2011). Despite these efforts, managing the expectation gap will likely remain an important issue to auditors and regulators.

Finally, because detecting fraud is such a difficult task, practitioners, researchers, and regulators must work together to improve auditors' ability to detect fraud. As an example of collaboration, four of the nation's leading professional associations, the CAQ, the National Association of Corporate Directors (NACD), Financial Executives International, and the Institute of Internal Auditors, are partnering to discuss a series of fraud topics such as the use of skepticism within the financial reporting arena (NACD 2012). Additionally, audit researchers are utilizing psychology theories to explain why fraudsters decide to commit fraud and what psychological biases may prevent auditors from detecting fraud. Working together to "think like a fraudster" and improve auditors' fraud detection tools continues to be a current issue for the auditing community.

History of auditors' responsibility for fraud

Looking at the major news headlines over the past decade, fraud followed by increased regulatory scrutiny seems like a new phenomenon. Stepping back 100 years, however, there seems to be a recurring pattern of large frauds spurring public outrage (partly due to the expectation gap) and resulting in actions by regulatory and standard setting bodies, as presented in Figure 9.1. In the early 1900s, audit textbooks described the detection of fraud and errors as only a *minor* objective

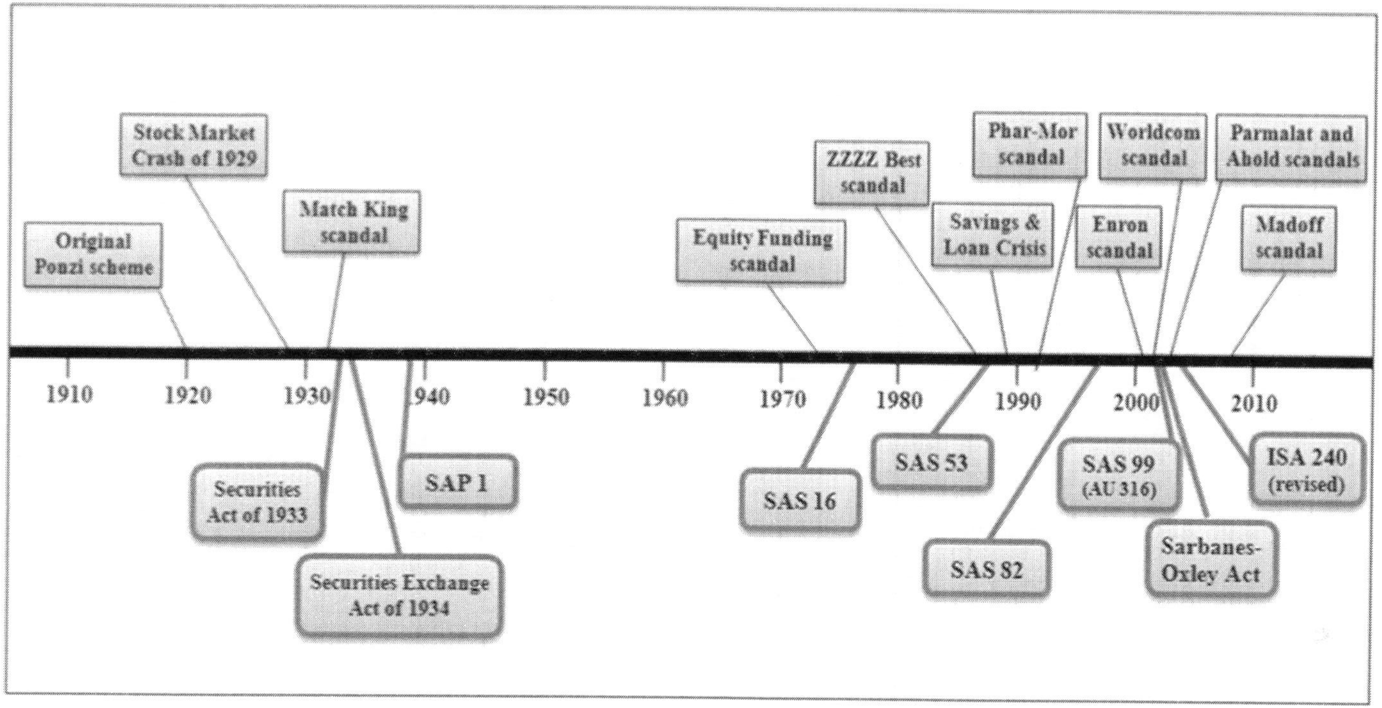

This figure presents a timeline with some of the most significant frauds over the past hundred years, as well as the major regulatory and auditing standard changes which followed these scandals.

Figure 9.1 Timeline of major fraud scandals and regulatory responses

of an audit (Montgomery 1912), but due to the cycle of fraud and regulatory response over the past 100 years, auditors' responsibility for fraud has greatly increased.

Beginning as far back as 1920 when Charles Ponzi fooled investors into purchasing his postal coupons (the original "Ponzi scheme"), investors have lost millions to fraudsters carrying out complicated and careful schemes. During the late 1920s Ivar Krueger, nicknamed "The Match King", collected investor money from around the world to form a monopoly on manufacturing and distributing safety matches, but in 1932 it was discovered that because of Krueger's fraudulent and aggressive accounting methods, most of the company's assets existed only on paper; American investors lost $250 million. In response to the stock market crash of 1929 and the Match King scandal in 1932, Congress enacted the Securities Act of 1933 and the Securities Exchange Act of 1934 to protect investors. These acts established the SEC and required companies to fully disclose material information. In 1939, the first auditing standard, Statement on Auditing Procedure (SAP) No. 1, clarified the auditor's responsibility for fraud. SAP No. 1 stated that the independent auditor should be "on his guard" against fraud, but that "he relies upon the integrity of the client's organization unless circumstances are such as to arouse suspicion." Under SAP No. 1, auditors had no responsibility to detect fraud and provided no assurance as to the presence or absence of fraud.

After a long period without significant fraud headlines or changes in the audit standards regarding fraud,[3] the discovery of the Equity Funding scandal in 1973 prompted the newly formed American Institute of Certified Public Accountants (AICPA) to issue Statement on Auditing Standard (SAS) No. 16 in 1977. SAS No. 16 stated that the auditor has the responsibility to plan the audit to search for material errors or irregularities (fraud). Even with this new standard, the audit report still provided no assurance that the financial statements were free from material fraud, but the auditor now had a responsibility to consider the possibility of material fraud when planning and performing the audit.

In 1987, investors lost $100 million in the ZZZZ Best accounting scandal, attracting considerable media attention due to the massive size of the fraud and concerns about how multiple audits failed to detect it. In 1988, the AICPA responded by issuing SAS No. 53 which required auditors to provide *reasonable* assurance of detecting material errors and irregularities (fraud) by considering fraud as they plan, perform, and evaluate the results of the audit procedures. By clarifying auditors' responsibility for fraud with SAS No. 53, the AICPA hoped to narrow the expectation gap, but about a decade later events such as the Savings and Loan crisis and the Phar-Mor scandal again resulted in public outcry concerning the auditor's responsibility for fraud. The AICPA responded by issuing SAS No. 82 in 1997, which maintained the responsibility of reasonable assurance established by SAS No. 53 but also required auditors to consider specific fraud risk factors when assessing the risk of fraud.

As discussed in the earlier section entitled Current issues in auditors' responsibility for fraud, the accounting scandals of the early 2000s spurred several significant changes for auditors. Congress enacted SOX in July 2002, creating the PCAOB and introducing new standards for auditors on public engagements, including the assessment of internal control. A few months later, SAS No. 99 dramatically increased the procedures auditors must perform related to their consideration of fraud. The standard also emphasized the importance of maintaining professional skepticism during an audit, regardless of previous experience with the client. In 2007, the PCAOB adopted SAS No. 99 as AU Section 316. Accounting scandals and subsequent audit standard changes are not unique to the United States. For example, in 2003 Europe suffered from the Parmalat and Ahold scandals which prompted international standard setters in 2004 to revise their fraud standard, International Standard on Auditing (ISA) 240, adopting the basic principles and essential procedures of SAS No. 99. Despite this long history of regulatory and audit standard changes, massive accounting frauds are still going undetected by auditors. Research on how auditors can prevent, deter, and detect fraud remains as important as ever.

Summary of current state of research findings

Several fraud-related literature reviews have been published in the last decade. Some papers consider prior fraud literature more generally and others provide a more narrow focus related specifically to actions by auditors, or commentary on avenues for future research. Since the purpose of this chapter is not to provide a literature review per se, but to offer useful insights for academic researchers, doctoral students, practicing auditors, policy makers, and media, we will discuss and synthesize these literature reviews, rather than focus on individual papers. We consider five review papers.

Nieschwietz *et al.* (2000) examine research related to auditors' detection of fraudulent financial reporting published between 1980 and 2000; Hogan *et al.* (2008) review the fraud-related literature from 1996–2006; and Trompeter *et al.* (2013) extend their paper to literature from 2006–12. Trompeter *et al.* (2013) also summarize fraud literature published in non-accounting journals such as criminology, ethics, finance, sociology, psychology, and organizational behavior. Hammersley (2011) offers a unique perspective by developing a model of auditor judgments in fraud-related planning tasks in an effort to improve auditors' ability to identify conditions where fraud may be present, and to plan appropriate tests when they encounter these conditions. Finally, Nelson (2009) also makes a notable contribution to the literature with his focus on professional skepticism.

A model of auditors' responsibility for fraud detection

We develop a model of auditors' responsibility for fraud detection that integrates earlier academic work by Hammersley (2011), Brazel *et al.* (2010), and Nelson (2009) with descriptions of auditors in practice drawn from PCAOB inspections. The auditing profession is currently regulated by the PCAOB, which was created by SOX in 2002. The PCAOB, with its adoption of SAS No. 99 (AU Section 316), continues to emphasize the importance of auditors' fraud detection. Auditors are required to understand the fraud risk factors for a particular client, synthesize these risk factors with other information and evidence to develop a fraud risk assessment, and develop a response to these risk assessments by modifying audit procedures. Based on its recent inspections, however, the PCAOB has observed that audit testing in response to auditors' fraud risk assessments has failed to satisfy audit standards and cites an overall lack of professional skepticism as a serious problem in auditors' fraud investigations (PCAOB 2007, 2008, 2010).

As illustrated in Figure 9.2, our model depicts the auditor/audit team as the decision maker who, as required by SAS No. 99, examines the fraud risk factors of the client, uses these to create a fraud risk assessment, and then follows with a fraud risk response (i.e., a change to audit testing). During this process, the auditor/audit team is influenced by: (1) their own characteristics and incentives including: experience, knowledge, incentives, motivation, and ability; (2) training; and (3) consultation with forensic accounting experts. This model, which integrates the academic literature and findings from the PCAOB inspection reports, provides a comprehensive picture of the current state of auditors' responsibility for fraud detection, identifies where auditors are struggling in practice, and creates a foundation that highlights where researchers can help auditors improve their fraud detection.

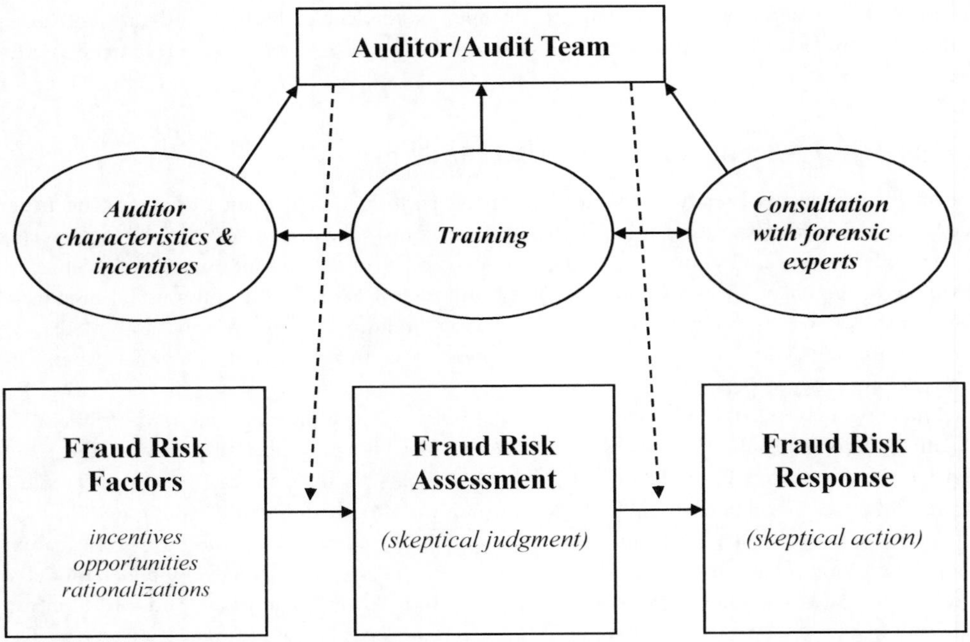

Figure 9.2 Auditors' responsibility for fraud detection

Fraud risk factors and fraud risk assessment

Nieschwietz *et al.* (2000) note that a substantial amount of research from 1980–2000 examines auditors' fraud risk assessments, finding that auditors generally increase their fraud risk assessments in response to fraud risk factors. However, they caution researchers on the importance of auditors assessing fraud risk accurately (not just higher) as auditors consider the cost of providing too much or too little investigation when fraud is present and when it is not. They suggest that auditors face two significant challenges when assessing fraud risk: a lack of experience with fraud; and difficulty determining how to properly weigh the fraud risk factors in their judgments.

Subsequent to Nieschwietz *et al.* (2000), SAS No. 99 provides a comprehensive list of fraud risk factors (i.e., red flags) that fall into the fraud triangle categories of incentives/pressures, opportunities, and attitudes/rationalizations. Hogan *et al.* (2008) suggest that, in general, academic research documents a relation between the existence of financial statement fraud and incentives/pressures, opportunities, and attitudes/rationalizations. They suggest that a checklist or decision aid with these fraud risk factors may be helpful to auditors, but they warn that the literature is mixed on the benefits to auditors of checklists.[4] Hammersley (2011) echoes this concern and notes that while the literature suggests that auditors generally increase their fraud risk assessments in response to fraud risk factors, if the use of a fraud risk checklist distracts auditors from identifying other fraud cues, then their fraud risk assessments can be impaired. She suggests that auditors might improve their fraud risk assessments if they focused more on linking fraud risk factors to the risk of fraud on specific accounts or assertions.

Nieschwietz *et al.* (2000) suggest that the value from the fraud risk assessment process may not be from the assessments themselves but rather from a heightened level of auditor skepticism when they are evaluating evidence. Nelson (2009) defines professional skepticism as "auditor judgments and decisions that reflect a heightened assessment of the risk that an assertion is incorrect, conditional on information available to the auditor" (Nelson 2009: 1). This definition reflects a more presumptive doubt perspective consistent with SAS No. 99's directive that it is important for the auditor to exercise professional skepticism when considering the risk of material misstatement due to fraud and that the auditor should "conduct the engagement with a mindset that recognizes the possibility that a material misstatement due to fraud could be present, regardless of any past experience with the entity and regardless of the auditor's beliefs about management's honesty and integrity" (AU 316.13). In the eyes of regulators, auditors do not always maintain the appropriate level of skepticism, as the PCAOB notes that "observations from the PCAOB's oversight activities continue to raise concerns about whether auditors consistently and diligently apply professional skepticism" (PCAOB 2012b). More specifically, PCAOB inspections report that procedures performed during the testwork phase of the audit sometimes do not appropriately reflect the fraud risk assessments auditors made during the planning phase (PCAOB 2007, 2008, 2010).

Fraud risk response (audit testing)

Auditors should respond to the risk of fraud by increasing the unpredictability of audit procedures (AU 316.50). The goal of fraud risk assessments is to make auditors sensitive to fraud risk so that they modify the nature or extent of their audit plans to improve their ability to detect fraud. However, the general consensus in the literature is that auditors typically focus on modifying the extent, rather than the nature, of audit tests (Nieschwietz *et al.* 2000; Hogan *et al.* 2008; Hammersley 2011; Trompeter *et al.* 2013). Hammersley (2011) emphasizes the importance of understanding the conditions that determine whether to change the extent versus the nature of planned procedures. She argues that in circumstances where auditors are examining high-level fraud red flags that signal only general fraud concern, a reasonable response is to increase the extent of testing. Alternatively, if client-specific information provides the fraud signal, then auditors can more easily generate precise fraud hypotheses, leading them to modify the nature of the planned tests. Nelson (2009) defines fraud risk assessments as skeptical judgments and modifications of audit testing as skeptical actions; he suggests that whether skeptical judgments translate into skeptical actions depends on aspects of the auditor's knowledge, traits, and incentives.

Auditor/audit team

Trompeter *et al.* (2013) emphasize the importance of considering financial statement fraud from a group dynamic perspective. Most often, large financial statement frauds involve collusion among multiple individuals (i.e., CEO, CFO, controller, and staff accountants). For example, top management might have incentives to manipulate the stock price to meet analysts' expectations or benefit personally. Accordingly, they might put pressure on their staff to book a fraudulent journal entry in order to meet this goal. Nieschwietz *et al.* (2000) suggest that fraudulent financial reporting typically involves scheming by clever teams of knowledgeable managers and intimidation of employees and auditors. Each of these fraudsters has different characteristics, knowledge, and incentives that are important to the decision to commit fraud.

Likewise, auditors' characteristics (e.g., knowledge, experience, ability) and incentives are critical inputs to their fraud judgments and decisions. Further, the auditor is part of a team that typically includes staff, seniors, managers, and partners, who each have different knowledge, incentives, experience, and ability. Nieschwietz *et al.* (2000) point out that although highly experienced members of the team (e.g., partners) may make client retention decisions, less experienced audit team members actually conduct the audit. They conclude that:

> It is highly unlikely that any member of the team will ever encounter fraud. Faced with these complex tasks, auditors must also cultivate positive client relations (especially from the client personnel most likely to perpetrate the fraud). They need to accommodate different masters, and their mixed accountability may lead them to make judgments that are less skeptical than one might expect.
>
> *(Nieschwietz* et al. *2000: 236)*

Auditor characteristics and incentives

Nelson (2009) suggests that auditors' characteristics (including experience, knowledge, and traits) and incentives are important determinants of professional skepticism and therefore influence audit performance. Prior work on auditor incentives suggests that auditors are more likely to exhibit professional skepticism when focused more on concerns of litigation and reputation loss rather than on concerns about client retention. Hammersley (2011) extends Nelson's (2009) professional skepticism model to a fraud setting by suggesting that in addition to auditors' experience, their ability and epistemic motivation (the degree to which people develop accurate and rich understandings of situations) influence their knowledge, which in turn affects auditors' performance in fraud tasks. In addition, she suggests that epistemic motivation will enhance auditors' knowledge, as they will work hard to understand the evidence that is critical to better performance in fraud tasks. Importantly, however, she notes that academic research has not investigated the effects of any of these auditor characteristics. She also points out that while fraud training may be the primary way for auditors to enrich their fraud knowledge, there is little known about auditors' fraud training or whether auditors may benefit from forensic training.

Training and consultation with forensic experts

Nieschwietz *et al.* (2000) and Hogan *et al.* (2008) call for research on auditor training to help improve auditors' fraud judgments. However, Trompeter *et al.* (2013) suggest that there has been a very limited response to this call and suggest that research on auditor training remains a critical area for future research. The PCAOB is also interested in how and when to use forensic experts on the audit, and how forensic accounting experts' mindsets may differ from those of auditors (PCAOB 2007, 2008). Hogan *et al.* (2008) note the lack of research in this area and call for future research. However, Trompeter *et al.* (2013) suggest that there has been very little research in response to this call in the last five years, and make yet another call for future research in the area of consultation with forensic experts.[5]

Unresolved issues related to fraud

As mentioned during our earlier discussion, Summary of current state of research findings, there are several issues facing the profession that remain unresolved. We believe the unresolved issues related to fraud are concentrated in four areas: auditor fraud risk response (i.e., testing); auditor characteristics; training; and forensic specialists.

First, we do not know much about *why* auditors have difficulty linking fraud risk assessments to fraud risk responses. Although it has been shown that auditors have trouble appropriately modifying planned audit procedures in response to identified fraud risks, little is understood about what causes auditors to struggle with this task. It is possible that auditors have the necessary knowledge and ability to respond appropriately to the identified fraud risks but they lack the motivation to do so, or they face conflicting goals (such as time/budget pressures, lack of professional skepticism, etc.). Alternatively, auditors might attempt to design appropriate fraud risk responses, but due to a lack of ability and/or fraud knowledge, the audit tests they design are insufficient. It is important to distinguish between these two possibilities – that is, do auditors know how to respond, but fail to do so; or do auditors not know how to respond appropriately? Answering this question will help auditors improve their fraud risk responses.

Second, little is known about whether individual characteristics affect auditor judgments on fraud tasks. Researchers have suggested that individual characteristics such as problem solving ability, fraud knowledge, professional skepticism, and epistemic motivation may affect fraud judgments, but there is little empirical evidence to support this view. Experience likely plays a smaller role on fraud tasks than on other audit tasks because most auditors have never experienced fraud on an engagement. Future research could examine whether auditor characteristics like problem solving ability and professional skepticism are more important on fraud tasks than on other audit tasks (where auditors can rely more on experience). If fraud tasks are more sensitive to individual auditor differences than other audit tasks, then researchers, regulators, standard setters, and audit firms should keep this in mind as they try to improve auditor performance on fraud tasks.

Third, we know little about how best to utilize training programs to enhance auditor fraud judgments. Because experiencing fraud on an audit engagement is unlikely, auditors gain the majority of their fraud knowledge through training rather than experience. Researchers and audit firms should consider what types of training courses (e.g., national firm trainings, multi-disciplinary panels, fraud conferences) are most effective for each level at the firm (i.e., staff, managers, partners) and whether it would be useful to customize programs based on individual auditor characteristics (problem solving ability, professional skepticism, etc.).

Fourth, the issue of how and when auditors should consult with forensic specialists on an audit remains unresolved. The CEOs of the six largest global audit firms recognize the value of forensic auditing because in their discussion of ideas for enhancing fraud detection, they outline that all public companies could be subject to a forensic audit on either a regular, random, or board-chosen basis (DiPiazza *et al.* 2006). Forensic audits are costly, however, so it would be beneficial to first investigate how auditors can enhance fraud detection through consultation with forensic specialists, a more cost-effective alternative. We currently do not know the audit factors (e.g., client industry, complexity of transactions, audit team fraud experience) which determine whether the audit would benefit from the involvement of a forensic specialist. Other unanswered questions include: During what phase of the audit (planning, testing, etc.) should auditors consult forensic specialists? Do forensic specialists have the necessary audit knowledge to be helpful to auditors? Do auditors' mindsets differ from forensic specialists' mindsets? Once we know more about when and how to use forensic specialists effectively on audits, fraud detection should improve.

Conclusion

Within this chapter, we present an overview of the current state of knowledge on auditors' responsibility for fraud. We discuss the critical issues facing auditors today, consider the influence of historical frauds and responses, and develop a model of auditors' responsibility for fraud detection that integrates the academic literature with our understanding of auditors in practice. Based on this analysis, we identify four unresolved issues related to fraud in the areas of auditor fraud risk response, auditor characteristics, training, and forensic specialists. By taking a broad but focused perspective, we hope our conclusions and insights are informative to a variety of audiences, including students, media, policy makers, and researchers. We believe this chapter contributes to the literature by providing an integrated summary of the current challenges, historical trends, and prior research findings related to auditors' responsibility for fraud, as well as providing new directions for future research that can improve auditors' fraud investigations.

As researchers, policy makers, and auditors work to address the unresolved issues related to fraud, we encourage these parties to consider innovative solutions, collaborate with each other, and maintain a global perspective. First, in order to solve the complex and unique problems related to fraud detection, we will need innovative solutions. Fraudsters are themselves creative, so a similar level of creativity is likely needed in order to design audits to detect their schemes. For inspiration, those interested in fraud detection should review work in related disciplines like crime, psychology, and organizational behavior, which can offer new perspectives. Second, auditors, policy makers, and academics should collaborate to tackle these problems. Each of these groups has unique resources which they can share with each other in order to reach their common goal of improving auditors' fraud detection. Third, audits are becoming more global which likely creates new opportunities for fraudsters to conceal fraud, further increasing auditors' difficulties with detecting fraud. Since global audits propose new fraud challenges, we encourage parties to keep a global perspective as they work to solve fraud-related problems.

Going forward, we urge researchers to focus on improving auditors' fraud judgments and decisions. As noted in recent PCAOB inspection reports, auditors have difficulty fulfilling their responsibility for fraud and this is especially problematic considering that the public holds auditors to an even higher level of responsibility. To help auditors meet regulatory standards and close the expectation gap, we need high quality research that contributes to improving auditors' fraud detection. For example, it is not enough for research to conclude that auditors differ on certain characteristics, or that fraud training helps auditors, or that forensic specialists are different from auditors. Rather, researchers should focus on questions like: When do individual auditor characteristics like professional skepticism make a difference on fraud judgments? What types of fraud trainings are most effective for improving on-the-job auditor fraud performance? How can forensic specialists cost-effectively assist auditors on their fraud tasks? Carefully designed studies that focus on these types of questions will provide a contribution to the main goal of improving auditor fraud detection and will thus provide promising insights to auditors, regulators, policy makers, and researchers.

Acknowledgements

We thank David Hay, Robert Knechel, and Marleen Willekens for inviting us to write this chapter. We also thank Michael Bamber, Jenny Gaver, and Jane Reimers for their insightful comments.

Notes

1 We estimate that the chance of an auditor working on a fraudulent client during a year is less than one percent. Our calculation was based on Beasley *et al.* (2010) reporting that 347 public companies were involved in alleged instances of fraudulent financial reporting during a ten-year time period, or about

35 fraudulent companies per year. Using a rough estimate of about 6,000 public companies in the US during that time, the chance per year of a public company being involved in fraud is less than one percent.

2 In this chapter, we focus on financial reporting fraud rather than misappropriation of assets. Although the two types can be linked, financial reporting fraud, or the intentional violation of Generally Accepted Accounting Principles (GAAP), is of primary concern to financial statement auditors because, while it occurs infrequently, it is extremely costly (Beasley *et al.* 2010). For ease of exposition, we use the label "fraud" to refer to financial reporting fraud throughout the chapter.

3 We chose to focus on the largest financial frauds over the past century, especially the frauds which led to regulatory reform, so we do not discuss any frauds from this time period. We note, however, that while no large-scale frauds were uncovered during this time period, fraudulent financial reporting and the detection of fraudulent activities still occurred during this time period.

4 For an example of how use of checklists can impair auditor performance, see Asare and Wright (2004).

5 Notable exceptions are Asare and Wright (2004) who examine the likelihood of consultation with forensic specialists and Gold *et al.* (2012) who investigate how the strictness of a requirement to consult on potential client fraud affects auditors' propensity to consult with firm forensic experts.

References

Asare, S. K. and A. M. Wright. 2004. "The Effectiveness of Alternative Risk Assessment and Program Planning Tools in a Fraud Setting", *Contemporary Accounting Research* 21(2): 325–52.

Beasley, M., J. Carcello, D. Hermanson, and T. Neal. 2010. *Fraudulent Financial Reporting, 1987–2007: An Analysis of U.S. Public Companies.* Durham, NC: Committee of Sponsoring Organizations of the Treadway Commission.

Brazel, J. F., T. D. Carpenter, and J. G. Jenkins. 2010. "Auditors' Use of Brainstorming in the Consideration of Fraud: Reports from the Field", *The Accounting Review* 85(4): 1273–1301.

Center for Audit Quality (CAQ). 2011. *In-Depth Guide to Public Company Auditing: The Financial Statement Audit.* Washington DC: CAQ.

DiPiazza, S. A., D. McDonnell, W. G. Parrett, M. D. Rake, F. Samyn, and J. S. Turley. 2006. *Global Capital Markets and the Global Economy: A Vision from the CEOs of the International Audit Network.* Available online at www.cybsoc.org/CEO_Vision.pdf (accessed 14 April 2014).

Gandel, S. 2008. "The Madoff Fraud: How Culpable were the Auditors?" *Time* (December 17). Available online at www.time.com/time/business/article/0,8599,1867092,00.html (accessed 14 April 2014).

Gold, A., W. R. Knechel, and P. Wallage. 2012. "The Effect of the Strictness of Consultation Requirements on Fraud Consultation", *The Accounting Review* 87(3): 925–49.

Hammersley, J. S. 2011. "A Review and Model of Auditor Judgments in Fraud-related Planning Tasks", *Auditing: A Journal of Practice & Theory* 30(4): 101–28.

Hogan, C. E., Z. Rezaee, R. A. Riley, and U. Velury. 2008. "Financial Statement Fraud: Insights from the Academic Literature", *Auditing: A Journal of Practice & Theory* 27(November): 231–52.

Montgomery, R. H. 1912. *Auditing Theory and Practice.* New York: Ronald Press.

National Association of Corporate Directors (NACD). 2012. "Anti-Fraud Collaboration Continues Battle against Financial Reporting Fraud with Release of Skepticism Webinar Series" October 1, 2012.

Nelson, M. 2009. "A Model and Literature Review of Professional Skepticism in Auditing", *Auditing: A Journal of Practice & Theory* 28(2): 1–34.

Nieschwietz, R., J. Schultz, and M. Zimbelman. 2000. "Empirical Research on External Auditors' Detection of Financial Statement Fraud", *Journal of Accounting Literature* 19: 190–246.

Public Company Accounting Oversight Board (PCAOB). 2007. *Observations of Auditors' Implementation of PCAOB Standards Relating to Auditors' Responsibilities with Respect to Fraud.* Release No. 2007–01, January 22, 2007. Washington DC: PCAOB.

Public Company Accounting Oversight Board (PCAOB). 2008. *Proposed Auditing Standards Related to the Auditor's Assessment of and Response to Risk.* Release No. 2008–006, October 21, 2008. Washington DC: PCAOB.

Public Company Accounting Oversight Board (PCAOB). 2010. *Report on Observations of PCAOB Inspectors Related to Audit Risk Areas Affected by the Economic Crisis.* Release No. 2010–06, September 29, 2010. Washington DC: PCAOB.

Public Company Accounting Oversight Board (PCAOB). 2011. *Concept Release on Possible Revisions to PCAOB Standards Related to Reports on Audited Financial Statements and Related Amendments to PCAOB Standards.* Release No. 2011–003, June 21, 2011. Washington DC: PCAOB.

Public Company Accounting Oversight Board (PCAOB). 2012a. *Report on the Progress of the Interim Inspection Program Related to Audits of Brokers and Dealers*. Release No. 2012–005, August 20, 2012. Washington DC: PCAOB.

Public Company Accounting Oversight Board (PCAOB). 2012b. *Staff Audit Practice Alert No. 10: Maintaining and Applying Professional Skepticism In Audits*. December 4, 2012. Washington DC: PCAOB.

Schapiro, M. 2011. "Speech by SEC Chairman: Remarks at Stanford Center on Longevity – FINRA Investor Education Foundation Conference", November 3. Available online at www.sec.gov/news/speech/2011/spch110311mls.htm (accessed 14 April 2014).

Trompeter, G., T. Carpenter, N. Desai, K. Jones, and R. A. Riley Jr. 2013. "A Synthesis of Fraud Related Research", *Auditing: A Journal of Practice & Theory* 32(Supp. 1): 287–321.

10

Earnings management and auditing

Steven F. Cahan

Introduction

Auditing evolved as a way to monitor the performance of a firm's managers (e.g., Jensen and Meckling 1976; Watts and Zimmerman 1983a). For example, merchant guilds in medieval England would require that "profits" arising during a year would be audited by an official such as an alderman (Watts and Zimmerman 1983a: 617). Thus, "auditors" have a long history in assuring that periodic measures of performance are free from errors or misstatements.

In the 1970s, academic researchers began to explore the incentives that managers have for reporting opportunistically. These researchers focus on contracts and the political process (e.g., Watts and Zimmerman 1983b). In the former case, accounting numbers are often used to specify the contract's terms or requirements. In the latter case, politicians target high income earning firms or industries for legislation or regulation because their wealth can be transferred to the voting public. According to "positive accounting theory", managers use the flexibility in generally accepted accounting principles (GAAP) to report higher income to increase their bonuses or loosen their firm's debt covenants, and to report lower income to reduce political costs (i.e., costly legislation and regulation). Thus, earnings management arises when managers opportunistically intervene in the financial reporting process in order to gain privately (e.g., Schipper 1989).

Auditors have incentives to discover and report breaches of GAAP (e.g., DeAngelo 1981). While earnings management represents more aggressive accounting treatments within GAAP rather than a breach of GAAP, DeAngelo's (1981) theory is instructive. Adapting her theory, the probability that earnings management is constrained depends on the likelihood that it is discovered and the likelihood that the auditor will oppose the client's desired accounting treatment. In other words, the auditor has to be competent and independent.

Numerous studies examine auditors' ability to constrain earnings management. These studies either examine competence-based or independence-based explanations (although the distinction is not always clear cut). Auditors with greater industry- and firm-specific knowledge should be more competent at spotting aggressive earnings management. For example, some studies examine whether firms with industry specialist auditors engage in less earnings management (e.g., see Chapter 15) while other studies find that earnings management decreases with auditor tenure, suggesting that client-specific experience and knowledge are important (e.g., see

Chapter 8). An auditor's independence from a client depends on the economic bond between the auditor and client, and on litigation risk. For instance, an auditor that receives a substantial amount of non-audit fees from a client might be more willing to acquiesce to the client's demands, although a majority of empirical studies do not support this supposition (e.g., see Chapter 7). In contrast, an auditor's independence may be enhanced by litigation risk. If auditors are more likely to be sued for overstated earnings, auditors have incentives to resist income increasing earnings management attempts (e.g., see Chapter 6).

To conduct research on the relation between auditors and earnings management, auditing researchers have generally adopted measures of earnings quality from financial accounting research. Earnings quality is an inverse measure of earnings management – less (more) earnings management is associated with higher (lower) earnings quality. However, it is worth noting that measures of earnings quality can also be affected by unintentional errors. The most commonly used earnings quality measures in auditing research are based on accruals, target beating, market pricing, and specific events. Real earnings management is another class of earnings management but affects both reported earnings and cash flows. The remainder of this chapter will focus on these measures.

Earnings quality measures

Accrual-based measures

Theoretically, a focus on accruals is attractive because accruals relate to a client's inherent risk (e.g., Francis and Krishnan 1999). Unlike cash flows which can be measured objectively with a high level of precision, accruals can introduce estimation errors into the accounting process, as they involve subjective judgments about the future and because managers have incentives to use accruals opportunistically. Francis and Krishnan (1999) contend that auditors respond to the added uncertainty by requiring accruals that are less income increasing. For example, auditors can interpret GAAP more tightly or apply more stringent thresholds when evaluating whether a proposed accrual is acceptable.

While earnings can be decomposed into cash flows and accruals, Jones (1991) recognizes that accruals can be further decomposed into a nondiscretionary piece and a discretionary piece. The nondiscretionary piece reflects the accruals that would be taken in normal circumstances, i.e., the amount that reflects the economic fundamentals of the underlying transaction. The discretionary piece reflects deviations around the normal or expected amount. Generally, researchers assume that the discretionary piece is the result of managers' opportunism; however, it is possible that the discretionary piece may also reflect measurement system error (e.g., incorrect estimates of future events).

Although Jones (1991) is not the first to recognize that accruals contain a discretionary component (e.g., see Healy 1985; DeAngelo 1986), she is the first to adopt a multivariate approach in modelling it. She expects that the normal level of accruals – i.e., nondiscretionary accruals – will be a function of the change in sales and plant, property, and equipment. Working capital accounts such as inventory and accounts payable vary with sales. Depreciation expense (a non-current accrual) is based on the gross balance of plant, property, and equipment. Thus, Jones (1991) regresses total accruals (*Acc*) on the change in sales (*ΔSales*) and the gross plant, property, and equipment (*PPE*), where all the variables are scaled by total assets to address heteroscedasticity:

$$Acc_t = \alpha + \beta_1 \Delta Sales_t + \beta_2 PPE_t + \varepsilon_t \qquad (1)$$

Jones (1991) uses seven years of data and estimates eq. (1) for every firm in her sample. She uses the estimated coefficients from eq. (1) to compute the expected nondiscretionary accruals in a subsequent test period. The difference between total accruals in the test period and the computed nondiscretionary accruals is an estimate of discretionary accruals in the test period.

As Jones's (1991) approach requires extensive time-series data prior to the test period, following DeFond and Jiambalvo (1994), researchers generally estimate the Jones model on a cross-sectional basis where eq. (1) is estimated for each industry on a year-by-year basis. When the cross-sectional approach is used, researchers can use the residual from the Jones model as an estimate of discretionary accruals.

Subsequent research has refined the Jones model. For example, Dechow *et al.* (1995) subtract the change in accounts receivable from the change in sales when computing discretionary accruals in the test period, since credit sales can be manipulated. Kothari *et al.* (2005) address concerns about the relation between discretionary accruals and performance documented by Dechow *et al.* (1995) and others. Kothari *et al.* (2005) recommend "performance-adjusting" discretionary accruals where each firm's discretionary accruals are adjusted by subtracting out the discretionary accruals from another firm that is matched on size and performance (return on assets [*ROA*]). Ashbaugh-Skaife *et al.* (2008) include the annual market adjusted buy and hold return, an indicator for negative abnormal returns, and the interaction of these two variables to control for conditional conservatism. One issue that researchers need to consider when using discretionary accruals is whether a signed or absolute value should be used. Although most studies assume that the auditor has a preference for income-decreasing accruals and uses the signed discretionary accruals, other studies view upward and downward earnings management as equally problematic and, hence, rely on the absolute value of discretionary accruals. In addition, the reversing nature of accruals means that an income-decreasing accrual in one period becomes an income-increasing accrual in a subsequent period. As a result, the absolute value can better capture the general propensity to manage earnings. In general, if the researcher has strong priors about the direction of the earnings management, the signed discretionary accruals should be used. For example, DeFond and Subramanyam (1998) examine whether clients switch auditors in order to find one who is less conservative. They find that the signed discretionary accruals in the year before the switch are negative but increase once the new auditor is in place. In contrast, Chung and Kallapur (2003) justify their use of the absolute value of discretionary accruals by referring to the former SEC (Securities and Exchange Commission) chief Arthur Levitt who criticized "cookie jar" accounting that could increase or decrease reported earnings.

However, Hribar and Nichols (2007) show that tests involving the absolute value of discretionary accruals are biased toward rejecting the null of no earnings management. In particular, they show that the unsigned value is highly correlated with operating volatility, and suggest that researchers can minimize the effect of this correlation by including measures of operating volatility such as total assets, cash flows from operations, and the standard deviations of cash flows and revenues in their tests.

Although widely used, the Jones-model-based measures of discretionary accruals are not without criticism. Dechow *et al.* (1995) find the null that discretionary accruals are less than or equal to zero is over-rejected when performance is extremely poor. Subramanyam (1996) and Guay *et al.* (1996) find that managers may use discretionary accruals to convey information to the market, i.e., to enhance earnings as a measure of performance. More recently, Dechow *et al.* (2010) find that discretionary accruals from the Jones model have less power than simple measures of accruals (e.g., working capital accruals) in predicting accounting manipulations.

Dechow and Dichev (2002) develop an alternative model of accruals based on the relation between working capital accruals and cash flows. That is, an accrual may relate to a future cash flow (e.g., an account receivable or account payable) or may arise because of a past cash flow (e.g., unearned revenue or a prepaid expense). Thus, they examine how past, current, and future cash flows map into current working capital accruals by regressing the change in working capital (ΔWC) on lagged, current, and future cash flows from operations (CFO):

$$\Delta WC_t = = = \alpha + \beta_1 CFO_{t-1} + \beta_2 CFO_t + \beta_3 CFO_{t+1} + \varepsilon_t \tag{2}$$

Dechow and Dichev (2002) estimate eq. (2) using firm-wise, time-series regressions. Later studies such as Francis *et al.* (2005) estimate eq. (2) on a cross-sectional basis by industry.

Dechow and Dichev (2002) propose two measures of earnings quality based on eq. (2). First, they suggest using the standard deviation of the residual for each firm. A smaller standard deviation reflects more predictable mapping of cash flows into accruals, suggesting higher earnings quality. Second, they suggest the absolute value of the firm-year residual as an alternative measure.

Srinidhi and Gul (2007) use Dechow and Dichev's (2002) measure to examine whether non-audit fees impair auditor's independence and reduce earnings quality. They argue that the Dechow-Dichev measure is superior to the Jones model in separating informative accruals from non-informative ones and "is more directly related to estimation errors that auditors are entrusted to reduce" (Srinidhi and Gul 2007: 597). However, other researchers use the Dechow-Dichev measure because they view it as a broader measure of earnings quality that does not just capture earnings management. For example, Doyle *et al.* (2007: 1150) argue that in their context, when examining the earnings quality of firms with weak internal controls, the Dechow-Dichev measure captures "both biased 'discretionary' accruals and unintentionally poorly estimated accruals, which we predict will be the result of an internal control system with material weaknesses." This may explain why the Dechow-Dichev measure is not widely used as a measure of earnings management in the auditing literature.

Target-based measures

Since the publication of Burgstahler and Dichev (1997), researchers have been attracted to target beating as a measure of earnings management. Burgstahler and Dichev (1997) find that there is a discontinuity around zero earnings and no change in earnings if earnings for a broad sample of firms are plotted around these thresholds. Specifically, they find too many small positive earnings observations relative to small negative earnings, and too many small increases in earnings relative to small decreases in earnings. They interpret this as evidence that managers manipulate earnings to surpass these key indicators. Degeorge *et al.* (1999) find a similar discontinuity around analysts' forecasts.

Target beating is attractive as a measure of earnings management because the researcher does not have to identify how earnings were managed. Thus, it is not necessary to develop models that capture different aspects of earnings such as the Jones model or Dechow-Dichev model. Instead, the researcher just has to determine an appropriate threshold, or bin width, for identifying "small" profits, changes in profits, or increments over analysts' forecasts.

An example of an auditing study using target beating is Reichelt and Wang (2010) who examine the role of industry expertise, measured at the national level and office level, in constraining earnings management. They find that firms which are clients of an auditor who has both national- and office-level industry expertise are less likely to meet or just beat analysts' forecasts by one penny, consistent with these auditors constraining aggressive earnings management. Davis *et al.* (2009) examine target beating in relation to auditor tenure, but they incorporate discretionary accruals in the analysis. Specifically, they examine whether firms that had earnings before discretionary accruals that were below the forecast used discretionary accruals to beat the forecast. They find clients with both short and long audit tenure are more likely to beat their forecasts. However, this U-shaped relation holds only in the period before the Sarbanes-Oxley Act (SOX) was passed in 2002. In the post-SOX period, auditor tenure is unrelated to meeting or beating analysts' forecasts.

Although intuitively appealing, the target beating metric has its own problems. Dechow *et al.* (2003) find that small loss and small profit firms have similar discretionary accruals, suggesting that the discontinuity is driven by something other than earnings management. Beaver *et al.* (2007) find evidence that asymmetric taxes, not earnings management, is driving the observed distribution, while Durtschi and Easton (2009) find that the discontinuity is an artifact of design issues, specifically scaling earnings by price.

Market-based measures

As an alternative to accrual- and target-based measures, some researchers have relied on the concept of earnings conservatism developed by Basu (1997). The central feature of earnings conservatism is that losses are recognized more quickly than gains. Moreover, Watts (2003) and LaFond and Watts (2008) argue that conservative earnings play an important role in contracting and reducing information asymmetry. Basu's (1997) approach relies on a reverse regression of earnings (*Earn*) on annual returns (*Ret*) that uses a dummy variable (*D*) to allow for separate slope coefficients for positive and negative returns:

$$Earn_{t+1} = \alpha_0 + \alpha_1 D_t + \beta_0 Ret_t + \beta_1 D_t \text{ x } Ret_t + \varepsilon_t \quad (3)$$

As D equals 1 if returns are negative, a positive and significant β_1 indicates that losses are recognized in earnings on a more timely basis than gains, i.e., earnings are of higher quality.

Francis and Wang (2008) use timely loss recognition in examining the role of Big 4 auditors in curbing earnings management in a sample of 42 countries. More conservative earnings provide implicit evidence that there is less income-increasing earnings management. Ruddock *et al.* (2006) use timely loss recognition in a test of the relation between non-audit services and earnings quality.

However, as Dechow *et al.* (2010) note, there are several issues that reduce the usefulness of timely loss recognition as a measure of earnings management. First, the relation between earnings and returns might not be the same for all firms. Second, the return reflects all information, not just information in earnings. For example, firms with more conservative earnings might provide additional information to augment their financial reports. Further, Penman and Zhang (2002) argue that conservative accounting actually increases earnings management by creating reserves that can be manipulated by managers. Francis and Wang (2008) acknowledge these limitations and use timely loss recognition as one of three measures of earnings quality.

Another market-based approach to measuring earnings quality is the earnings response coefficient (ERC). The ERC is simply the coefficient on unexpected earnings from a regression of returns on unexpected earnings where unexpected earnings are either current earnings less prior earnings or current earnings less forecasted earnings. The ERC should be increasing in earnings quality. If earnings are garbled by earnings management, the ERC should decrease.

Teoh and Wong (1993) is the first auditing study to use the ERC. They contend that financial statements audited by the largest audit firms (then the Big 8) would be more credible due to their reputation, training, and resources. As expected, they find a higher ERC for clients of the Big 8, indicating that the earnings of these firms are less noisy and more credible. In a more recent example, Nelson *et al.* (2008) use the ERC to examine whether the earnings of Andersen clients were viewed as being less credible after 10 January 2002 when Andersen acknowledged that it had shredded documents related to the Enron audit. This would be the case if news about the shredding led investors to question Andersen's ability to constrain earnings management. They find that the ERC for Andersen clients did not decline in the post-shredding period relative to clients of the Big 4 and conclude that Andersen's overall reputation was not impaired.

Similar to timely loss recognition, using the ERC as a measure of earnings management is problematic. First, the ability of the ERC to capture earnings management is debatable. For example, Altamuro *et al.* (2005) find that the ERC of firms that accelerated the recognition of revenue – an approach typically associated with earnings management – decreased (rather than increased) after Staff Accounting Bulletin No. 101, which prohibited such treatment, came into effect. Second, like the timely loss recognition measure, the ERC is a conditional measure of earnings quality because it is affected by multiple factors. As Dechow *et al.* (2011: 26) state:

> [I]f one wanted to test whether auditors improve earnings quality by decreasing errors in the financial statements, then the ERC would not be an appropriate proxy for this notion of quality because it does not necessarily reflect variation in the types of errors that auditors can control or affect.

Third, the ERC is related to the firm's information environment, leading to an omitted variable problem if the latter is not controlled for; and fourth, the returns generating process can be affected by market factors (e.g., trading frequency) and macroeconomic factors (e.g., Dechow *et al.* 2010).

Event-based measures

The measures discussed do not actually identify specific instances of earnings management. Two measures that can provide specific evidence of earnings management are restatements and Accounting and Auditing Enforcement Releases (AAERs) issued by the SEC. In other words, they are direct measures of aggressive earnings management, and as a result, the researcher does not need to model the extent of earnings management behavior.

Restatements are an obvious candidate as a measure of earnings management, since they represent the correction of financial statements that have been released previously. The SEC described accounting restatements as "the most viable indicator of improper accounting" (Schroeder 2001: C1) and the General Accounting Office (GAO) created the Financial Statement Database in response to Congressional interest. Most studies select their sample using the GAO's database, which contains 2,309 restatements from 1 January 1997 to 30 September 2005 (Hennes *et al.* 2008), although more current restatement data are available through Audit Analytics. However, it is important to note that restatements can be of two types: restatements due to errors (unintentional misstatements) and restatements due to irregularities (intentional misstatements). In fact, Hennes *et al.* (2008) classify only 24 percent of the restatements in the GAO database as irregularities. They classify a restatement as an irregularity if "fraud" or "irregularity" is mentioned in the firm's discussion of the restatement or if the restatement was associated with an SEC, Department of Justice, or other independent investigation.

Romanus *et al.* (2008) use restatements to examine the effectiveness of industry specialist auditors. They find that the likelihood of a restatement is lower if the client is audited by an industry specialist auditor. They also find that industry specialists are associated with fewer restatements involving core operating accounts, and they find that a change from a non-specialist auditor to a specialist lowers the likelihood of a restatement, while a switch in the opposite direction increases that likelihood. Kinney *et al.* (2004) compare non-audit fees for a sample of restating and non-restating firms to add to the debate on non-audit fees and auditor independence. They consider six categories of non-audit fees and find only two are significantly related to restatements – tax fees are negatively related to restatements, while unspecified fees are positively related. The latter result suggests some non-audit fees can create an economic bond between auditor and client.

There are several limitations in using restatements as a measure of earnings management. As Hennes *et al.* (2008) discuss, identifying restatements that are due to irregularities is not straightforward. Misclassification introduces noise in the restatement measure and reduces the power of the tests. In addition, the initiator of the restatement can be either the client, the auditor, or the SEC. Palmrose *et al.* (2004) find different market reactions to the restatement announcement depending on the initiating party, suggesting that the source is important. Finally, restatements are discrete and capture only those irregularities (and errors) that were large and were detected, making it difficult to address earnings management behavior in the general population.

AAERs result from SEC investigations of securities law violations. At the end of the process, the SEC issues an AAER that describes the misconduct and the settlement, which can include civil actions (e.g., a permanent injunction, consent agreements) and administrative proceedings. Thus, AAERs provide a direct link with accounting misconduct. Since the SEC has limited resources, it will pursue only cases that are significant and likely to be successful. As Dechow *et al.* (1996: 2) state, AAERs are related to the "more obvious and spectacular cases of earnings manipulation". The flip side is that the SEC cannot identify all serious cases of accounting manipulation so some will go undetected.

Carcello and Nagy (2004) use a sample of AAER firms to examine the relation between auditor tenure and fraudulent financial reporting. They find no relation between long auditor tenure and fraud, but instead find evidence that fraud is more likely to occur in the initial three years of an auditor's tenure. Their evidence suggests that client-specific knowledge gained over a long period increases the likelihood of the auditor resisting overly aggressive earnings management attempts. Geiger *et al.* (2008) find that firms which hire accounting and finance officers directly from their external auditor (a revolving door hire) are less likely to receive an AAER. Cahan *et al.* (2011) examine whether clients of Arthur Andersen received more AAERs in the ten years before Enron compared to the clients of the Big 4. They find that, in general, the frequency of AAERs was similar, suggesting that Andersen was equally likely to resist aggressive earnings management attempts during this period.

The limitations of using AAERs relate to the number of AAERs, selection issues, and the generalizability of the tests. For example, Carcello and Nagy (2004) find only 267 AAERs related to fraudulent reporting in the period 1990–2001, which is an average of only 22 AAERs per year. As a result, tests using AAERs will have low statistical power. Also, Dechow *et al.* (2010) note that the SEC may target certain types of firms, meaning that they may be similar across a number of dimensions leading to a possible correlated omitted variables problem. Finally, like restatements, AAER tests can be misleading because they say nothing about more innocuous, pervasive methods of earnings management.

New measures

Dechow *et al.* (2012) develop a new measure of earnings management. Their measure is based on the reversing nature of accruals. Specifically, they argue that the power of the typical earnings management test can be increased by around 40 percent if the researcher includes an additional dummy variable to capture the reversal year. If the researcher cannot predict when the reversal will occur, they assume that working capital accruals will reverse in the subsequent year. Thus, they compare the rejection rates for the null of no earnings management using eqs. (4) and (5):

$$WC\_Acc_t = \alpha + \beta_1 Part_t + \text{NDA\_controls} + \varepsilon_t \tag{4}$$

$$WC\_Acc_t = \alpha + \beta_1 Part_t + \beta_2 PartR_t + \text{NDA\_controls} + \varepsilon_t \tag{5}$$

where *WC_Acc* is working capital accruals, *Part* is 1 in the manipulation period, *PartR* is 1 in the reversal period, and NDA_controls is a vector of controls for the nondiscretionary portion of working capital accruals. They compare the performance of the two models using randomly assigned earnings management years, induced earnings management, and an AAER sample where period of manipulation is identified by the SEC. NDA_controls is based on several models including the Jones model. In addition to increasing the power of the tests by around 40 percent, Dechow *et al.* (2012) claim that their approach reduces mis-specification due to omitted correlated variables.

Hribar *et al.* (2010) contend that unexpected audit fees can be used as a measure of accounting quality. Specifically, they argue that auditors charge higher fees when the client has poor accounting quality. In their view, the increase in fees is not a risk premium, but instead reflects the increased audit scope and hours that the auditor will incur to address the issues and risks associated with the lower accounting quality. They find their measure is correlated with other measures of earnings quality such as the absolute value of discretionary accruals, the Dechow-Dichev measure of accruals quality, internal control deficiencies, and accounting restatements. Further, they argue that their measure is less affected by innate firm characteristics, reducing the likelihood of omitted variables. At the same time, they note that their measure captures accounting quality more generally, e.g., it can reflect misstatements in any of the financial statements including the notes to the financial statements, as well as legal and reputational costs. Consequently, from the standpoint of earnings management research, the Hribar *et al.* (2010) measure may be less useful than other measures that are more closely linked to earnings.

Real earnings management

A discussion of earnings management would not be complete without mention of real earnings management. In addition to adjusting accruals, managers can also engage in actual operating transactions that can lead to higher or lower levels of reported income. Thus, unlike accruals earnings management, real earnings management can alter current or future cash flows. As Roychowdhury (2006) points out, real earnings management can be more costly than accruals earnings management because the firm enters into real transactions for opportunistic, rather than business, reasons. In this sense, those transactions are sub-optimal. The advantage of real earnings management is that such actions are less likely to be detected by auditors, regulators, and shareholders (e.g., Cohen *et al.* 2008). In fact, auditors might not care about real earnings management since it is not their role to distinguish between optimal and opportunistic operating decisions. However, if the presence of real earnings management makes it more difficult to detect accruals earnings management, auditors might have to exert more effort when real earnings management is high. Also, litigation risk may be higher for firms that opportunistically use real earnings management (e.g., Sohn 2011).

Roychowdhury (2006) identifies three channels that can be used to manage earnings using real transactions: (1) increasing sales revenue at the end of the period by offering excessive sales discounts or easy credit terms; (2) engaging in overproduction which leads to a lower cost of goods sold; and (3) reducing discretionary expenses. He develops three models to capture the normal or expected portion of cash flows (*CFO*), production costs (*Prod*), and discretionary expenses (*DiscExp*):

$$CFO_t/A_{t-1} = \alpha_0 + \alpha_1(1/A_{t-1}) + \beta_1(S_t/A_{t-1}) + \beta_2(\Delta S_t/A_{t-1}) + \varepsilon_t \quad (6)$$

$$Prod/A_{t-1} = \alpha_0 + \alpha_1(1/A_{t-1}) + \beta_1(S_t/A_{t-1}) + \beta_2(\Delta S_t/A_{t-1}) + \beta_3(\Delta S_{t-1}/A_{t-1}) + \varepsilon_t \quad (7)$$

$$DiscExp_t/A_{t-1} = \alpha_0 + \alpha_1(1/A_{t-1}) + \beta_1(S_{t-1}/A_{t-1}) + \varepsilon_t \quad (8)$$

where A is total assets at the end of the period and S is sales revenue during the period. These equations are estimated for each industry year, and the estimated coefficients are used to compute the abnormal *CFO*, *Prod*, and *DiscExp* for each firm. These abnormal amounts represent the deviation from the expected amount and are analogous to the discretionary accruals from the Jones model.

The use of real versus accruals earnings management is likely to be affected by the level of scrutiny that is put on the latter, since accruals are always of direct interest to auditors. This level of scrutiny can vary over time. For example, Cohen *et al.* (2008) expect that managers of US firms would have shifted to greater use of real earnings management after the collapse of Enron and the passage of the SOX in 2002, since the implicit and explicit penalties associated with accruals earnings management increased after those events. They find a significant decrease in accruals earnings management and a significant increase in real earnings management after SOX, consistent with a trade-off between the two.

More recently, Burnett *et al.* (2012) examine the effect of audit quality on the trade-off between real and accruals earnings management more directly. They focus on target beating and expect that firms are more likely to use accretive stock repurchases – a form of real earnings management – to beat analysts' forecasts when audit quality is high. They use auditor industry specialization to measure audit quality. Consistent with their expectations, auditor industry specialization is positively related to the use of accretive stock repurchases and negatively related to discretionary accruals for firms that just meet or beat their consensus analyst forecast.

Conclusion

The interest of auditing researchers in earnings management is not surprising given the role that auditors play in constraining opportunistic reporting. Auditing researchers have generally borrowed measures of earnings management from the financial accounting literature. These measures can be classified as accruals-based, target-based, market-based, or event-based. In addition, auditing researchers are interested in the trade-off between accruals related forms of earnings management and real earnings management. Real earnings management arises when managers enter into actual transactions in order to report a more favorable earnings figure. The ability of auditors to constrain earnings management is related to their competence and independence.

References

Altamuro, J., Beatty, A. and Weber, J. 2005. "The Effects of Accelerated Revenue Recognition on Earnings Management: Evidence from SEC Accounting Bulletin No. 101", *The Accounting Review* 80: 373–401.

Ashbaugh-Skaife, H., Collins, D., Kinney, W. and LaFond, R. 2008. "The Effect of SOX Internal Control Deficiencies and their Remediation on Accrual Quality", *The Accounting Review* 83: 217–50.

Basu, S. 1997. "The Conservatism Principle and the Asymmetric Timeliness of Earnings", *Journal of Accounting and Economics* 24: 3–37.

Beaver, W., McNichols, M. and Nelson, K. 2007. "An Alternative Interpretation of the Discontinuity in Earnings Distributions", *Review of Accounting Studies* 12: 525–56.

Burgstahler, D. and Dichev, I. 1997. "Earnings Management to Avoid Earnings Decreases and Losses", *Journal of Accounting and Economics* 24: 99–126.

Burnett, B., Cripe, B., Martin, G. and McAllister, B. 2012. "Audit Quality and the Trade-off between Accretive Stock Repurchases and Accruals-based Earnings Management", *The Accounting Review* 24: 1861–84.

Cahan, S., Veenman, D. and Zhang, W. 2011. "Did the Waste Management Audit Failures Signal Deteriorating Firm-wide Audit Quality at Arthur Andersen?" *Contemporary Accounting Research* 28: 859–91.

Carcello, J. and Nagy, A. 2004. "Audit Firm Tenure and Fraudulent Financial Reporting", *Auditing: A Journal of Practice and Theory* 23: 55–69.

Chung, H. and Kallapur, S. 2003. "Client Importance, Nonaudit Services, and Abnormal Accruals", *The Accounting Review* 78: 931–55.

Cohen, D., Dey, A. and Lys, T. 2008. "Real and Accruals-based Earnings Management in the Pre- and Post-Sarbanes-Oxley Periods", *The Accounting Review* 83: 757–87.

Davis, L., Soo, B. and Trompeter, G. 2009. "Auditor Tenure and the Ability to Meet or Beat Earnings Forecasts", *Contemporary Accounting Research* 26: 517–48.

DeAngelo, L. 1981. "Auditor Size and Audit Quality", *Journal of Accounting and Economics* 3: 183–99.

DeAngelo, L. 1986. "Accounting Numbers as Market Valuation Substitutes: A Study of Management Buyouts of Public Stakeholders", *The Accounting Review* 61: 400–20.

Dechow, P. and Dichev, I. 2002. "The Quality of Accruals and Earnings: The Role of Accrual Estimation Errors", *The Accounting Review* 77(Supplement): 35–59.

Dechow, P., Sloan, R. and Sweeney, A. 1995. "Detecting Earnings Management", *The Accounting Review* 70: 193–225.

Dechow, P., Sloan, R. and Sweeney, A. 1996. "Causes and Consequences of Earnings Manipulation: An Analysis of Firms Subject to Enforcement Actions by the SEC", *Contemporary Accounting Research* 13: 1–36.

Dechow, P., Richardson, S. and Tuna, I. 2003. "Why are Earnings Kinky? An Examination of the Earnings Management Explanation", *Review of Accounting Studies* 8: 355–84.

Dechow, P., Ge, W. and Schrand, C. 2010. "Understanding Earnings Quality: A Review of the Proxies, Their Determinants and Consequences", *Journal of Accounting and Economics* 50: 344–401.

Dechow, P. M., Ge, W., Larson, C. R. and Sloan, R. G. 2011. "Predicting Material Accounting Misstatements", *Contemporary Accounting Research* 28: 17–82.

Dechow, P., Hutton, A., Kim, J. and Sloan, R. 2012. "Detecting Earnings Management: A New Approach", *Journal of Accounting Research* 50: 275–334.

DeFond, M. and Jiambalvo, J. 1994. "Debt Covenant Violation and Manipulation of Accruals", *Journal of Accounting and Economics* 17: 145–76.

DeFond, M. and Subramanyam, K. 1998. "Auditor Changes and Discretionary Accruals", *Journal of Accounting and Economics* 25: 35–67.

Degeorge, F., Patel, J. and Zeckhauser, R. 1999. "Earnings Management to Exceed Thresholds", *Journal of Business* 72: 1–33.

Doyle, J., Ge, W. and McVay, S. 2007. "Accruals Quality and Internal Control over Financial Reporting", *The Accounting Review* 82: 1141–70.

Durtschi, C. and Easton, P. 2009. "Earnings Management? Erroneous Inferences Based on Earnings Frequency Distributions", *Journal of Accounting Research* 47: 1249–82.

Francis, J. and Krishnan, J. 1999. "Accounting Accruals and Auditor Reporting Conservatism", *Contemporary Accounting Research* 16: 135–65.

Francis, J., LaFond, R., Olsson, P. and Schipper, K. 2005. "The Market Pricing of Accruals Quality", *Journal of Accounting and Economics* 39: 295–327.

Francis, J. R. and Wang, D. 2008. "The Joint Effect of Investor Protection and the Big 4 Audits on Earnings Quality around the World", *Contemporary Accounting Research* 25: 157–91.

Geiger, M., Lennox, C. and North, D. 2008. "The Hiring of Accounting and Finance Officers from Audit Firms: How did the Market React?" *Review of Accounting Studies* 13: 55–86.

Guay, W., Kothari, S. and Watts, R. 1996. "A Market-based Evaluation of Discretionary Accrual Models", *Journal of Accounting Research* 34(Supplement): 83–105.

Healy, P. 1985. "The Effect of Bonus Schemes on Accounting Decisions", *Journal of Accounting and Economics* 7: 85–107.

Hennes, K., Leone, A. and Miller, B. 2008. "The Importance of Distinguishing Errors for Irregularities in Restatement Research: The Case of Restatements and CEO/CFO Turnover", *The Accounting Review* 83: 1487–1519.

Hribar, P. and Nichols, D. 2007. "The Use of Unsigned Earnings Quality Measures in Tests of Earnings Management", *Journal of Accounting Research* 45: 1017–53.

Hribar, P., Kravet, T. and Wilson, R. 2010. "A New Measure of Accounting Quality", working paper. Iowa City, I.A.: University of Iowa.

Kinney, W., Palmrose, Z. and Scholz, S. 2004. "Auditor Independence, Non-audit Services, and Restatements: Was the U.S. Government Right?" *Journal of Accounting Research* 42: 561–88.

Kothari, S., Leone, A. and Wasley, C. 2005. "Performance Matched Discretionary Accrual Measures", *Journal of Accounting and Economics* 39: 163–97.

Jensen, M. and Meckling, W. 1976. "Theory of the Firm: Managerial Behavior, Agency Costs and Ownership Structure", *Journal of Financial Economics* 3: 305–60.

Jones, J. 1991. "Earnings Management during Import Relief Investigations", *Journal of Accounting Research* 29: 193–228.

LaFond, R. and Watts, R. 2008. "The Information Role of Conservatism", *The Accounting Review* 83: 447–78.

Nelson, K., Price, R. and Rountree, B. 2008. "The Market Reaction to Arthur Andersen's Role in the Enron Scandal: Loss of Reputation or Confounding Effects?" *Journal of Accounting and Economics* 46: 279–93.

Palmrose, Z., Richardson, V. and Scholz, S. 2004. "Determinants of Market Reactions to Restatement Announcements", *Journal of Accounting and Economics* 37: 59–89.

Penman, S. and Zhang, X. 2002. "Accounting Conservatism, the Quality of Earnings, and Stock Returns", *The Accounting Review* 77: 157–79.

Reichelt, K. and Wang, D. 2010. "National and Office-specific Measures of Auditor Industry Expertise and Effects on Audit Quality", *Journal of Accounting Research* 48: 647–86.

Romanus, R., Maher, J. and Fleming, D. 2008. "Auditor Industry Specialization, Auditor Changes, and Accounting Restatements", *Accounting Horizons* 22: 389–413.

Roychowdhury, S. 2006. "Earnings Management through Real Activities Manipulation", *Journal of Accounting and Economics* 42: 335–70.

Ruddock, C., Taylor, S. and Taylor, S. 2006. "Nonaudit Services and Earnings Conservatism: Is Auditor Independence Impaired?" *Contemporary Accounting Research* 23: 701–46.

Schipper, K. 1989. "Commentary on Earnings Management", *Accounting Horizons* 3: 91–102.

Schroeder, M. 2001. "SEC List of Accounting-fraud Probe Grows", *Wall Street Journal* (July 6): C7.

Sohn, B. 2011. "Do Auditors Care about Real Earnings Management in their Audit Fee Decisions?", working paper. Kowloon: City University of Hong Kong.

Srinidhi, B. and Gul, F. 2007. "The Differential Effects of Auditors' Nonaudit and Audit Fees on Accrual Quality", *Contemporary Accounting Research* 24: 595–629.

Subramanyam, K. 1996. "The Pricing of Discretionary Accruals", *Journal of Accounting and Economics* 22: 249–81.

Teoh, S. and Wong, T. 1993. "Perceived Auditor Quality and the Earnings Response Coefficient", *The Accounting Review* 68: 346–66.

Watts, R. 2003. "Conservatism in Accounting, Part I: Explanations and Implications", *Accounting Horizons* 17: 207–21.

Watts, R. and Zimmerman, J. 1983a. "Agency Problems, Auditing, and the Theory of the Firm: Some Evidence", *Journal of Law and Economics* 26: 613–33.

Watts, R. and Zimmerman, J. 1983b. *Positive Accounting Theory*. Englewood Cliffs, NJ: Prentice-Hall.

11
Audit quality

W. Robert Knechel and Lori B. Shefchik

Introduction

In order to discuss audit quality, it is necessary to first define what we mean by an audit. Knechel *et al.* (2013a: 2) describe an audit as "a professional service delivered by experts in response to economic and regulatory demand." They then go on to discuss a number of multi-dimensional attributes that define an audit.[1] First, demand for an audit is driven by economic risks; therefore, *incentives* are influential. Second, audits are not designed to provide absolute assurance; thus, the outcome of an audit is uncertain. This *uncertainty* plays a role in the audit process. Third, due to variations in client characteristics, audit teams, and other environmental factors, each audit engagement is unique so the *idiosyncratic* nature of engagements matters. Fourth, an audit is a systematic process used to obtain reasonable assurance, i.e., the *process* is important. Finally, successful execution of an audit requires a great deal of judgment by professionals with adequate knowledge and expertise – i.e., *professional judgment* matters. As will be discussed, each of these characteristics plays a role in the audit process and uniquely influences audit quality.

Stating a definition of audit quality is even more difficult. Despite decades of research, a consensus as to what constitutes audit quality has not been reached. Rather, various divergent definitions of audit quality remain in the literature. In a seminal paper, DeAngelo (1981) defines audit quality in terms of two components: the likelihood that an auditor will (1) discover a breach (i.e., an existing misstatement); and (2) appropriately report the breach if discovered. The first component links audit quality to an auditor's competence and level of effort while the latter refers to audit quality in terms of an auditor's independence and professional skepticism. While this definition continues to be applied in current research, various definitions have also emerged in subsequent research.

First, audit quality has been defined in terms of the audit process carried out by auditors – i.e., that the audit was performed in accordance with Generally Accepted Auditing Standards (GAAS) (Tie 1999; Krishnan and Schauer 2001; GAO 2003). Second, the quality of an audit has been defined in terms of the financial statement outcome. From this perspective, the quality of reported earnings (i.e., the reliability of the financial statements) represents the quality of the audit and any error in reported earnings represents an audit failure (e.g., Chan and Wong 2002;

Gul *et al.* 2002; Behn *et al.* 2008; Chang *et al.* 2009). Third, audit quality has been defined by the amount of audit work performed whereby higher amounts of effort represent high audit quality (Carcello *et al.* 2002). Finally, some researchers focus on defining "poor audit quality" by identifying what audit quality is "not" (e.g., financial statement restatements, litigation against the auditor).[2] In summary, there is currently no unified definition of audit quality.

The divergent views as to what constitute audit quality are partly attributable to varying perceptions of audit quality by different stakeholders in the financial reporting process (Knechel *et al.* 2013a). For example, users of financial reports may perceive a high quality audit as one without financial statement misstatements, whereas audit firms may define audit quality as satisfactorily completing the audit process in accordance with the firm's audit methodology. Additionally, regulators may judge audit quality in terms of compliance with the professional auditing standards. In the end, different stakeholders appear to have come to one agreement – that a single definition of audit quality may be impossible (e.g., FRC 2008; IOSCO 2009; Francis 2011; Knechel *et al.* 2013a).

As a result, frameworks for gauging overall audit quality have become increasingly popular.[3] Accordingly, we develop a framework for audit quality. The framework incorporates indicators of audit quality from various viewpoints in an attempt to capture different stakeholders' perceptions of audit quality. Specifically, the framework includes antecedents of audit quality – factors that lead to higher or lower audit quality (i.e., audit inputs and the audit process) as well as consequences of audit quality – *ex post* factors used to measure audit quality (i.e., outcomes). Reference to Figure 11.1 will provide a summary of the framework.

In this chapter, we briefly summarize the related research for each factor in the audit quality framework. In so doing, we also describe how the characteristics of an audit (e.g., incentives, uncertainty, idiosyncrasies, process, and professional judgment) interact with the factors to influence audit quality. For example, we explain how auditor incentives influence the various audit inputs (e.g., auditor independence) which in turn affect audit quality. Likewise, we explain how the idiosyncratic nature of an audit influences the various factors in the audit process, and so forth.

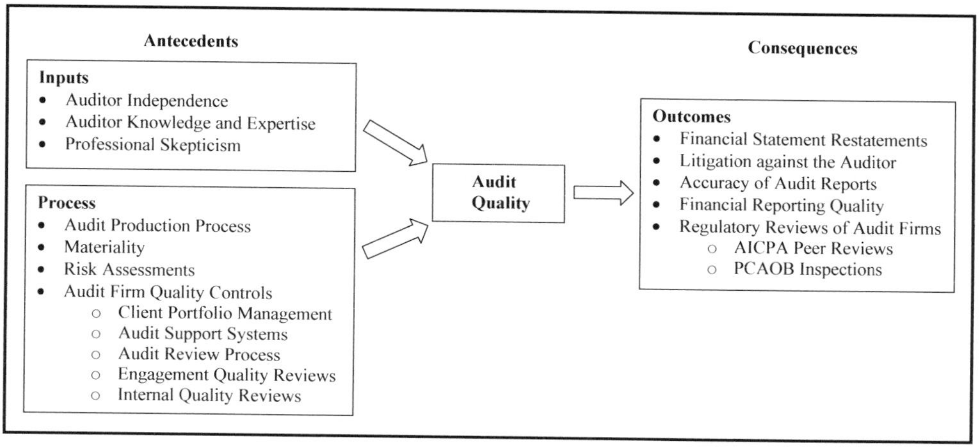

Figure 11.1 Framework for audit quality

Audit inputs

Audit inputs are primarily reflected in individual characteristics of auditors. Varying levels of inputs contribute to the level of audit quality achieved. Due to the idiosyncratic nature of each audit engagement (e.g., client risk, audit complexity, environmental uncertainty, etc.) the level of audit inputs required to reach "reasonable assurance" varies for each audit engagement. Accordingly, auditors must use professional judgment to tailor audit inputs for each client. For example, auditors determine who ought to be assigned to a specific engagement and how much work they ought to do. When deciding "who" is appropriate for certain engagements, auditors consider staff independence and level of auditor knowledge and expertise. These factors help ensure that auditors are willing to make objective judgments and that they have the ability to make high quality judgments. Another audit input is the extent to which auditors exercise professional skepticism. Professional skepticism requires a great deal of professional judgment and it influences audit quality by determining how much work is done to support an auditor's conclusions.[4] We discuss the importance of each of these audit inputs in turn. We also summarize the literature related to these audit inputs and their links with audit quality.

Auditor independence

Independence is a capstone of auditing and a necessary condition to achieving high audit quality (Mautz and Sharaf 1961). Independence promotes an objective mindset which helps to reduce bias in auditor judgments. Bias in auditor judgments often results from conflicting incentives that naturally occur in the audit market. Indeed some argue that because of these naturally occurring incentives, auditors can never truly be independent. They argue that economic and social bonds with the client lead to conscious or unconscious bias resulting in favorable audit judgments for the client (Bazerman *et al.* 1997, 2002; Moore *et al.* 2006).

Economic bonding occurs when an auditor becomes economically tied to a client. Economic bonding can undermine auditor independence by influencing auditors' judgments (Antle 1982). In general, the magnitude of audit fees can create a conflict of interest for the auditor (Zeff 2003; Church *et al.* 2012). Research in auditing shows that audit partner's judgments can be compromised when the client is more economically important to the partner's compensation (e.g., Trompeter 1994; Carcello *et al.* 2000; Knechel *et al.* 2013b). For example, audit partners were found to be less likely to require income-decreasing adjustments (Trompeter 1994) and less likely to issue going-concern opinions (Knechel *et al.* 2013b) for clients that were more economically important.

Regulators, including the SEC (Securities and Exchange Commission) and the Public Company Accounting Oversight Board (PCAOB), have attempted to limit economic bonding by reducing the amount of non-audit services that auditors are allowed to provide to their audit clients. Much research in auditing has examined the effect of non-audit services on audit quality. The findings are mixed. A few early studies suggest that non-audit service fees compromise auditors' independence. Specifically, they find a positive association between non-audit service fees and proxies for negative audit quality including earnings management (Frankel *et al.* 2002) and financial statement restatements (Ferguson *et al.* 2004). However, the majority of subsequent research fails to support this claim, using proxies for negative audit quality that include earnings management, the auditor's propensity to issue going-concern reports, and financial statement restatements.[5] Further, some argue that non-audit services are beneficial, claiming that non-audit services provide knowledge spillovers that lead to improvements in audit quality (Simunic 1984; Kinney *et al.* 2004; Krishnan and Yu 2011; Bell *et al.* 2013). For example, studies show positive relationships between auditor-provided tax services and proxies for audit quality (Kinney *et al.* 2004; Robinson 2008; Gleason and Mills 2011; Krishnan and Visvanathan 2011). Likewise, Bell *et al.* (2013) find positive associations between certain types of non-audit services (e.g., fees received from management advisory services and fees from services related to new equity offerings) and firm's internal quality review results (i.e., a direct proxy for audit quality).

Social bonding is believed to compromise auditor independence by creating incentives for the auditor to maintain a long-term future relationship, i.e., to receive future audit fees. This creates an incentive for auditors to advocate for the client in hopes of maintaining a long-term relationship. In support of this claim, survey and experimental research find that the auditors' perceived risk of losing a client leads to adverse effects on the quality of auditor judgments (e.g., Farmer *et al.* 1987; Blay 2005).

Relatedly, there is some concern that the length of the auditor–client relationship may impair the quality of audits; however, the issue is intensely debated. On one side, the argument is that shorter tenure results in lower audit quality because the auditor has less knowledge and familiarity with a client. On the other side, the argument is that longer tenure strengthens the auditor–client bond which can impair the auditor's objectivity resulting in lower audit quality. Research in this area provides evidence of both a positive (e.g., Johnson *et al.* 2002; Myers *et al.* 2003; Chen *et al.* 2008; Chi *et al.* 2009; Bell *et al.* 2013) and a negative (e.g., Carey and Simnett 2006; Davis *et al.* 2009; Lin and Hwang 2010) association between auditor tenure and proxies for audit quality (e.g., financial reporting and earnings quality).[6]

As discussed, incentives from economic and social bonding can threaten independence; however, it is important to note that several countervailing forces promote independence (Church *et al.* 2012). For example, concerns about maintaining a positive reputation in the audit market provide a strong incentive for auditors to remain independent (DeAngelo 1981). Empirical research supports the validity of this concern given that audit firms incur significant reputational costs (i.e., loss of clients) following audit failures (e.g., Barton 2005; Weber *et al.* 2008). Other factors that provide auditors with incentives to maintain independence include litigation concerns (e.g., Chen *et al.* 2012); professional and regulatory oversight (Hilary and Lennox 2005; Kinney 2005; Carcello *et al.* 2011); and audit firm quality controls (e.g., partner rotation and consultation units). Additional discussion related to these latter factors and audit quality is included in the respective sections below.

Auditor knowledge and expertise

As a professional service that requires extensive judgment, auditing requires adequate knowledge and expertise for achieving high quality. Many experimental studies have documented a positive effect of auditing and accounting knowledge on auditor performance. For example, auditors with relatively more auditing and accounting knowledge make judgments that are more consistent with auditing theory and are more accurate (Choo 1986; Frederick and Libby 1986; Bonner 1990; Bonner and Lewis 1990). Auditor knowledge is gained through experience, so experience is necessary for developing auditing expertise (Frederick and Libby 1986; Bedard 1989). Indeed, studies find benefits of experience on audit judgment performance. For example, audit managers outperform audit seniors at detecting conceptual errors (Ramsay 1994; Rich *et al.* 1997; Owhoso *et al.* 2002).

Many associate Big N auditors with having higher expertise relative to non-Big N auditors claiming that large accounting firms have more resources to devote to developing expertise. Consistent with this notion, empirical archival studies document that Big N auditors earn higher audit fees than non-Big N auditors (e.g., Francis and Wang 2008; Francis and Yu 2009).[7] Indeed, a positive relationship has been established between Big N auditors and proxies for audit quality including lower levels of client's abnormal discretionary accruals (Francis 2004) and a lower propensity to waive financial statement adjustments (Nelson *et al.* 2002).[8] Further, Big N auditors are sued less frequently and are sanctioned less frequently by the SEC (see review in Francis [2004]).

Finally, the academic literature also associates specialized industry expertise with higher levels of audit expertise. Specialized industry expertise is associated with higher auditing performance (Bonner and Lewis 1990; Bedard 1991; Wright and Wright 1997; Owhoso *et al.* 2002). For example, Owhoso *et al.* (2002) find that auditors with specialized industry expertise detect more errors than do auditors at the same experience level who do not have specialized industry expertise. Relatedly, empirical archival studies find that auditors with greater industry expertise earn higher audit fees, suggesting that audit quality may be higher (e.g., Francis 2004; Carson and Fargher 2007; Carson 2009). This theory is somewhat supported in that clients of auditors with higher industry specialization have lower discretionary accruals (i.e., a proxy for earnings and audit quality) (Nagy 2012).

Professional skepticism

Professional skepticism is "an attitude that includes a questioning mind and a critical assessment of audit evidence" (PCAOB 2006) and it is required by US GAAS throughout the audit. Despite the importance of, and focus on, professional skepticism in auditing, a lack of professional skepticism is often cited as a number one cause of auditing deficiencies and auditing failures, e.g., fraud-related SEC cases (Beasley *et al.* 2001); SEC engagement quality review enforcements (Messier *et al.* 2010); and PCAOB inspection findings for large accounting firms (PCAOB 2008).

As with audit quality, due to the uniqueness of each engagement, professional skepticism is difficult to measure. As a result, the level of aggressiveness or conservatism in auditor judgments is often used as a measure of professional skepticism (i.e., more conservative decisions reflect greater skepticism) (Nelson 2009). Other measures of professional skepticism found in the literature include auditors' likelihood of performing additional procedures following an accounting irregularity (Shaub and Lawrence 1996), auditors' likelihood of detecting fraud (Bernardi 1994), and auditors' likelihood of thoroughly assessing and questioning audit evidence (Hurtt *et al.* 2008).

Research indicates that professional skepticism is influenced by many environmental and situational factors (e.g., client risk, integrity of management, the degree of uncertainty) and also by auditors' dispositional traits (e.g., ethical development, professional identification, and skepticism measures as an individual trait).[9] Due to the high degree of judgment required, professional skepticism has been found to be unduly influenced by auditor incentives. For example, auditors have been found to make auditor judgments that are perceived as less skeptical when faced with conflicting incentives resulting from various factors such as client fee pressures (Gramling 1999; Houston 1999), lower client risk (Hackenbrack and Nelson 1996; Braun 2001; Blay 2005), and perceived importance of client's fees (Trompeter 1994).

Audit process

An audit is a systematic process. However, due to idiosyncrasies of clients, auditors use a risk-based process that is uniquely tailored for each audit. For example, given varying levels of client risk and complexity as well as varying levels of audit inputs available, auditors adjust the audit process in order to achieve a desired level of assurance. Accordingly, the audit process requires extensive auditor judgment and the quality of an audit depends on the quality of the audit process, i.e., how the auditor adjusts the process based on identified risks and other factors. Integral components of the audit process include setting materiality, assessing risks, obtaining and evaluating audit evidence, etc. These components directly impact the audit production process (i.e., the nature, extent, and timing of testing). Also, audit firms have quality control mechanisms to ensure sufficient levels of quality are achieved throughout the audit process (e.g., reviews and consultation units).

Audit production process

The literature documents that auditors respond to risks and other factors by altering the audit production process. For example, to increase the effectiveness of an audit, auditors have been found to increase the planned amount of audit hours (audit effort) (O'Keefe *et al.* 1994; Caramanis and Lennox 2011; Calderon *et al.* 2012); modify the nature of the planned testing (Hackenbrack and Knechel 1997); modify the timing of planned tests (e.g., more testing closer to the year-end); and/or assign more experienced auditors or specialists to the audit engagement (e.g., Johnstone and Bedard 2001, 2003).

However, given the extent of judgment involved in the audit production process, the quality of related auditor judgments has been found to be compromised under conditions that create conflicting incentives for auditors, e.g. high fee pressure and budget pressure. For instance, Houston (1999) finds that auditors are less likely to increase planned audit effort in response to increases in audit risk when auditors have high fee pressures. Similarly, time budget pressures on auditors lead to lower audit effectiveness (e.g., McDaniel 1990; Asare *et al.* 2000).

Materiality

Setting and assessing materiality is a subjective judgment that requires qualitative and quantitative assessments, e.g., whether the magnitude of a misstatement would influence the judgment of a reasonable person relying on the information (PCAOB 2010). Materiality judgments influence both the audit production process and auditor conclusions. Given the level of judgment and uncertainty involved, research finds that materiality assessments can be influenced by auditor incentives. For example, studies find that auditors are more likely to conclude a misstatement is immaterial (i.e., waive a proposed adjustment) when recording the misstatement would result in the client missing an earnings target as compared to when recording the same misstatement would not result in the client missing an earnings target (Libby and Kinney 2000; Ng 2007; Ng and Tan 2007).

Risk assessments

Assessing audit risk is a vital component of the audit process which influences the nature, timing, and extent of audit procedures required to achieve reasonable assurance. In their synthesis of the audit risk literature, Allen *et al.* (2006) make a number of conclusions related to audit risk assessments: (1) industry expertise and specialization are critical to effective risk assessments; (2) using a business risk focus has positive effects on assessing risk; and (3) fraud risk assessments are enhanced by considering fraud risks separately from misstatements due to error, by engaging in fraud brainstorming discussions, and by thinking strategically about management's possible efforts to commit or conceal fraud. Another stream of literature documents that the use of analytical procedures greatly improves the effectiveness of auditors' risk assessment process (see Koonce [1993] and Messier *et al.* [2013] for reviews). The auditing literature documents that auditors are generally effective at assessing risks; however, they often have difficulties appropriately responding to risks during subsequent audit testing (see Allen *et al.* [2006] for a review).

Audit firm quality controls

Audit firms have many quality control mechanisms used to assess, monitor, and control risks. These quality controls are vital in enhancing audit quality in the audit process. Quality control mechanisms include (1) pre-engagement risk management such as the composition of the firm's client portfolio and maintaining auditor independence; (2) risk management mechanisms during the engagement, e.g., audit support systems, audit review processes, consultation units; and (3) risk management after the engagement including internal quality reviews. We discuss some of the related auditing literature that links these quality control processes to audit quality.

Client portfolio management

Audit firms use a portfolio approach to manage their audit risk (Simunic and Stein 1990). To manage their overall exposure to potential audit failures, often referred to as auditor's business risk (Asare *et al.* 1994), audit firms are selective in their choice of new and continuing clients. This approach helps ensure sufficient audit quality for the firm as a whole. Indeed, empirical studies find that audit firms' client portfolios decline with client financial reporting risk (Johnstone and Bedard 2004). Likewise, client acceptance decisions (Johnstone 2000) and client termination decisions (Krishnan and Krishnan 1997; Shu 2000) are influenced by client litigation risk.

Audit support systems

Firm's audit methodology and audit support systems are designed to help auditors cope with uncertainty in an audit in a systematic manner. Studies show that audit support systems and decision aids (e.g., checklists, audit programs) are especially beneficial for auditors who lack expertise or who are susceptible to performance deficiencies (Nelson and Tan 2005). Challenges of decision aids however include getting auditors (1) to rely on aids when using aids would improve their decisions (Kachelmeier and Messier 1990; Whitecotton 1996; Eining *et al.* 1997; Messier *et al.* 2001) and (2) not to use aids when professional judgment is necessary to make high quality decisions (Pincus 1989; Ashton 1990; Arnold and Sutton 1998; Asare and Wright 2004; Dowling and Leech 2007).

Audit review process

The audit review process is an important quality control mechanism that is beneficial to audit quality. The review process serves as a means of detecting errors made by preparers (Bamber 1983; Rich *et al.* 1997; Owhoso *et al.* 2002). Further, the multi-person nature of the review process allows for higher quality judgments (e.g., greater auditor consensus and improved accuracy) (Trotman and Yetton 1985; Solomon 1987). In addition, the review process imposes accountability on preparers which generally leads to enhanced auditor performance and higher quality judgments (e.g., Johnson and Kaplan 1991; Kennedy 1995; Koonce *et al.* 1995).

When subjective auditor judgments are being made, a few factors have been found to negatively impact the effectiveness of the review process. First, knowledge of the reviewer's preferences for an outcome can lead to biased preparer judgments (Peecher 1996, Turner 2001; Wilks 2002; Shankar and Tan 2006). For example, Wilks (2002) finds that audit preparers who learn the partner's view about a going-concern judgment tend to evaluate audit evidence in a manner that is consistent with the partner's view. Further, the quality of audit reviews has been found to be negatively influenced by the reviewer's familiarity (i.e., positive perceptions) with the preparer (Asare and McDaniel 1996).

Engagement quality reviews

Engagement quality reviews (also known as concurring or second partner reviews) are another type of quality control used to monitor the quality of individual audit engagements. Engagement quality reviewers provide an objective look at the significant judgments made and conclusions reached during the audit. This objective review can help reduce bias or errors in auditor judgments that result from engagement team auditor incentives. Indeed, the literature finds that engagement quality reviews improve the quality of audits. For example, engagement quality reviews result in more effective risk assessment judgments, increased planned audit investment, and higher quality of audit evidence evaluation (see reviews of the literature in Epps and Messier [2007] and Bedard *et al.* [2008]).

Internal quality reviews

As another quality control mechanism, audit firms conduct internal quality reviews. Internal quality reviews are performed on a limited sample of audit engagements and are performed after the audit is complete. The reviews are designed as monitoring mechanisms to assess the engagement teams' compliance with firm methodologies. Due to the private nature of the process, relatively little research has been conducted on internal quality reviews and audit quality. However, in an experimental study, Stefaniak and Houston (2013) find that when auditors are anticipating an internal quality review, they increase planned audit effort and audit fees. The finding suggests that this quality control process does contribute to higher levels of audit quality. Further, using a propriety dataset from one of the Big 4 firms, Bell *et al.* (2013) are able to use internal quality reviews as a proxy for audit quality finding positive associations with audit firm tenure and non-audit services.

Audit outcomes

Up to this point, the audit quality indicators discussed were factors that led to higher or lower audit quality. In this section, we discuss factors that have been used to measure actual audit quality (i.e., outcomes of an audit). Recall, that the outcome of an audit is uncertain and unobservable. While audit quality might be believed to be high or low, due to uncertainty it is not possible to "know" the outcome of an audit (e.g., the level of audit assurance obtained). Accordingly, researchers use proxies for audit outcomes to assess actual audit quality. The various proxies used are observable characteristics that are associated with high or low audit quality. Examples of proxies for audit outcomes include the quality of a firm's financial reporting, the accuracy of audit reports, and results of regulatory reviews. Further, because high audit quality is difficult to observe, it is common to identify what audit quality "is not." For example, subsequent financial statement restatements and litigation against the auditor are often indicators of poor audit quality.

These observable proxies for audit outcomes are measured *ex post*. That is, the outcomes are measured after the audit has been completed. Due to the uncertainty of an audit, there are some issues with using such *ex post* measures of outcomes as indicators of audit quality at the time of the audit. For example, *ex post* assessments of audit judgments are subject to hindsight and outcome biases (Hawkins and Hastie 1990). Jurors, judges, and regulators assessing the quality of auditor judgments may be biased by their knowledge of the *ex post* outcomes whereas auditors made their judgments based on the (limited) information provided at the time of the judgment (e.g., Kadous 2000, 2001; Peecher and Piercey 2008; Casterella *et al.* 2009). Nonetheless, in general, *ex post* outcomes are thought to provide indications of high or low audit quality. We discuss in turn the use of various *ex post* outcomes as indicators of audit quality.

Financial statement restatements

The presence of a financial statement restatement is often used as an indicator for poor audit quality. However, there are several limitations to using restatements as proxies for audit quality. For example, the audit approach is not designed to provide absolute assurance. Therefore, even when auditors properly complete an audit in accordance with GAAS, there is a risk that a material misstatement may not be identified.[10] Nonetheless, the presence of a restatement is often associated with negative audit quality. Indeed, researchers find that restatements are negatively associated with other proxies for high audit quality, including auditor industry expertise, auditor tenure, and audit team experience (refer to Knechel *et al.* [2013a] for a review). The findings in the literature suggest the presence of a restatement is generally indicative of low audit quality.

Litigation against the auditor

Litigation against an auditor indicates an accusation of poor audit quality. However, research related to auditor litigation is somewhat limited. First, auditors are typically only sued when there is very strong evidence of negligence which is not necessarily representative of all audits, or even of poor quality audits. Second, auditors are named in a relatively small number of class-action lawsuits and a majority of lawsuits are settled out of court (Palmrose 1988). Palmrose (2000) reports that during the period 1960 to 1995 there were, on average, only 28 lawsuits per year for large national accounting firms. Further, the number of successful lawsuits is even smaller, approximately 50 percent (Palmrose 1997). In a review of the literature, Francis (2004: 347) reports that the number of proven audit failures from litigation is so small it approaches a rate of zero.

Accuracy of audit reports

The accuracy of audit reports is often viewed as a signal for audit quality. Much research examines whether auditors correctly issue a modified report for going concern uncertainty. A relatively low percent of firms receive going concern opinions (i.e., less than 10 percent) (Francis 2004). Due to the high level of uncertainty involved in making going concern judgments, going concern opinion judgments have a relatively high error rate.[11] In their review of the literature, Carson *et al.* (2013) report that, on average, 40 to 50 percent of bankrupt companies in the US did not receive a prior going concern opinion (i.e., a Type II error) and 80 to

90 percent of companies who received a going concern opinion did not enter bankruptcy in the subsequent year (i.e., a Type 1 error). The high error rate for Type I errors is indicative of auditor conservatism when making going concern judgments. Finally, it is important to note that not all inaccurate going concern opinions are audit failures. Related to Type II errors, the objective of the audit is not to predict bankruptcies (Francis 2004).

Despite high error rates, inaccurate going concern reports are often perceived as audit failures. For example, auditors are more likely to be dismissed by the client following a false going concern report (Krishnan 1994). Also, compared to auditors who issue a going concern report, auditors who fail to issue a going concern report before a client's bankruptcy are sued twice as often, have lower lawsuit dismissal rates, and have higher resolution payments (Carcello and Palmrose 1994). Further, investors negatively react to going concern audit reports suggesting that they perceive the reports as beneficial and as a signal of high audit quality (e.g., Chen and Church 1996). The use of going concern reporting as a proxy for audit quality is somewhat validated by empirical studies which find that higher quality auditors (e.g., Big 4 auditors and auditors with longer tenure) are more accurate in issuing going concern reports (Geiger and Raghunandan 2002; Geiger and Rama 2006).

Financial reporting quality

As an observable outcome of the audit process, the client's audited financial statements are often used to signal audit quality. However, because there is no comprehensive or generally accepted measure for financial reporting quality, various proxies for earnings quality are used. Common proxies for high earnings quality include measures of earnings credibility and earnings conservatism. Common proxies for poor earnings quality include measures of earnings management behavior including abnormal discretionary accruals and whether clients meet or beat earnings targets. While each of these earnings measures have limitations as indicators of audit quality (see Francis [2004] for a review), research indicates these measures are associated with proxies for audit quality. For example, accounting conservatism has been positively linked with indicators of high audit quality (e.g., Big N auditors, auditor specialization, and auditor tenure). Likewise, clients' abnormal discretionary accruals levels are negatively associated with similar proxies for high audit quality (see Knechel *et al.* [2013a] for a review). Further, evidence of client earnings management is more likely for auditors who exert lower effort (Caramanis and Lennox 2011). The findings suggest that high quality auditors are better able to inhibit clients' attempts to manage earnings through discretionary accruals and/or aggressive accounting treatments.

Regulatory reviews of audit firms

The results of regulatory reviews represent direct measures of audit quality. In the US, audit firms participate in self-regulation through the American Institute of Certified Public Accountants (AICPA) peer review process and in statutory regulation through the PCAOB inspection process.[12] Despite limitations in the results of the reviews that are publicly disclosed, the outcomes of these reviews shed light on audit firm quality.

AICPA peer reviews

The outcome of a peer review is a report with a rating of pass (i.e., unqualified, clean report), pass with deficiencies, or fail. Historically, the outcomes of peer reviews are largely positive, i.e., the overwhelming majority of firms receive unqualified reports (Wallace 1991). Despite the small number of negative peer reviews, there is some evidence documenting a link between outcomes of peer reviews and proxies for audit quality. For example, Casterella *et al.* (2009) provide evidence that negative peer review outcomes are effective signals for poor audit firm quality. Specifically, they find that negative findings are associated with subsequent audit failures (e.g., malpractice claims alleging auditor negligence). Further, audit firms receiving negative peer reviews are more likely to lose clients, whereas audit firms receiving positive reviews are more likely to attract and retain clients (Hilary and Lennox 2005).

PCAOB inspections

Post-SOX (Sarbanes–Oxley Act), all accounting firms who audit US public companies are subject to mandatory inspections by the PCAOB. Compared to AICPA peer reviews, PCAOB inspections are thought to be somewhat more effective at improving audit quality because they are conducted by independent reviewers and the PCAOB can impose larger sanctions against audit firms for poor audit quality (DeFond 2010). Descriptive analysis of the inspection results indicate that auditing deficiencies had significantly decreased over time through 2009 (Hermanson *et al.* 2007; Church and Shefchik 2012); however, reports indicate that auditing deficiencies have significantly spiked during the most recent audits (PCAOB 2012). Likewise, reviews of large accounting firms' quality controls suggest negative quality in recent years.[13] Yet, empirical evidence documenting a link between PCAOB inspections and audit quality is limited.

Gunny and Zhang (2012) find that clients of audit firms with serious inspection deficiencies are associated with proxies for lower audit quality (i.e., higher abnormal accruals and financial statement restatements). The findings suggest that inspection results are beneficial at signaling audit quality. Further, the outcomes of PCAOB inspections appear to have information value. For example, audit firms are more likely to be dismissed following negative PCAOB inspection results (Dougherty *et al.* 2011; Abbott *et al.* 2013). Also, clients of audit firms who receive negative inspection reports in terms of disclosed auditing deficiencies (Offermanns and Peek 2011) and disclosed quality control defects (Dee *et al.* 2011) experience abnormal, negative market reactions.

Finally, there is some evidence that the PCAOB inspection process, alone, promotes and enhances audit quality. First, there is evidence that smaller, low quality audit firms are more likely to exit the market following the inception of the PCAOB (DeFond and Lennox 2011). Second, audit firms are more likely to report going concern opinions and material weaknesses (i.e., signals for high audit quality) for clients in jurisdictions that allow PCAOB inspections relative to those in jurisdictions barring PCAOB inspections (Lamoreaux 2013). Third, there is evidence that over time the PCAOB inspection process has contributed to improved audit quality, in terms of going concern reporting (Gramling *et al.* 2011), increased auditor effort (Knechel *et al.* 2012), and lower levels of clients' abnormal accruals (Carcello *et al.* 2011).

Discussion and conclusions

An audit is a multifaceted concept that includes incentives, uncertainty, idiosyncrasies, a unique process, and professional judgment. Each of these characteristics influences audit quality. In this chapter, we synthesized the literature related to audit quality. We developed a framework for audit quality that includes the different attributes or indicators of audit quality. The framework provides insight as to what factors contribute to high or low audit quality (i.e., audit inputs and process) as well as what factors can be used to measure audit quality (i.e., outcomes).

While much research has been conducted related to audit quality, there is still a great amount left to be done. Future research can continue to enhance our knowledge as to how the primary attributes of an audit (incentives, uncertainty, idiosyncrasies, process, and professional judgment) affect the different indicators of audit quality (inputs, process, and outcomes). For example, how can auditors mitigate the negative effects of conflicted incentives on judgments related to audit inputs and the audit process to improve audit outcomes? Likewise, how can the audit process be modified to appropriately respond to changes in the environment (e.g., increased use of fair value accounting) that add to the uncertainty of audits? We also encourage future research to enhance our understanding about the links between the different indicators of audit quality. For example, to what extent do changes in audit inputs (e.g., more or less professional skepticism) affect the audit process and audit outcomes? Finally, we encourage researchers to continue to develop new metrics for measuring audit quality. Continued research will help to provide a better understanding of audit quality.

Notes

1 Auditing textbooks also define an audit as a multidimensional process. Messier *et al.* (2012: 12) define an audit as "a systematic process of objectively obtaining and evaluating evidence regarding assertions about economic actions and events to ascertain the degree of correspondence between those assertions and established criteria and communicating the results to interested users."

2 See Palmrose 1988; Carcello and Palmrose 1994; Kinney *et al.* 2004; Peecher and Piercey 2008.

3 Audit quality frameworks have been established by several regulatory bodies including the UK's Financial Reporting Council (FRC 2008), the Australian Treasury (Commonwealth of Australia 2010), and the International Auditing and Assurance Standards Board (IAASB 2011), as well as by several academics (e.g., Arrunada 2000; Francis 2011; Knechel *et al.* 2013a).

4 We discuss other non-personal factors that influence how much work ought to be performed in the audit process section (e.g., audit risk).

5 See reviews in Bedard *et al.* (2008) and Church *et al.* (2012).

6 See Lin and Hwang (2010) for a recent meta-analysis of studies in the auditing literature. Ultimately, they identify auditor tenure as a factor that positively influences accounting quality. Likewise, using a direct measure of audit quality (internal quality reviews), Bell *et al.* (2013) provide empirical evidence that links audit firm tenure with audit quality. Specifically, they find that first year audits have lower audit quality; but quality increases to an average level starting in the second year and sustains for long tenure engagements. Further, their findings support that audit firm tenure improves client-specific knowledge which increases audit quality.

7 Big N auditors are also thought to earn a fee premium for reasons other than greater expertise including (1) that they can charge a higher fee because of their market (monopolistic) power (Palmrose 1986), and/or (2) that they provide more effort to preserve their reputational capital (Francis 2004).

8 Not all academics are in agreement on the findings that Big N auditors result in higher earnings quality. It is possible that clients of Big N auditors have higher earnings quality than clients of non-Big N auditors (Francis 2004). To this point, a recent study provides some evidence and contends that the difference in audit quality reflects client characteristics (e.g., client size) rather than differences in audit quality between the Big 4 and non-Big 4 firms (Lawrence *et al.* 2011).

9 See Nelson (2009), Hurtt *et al.* (2013) and Knechel *et al.* (2013a) for detailed summaries of the literature.

10 Other limitations of using restatements as a proxy for audit quality include but are not limited to the following: the use of restatements focuses on extreme events of poor audit quality and does not allow for capturing audit deficiencies of lower magnitude; not all misstatements are detected (i.e., not identifying a misstatement does not necessarily mean that one does not exist); a lack of restatement is not necessarily indicative of high audit quality (i.e., an auditor could have done a poor job but there were no misstatements in the financial statements); and many restatements include adjustments of accounting 'estimations' in prior-year financial statements which are not audit failures.

11 See Francis (2004), Carson *et al.* (2013), and Knechel *et al.* (2013a) for reviews.

12 AICPA peer reviews covered all audits prior to SOX and remain in place for private clients after SOX. Post-SOX, all public company audits are subject to PCAOB inspections. Both systems conduct reviews on a test basis.

13 Through 2009, no large accounting firm had received quality control criticisms warranting public disclosure, indicating that firms had made reasonable progress in addressing the criticisms within a 12-month period following the inspection report (Church and Shefchik 2012). Subsequent to 2009, two large accounting firms (Deloitte and PricewaterhouseCoopers) had their quality control criticism released to the public.

References

Abbott, L., K. Gunny, and T. C. Zhang. 2013. "When the PCAOB talks, who listens? Evidence from client firm reaction to GAAP-deficient PCAOB inspection reports of small auditors", *Auditing: A Journal of Practice & Theory* 32(May): 1–31.

Allen, R. D., D. R. Hermanson, T. M. Kozloski, and R. J. Ramsay. 2006. "Auditor risk assessment: Insights from the academic literature", *Accounting Horizons* 20(2): 157–77.

Antle, R. 1982. "The auditor as an economic agent", *Journal of Accounting Research* 20(2): 503–27.

Arnold, V. and G. Sutton. 1998. "The theory of technology dominance: Understanding the impact of intelligent aids on decision maker's judgment", *Advances in Accounting Behavior Research* 1: 175–94.

Arrunada, B. 2000. "Audit quality: Attributes, private safeguards and the role of regulation", *European Accounting Review* 9(2): 205–24.

Asare, S. K. and L. S. McDaniel. 1996. "The effects of familiarity with the preparer and task complexity on the effectiveness of the audit review process", *The Accounting Review* 71(2): 139–59.

Asare, S. K. and A. M. Wright. 2004. "The effectiveness of alternative risk assessment and program planning tools in a fraud setting", *Contemporary Accounting Research* (Summer): 325–52.

Asare, S. K., K. Hackenbrack, and W. R. Knechel. 1994. "Client acceptance and continuation decisions", in R. P. Srivatava (ed.) *Auditing Symposium XII: Proceedings of the 1994 Deloitte & Touche/University of Kansas Symposium on Auditing Problems*, pp. 163–78. Lawrence, KS: University of Kansas.

Asare, S. K., G. M. Trompeter, and A. M. Wright. 2000. "The effect of accountability and time budgets on auditors' testing strategies", *Contemporary Accounting Research* 17(4): 539–60.

Ashton, R. H. 1990. "Pressure and performance in accounting decision settings: Paradoxical effects of incentives, feedback, and justification", *Journal of Accounting Research* 28(Supplement): 148–80.

Bamber, M. 1983. "Expert judgment in the audit team: A source reliability approach", *Journal of Accounting Research* 21(Autumn): 396–412.

Barton, J. 2005. "Who cares about auditor reputation?", *Contemporary Accounting Research* 22(3): 549–86.

Bazerman, M. H., K. P. Morgan, and G. F. Loewenstein. 1997. "The impossibility of auditor independence", *Sloan Management Review* 38(4): 89–94.

Bazerman, M. H., G. F. Loewenstein, and D. A. Moore. 2002. "Why good accountants do bad audits", *Harvard Business Review* 80(11): 96–103.

Beasley, M. S., J. V. Carcello, and D. R. Hermanson. 2001. "Top 10 audit deficiencies", *Journal of Accountancy* 191(4): 63–6.

Bedard, J. 1989. "Expertise in auditing: Myth or reality", *Accounting, Organizations and Society* 14(1/2): 113–32.

Bedard, J. 1991. "Expertise and its relation to audit decision quality", *Contemporary Accounting Research* 8(1): 198–222.

Bedard, J., D. Deis, M. Curtis, and J. G. Jenkins. 2008. "Risk monitoring and control in audit firms: A research synthesis", *Auditing: Journal of Practice & Theory* 27(1): 187–218.

Behn, B., J. Choi, and T. Kang. 2008. "Audit quality and properties of analyst earnings forecasts", *The Accounting Review* 83(3): 327–49.

Bell, T., M. Causholli, and W. R. Knechel. 2013. "Audit firm tenure, non-audit services and internal assessments of audit quality", working paper. Jacksonville, FL: University of North Florida; Lexington, KY: University of Kentucky; Gainesville, FL: University of Florida.

Bernardi, R. 1994. "Fraud detection: The effect of client integrity and competence and auditor cognitive style", *Auditing: A Journal of Practice & Theory* 13(Supplement): 68–84.

Blay, A. D. 2005. "Independence threats, litigation risk, and the auditor's decision process", *Contemporary Accounting Research* (Winter): 759–89.

Bonner, S. E. 1990. "Experience effects in auditing: The role of task-specific knowledge", *The Accounting Review* 65(January): 72–92.

Bonner, S. E. and B. L. Lewis. 1990. "Determinants of auditor expertise", *Journal of Accounting Research* 28(Supplement): 1–20.

Braun, K. W. 2001. "The disposition of audit-detected misstatements: An examination of risk and reward factors and aggregation effects", *Contemporary Accounting Research* (Spring): 71–99.

Calderon, T., L. Wang, and T. Klenotic. 2012. "Past control risk and current audit fees", *Managerial Auditing Journal* 27(2): 693–708.

Caramanis, C. and C. Lennox. 2011. "Audit effort and earnings management", *Journal of Accounting and Economics* 45(1): 116–38.

Carcello, J. V. and J. Palmrose. 1994. "Auditor litigation and modified reporting on bankrupt clients", *Journal of Accounting Research* (Supplement): 1–30.

Carcello, J. V., D. R. Hermanson, and H. F. Huss. 2000. "Going-concern opinions: The effects of partner compensation plans and client size", *Auditing: A Journal of Practice & Theory* 19(1): 67–77.

Carcello, J. V., D. R. Hermanson, and R. A. Riley. 2002. "Board characteristics and audit fees", *Contemporary Accounting Research* 19(3): 365–84.

Carcello, J. V., C. Hollingsworth, and S. Mastrolia. 2011. "The effect of PCAOB inspections on Big 4 audit quality", *Research in Accounting Regulation* 23: 85–96.

Carey, P. and R. Simnett. 2006. "Audit partner rotation and audit quality", *The Accounting Review* 81(3): 653–6.

Carson, E. 2009. "Industry specialization by global audit firm networks", *The Accounting Review* 84(2): 355–82.

Carson, E. and N. Fargher. 2007. "Note on audit fee premiums to client size and industry specialization", *Accounting and Finance* 47(3): 423–46.

Carson, E., N. Fargher, M. Geiger, C. Lennox, K. Raghunandan, and M. Willekens. 2013. "Auditor reporting on going-concern uncertainty: A research synthesis", *Auditing: A Journal of Practice & Theory* 32(Special Issue): 353–84.

Casterella, J. R., K. L. Jensen, and R. Knechel. 2009. "Is self-regulated peer review effective at signaling audit quality?", *The Accounting Review* 84(May): 713–35.

Chan, D. and K. Wong. 2002. "Scope of auditors' liability, audit quality, and capital investment", *Review of Accounting Studies* 7(2): 97–122.

Chang, X., S. Dasgupta, and G. Hilary. 2009. "The effect of auditor quality on financing decisions", *The Accounting Review* 84(4): 1085–117.

Chen, C., C. Lin, and Y. Lin. 2008. "Audit partner tenure, audit firm tenure, and discretionary accruals: Does long auditor tenure impair earnings quality?" *Contemporary Accounting Research* 25(2): 215–45.

Chen, C., X. Martin, and X. Wang. 2012. "Insider trading, litigation concerns, and auditor going-concern opinions", *The Accounting Review* 88(2): 365–93.

Chen, K. and B. K. Church. 1996. "Going concern opinions and the market's reaction to bankruptcy filings", *The Accounting Review* (January): 117–28.

Chi, W., H. Huang, Y. Liao, and H. Xie. 2009. "Mandatory audit partner rotation, audit quality, and market perception: Evidence from Taiwan", *Contemporary Accounting Research* 26(4): 359–91.

Choo, F. 1986. "Job stress, job performance, and auditor personality characteristics", *Auditing: A Journal of Practice & Theory* 5(Spring): 17–34.

Church, B. K. and L. B. Shefchik. 2012. "PCAOB inspections and large accounting firms", *Accounting Horizons* 26(March): 43–63.

Church, B. K., J. G. Jenkins, S. McCracken, P. B. Roush, and J. D. Stanley. 2012. "A consideration of forces surrounding auditor independence in fact: A literature synthesis and review", working paper. Atlanta, GA: Georgia Tech; Blacksburg, VA: Virginia Tech; Hamilton, ON: McMaster University; Orlando, FL: University of Central Florida; Auburn, AL: Auburn University.

Commonwealth of Australia. 2010. "Audit quality in Australia". Available online at http://archive.treasury.gov.au/documents/1745/PDF/Audit_Quality_in_Australia.pdf (accessed 22 April 2014).

Davis, L., B. Soo, and G. Trompeter. 2009. "Auditor tenure and the ability to meet or beat earnings forecasts", *Contemporary Accounting Research* 26(2): 517–48.

DeAngelo, L. E. 1981. "Auditor size and auditor quality", *Journal of Accounting and Economics* 3(December): 183–99.

Dee, C., A. Lulseged, and T. Zhang. 2011. "Client stock market reaction to PCAOB sanctions against a Big 4 auditor", *Contemporary Accounting Research* 28(1): 263–91.

DeFond, M. L. 2010. "How should the auditors be audited? Comparing the PCAOB inspections with the AICPA peer reviews", *Journal of Accounting and Economics* 49(February): 104–8.

DeFond, M. L. and C. S. Lennox. 2011. "The effect of SOX on small auditor exits and audit quality", *Journal of Accounting & Economics* 52(1): 21–40.

Dougherty, B., D. Dickins, and W. Tervo. 2011. "Negative PCAOB inspections of triennially inspected auditors and involuntary and voluntary client losses", *International Journal of Auditing* 15(3): 231–46.

Dowling, C. and S. Leech. 2007. "Audit support systems and decision aids: Current practice and opportunities for future research", *International Journal of Accounting Information Systems* 8: 92–116.

Eining, M. M., D. R. Jones, and J. K. Loebbecke. 1997. "Reliance on decision aids: An examination of auditors' assessment of management fraud", *Auditing: A Journal of Practice & Theory* 16(Fall): 1–19.

Epps, K. K. and W. F. Messier Jr. 2007. "Engagement quality reviews: A comparison of audit firm practices", *Auditing: A Journal of Practice & Theory* 26(November): 167–81.

Farmer, T. A., L. E. Rittenberg, and G. M. Trompeter. 1987. "An investigation of the impact of economic and organizational factors on auditor independence", *Auditing: A Journal of Practice & Theory* 7(Fall): 1–14.

Ferguson, M. J., G. S. Seow, and D. Young. 2004. "Nonaudit services and earnings management: UK evidence", *Contemporary Accounting Research* 21(Winter): 813–41.

Financial Reporting Council (FRC). 2008. "The audit quality framework". Available online at www.frc.org.uk/Our-Work/Publications/FRC-Board/The-Audit-Quality-Framework-%281%29.aspx (accessed 22 April 2014).

Francis, J. R. 2004. "What do we know about audit quality?", *British Accounting Review* 36: 345–68.

Francis, J. R. 2011. "A framework for understanding and researching audit quality", *Auditing: A Journal of Practice & Theory* 30(2): 125–52.

Francis, J. R. and D. Wang. 2008. "The joint effect of investor protection and Big 4 audits on earnings quality around the world", *Contemporary Accounting Research* 25(1): 157–91.

Francis, J. R. and M. Yu. 2009. "Big 4 office size and audit quality", *The Accounting Review* 84(1): 1521–52.

Frankel, R. M., M. F. Johnson, and K. K. Nelson. 2002. "The association between auditors' fees for non-audit services and earnings management", *The Accounting Review* 77(Supplement): 71–105.

Frederick, D. M. and R. Libby. 1986. "Expertise and auditors' judgments of conjunctive events", *Journal of Accounting Research* 24(Autumn): 270–90.

Geiger, M. A. and K. Raghunandan. 2002. "Auditor tenure and audit reporting failures", *Auditing: A Journal of Practice & Theory* 21(1): 67–78.

Geiger, M. A. and D. V. Rama. 2006. "Audit firm size and going-concern reporting accuracy", *Accounting Horizons* 20(1): 1–17.

Gleason, C. A. and L. F. Mills. 2011. "Do auditor-provided tax services improve the estimate of tax reserves?", *Contemporary Accounting Research* 28(5):1484–509.

Government Accounting Office (GAO). 2003. "Public accounting firms: Required study on the potential effects of mandatory audit firm rotation". United States General Accounting Office. Available online at www.gao.gov/assets/250/240736.pdf (accessed 22 April 2014).

Gramling, A. A. 1999. "External auditors' reliance on work performed by internal auditors: The influence of fee pressure on this reliance decision", *Auditing: A Journal of Practice & Theory* 18(Supplement): 117–35.

Gramling, A. A., J. Krishnan, and Y. Zhang. 2011. "Are PCAOB-identified audit deficiencies associated with a change in reporting decisions of triennially inspected audit firms?", *Auditing: A Journal of Practice & Theory* 30(3): 59–79.

Gul, F., S. G. Lynn, and J. Tsui. 2002. "Audit quality, management ownership, and the informativeness of accounting earnings", *Journal of Accounting, Auditing and Finance* 17(Winter): 25–49.

Gunny, K. A. and T. C. Zhang. 2012. "PCAOB inspection reports and audit quality", *Journal of Accounting and Public Policy* 32(2): 136–60.

Hackenbrack, K. and W. R. Knechel. 1997. "Resource allocation decisions in audit engagements", *Contemporary Accounting Research* (Fall): 481–99.

Hackenbrack, K. and M. W. Nelson. 1996. "Auditors' incentives and their application of financial accounting standards", *The Accounting Review* 71(January): 43–59.

Hawkins, S. A. and R. Hastie. 1990. "Hindsight: Biased judgments of past events after the outcomes are known", *Psychological Bulletin* 107(3): 311.

Hermanson, D. R., R. W. Houston, and J. Rice. 2007. "PCAOB inspections of smaller CPA firms: Initial evidence from inspection reports", *Accounting Horizons* 21(2): 137–52.

Hilary, G. and C. Lennox. 2005. "The credibility of self-regulation: Evidence from the accounting profession's peer review program", *Journal of Accounting and Economics* 40: 211–29.

Houston, R. W. 1999. "The effects of fee pressure and client risk on audit seniors' time budget decisions", *Auditing: A Journal of Practice & Theory* 18(Fall): 70–86.

Hurtt, K. R., M. Eining, and D. Plumlee. 2008. "An experimental examination of professional skepticism", working paper. Available online at: http://papers.ssrn.com/sol3/papers.cfm?abstract_id=1140267 (accessed 22 April 2014).

Hurtt, K. R., H. L. Brown-Liburd, C. E. Earley, and G. Krishnamoorthy. 2013. "Research on auditor professional skepticism-literature synthesis and opportunities for future research", *Auditing: A Journal of Practice & Theory* (Special Issues): 45–97.

International Auditing and Assurance Standards Board (IAASB). 2011. *Audit Quality: An IAASB Perspective.* Available online at www.ifac.org/sites/default/files/publications/files/audit-quality-an-iaasb-per.pdf (accessed 22 April 2014).

International Organization of Securities Commissions (IOSCO). 2009. *Consultation Report on Transparency of Firms that Audit Public Companies.* Available online at www.iosco.org/library/pubdocs/pdf/IOSCOPD302.pdf (accessed 22 April 2014).

Johnson, E., I. Khurana, and K. Reynolds. 2002. "Audit firm tenure and quality of financial reports", *Contemporary Accounting Research* 19(4): 637–60.

Johnson, V. and S. Kaplan. 1991. "Experimental evidence on the effects of accountability on auditor judgments", *Auditing: A Journal of Practice & Theory* 10: 96 – 107.

Johnstone, K. 2000. "Client-acceptance decisions: Simultaneous effects of client business risk, audit risk, auditor business risk, and risk adaptation", *Auditing: A Journal of Practice & Theory* 19(1): 1–25.

Johnstone, K. and J. Bedard. 2003. "Risk management in client acceptance decisions", *The Accounting Review* 78(4): 1003–25.

Johnstone, K. and J. Bedard. 2004. "Earnings manipulation risk, corporate governance risk, and auditors' planning and pricing decisions", *The Accounting Review* 79(2): 277–304.

Johnstone, K. M. and J. Bedard. 2001. "Engagement planning, bid pricing, and client response to initial attest engagements", *The Accounting Review* 76(2): 199–220.

Kachelmeier, S. J. and W. F. Messier. 1990. "An investigation of the influence of a nonstatistical decision aid on auditor sample size decisions", *The Accounting Review* 65(January): 209–26.

Kadous, K. 2000. "The effects of audit quality and consequence severity on juror evaluations of auditor responsibility for plaintiff losses", *The Accounting Review* 75(3): 327–41.

Kadous, K. 2001. "Improving jurors' evaluations of auditors in negligence cases", *Contemporary Accounting Research* 18(3): 425–44.

Kennedy, J. 1995. "Debiasing the curse of knowledge in audit judgment", *The Accounting Review* 70(April): 249–73.

Kinney, W. R. 2005. "Twenty-five years of audit deregulation and re-regulation: What does it mean for 2005 and beyond?", *Auditing: A Journal of Practice & Theory* 24(Supplement): 89–109.

Kinney, W. R., Z. V. Palmrose, and S. Scholz. 2004. "Auditor independence, non-audit services, and restatements: Was the U.S. government right?", *Journal of Accounting Research* 42(3): 561–88.

Knechel, W. R., M. Offermanns, and A. Vanstraelen. 2012. "Audit firm inspections and audit fees", working paper. Maastricht: University of Maastricht.

Knechel, W. R., G. V. Krishnan, M. Pevzner, L. B. Shefchik, and U. K. Velury. 2013a. "Audit quality: Insights from the academic literature", *Auditing: A Journal of Practice & Theory* 32(Special Issue): 385–421.

Knechel, W. R., L. Niemi, and M. Zerni. 2013b. "Empirical evidence on the implicit determinants of compensation in Big 4 audit partnerships", *Journal of Accounting Research* 51(2): 349–87.

Koonce, L. 1993. "A cognitive characterization of audit analytical review", *Auditing: A Journal of Practice & Theory* 12(Supplement): 57–76.

Koonce, L., U. Anderson, and G. Marchant. 1995. "Justification of decisions in auditing", *Journal of Accounting Research* (Autumn): 369–84.

Krishnan, J. 1994. "Auditor switching and conservatism", *The Accounting Review* 69(1): 200–15.

Krishnan, J. and J. Krishnan. 1997. "Litigation risk and auditor resignations", *The Accounting Review* 72(4): 539–60.

Krishnan, J. and P. C. Schauer. 2001. "Differences in quality among audit firms", *Journal of Accountancy* (July): 85.

Krishnan, G. and G. Visvanathan. 2011. "Is there an association between earnings management and auditor-provided tax services?", *Journal of the American Taxation Association* 33(Fall): 111–35.

Krishnan, G. and W. Yu. 2011. "Further evidence on knowledge spillover and the joint determination of audit and non-audit fees", *Managerial Auditing Journal* 26(3): 230–47.

Lamoreaux, P. T. 2013. "Does PCAOB inspection exposure affect auditor reporting decisions?", working paper. Tucson, AZ: University of Arizona.

Lawrence, A., M. Minutti-Meza, and P. Zhang. 2011. "Can Big 4 versus non-Big 4 differences in audit-quality proxies be attributed to client characteristics?", *The Accounting Review* 86(1): 259–86.

Libby, R. and W. R. Kinney Jr. 2000. "Does mandated audit communication reduce opportunistic corrections to manage earnings to forecasts", *The Accounting Review* (October): 383–404.

Lin, J. and M. Hwang. 2010. "Audit quality, corporate governance, and earnings management: A meta-analysis", *International Journal of Auditing* 14(1): 57–77.

McDaniel, L. S. 1990. "The effects of time pressure and audit program structure on audit performance", *Journal of Accounting Research* (Autumn): 267–85.

Mautz, R. K. and H. A. Sharaf. 1961. *The Philosophy of Auditing*. Sarasota, FL: American Accounting Association.

Messier, W. F., S. J. Kachelmeier, and K. L. Jensen. 2001. "An experimental assessment of recent professional developments in nonstatistical audit sampling guidance", *Auditing: A Journal of Practice & Theory* 20(1): 81–96.

Messier, W. F., T. M. Kozloski, and N. Kochetova-Kozloski. 2010. "An analysis of SEC and PCAOB enforcement actions against engagement quality reviewers", *Auditing: A Journal of Practice & Theory* 29(2): 233–52.

Messier, W. F., S. M. Glover, and D. F. Prawitt. 2012. *Auditing & Assurance Services: A Systematic Approach*, 8th ed. New York: McGraw-Hill.

Messier, W. F., C. A. Simon, and J. L. Smith. 2013. "Two decades of behavioral research on analytical procedures: What have we learned?", *Auditing: A Journal of Practice & Theory* 32(1): 139–81.

Moore, D. A., P. E. Tetlock, L. Tanlu, and M. H. Bazerman. 2006. "Conflicts of interest and the case of auditor independence: Moral seduction and strategic issue cycling", *Academy of Management Review* 31(January): 10–29.

Myers, J., L. Myers, and T. Omer. 2003. "Exploring the term of the auditor-client relationship and quality of earnings: A case for mandatory auditor rotation?", *The Accounting Review* 78(3): 779–99.

Nagy, A. 2012. "Audit partner specialization: The case of Andersen followers", *Managerial Auditing Journal* 27(3): 251–62.

Nelson, M. W. 2009. "A model and literature review of professional skepticism in auditing", *Auditing: A Journal of Practice & Theory* 28(November): 1–34.

Nelson, M. W. and H-T. Tan. 2005. "Judgment and decision making research in auditing: A task, person, and interpersonal interaction perspective", *Auditing: A Journal of Practice & Theory* (Supplement): 41–72.

Nelson, M. W., J. A. Elliott, and R. L. Tarpley. 2002. "Evidence from auditors about managers' and auditors' earnings management decisions", *The Accounting Review* (Supplement): 175–202.

Ng, T. B-P. 2007. "Auditor's decision on audit differences that affect significant earnings thresholds", *Auditing: A Journal of Practice & Theory* (May): 71–89.

Ng, T. B-P. and H-T. Tan. 2007. "Effects of qualitative factor salience, expressed client concern, and qualitative materiality thresholds on auditors' audit adjustment decisions", *Contemporary Accounting Research* (Winter): 1171–92.

Offermanns, M. and E. Peek. 2011. "Investor reactions to PCAOB inspection reports", working paper. Maastricht: Maastricht University; Rotterdam: Erasmus University.

O'Keefe, T. G., R. D. King, and K. M. Gaver. 1994. "Audit fees, industry specialization, and compliance with GAAS reporting standards", *Auditing: A Journal of Practice & Theory* 13(2): 41–55.

Owhoso, V. E., W. F. Messier, and J. G. Lynch. 2002. "Error detection by industry-specialized teams during sequential audit review", *Journal of Accounting Research* 40(3): 883–900.

Palmrose, Z-V. 1986. "Audit fees and auditor size: Further evidence", *Journal of Accounting Research* 24(1): 97–110.

Palmrose, Z-V. 1988. "An analysis of auditor litigation and audit service quality", *The Accounting Review* (January): 55–73.

Palmrose, Z-V. 1997. "Who got sued?", *Journal of Accountancy* 183(3): 67–69.

Palmrose, Z.-V. 2000. *Empirical Research in Auditor Litigation: Considerations and Data*. Studies in Accounting Research No. 33. Sarasota, FL: American Accounting Association.

Peecher, M. E. 1996. "The influence of auditors' justification processes on their decisions: A cognitive model and experimental evidence", *Journal of Accounting Research* 34(Spring): 125–40.

Peecher, M. E. and D. Piercey. 2008. "Judging audit quality in light of adverse outcomes: Evidence of outcome bias and reverse outcome bias", *Contemporary Accounting Research* 25(1): 243–74.

Pincus, K. V. 1989. "The efficacy of a red flags questionnaire for assessing the possibility of fraud", *Accounting, Organizations and Society* 14(1/2): 153–64.

Public Company Accounting Oversight Board (PCAOB). 2006. *Due Professional Care in the Performance of Work*. AU Section 230. Available online at http://pcaobus.org/Standards/Auditing/Pages/AU230.aspx (accessed 22 April 2014).

Public Company Accounting Oversight Board (PCAOB). 2008. "Report on the PCAOB's 2004, 2005, 2006, and 2007 inspections of domestic annually inspected firms". PCAOB Release No. 2008–08. Washington DC: PCAOB.

Public Company Accounting Oversight Board (PCAOB). 2010. *Consideration of Materiality in Planning and Performing and Audit*. Audit Standard No. 11. Available online at http://pcaobus.org/Standards/Auditing/Pages/Auditing_Standard_11.aspx (accessed 22 April 2014).

Public Company Accounting Oversight Board (PCAOB). 2012. "Observations from 2010 inspections of domestic annually inspected firms regarding deficiencies in audits of internal control over financial reporting", PCAOB Release No. 2012–006. Washington DC: PCAOB.

Ramsay, R. J. 1994. "Senior/manager differences in audit workpaper review performance", *Journal of Accounting Research* 32(Spring): 127–35.

Rich, J. S., I. Solomon, and K. T. Trotman. 1997. "The audit review process: A characterization from the persuasion perspective", *Accounting, Organizations and Society* 22(5): 481–505.

Robinson, D. 2008. "Auditor independence and auditor-provided tax service: Evidence from going-concern audit opinions prior to bankruptcy filings", *Auditing: A Journal of Practice & Theory* 27(November): 31–54.

Shankar, P. G. and H-T. Tan. 2006. "Determinants of audit preparers' workpaper justifications", *The Accounting Review* (March): 473–95.

Shaub, M. K. and J. E. Lawrence. 1996. "Ethics, experience, and professional skepticism: A situational analysis", *Behavioral Research in Accounting* 8(Supplement): 124–57.

Shu, S. Z. 2000. "Auditor resignations: Clientele effects and legal liability", *Journal of Accounting and Economics* 29(April): 173–205.

Simunic, D. A. 1984. "Auditing, consulting, and auditor independence", *Journal of Accounting Research* 22(2): 679–702.

Simunic, D. A. and M. T. Stein. 1990. "Audit risk in a client portfolio context", *Contemporary Accounting Research* 6(2): 329–43.

Solomon, I. 1987. "Multi-auditor judgment/decision making research", *Journal of Accounting Literature* 6: 1–25.

Stefaniak, C. M. and R. W. Houston. 2013. "Investigating the effects of post-audit reviews: A comparative analysis of PCAOB inspections and internal quality reviews", working paper. Stillwater, OK: Oklahoma State University; Tuscaloosa, AL: University of Alabama.

Tie, R. 1999. "Concerns over auditing quality complicate the future of accounting", *Journal of Accountancy* (December): 14–15.

Trompeter, G. 1994. "The effect of partner compensation schemes and generally accepted accounting principles on audit partner judgment", *Auditing: A Journal of Practice & Theory* 13(Fall): 56–68.

Trotman, K. T. and P. W. Yetton. 1985. "The effect of the review process on auditor judgments", *Journal of Accounting Research* 23(1): 256–67.

Turner, W. C. 2001. "Accountability demands and the auditor's evidence search strategy: The influence of reviewer preferences and the nature of the response (belief vs action)", *Journal of Accounting Research* (December): 683–706.

Wallace, W. A. 1991. "Peer review filings and their implications in evaluating self-regulation", *Auditing: A Journal of Practice & Theory* 10(Spring): 53–68.

Weber, J., M. Willenborg, and J. Zhang. 2008. "Does auditor reputation matter? The case of KPMG Germany and ComROAD AG", *Journal of Accounting Research* 46(4): 941–72.

Whitecotton, S. M. 1996. "The effects of experience and confidence on decision aid reliance: A causal model", *Behavioral Research in Accounting* (8): 194–216.

Wilks, T. J. 2002. "Predecisional distortion of evidence as a consequence of real-time audit review", *The Accounting Review* 77(1): 51–71.

Wright, S. and A. M. Wright. 1997. "The effect of industry experience on hypothesis generation and audit planning decisions", *Behavioral Research in Accounting* 9: 273–94.

Zeff, S.A. 2003. "How the US accounting profession got where it is today: Part II", *Accounting Horizons* 17(4): 267–86.

12

Audits of private companies

John Christian Langli and Tobias Svanström

Introduction

In this chapter we review research on audits of private companies.[1] The topic is important for several reasons. One is that research focusing on public companies may not be generalizable to private companies since public companies differ from private companies along a number of important dimensions (which we discuss in the next section). Thus, it is not clear to what extent findings based on public companies can provide insight and guidance for regulators, standard setters, researchers and users of (audited) financial statements when it comes to auditing in the private sector.

A second reason is the economic importance of private companies and the role that auditors may play as verifier of financial information and provider of advisory services. Private companies are unlisted and represent more than 99 per cent of all companies in the US and account for more than 50 per cent of the private sector's gross domestic product (GDP) (Minnis 2011). In the EU, small and medium-sized companies (SMEs) accounted for 67 per cent of total employment and 58 per cent of gross value added (Wymenga *et al.* 2012). Understanding how auditors may contribute to governance and growth for these companies is thus of great importance for the society.

A third reason is the opportunities that the private sector provides for the development and testing of new theories. Researchers have so far mostly chosen topics that have previously been analyzed for public companies. However, it is possible to further advance the literature by asking questions that are more relevant for private companies and also to conduct tests that are not feasible in a public company setting. The private company segment of the economy is thus an underutilized research area.

The structure of the chapter is as follows. We start by highlighting the differences between private and public companies and proceed by providing an overview of existing research. Then we briefly discuss directions for future research before a short summary concludes the chapter.

What is special about private companies and their audit?

Compared with public companies, the nature of agency conflict is different in private companies as they have much more concentrated ownership; family ties between CEOs and shareholders and between CEOs and board members are much more common, and major capital providers may have better access to information. Besides, private companies operate in a substantially poorer information environment, disclose less non-financial information, are less scrutinized by market participants and have little capital-market pressure to hire high quality auditors. Furthermore, their financial statements may be more influenced by taxation, dividend and other political issues such as the intention to transfer the company to the next generation. In sum, this means weaker incentives for private companies to produce high quality financial statements and less agency conflict between shareholders and managers, but potentially more agency conflict between majority owners and minority owners and/or between owners and creditors and tax authorities.

Another difference is that private companies may choose not to engage an auditor (depending on national legislation); those that do engage an auditor may demand auditing because it is statutory or for reasons not related to agency conflicts. For instance many companies demand external auditors to compensate for the loss of control that is inherent in hierarchical organizations as a longer chain of command reduces the top manager's ability to observe subordinates' actions or to improve operational efficiency and effectiveness as auditors evaluate internal procedures in the audit process. Audit demand could also be driven by access to competences not available in house, as private companies may not be able to afford their own staff with expertise in accounting, taxation and other business issues. Thus, compared to public companies there is much greater heterogeneity in the reasons why private companies hire auditors (or voluntarily hire a high quality auditor when auditing is mandatory).

Substantial differences also exist on the supply side. Among listed companies, the market for auditors may be characterized as an oligopoly as the large international audit firms, currently Ernst & Young, KPMG, Deloitte and PwC (henceforth Big N), dominate.[2] The dominance of Big N, particularly among listed companies, has led regulators to worry about market concentration and how this may affect audit quality (EC 2010). In the private sector audit firms are mostly small with a local anchor, and market concentration is of less concern. However, a large number of mostly small audit firms, where auditors work alone or in teams with few members, create other threats to audit quality. The incentive to provide audits of high quality decreases because the reputational capital at risk and the risk of litigation is reduced when auditing small clients with low publicity. Additionally, the pool of colleagues to consult is smaller and the internal monitoring mechanisms are likely to be weaker and less thorough compared to larger audit firms.

Furthermore, the risk of social bonding – a potential threat to independence – between the auditor and the client due to long-term relationships, local anchoring and familiarity is higher compared to public companies. As an auditor's reputation risk falls, impaired independence due to economic bonding may also increase. On the other hand, economic bonding may be of less concern since the fee from each client is often insignificant (due to smaller clients). Furthermore, the small size of the audit team makes potential synergies and spillovers gained from providing non-audit services (NAS) more easily transferable to the audit. In sum, audit quality may be much more dependent on the experience, competence, judgment and integrity of the individual auditor in charge in smaller audit firms compared to large audit firms, and in particular compared to those that have been subject to extensive research: the auditors of public companies.

Taken together, the differences that exist between private and public companies are so large and fundamental that without careful consideration we cannot rely on findings for public companies when we want to understand the role of auditing in private companies.

Review of the literature

We organize the review around the concept of audit quality. First, we review studies that look at input factors, i.e. factors that are critical for the auditors' ability to deliver audits of high quality. Here we use DeAngelo's (1981) two-dimensional model as a point of reference. In the DeAngelo model, audit quality is related to the auditors' ability to detect material misstatements (competence and level of effort) *and* willingness to issue an audit report that reveals these findings (independence). Next we review studies that analyze how measures that may proxy for actual or perceived audit quality (financial reporting quality, the accuracy of the audit report, disciplinary sanctions against auditors, audit fees, access to credit, interest rates on debt, and proceeds from sale of shares) relate to characteristics of the auditor or whether the companies are audited or not. Last, we review studies on audit choices.

Ability to detect misstatements

The likelihood that an auditor discovers material misstatements depends on the auditor's competence and the level of effort. Since auditing decisions are ultimately judgmental, understanding how competence and effort relates to audit quality is important, particularly in the private sector (as explained in the previous two sections).

Competence

The competence needed to detect material misstatements can be divided into general knowledge, domain-specific knowledge and client-specific knowledge. Work experience, participation in courses, seminars and other training activities are positively associated with an auditor's ability to detect misstatements in general. Prior experience of auditing companies in the same industry generates domain-specific knowledge that improves auditor judgment. Evidence from public companies supports the view that industry experts outperform non-specialists in e.g. error-detection, in performing analytical procedures and in assessing components of audit risk (Knechel *et al.* 2013). Auditors of small private companies typically audit a large number of clients and it is less likely that they are industry specialist compared with auditors of public companies. The potential relationship between industry expertise and audit quality has not gained much attention in private company research. Hay and Jeter (2011) report that industry specialists earn an audit fee premium from listed and large unlisted firms in New Zealand at the city level, but not at the national level. Dutillieux and Willekens (2009) analyze private Belgium companies and document a fee premium for industry specialists.

Client-specific knowledge is of vital importance when conducting private company audits, given that often only one or very few persons are involved throughout the whole audit process. Client-specific knowledge, such as knowledge of the client's accounting system and internal control structure, gives auditors comparative advantages in detecting errors, creates a significant learning curve for new auditors and significantly reduces start-up costs (DeAngelo 1981; Johnson *et al.* 2002). Client-specific knowledge, and thus audit quality, can be expected to increase with tenure and the provision of NAS. The evidence, however, is limited and mixed: Knechel and Vanstraelen (2007), analysing bankrupt and non-bankrupt private companies in Belgium, find no association between tenure and the ability to predict bankruptcy or independence. Svanström (2012) finds a positive association between provision of NAS and audit quality in Sweden. The importance of client-specific knowledge is also supported by Svanström and Sundgren (2012). They show that the purchase of NAS from the incumbent auditor is positively associated with tenure and the perceived quality of the auditing services.

Level of effort

Competence must be accompanied by effort for the audit programme to be properly planned and executed. Several factors influence how thoroughly this is achieved, among them the auditor's judgments about how agency conflicts influence the risk of material misstatements in financial statements, the size of the auditor's portfolio, the incentives facing the auditor and the auditor's working environment.

The International Standards on Auditing (ISA) require auditors to assess several agency conflicts when determining risk of material misstatements, for instance agency conflicts related to the companies' ownership and governance structures (e.g. ISA 315. 11, 14, A17, A30). Hope *et al.* (2012) analyze how auditors respond in the presence of agency conflicts using confidential data on family relationships between all owners, board members and CEOs for a large sample of Norwegian companies. They document that auditors adjust their level of effort as predicted by agency theory and the ISAs. For instance they document that family relationships between major shareholders and the CEO are positively associated with auditor effort, consistent with kinship and marriage resulting in reduced monitoring by owners and thus increased need for auditing. They also find that audit effort is negatively associated with the proportion of board members from the largest family owners (consistent with fewer agency conflicts between owners and the board, which reduces the need for auditing) and positively associated with family relationships between board members and the CEO (suggesting a less independent board, thus increasing the need for auditing).

The size of an engagement partner's portfolio is related to effort since one engagement partner has a limited number of hours available. Therefore, having too many clients may force the engagement partner or members of the audit team to cut corners and simplify test procedures, which increases the risk of material misstatements and erroneous audit reports. Analyzing public companies, Coram *et al.* (2004) show that tight reporting deadlines following from time and budget pressure have the potential to compromise auditor scepticism and professional judgment and López and Peters (2012) documents that increased workload impair audit quality and increase earnings management. As private company auditors are less exposed to risks of litigation and loss of reputation, it is reasonable to expect that business may have at least the same negative effect on audit quality for private companies. The level of effort may also depend on where the engagement partner is in his or her career, as young persons may be more willing to put in effort in order to achieve promotions and wage increases compared to persons approaching retirement. Consistent with the above, Sundgren and Svanström (2014) find that audit quality relates negatively to the number of assignments held by the audit partner and closeness to the retirement age. Gaeremynck *et al.* (2008) find no relationships between the size of the audit firm's client portfolio and measures of audit quality.

Auditor independence

The second component in DeAngelo's model of audit quality is the likelihood that an auditor will uncover material misstatements and weaknesses in the audit report. This likelihood depends on professional scepticism, objectivity and independence. The threats to independence in the private sector are somewhat different compared to those related to public companies. In general, auditors of private companies audit predominantly small companies, and fees from auditing and NAS from a single client are unlikely to significantly impact an auditor's total compensation. At the same time, the risks of litigation and loss of reputation that act as guards of independence for public companies are substantially lower in private companies. As the expected cost caused by loss of reputation and litigation falls, lower future fees are necessary in order for the auditor to be willing to compromise integrity. Furthermore, since the fees from auditing may be limited, future fees from providing NAS may become more important. Social bonding due to long-standing relationships between the auditor and client may reinforce the risk of impaired independence, particularly if the auditor provides NAS and assumes to a larger extent a managerial role. However, whether impaired independence due to economic and social bonding results in reduced audit quality is uncertain since better client-specific knowledge may increase the auditors' ability to deliver audits of high quality.

A few private company studies analyze auditor independence and no indication of impaired independence is documented, whether caused by social or economic bonding. The results in Venkatamaran and Rama (2004) suggest that auditors are most susceptible to be influenced by the clients in the early years of the engagement and that long auditor tenures do not adversely affect audit quality. Davis *et al.* (1993) find that purchasers of NAS require more audit effort, but report no evidence that auditors would compromise their independence for these clients. Hope and Langli (2010) find no association between auditors' fees and audit quality, while Svanström (2012) documents a *positive* association between provision of NAS and audit quality.

Audit quality inferred from proxy measures

For public companies, it is well documented that there are quality differences between audit firms, and that large audit firms, typically operationalized as the Big N audit firms, provide audits of higher quality than other auditors (Knechel *et al.* 2013). The evidence in the private company setting is sparse in comparison.[3]

Financial reporting quality

High quality auditors should promote high financial reporting quality, for instance by preventing earnings management. Vander Bauwhede and Willekens (2004) found no evidence that clients of Big N auditors engaged less in earnings management than did clients of other auditors. However, Vander Bauwhede *et al.* (2003) reported that Big N auditors constrained income-decreasing earnings management to a higher extent than did non-Big N auditors, but no differences were found for income-increasing earnings management. Van Tendeloo and Vanstraelen (2008) documented lower levels of earnings management among clients of Big N auditors compared to clients of other auditors in high book-tax alignment countries (Belgium, France, Finland, Spain), but no such evidence was found in low book-tax alignment countries (UK and Netherlands). Van Tendeloo and Vanstraelen (2008) suggest that Big N auditors constrain earnings management in high-tax alignment countries because financial statements are more closely scrutinized by tax authorities in these countries. As such, the likelihood of detecting audit failures is higher in high-tax alignment countries, which gives Big N audit firms stronger incentives to restrain companies from aggressive earnings management in order to protect their own reputation. The argument that auditors take reputation and litigation risk into account when auditing private companies is also supported by Cano-Rodrígues (2010), Ajona *et al.* (2008) and Gaeremynck *et al.* (2008).

The accuracy of the audit report

Upon completion of the audit, the auditor issues an audit report that is publicly available. Researchers have been particularly interested in the accuracy of the reports with respect to going concern qualifications. Evidence suggests that Big N auditors more often issue going concern reports, consistent with protecting themselves from the risk described above (Keasey *et al.* 1988; Ireland 2003; Ajona *et al.* 2008). Gaeremynck and Willekens (2003) document no difference between Big N and non-Big N auditors when analyzing auditees going bankrupt. However, when analyzing companies that liquidate voluntarily, their results suggest Big N auditors being more sophisticated in detecting companies with financial problems.[4]

Regulatory sanctions

Quality differences between auditors may also be studied by analyzing disciplinary sanctions from public oversight boards against auditors. Sundgren and Svanström (2013) find that auditors of non-Big N audit firms working at larger offices were significantly less likely to be subject to disciplinary sanctions compared with auditors at smaller offices. For Big N audit firms, there was no relationship between office size and disciplinary sanctions.

Audit fees

There is ample evidence using public company data that large auditors charge significantly higher fees than smaller auditors (Causholli *et al.* 2010). The fee premium can be caused by for example: lack of competition among auditors; reputation and brand name effects; higher quality audits; higher production cost, better trained staff and more advanced technology; and higher potential losses in the event of litigation (large audit firms have 'deep pockets') (Chaney *et al.* 2004; Clatworthy *et al.* 2009). Compared with studying audit fees in public companies, analyzing the fee premium in private companies significantly reduces the effects that 'deep pockets', litigation risk, loss of reputation, and market concentration have on fees, since non-listed clients reduce litigation and reputation risk, and market concentration is of less concern. However, the results indicate that large audit firms earn higher fees also in the private sector (Willekens and Achmadi 2003; Clatworthy *et al.* 2009; Dutillieux and Willekens 2009; Hope *et al.* 2012; Sundgren and Svanström 2012) and that industry specialists (Big N as well as non-Big N) earn higher fees than non-specialists (Dutillieux and Willekens 2009).[5]

Access to credit, financing costs and credit ratings

Most private companies need external financing, and their ability to raise equity may be limited by e.g. insufficient private wealth or reluctance to open up for new owners by selling shares. Therefore, access to credit can be of vital importance. Researchers have investigated whether engaging an auditor in a voluntarily audit regime, or engaging a high quality auditor in a statutory audit regime, eases auditee access to credit or lowers the financing costs.

Hope *et al.* (2011) use survey data from 68 countries and find that audited financial information is associated with lower perceived financing constraints. Allee and Yohn (2009) document that audited financial statements reduces the probability of having a loan denied compared to companies with non-audited financial statements.

One effect of reduced agency costs from auditing is that it reduces financiers' lending costs. In a competitive market, this reduction will be passed on to lenders. Thus companies that voluntarily engage an external auditor are expected to obtain loans at lower interest rates than companies without an auditor. Lower interest rates for companies that voluntarily subject themselves to auditing are documented in Blackwell *et al.* (1998), Minnis (2011) and Kim *et al.* (2011), but not in Allee and Yohn (2009) and Cassar (2011). In regimes with statutory auditing, Karjalainen (2011) and Cano-Rodriguez and Alegria (2012) find that Big N auditors are associated with lower interest rates. Thus, the majority of studies indicate that voluntarily engaging an auditor (or a high quality auditor when auditing is mandatory) ease companies' access to credit and reduce interest rates.

Lennox and Pittman (2011) utilize the change in audit regulation in the UK in 2004 that made it possible for a number of private companies for the first time to opt out of an audit. Results show that companies that remain audited receive a significant upgrade in credit rating while those that opt out get an even larger downgrade. Since there is no change in the assurance effect of auditing for those that remain audited, the upgrade can be attributed to a signalling effect (i.e. the willingness to be audited). The opt-out companies were less likely to appoint Big N auditors and paid lower audit fees under the mandatory regime relative to the companies that remained audited. The authors suggest that the benefits from requiring these companies to be audited are likely to be small since they privately contract for a low level of audit assurance when audits are legally required. The notion that auditing matters and is valued by credit rating agencies is further supported by Zerni *et al.* (2012). The positive effect of engaging a high quality auditor is also supported by De Franco *et al.* (2011) who find that owners of a firm who sell all shares or assets obtain significantly higher proceeds if the firm is audited by a Big N auditor.

Auditor choice and client characteristics

The reasons why companies voluntarily engage an auditor, or choose a specific auditor type in a statutory auditing regime, are complex and likely to vary across companies and countries. Many of the characteristics that are associated with auditor choices in public companies are also relevant for private companies, but there are noteworthy differences.

Similar to findings on public companies, research on private companies documents positive associations between voluntarily hiring an auditor or a high quality auditor, and agency conflicts (e.g. Carey *et al.* 2000; Knechel *et al.* 2008). However, because of greater variation in the data, the private company setting has enabled researchers to advance our understanding of agency conflicts beyond what is possible when using public companies. Lennox (2005) reports that the demand for high quality auditors is highest both at the low and at the high end region of managerial ownership because of the divergence-of-interest effects in the tails and the entrenchment effect within intermediate regions of CEO ownership. Hope *et al.* (2012) find that the likelihood of choosing a Big N auditor decreases with concentrated ownership, the size of the second largest owner, and family relationships between the board and the largest owner.

Due to the multifaceted value of auditing, an audit may be demanded for reasons other than reducing agency costs. The positive relationship between firm size and the voluntary hiring of an auditor (Collis *et al.* 2004; Francis *et al.* 2011; Niemi *et al.* 2012) could be caused by auditing generating a more multidimensional value for larger and more complex companies (Abdel-Khalik 1993; Knechel *et al.* 2008). Collis *et al.* (2004) show that for small companies the main users of statutory accounts are the directors and that the primary determinants of auditing are managers' perceptions of the degree to which audits improve the quality of information and provide a check on internal records. Even though the evidence is limited, the results suggest that in private companies audits have a wider function than just being a monitoring device for controls of agency conflicts.

Future research

The review above shows that the available research covers a limited set of topics. Given the importance of private companies, more research should be directed towards understanding the role played by financial statements and auditors. What are the costs and benefits of auditing? When should auditing be made mandatory? How do audit firms, audit offices and individual partners perform their audit? How important are auditing standards and audit procedures compared to characteristics of the individual auditor or members of the audit team? There are numerous questions that should be addressed, and the reviews and frameworks in e.g. Eilifsen and Willekens (2008), Francis (2011) and Knechel *et al.* (2013) provide useful suggestions for future research.

In pursuing private company auditing research, we believe it is decisive to carefully consider the impact of the greater heterogeneity that exists in the private sector. Furthermore, researchers need to address issues with theories and tests that embrace the particularities of private companies in institutional settings and environments that differ from country to country.

For the most part the available empirical evidence deals with topics that have been addressed for public companies (adjusted for the particularities of the private company setting). This is a valid and important approach due to the need to verify if findings for public companies are generalizable to private companies. However, such a strategy does not take full advantage of the unique opportunities provided by the private sector, such as lower level of market concentration, different auditor incentives, and overall a greater flexibility. Thus, we call for greater ingenuity in the choices of topics and research designs.

Data on private company may be harder to obtain than public company data. This calls for a wider search for available data sources. For instance do banks, credit agencies, tax authorities and other governmental agencies and international organizations collect data which should be utilized by researchers?[6] Another option is to collect data through surveys or field research. Cooperation with audit firms and regulatory bodies may also give access to new and relevant data (it may be easier to guarantee anonymity as there are many more audit firms and auditees).

Summary

In this chapter, we highlight the differences between audits of private and public companies and review and synthesize the relatively sparse empirical evidence on audits of private companies. Existing studies have used data from countries that differ with regard to important factors such as investor protection, tort law, market concentration among auditors, regulatory oversight of auditors and the relationship between accounting rules and taxation. The topics covered by the researchers are fragmented compared to public company research and it is an unresolved question as to what extent results are country specific.

The fragmented evidence makes it premature to generalize. However, the majority of the evidence suggests that Big N firms are more sophisticated, charge higher fees than non-Big N firms, and that the Big N firms' incentives to deliver audits of higher quality increase with the extent to which the auditee exposes the audit firm to risk. Furthermore, results indicate that auditors increase their effort with higher level of agency conflicts, and that provision of NAS have no negative effect (or perhaps a positive effect) on audit quality. The perception that large audit firms deliver audits of higher quality than do small audit firms does not receive unanimous support.

The benefits of private company audits are multifaceted and vary considerably across companies. While agency factors are important drivers of voluntary audits and the choice of high quality auditors, there are also other drivers. The evidence suggests that voluntary audit eases access to credit, reduces the cost of capital and improves credit ratings; and can also to some extent be of internal value to the auditee.

The private company setting is different from that of the more homogeneous public company. This makes it necessary to verify the generalizability of results from public company studies. The uniqueness of the private company setting also provides researchers with opportunities to investigate questions that cannot be addressed using public company data. Some of these questions may provide regulators with useful insights; for instance related to the provision of NAS (no detrimental effect of NAS has so far been found), the imposition of statutory auditing (which suppresses companies' abilities to signal their type because they are denied the option of voluntarily engaging an auditor) and the costs and benefits of auditing. Thus, by exploiting the particularities of the private sector, we believe there is potential for advancing our understanding of the role of auditing for both public and private companies.

Notes

1 By public companies we mean firms that sell stocks or bonds to individual investors in public markets or have their stocks or bonds traded in organized markets. Private companies are non-public companies. The legal definition of public companies varies between jurisdictions, and in many countries public companies encompass more firms than those that are listed (Nobes 2010). Businesses may be organized in different legal forms and for non-listed firms a variety of legal forms are possible subject to national legislation. We restrict our discussion to firms with limited liability in order to facilitate the exposition. For the same reason we disregard not-for-profit organizations, municipalities, and firms that operate in industries with specific regulation due to their significance to the society or because they hold assets for a broad group of outsiders (e.g. financial institutions as banks and insurance companies, utilities, trade unions and charities).

2 The Big N's market share is over 90 percent of public companies in most EU member states (ESCP Europe 2011) and 98 percent among the 1,500 largest public US firms (Government Accounting Office 2008). When public and private companies are viewed as a whole, the market share of Big N firms is less than 26 percent in 19 EU member states and between 35 and 44 percent in Denmark, Luxembourg, Sweden and the UK (ESCP Europe 2011).

3 Eilifsen and Willekens (2008) review the European evidence prior to 2007 and we refer to their study for a more thorough coverage of the European evidence.

4 The results in Hope *et al.* (2012) also indicate that Big-N auditors are more sophisticated.

5 Chaney *et al.* (2004) analyze the fee premium in the UK and the existence of the fee premium depends on the estimation method employed.

6 With the exception of Hope *et al.* (2011), who use data from 68 countries, the empirical evidence we cover in this chapter uses data from Belgium, Korea, Finland, France, the Netherlands, New Zealand, Norway, Spain, Sweden, UK, and US.

References

Abdel-Khalik, A. R. 1993. 'Why Do Private Companies Demand Auditing? A Case for Organizational Loss of Control', *Journal of Accounting, Auditing & Finance* 8(1): 31–52.

Ajona, L. A., F. L. Dallo, and S. S. Alegría, 2008. 'Discretionary Accruals and Auditor Behaviour in Code-law Contexts: An Application to Failing Spanish Firms', *European Accounting Review* 17(4): 641–66.

Allee, K. D. and T. L. Yohn, 2009. 'The Demand for Financial Statements in an Unregulated Environment: An Examination of the Production and use of Financial Statements by Privately Held Small Businesses', *The Accounting Review* 84(1): 1–25.

Blackwell, D., T. Noland, and D. Winters, 1998. 'The Value of Auditor Assurance: Evidence from Loan Pricing', *Journal of Accounting Research* 36: 57–70.

Cano-Rodriguez, M., 2010. 'Big Auditors, Private Firms and Accounting Conservatism: Spanish Evidence', *European Accounting Review* 19(1): 131–59.

Cano-Rodriguez, M. and S. S. Alegria, 2012. 'The Value of Audit Quality in Public and Private Companies: Evidence from Spain', *Journal of Management & Governance* 16(4): 683–706.

Carey, P., R. Simnett, and G. Tanewski, 2000. 'Voluntary Demand for Internal and External Auditing by Family Businesses', *Auditing: A Journal of Practice and Theory* 19(Supplement): 37–51.

Cassar, G., 2011. Discussion of the Value of Financial Statement Verification in Debt Financing: Evidence from Private U.S. Firms. *Journal of Accounting Research* 49(2): 507–28.

Causholli, M., M. de Martinis, D. Hay, and W. R. Knechel, 2010. 'Audit Markets, Fees and Production: Towards an Integrated View of Empirical Audit Research', *Journal of Accounting Literature* 29: 167–215.

Chaney P., D. Jeter, and L. Shivakumar, 2004. 'Self-selection of Auditors and Audit Pricing in Private Firms', *The Accounting Review* 79(1): 51–72.

Clatworthy, M. A., G. H. Makepeace, and M. J. Peel, 2009. 'Selection Bias and the Big Four Premium: New Evidence using Heckman and Matching Models', *Accounting and Business Research* 39(2): 139–66.

Collis, J., R. Jarvis, and L. Skerratt, 2004. 'The Demand for the Audit in Small Companies in the UK', *Accounting and Business Research* 34(2): 87–100.

Coram, P., J. Ng, and D. R. Woodliff, 2004. 'The Effect of Risk of Misstatement on the Propensity to Commit Reduced Audit Quality Acts under Time Budget Pressure', *Auditing: A Journal of Practice & Theory* 23(2): 159–67.

Davis, L. R., D. N. Ricchiute, and G.Trumpeter, 1993. 'Audit Effort, Audit Fees and the Provision of Nonaudit Services to Audit Clients', *The Accounting Review* 68 (1): 35–50.

De Franco, G., I. Gavious, J. Y. Jin, and G. D. Richardson, 2011. 'Do Private Company Targets that Hire Big 4 Auditors Receive Higher Proceeds?', *Contemporary Accounting Research* 28(1): 215–62.

DeAngelo, L., 1981. 'Auditor Size and Audit Quality', *Journal of Accounting and Economics* 3: 183–99.

Dutillieux, W. and M. Willekens, 2009. 'The Effect of Auditor Industry Specialization on Audit Pricing in Belgium', *Review of Business and Economics* 54(2): 129–46.

Eilifsen, A. and M. Willekens, 2008. 'In the Name of Trust: Some Thoughts about Trust, Audit Quality and Audit Regulation in Europe', in R. Quick, S. Turley and M. Willekens (eds) *Auditing, Trust and Governance – Developing Regulation in Europe,* pp. 1–18. Oxford: Routledge.

ESCP Europe, 2011. 'Study on the Effects of the Implementation of the Acquis on Statutory Audits of Annual and Consolidated Accounts including the Consequences on the Audit Market', final Report, 9 November. Paris: ESCP Europe.

European Commission (EC), 2010. 'Green Paper: Audit Policy: Lessons from the Crisis'. Brussels: EC.

Francis, J. R., 2011. 'A Framework for Understanding and Researching Audit Quality', *Auditing: A Journal of Practice & Theory* 30(2): 125–52.

Francis, J. R., I. K. Khurana, X. Martin, and R. Pereira, 2011. 'The Relative Importance of Firm Incentives versus Country Factors in the Demand for Assurance Services by Private Entities', *Contemporary Accounting Research* 28(2): 487–516.

Gaeremynck, A. and M. Willekens, 2003. 'The Endogenous Relationship between Audit-report Type and Business Termination: Evidence on Private Firms in a non-Litigious Environment', *Accounting and Business Research* 33(1): 65–79.

Gaeremynck, A., S. Van Der Meulen and M. Willekens, 2008. 'Audit Portfolio Characteristics and Client Financial Reporting Quality', *European Accounting Review* 17(2): 243–70.

Government Accountability Office (GAO), 2008. *Audits of Public Companies: Continued Concentration in Audit Market for Large Public Companies Does Not Call for Immediate Action*, Washington DC: United States GAO.

Hay, D. and D. Jeter, 2011. 'The Pricing of Industry Specialization by Auditors in New Zealand', *Accounting and Business Research* 41(2): 171–95.

Hope, O.-K. and J. C. Langli, 2010. 'Auditor Independence in a Private Firm and Low Litigation Setting', *The Accounting Review* 85(2): 573–605.

Hope, O.-K., W. B. Thomas, and D. Vyas, 2011. 'Financial Credibility, Ownership and Financing Constraints in Private Firms', *Journal of International Business Studies* 42: 935–57.

Hope, O.-K., J. C. Langli, and W. B. Thomas, 2012. 'Agency Conflicts and Auditing in Private Firms', *Accounting, Organizations, and Society* 37: 500–17.

Ireland, J., 2003. 'An Emprical Investigation of Determinants of Audit Reports in the UK', *Journal of Business Finance and Accounting* 30(7–8): 975–1016.

Johnson, E., I. K. Khurana, and K. J. Reynolds, 2002. 'Audit-firm Tenure and the Quality of Financial Reports', *Contemporary Accounting Research* 19(4): 637–60.

Karjalainen, J., 2011. 'Audit Quality and Cost of Debt Capital for Private Firms: Evidence from Finland', *International Journal of Auditing* 15: 88–108.

Keasey, K., R. Watson, and P. Wynarczyk, 1988. 'The Small Company Audit Qualification: A Preliminary Investigation', *Accounting and Business Research* 18(72): 323–33.

Kim, J.-B., D. A. Simunic, M. T. Stein, and C. H. Yi, 2011. 'Voluntary Audits and the Cost of Debt Capital for Privately Held Firms: Korean Evidence', *Contemporary Accounting Research* 28(2): 585–615.

Knechel, W. R. and A.Vanstraelen, 2007. 'The Relationship between Auditor Tenure and Audit Quality Implied by Going Concern Opinions', *Auditing: A Journal of Practice and Theory* 26(1): 113–31.

Knechel, W. R., L. Niemi, and S. Sundgren, 2008. 'Determinants of Auditor Choice: Evidence from a Small Client Market', *International Journal of Auditing* 12: 65–88.

Knechel, W. R., G. V. Krishnan, M. B. Pevzner, L. Shefchik, and U. Velury, 2013. 'Audit Quality: Insights from the Academic Literature', *Auditing: A Journal of Practice & Theory* 32(Supplement 1): 385–421.

Lennox, C., 2005. 'Management Ownership and Audit Firm Size', *Contemporary Accounting Research* 22(1): 205–27.

Lennox, C. S. and J. A. Pittman, 2011. 'Voluntary Audits versus Mandatory Audits', *The Accounting Review* 86(5): 1655–78.

López, D. and G. F. Peters, 2012. 'The Effect of Workload Compression on Audit Quality', *Auditing: A Journal of Practice & Theory* 31(4): 139–65.

Minnis, M., 2011. 'The Value of Financial Statement Verification in Debt Financing: Evidence from Private Firms', *Journal of Accounting Research* 49: 457–506.

Niemi, L., J. Kinnunen, H. Ojala, and P. Troberg, 2012. 'Drivers of Voluntary Audits in Finland: To be Audited or Not?', *Accounting and Business Research* 42(2): 169–96.

Nobes, C., 2010. 'On Researching into the Use of IFRS by Private Entities in Europe', *Accounting in Europe* 7(1): 213–17.

Sundgren, S. and T. Svanström, 2013. 'Audit Office Size, Audit Quality, and Audit Pricing: Evidence from Private Firms', *Accounting and Business Research* 43(1): 31–55.

Sundgren, S. and T. Svanström, 2014. 'Auditor-in-charge Characteristics and Going Concern Reporting', *Contemporary Accounting Research*, doi: 10.1111/1911-3846.12035.

Svanström, T., 2012. 'Non-audit Services and Audit Quality: Evidence from Private Firms', *European Accounting Review* 22(2): 337–66.

Svanström, T. and S. Sundgren, 2012. 'The Demand for Non-audit Services and Auditor-Client Relationships – Evidence from Swedish Small and Medium-sized Companies', *International Journal of Auditing* 16: 54–78.

Van Tendeloo, B. and A. Vanstraelen, 2008. 'Earnings Management and Audit Quality in Europe: Evidence from the Private Client Segment Market', *European Accounting Review* 17(3): 447–69.

Vander Bauwhede, H. and M. Willekens, 2004. 'Evidence on the Lack of Audit-quality Differentiation in the Private Client Segment of the Belgian Audit Market', *European Accounting Review* 13(3): 501–22.

Vander Bauwhede, H., M. Willekens, and A. Gaeremynck, 2003. 'Audit Firm Size, Public Ownership, and Firms' Discretionary Accruals Management', *International Journal of Accounting* 38(1): 1–22.

Venkatamaran, M. I. and D. V. Rama, 2004. 'Clients' Expectations on Audit Judgment: A Note', *Behavioural Research in Accounting* 16 (1): 63–74.

Willekens, M. and C. Achmadi, 2003. 'Pricing and Supplier Concentration in the Private Client Segment of the Audit Market: Market Power or Competition?', *International Journal of Accounting* 38: 431–55.

Wymenga, P., V. Spanikova, A. Barker, J. Konings, and E. Canton, 2012. *EU SMEs in 2012: at the Crossroads. Annual Report on Small and Medium-sized Enterprises in the EU, 2011/12.* Rotterdam: Ecorys.

Zerni, M., E. Haapama, T. Jarvinen, and L. Niemi, 2012. 'Do Joint Audits Improve Audit Quality? Evidence from Voluntary Joint Audits', *European Accounting Review* 21(4): 731–65.

Part II

The impact of regulation of auditing

13

Not just a standard story

The rise of international standards on auditing

Christopher Humphrey, Anne Loft and Anna Samsonova-Taddei

Introduction

> An outside observer who looks at matters from a global perspective would think of the need for uniform quality of audits as a necessary condition for a world economy and highly interconnected international markets.

The above statement, made by Stavros Thomadakis, the first Chairman of the Public Interest Oversight Board[1] (PIOB) of the International Federation of Accountants (IFAC), speaking in 2005, may appear obvious today, but it was not so obvious back in 1977 when IFAC was formed. The International Auditing Practices Committee (IAPC) that IFAC established to address auditing issues was arguably one of its most important committees. It set out to produce International Auditing Guidelines (IAGs) rather than standards. IAPC initially found that it was mostly developing and emerging economies that had an interest in the guidelines being developed. Such perceptions started gradually to change in the 1990s, when International Standards on Auditing (ISAs) replaced IAGs and some of IFAC's more prominent national professional associations (who were IFAC member bodies) started to consider them as legitimate competitors to their own national standards. The interest in ISAs was further fuelled by the Asian financial crisis of the late 1990s, the collapse of US energy giant Enron in 2001 and (subsequent) important structural changes within IFAC, including the reorganization in 2002 of IAPC into the International Auditing and Assurance Standards Board (IAASB).

Audit researchers and some standard setting bodies have recognized that audit quality is a socially constructed phenomenon (see Power, 1997; 2003; Humphrey, 2008; Holm and Zaman, 2012). Such recognition is significant for an analysis of the rise of international auditing standards, as it suggests strongly that attention needs to be focused on the way in which such standards have shaped and influenced what is accepted internationally as quality auditing practice. This requires consideration of the rise of IAASB, its growing status in the international financial regulatory arena, together with an analysis of the practical significance of ISAs and their influence on international audit practice. Accordingly, in this chapter, we first explore the rise of the IAASB on the global regulatory stage, where its only major visible 'competitor' is the

US Public Company Accounting Oversight Board (PCAOB) which issues auditing standards for US publicly listed companies.

The second half of the chapter focuses more explicitly on the capability of ISAs to reshape audit practice and redefine accepted notions of 'quality' auditing. We do this by considering both cases made in support of their adoption in particular national settings and issues arising from their application, including processes of compliance and translation, and encounters with different practice traditions, demands and contexts. We also discuss ongoing strategies and collaboration at national, regional (such as the EU) and international levels that serve to reinforce the application of ISAs. The chapter concludes by identifying a number of interesting and topical research and related public policy questions regarding audit practice development.

A world of standards, the world of ISAs

When audit practice standards were in their infancy, the largest and most highly respected audit firms internationally would have seen their practices as always being ahead of standards – the role of standards was to bring audit practice up to some common, basic level of practice; a professionally expected minimum above which the better firms could certainly be expected to be operating. Audit firms spoke of their own distinctive methodologies. At present, as Catasús *et al.* (2013) recently emphasized, the same leading international audit firms define and categorize their practices very directly as being in compliance with (international) standards on auditing. In short, standards matter these days (Knechel, 2010).

Modern ISAs are 'process' standards in the sense that they provide guidance on how to carry out various steps of the audit process with an implicit expectation that following such steps should enable an auditor to provide a high-quality service. ISAs are presented in groups. ISAs 200–299, for example, outline the auditors' responsibilities as well as the nature and general organization of an audit, including audit documentation and internal quality control. Other groups of ISAs provide technical guidance on specific aspects of the audit, such as audit planning (ISAs 300–499), evidence gathering (ISAs 500–599), using the work of others during the audit (ISAs 600–699), and the preparation of an auditor's report (ISAs 700–799).

Over the last 30–40 years, we have witnessed not just growth in the number of ISAs but also a rise in their significance and influence. The success of IAASB as a standard setter is evident from the fact that ISAs have been adopted, albeit in varying forms, by 126 countries around the world.[2] Additionally, the support of convergence of national audit standards with ISAs and the commitment to conducting transnational audits using policies and methodologies based on ISAs are central membership requirements of the Forum of Firms, a body formed in 2002 and of which the leading global firms and international network firms are members.[3]

Fraser[4] (2010) neatly summarizes key points frequently made in support of the ongoing global convergence towards a single set of standards. For instance, he stresses that the commercial world (and the world of auditing) is much more complex than in the past, with a growth in the global, integrated, interconnected nature of business, an increasing sophistication of IT systems, the substantially more complicated nature of accounting practices (given the need to account for an increasingly complicated set of investment products and associated asset values) and a larger number of (more detailed) auditing standards. The uneasy coexistence of different sets of national and international auditing standards is said to have had numerous unfortunate and costly consequences, with Fraser claiming that the work of both auditors and audit regulators/inspectors would be much easier and more effective if there was just one accepted worldwide set of auditing standards, with ISAs as set by IAASB being his preferred option. He justifies his position by emphasizing the number of international bodies that have formally endorsed ISAs and the support that ISAs received from a detailed academic study funded by the European Commission (EC) which had concluded that

> [o]n balance, an adoption of the clarified ISAs through the EU would contribute to the credibility and quality of financial statements and to audit quality in the EU, and to a greater acceptance of audit reports outside of their home jurisdictions within and outside of the EU.
>
> *(Duisberg-Essen, 2009: 9)*

A short history of a long rise to global significance – The case of IAASB

The notion of establishing international standards for accounting and auditing developed on the back of the growth of international trade in the 1960s and the resulting internationalizing tendencies in the accounting profession. In 1973, the International Accounting Standards Committee (IASC) was established with headquarters in London, while an international body for the development of international auditing guidance was established in 1977, shortly after the formation of IFAC, with a small secretariat based in New York. IAPC formally started its work in March 1978 with its terms of reference being to 'develop guidelines on generally accepted auditing practices, auditing procedures and methods, and the form and content of audit reports' (IAPC minutes, March 1978: 2) which would be 'helpful to member bodies of IFAC and in achieving the objective of a coordinated worldwide accountancy profession (1978: 7).[5]

The first IAG was released in 1980, entitled 'Objective and Scope of the Audit of Financial Statements'. IAPC met three times a year in different places around the world so that it could interact with local professional associations on a regular basis and promote the importance of IAGs. When Justin Fryer became the new chair in June 1985, he commented that he saw IAPC as an international committee deserving of international recognition, and that the first duty of the committee should be the interest of the public. He felt that the members should represent not just their home country but the public interest in general and was critical of the quality of certain existing guidelines. IAPC gradually developed interactions with international regulators, including the Basel Committee on Banking Supervision (BCBS), the United Nations and the International Organization of Securities Commissions (IOSCO), the body representing governmental regulators of securities markets (see Camfferman and Zeff, 2007). While the IASC attempted to get IOSCO recognition of IASs for cross-border listings, IFAC started to seek IOSCO recognition for its IAGs. Linked to this pursuit was the decision in 1991 (by which time IAPC had issued 28 IAGs) to rename existing guidelines and future statements as ISAs on the basis that the term 'standard' more appropriately reflected IFAC's position and authority. IAPC also committed itself to a major codification and assessment of these standards, with it being felt that the switch would improve perceptions as to the status of such documents and encourage their usage.

The second phase: 1992–2001

In 1992, IOSCO issued a resolution that recommended that members of IOSCO accept 24 specified ISAs (and three exposure drafts expected to be published as standards in 1993) as an 'acceptable basis for use in cross-border offerings and continuous reporting by foreign issuers'. IAPC duly issued in 1994 its updated codified version of ISAs. This had involved much committee work and sought to make the standards easier to understand and use. IOSCO, however, had chosen to express concern over the division of text in the standards between basic principles and essential procedures (identified by the use of bold black lettering) and related guidance and explanation.

IOSCO saw such a division as weakening the standards (claiming that a significant component now appeared to be advisory rather than mandatory), and deemed them to be insufficient for the audit of quoted companies with cross-border listings. IAPC (and IFAC) decided not to make the requisite changes and IOSCO's endorsement of ISAs duly lapsed, although discussions between the two bodies continued. In December 1996, the World Trade Organization (WTO) gave a significant boost to the effort to harmonize international accounting and auditing standards by issuing a statement of support for the work of IASC and IFAC and their capacity to provide benchmark international standards for the accountancy profession. In December 1996, in the wake of a major conference on the role of the statutory auditor in the EU, the EC decided to consider using ISAs as EU-wide auditing standards. A 1998 study by FEE (a representative body for the European accounting profession) subsequently showed that most European countries had either adopted ISAs as national standards or adapted them to suit their local circumstances.

However, the 1997–8 Asian crisis raised serious questions about the overall consistency and quality of the audits being undertaken in the region by the large international audit firms (Loft *et al.* 2006). It was also formally recognized that the work of IAPC was being hampered by a lack of funds and by being heavily dependent on the unpaid commitment of its committee members. In 1998, IAPC was granted 60 per cent more funds by IFAC (supported by the large firms) to assist with the development of its core standards. According to Jim Sylph, the first technical director of IFAC, his most pressing task on being appointed in 1999 was to recruit good international technical staff with whom he could work 'to get the agenda of IAPC (back) on track' for approval by IOSCO.[6] The Asian crisis brought calls for a new global financial architecture to prevent future financial crises as well as a system of global governance through the use of (global) standards. To coordinate this new financial 'architecture', a Financial Stability Forum (FSF) was established with a set of 12 recognized standards for enhancing financial stability, including IAPC's ISAs and IASB's IASs.

James Wolfensohn, then president of the World Bank, had made a particularly strong critique of the accounting profession in a speech to the 1997 World Accounting Congress in Paris, emphasizing the need for harmonized international standards (Wolfensohn, 1997). With related expressions of concern from international financial and regulatory agencies, IFAC made major strategic changes and sought to ensure that ISAs became more globally significant in terms of their practical operation and impact. Many countries were still using their own auditing standards, with the main take-up of ISAs being with developing and emerging economies. At an IFAC Board meeting in Edinburgh in May 2000, a new strategic plan was discussed, with one key element being to develop IAPC's position as a global standard setter. Commitments were made to put additional resources into audit standard setting and to revising the membership, operational and governance procedures of IAPC. The reforms were agreed in 2001, and the new IAASB formally began operating in April 2002, with a larger support staff and a full-time chair, John Kellas.

2002–14: The third phase and beyond

As the reform of IAASB was being finalized, the Enron scandal broke in late 2001. IFAC adopted a relatively quiet profile in the immediate aftermath of the scandal but, as revelations of poor audit work grew and Enron's auditor Arthur Andersen collapsed, it became clear that further fundamental reform was required at IFAC. In January 2003, IFAC brought together the chief executives of various IFAC member bodies and others to discuss IFAC's strategic direction and it was agreed that high-quality standard setting and international regulatory endorsement for ISA had to be assigned the highest priority. In February 2003, a meeting was held between IFAC and representatives of the international regulatory community drawn from IOSCO, the BCBS, the International Association of Insurance Supervisors (IAIS), the FSF, the EC and the World Bank. This group (duly becoming known as the 'Monitoring Group'), exerted pressure on IFAC for improvements to be made in international audits, setting in motion a move from self-regulation to independent oversight (see Loft *et al.*, 2006).

In 2003–4, regulatory agencies and institutions such as the FSF and the EC were pressing for greater public oversight of international audit standard setting and the creation of an independent, external body acting in the public interest to oversee the work of the IAASB. The EC, for example, emphasized the need for ISAs to be 'developed with proper due process, public oversight and transparency'; IFAC's governance arrangements had to be deemed to be adequate to ensure the pursuit of the public interest, with ISAs having to be 'conducive to the European public good' (EC, 2004: 7).

In response to such calls, and in order to retain IAASB within its organizational structures, IFAC instigated further reform (see IFAC, 2003) which established, in 2005, a PIOB to serve as an independent body charged with the oversight of the public interest activities of IFAC. IFAC's reform document also regularly emphasized the need to be responsive to the public interest agendas and to achieve a 'global convergence to high quality standards'. IFAC's increasing reference to serving the public interest is one example of the strategies that standard setting organizations such as IAASB rely on in an attempt to gain greater recognition of their standards by potential adopters and regulators (Schockaert and Houyoux, 2007; see also Jeppesen (2010) for similar trends in audit standard setting in Denmark).

In 2004, IAASB began a comprehensive programme to enhance the clarity of ISAs. The aim of the 'Clarity Project', as it was called, was to update all the ISAs in a consistent format such that the requirement of each standard and the obligations on auditors were clear. In the process of carrying out this project, more than half of the 36 ISAs were subject not just to clarification, but also to substantive changes to improve practice. The Clarity Project was completed early in 2009, with the clarified standards being effective for the audits of financial statements for periods beginning on or after 15 December 2009.

In the wake of the completion of the Clarity Project, IOSCO, in June 2009, finally endorsed the ISAs for cross-border offerings and listings. IOSCO itself has limited enforcement powers over its members, and thus it is not certain that all countries will follow the recommendation. One important player that is not following ISAs is the US. The Securities Exchange Commission (SEC) has not endorsed ISAs for the audit of listed companies in the US, with approved auditing standards being set by the PCAOB. The establishment of the PIOB and the issuing of clarified ISAs did bring ISAs closer to being endorsed as EU-wide accepted auditing standards but the matter is still not totally resolved. In its 2006 Statutory Audit Directive (Directive 2006/43/EC), the EC had appeared positive towards ISAs, stating in Article 26 of the Directive that 'Member States shall require statutory auditors and audit firms to carry out statutory audits in compliance with international auditing standards adopted by the Commission'. However, the additional (above noted) demands by the Commission (for the ISAs to be developed with proper due process, public oversight and transparency, generally accepted internationally, and conducive to the European public good), do appear to have been a considerable stumbling block to their official, practical endorsement by the EU.

By 2008 a new (global) financial crisis had hit. While to start with this had little effect on the auditing profession, as the crisis grew, the role of auditors was seriously questioned (see Humphrey *et al.*, 2009). The new EU Commissioner, Michel Barnier, weighed in at this time with an agenda for a 'real debate at European level on the subject of audit' and an accompanying new Green Paper (see Humphrey *et al.*, 2011). The radical nature of the Green Paper came as something of a shock to the auditing profession as the new Statutory Audit Directive had only been finalized in 2010. The Green Paper put a range of auditing topics firmly on the regulatory agenda, including compulsory rotation of audit firms and proposals to split the Big 4 up into smaller entities so as to bring more competition to the audit market. Following extensive discussion and consultation, revised EC proposals were issued and duly debated further, with a preliminary agreement on the framework of EU audit reform not being reached until late December 2013 between the trialogue of the EU Council Presidency, the European Parliament and the EC.[7] The agreed regulatory changes are less exacting than initially constructed,[8] but Commissioner Barnier still welcomed the agreement, calling it 'a first step towards increasing audit quality and re-establishing investor confidence in financial information' and emphasizing that it 'is now high time for auditors to meet the challenges of their role – a societal role'.[9]

From the point of view of IAASB, the most important item on the EU agenda for reform of auditing was the acceptance of ISA as the standards for audits in the EU. In the press release announcing the agreement, Barnier was noted as particularly welcoming 'the agreement on the harmonization of the international standards on auditing (ISAs)' (see http://europa.eu/rapid/press-release_MEMO-13-1171_en.htm?locale=en (accessed 2 February 2014)). The amended Directive on Statutory Audit retains the various clauses of the original 2006 Directive, requiring ISAs to be developed with proper due process and public oversight and in accordance with the European (now stated as 'Union') public good and continues to note that ISAs may be applied in a proportionate fashion in the case of the audits of smaller entities. However, the tone of the amended Directive is stronger in terms of the general utilization of ISAs, with the revised Article 26 speaking of the EC being 'empowered' to adopt ISAs, rather than, as previously stated, saying that it 'may decide on the applicability' of ISAs.

There is no utilization of the term 'carve out', as there was in Article 26 in the 2006 Directive, when discussing the capacity, in exceptional circumstances, of Member States choosing not to apply elements of ISAs – with the received impression here being more clearly one of 'ISA plus' rather than 'ISA less'. The amended Directive also talks of the Commission continuing 'to be involved in the monitoring of the content of the international auditing standards and the process for their adoption by the International Federation of Accountants (IFAC)' (para. 12), but no longer explicitly states that 'a technical committee or group on auditing should assist the Commission in the assessment of the technical soundness of all the international auditing standards' (para. 13 of the 2006 Directive). Related to these events, the EU has agreed to contribute resources to IFAC's International Public Interest Oversight Board (PIOB), a move which is further indicative of the EU's recognition of ISAs and the accompanying work and standing of IAASB.

One of the most important technical projects in which IAASB has been involved since the Clarity Project is dealing with revisions to standard audit reporting formats, an initiative driven by the belief that the audit report could be more informative. The IAASB has badged its proposals for a new, longer form audit report as a direct response to 'calls from investors, analysts, and other users of financial statements in the wake of the global financial crisis for the auditor to provide more relevant information in the auditor's report' (IAASB, 2013).[10] At the time of writing, IAASB is studying comments on the latest Exposure Draft on this issue with plans to issue revised audit reporting standards later in 2014. It is a fascinating project in the context of audit standard setting, inviting debate as to whether the value of the audit is strengthened or undermined by an enhanced capacity for auditors to demonstrate more clearly the nature of (and potential difference in) their professional judgments.[11]

The above acknowledgement of the importance of responding to public demand is consistent with what, over the years, has become a very clearly stated intent on the part of IAASB – namely, to serve the public interest. IAASB's recently published proposed strategy for 2015–19, entitled 'Fulfilling our Public Interest Mandate in an Evolving World', saw this commitment as now having three key objectives: to develop and maintain high-quality ISAs that are accepted as the basis for high-quality financial statement audits; to ensure IAASB's suite of standards continues to be relevant in a changing world by responding to stakeholder needs; and to collaborate and cooperate with contributors to the financial reporting supply chain to foster audit quality and stay informed.[12] In the accompanying press release, IAASB chair, Arnold Schilder,[13] commented that:

> Stakeholders internationally expect the IAASB to not only produce high-quality standards ... but also to carry out its efforts in coordination and cooperation with key stakeholders so that the standards it develops can achieve global acceptance and work, and can be seen to work, internationally ... Our strategic objectives help meet these important expectations and provide the basis upon which the IAASB can effectively identify and respond to the most pertinent public interest issues.
>
> *(IAASB 2013: 1)*

According to the United Nations Conference on Trade and Development (UNCTAD) (2008), a key dimension to IAASB's public interest orientation has been to reform the process by which ISAs are set. UNCTAD observed that IAASB

> has implemented a number of changes to its processes with a view to becoming one of the most transparent standard setters in the world. IAASB's meetings are open to the public, and agenda papers, meeting summaries, and final pronouncements are freely available on its website. Visitors can download audio recordings of IAASB meetings, exposure drafts of proposed standards and other consultative documents, and view all comments received on those documents. ... IAASB has made public interest input into its standard-setting process a priority. It has established a formal Consultative Advisory Group (CAG) to provide it with broad-based and continuous input on its work programme, project priorities and technical issues.
>
> *(UNCTAD, 2008: paras 16–17)*[14]

The reform process at IAASB (and IFAC more generally) has been subject to a considerable degree of analysis, particularly in terms of the shifting reliance on experts as against operational and governance modes that prioritize geographical representation, and the contrast between appeals to transparency and the growing institutional influence of the large global accounting firms (for discussions, see Loft *et al.*, 2006; Humphrey and Loft, 2009). Any diversity of views regarding the strength of stated public interest commitments, however, contrasts with a widespread acknowledgement that assessments of standard setting processes have to be accompanied by consideration of levels of compliance with standards and it is to this issue that we now turn.

Considering the impact of ISAs

Any attempt to provide a definitive view of the impact of ISAs on the field of audit practice is always likely to be fraught with difficulties given that there is such a diversity of opinion, subjectivity, and even lack of understanding about the concept of audit quality. As Knechel *et al.*'s (2013) review of the insights provided by the academic literature on audit quality opens up 'Audit quality is much debated but little understood. Despite more than two decades of research, there remains little consensus about how to define, let alone measure, audit quality' (2013: 385). After a detailed analysis and categorization of such research, Knechel *et al.* concluded that

> there is little consensus about how to define audit quality and various frameworks and disclosures that exist are incomplete. The range of definitions is quite broad because they focus on different attributes of the audit, such as outcomes, processes and judgments.
>
> *(Knechel* et al. *2013: 407)*

Further, it also has to be acknowledged that despite the volume of research on audit quality, studies of the particular impact of auditing standards, and more precisely ISAs, are quite limited in number.

A pertinent illustration of the difficulties in making formal assessments of the impact of standards on audit quality is provided by Catasús *et al.* (2013) in their reflections on the lack of innovation in auditing practice and review of the first ever global survey of inspection findings (covering 22 national audit inspection bodies), published by the International Forum of Independent Audit Regulators (IFIAR, 2012). This survey concluded that audit firms globally needed to do more to improve the consistency of auditor performance and to operationalize enhanced levels of professional scepticism. Of critical importance here is the way in which IFIAR defines an 'inspection finding'.[15] As Catasús *et al.*, (2013: 50) highlighted, findings for IFIAR are not about positive or innovative audit practice but about 'where the auditor did not perform sufficient work to meet the applicable auditing standards and other related requirements ... (with the corollary that). ... a finding should not be interpreted to imply that the financial statements were necessarily materially misstated' (IFIAR, 2012: 6). They also noted the observations of Bedard *et al.* (2010) that internal audit firm inspections outnumber PCAOB inspections by a multiple of four or five, and concluded that the realities of audit practice seem to be

> dominated by a concern with compliance with standards and/or standard procedures ... the dominant focus appears to be one that is intent on avoiding deficient performance or justifying existing performance. Audits in compliance with standards or audits that set new standards of excellence are not ones that are of central concern; audit quality improvement looks to rest more in making deficient audits 'standard', not making 'standard' audits 'better'
>
> *(Catasús* et al. *2013: 55–6)*

Accordingly, it is important to recognize that an assessment of the impact of ISAs, whether by formal inspections or other means, is always likely to be partial or selective, dependent on the interests and the assumptions and perspectives adopted by those providing the assessment. In contemplating the practical impact of ISAs, we present in this second part of the chapter a series of reflections drawn from the auditing literature. We hope that such reflections and related analysis will provide a flavour of some of the dimensions across which the impact of ISAs can be considered – as well as helping to explain both our closing proposed research agenda and the primary sources of variation in the views and opinions that currently exist regarding the impact of, and support for, ISAs.

Deciding to endorse and/or adopt ISAs – and the push for global convergence

Probably one of the most vivid sources of evidence of the impact and quality of ISAs, or at least of possible frameworks for evaluating differences in audit quality across different standard-setting regimes, are the formal cases made for ISA adoption and the decision-making processes (and supporting material considered by policymakers) involved in making any formal, institutional endorsement of ISAs. In this regard, Simunic's (2003) analysis of the case for Canada to adopt ISAs is an exemplar of the issues that policymakers need to contemplate and assess. Simunic regarded ISAs as comprehensive in scope, and principles-based in nature, viewing them as meeting the essential elements of what the Canadian context would define as 'high quality' standards: 'Principles based standards serve to support and enhance the exercise of an auditor's professional judgement, while avoiding excessively prescriptive detail that can serve as an inappropriate substitute for well reasoned professional judgement' (Simunic, 2003: 13). He saw members of IAPC (now IAASB) as likely to be of high technical competence, with some outside representation on the standard setting board. He also saw the momentum behind ISAs as important, noting the substantial degree of support for ISAs across IFAC member bodies and drawing on a persuasive published commentary by Robert Roussey, a former IAPC chair (see Roussey, 1999). Roussey had reported that: a number of the large international accounting firms were now using ISAs as the basis for their worldwide practice standards, numerous regulatory bodies were now accepting financial statements audited using ISAs for regulatory filings; and that various international bodies had either endorsed or were working towards formal endorsement of ISAs. Simunic also saw it as particularly compelling that auditing standard setters in countries such as the UK, Netherlands and Australia had recently abandoned structures that saw them setting domestic auditing standards independent of ISAs, while emerging market economies (such as Russia and China) were choosing ISAs, modified for local conditions, as their domestic standards.

Attitudes towards the adoption of ISAs also appear to be shaped by a range of national and regional agendas and perspectives as to what counts as 'quality' standards. For example, Duhovnik (2012) argued that European-wide ISA adoption was vital for the relative standing of the European auditing profession, arguing that

> clarified ISAs are the best instrument available to unify the auditing approach in the European environment and to take the necessary second step after the endorsement of the IFRSs. If Europe waits for an alternative solution it may happen that, due to the time lag in its application, the overall quality of the European audit profession will be not on a par with the quality of audits in the rest of the world.
>
> *(Duhovnik, 2012: 138–9)*

From an alternative perspective, it has been said that the EU's experiences with IASB and an increasing politicization of the standard-setting arena, especially in terms of fair value accounting opt-outs in the financial services sector, may have made it that much more difficult to secure any endorsement of ISAs as issued by IAASB (Humphrey *et al.*, 2011; Smith-Lacroix *et al.*, 2012).[16]

Interestingly, this is despite clear evidence that ISAs have been adopted by many international auditing firms and by a good number of national standard setters in the EU.[17] This scale of support does suggest that the significance of the regional or national context to attempts to secure transnational reform extends well beyond arguments concerning the interested nature of private standard setting bodies. For instance, the PCAOB has been under some substantial pressure from the major audit firms to make a faster move towards convergence with ISAs.[18] However, such lobbying has not yet produced a response that the firms would render satisfactory and the PCAOB, despite promising to keep the possibility of ISA adoption under review as part of its post-2008 strategy, is holding a strong line with respect to the importance of having US auditing standards set by a US-based body. Interestingly, this is despite a study funded by the EC on the differences between clarified ISAs and PCAOB Auditing Standards (see MARC, 2009) finding that, notwithstanding frequently drawn contrasts between such standards, substantive differences were limited. The study concluded that 'the differences between US-based PCAOB auditing standards and the ISAs issued by IAASB may be less important than the actual practice of auditing based on those standards as subject to inspection and enforcement by regulators in different jurisdictions' (MARC, 2009: 9–10). In other words, processes of adoption and any subsequent impact of ISAs (or any other set of auditing standards) are going to depend significantly on the environment and context within which the standards are being applied, and not just their formal content.

Dimensions of variation in the utilization of ISAs: The importance of looking beyond the standards

The above urgings that quality auditing practice depends on more than the establishment and adoption of quality auditing standards emphasize the importance of studying the utilization of standards in (differing) practice environments. This opens up a number of additional ways of analysing the significance, development and application of ISAs.

For instance, through a tightly specified theoretical modelling approach, Simunic *et al.* (2013) conclude that different countries can be expected to have different preferences regarding the exactitude of auditing standards. Thus, countries with strict legal systems and a high degree of litigation risk for auditors will prefer quite strict auditing standards in order to induce 'optimal' audit quality, while countries with weak legal systems and less well developed auditing institutions can be expected to prefer vaguer, less tough standards. They conclude, in considering the global adoption of ISAs that 'imposing an initially non-optimal set of auditing standards on a country will require concurrent changes in the legal environment if those standards are expected to be effective (e.g. elicit auditor compliance with the rules)' (Simunic *et al.*, 2013: 22). While assumptions that 'optimal' levels of audit quality can be determined in any national audit regime are clearly highly questionable, the spirit of Simunic *et al.*'s analysis is interesting in that it introduces an alternative rhetoric (of a national compatibility of standards and of any associated field of audit practice) to stand alongside the claims that globalization necessitates the adoption of global standards. Their point is that global standards have to have a compatibility with the national audit regime and associated legal culture, and if such standards are introduced, the latter regime may well need to change to ensure that the maximum benefit is gained from such global adoption. Whether such changes are then, in turn, compatible with other national social and cultural characteristics and qualities is not considered by Simunic *et al.* but their work is an important reminder that standard setters, and those making the case for global convergence in auditing standards, must reflect critically on the potential unintended consequences of such calls (also see Hatherly (2009: 212) and Power (1997) for a discussion of the broader social impacts of audit).

Such considerations emphasize that deliberations on the relative quality of auditing standards need to retain a strong focus on the practice arena and patterns of practice development. There continues to be a serious need to

> undertake more detailed research examining the connections between individual standards and the regulatory context in which they are developed. A particularly crucial test here is not so much standard setting, but standard use and, in particular, enforcement ... While 'professional judgement' may well be an essentially indeterminate or subjective concept, it is capable of being shaped by particular contexts and influences – and a priority for those interested in the international standardization of practices such as auditing is to investigate how regulatory actions are, indeed, reconstructing and reshaping what is deemed to be 'legitimate' audit work and the exercising of 'appropriate' professional judgement.
>
> *(Humphrey and Loft, 2011: 122–3)*

Standards in auditing are very much about providing an outline, structuring of the audit process (even in regimes where the level of strictness or toughness is higher). In many jurisdictions, they are far removed from the type of manufacturing standards formulated to produce industrial 'nuts and bolts'. As Humphrey and Loft (2011), writing in an EU context, observed

> ISAs are strong on process and general procedures, but light on anything relating to the particular ways of exercising professional judgement as is required for the overall realization of the ISAs programme. The emphasis on professional judgement and skepticism in ISAs fits with the nature of principled-based standards, which require interpretation and elaboration before they can be used.
>
> *(Humphrey and Loft, 2011: 120)*

Further, professional judgement is only loosely defined under ISAs as 'the application of relevant training, knowledge, and experience, within the context provided by auditing, accounting and ethical standards, in making informed decisions about the courses of action that are appropriate in the circumstances of the audit engagement' (IFAC 2010: 26). Similarly, Knechel *et al.* (2013), writing in a US context, essentially represent auditing standards as a structuring process that attempts to compensate for or accommodate a range of uncertainties that confront the auditing function, but leaving open a considerable degree of scope for professional judgment and differentiation across audit teams.

Identifying research opportunities

From such an analytical position, the potential for research is vast. For instance, Peecher *et al.* (2013) have sought to build a new accountability framework for auditors as a way of motivating them to deliver higher quality audits and to facilitate the evaluations as to how well auditors are carrying out their duties. This involves rethinking the reward–penalty and outcome–process dimensions associated with existing auditor accountability frameworks and proposes various developments to incentivize auditors to exceed minimum quality thresholds for compliance and develop fraud-detection procedures. Underlying such analysis is a concern that current standard setting, regulatory and professional practice regimes are not delivering, or at least merit much more in-depth inquiry – concerns and conclusions delineated in numerous studies and surveys concerned with: shifting conceptions of audit quality (Humphrey, 2008); the effectiveness of independent regulatory oversight (see Humphrey, 2008; DeFond, 2010; Lennox and Pittman, 2010; Malsch and Gendron, 2011); the relationship between transparency, competition and audit quality (Maijoor and Vanstraelen, 2012); and the prospects and scope for innovation in audit practice (see Humphrey *et al.*, 2011; Catasús *et al.*, 2013).

Probably the most polemical issue in relation to the rise of (global) auditing standards and associated independent regulatory oversight and inspection is whether they have gradually instilled a check-list, overly compliance, rules-oriented view of audit quality that has severely constrained the exercising of professional judgment and in the process lowered overall levels of audit quality. Any such claims by the auditing profession are hotly disputed by regulatory bodies, who point to evident failures on the part of auditing professionals to do what is required by auditing standards. Regulators criticize auditors for applying lower levels of scepticism, while the profession responds by asserting that any loss of scepticism is either (a) not proven or (b) has happened under the watch of audit regulators and cannot be solely attributed to the actions and motives of audit practitioners. Global standards are represented as being too lengthy, complex, unwieldy and not respecting of the spirit and value of professional judgment; but standard setters complain that audit firms continually request the provision of more, rule-oriented, interpretations of the requirements of 'vague' standards, with it also being suggested that the profession has seemed to prosper financially on the back of such an international standards regime. Humphrey *et al.* (2011) sought to capture the perennial tension evident in such discussions when noting that a central dilemma for the auditing profession was that a 'professional imperative potentially encourages openness and transparency over levels of audit quality, while the commercial imperative traditionally points to camouflage, secrecy and the maintenance of the audit mystique' (2011: 451).

Catasús *et al.* (2013) recently sought to capture some of this intrigue and to stimulate a greater professional focus on practice development by calling for audit innovation to become the new 'practice standard'. It is evident that the tone of the professional response has started to shift in recent years from a stubborn defence of the quality of audit practice in the aftermath of the global financial crisis to a more open contemplation as to the possibilities for innovation in practice. International standard-setting bodies such as IAASB are in recent proposed revisions to audit reporting standards themselves advocating experimentation and promoting new, more lengthy forms of audit reporting (see IAASB, 2013). There are also innovation projects and initiatives at the level of audit firms and professional institutes, including collaborations between the accounting profession and bodies such as the World Wildlife Foundation (WWF) and the Royal Society of Arts (RSA) in the pursuit of new 'audit futures'.[19]

Interestingly, in developing nations, notions of compliance with ISAs are less likely to be viewed or represented in a negative sense, as an intrusion in the sphere of professional auditor judgment, but are seen as an essential next step in the building of more vibrant and sustainable professional auditing (and accounting) regimes. As 'capacity building' projects, they are portrayed as critical elements to growing global commitments to financial transparency and stability and the closing of key gaps in countries' financial reporting infrastructure. Highly active in this field are bodies such as the World Bank and the IMF in their Accounting and Auditing Reports on Standards and Codes (AA ROSCs). Furthermore, the issue of compliance with the standards is of great importance to IFAC in terms of demonstrating that ISAs can be successfully applied in a wide variety of contexts. Since 2003, IFAC's Compliance Advisory Panel has operated a Member Body Compliance Programme whereby the national professional accounting organizations that are IFAC members are required to report regularly on how ISAs are adhered to in relation to audit practice in their respective jurisdictions. Linkages and a mutual compatibility of interests between IFAC and the international donor and development community were recently vividly demonstrated through a claimed historic Memorandum of Understanding to Strengthen Accountancy and Improve Collaboration (known as MOSAIC). This agreement detailed mutual, collaborative commitments to enhance the capacity of professional accountancy organizations in developing nations.[20]

The growing emphasis on compliance placed in the context of international audit standardization has come amid significant concerns over the last two decades (especially since the Asian crisis of the late 1990s) that the outcomes of the adoption of ISAs across national jurisdictions does not just vary but '[are] significantly different from those intended ... despite significant pressure from the global regulatory and market institutions' (Samsonova-Taddei, 2013: 507). One of the challenges of standardization has been to understand what determines local adopters' attitudes to international standards and consequently, their actual compliance with such standards. Notably, the degree of compliance has been found to differ not just among countries but also within a given national jurisdiction. Illustrative in this regard is the case of Russia where ISAs have been represented as 'a mechanism through which new audit professionalism could be articulated and demonstrated' (Mennicken, 2008: 393).

However, nearly 20 years of reforms wherein Russian auditing standards were being gradually converged with ISAs failed to achieve a broad level of consistency in local audit practice. As Samsonova-Taddei (2013) demonstrates, local auditors' commitment to following auditing standards continued to differ depending on their specific (existing) professional identities and practice norms. Her findings echoed those of Mennicken (2008) who acknowledged that 'it is the specificities of the "practice communities" ... within which the standards become circulated that define how ISAs should be used and interpreted' (2008: 390). Samsonova-Taddei found that auditors less socially connected with members of international audit firms (which first introduced ISAs to Russia) tended to be slower learners about ISAs compared to those more socially connected to their 'international' colleagues. Evident cases of non-compliance with ISAs were not expected to decline significantly given the continuing scale of the Russian 'shadow' economy.

Such work has sought to highlight the importance of the translation processes that ISAs undergo in different national contexts in order to make them operational. As Mennicken (2008: 239) emphasized, 'defining what it means to work in accordance with international standards' can vary significantly across different contexts. The emerging evidence about the implementation of ISAs in Russia shows that such processes can be influenced significantly by auditors' past professional experiences and habits, particularly in areas which require the most audit judgment, such as the determination of materiality thresholds (see Samsonova-Taddei, 2013). Some Russian auditors expected there would be some universal formula that would magically produce a precise figure for materiality, and that it was just a matter of one's experience to find that; a sentiment that was seen to reflect the substantial gap between the 'professional' mindset used to construct principle-based ISAs and local auditors' strong preference for more quantifiable (and what they deemed as more reliable), Soviet-style audit techniques.[21]

UNCTAD (2008), in drawing conclusions from its review of the institutional dimensions of international auditing standard setting, argued that the chances of successful ISA implementation depended fundamentally on the existence of: a robust implementation strategy and action plan; adequate implementation support infrastructure; appropriate training and education; and timely and high-quality translations of ISAs.[22] Subsequent to UNCTAD's study, IAASB's concerns as to whether ISAs were being applied in practice led to the establishment of an 'ISA Implementation Monitoring' project. This was implemented in two phases: the first being 'pre-implementation monitoring', where the experiences of introducing clarified ISAs were studied; and the second being 'post-implementation monitoring', focusing on whether the standards were being consistently understood and implemented. A 2010 report spoke positively of the implementation process but highlighted that auditors of small and medium-sized firms were having difficulty with the clarified ISAs. A final report on the second phase of monitoring,[23] issued in July 2013, concluded that the clarified ISAs were generally understood by respondents (mainly auditors and regulators), and the revised standards appeared to have achieved the aims of the Clarity Project. However, the consultation process did reveal some divergence in views as to whether full harmonization in audit practices globally is achievable and the extent to which clarified ISAs had secured the right balance between principles and rules. IAASB has committed to investigating these issues further as part of its proposed 2015–19 strategic plan.

Humphrey and Loft (2011: 119) argued that '[b]eing a member of a profession, using professional standards, making professional judgments, and retaining professional scepticism embodies a discourse of professionalism that has a range of implications for the production, adoption, usage and enforcement of the standards'. Whether (international) auditing standards can transform varying practice environments, and control and inspection regimes can accommodate diversity in auditor judgment processes are, as we have just seen, still very dependent on interpretation. Indeed, a growing compliance mentality among auditors could easily be regarded as a direct consequence of a trend towards a more 'controlled' audit function rather than the dominant existence of 'rules-based' standards (see Gendron and Spira, 2009; Beattie *et al.*, 2011).

Concluding comments

The analysis presented in the chapter has sought to develop a better appreciation of the relative significance of ISAs, the motivations underlying their promotion, and the interests and factors that have shaped their development, application and impact on practice. We have seen examples of strong support for ISAs, most notably in the case of an EU-commissioned research (see Duisberg-Essen, 2009), although this has yet to produce a fully confirmed EU-wide endorsement of ISAs. While there has been an impressive growth in the adoption and utilization of ISAs, important questions still remain about the value of a globally standardized audit, the scale of compliance with ISAs and the capacity of standards to avert audit failure. For example, critics of ISAs will claim that the advance of ISAs globally did not prevent the discontent that has come to be expressed about the role of the audit profession in relation to the recent global financial crises.

The world of ISAs can give an impression of auditing as being increasingly sophisticated, technically demanding and expert-driven. However, behind this aura of complexity surrounding modern audit practice, the same kind of issues highlighted decades ago are arguably still lurking with regard to ensuring auditor independence, rethinking audit training and revisiting the dynamics of audit team workings (see, for example, Humphrey *et al.*, 2013). While the key motivations for and benefits of adopting the standards have been delineated in some depth (Roussey, 1992; 1996; Fraser, 2010), there is still a profound lack of contextualized knowledge and understanding of the extent to which ISAs function mainly as legitimizing tools or as means to improve performance and, consequently, whether standardization has been able to invoke substantive changes in auditors' mindsets and routines.

While the case for ISAs has been frequently made on the grounds that audit practice needs to be consistent throughout international audit firms and across national jurisdictions, it is noticeable that when an audit scandal breaks, questions of concern or accusations of blame are directed at the locally based auditors, with little reference being made to the extent to which the auditors had applied ISAs in their work. Possibly the new draft audit reporting standard being developed by IAASB (and related variants in certain national jurisdictions) will give auditors the opportunity, through the desired expanded reporting format, to demonstrate more clearly the quality and impact of their work. If it succeeds, it will start to set a new precedent, namely that in a world of standards, the standard requirement for auditors is not to be standard, but to show their special and distinctive contribution.

Notes

1 Presentation at the GPPS Symposium, London, 19–20 October 2005.
2 Available online at www.ifac.org/about-ifac/membership/compliance-program/basis-isa-adoption (accessed 2 February 2014). The key adoption categories are: ISAs are required by national law or regulation; ISAs are adopted by the national audit standard setter; national standards are essentially ISAs, with modifications consistent with IAASBs modifications policy; and others, where there are information inadequacies with respect to the utilized translation process for ISAs, the adopted modifications policy and/or where it is known that despite declared commitments to convergence with ISAs, such processes have some way still to go in practice. On the basis of IFAC's categorization, as of early 2014, 58 per cent of the 126 countries were classified into the first three categories.
3 Available online at www.ifac.org/about-ifac/forum-firms (accessed 2 February 2014). The Forum of Firms is formally connected to IFAC through IFAC's Transnational Auditors Committee (TAC). The TAC effectively acts as the executive arm of the Forum of Firms, with a remit to promote, among other things, the conducting of high quality audits – see www.ifac.org/about-ifac/transnational-auditors-committee (accessed 2 February 2014).
4 At the time of publication of his article, Nicholas Fraser was chair of IFAC's Transnational Auditors' Committee.
5 IAPC minutes were not formally published.
6 Jim Sylph, interviewed in *The Accountant*, 1 May 1999.
7 The EU Parliament subsequently formally adopted the amended Directive on Statutory Audit and the Regulation on specific requirements regarding the statutory audit of public-interest entities in plenary session on 3 April 2014 (see http://europa.eu/rapid/press-release_STATEMENT-14-104_en.htm (accessed 3 April 2014)). The Council of the EU subsequently adopted the audit reform package on 14 April 2014 (see www.consilium.europa.eu/uedocs/cms_data/docs/pressdata/en/intm/142180.pdf (accessed 14 April 2014)). Helpful website links detailing historical progress with the EU audit reforms can be found at http://ec.europa.eu/internal_market/auditing/reform/ and www.iasplus.com/en-gb/news/2014/04/eu-audit-reform-eu-council-adoption (both accessed 14 April 2014).
8 The agreed mandatory EU auditor rotation rules will require public-interest entities to change their statutory auditors after a maximum engagement period of ten years, although Member States can choose to extend this period by a maximum of ten additional years if the audit is put out to tender and by up to a further 14 years in the case of joint audits. The reforms also include additional restrictions on the provision of non-audit services to audit clients (including the establishment of a cap on the scale of permitted non-audit fees that can be earned by auditors of public-interest entities) and prohibit the use of restrictive clauses in contracts which limit a company's choice of auditor (e.g. to a Big 4 firm). The Commission had wanted a shorter mandatory rotation period but the agreed limits represent a compromise position following extensive lobbying by the profession. Commission proposals for splitting up the Big 4 audit firms were also dropped.
9 Available online at http://ec.europa.eu/commission_2010–14/barnier/headlines/speeches/2013/12/20131217_en.htm (accessed 2 February 2014).
10 Similar initiatives have been pursued by bodies such as the UK's Financial Reporting Council (FRC) and the PCAOB. The press release announcing the issuing of the exposure draft is available online at www.ifac.org/news-events/2013-07/iaasb-proposes-standards-fundamentally-transform-auditors-report-focuses-communi (accessed 2 February 2014).
11 For a recent consideration of the threats to the social relevance of audit in regimes where rules-based standards are increasingly dominant, see Tarr and Mack, 2013.
12 Available online at www.ifac.org/news-events/2013–12/iaasb-consults-five-year-strategic-objectives-and-work-priorities (accessed 2 February 2014).
13 See www.ifac.org/news-events/2013-12/iaasb-consults-five-year-strategic-objectives-and-work-priorities (accessed 2 February 2014).
14 UNCTAD did acknowledge that its report was prepared with substantive input from IAASB staff.
15 A definition that it continues to apply in its second global survey – see www.ifiar.org/IFIAR/media/Documents/IFIARMembersArea/MemberUpdates/IFIAR-Inspection-Survey-9-April-2014_1.pdf (accessed 9 April 2014).
16 For a broader, historical analysis of the politicization of accounting standard settings and its implications for audit standard setting, see Jeppesen and van Liempd, 2014.

17 Indeed, as Humphrey *et al.* (2011) observed, a subsequent consultation by the EU's own Directorate-General on the adoption of ISAs 'found an overwhelming majority in support of such actions from respondents (the majority of whom were from the accounting profession but the remainder were acknowledged as covering a wide range of stakeholders)' (2011: 446).
18 See http://pcaobus.org/Rules/Rulemaking/Docket040/002_CAQ.pdf (accessed 2 February 2014).
19 Available online at www.auditfutures.org (accessed 2 February 2014).
20 www.ifac.org/about-ifac/professional-accountancy-organization-development-committee/mosaic (accessed 2 February 2014).
21 For related findings in the context of Egypt and the use by auditors of analytical procedures, see Samaha and Hegazy, 2010.
22 Following the Wong report (2004), translations of standards and associated publications is an area where IFAC has made significant advances over recent years and has clearly helped to contribute to the global application of ISAs – both in terms of making material available in different languages and establishing a formal translations policy. For an example of the Spanish translation of ISAs, see http://incp.org.co/Site/2012/news/archivos/708a.pdf (accessed 2 February 2014). For IFAC's official translations policy, see www.ifac.org/about-ifac/translations-permissions (accessed 2 February 2014).
23 Available online at www.ifac.org/sites/default/files/publications/files/Implementation-Review-of-the-Clarified-ISAs.pdf (accessed 2 February 2014).

References

Beattie, V., Fearnley, S. and Hines, T. (2011) *Reaching Key Financial Reporting Decisions: How Directors and Auditors Interact*. Chichester: John Wiley.

Bedard, J.C., Johnstone, K.M. and Smith, E.F. (2010) 'Audit Quality Indicators: A Status Update on Possible Public Disclosures and Insights from Audit Practice; Commentary', *Current Issues in Auditing* 4 (1): C12–C19.

Camfferman, K. and Zeff, S.A. (2007) *Financial Reporting and Global Capital Markets: A History of the International Accounting Standards Committee, 1973–2000*. Oxford: Oxford University Press.

Catasús, B., Hellman, N. and Humphrey, C. (2013) 'Thinking Differently: Making Audit Innovation the New Practice Standard', in *Revisiones Roll i Bolagsstyrningen*, pp. 32–60. Stockholm: SNS Förlag.

DeFond, M.L. (2010) 'How Should the Auditors be Audited? Comparing the PCAOB Inspections with the AICPA Peer Reviews', *Journal of Accounting and Economics* 49(1–2): 104–8.

Duhovnik, M. (2012) 'Time to Endorse the ISAs for European Use: The Emerging Markets Perspective', *Accounting in Europe* 8(1–2): 129–40.

Duisburg-Essen (2009) *Evaluation of the Possible Adoption of International Standards on Auditing (ISAs) in the EU*. Executive Summary. Essen: University of Duisburg-Essen.

European Commission (EC) (2004) *52004PC0177 Proposal for a Directive of the European Parliament and of the Council on Statutory Audit of Annual Accounts and Consolidated Accounts and Amending Council Directives* 78/660/EEC and 83/349/EEC/* COM/2004/0177 final – COD 2004/0065 */. Brussels: EC.

Fraser, N.P. (2010) 'A Single Set of Worldwide Auditing Standards: The Road is Long … ', *International Journal of Disclosure and Governance* 7: 289–3079.

Gendron, Y. and Spira, L. (2009) 'What Went Wrong? The Downfall of Arthur Andersen and the Construction of Controllability Boundaries Surrounding Financial Auditing', *Contemporary Accounting Research* 26(4): 987–1027.

Hatherly, D.J. (2009) 'Travelling Audit Fault's Lines: A New Architecture for Auditing Standards', *Managerial Auditing Journal* 24(2): 204–15.

Holm, C. and Zaman, M. (2012) 'Regulating Audit Quality: Restoring Trust and Legitimacy', *Accounting Forum* 36(1): 51–61.

Humphrey, C. (2008) 'Auditing Research: A Review across the Disciplinary Divide', *Accounting, Auditing & Accountability Journal* 21(2): 170–203.

Humphrey, C. and Loft, A. (2009) 'Governing Audit Globally: IFAC, the New International Financial Architecture and the Auditing Profession', in C. S. Chapman, D. J. Cooper and P. B. Miller (eds) *Accounting, Organizations, & Institutions, Essays in Honour of Anthony Hopwood*, pp. 205–32. Oxford: Oxford University Press.

Humphrey, C. and Loft, A. (2011) 'Moving beyond Nuts and Bolts: The Complexities of Governing a Global Profession through International Standards', in S. Ponte, P. Gibbon and J. Vestergaard (eds)

Governing through Standards: Origins, Drivers and Limitations, pp. 102–29. London; New York: Palgrave MacMillan.

Humphrey, C., Loft, A. and Woods, M. (2009) 'The Global Audit Profession and the International Financial Architecture: Understanding Regulatory Relationships at a Time of Financial Crisis', *Accounting, Organizations and Society* 34(6–7): 810–25.

Humphrey, C., Kausar, A., Loft, A. and Woods, M. (2011) 'Regulating Audit beyond the Crisis: A Critical Discussion of the EU Green Paper', *European Accounting Review* 20(3): 431–57.

Humphrey, C., Samsonova, A. and Siddiqui, J. (2013) 'Auditing, Regulation and the Persistence of the Expectation Gap', in C. van Mourik and P. Walton (eds) *The Routledge Companion to Accounting, Reporting and Regulation*, pp. 163–84. Abingdon: Routledge.

International Auditing and Assurance Standards Board (IAASB) (2013) *Reporting on Audited Financial Statements: Proposed New and Revised International Standards on Auditing (ISAs)*, Exposure draft. New York: (IAASB), IFAC.

International Federation of Accountants (IFAC) (2003) *Reform Proposals*. New York: IFAC.

International Federation of Accountants (IFAC) (2010) *Handbook of International Quality Control, Auditing, Review, Other Assurance, and Related Services Pronouncements*. New York: IFAC.

International Forum of Independent Audit Regulators (IFIAR) (2012) *2012 Summary Report of Inspection Findings*. London: IFIAR, 18 December. Available online at www. ifiar.org (accessed 11 November 2013).

Jeppesen, K.K. (2010) 'Strategies for Dealing with Standard-setting Resistance', *Accounting, Auditing & Accountability Journal* 23(2): 175–200.

Jeppesen, K.K. and van Liempd, D. (2014) 'Turning Points in the Correspondence between Accounting and Auditing Thought', working paper. Copenhagen: Copenhagen Business School/ Department of Entrepreneurship and Relationship Management, University of Southern Denmark.

Knechel, R.W. (2010) 'Why Standards Matter', in *Zicht op Schilder: Ethiek, controle en toezicht (Libor amicorum voor prof. dr Arnold Schilder)*. Amsterdam: University of Amsterdam Business School.

Knechel, R.W., Krishnan, G.V., Pevzner, M., Shlefchik, L.B. and Uma, K. (2013) 'Audit Quality: Insights from the Academic Literature', *Auditing: A Journal of Practice and Theory* 32(1): 385–421.

Lennox, C. and Pittman, J. (2010) 'Auditing the Auditors: Evidence on the Recent Reforms to the External Monitoring of Audit Firms', *Journal of Accounting and Economics* 49(1/2): 84–103.

Loft, A., Humphrey, C. and Turley, S. (2006) 'In Pursuit of Global Regulation: Changing Governance and Accountability Structures at the International Federation of Accountants (IFAC)', *Accounting, Auditing and Accountability Journal* 19(3): 428–51.

Maijoor, S. and Vanstraelen, A. (2012) 'Research Opportunities in Auditing in the EU, Revisited', *Auditing: A Journal of Practice & Theory* 31(1): 115–26.

Malsch, B. and Gendron, Y. (2011) 'Reining in Auditors: On the Dynamics of Power Surrounding an "Innovation" in the Regulatory Space', *Accounting, Organizations and Society* 36(7): 135–55.

Maastricht Accounting, Auditing and Information Management Research Centre (MARC) (2009) *Evaluation of the Differences between International Standards on Auditing (ISA) and the standards of the US Public Company Accounting Oversight Board (PCAOB)*. Maastricht: MARC.

Mennicken, A. (2008) 'Connecting Worlds: The Translation of International Auditing Standards into Post-Soviet Audit Practice', *Accounting, Organizations and Society* 33(4/5): 384–414.

Peecher, M.E., Solomon, I. and Trotman, K.T. (2013) 'An Accountability Framework for Financial Statement Auditors and Related Research Questions', *Accounting, Organizations and Society* 38(8): 596–620.

Power, M. (1997) *The Audit Society: Rituals of Verification*. Oxford: Oxford University Press.

Power, M. (2003) 'Auditing and the Production of Legitimacy', *Accounting, Organizations and Society* 28(4): 379–94.

Roussey, R.S. (1992) 'Developing International Accounting and Auditing Standards for World Markets', *Journal of International Accounting, Auditing and Taxation* 1(1): 1–11.

Roussey, R.S. (1996) 'New Focus for the International Standards on Auditing', *Journal of International Accounting and Taxation* 5(1): 133–46.

Roussey, R.S. (1999) 'The Development of International Standards on Auditing', *The CPA Journal* 69(10): 14–20.

Samaha, K. and Hegazy, M. (2010) 'An Empirical Investigation of the Use of ISA 520 "Analytical procedures" among Big 4 versus non-Big 4 Audit Firms in Egypt', *Managerial Auditing Journal* 25(9): 882–911.

Samsonova-Taddei, A. (2013) 'Social Relations and the Differential Local Impact of Global Standards: The Case of International Standards on Auditing', *Abacus: A Journal of Accounting, Finance and Business Studies* 49(4): 506–38.

Schockaert, D. and Houyoux, N. (2007) 'International Standards on Auditing within the European Union', *Revue bancaire et financière* 72(8): 515–29.

Simunic, D.A. (2003) *The Adoption of International Auditing Standards in Canada*. Burnaby, BC: Certified General Accountants Association of Canada, British Columbia.

Simunic, D.A., Ye, M. and Zhang, P. (2013) 'The Economics of Setting Auditing Standards under Different Legal Regimes: Implications for International Standards on Auditing', Working Paper No. 2281270. Toronto, ON: Rotman School of Management.

Smith-Lacroix, J-H., Durocher, S. and Gendron, Y. (2012) 'The Erosion of Jurisdiction: Auditing in a Market Value Accounting Regime', *Critical Perspectives on Accounting* 23(1): 36–53.

Tarr, J-A. and Mack, J. (2013) 'Auditor Obligations in an Evolving Legal Landscape', *Accounting, Auditing and Accountability Journal* 26(6): 1009–26.

United Nations Conference on Trade and Development (UNCTAD) (2008) *Practical Challenges and Related Considerations in Implementing International Standards on Auditing* Geneva: UNCTAD.

Wolfensohn, J. (1997) 'Accountants and Society: Serving the Public Interest. Remarks to the World Congress of Accountants'. Speech made to World Congress of Accountants, Paris, 26 October. Available online at http://web.worldbank.org/WBSITE/EXTERNAL/NEWS/0,contentMDK:20025564~pagePK:34370~piPK:42770~theSitePK:4607,00.html (accessed 2 February 2014).

14
Oversight and inspection of auditing

Mona Offermanns and Ann Vanstraelen[1]

Introduction

With the rising importance of global capital markets in today's economy, mechanisms designed to secure their proper functioning become increasingly important. The use of external sources of financing, especially via the stock market, is based on the concept that firms can credibly communicate their true economic performance by means of audited financial statements. If investors lose confidence in the reliability of audited financial information, market participation and the availability of capital will decrease, harming financial stability.

Public oversight of the auditing profession represents a mechanism intended to ensure high audit quality and was installed in response to loss of investor confidence resulting from high-profile financial reporting scandals in which auditors were also blamed (e.g., Enron and Worldcom in the US, Ahold in the Netherlands, Lernout and Hauspie in Belgium, Parmalat in Italy). The idea of regulatory, in contrast to private, oversight relies on the existence of a public regulatory authority that is independent of the auditing profession. Independence can be defined with respect to various elements including financing, staffing, and enforcement power. Ideally, the oversight body is independent with respect to all of these elements.

The tasks taken up by public oversight bodies can be numerous including registration of auditors, establishment of standards governing the audit process, quality assurance and disciplinary actions. As part of quality control and quality assurance, in most cases, a system of regularly conducted inspections of audit firms has been established. The inspections are perceived to be one of the key responsibilities of public oversight bodies. Depending on the size of the audit firm, the frequency and extent of inspections may vary. The Public Company Accounting Oversight Board (PCAOB) in the US, for example, performs annual inspections of audit firms having more than 100 clients with publicly traded debt or equity, while the remaining smaller audit firms are inspected every three years. In continental Europe, inspections are generally performed every three years for audit firms with public interest entities (PIE), and every six years for non-PIE audit firms. According to the PCAOB, the 'inspections are risk-based and often focused on key areas in particular audits that pose risk to investors' (Franzel 2012: 3).

The US is one of the few countries that publicly disclose their inspection reports, but other countries seem to be starting to follow. For example, in continental Europe, the Netherlands recently announced that as of 2014 the Dutch Oversight Body (AFM) will be allowed to publish its findings on individual audit firms. An analysis of inspection reports over time reveals that the PCAOB continues to detect serious audit deficiencies in public company audits. A deficiency is flagged when the PCAOB believes that the audit opinion is not supported by sufficient, appropriate audit evidence. While often related, a distinction is made between audit performance deficiencies (which are always made public) and audit firm's quality control system deficiencies (which are only made public if not satisfactorily addressed within 12 months). While one would expect that learning effects cause the percentage of audits with deficiencies to decrease over time, it turns out to be rather the opposite. For example, the average failure rate of the Big 4 in 2009 was 13.5% and jumped to 32.2% in 2010 and 33% in 2011 (based on the two reports that are currently available for 2011).[2] This would suggest that the auditor's learning curve may be lagging behind the inspector's learning curve. Our analysis of the Big 4 inspection reports from 2007–11 further indicates that over time Big 4 audit firms continue to have the same deficiencies. This finding could also be attributed to the PCAOB increasing the bar of what is acceptable. For example, in every single year, the PCAOB noted deficiencies in PwC's audit procedures related to revenue recognition. Similarly, the PCAOB repeatedly noted shortcomings in the analytical procedures in audit engagements of Ernst & Young. While many of the shortcomings identified are associated with more complex matters like fair value of financial instruments, goodwill and impairment, a substantial number of shortcomings also appear to relate to quite basic auditing issues and related procedures. This observation is confirmed by public oversight bodies in other countries (Maijoor 2012).

In the remainder of this chapter, we outline the development of public oversight in the US and internationally, discuss current issues on the agenda of regulators, provide an overview of research findings on public oversight and suggest areas for future research.

Historical development

Traditionally, the auditing profession had mainly been subject to self-regulation with quality control being achieved by peer and internal reviews. There used to be a common notion that the threat of reputational losses and litigation from investors in case of audit failure would be sufficient to keep audit firms from providing substandard audit quality. The collapse in 2002 of Enron and its auditor Arthur Andersen – once one of the Big 5 audit firms in the world – was used by regulators, politicians and the media to make a case that self-regulation of the auditing profession and audit market mechanisms appeared ineffective. As a result, there has been moves towards stricter regulation, one of which was the creation of a public oversight system of the auditing profession.

By means of the Sarbanes-Oxley Act (hereafter referred to as SOX) in 2002, US Congress created the PCAOB to 'oversee the audits of public companies in order to protect the interests of investors' (PCAOB 2011). Subsequent to developments in the US, changes to the established systems of oversight of the auditing profession were also established in other parts of the world. Currently, there is still a high degree of variation in oversight models, for example with regard to powers and sanctions of oversight bodies and the role of the profession and practitioners in inspections (Maijoor and Vanstraelen 2012). To illustrate the latter, the revised Eighth EU Council Directive of 2006 (Directive 2006/43/EC) allows EU member states to choose between two options (or a combination of the two) for public inspections: either they are performed by full-time inspectors; or alternatively by peer reviewers with an independent commission monitoring the process.

The rising number of national oversight bodies led to an increasing need to coordinate and harmonize the various oversight activities. As a result, organizations were established to promote effective public audit oversight across countries. At a European level, the European Group of Auditors' Oversight Bodies (EGAOB) was founded in 2005, and recently replaced by the Committee of European Auditing Oversight Bodies (CEAOB) in 2014. The tasks of the CEAOB include facilitating the exchange of information, expertise and best practices of public oversight and contributing to the improvement of cooperation mechanisms. At an international level, the International Forum of Independent Audit Regulators (IFIAR) was formed in 2006. The organization began with independent audit regulators from 18 jurisdictions and currently counts 44 members. IFIAR membership requires an independent regulatory agency in terms of funding and composition of the governing body, and periodic inspections of audit firms undertaking audits of PIE.

Current issues

The development of public oversight has certainly not yet reached its limit. The financial crisis and its aftermath have fuelled the debate regarding how to regulate financial markets. In that context, regulators are again considering potential enhancements to the audit function with the main objective of strengthening the role of the auditor in ensuring trust in the financial markets (e.g., Doty 2011). The problem areas, mainly stemming from common inspection findings, where improvement is considered desirable include auditors' professional scepticism and tone at the top; group audits (e.g., global consistency of audit quality); revenue recognition; internal control testing; and engagement quality control review (IFIAR 2012 Global Survey of Audit Inspection Findings, www.ifiar.org). Other audit policy issues on the agenda of regulators in response to the financial crisis and the economic downturn comprise audit risks associated with sovereign debt exposure, fair value measurements, changes to the auditor's reporting model to make it more relevant for the investor (e.g., by providing additional information on the auditor's view of significant risks and key judgements; or audit reporting on integrated reports of financial, environmental, and social corporate information),[3] improving audit transparency,[4] and auditor independence (IFIAR 2011, 2012).

Also, the scope of oversight is still subject to refinements. For example, after the revelation of Bernard Madoff's Ponzi scheme, regulators were pressured to strengthen oversight of securities industry auditors. To this end, the PCAOB received authority to oversee audits of broker–dealers through the Dodd-Frank Act of 2011. Furthermore, discussions regarding the necessary and achieved degree of independence of oversight bodies from the auditing profession are continuing.

Finally, an important issue on the agenda of public oversight bodies is to establish cross-border regulatory cooperative inspection agreements since the lack thereof hampers the effectiveness of audit oversight in a global context. To promote a more effective and efficient oversight of global audit firms, some countries have recognized the equivalence of audit oversight systems and mutually rely on each other's inspection of audit firms (Maijoor and Vanstraelen 2012). In a similar vein, the PCAOB established in 2011 a separate Global Network Firm (GNF) inspection programme taking into account some of the unique aspects of global audit practice (Franzel 2012). Despite these important steps forward in international regulatory cooperation, public oversight bodies are still confronted with obstacles preventing inspections in certain foreign jurisdictions. In this regard, the current chair of ESMA, Steven Maijoor, stated that there appears to be 'a large gap between the level of cooperation and integration of auditing regulators compared with that of international networks of audit firms to oversee' and therefore urges them to be much more ambitious for international cooperation in audit oversight (Maijoor 2012: 15–16).

Summary of current state of research findings

Existing studies on public oversight focus to a large extent on the US, as the PCAOB is one of the few public oversight bodies that publicly discloses inspection findings. Nevertheless, a few interesting insights are available from studies conducted within an international context. Researchers have addressed public oversight at various levels of detail: (1) the existence of an independent inspection process; (2) audit firm inspection outcomes; and (3) enforcement.

Existence of an independent inspection process

A number of arguments have been voiced as to why the public inspection process may be superior to a peer review system, as for example independence and objectivity, expertise, and availability of resources (Carcello *et al.* 2011a). Also, the inspections performed by an independent oversight body may provide an ex-ante incentive to improve audit quality because large penalties can follow from observed deficiencies (DeFond 2010). This point of view is supported by a considerable number of studies.

Beginning with the impact of the presence of a public oversight body, Ernstberger *et al.* (2012) find that the creation of the German Auditor Oversight Commission (Abschlussprüferaufsichtskommission) in combination with other enforcement reforms in 2005 has reduced the level of earnings management and has increased stock liquidity and market valuation. Similarly, Fuentes *et al.* (2010) find that earnings quality has improved since the beginning of inspections conducted by the Spanish Institute of Accounting and Audit (Instituto de Contabilidad y Auditoría de Cuentas) as a result of Big-N auditors adjusting their client selection and Non-Big N auditors restricting earnings management. In the US, Carcello *et al.* (2011a) show that absolute abnormal accruals decrease following PCAOB inspections. Read *et al.* (2004) show that audit firms without public clients voluntarily adhere to stricter standards than necessary by registering with the PCAOB in order to signal audit quality. Overall, the results suggest that the existence of a public oversight body performing inspections leads to desirable effects.

A positive perception of the usefulness of inspections also appears to be held by the majority of investors. Offermanns and Peek (2011) show that inspection reports are informative to investors and are associated with changes in perceived uncertainty about financial reporting quality. Further, markets react negatively to announcements that PCAOB inspections of audit firms located in certain foreign countries are not permitted, while disclosure that inspections are no longer blocked in one of these countries leads to a positive market reaction (Carcello *et al.* 2011b).

Despite its merits, public oversight has been subject to criticism and scepticism. For example, in the US, the inspection process has been heavily criticized because of insufficient staff, staff with limited expertise, inadequate transparency of procedures and inspection outcomes, and slow feedback (e.g., Glover *et al.* 2009). This critical view is also taken by audit firms, as small US audit firms see neither an improvement in audit quality nor increased public confidence in the auditing profession arising from the inspection process (Daugherty and Tervo 2010).

Audit firm inspection outcomes

Inspection outcomes and types of deficiencies have been descriptively analysed and summarized in prior literature (e.g., Roybark 2009). Both US and international audit firms with a deficient

PCAOB inspection result have been found to be smaller, have a larger number of issuer clients, and show more rapid growth (Hermanson *et al.* 2007; Bishop *et al.* 2013). Furthermore, US accounting firms display a declining number of deficiencies over time, while annually inspected firms continue to have quality control deficiencies (Church and Shefchik 2012).

Inspection results have also been linked to their antecedents and consequences. Among the literature investigating the antecedents of the inspection outcome, a number of studies examine the association between inspection outcomes and audit quality characteristics to address the question of whether the inspection process effectively identifies cases of structural audit problems. For example, clients of audit firms with deficiencies discovered during the PCAOB inspection process display higher levels of abnormal accruals (Gunny and Zhang 2013). On the other hand, clients of auditors with deficiencies are not more likely to meet analyst forecasts and the available evidence is inconclusive on whether they are less likely to receive a going-concern opinion (Gramling *et al.* 2011; Gunny and Zhang 2013). Hence, the PCAOB inspection process does not seem to clearly differentiate audit quality using common measures of audit quality except for client earnings quality based on abnormal accruals.

Insights from an international context are scarce. Notable exceptions are a study by Carson *et al.* (2013) examining the effectiveness of public oversight in its different forms at an international level. Van Opijnen *et al.* (2011) focus on the Dutch public oversight body and show that companies audited by an audit firm with a negative inspection outcome are associated with higher abnormal accruals. Furthermore, they find that the types of weaknesses that are most able to discriminate audit quality are related to the design of the audit firm's quality control system and independence.

Inspection outcomes do not appear to be inconsequential. For example, some audit firms, in particular smaller ones, have deregistered from the PCAOB (Read *et al.* 2004; Daugherty *et al.* 2011). DeFond and Lennox (2011) conclude that especially low quality audit firms deregister in response to inspections, with quality measured in terms of non-compliance, negative peer review and inspection results, and a higher likelihood that clients receive a going-concern opinion from a successor auditor.

To obtain a more direct measure of changes in audit procedures, researchers have examined changes in audit fees. Based on a client-level analysis, Knechel *et al.* (2012) find that audit fees increase in response to deficient inspection results. Also, Knechel *et al.* (2012) observe that deficient firms increase the number of professionals employed and develop more specialized client portfolios, indicating that audit firms take measures to improve audit quality in response to deficient inspection results.

Next to audit firm reactions, clients' sensitivity to inspection outcomes has been looked at. This is of particular importance given that anecdotal deficiencies currently presented in the PCAOB inspection reports could lead to incorrect perceptions of audit firms (Wainberg *et al.*, 2013). Lennox and Pittman (2010) find no indication for changes in audit firm market shares as a result of deficient inspection results, which would imply that clients do not adjust their audit firm choices based on the inspections. This can partly be explained by the fact that inspections are not intended to categorize audit firms into high and low quality firms, because reviewed engagements and audit issues are not selected randomly.

However, Daugherty *et al.* (2011) find that clients of triennially inspected auditors with deficient inspection reports dismiss their auditor and are more likely afterwards to hire a new auditor without deficiencies. Also, Abbott *et al.* (2013) show that clients with effective audit committees or high potential agency conflicts are more likely to switch to a successor auditor without GAAP (generally accepted accounting principles) related deficiencies. Hence, the PCAOB inspection results seem relevant at least for a subgroup of clients or audit firms.

Enforcement

Finally, there is some literature on the enforcement powers of public oversight bodies, which can include civil monetary penalties or disciplinary proceedings ranging from censuring, suspending or barring of auditors, to revoking the registration of audit firms. Gilbertson and Herron (2009) describe PCAOB enforcement actions and find that sanctioned firms tend to have longer inspections, more audit deficiencies, fewer partners, more SEC issuers and clients that are smaller and less financially sound. Dee *et al.* (2011) find that stock markets react negatively to news of PCAOB sanctions imposed upon one of the Big 4 audit firms, which is likely to be attributed to the public disclosure of severe quality control problems. This would also be in line with an analysis of quality control defects disclosed in peer review reports by Lennox and Pittman (2010), showing that this type of information is value relevant. Interestingly, Dee *et al.* (2011) suggest that the negative effects of news on sanctions outweigh the possible remedial effects of news on corrective actions.

Overall, the available studies indicate that actions taken by oversight bodies are sufficiently important to be both noticed and valued by market participants. The key question underlying the majority of the existing research studies relates to the effectiveness of the inspection process, i.e., whether the process is able to identify meaningful audit deficiencies and lead to improvements in audit quality. With few exceptions, existing research studies indicate that the inspection activity effectively identifies instances of structurally low audit quality as measured in terms of abnormal accruals, is relevant for clients and investors, and causes audit firms to take audit quality improving measures. However, it needs to be borne in mind that the lack of information about many of the processes taking place at regulatory oversight bodies limits the availability to judge the quality of their methodologies. Remaining uncertainty regarding numerous aspects of public oversight including possibilities for improvement leaves ample room for future research, which we address in the next section, 'Unresolved issues related to inspections'.

Unresolved issues related to inspections

While we have provided some insights on the impact and effectiveness of public oversight, there are still many things that are unknown related to how public oversight affects auditor incentives and behaviour. Specifically, as outlined in the previous section, 'Summary of current state of research findings', while a number of existing research studies examine public oversight in the US, we have only limited insights from other countries. Even though oversight systems in many countries were shaped to mimic the structure of the already established US oversight system, there still exist major differences across countries. Currently, we do not know much about the efficiency and effectiveness of different forms of public oversight but insights on this would be helpful for at least three reasons. First, it can help to evaluate which elements of public oversight are more critical in achieving the desired objectives. Second, it might be possible to achieve the desired improvements in audit quality and investor confidence in a less costly way. Third, better knowledge regarding the critical elements can help mutual reliance and harmonization of key features of public oversight systems across countries. In this regard, it is currently not known whether different forms of international cooperation (in terms of mutual reliance, extent of communication, and exchange of information) affect their effectiveness (Maijoor and Vanstraelen 2012).

To learn more about the role of the inspection as a key element of public oversight, it would be informative to examine differences between inspection regimes that do or do not disclose inspection outcomes to the public. As Maijoor and Vanstraelen (2012: 120) state:

It is currently not clear what the impact is of the level of transparency on inspection outcomes on the functioning of the audit market, in terms of competition and quality, and how it affects the interaction between the oversight body and the audit firm.

At the same time, it would be relevant to know whether certain additions to the inspection report make it more informative to the investor. For example, detected quality control deficiencies are likely to permeate throughout the whole audit firm and are likely relevant for all of an audit firm's clients. Hence, more timely disclosure of detailed quality control deficiency descriptions might be useful to investors (Lennox and Pittman 2010).

We would also like to know more about the implications of changes in the audit process brought about by inspections. For example, inspections may cause the audit to become more compliance or rules oriented, actually undermining the auditor's ability to exercise judgement in the event of unusual idiosyncratic risk. Further, inspectors' and investors' views of costs and benefits of additional audit effort need not be fully aligned and it would be useful to examine potential differences between the two. With regard to costs and benefits, we currently do not know whether smaller audit firms face higher cost compared to larger firms in proportion to the benefits accruing to them. Although inspection reports indicate that some audit firms continue to have the same deficiencies over time, it is unclear to what extent audit firms learn about inspector attitudes and likely inspection targets. In this way, and with an increasing number of inspection rounds, anticipation of the inspection approach and its strictness could decrease detected deficiencies.

Conclusion

One of the most profound changes in the history of audit regulation is the instalment of public oversight, putting an end to the dominant model of self-regulation of the auditing profession. The ultimate goal of public oversight bodies is to ensure trust in the financial markets and to protect investors and the public interest. Given that the role of public oversight is not uncontested, the creation of public oversight bodies and their inspections have triggered academic research, focusing mainly on their effectiveness. This chapter has demonstrated that public oversight is still in development. There are many challenges ahead, not only for regulators but also for audit firms. We have outlined a research agenda for academic scholars of which the findings may also be helpful for policymakers.

Notes

1 The authors gratefully acknowledge research assistance from Lei Zou.
2 The PCAOB began by disclosing the number of audits inspected in 2009, allowing calculation of the failure rates from 2009 onwards.
3 We refer to Vanstraelen *et al.* (2012) for a recent study on the audit reporting debate.
4 We refer to Deumes *et al.* (2012) for a study on transparency on audit firm governance.

References

Abbott, L.J., Gunny, K. and Zhang, T.C. (2013). 'When the PCAOB Talks, Who Listens? Evidence from Client Firm Reactions to Adverse, GAAP-deficient PCAOB Inspection Reports', *Auditing: A Journal of Practice & Theory* 32(2): 1–31.

Bishop, C.C., Hermanson, D.R. and Houston, R.W. (2013). 'PCAOB Inspections of International Audit Firms: Initial Evidence', *International Journal of Auditing* 17(1): 1–18.

Carcello, J.V., Hollingsworth, C. and Mastrolia, S. (2011a). 'The Effect of PCAOB Inspections on Big 4 Audit Quality', *Research in Accounting Regulation* 23(2): 85–96.

Carcello, J.V., Carver, B.T. and Neal, T.L. (2011b). 'Market Reaction to the PCAOB's Inability to Conduct Foreign Inspections', working paper. Available online at http://ssrn.com/abstract=1911388 or http://dx.doi.org/10.2139/ssrn.1911388 (accessed 5 May 2014).

Carson, E., Simnett, R. and Vanstraelen, A. (2013). 'Is Public Oversight of the Auditing Profession Effective? Insights from an International Study', working paper. Sydney: NSW: University of New South Wales; Maastricht: Maastricht University.

Church, B.K. and Shefchik, L.B. (2012). 'PCAOB Inspections and Large Accounting Firms', *Accounting Horizons* 26(1): 43–63.

Daugherty, B. and Tervo, W. (2010). 'PCAOB Inspections of Smaller CPA Firms: The Perspective of Inspected Firms', *Accounting Horizons* 24(2): 189–219.

Daugherty, B., Dickins, D. and Tervo, W.A. (2011). 'Negative PCAOB Inspections of Triennially Inspected Auditors and Involuntary and Voluntary Client Losses', *International Journal of Auditing* 15(3): 231–46.

Dee, C.C., Lulseged, A. and Zhang, T. (2011). 'Client Stock Market Reaction to PCAOB Sanctions against a Big Four Auditor', *Contemporary Accounting Research* 28(1): 263–91.

DeFond, M.L. (2010). 'How Should the Auditors be Audited? Comparing the PCAOB Inspections with the AICPA Peer Reviews', *Journal of Accounting and Economics* 49(1/2): 104–8.

DeFond, M.L. and Lennox, C.S. (2011). 'The Effect of SOX on Small Auditor Exits and Audit Quality', *Journal of Accounting and Economics* 52(1): 21–40.

Deumes, R., Schelleman, C., Vander Bauwhede, H. and Vanstraelen, A. (2012). 'Audit Firm Governance: Do Transparency Reports Reveal Audit Quality?' *Auditing: A Journal of Practice and Theory* 31(4): 193–214.

Doty, J.R. (2011). 'Testimony Concerning the Role of the Accounting Profession in Preventing another Financial Crisis', in *United States Senate Committee on Banking, Housing and Urban Affairs, Subcommittee on Securities, Insurance, and Investment*. Washington, DC: PCAOB. Available online at http://pcaobus.org/News/Speech/Pages/04062011_DotyTestimony.aspx (accessed 5 May 2014).

Ernstberger, J., Stich, M. and Vogler, O. (2012). 'Economic Consequences of Accounting Enforcement Reforms: The Case of Germany', *European Accounting Review* 21(2): 217–51.

Franzel, J.M. (2012). *Keynote Address – PCAOB: Protecting Investors and the Public Interest*. ALI CLE Conference, Chicago, IL, 13 September.

Fuentes Barbera, C.D., Illueca, M. and Pucheta-Martinez, M.C. (2010). 'Disciplinary Sanctions and Audit Quality: Empirical Evidence from an External Oversight System' (9 July 2010), working paper. Available online at http://ssrn.com/abstract=1636730 or http://dx.doi.org/10.2139/ssrn.1636730 (accessed 5 May 2014).

Gilbertson, D.L. and Herron, T.L. (2009). 'PCAOB Enforcements: A Review of the First Three Years', *Current Issues in Auditing* 3(2): A15–A34.

Glover, S.M., Prawitt, D.F. and Taylor, M.H. (2009). 'Audit Standard Setting and Inspection for US Public Companies: A Critical Assessment and Recommendations for Fundamental Change', *Accounting Horizons* 23(2): 221–37.

Gramling, A.A., Krishnan, J. and Zhang, Y. (2011). 'Are PCAOB Identified Audit Deficiencies Associated with a Change in Reporting Decisions of Triennially Inspected Audit Firms?', *Auditing: A Journal of Practice & Theory* 30(3): 59–79.

Gunny, K. and Zhang, T.C. (2013). 'PCAOB Inspection Reports and Audit Quality', *Journal of Accounting and Public Policy* 32(March–April): 136–60.

Hermanson, D.R., Houston, R.W. and Rice, J.C. (2007). 'PCAOB Inspections of Smaller CPA Firms: Initial Evidence from Inspection Reports', *Accounting Horizons* 21(2): 137–52.

International Forum of Independent Audit Regulators (IFIAR) (2011). *Activity Report*. Available online at www.ifiar.org/IFIAR/media/Documents/General/Reports/IFIAR-Activity-Report-2011.pdf (accessed 5 May 2014).

International Forum of Independent Audit Regulators (IFIAR) (2012). *Annual Report*. Available online at www.ifiar.org/IFIAR/media/Documents/General/About%20Us/IFIAR%20Member%20Updates%202013/IFIAR-Annual-Report-2012.pdf (accessed 5 May 2014).

Knechel, W.R., Offermanns, M. and Vanstraelen, A. (2012). 'PCAOB Inspections and Audit Firm Behavior: An Analysis of Audit Fees, Audit Effort and Industry Specialization', working paper. Maastricht: Maastricht University.

Lennox, C. and Pittman, J. (2010). 'Auditing the Auditors: Evidence on the Recent Reforms to the External Monitoring of Audit Firms', *Journal of Accounting and Economics* 49(1/2): 84–103.

Maijoor, S. (2012). *Keynote Speech*. Audit Quality Symposium – Canadian Public Accountability Board, Toronto, ON, 29 November, European Securities Market Authority (ESMA) ESMA/2012/797.

Available online at www.esma.europa.eu/system/files/cpab_maijoor_esma_29_nov.pdf (accessed 5 May 2014).
Maijoor, S. & Vanstraelen, A. (2012). 'Research Opportunities in Auditing in the EU', Revisited. *Auditing: A Journal of Practice & Theory* 31(1): 115–26.
Offermanns, M. and Peek, E. (2011). 'Investor Reactions to PCAOB Inspection Reports', *working paper.* Maastricht: Maastricht University.
Read, W.J., Rama, D.V. and Raghunandan, K. (2004). 'Local and Regional Audit Firms and the Market for SEC Audits', *Accounting Horizons* 18(4): 241–54.
Public Company Accounting Oversight Board (PCAOB) (2011) *Mission Statement.* PCAOB. Available online at http://pcaobus.org/About/History/Pages/default.aspx (accessed 5 May 2014).
Roybark, H.M. (2009). 'An Analysis of Audit Deficiencies Based on Section 104 Inspection Reports Issued by the PCAOB during 2004–2007', *Journal of Accounting, Ethics and Public Policy* 10(1): 1–81.
Van Opijnen, M., Van de Poel, K. and Vanstraelen, A. (2011). 'Public Oversight and Audit Quality: Evidence from Public Oversight of Audit Firms in the Netherlands', working paper. Available online at http://ssrn.com/abstract=1916558 (accessed 5 May 2014).
Vanstraelen, A., Schelleman, C., Meuwissen, R. and Hofmann, I. (2012). 'The Audit Reporting Debate: Seemingly Intractable Problems and Feasible Solutions', *European Accounting Review* 21(2): 193–215.
Wainberg, J., Kida, T., Piercey, M.D. and Smith, J.F. (2013). 'The Impact of Anecdotal Data in Regulatory Audit Firm Inspection Reports', *Accounting, Organizations and Society* 38(8): 621-636.

Part III

Research on the process of auditing

15 Auditor industry specialization

Debra Jeter

Overview

Specialization by auditors to enhance their technological expertise could be defined in a variety of ways, such as specialization in particular income statement or balance sheet accounts (net pension liability, for example, or valuation of intangibles); or in specific aspects of the audit engagement (e.g., the accounting for foreign subsidiaries, mergers, or research and development expenditures). It has most often, however, been defined in the literature as industry specialization.

Audit firms have incentives to differentiate themselves by investing in technology and human capital that are specific to their chosen sets of specializations. To do so, they invest in the attainment of superior knowledge in order to provide services that other audit firms cannot easily replicate. Mayhew and Wilkins (2003) and Cahan *et al.* (2008) present arguments that these investments are most beneficial in offering services to a fairly homogeneous group of clients, such as same-industry firms. Knowledge specialization facilitates the development of a more clearly differentiated audit product, as well as superior related services, such as the provision of advice and counsel to audit clientele. At the office level, industry expertise may be linked to individual auditors' deep personal knowledge of their clients and their clients' industries, which is less easily disseminated to other individuals (Ferguson *et al.* 2003; Francis *et al.* 2005). By drawing on this deeper knowledge, industry specialists may provide better recommendations to clients, thus positively influencing business and industry risk reporting.

While the exact nature of the benefits to the auditors investing in the acquisition of industry-specific knowledge has not been clearly established – whether specialization leads to higher fees, greater market share, lowered probability of audit failure, or an improved ability to retain desirable clientele – evidence indicates industry expertise, or the perception of such, to be a priority for most large auditors (e.g., Hogan and Jeter 1999; Cahan *et al.* 2011).

A question often examined is whether industry specialization leads to fee premiums paid by clients hiring specialists. Here the evidence is mixed with respect to whether such premiums are widely paid or only in some instances; whether the premiums are being accurately measured given the current state of the methodology applied; and, in the event that they are paid by some but not all clients, the nature of client characteristics most compatible with the existence of fee premiums for industry specialists.

Current issues

Current issues include:

- Is industry specialization by auditors associated with either (or both) higher quality audits or higher quality financial reporting by clientele?

Conversely, the General Accounting Office (GAO) issued two reports (GAO 2003, 2008) in which it expressed some concern that the high levels of concentration in the audit market resulting from the mergers of the largest auditors could lead to inadequate competition and lowered quality. Investigation of these questions entails not only finding an appropriate way to gauge industry specialization and concentration, but also how best to capture the elusive quality aspects. While discretionary accruals are most often used to proxy for earnings quality, they have often been assumed to proxy for audit quality as well. However, this assumption is admittedly a dubious one, since the auditors' role in the reporting of discretionary accruals is a secondary one; discretionary accruals models are imperfect; and discretionary accruals choices, like auditor choices, are endogenous. Other proxies in the literature include the propensity of the auditor to issue non-standard audit opinions and their clients' propensity to just meet or beat analysts' expectations (see also Chapter 10, Earnings management and auditing).

- Is industry specialization priced by auditors, and if so, how?

While specialist auditors have incentives to recoup their investment in attaining industry-specific expertise, pricing is also a function of competitive forces. As a result, specialists may not be able to price their expertise to the extent desired unless the client perceives sufficient benefits to warrant higher prices for specialist auditors.

- Do industry specialists charge a fee premium or pass along cost savings, if any, to clients?

This question is related to the previous one. Further, it is conceivable that specialist auditors are able to perform audits with significantly greater efficiency than non-specialists, leading to fewer chargeable hours and hence lower, rather than higher, fees, even in the face of higher hourly rates. These detailed data are rarely available to researchers, however, making these questions challenging ones to investigate.

- How is industry specialization best captured empirically?

Market share measures, either at the city or national level, have been most often used in the literature. Some recent studies (e.g., Ferguson *et al.* 2003; Francis *et al.* 2005) suggest that audit markets are better defined at the local level than at the national level. The typical argument is that local markets are important if industry expertise resides with personnel in specific offices and if such knowledge cannot be easily transferred to other offices in the same audit firm. On the other hand, if this information can easily be transferred to other offices, then national level measures may be more appropriate. Market share measures may preclude small auditors from qualifying as specialists. Alternative portfolio approaches will be discussed in the subsection 'How can industry specialization best be captured?' (p. 195)

- How does self-selection affect the interpretation of the results presented in the literature?

Typical models include specialization as an independent variable in a standard OLS (ordinary least squares) regression with either fees or a proxy for quality as the dependent variable. Since specialization is a choice, these models may be argued to lead in some instances to incorrect inferences.

Historical development

Early work on audit specialists assumed a non-differentiated product (e.g., Eichenseher and Danos 1981), and researchers generally attributed pricing effects to market structure. For example, building on earlier work by economists in the structure–conduct–performance paradigm, Pearson and Trompeter (1994) argue that when there are a few dominant auditors (specialists) who have greater bargaining power, these auditors will be price setters, leading to oligopolistic rents.[1]

However, market structure can also be used to explain fee discounts. As Eichenseher and Danos (1981) suggest, specialists can benefit from economies of scale, since specialists can spread the cost of acquiring industry-specific knowledge across a larger set of clients. To the extent that the cost savings are passed on to the client as would be expected in more competitive markets, this can lead to lower fees. Another reason why specialists may on occasion offer lower fees is monopsony power on the part of the client in situations where there are limited buyers of the auditor's specialized knowledge. This shifts the bargaining advantage to the client, allowing the client to bargain away any oligopolistic rents and, possibly, to obtain fee discounts from the specialist.

Later papers (e.g., Craswell *et al.* 1995; Mayhew and Wilkins 2003) relax the homogeneity assumption and recognize that a positive relation between specialization and audit fees could be reflective of a higher quality audit conducted by a specialist.

State of research

Is industry specialization by auditors associated with either (or both) higher quality audits or higher quality financial reporting by clientele?

Industry specialization has been argued to benefit clients in a number of ways. Industry specialists may be able to provide higher levels of assurance because they are more likely to assess risks, and detect financial reporting errors and irregularities, thereby providing better planned and more effective audits. Industry specialization can positively affect the quality of the financial reports because specialists are associated with higher earnings quality, whether due to their intervention in the reporting process, or because management anticipates such intervention and constrains opportunistic or aggressive earnings management.

Studies using experimental research find that specialist auditors can lower audit costs through more effective and efficient audits. Low (2004), for example, finds that specialist auditors are likely to make better risk assessments and to develop better audit plans and time budgets than do non-specialist auditors. Low (2004) also finds that specialist auditors are capable of making higher quality changes to inherited audit programs. Similarly, Owhoso *et al.* (2002) find that audit seniors and managers within specialist teams detect errors in work papers in a complementary way.

Balsam *et al.* (2003) find that firms employing industry specialist auditors have higher earnings quality where earnings quality is measured using discretionary accruals and the earnings response coefficient; Dunn and Mayhew (2004) find that the quality of disclosures is positively associated with auditor industry specialization. In addition, auditors often help their clients to deal with strategic and operating business issues in ways that clients value. Industry knowledge and expertise have been identified in various surveys as primary factors in assessing audit quality, and Behn *et al.* (1997) find a link between industry specialization and client satisfaction.

Furthermore, within-client perceptions that an auditor offers higher quality by virtue of its industry specialization may deter employees from acting contrary to shareholders' interests regardless of whether the auditor is perceived to provide a higher quality audit, better operational or reporting advice, or lower fees from economies of scale. Capital market perceptions that an auditor provides high quality by virtue of his or her industry specialization may encourage confidence in the client's audited financial statements, and possibly lower estimated risk levels associated with the firm, thereby leading to a potentially lower cost of capital. In summary, the literature provides evidence of improved audit quality on various dimensions including audit efficiency (Owhoso *et al.* 2002); disclosure quality (Dunn and Mayhew, 2004); and the market's responsiveness to clients' earnings (Balsam *et al.* 2003).

Is industry specialization priced by auditors and, if so, how? Do industry specialists earn a fee premium?

Although the relation between audit fees and specialization has been widely examined, the results are inconclusive. While many studies find a positive relation, others find no relation, a negative relationship, or some combination, with fee premiums accruing only to certain types of specialists or paid by certain types of clients. Hay and Jeter (2011) list 32 published studies showing a variety of mixed results.

In an early study of audit pricing by industry specialists, Craswell *et al.* (1995) find that industry specialist auditors receive fee premiums in excess of their brand name premiums. They argue that the fee premiums could be compensation for the specialists' investment in industry-specific knowledge, while positing an alternative explanation that specialists provide a higher quality audit (i.e., a differentiated product). However, while Craswell *et al.* (1995) define an industry specialist as an auditor having a market share of at least 10 percent of an industry, Ferguson and Stokes (2002), using different definitions of specialists, find limited evidence of specialist premiums. In the face of fewer large auditors, more recent studies generally use higher cut-offs such as 20 to 30 percent of the market share in an industry.

Ferguson *et al.* (2003) and Francis *et al.* (2005) extend Craswell *et al.* (1995) and consider industry specialization at national and city levels. Using Australian and US data respectively, these studies find evidence of fee premiums when the auditor is an industry leader at both the national and city levels. Mayhew and Wilkins (2003) attempt to tease out the premium and discount pricing effects. They argue that an increasing market share in an industry gives rise to production economies that should lead to lower fees. They contend, however, that a market share *significantly higher* than that of competitors provides evidence that an industry specialist auditor offers a differentiated product. Using IPO (initial public offering) data, they find that audit fees decrease as the auditor's industry market share grows but increase if the auditor has a dominant share.

Casterella *et al.* (2004) find that small clients pay a specialist premium while large clients do not. They interpret this as evidence that large clients have sufficient bargaining power to negotiate away any specialist premium. In contrast, Hay and Jeter (2011) find that in a sample of New Zealand audits, specialist audits of both larger clients and low-risk auditees are more likely to exhibit a fee premium relative to audits by non-specialists. They argue that in their setting, non-specialist auditors have to offer fee discounts to attract the most desirable clients. (The typical methodology applied in pricing studies to establish the existence of a fee premium does not distinguish between a premium to specialists versus a discount to non-specialists.)

Pricing studies vary with respect to the assumptions made about the audit quality provided by specialists. Pearson and Trompeter (1994), for example, assume homogeneous audit quality for specialists and non-specialists. Craswell *et al.* (1995) assume higher quality audits for specialists, and Mayhew and Wilkins (2003) assume higher audit quality for those specialists who dominate their industry. Cahan *et al.* (2011) argue that the audit market is characterized by a type of segmentation in which some specialists pursue a product differentiation strategy, focusing more extensively on the acquisition of requisite skills and expertise, while other specialists pursue a cost minimization strategy, producing lower cost, lower quality audits. Numan and Willekens (2012) argue that when competitors are close or similar in their levels of specialization or market share, the client is less willing to pay a fee premium for the delivered quality related to industry specialization since a competitor can deliver much the same value.

How can industry specialization best be captured empirically?

Auditor specialization may be actual, perceived, or both. Big 4 firms' websites suggest claims to specialization in most, if not all, industries (Hogan and Jeter 1999; Cahan *et al.* 2011); and they are indeed likely to be "actual" specialists in several industries in the sense of having teams devoted to multiple industries. Market share based on either client sales or client assets has been widely used in prior studies (Palmrose, 1986; Hogan and Jeter, 1999; Mayhew and Wilkins, 2003; Dunn and Mayhew, 2004, among others). Along this line of thinking, market leaders (as measured by market share) are presumed to have superior industry-specific skills in monitoring and advising with respect to internal controls and external financial reporting. Studies often use an arbitrary cut-off to establish specialization, such as 25 percent or 30 percent of the market share in an industry, based on audit fees, client assets, or client revenues, all of which tend to be highly correlated. In some studies, an alternative measure is to consider only the market leader or the top two, based on market share, as the specialists. These measures may be based on either national or city level market share.

Market-share based measures of industry specialization have been used to examine a variety of issues, including the relation between industry specialization and disclosures (Dunn and Mayhew 2004); the market's reaction to auditor switches (Knechel *et al.* 2007); legal systems and earnings quality (Kwon *et al.* 2007); audit committees (Chen *et al.* 2005); auditor resignations (Cenker and Nagy 2008); non-audit fees (Lim and Tan 2008); investment opportunities (Cahan *et al.* 2008); and analysts' forecasts (Behn *et al.* 2008; Payne 2008).

However, such measures for auditor specialization are likely to exclude small audit firms that are quite specialized in the sense that they may audit primarily clients in a given industry and focus largely on honing their knowledge and skills about that specific industry. For example, suppose a small local auditor audits firms exclusively in the healthcare industry. Yet, because of the size of the audit firm, the market share proxy would rarely capture this firm as a leader. Williams (1991) suggests a continuous measure of audit specialization based on the difference between the audit firm's market share of the client's industry and the audit firm's market share of the total audit market. Neal and Riley (2004) present a portfolio share approach; if the proportion of the auditor's work in a particular industry exceeds the auditor's share of the total market, an audit firm is considered a specialist, since it has a particular industry focus not representative of the general market. Applying this measure, an audit firm specializes in an industry to the extent that it audits a greater proportion of that industry than the proportion of the total market that it audits. For example, an audit firm that audits 20 percent of an industry but only 10 percent of the total market is deemed to specialize in that industry.

How does self-selection affect the interpretation of the results presented in the literature?

Clearly, clients are not randomly assigned to audit firms, but select their auditors. Client firm characteristics that affect auditor choice are quite similar to the characteristics that determine audit fees (the variables in the typical audit fee models). Some analytical studies (see Hogan 1997, for instance) develop theoretical models to explore the self-selection of auditors by clients. In these models, clients with favorable private information choose higher quality auditors despite higher costs.

From an econometric perspective, self-selection introduces a bias in the standard OLS regressions. The self-selection problem arises because fees are observable only after a firm has chosen its auditor, while the fees under an alternative auditor choice remain unobserved. As a result, the expected error in the standard OLS specification of audit fees is non-zero and the auditor choice (specialization) variable is endogenous. A number of researchers, however, suggest pitfalls in applying selection models, which can yield a wide range of outcomes in response to minor changes in model specification. It is thus an unresolved issue as to whether the benefits of the self-selection models outweigh the challenges with respect to addressing the questions of interest.

Unresolved issues requiring future research

The literature has not yet clearly established whether specialization fee premiums are more likely to be paid by larger clients or by smaller ones. Also, it is conceivable that larger clients could appear to be more likely to pay specialization premiums for one of the following reasons:

a) The impact of client size on fees is not adequately controlled for in the audit fee models.
b) It is extremely difficult to construct a matched sample design with sufficient data for analyses in which clients hiring non-specialist auditors are very similar to those hiring specialists.
c) Non-specialist auditors must offer fee discounts to attract the largest, most desirable clients; but, in so doing, they are likely to offer lower quality.

Also, there may be other observable client characteristics that make some clients more or less likely to benefit from industry specialization and thus more likely to be willing to pay fee premiums.

Future research should continue to seek out identifiable characteristics of the industry, or of the marketplace, indicative of when and where industry specialization is most likely to occur, and to result in fee premiums, while also recognizing that specialist auditors may on occasion offer fee discounts. Further, it is important to distinguish under which circumstances discounts represent economies of scale being passed on to the clients (for example, Bills *et al.* 2013), as opposed to those where they are reflective of lowered audit quality resulting from competitive pressures (Cahan *et al.* 2011).

The literature has not yet established how industry specialists are most appropriately identified, though various approaches have been suggested and tried; nor is it clear whether specialization is captured better at the city or national level (or whether, as some studies suggest, an auditor needs to qualify as a specialist at both levels to benefit from fee premiums).

Finally, researchers may wish to consider new approaches to differentiate empirically between actual and perceived quality by industry specialists.

Conclusion

While auditor industry specialization has attracted considerable attention in the literature, the role of industry specialization in audit pricing remains unresolved. A number of studies find evidence of specialist premiums, but others do not. Nonetheless, large auditors are virtually unanimous in their acknowledgement of the importance of industry specialization to their respective firms.

The literature has not established conclusively how industry specialists should be identified, though the majority of researchers continue to use some variation of market share measures based on client asset, revenues, or audit fees. Further, it is not clear whether specialization is captured better at the city or national level, as arguments have been presented for both. The essence of this distinction appears to rest on the ease of information transfer across offices within the same audit firm. If transfer is considered relatively easy, then national level measures are logical; however, if deep personal or locale-specific knowledge is crucial and is not easily disseminated, then city level measures may be more relevant.

In an informal survey, practitioners defined industry specialization as it pertained to their firms to involve "knowledge specific to a client's industry," "an understanding of how general and specific accounting guidance applies to the client's industry," and "an understanding of operational nuances and challenges," with one practitioner volunteering that industry knowledge was more important to his clients than auditing knowledge (Cahan *et al.* 2011).

Pricing studies vary with respect to the assumptions made about the audit quality provided by specialists. Whereas Pearson and Trompeter (1994) assume homogeneous audit quality for both specialists and non-specialists, Craswell *et al.* (1995) assume higher quality audits for specialists, and Mayhew and Wilkins (2003) assume higher audit quality only for those specialists who dominate their industry. Cahan *et al.* (2011) argue that the audit market is characterized by a type of segmentation in which some specialists pursue a product differentiation strategy, focusing more extensively on the acquisition of requisite skills and expertise, while other specialists pursue a cost minimization strategy, producing lower cost, lower quality audits.

Although concerns have been voiced that high auditor concentration (resulting from the audit firm mergers and the demise of Arthur Andersen) could lead to oligopolistic pricing in some industries, most researchers find little evidence of such an impact. As audit quality is paramount in returning the profession to the "priesthood" in the wake of accounting scandals such as Enron and bank failures, the question that perhaps most needs to be addressed is whether specialists provide truly superior quality audits. If specialists take advantage of their reputation to deliver low quality audits – for example, by substituting junior staff hours for senior or partner hours – then specialization (and high concentration) could become problematic. On the other hand, if specialists are motivated to protect their reputation by providing quality services, the increasing industry and business complexity in today's economy would seem to dictate a continuing need for industry specialist auditors. The bulk of the extant research is generally consistent with the latter view.

Industry specialization, if pursued as a means of enhancing the knowledge and understanding necessary to conduct superior audits, should result in benefits to both client and auditor. First, from the client's perspective, industry specialists may be able to provide higher levels of assurance because they are more likely to assess risks, and to detect financial reporting errors and irregularities, and are thus equipped to deliver better planned and more effective audits. Research suggests that specialists are associated with higher earnings quality for their auditees, whether due to intervention in the reporting process, or because management anticipates such intervention and constrains opportunistic earnings management. For the auditors investing in the acquisition of industry-specific knowledge, benefits of successful differentiation via specialization are likely to include higher fees, greater market share, lowered probability of audit failure, and an improved ability to retain desirable clientele.

Note

1 At a more general level, this is one of the arguments used to explain a large body of evidence that consistently finds audit fee premiums for Big N audit firms (see Hay *et al.*, 2006, for a review).

References

Balsam, S., J. Krishnan and J.S. Yang. 2003. "Auditor Industry Specialization and Earnings Quality", *Auditing: A Journal of Practice & Theory* 22(September): 71–97.

Behn, B.K., J.V. Carcello, D.R. Hermanson and R.H. Hermanson. 1997. "The Determinants of Audit Client Satisfaction among Clients of Big 6 Firms", *Accounting Horizons* 11: 7–24.

Behn, B.K., J.-H. Choi and T. Kang. 2008. "Audit Quality and Properties of Analyst Earnings Forecasts", *The Accounting Review* 83(April): 327–49.

Bills, K., D. Jeter and S. Stein. 2013. "Auditor Industry Specialization and Evidence of Cost Efficiencies in Homogenous Industries", working paper. Available online at http://ssrn.com/abstract=2321741 or http://dx.doi.org/10.2139/ssrn.2321741 (both accessed 21 May 2014).

Cahan, S.F., J.M. Godfrey, J. Hamilton and D.C. Jeter. 2008. "Auditor Specialization, Auditor Dominance, and Audit Fees: The Role of Investment Opportunities", *The Accounting Review* 83(November): 1393–423.

Cahan, S.F., D. Jeter and V. Naiker. 2011. "Are all Industry Specialist Auditors the Same?" *Auditing: A Journal of Practice & Theory* 30(4, November): 191–222.

Carson, E. 2009. "Industry Specialization by Global Audit Firm Networks", *The Accounting Review* 84(March): 355–82.

Casterella, J.R., J.R. Francis, B.L. Lewis and P.L. Walker. 2004. "Auditor Industry Specialization, Client Bargaining Power, and Audit Pricing", *Auditing: A Journal of Theory and Practice* 23(March): 123–40.

Cenker, W. and A. Nagy. 2008. "Auditor Resignations and Auditor Industry Specialization", *Accounting Horizons* 22(September): 279–95.

Chen, Y.M., R. Moroney and K. Houghton. 2005. "Audit Committee Composition and the Use of an Industry Specialist Audit Firm", *Accounting and Finance* 45(July): 217–39.

Craswell, A., J. Francis and S. Taylor. 1995. "Auditor Brand Name Reputation and Industry Specialization", *Journal of Accounting and Economics* 20(December): 297–322.

Dunn, K.A. and B.W. Mayhew. 2004. "Audit Firm Industry Specialization and Client Disclosure Quality", *Review of Accounting Studies* 9(March): 35–58.

Eichenseher, J.W., and P. Danos. 1981. "The Analysis of Industry-specific Auditor Concentration: Towards an Explanatory Model", *The Accounting Review* 56(July): 479–92.

Ferguson, A. and D. Stokes. 2002. "Brand Name Audit Pricing, Industry Specialization and Industry Leadership Premiums Post Big 8 and Big 6 Mergers", *Contemporary Accounting Research* 19(Spring): 77–110.

Ferguson, A., J. Francis and D. Stokes. 2003. "The Effect of Firm-wide and Office-level Industry Expertise on Audit Pricing", *The Accounting Review* 78(April): 428–48.

Francis, J.R., K. Reichelt and D. Wang. 2005. "The Pricing of National and City-specific Reputations for Industry Expertise in the U.S. Audit Market", *The Accounting Review* 80(1, January): 113–36.

General Accountability Office (GAO). 2003. *Public Accounting Firms: Mandated Study on Consolidation and Competition*. GAO report 03–864. Washington, DC: GAO.

General Accountability Office (GAO). 2008. *Audits of Public Companies: Continued Concentration in Audit Market for Large Public Companies Does Not Call for Immediate Action*. GAO report 08–163. Washington, DC: GAO.

Hay, D.C. and D. Jeter. 2011. "The Pricing of Industry Specialization by Auditors in New Zealand", *Accounting and Business Research* 41(2, June): 171–95.

Hay, D.C., W.R. Knechel and N. Wong. 2006. "Audit Fees: A Meta-analysis of the Effect of Supply and Demand Attributes", *Contemporary Accounting Research* 23(Spring): 141–91.

Hogan, C. 1997. "Costs and Benefits of Audit Quality in the IPO Market: A Self-selection Analysis", *Accounting Review* 72(1): 67–86.

Hogan, C.E. and D.C. Jeter. 1999. "Industry Specialization by Auditors", *Auditing: A Journal of Practice and Theory* 18(Spring): 1–17.

Knechel, R.W., V. Naiker and G. Pacheco. 2007. "Does Auditor Industry Specialization Matter? Evidence from Market Reaction to Auditor Switches", *Auditing: A Journal of Theory and Practice* 26(May): 19–45.

Kwon, S.Y., C.Y. Lim and P.M.-S. Tan. 2007. "Legal Systems and Earnings Quality: The Role of Auditor Industry Specialization", *Auditing: A Journal of Practice & Theory* 26(2): 25–55.

Lim, C.-Y. and H.-T. Tan. 2008. "Non-audit Service Fees and Audit Quality: The Impact of Auditor Specialization", *Journal of Accounting Research* 46(March): 199–246.

Low, K.Y. 2004. "The Effect of Industry Specialization on Audit Risk Assessments and Audit-planning Decisions", *The Accounting Review* 79: 201–9.

Mayhew, B.W. and M.S. Wilkins. 2003. "Audit Firm Industry Specialization as a Differentiation Strategy: Evidence from Fees Charged to Firms Going Public", *Auditing: A Journal of Theory and Practice* 22(September): 33–52.

Neal, T.L. and R.R. Riley. 2004. "Auditor Industry Specialist Research Design", *Auditing: A Journal of Practice and Theory* 23: 169–77.

Numan, W. and M. Willekens. 2012. "Competitive Pressure, Audit Quality, and Industry Specialization", working paper. Leuven: Katholieke Universiteit Leuven.

Owhoso, V.E., W.F. Messier and J. Lynch. 2002. "Error Detection by Industry-specialized Teams during the Sequential Audit Review", *Journal of Accounting Research* 40: 883–900.

Palmrose, Z.-V. 1986. "Audit Fees and Auditor Size: Further Evidence", *Journal of Accounting Research* 24(Autumn): 97–110.

Payne, J. 2008. "The Influence of Audit Firm Specialization on Analysts' Forecast Errors", *Auditing: A Journal of Theory and Practice* 27(November): 109–36.

Pearson, T. and G. Trompeter. 1994. "Competition in the Market for Audit Services: The Effect of Supplier Concentration on Audit Fees", *Contemporary Accounting Research* 11: 115–35.

Williams, R.A. 1991. "Measuring Submarket Specialization by Firms", *Economics Letters* 36: 291–4.

16

Judgment and decision making

Ken Trotman

Introduction

Judgment and decision making (JDM) research in auditing[1] is undertaken to understand how individual and group judgments and decisions[2] in auditing are made and how to improve those judgments. References to the need for judgments are very common in auditing standards and, in fact, the whole process of auditing is permeated by professional judgment. For example, consider the broad range of judgments and decisions auditors make: plan the amount and type of evidence to collect; determine fraud risk factors; search for and obtain evidence; determine the level of professional skepticism to exercise; review the work of others; and make assessments of internal control, materiality, fair value, going concern and the reliance to be placed on the work of internal auditors and other experts.

This is an extremely broad topic covering almost 40 years of published research. Some indicators of this breadth are that there were 303 JDM audit papers published between 1970 and 2009 in just four leading journals: *Accounting, Organizations and Society*; *Contemporary Accounting Research*; *Journal of Accounting Research;* and *The Accounting Review* (Trotman *et al.*, 2011: Table 1). The leading specialist journal in auditing, *Auditing: A Journal of Practice & Theory*, also contains numerous JDM papers. In fact, a recent edition of *Auditing: A Journal of Practice & Theory* contains nine papers which were part of the Public Company Accounting Oversight Board (PCAOB) synthesis project (Cohen and Knechel, 2013) and cover the following aspects of auditor judgments: fair value and other estimates; professional skepticism; audit sampling; the approach to subsequent events; the effect of client's use of service organizations; reliance on the internal audit function; fraud-related research; and the auditor-reporting model. These synthesis papers cover an extensive range of literature in over 350 pages of text, much of which is not included in this paper. The remainder of this chapter aims to provide a background for these and other recent synthesis papers by describing the purpose of JDM research in auditing, the types of research that have been carried out, including the historical development and current issues addressed.[3] It then considers some of the unresolved issues that future research might address.

Purpose of JDM research[4]

JDM research in auditing has four main purposes: (1) it evaluates the quality of auditor judgments; (2) it attempts to describe how auditors make judgments and how these judgments are affected by various factors; (3) it tests theories of the cognitive processes that produce auditors' judgments and decisions, including the role of knowledge and memory in audit judgments; and (4) it develops and tests decision aids designed to overcome any deficiencies found in research on auditor judgments (Libby, 1981).

There is a variety of issues examined under each of these four purposes. First, under the category evaluating the quality of auditor judgments, issues include the accuracy of auditors' judgments, the level of consensus between auditors, the consistency of auditors' judgments across time, and the level of bias in auditor judgments due to the use of heuristics (simplified judgmental rules including representations, availability, and anchoring and adjustment). Understanding the results of this research provides information on where improvements are necessary and under what circumstances decision aids are likely to be useful. In fact, recent professional publications (e.g. KPMG, 2011: 23) outline potential biases in auditor judgments including those related to anchoring, availability and confirmation. For example, a confirmation bias is where individuals preferentially collect evidence to confirm rather than disconfirm their hypotheses (see Smith and Kida, 1991 for other examples).

The second purpose is to describe how auditors make judgments and which factors affect judgment performance. The research considers such questions as: What information cues do auditors use in making judgments? On which of these cues do auditors place the most reliance; and whether auditors combine information cues configurally or non-configurally (linearly) and under what circumstances do they process configurally? Another question is what factors affect the reliance that auditors place on information cues (e.g. source credibility)? Further questions include: Is it information selection, hypothesis generation or information processing that has the most effect on auditors' judgment performance? Under what circumstances do judgment biases occur? What factors determine whether auditors' judgments are biased? An understanding of the above factors provides insights into explaining potential deficiencies in judgments and assists in the development of possible remedies.

The third purpose is to test theories of the cognitive processes which produce auditor judgments. This research examines the role of knowledge and memory in auditor judgments including the differences in knowledge structures between experts and novices, and more recently the role of industry expertise. It considers the cognitive processes through which knowledge is incorporated into judgments. Some of the questions addressed include: What knowledge is needed to make different judgments and when, how and how well is this knowledge acquired and later used? What is the role of the auditors' task specific knowledge and information processing in problem recognition, hypothesis generation and information search? What factors affect auditor memory for audit evidence and what is the relationship of memory to auditor judgments (Libby, 1995)? The benefits of understanding these knowledge and memory differences between experts and novices is to help practitioners to develop training and new decision aids to assist novices to make judgments more like those of experts. It also provides insights into why particular organizational arrangements (such as the review process) are applied in particular accounting settings (Libby and Luft, 1993; Libby and Trotman, 1993). Overall, understanding cognitive processes better allows us to answer 'why' and 'how' questions which are an important step in the ultimate improvement of professional judgments.

Fourth, audit JDM research provides insights into potential remedies for identified deficiencies, since it is necessary to understand a decision process in order to improve it. Possible methods of improving decision making that have been addressed include changing the framing of the question, changing the format of the information provided, providing feedback, using interacting and nominal groups and using decision aids, and the decomposition of how judgments are made. Overall, the ultimate aim of research on auditor judgments is to improve judgments. Consequently, this area of research has significant scope to impact the practice of auditing (see Bell and Wright, 1995; Cohen and Knechel, 2013).

While JDM research can sometimes directly address current questions that regulators and auditors want answered, it has an important role in basic research and providing building blocks to address more applied questions. Examples of this type of research would include research on cognitive processes which consider how information is encoded, stored and retrieved from memory (e.g. Libby and Luft, 1993). JDM researchers have the opportunity to move beyond examining the effects of structures that practitioners presently use, to testing the effects of structures, formats and processes not presently used. For example, if audit firms moved from a review process to some other form of group processing, how would this new type of group structure impact judgments related to the search for and processing of evidence, professional skepticism, etc.? Similarly, how would new types of accountability structures impact auditors' and inspectors' judgments (e.g. Peecher *et al.*, 2013)?

Use of experiments

Most JDM audit research has been conducted using experiments. Experiments involve the researcher providing appropriate background material to participants, manipulating one or more independent variables and measuring the effect on one or more dependent variables. Individuals or groups are randomly assigned to the treatments while other factors are controlled (e.g. background information) or measured (e.g. experience of the participants). An experiment addresses the following key questions: whether there is an effect; under what circumstances is there an effect (i.e. when); how and why there is an effect (e.g. cognitive processes). Thus, experiments are useful to see if and when there is an effect, and to identify what causes that effect. They are less beneficial in determining the amount of an effect as the results will be impacted by the level at which the variables are set.

There are a number of benefits of using experimental methods in audit JDM research. A key strength of experiments is that they allow strong causal inferences to be made. Experiments can also be used to separate out interrelated factors that coexist in the natural environment to examine which of a number of potential factors cause a change in an auditor judgment (Joe, 2003; Ng and Tan, 2007). As noted by Libby and Luft (1993), 'the experimentalist's comparative advantage lies in the ability to abstract and control other potentially influential variables'. Experiments also have the advantage of testing the effects of conditions that do not presently exist in practice or exist but not in sufficient volume to examine archivally (e.g. proposed new standards, new audit methods).[5]

Most JDM research is based on theory from psychology. These theories include information processing, including the lens model framework (e.g. Ashton, 1974); heuristics and biases (e.g. Joyce and Biddle, 1981); auditor expertise (e.g. Libby, 1985); decision aids (e.g. Messier, 1995); motivated reasoning (e.g. Kadous *et al.*, 2003); accountability (e.g. Kennedy, 1993; Tan, 1995); groups theory (e.g. Trotman and Yetton, 1985); negotiation theory (e.g. Gibbins *et al.*, 2001); prospect theory (e.g. Peecher and Piercey, 2008); reciprocity theory (e.g. Hatfield *et al.*, 2008); attribution theory (e.g. Kaplan and Reckers, 1985); framing (e.g. Kida, 1984); and persuasion theories (e.g. Rich *et al.*, 1997). Even within these groups of theories there are many individual theories, for example, the social psychology research on groups provides numerous theories on the ways groups combine individual judgments and what types of group structures lead to better decisions under different circumstances.

Theory can also be based on research in a range of other disciplines including economics (e.g. economic theories related to incentives, especially as they apply to the audit domain) and knowledge of the audit domain (e.g. Bell *et al.*, 2005 on the use of different forms of evidence and the likely effect of different forms of professional skepticism). Peecher *et al.* (2013), in addressing the question of what kind of accountability system would motivate auditors to improve quality, outline potential changes for improvement in audit quality based on a two-dimensional framework of process/outcome accountabilities and rewards/penalties. They put forward a range of research questions supported by theory and research in accounting, economics, psychology and neuroscience. Similarly, theory-based papers such as Nelson (2009) on professional skepticism and Hammersley (2011) on fraud develop models based mainly on past research in auditing and psychology. Interview data can also be useful in model building and development of theory (e.g. Cohen *et al.*, 2010; Trompeter and Wright, 2010).

Theoretical frameworks for considering JDM research in auditing

Four theoretical frameworks for the consideration of previous JDM audit research are presented in Libby and Luft (1993), Solomon and Shields (1995), Nelson and Tan (2005) and Bonner (2008). Libby and Luft considered four categories of JDM audit research noting that performance is a function of ability, knowledge, environment and motivation. Solomon and Shields separate individual and group judgments as well as dividing ability into three categories: policy capturing, probabilistic judgment and heuristics and biases. This results in six categories of JDM research: policy capturing, probabilistic judgment, heuristics and biases, cognitive processes, environment and motivation and multi-person judgments. Nelson and Tan (2005) classify JDM research by the audit task, the auditor and interpersonal interactions. Their emphasis on task is important if one of the ultimate goals is to inform policy makers. For example, JDM research may be motivated around such audit tasks as the audit of fair values, audit sampling, internal control, subsequent events, reliance on the internal audit function and fraud assessments (Cohen and Knechel, 2013). Nelson and Tan's (2005) category of 'the auditor' covers much of the earlier research on ability (including cognitive limitations) and knowledge. Their third category of interpersonal relationship considers a much broader coverage than previous categorizations due to new topics introduced to the literature (for example, negotiation between auditors and clients; consultation within audit firms). Finally, the framework adopted in Bonner (2008) considers three types of factors (person, task and environment) that create differences on particular dimensions of JDM quality.

For the remainder of this chapter I will adopt a characterization based on (1) policy capturing; (2) heuristics and bias; (3) knowledge and memory; (4) environmental and motivation factors; and (5) group decision making. It is based on a combination of the earlier frameworks discussed above. I use the Nelson and Tan (2005) framework in discussing current research and unanswered questions.

Historical overview of JDM audit research

Policy capturing research

The aim of policy capturing research is to develop a mathematical representation of the judgment policies of auditors to determine judgment strategy ('policy'). This is generally achieved by providing participants with a series of judgment situations in which various combinations of cues (i.e. information) are presented. The relationships among the cues presented and the judgments made are derived using statistical methods such as ANOVA (analysis of variance) to infer an individual's judgment strategy. Most of the policy capturing research considered internal control judgments and followed Ashton (1974). The main issues addressed by policy capturing research are consensus among different auditors, the relative importance of individual cues to auditors, the stability of auditor judgments over time and the extent of self-insight auditors have into their own judgment policies (Ashton, 1974). Another primary issue addressed in the policy capturing research is whether auditors combine information configurally, that is, does an auditor's reaction to one piece of information depend on the presence or absence of other pieces of information. Configural information processing is 'cognition in which the pattern (or configuration) of stimuli is important to the subsequent judgment/decision' (Brown and Solomon, 1991). Knowledge of the relative importance of individual cues and the functional form of the judgment rule used (linear versus configural) can be a basis for the evaluation of policies used, provide an explanation for disagreements between auditors and assist in the design of training and decision aids. The level of such configural information processing is impacted by the level of risk (Maletta and Kida, 1993).

There has been considerable research, most of which was conducted prior to 1990, on the level of consensus of experienced auditors. Solomon and Shields (1995) report that the mean correlation between pairs of auditors in 22 studies of auditor judgment was +0.59 (with a range from +0.28 to +0.93). It should also be noted that disagreements both between individual auditors and between auditors and inspectors are still important today (Pozen, 2008; Peecher *et al.*, 2013). Reasons why experts disagree include using different information sets, having different mental models, combining information and weighting of diverse information in different ways, different propensity to be biased, and different timing of making a judgment (Mumpower and Stewart, 1996; Peecher *et al.*, 2013).

Heuristics and biases

The psychology literature in the early 1970s suggested that individuals do not always act normatively and that they often use a range of heuristics (that is, simplified judgmental rules). A number of decision heuristics, which were considered to be more accurate descriptions of human judgments, were developed and formulated by Tversky and Kahneman (1974), who suggested that these heuristics reduce the cognitively complex task of assessing probabilities and predicting values to simpler judgmental operations. While these heuristics can be useful, they can lead to severe and systematic errors.

There are three main heuristics, namely, representativeness, anchoring and adjustment, and availability that have been the main focus of research in this area. First, the representativeness heuristic suggests that when individuals make assessments of the probability that A comes from population B, the assessment will often be based on the extent to which A is similar to B. Events which are more representative tend to be judged as having an increased likelihood of occurrence than do less representative events. However, these judgments often ignore relevant information such as base rates, reliability of data (Joyce and Biddle, 1981) and source credibility (Bamber, 1983). Second, the anchoring and adjustment heuristic suggests that in many situations individuals make estimates by starting from an initial value (e.g. suggested by the formulation of the problem or by the result of a partial computation) and then adjusting this number to yield a final answer. The adjustment from this anchor, although it may be in the appropriate direction, is often insufficient. Third, the availability heuristic suggests that the frequency of certain events occurring is impacted by how easy it is for similar events to be brought to mind. Experimental research has shown that auditors use these heuristics but the effects were often less than in general psychology studies where participations are not dealing with professional decisions (Smith and Kida, 1991).

Hogarth and Einhorn's (1992) belief-adjustment model (and earlier working paper versions in the 1980s) provided a theoretical framework for considering the sequential nature in which information is received. The model assumes that belief-adjustment follows an anchoring and adjustment process and predicts that when both confirming and disconfirming information are received, there will be an order effect. Under this model the disconfirming/confirming order is hypothesized to lead to higher final beliefs than the confirming/disconfirming order. While initial studies (for example, Ashton and Ashton, 1988; Knechel and Messier, 1990) found the model applied in auditing, subsequent research considered under what circumstances the confirmation bias exists (for example, more experienced auditors, more complex judgments, with or without the review process, etc.) (Messier and Tubbs, 1994) and the descriptive validity of this model (Bamber *et al.*, 1997).

The issue of biases was extended into predecisional behavior. Audit tasks require auditors to consider a range of information, consisting of confirming evidence and disconfirming evidence. Kida (1984) examined the effect of hypothesis framing on auditors' search for, and attention to the use of, judgmental data. While Kida (1984) found some limited support for the use of confirmatory strategies among auditors, the effect was weaker than in the psychology literature. The fact that many general psychology findings only hold under limited circumstances when decision makers are dealing with professional issues is reasonably common within the audit literature (Smith and Kida, 1991). Subsequent research examined the impact of hypothesis generation on other judgments in the audit process (e.g. Heiman-Hoffman *et al.*, 1995; Asare and Wright, 1997).

Knowledge and memory

The fundamental model that *Performance* is a function of *Ability, Knowledge, Environment* and *Motivation*, was suggested by Libby (1983) in the context of considering the determinants of judgment performance. The important role of memory in accounting decisions, was outlined in Birnberg and Shields (1984). While early JDM research addressed the issue of ability, over the following two decades a large percentage of JDM research in auditing addressed the latter three determinants of performance, and the interactions among the four determinants. In particular, the emphasis was on knowledge and memory issues and how these knowledge differences, and their interactions with other variables, lead to performance differences. Research relating to knowledge of financial statement errors examined both learning based on experiences in the laboratory (Nelson, 1993) and experiences accumulated in practice (Libby and Frederick, 1990).

How knowledge is acquired and what experiences lead to gaining this knowledge were also being examined. This research examines how auditors with different levels and types of experience encode, store and retrieve information from memory and how these knowledge structure differences are related to performance differences (e.g. Choo and Trotman, 1991). The motivation for research on knowledge is that this research allows us to better understand the knowledge structures of an expert auditor, and how that knowledge is acquired. In turn, this assists in the development of training and decision aids which improve the performance of novices (Libby and Luft, 1993).

Experimental studies examined a range of topics including: the importance of the hypothesis generation stage in diagnosing problems and the interactions of environmental cues with the decision makers' knowledge structure (e.g. Libby, 1985); the influence of experience levels together with task complexity for specific tasks, including less structured tasks (Abdolmohammadi and Wright, 1987); development of models of auditor performance (Bonner and Lewis, 1990); the relationship between experience and knowledge. For example, Libby and

Frederick (1990) found that as auditors become more experienced their knowledge of financial statements becomes more complete, they learn error occurrence rates and they organize their knowledge of financial statement errors along different dimensions. Further evidence on knowledge differences have been found in protocol studies where auditors are asked to 'think aloud' while making judgments (Biggs and Mock, 1983; Bedard and Biggs, 1991), and studies of auditor memory (Plumlee, 1985; Moeckel and Plumlee, 1989).

Libby and Luft (1993) outlined previous and future audit JDM research using the *Performance* = f(*Ability, Knowledge, Environment, Motivation*) framework. They provide a model examining the relationship between knowledge and performance and outline the requirements of the expertise paradigm for conducting experimental research involving expertise. Libby (1995) extended the model of the antecedents and consequences of knowledge and suggested that these relations are complicated by the fact that knowledge is determined by experience and abilities. Tan and Libby (1997) expand the concept of expertise from a consideration of technical dimensions to include managerial dimensions. They examine how managerial components of knowledge, together with technical knowledge and problem solving abilities, distinguish auditors with superior performance from those with less superior performance. Solomon *et al.* (1999) compared the knowledge of industry specialists with non-specialists. They found that training and concentrated experiences of industry specialists primarily enhanced non-error knowledge.

Group decision making

There are two main types of multi-person processes: audit teams and audit groups (Solomon, 1987; Rich *et al.*, 1997). Audit teams refer to the audit judgments made in a hierarchical, sequential and iterative audit review process. The term audit groups refers to joint multi-person JDM. These groups can be interacting groups (group members interact with each other) or nominal groups (when their judgments are combined statistically and there is no interaction between group members). The relative performance of individuals is then compared to nominal and interacting groups and the review process. The comparison of individual with nominal group performance indicates whether there is any benefit from group decision making (i.e. a diversification effect). The comparison of nominal with interacting groups provides evidence regarding additional interaction effects. Finally, the comparison of interacting groups with the review process provides evidence on additional gains to the interacting group related to the hierarchical iterative nature of the review process.

The earlier literature on multi-person processes considered individual versus group performance (Schultz and Reckers, 1981; Solomon, 1982). Research then moved to address questions such as whether the review process improves auditor judgments, and whether that improvement is incremental to what would occur if some other form of group decision making, such as interacting or nominal groups, was used (Trotman, 1985; Trotman and Yetton, 1985). Later studies examined the specific sources of gain that result from the review process and under what circumstances these gains occur (e.g. Libby and Trotman, 1993; Ramsay, 1994; Bamber and Ramsay, 1997).

Decision aids

Studies on decision aids have examined the performance of decision aids that were developed to overcome the deficiencies found in auditor judgments in policy capturing research and heuristics and biases research. A significant proportion of this research addresses whether a particular decision aid improves performance or not, how this effect varies with environmental and motivation issues and what are the cognitive mechanisms leading to those effects (see Messier, 1995 for a summary of earlier research).

Kachelmeier and Messier (1990) document that decision aids can have unintended negative effects. They found that auditors provided with the decision aid showed greater variability in their sample sizes than auditors in an intuitive judgment group, and some auditors circumvented the decision aid by working backwards from their desired sample sizes. Ashton (1990) also documents negative effects of decision aids, showing that the positive effects of financial incentives, performance feedback and justification can be decreased and sometimes reversed by the use of a decision aid. Nelson *et al.* (1995) suggested that auditors often had difficulty in applying the error frequencies they have previously experienced because of a mismatch between the organization of the judgment task and the organization of auditors' knowledge. They developed and tested a decision aid to overcome deficiencies in knowledge organization.

Environmental and motivational factors

Environment was part of the Libby and Luft (1993) model and environmental factors, such as the need for justification of decisions, accountability, prior involvement in the audit, time pressure, source credibility and precedents, were the focus of a large amount of JDM research in auditing in the 1990s. For example, Peecher (1996) presented a cognitive model of how justification influences auditors' decisions and conducted an experiment that examined how auditors' justification processes influence their analytical procedures performance. Koonce *et al.* (1995) examined the role of justification in the review process. A number of studies considered alternative ways of mitigating biases previously found in audit JDM research as well as examining the moderating effects of other variables. For example, studies examined the impact of accountability on reducing biases (Kennedy, 1993; Glover, 1997; Hoffman and Patton, 1997); the effects of time pressure (McDaniel, 1990; Glover, 1997); and the effect of audit program structure on the effectiveness and efficiency of auditors' judgments (Bamber and Snowball, 1988; McDaniel, 1990). Tan (1995) considered auditors' prior involvement in the audit process by examining whether repeat engagements increased the likelihood that auditors' judgments remain consistent with prior findings and whether staff rotations reduce such tendencies. It should be noted that many of the above studies contributed both to the accounting and to psychology literature because they examined decision making in a professional environment in contrast to the more general setting of psychology.

Evidence is key to the audit process, and in the 1990s an important line of research considered various attributes of evidence. For example, Hirst (1994) considered both the competency of the source and the objectivity of the source of the evidence. The persuasiveness of evidence is important and Salterio and Koonce (1997) considered the role of precedents provided by national audit firm offices in accounting situations where authoritative guidance is not present.

Libby and Luft (1993) suggest that a motivational factor, monetary incentives, is an important characteristic of auditing that may affect performance. Libby and Lipe (1992) show that cognitive processes are not equally sensitive to effort changes and therefore increasing effort often does not improve performance on all tasks to a similar extent. Hackenbrack and Nelson (1996) found that auditors' incentives influence their reporting decisions between aggressive and conservative and these decisions were justified with aggressive/conservative interpretations of accounting standards.

Current state of JDM research

Since 2000 many of the themes in earlier research have continued often with the introduction of new variables, sometimes establishing boundary conditions from earlier findings or providing a better understanding of the cognitive processes operating. Much of this research arose because of changes in the audit environment. Examples include the increased emphasis on audit quality, decision aids related to fraud identification and industry specialization, new audit standards on internal control over financial reporting (ICFR) and independence. Three such examples were: addressing new fraud audit standards has resulted in studies that examine decision aids aimed at improving fraud judgments (Asare and Wright, 2004; Wilks and Zimbelman, 2004); extending the expertise literature to examine mental models has resulted in research on how auditors who are industry experts differ from non-industry experts in interpreting incomplete patterns of cues (Hammersley, 2006); research on the curse of knowledge bias and a new audit standard on ICFR examined the effect of cognitively restructuring the ICFR assessment task (Earley *et al.*, 2008).

Changing expectations of auditors and changing audit standards have resulted in greater attention to such fundamental audit issues as audit evidence (e.g. Bell *et al.*, 2005; O'Donnell and Schultz, 2005); materiality (Libby and Brown, 2013); professional skepticism (Nelson, 2009); and fraud (Carpenter, 2007; Hammersley, 2011). Bell *et al.* (2005) suggest that the changed regulatory environment for auditors includes increasing the minimum evidence requirements and increased auditor responsibilities related to fraud detection and a greater focus on how auditors respond to different types and forms of audit evidence. Links between fraud risk, professional skepticism and evidence collection are important and have started to be addressed (e.g. Hoffman and Zimbelman, 2009; Hammersley *et al.*, 2010).

PCAOB synthesis papers (Cohen and Knechel, 2013) show the importance of environment factors in recent JDM research. Following Bonner (2008), environmental factors are considered those that surround the auditor but are not specific either to the task being completed or to the individual making the judgment. For example, environmental factors for the audit of fair values include measurement uncertainty; macroeconomic risks and regulatory/legal influences (Bratten *et al.*, 2013); accountability, client characteristics, audit standards and frequency of risk assessments (Hurtt *et al.*, 2013); and governance characteristics (Bame-Aldred *et al.*, 2013).

As noted earlier, Nelson and Tan (2005) divide the JDM research for the period 1980–2005 into three categories: task, auditor and interpersonal interactions. A considerable amount of research since their overview paper has addressed a whole new range of tasks and new interpersonal interactions. For example, there has been research on the emotions and mood of auditors (Bhattacharjee and Moreno, 2002; Chung *et al.*, 2008). Importantly, research has also moved toward looking at the interaction between task, auditor and interpersonal interactions. We conclude this section on issues related to task and interpersonal interactions.

Nelson and Tan (2005) divide up audit tasks between risk assessments (including the audit risk model and audit planning), analytical procedures and evidence evaluation, 'correction' decisions and going concern judgments. Generally, audit JDM experiments have given very limited attention to tasks, even though there had been significant evidence of the importance of differences in tasks (e.g. Abdolmohammadi and Wright, 1987; Asare and McDaniel, 1996; Simnett, 1996; Tan and Kao, 1999). One notable exception is Koonce (1993) who broke down analytical procedures into five categories: mental representation, hypothesis generation, information search, hypothesis evaluation and action decision.[6] In fact, over the last three decades numerous JDM tasks have involved analytical procedures tasks (e.g. Biggs *et al.*, 1988; Cohen and Kida, 1989; Koonce, 1992; McDaniel and Kinney, 1995; Asare and Wright, 2004; Moreno *et al.*, 2007).

Research on interpersonal interactions has expanded considerably through four main avenues: conditions under which different forms of the review process have different effects; auditor–client negotiations; fraud brainstorming discussions; auditors' interactions with other parties including juror decisions in matters concerning auditors and relationships between auditors and the audit committee.

The review process is a critical aspect of quality control within audit firms. Various aspects of the review process have been investigated for over 25 years. More recent research on the review process has considered a number of themes. First, the judgments of both preparers and reviewers are affected by actions of others, for example, alternative justification memos (e.g. Agoglia *et al.*, 2003; Shankar and Tan, 2006; Tan and Trotman, 2003). Second, an important part of the review process is the ability of reviewers to assess the quality of preparers (e.g. Kennedy and Peecher, 1997; Jamal and Tan, 2001; Messier *et al.*, 2008). Third, consideration of motivation factors is impacting the review process. For example, research based on motivation theory from psychology shows that auditors who overweight evidence that supports the conclusions of the reviewer adds this bias onto the direction of a supervisor's preferences (Wilks, 2002). This study found that predecisional distortion of information was due to subordinates unconsciously interpreting evidence to be consistent with the views of the reviewer. Fourth, there has been research that compares the effectiveness of different forms of review, such as electronic versus face-to-face review (Brazel *et al.*, 2004). Fifth, Lambert and Agoglia (2011) find that review timeliness and the framing of the review notes affects reviewee responses to comments provided by their reviewers.

Another major line of JDM research on auditor–client negotiations has been largely based on Gibbins *et al.* (2001) who developed an accounting negotiation model consisting of three elements: (1) an accounting issue; (2) the auditor–client process; and (3) the accounting outcome. He also discussed various contextual factors related to auditor–client negotiations. The model recognizes that negotiations between auditors and management often arise with respect to disagreements over accounting policies, financial statement disclosures and accounting estimates. A wide range of experiments have addressed relationships in the Gibbins *et al.* (2001) model. These experiments generally involve very experienced participants, either CFOs or audit managers/partners, and have used a variety of innovative methods to achieve the negotiations including interactive computer programs, emails and the use of confederate negotiations. A considerable amount of focus has been on the effect of different forms of strategies and tactics and the outcomes of the negotiations (Bame-Aldred and Kida, 2007). Research has shown that altering the auditor's approach to the negotiation process can affect outcomes of the negotiation process (e.g. Trotman *et al.*, 2005; Sanchez *et al.*, 2007; Hatfield *et al.*, 2008; Tan and Trotman, 2010).

Another area of interpersonal interaction is the discussion groups, often referred to as brainstorming groups, that are required under recent auditing standards related to auditors' responsibilities for the detection of fraud. These standards suggest that brainstorming sessions place emphasis on how and why the financial statement may be susceptible to material misstatement due to fraud and also how fraud could occur. Two main lines of research are what forms of brainstorming groups (e.g. nominal or interacting) result in a greater quantity and quality of potential fraud for an auditor to consider in their planning (e.g. Carpenter, 2007) and how auditors respond to higher risk of fraud through planning effective audit procedures (e.g. Hoffman and Zimbelman, 2009).

JDM audit research has also considered interpersonal interactions between auditors and other parties. One such line of research is the evaluation of auditor performance by jurors. In the USA, jurors evaluate auditors' performance in negligence lawsuits and are involved in comparing the audit actually performed with what others would likely have done in the circumstances (Kadous, 2000). Subsequent research has addressed how task and environment factors affect jurors' judgments and the implications for auditors (e.g. Kadous and Mercer, 2012). Research has also considered the judgments of audit committee members (e.g. Gaynor *et al.*, 2006).

Issues to be addressed

Auditing ceased to be self-regulated with the passing of the Sarbanes-Oxley Act of 2002, the establishment of the PCAOB in the USA and similar organizations in many countries (e.g. International Forum of Independent Audit Regulators). Regulatory inspections of audit firms now cover both the quality of audit work (e.g. has sufficient appropriate evidence been collected?) as well as quality controls (supervision, review and independence issues). Some reports have been critical of auditing (e.g. EC, 2010; IFAC, 2011) and there has also been recognition of the importance of a professional judgment framework (Pozen, 2008; KPMG, 2011). These changes have led to suggestions for consideration of a new accountability framework that regulators could use to (a) motivate auditors to improve audit quality, and (b) evaluate how well auditors have carried out their duties (Peecher *et al.*, 2013). Peecher *et al.* (2013) provide a two-dimensional auditor accountability framework. The first dimension considers whether auditors are accountable for outcomes versus judgment processes. The second dimension considers the degree to which auditors' accountabilities are in the form of penalties versus rewards. They identify four potential changes to the existing framework with the aim of moving accountabilities to be more reward based and more process accountable. The four potential changes include introducing an auditors' judgment rule, encouraging auditors to be skeptical of their own judgments, adding a concurrent element to the inspection process and rewarding auditors for the detection of fraud, and improving the quality of financial statements. They suggest 36 potential research questions all aimed at improving audit quality. More generally, Knechel *et al.* (2013) provide insights into frameworks for establishing audit quality and summarize input, process and output audit quality indicators. They also provide suggestions for future research on the important question of 'How can quality be increased?'.

With changing expectations of society with respect to auditing, increased regulation of auditing, and substantial criticism of audits by regulatory inspectors, future research is clearly needed to examine those areas where concerns have been expressed, including the audit of fair values and estimates, the level of professional skepticism and detection of financial statement fraud. Each of these three areas is discussed in PCAOB synthesis papers (Bratten *et al.*, 2013; Hurtt *et al.*, 2013; Trompeter *et al.*, 2013), which provide very useful insights into the important issues to be addressed.

Further insights on the above key issues are provided by the Bell *et al.* (2005) monograph which introduces the concept of evidentiary triangulation by comparing the implications of external evidence on the economic state of the client's business (EBS evidence) with the implications of evidence obtained from the client's financial accounting system and evidence from other internal information sources. Use of EBS evidence is of particular importance because this evidence is likely to be more diagnostic than other forms of evidence as it is much more difficult for it to be manipulated by management. The monograph raises such questions as what factors (do and should) heighten auditors' skepticism? While auditors are traditionally encouraged to adopt an outward orientation in which the focus is on the doubt with which management representations should be viewed, Bell *et al.* (2005) propose an alternative inward orientation in which the focus of an auditor's doubt is directed inward to their own fallible judgments. Inward directed skepticism includes being self-critical in anticipation of arguments of others concerning the evidence they have or have not relied on.

On a number of occasions in this paper I have referred to the Nelson and Tan (2005) framework classifying JDM audit research across audit task, auditor attributes and interpersonal interactions. As noted by Nelson and Tan (2005), there are interdependencies between these areas, and future research could benefit considerably from considering these interactions. In particular, auditor interpersonal interaction research (e.g. between auditors, audit–client negotiations and auditor/audit committee interactions) will benefit by considering both task and auditor attributes (e.g. knowledge, trait skepticism). To make this manageable, manipulating the type of interaction (e.g. the form of brainstorming) across different tasks while measuring individual attributes has potential.

In the area of interpersonal interactions there are important contributions to be made. Gibbins *et al.* (2001) developed a model of the audit–client interaction process based on retrospective recalls of senior professionals (see Brown and Wright, 2008 for subsequent research). However, only a small number of the links in this model have been examined experimentally. Second, with the increased emphasis on fraud detection by auditors there has also been increased emphasis on the group discussion process in the planning stage of the audit referred to as 'fraud brainstorming'. While some important early research has been completed (see Hammersley, 2011 for a review) there are opportunities to examine alternate brainstorming structures to those presently used in practice and to examine how effective they are under different environmental conditions, different task structures and different combinations of individual attributes. Another important potential area of interactions is between auditors and inspectors. The research questions on audit inspection processes developed by Peecher *et al.* (2013) can be experimentally tested. However, it should be noted that there are difficulties in conducting interpersonal interaction research as ideally they involve discussions between more than one participant, which creates logistical problems in organizing different participants to be present at the same time (e.g. CFO and auditor or a group of audit team members).

There has been considerable debate and proposals for a variety of changes to the audit reporting model (see discussion in Mock *et al.*, 2013). Numerous potential modifications have been suggested and experiments allow the researcher to examine the likely effects of potential changes on users, preparers, audit committee members and auditor judgments prior to implementation. Extant research is discussed by Mock *et al.* (2013) and there is substantial scope for research to address 'when' and 'why' questions related to changes in auditors' reports.

Earlier in this section I suggested the desirability of manipulating task factors within subjects, where appropriate, to gain a much better knowledge of task effects which have been suggested could be as important as experience effects. This requires special care by the researcher in theory development and design in order to predict what differences would be expected between tasks. While the difficulty of predicting task differences should not be underestimated (and resulting difficulties for publication), on the positive side, such risks are most likely to lead to a much better understanding of how effects vary across individuals and tasks, and ultimately a much richer understanding of the research area.

Conclusion

Historically, JDM audit research has progressed by extending major prior studies (for example, see the progress of studies as outlined in Solomon and Shields (1995) and Libby and Luft (1993)). Similarly, psychology research has typically gradually built on seminal papers. I see the recent audit JDM research as more fragmented. It is always a difficult judgment on what is sufficient 'incremental contribution' but there needs to be a balance between originality and building on the existing body of knowledge. Our contribution to knowledge and practice can be enhanced by a concentration on some central themes and incrementally building on previous research. I believe the discipline may benefit more from theory refinement rather than individual papers all looking to be the 'first' in some way. A single experiment may be able to show an effect and the reason for the effect ('the why question'); but to answer questions related to 'under what circumstances does the effect hold?' requires a series of experiments building on earlier studies where theory is refined as we learn more from earlier studies about unique attributes of the audit setting including task effects, individual effects and interpersonal effects (see Nelson and Tan, 2005 for a discussion of these effects).

If the above approach is to be considered, audit JDM researchers as a group can learn from psychology. Psychology, and some other experimentally based research disciplines, regularly progresses by earlier studies being extended to consider under what environmental conditions the results hold. In general, there is much greater emphasis on boundary conditions. For example, the research literature on group decision making and negotiations includes many hundreds of experiments. Meta analyses and detailed literature reviews (see *Psychological Review*) are regularly produced providing insights on past conclusions and future areas of research. This leads to new research thoroughly entrenched in the previous literature. These extension papers are often shorter in length by providing the link to previous research, a clear statement of the research questions discussed, a series of experiments with research methods described (full details for experiment 1 and the changes made in subsequent experiments), a short description of the results and an overall discussion of the combined results. Should this be a model adopted by at least some of our accounting journals? I certainly believe this model has merit and it is worthy of debate in the auditing arena.

My view is that audit JDM research is at a critical time in its history. Particularly in the US, participants are becoming more difficult to obtain and difficult choices need to be made over the best use of these participants. On the one hand, we have numerous important audit issues where the research is only in its infancy (e.g. professional skepticism) and new important issues continually arising with changes (or proposed changes) in regulation. Practitioners, researchers and the editorial process all have an important role to play. Any vibrant profession needs to take advantage of the opportunity to learn from new and well-designed research and the auditing profession is no exception.

If researchers want access to costly participants, it is not unreasonable for practitioners to expect that important practical questions be addressed. However, it is important that practitioners recognize that research has both short- and long-term benefits and it is essential that basic research, which builds the foundation for subsequent applied research, is not overlooked. Much of the research on the expertise paradigm in auditing in the 1980s followed this approach (see Libby and Luft, 1993). This has also been the model used in many areas of science including medicine. For example, before carrying out medical experiments on humans to test the benefits and side effects of certain drugs, there may have been decades of basic research learning about a disease, cell structure, etc. While audit researchers can benefit from some basic research done in other disciplines (e.g. psychology, economics) invariably this does not address issues connected to the audit environment, so that basic research is also needed within the audit discipline.

In conclusion, while there are challenges, I expect a bright future ahead for JDM research in auditing. There is no shortage of important questions and new researchers are well trained and enthusiastic. Audit firms face challenges and opportunities from cost pressures, regulatory pressures, new products and a changing expectation from society. The opportunity is there for greater cooperation between practitioners and researchers in addressing the important issues.

Acknowledgements

Helpful comments have been provided by Robert Knechel, Anna Huggins and Hun-Tong Tan. I also thank my co-authors and friends who over a number of decades have influenced my thinking about JDM research. The financial support of the Australian Research Council via an Australian Professorial Fellowship is gratefully acknowledged.

Notes

1 Given this is a synthesis paper, parts of this chapter rely heavily on previous papers written by the author including Trotman (1998) and Trotman *et al.* (2011).

2 The terms judgment and decision-making are sometimes used interchangeably. When distinguished, judgment usually refers to the process of estimating outcomes and their consequences (e.g. the assessment of the likelihood of a material misstatement, evaluation of internal controls, risk assessments, estimates of future cash flows and future profitability), while decision-making generally involves an evaluation of these consequences which leads to an action (e.g. accept/retain an audit client, selection of a type of audit report) (Libby, 1981). Judgments are usually an input for decisions.

3 Given the vast literature, I often cite these synthesis papers and leave it to the reader to refer to these papers for more detailed citations. Many of my citations are to the earlier literature to help newer researchers become aware of this literature.

4,5 For further explanations of the benefits of experiments, see Libby and Luft (1993) and Libby *et al.* (2002).

6 Libby and Luft (1993) outline some salient features of audit tasks, including: learning opportunities, judgment guidance, hierarchical group settings, and sequential multi-period tasks.

References

Abdolmohammadi, M. and Wright, A. 1987. 'An Examination of the Effects of Experience and Task Complexity on Audit Judgments', *The Accounting Review* 62(1): 1–13.

Agoglia, C. P., Kida, T. and Hanno, D. M. 2003. 'The Effects of Alternative Justification Memos on the Judgments of Audit Reviewees and Reviewers', *Journal of Accounting Research* 41(1): 33–46.

Asare, S. K. and McDaniel, L. S. 1996. 'The Effects of Familiarity with the Preparer and Task Complexity on the Effectiveness of the Audit Review Process', *The Accounting Review* 71(2): 139–59.

Asare, S. K. and Wright, A. 1997. 'Hypothesis Revision Strategies in Conducting Analytical Procedures', *Accounting, Organizations and Society* 22(8): 737–55.

Asare, S. K. and Wright, A. M. 2004. 'The Effectiveness of Alternative Risk Assessment and Program Planning Tools in a Fraud Setting', *Contemporary Accounting Research* 21(2): 325–52.

Ashton, A. H. and Ashton, R. H. 1988. 'Sequential Belief Revision in Auditing', *The Accounting Review* 63(4): 623–41.

Ashton, R. H. 1974. 'An Experimental Study of Internal Control Judgments', *Journal of Accounting Research* 12(1): 143–57.

Ashton, R. H. 1990. 'Pressure and Performance in Accounting Decision Settings: Paradoxical Effects of Incentives, Feedback, and Justification', *Journal of Accounting Research* 28(3): 148–80.

Bamber, E. M. 1983. 'Expert Judgment in the Audit Team: A Source Reliability Approach', *Journal of Accounting Research* 21(2): 396–412.

Bamber, E. M. and Ramsay, R. J. 1997. 'An Investigation of the Effects of Specialization in Audit Workpaper Review', *Contemporary Accounting Research* 14(3): 501–13.

Bamber, E. M. and Snowball, D. 1988. 'An Experimental Study of the Effects of Audit Structure in Uncertain Task Environments', *The Accounting Review* 63(3): 490–504.

Bamber, E. M., Ramsay, R. J. and Tubbs, R. M. 1997. 'An Examination of the Descriptive Validity of the Belief-adjustment Model and Alternative Attitudes to Evidence in Auditing', *Accounting, Organizations and Society* 22(3–4): 249–68.

Bame-Aldred, C. W. and Kida, T. 2007. 'A Comparison of Auditor and Client Initial Negotiation Positions and Tactics', *Accounting, Organizations and Society* 32(6): 497–511.

Bame-Aldred, C. W., Brandon, D. M., Messier, W. F. Jr, Rittenberg, L. E. and Stefaniak, C. M. 2013. 'A Summary of Research on External Auditor Reliance on the Internal Audit Function', *Auditing: A Journal of Practice & Theory* 32: 251–86.

Bedard, J. C. and Biggs, S. F. 1991. 'Pattern Recognition, Hypotheses Generation, and Auditor Performance in an Analytical Task', *The Accounting Review* 66(3): 622–42.

Bell, T. B. and Wright, A. M. 1995. *Audit Practice, Research and Education: A Productive Collaboration*. American Institute of Certified Public Accountants (AICPA).

Bell, T. B., Peecher, M. E. and Solomon, I. 2005. *The 21st Century Public Company Audit: Conceptual Elements of KPMG's Global Audit Methodology*. Montvale, NJ: KPMG.

Bhattacharjee, S. and Moreno, K. 2002. 'The Impact of Affective Information on the Professional Judgments of More Experienced and Less Experienced Auditors', *Journal of Behavioral Decision Making* 15(4): 361–77.

Biggs, S. F. and Mock, T. J. 1983. 'An Investigation of Auditor Decision Processes in the Evaluation of Internal Controls and Audit Scope Decisions', *Journal of Accounting Research* 21(1): 234–55.

Biggs, S. F., Mock, T. J. and Watkins, P. R. 1988. 'Auditor's Use of Analytical Review in Audit Program Design', *The Accounting Review* 63(1): 148–61.

Birnberg, J. G. and Shields, M. D. 1984. 'The Role of Attention and Memory in Accounting Decisions', *Accounting, Organizations and Society* 9(3–4): 365–82.

Bonner, S. E. 2008. *Judgment and Decision Making in Accounting*. Upper Saddle River, NJ: Pearson Prentice Hall.

Bonner, S. E. and Lewis, B. L. 1990. 'Determinants of Auditor Expertise', *Journal of Accounting Research* 28(3): 1–20.

Bratten, B., Gaynor, L. M., McDaniel, L., Montague, N. R. and Sierra, G. E. 2013. 'The Audit of Fair Values and Other Estimates: The Effects of Underlying Environmental, Task, and Auditor-specific Factors', *Auditing: A Journal of Practice & Theory* 32(Supplement 1): 7–44.

Brazel, J. F., Agoglia, C. P. and Hatfield, R. C. 2004. 'Electronic versus Face-to-Face Review: The Effects of Alternative Forms of Review on Auditors' Performance', *The Accounting Review* 79(4): 949–66.

Brown, C. E. and Solomon, I. 1991. 'Configural Information Processing in Auditing: The Role of Domain-specific Knowledge', *The Accounting Review* 66(1): 100–119.

Brown, H. L. and Wright, A. M. 2008. 'Negotiation Research in Auditing', *Accounting Horizons* 22(1): 91–109.

Carpenter, T. D. 2007. 'Audit Team Brainstorming, Fraud Risk Identification, and Fraud Risk Assessment: Implications of Sas No. 99', *The Accounting Review* 82(5): 1119–40.

Choo, F. and Trotman, K. T. 1991. 'The Relationship between Knowledge Structure and Judgments for Experienced and Inexperienced Auditors', *The Accounting Review* 66(3): 464–85.

Chung, J. O. Y., Cohen, J. R. and Monroe, G. S. 2008. 'The Effect of Moods on Auditors' Inventory Valuation Decisions', *Auditing: A Journal of Practice & Theory* 27(2): 137–59.

Cohen, J. and Kida, T. 1989. 'The Impact of Analytical Review Results, Internal Control Reliability, and Experience on Auditors' Use of Analytical Review', *Journal of Accounting Research* 27(2): 263–76.

Cohen, J. R. and Knechel, W. R. 2013. 'A Call for Academic Inquiry: Challenges and Opportunities from the PCAOB Synthesis Projects', *Auditing: A Journal of Practice & Theory* 32(Supplement 1): 1–5.

Cohen, J., Krishnamoorthy, G. and Wright, A. 2010. 'Corporate Governance in the Post-Sarbanes-Oxley Era: Auditors' Experiences', *Contemporary Accounting Research* 27(3): 751–86.

Earley, C. E., Hoffman, V. B. and Joe, J. R. 2008. 'Reducing Management's Influence on Auditors' Judgments: An Experimental Investigation of SOX 404 Assessments', *The Accounting Review* 83(6): 1461–85.

European Commission (EC). 2010. *Green Paper – Audit Policy: Lessons from the Crisis*. Brussels: EC. Available online at http://eur-lex.europa.eu/LexUriServ/LexUriServ.do?uri=COM:2010:0561:FIN:EN:PDF (accessed November 2012).

Gaynor, L. M., McDaniel, L. S. and Neal, T. L. 2006. 'The Effects of Joint Provision and Disclosure of Nonaudit Services on Audit Committee Members' Decisions and Investors' Preferences', *The Accounting Review* 81(4): 873–96.

Gibbins, M., Salterio, S. and Webb, A. 2001. 'Evidence About Auditor-Client Management Negotiation Concerning Client's Financial Reporting', *Journal of Accounting Research* 39(3): 535–63.

Glover, S. M. 1997. 'The Influence of Time Pressure and Accountability on Auditors' Processing of Nondiagnostic Information', *Journal of Accounting Research* 35(2): 213–26.

Hackenbrack, K. and Nelson, M. W. 1996. 'Auditors' Incentives and their Application of Financial Accounting Standards', *The Accounting Review* 71(1): 43–59.

Hammersley, J. S. 2006. 'Pattern Identification and Industry-specialist Auditors', *The Accounting Review* 81(2): 309–36.

Hammersley, J. S. 2011. 'A Review and Model of Auditor Judgments in Fraud-related Planning Tasks', *Auditing: A Journal of Practice & Theory* 30(4): 101–28.

Hammersley, J. S., Bamber, E. M. and Carpenter, T. D. 2010. 'The Influence of Documentation Specificity and Priming on Auditors' Fraud Risk Assessments and Evidence Evaluation Decisions', *The Accounting Review* 85(2): 547–71.

Hatfield, R. C., Agoglia, C. P. and Sanchez, M. H. 2008. 'Client Characteristics and the Negotiation Tactics of Auditors: Implications for Financial Reporting', *Journal of Accounting Research* 46(5): 1183–207.

Heiman-Hoffman, V. B., Moser, D. V. and Joseph, J. A. 1995. 'The Impact of an Auditor's Initial Hypothesis on Subsequent Performance at Identifying Actual Errors', *Contemporary Accounting Research* 11(2): 763–79.

Hirst, D. E. 1994. 'Auditors' Sensitivity to Source Reliability', *Journal of Accounting Research* 32(1): 113–26.

Hoffman, V. B. and Patton, J. M. 1997. 'Accountability, the Dilution Effect, and Conservatism in Auditors' Fraud Judgments', *Journal of Accounting Research* 35(2): 227–37.

Hoffman, V. B. and Zimbelman, M. F. 2009. 'Do Strategic Reasoning and Brainstorming Help Auditors Change their Standard Audit Procedures in Response to Fraud Risk?', *The Accounting Review* 84(3): 811–37.

Hogarth, R. M. and Einhorn, H. J. 1992. 'Order Effects in Belief Updating: The Belief-adjustment Model', *Cognitive Psychology* 24(1): 1–55.

Hurtt, R. K., Brown-Liburd, H., Earley, C. E. and Krishnamoorthy, G. 2013. 'Research on Auditor Professional Skepticism: Literature Synthesis and Opportunities for Future Research', *Auditing: A Journal of Practice & Theory* 32(Supplement 1): 45–97.

International Federation of Accountants (IFAC) 2011. *Audit Quality: An IAASB Perspective*. New York: IFAC.

Jamal, K. and Tan, H. T. 2001. 'Can Auditors Predict the Choices Made by Other Auditors?', *Journal of Accounting Research* 39(3): 583–97.

Joe, J. R. 2003. 'Why Press Coverage of a Client Influences the Audit Opinion', *Journal of Accounting Research* 41(1): 109–33.

Joyce, E. J. and Biddle, G. C. 1981. 'Are Auditor's Judgments Sufficiently Regressive?', *Journal of Accounting Research* 19(2): 323–49.

Kachelmeier, S. J. and Messier, W. F. Jr 1990. 'An Investigation of the Influence of a Nonstatistical Decision Aid on Auditor Sample Size Decisions', *The Accounting Review* 65(1): 209–26.

Kadous, K. 2000. 'The Effects of Audit Quality and Consequence Severity on Juror Evaluations of Auditor Responsibility for Plaintiff Losses', *The Accounting Review* 75(3): 327–41.

Kadous, K. and Mercer, M. 2012. 'Can Reporting Norms Create a Safe Harbor? Jury Verdicts against Auditors under Precise and Imprecise Accounting Standards', *The Accounting Review* 87(2): 565–87.

Kadous, K., Kennedy, S. J. and Peecher, M. E. 2003. 'The Effect of Quality Assessment and Directional Goal Commitment on Auditors' Acceptance of Client-preferred Accounting Methods', *The Accounting Review* 78(3): 759–78.

Kaplan, S. E. and Reckers, P. M. J. 1985. 'An Examination of Auditor Performance Evaluation', *The Accounting Review* 60(3): 477–87.

Kennedy, J. 1993. 'Debiasing Audit Judgment with Accountability: A Framework and Experimental Results', *Journal of Accounting Research* 31(2): 231–45.

Kennedy, J. and Peecher, M. E. 1997. 'Judging Auditors' Technical Knowledge', *Journal of Accounting Research* 35(2): 279–93.

Kida, T. 1984. 'The Impact of Hypothesis-testing Strategies on Auditors' Use of Judgment Data', *Journal of Accounting Research* 22(1): 332–40.

Knechel, W. R. and Messier, W. F. Jr 1990. 'Sequential Auditor Decision Making: Information Search and Evidence Evaluation', *Contemporary Accounting Research* 6(2): 386–406.

Knechel, W. R., Krishnan, G. V., Pevzner, M., Shefchik, L. B. and Velury, U. K. 2013. 'Audit Quality: Insights from the Academic Literature', *Auditing: A Journal of Practice & Theory* 32(Supplement 1): 385–421.

Koonce, L. 1992. 'Explanation and Counterexplanation during Audit Analytical Review', *The Accounting Review* 67(1): 59–76.

Koonce, L. 1993. 'A Cognitive Characterization of Audit Analytical Review', *Auditing: A Journal of Practice & Theory* 12(2): 57–76.

Koonce, L., Anderson, U. and Marchant, G. 1995. 'Justification of Decisions in Auditing', *Journal of Accounting Research* 33(2): 369–84.

KPMG 2011. *Elevating Professional Judgment in Auditing: The KPMG Professional Judgment Framework*. KPMG.

Lambert, T. A. and Agoglia, C. P. 2011. 'Closing the Loop: Review Process Factors Affecting Audit Staff Follow-through', *Journal of Accounting Research* 49(5): 1275–306.

Libby, R. 1981. *Accounting and Human Information Processing: Theory and Applications*. Englewood Cliffs, NJ: Prentice Hall.

Libby, R. 1983. 'Determinants of Performance in Accounting Decisions', in K. R. Bindon (ed.) *1983 Accounting Research Convocation*, pp. 77–88. Tuscaloosa, AL: University of Alabama.

Libby, R. 1985. 'Availability and the Generation of Hypotheses in Analytical Review', *Journal of Accounting Research* 23(2): 648–67.

Libby, R. 1995. 'The Role of Knowledge and Memory in Audit Judgment', in R. H. Ashton and A. H. Ashton (eds) *Judgment and Decision-making Research in Accounting and Auditing*, pp. 176–206. New York: Cambridge University Press.

Libby, R. and Brown, T. 2013. 'Financial Statement Disaggregation Decisions and Auditors' Tolerance for Misstatement', *The Accounting Review* 88(2): 641–65.

Libby, R. and Frederick, D. M. 1990. 'Experience and the Ability to Explain Audit Findings', *Journal of Accounting Research* 28(2): 348–67.

Libby, R. and Lipe, M. G. 1992. 'Incentives, Effort, and the Cognitive Processes Involved in Accounting-related Judgments', *Journal of Accounting Research* 30(2): 249–73.

Libby, R. and Luft, J. 1993. 'Determinants of Judgment Performance in Accounting Settings: Ability, Knowledge, Motivation, and Environment', *Accounting, Organizations and Society* 18(5): 425–50.

Libby, R. and Trotman, K. T. 1993. 'The Review Process as a Control for Differential Recall of Evidence in Auditor Judgments', *Accounting, Organizations and Society* 18(6): 559–74.

Libby, R., Bloomfield, R. and Nelson, M. W. 2002. 'Experimental Research in Financial Accounting', *Accounting, Organizations and Society* 27(8): 775–810.

McDaniel, L. S. 1990. 'The Effects of Time Pressure and Audit Program Structure on Audit Performance', *Journal of Accounting Research* 28(2): 267–85.

McDaniel, L. S. and Kinney, W. R. Jr 1995. 'Expectation-Formation Guidance in the Auditor's Review of Interim Financial Information', *Journal of Accounting Research* 33(1): 59–76.

Maletta, M. J. and Kida, T. 1993. 'The Effect of Risk Factors on Auditors' Configural Information Processing', *The Accounting Review* 68(3): 681–91.

Messier, W. F. Jr 1995. 'Research in and Development of Audit Decision Aids: A Review', in R. H. Ashton and A. H. Ashton (eds) *Judgment and Decision-making Research in Accounting and Auditing*, pp. 205–28. New York: Cambridge University Press.

Messier, W. F. Jr and Tubbs, R. M. 1994. 'Recency Effects in Belief Revision: The Impact of Audit Experience and the Review Process', *Auditing: A Journal of Practice & Theory* 13(1): 57–72.

Messier, W. F. Jr, Owhoso, V. and Rakovski, C. 2008. 'Can Audit Partners Predict Subordinates' Ability to Detect Errors?', *Journal of Accounting Research* 46(5): 1241–64.

Mock, T. J., Bédard, J., Coram, P. J., Davis, S. M., Espahbodi, R. and Warne, R. C. 2013. 'The Audit Reporting Model: Current Research Synthesis and Implications', *Auditing: A Journal of Practice & Theory* 32(Supplement 1): 323–51.

Moeckel, C. and Plumlee, R. D. 1989. 'Auditors' Confidence in Recognition of Audit Evidence', *The Accounting Review* 64(4): 653.

Moreno, K. K., Bhattacharjee, S. and Brandon, D. M. 2007. 'The Effectiveness of Alternative Training Techniques on Analytical Procedures Performance', *Contemporary Accounting Research* 24(3): 983–1014.

Mumpower, J. L. and Stewart, T. R. 1996. 'Expert Judgment and Expert Disagreement', *Thinking and Reasoning* 2(2/3): 191–211.

Nelson, M. and Tan, H.-T. 2005. 'Judgment and Decision Making Research in Auditing: A Task, Person, and Interpersonal Interaction Perspective', *Auditing: A Journal of Practice & Theory* 24: 41–71.

Nelson, M. W. 1993. 'The Effects of Error Frequency and Accounting Knowledge on Error Diagnosis in Analytical Review', *The Accounting Review* 68(4): 804–24.

Nelson, M. W. 2009. 'A Model and Literature Review of Professional Skepticism in Auditing', *Auditing: A Journal of Practice & Theory* 28(2): 1–34.

Nelson, M. W., Libby, R. and Bonner, S. E. 1995. 'Knowledge Structure and the Estimation of Conditional Probabilities in Audit Planning', *The Accounting Review* 70(1): 27–47.

Ng, T. B.-P. and Tan, H.-T. 2007. 'Effects of Qualitative Factor Salience, Expressed Client Concern, and Qualitative Materiality Thresholds on Auditors' Audit Adjustment Decisions', *Contemporary Accounting Research* 24(4): 1171–92.

O'Donnell, E. and Schultz, J. J. Jr 2005. 'The Halo Effect in Business Risk Audits: Can Strategic Risk Assessment Bias Auditor Judgment about Accounting Details?', *The Accounting Review* 80(3): 921–39.

Peecher, M. E. 1996. 'The Influence of Auditors' Justification Processes on their Decisions: A Cognitive Model and Experimental Evidence', *Journal of Accounting Research* 34(1): 125–40.

Peecher, M. E. and Piercey, M. D. 2008. 'Judging Audit Quality in Light of Adverse Outcomes: Evidence of Outcome Bias and Reverse Outcome Bias', *Contemporary Accounting Research* 25(1): 243–74.

Peecher, M. E., Solomon, I. and Trotman, K. T. 2013. 'An Accountability Framework for Financial Statement Auditors and Related Research Questions', *Accounting Organizations and Society,* 38(8): 596–620.

Plumlee, R. D. 1985. 'The Standard of Objectivity for Internal Auditors: Memory and Bias Effects', *Journal of Accounting Research* 23(2): 683–99.

Pozen, R. 2008. *Final Report of the Advisory Committee on Improvements to Financial Reporting to the United States Securities and Exchange Commission.* Washington DC: Securities and Exchange Commission Advisory Committee.

Ramsay, R. J. 1994. 'Senior/Manager Differences in Audit Workpaper Review Performance', *Journal of Accounting Research* 32(1): 127–35.

Rich, J. S., Solomon, I. and Trotman, K. T. 1997. 'The Audit Review Process: A Characterization from the Persuasion Perspective', *Accounting, Organizations and Society* 22(5): 481–505.

Salterio, S. and Koonce, L. 1997. 'The Persuasiveness of Audit Evidence: The Case of Accounting Policy Decisions', *Accounting, Organizations and Society* 22(6): 573–87.

Sanchez, M. H., Agoglia, C. P. and Hatfield, R. C. 2007. 'The Effect of Auditors' Use of a Reciprocity-based Strategy on Auditor-Client Negotiations', *The Accounting Review* 82(1): 241–63.

Schultz, J. J. Jr and Reckers, P. M. J. 1981. 'The Impact of Group Processing on Selected Audit Disclosure Decisions', *Journal of Accounting Research* 19(2): 482–501.

Shankar, P. G. and Tan, H.-T. 2006. 'Determinants of Audit Preparers' Workpaper Justifications', *The Accounting Review* 81(2): 473–95.

Simnett, R. 1996. 'The Effect of Information Selection, Information Processing and Task Complexity on Predictive Accuracy of Auditors', *Accounting, Organizations and Society* 21(7/8): 699–719.

Smith, J. F. and Kida, T. 1991. 'Heuristics and Biases: Expertise and Task Realism in Auditing', *Psychological Bulletin* 109(3): 472–89.

Solomon, I. 1982. 'Probability of Assessment by Individual Auditors and Audit Teams: An Empirical Investigation', *Journal of Accounting Research* 20(2): 689–710.

Solomon, I. 1987. 'Multi-auditor Judgment/Decision Making Research', *Journal of Accounting Literature* 6: 1–25.

Solomon, I. and Shields, M. D. 1995. 'Judgment and Decision-making Research in Auditing', in R. H. Ashtonand A. H. Ashton (eds) *Judgment and Decision-making Research in Accounting and Auditing*, pp. 137–75. New York: Cambridge University Press.

Solomon, I., Shields, M. D. and Whittington, O. R. 1999. 'What Do Industry-specialist Auditors Know?', *Journal of Accounting Research* 37(1): 191–208.

Tan, H.-T. 1995. 'Effects of Expectations, Prior Involvement, and Review Awareness on Memory for Audit Evidence and Judgment', *Journal of Accounting Research* 33(1): 113–35.

Tan, H.-T. and Kao, A. 1999. 'Accountability Effects on Auditors' Performance: The Influence of Knowledge, Problem-solving Ability, and Task Complexity', *Journal of Accounting Research* 37(1): 209–23.

Tan, H.-T. and Libby, R. 1997. 'Tacit Managerial versus Technical Knowledge as Determinants of Audit Expertise in the Field', *Journal of Accounting Research* 35(1): 97–113.

Tan, H.-T. and Trotman, K. T. 2003. 'Reviewers' Responses to Anticipated Stylization Attempts by Preparers of Audit Workpapers', *The Accounting Review* 78(2): 581–605.

Tan, H.-T. and Trotman, K. T. 2010. 'Effects of the Timing of Auditors' Income-reducing Adjustment Concessions on Financial Officers' Negotiation Judgments', *Contemporary Accounting Research* 27(4): 1207–39.

Trompeter, G. and Wright, A. 2010. 'The World Has Changed – Have Analytical Procedure Practices?', *Contemporary Accounting Research* 27(2): 669–700.

Trompeter, G. M., Carpenter, T. D., Desai, N., Jones, K. L. and Riley, R. A. 2013. 'A Synthesis of Fraud-related Research', *Auditing: A Journal of Practice & Theory* 32(Supplement 1): 287–321.

Trotman, K. T. 1985. 'The Review Process and the Accuracy of Auditor Judgments', *Journal of Accounting Research* 23(2): 740–52.

Trotman, K. T. 1998. 'Audit Judgment Research – Issues Addressed, Research Methods and Future Directions', *Accounting & Finance* 38(2): 115–56.

Trotman, K. T. and Yetton, P. W. 1985. 'The Effect of the Review Process on Auditor Judgments', *Journal of Accounting Research* 23(1): 256–67.

Trotman, K. T., Wright, A. M. and Wright, S. 2005. 'Auditor Negotiations: An Examination of the Efficacy of Intervention Methods', *The Accounting Review* 80(1): 349–67.

Trotman, K. T., Tan, H. C. and Ang, N. 2011. 'Fifty-year Overview of Judgment and Decision-making Research in Accounting', *Accounting & Finance* 51(1): 278–360.

Tversky, A. and Kahneman, D. 1974. 'Judgment under Uncertainty: Heuristics and Biases', *Science* 185 (4157): 1124–31.

Wilks, T. J. 2002. 'Predecisional Distortion of Evidence as a Consequence of Real-time Audit Review', *The Accounting Review* 77(1): 51–72.

Wilks, T. J. and Zimbelman, M. F. 2004. 'Decomposition of Fraud-Risk Assessments and Auditors' Sensitivity to Fraud Cues', *Contemporary Accounting Research* 21(3): 719–45.

17
Analytical procedures

Stephen Kwaku Asare and Justin Leiby

Overview and importance of analytical procedures

Analytical procedures (APs) refer to a family of relatively inexpensive, expectation-based evidence-gathering tools available to an external auditor to efficiently provide assurance on a client's financial statements. In essence, APs consist of comparing a reported numeric value, such as an account balance or ratio, with an expected value to determine whether the account balance or ratio appears reasonable (PCAOB 2010a: AU 329). APs also encompass investigations, as is necessary, of identified fluctuations or relationships that differ from expected values by a significant amount (IAASB 2009: ISA 520). As an example, to test the reasonableness of an account balance such as commission expense, an auditor may compare the balance to an expected amount computed by multiplying audited sales by the average commission rate.

The use of APs in auditing rests on the reasonable expectation that plausible relationships among data exist and will continue to exist in the absence of known conditions to the contrary (PCAOB 2010a: AU 329). Conditions that can cause variations in these relationships include unusual transactions or events, accounting changes, business changes, random fluctuations, or misstatements (PCAOB 2010a: AU 329). APs are performed by developing expectations based on an understanding of the client and of the industry in which the client operates (PCAOB 2010a: AU 329). These expectations are then used to focus audit resources on areas with relatively higher risks of material misstatement and to evaluate the reasonableness of unaudited balances. Unaudited accounts that significantly depart from expectations are targeted for investigations, while those that are consistent with expectations are deemed reasonable. Developing expectations, setting investigation thresholds, and investigating significant differences all require the exercise of professional judgment.

In practice, APs range from simple comparisons – such as scanning transaction summaries for unusual items, ratio comparisons, trend analysis – to the use of complex models involving many relationships and elements of data (IAASB 2009: ISA 520; Trompeter and Wright 2010). APs are also important for testing assertions for which potential misstatements would not be apparent from an examination of the detailed evidence, or for which detailed evidence is not readily available (PCAOB 2010a: AU 329). For example, comparing aggregate salaries paid with the number of personnel may indicate unauthorized payments that may not be apparent from testing individual transactions. Differences from expected relationships may also indicate potential omissions when independent evidence that a transaction should have been recorded is not readily available (PCAOB 2010a: AU 329).

To the extent that expectations are precise (i.e., accurate), APs significantly enhance audit quality, assuming that unexpected fluctuations are competently investigated. Also, APs are versatile and can be used in multiple phases of the audit. Worldwide standards require auditors to use them as risk assessment procedures and in the overall review phase (IAASB 2009: ISA 520; PCAOB 2010a: AU 329; AICPA 2012: AU-C 520; AUASB 2009: ASA 520). The use of APs during substantive testing remains discretionary and may be combined with other tests of details to achieve the desired level of assurance. However, APs are a double-edged sword. If expectations are imprecise, then audit quality can be significantly compromised by accepting misstated unaudited balances and/or by investigating fairly stated balances.

Professional standards provide several prophylactic measures that auditors can take to enhance the precision of their expectations. First, auditors can root their expectations in multiple sources, including: (i) financial information for comparable prior period(s) giving consideration to known changes; (ii) anticipated results (e.g., budgets, or forecasts) including extrapolations from interim or annual data; (iii) relationships among elements of financial information within the period; (iv) information regarding the industry in which the client operates; (v) relationships of financial information with relevant non-financial information (PCAOB 2010a: AU 329). Second, auditors should assess the availability and test the reliability of the underlying data used to develop the expectations. Third, auditors should identify and consider factors that significantly affect the unaudited amount. For example, in setting an expectation for sales, auditors will consider prices, volume, product mix, etc. Fourth, the use of disaggregated data, rather than broad comparisons (e.g., monthly expectations rather than annual expectations) is necessary for applications requiring a higher level of assurance.

In the next section, "Historical developments", we discuss the historical development of the use of APs in the profession. This is followed by a review of current issues on regulators' agendas. We then transition to highlights of current research findings, which are of necessity brief (see Messier *et al.* 2013 for a detailed literature review). In the penultimate section, "Unresolved issues", we underscore unresolved issues in need of further research, followed by our concluding comments.

Historical development

The accounting profession has long recognized that the proper use of APs can lead to more efficient and effective audits. For instance, an *Accounting Review* editorial written in 1934 compared scanning (a type of AP) to account analyses (a type of test of details) and noted: "a few moments' judicious probing and questioning will yield results that account analyses, no matter how painstakingly made, will never yield, notwithstanding the effort to get at the sources" (AAA 1934). This editorial not only points out the benefits of using AP, but also makes the case that exceptionally well trained auditors are good scanners who see "many things quickly – in their relationship to other things." The editorial also highlights the importance of knowledge, training, and experience in the effective use of APs by noting that a good scanner's "judgment has ripened by constant contact with the practical affairs of many business enterprises." To use scanning effectively, the editorial continues, is to acquire a "store of valuable and amazing information," and to "exercise intellectual capacity and to enjoy oneself thoroughly."

Statement on Auditing Standards No. 1 (SAS 1) lists "analytical review of significant ratios and trends and resulting investigation of unusual fluctuations and questionable items" as one of two general classes of auditing procedures for obtaining the evidential matter required by the third standard of fieldwork (AICPA 1972: SAS 1). However, SAS 1 did not give specific guidance on the use of AP beyond mentioning that its use relates to the quality of internal controls and other substantive tests. SAS 23 provides the first formal guidance on the use of AP (AICPA 1978). While this standard did not require the use of APs, it provided general guidance for consideration by the auditor who is going to use APs: the auditor should investigate unusual fluctuations; APs may be performed during the risk assessment and planning, substantive testing, and review stages; APs can take many forms, and may be applied to the overall financial information of the entity or to its components (e.g., subsidiaries or divisions). Two members of the Auditing Standards Board (ASB) dissented because they believed the standard did not offer specific guidance on how it should be implemented and documented. By and large, the emphasis on APs during this period was on their ability to increase cost and audit efficiency.

The Treadway Commission observed that auditors can and should do more to improve their fraud detection capabilities and recommended that the ASB should establish standards to require auditors to perform analytical review procedures in all audits (NCFFR 1987: 52). It was this recommendation that gave impetus to the promulgation of SAS 56 which, among other things, required the use of APs in the planning and overall review phases of an audit (AICPA 1988: AU 329). The use of substantive APs remained optional. The PCAOB also adopted SAS 56 as part of its interim standards (PCAOB 2003).

Based on these developments, APs are performed during the risk assessment and planning, testing, and final review phases of the audit. Current guidance on the use of APs on the audit of public companies in the US can be found in AS 12 (PCAOB 2010b), AU 329 (PCAOB 2010a) and AS 14 (PCAOB 2010c).[1] AS 12 provides guidance for the use of APs in the planning and risk assessment phase, in which APs should be designed (1) to enhance the auditor's understanding of the client's business and the significant transactions and events that have occurred since the prior year end; and (2) to identify areas that might represent specific risks relevant to the audit (PCAOB 2010b). In essence, APs play an attention-directing role in the planning and risk assessment phase, leading the auditors away from low risk areas towards potentially troubling aspects of the audit. It is in this sense that the standards describe APs as "risk assessment procedures."

AU 329 provides guidance on APs used as substantive tests of the reasonableness of an account balance (PCAOB 2010a). For example, an auditor might compare hotel revenues with an expected amount computed by multiplying the number of rooms, the occupancy rate and average per room rates. If the difference between the two is within a predetermined acceptable range, the auditor can accept the hotel revenue as reasonable. There is obvious efficiency in this approach to testing the reasonableness of an account balance relative to tests of details, which require vouching and tracing of detailed accounts. However, the proper use of APs as substantive tests requires compliance with stringent requirements, including (1) developing an expectation for the amount or ratio that is precise enough to provide the desired level of assurance; (2) determining the amount of difference from the expectation that can be accepted without further investigation; and (3) evaluating significant unexpected differences. In this evaluation, the auditor may consider management's responses to the auditor's inquiries, but the auditor ordinarily should obtain other evidence to corroborate the information that is received (PCAOB 2010a: AU 329).

AS 14 provides guidance on APs during the review phase. In this phase, APs are to be designed to evaluate the auditor's conclusions about significant accounts and disclosures and to assist in forming an opinion on whether the financial statements as a whole are free from material misstatements (PCAOB 2010c: AS 14). The nature and extent of APs performed in the review phase may be similar to APs used in the risk assessment phase, and should include APs relating to revenue and whether there is a previously unrecognized fraud risk.

Despite the guidance that is provided in the standards, the use of APs in practice involves the exercise of considerable professional judgment by the auditor. As noted above, the use of professional judgment may allow auditors to detect misstatements that they would otherwise miss using more mechanistic tests of details. However, these judgment are also more open to scrutiny and second-guessing during peer reviews, regulatory inspections, etc. In the next section, "Current issues", we provide an overview of issues that regulators argue arise in the performance of APs in practice.

Current issues

Although no standard setter has the use of APs on its current agenda, regulatory inspection reports, primarily from the US, raise questions about whether APs are being properly designed and applied in practice. In the opinions of the inspectors, there are two types of problems: (i) the auditor determining that conditions justify the use of APs when regulators believe that conditions do not justify their use; and (ii) the auditor applying APs when conditions do justify their use, but in a manner that regulators believe is improper. Regulators do appear to acknowledge the potential power of APs, as their concerns focus on the use of APs in improper conditions or on improper application and not on inherent deficiencies in APs.

With respect to the use of APs in improper conditions, inspectors focus on instances in which auditors used APs for substantive testing even though the underlying internal controls were not strong enough to justify such usage (PCAOB 2011). With respect to the improper application of APs, the inspection reports highlight problems in all phases of the audit. In some instances, auditors do not set expectations, or set expectations that are not sufficiently precise to provide the desired level of assurance that differences are not potential misstatements (PCAOB 2007, 2008). Some auditors set expectations based on their clients' competitors without determining whether the competitors' numbers are predictive of their clients (PCAOB 2011). There are also instances in which expectations have been set based on data whose completeness and accuracy had not been tested (PCAOB 2011).

Inspectors also claim that there are instances in which firms failed to establish the threshold for investigation. Also, regulators contend that firms have failed to consider the possibility that a combination of misstatements could aggregate to an unexpected amount, which results in auditors failing to investigate differences that, in combination, exceed materiality (PCAOB 2011). Auditors also fail to evaluate significant variances identified by APs (PCAOB 2012). When evaluating significant variances, there are instances in which auditors fail to obtain corroboration of management explanations or do not go beyond reading reports that management provides to the Board of Directors (PCAOB 2012). Other concerns have been raised about the improper application of APs to detect intentional misstatements, a purpose of for which APs are arguably well suited. These concerns are crystallized by the testimony of Mel Dick (2002) to the US Congress in the WorldCom fraud:

> Additionally, we performed numerous APs of the various financial statement line items, including line costs, revenues, and plant and service in order to determine if there were any significant variations that required additional work. We also utilized sophisticated auditing software to study WorldCom's financial statement line items, which did not trigger any indication that there was a need for additional work.
>
> *(Dick 2002: 3)*

The Securities and Exchange Commission (SEC) has also weighed in. For instance, a study by the Commission found that audit failures most often arise from auditors accepting management representations without verification, truncating analytical and substantive procedures, and failing to gain sufficient evidence to support the numbers in the financial statements (SEC 2012: 44). Schuetze (1998) puts it more vividly:

> Auditors not doing substantive audit work but relying on so-called APs where the evidence, or lack thereof, cries out for substantive audit work. In one case, the physical inventory test counts showed a large shortfall from the inventory amount in the general ledger. Rather than requiring a complete physical count of the inventory or qualifying the audit opinion, the auditor relied on so-called "analytical procedures" which led to acceptance of an erroneous book amount for the inventory.
>
> *(Schuetze 1998: penult. para)*

Other current concerns revolve around how emerging regulations (e.g., the Sarbanes-Oxley Act), technological changes (allowing auditors to mine significant databases), and financial scandals (e.g., Enron, WorldCom) are affecting the use of AP in practice (see e.g., Trompeter and Wright 2010). Last, there is growing interest in finding ways to leverage the use of APs in the auditing of accounting estimates. However, as is the case with APs in other areas, the effective use of APs in auditing estimates requires the formation of independent and sufficiently precise expectations. Recent regulatory inspection reports contend that auditors have difficulty doing so.

Regardless of the validity of the criticisms by regulators, they highlight the diversity of practices in which the application of APs continues to be problematic. In the next section, "Current state of research findings", we review findings from academic research that examine how some of the variables that auditors confront in the field are likely to influence their performance of APs. This research highlights the fact that APs require the exercise of professional judgment and are, thus, subject to the same limitations as any human judgment. This research offers insights into the circumstances in which APs are more or less likely to be effective in practice, and identifies potential ways in which APs can be improved.

Current state of research findings

There has been a large volume of research on APs during the past two decades. We first discuss research related to the use of APs in practice, followed by research related to the determinants of APs performance. With respect to the former, two comprehensive interview studies published 14 years apart provide important insights (Hirst and Koonce 1996; and Trompeter and Wright 2010). Despite the relatively long interim between these studies, there is considerable consistency in the practical issues that they documented. Auditors in both studies report the use of relatively simple techniques, such as the use of prior year balances, to develop expectations for the current year's balances. In the investigation phase, auditors in both studies report that they did not generate their own independent explanations, and instead focused on assessing the reasonableness of clients' explanations.

In the intervening years, there were a few noteworthy changes in practice. For instance, Trompeter and Wright (2010) report heavier reliance on APs due to technological advances and stronger client internal controls, and heavier usage of lower level auditors to perform APs. Moreover, multiple developments have increased the volume of information that is available for use in APs. Inquiries of non-accounting personnel – who are potentially more objective or less likely to have an understanding of the financial statement implications of intentional errors – are increasingly common, whereas auditors had previously avoided such discussions because they tended to provide too much irrelevant information. In general, non-financial information is more widely used, perhaps as a response to the AICPA's (2008) guidance to make greater use of non-financial information in APs. To cope with these larger information sets, advances in technology, including more sophisticated analytical software, have enabled more appropriate benchmarking and, in turn, the development of more precise expectations.

With respect to determinants of APs performance, research has focused on characteristics of the auditor (e.g., knowledge and motivation) and auditee (e.g., integrity); interactions of the auditor with clients and other auditors (e.g., the review process); and how the procedure is performed (e.g., judgment aids). Juxtaposing these determinants and the phases of APs provides a framework for organizing prior research findings as illustrated in Table 17.1. The research has focused predominantly on auditors' development of expectations and investigations of significant differences, including the generation of hypotheses and assessment of alternatives. There are also multiple unpopulated cells in the table, which represent potentially significant unanswered questions.

Research on expectation development has focused primarily on how the procedure is performed, such as the presence of an unaudited book value, the steps used in the procedure, and the level of aggregation of data. Auditors' expectations can be biased by the presence of the client's unaudited balance, especially when the client's numbers appear to be reliable (e.g., when they have no history of prior adjustments [Heintz *et al.* 1999]). Moreover, APs increasingly necessitate the use of complex and interrelated information to form expectations and to identify possible misstatements. The use of this information may be facilitated by strategic risk assessment, which is a tool that is intended to help auditors identify and understand the complex relations between an auditee's business conditions and the risk of material misstatement. In a task in which auditors developed expectations based on a complex balanced scorecard, Knechel *et al.* (2010) found that auditors who had strategic information about a client made relatively

Table 17.1 Determinants of analytical procedures judgments

	Auditor Attributes	*Client Attributes*	*Auditor and Client Interactions*	*Task Attributes*
Develop expectations			Superiors' preferences	Book value Prior-year adjustments Holistic assessments Disaggregated data
Define investigation threshold	Auditor expectations			Quality of controls
Investigate Significant differences	Knowledge Industry specialization Pattern recognition	Integrity Competence	Source reliability Partner preferences Superiors' explanations Type of justification	Competing hypotheses Quantification of explanation

well-calibrated risk assessments, but those who did not have such information overemphasized certain incomplete benchmarked metrics.

However, there is also evidence that strategic assessment can hinder the performance of APs. For example, O'Donnell and Schultz (2005) found that, in response to a negative balance fluctuation, auditors assess misstatement risk as lower when they form relatively positive expectations based on a positive (as opposed to negative) strategic assessment of the auditee's business conditions. Thus, while strategic assessments can lead to a better, more balanced understanding of how business conditions may affect account balances, it may also lead to the development of overly positive expectations.

Regarding the setting of thresholds to determine what constitutes a "significant" difference, auditors may tolerate larger differences when they develop more positive expectations based on higher (unaudited) reported amounts (Heintz *et al.* 1999). However, there is also evidence that auditors rely less on these amounts when they observe a signal of potentially poor controls (e.g., recent information system changes).

In the subsequent investigation phase, research has documented the effects of knowledge on AP performance. For instance, the increase in the reliance on APs has coincided with increasing industry specialization among auditors. Research has examined how specialist training and direct experience influence the performance of auditors who have more expertise in an industry when performing APs. Solomon *et al.* (1999) found that industry specialists were more able than non-specialists at developing explanations for unusual fluctuations. However, because specialists' superiority is driven by their direct experience and because auditors rarely have direct experience with material misstatements, specialists were only superior at explaining why a difference *is not* the result of a misstatement (non-misstatement explanations). Thus, specialization may actually worsen the tendency to rationalize that unusual fluctuations are not the result of a misstatement, which could compromise audit quality.

In addition to potential limitations in auditors' development of explanations, there is also evidence that auditors often do not generate their own explanations. Instead, auditors simply borrow and test the explanations of others, including the client. Accordingly, research has examined whether the source of an explanation affects how heavily auditors rely on the explanation. Encouragingly, auditors do generate a greater number of alternative explanations when the source of an explanation is believed to lack integrity (Peecher 1996). More generally, auditors rely more on explanations as the source increases in objectivity, such as an audit team member versus the client CFO, and increases in competence, such as an industry specialist versus non-specialist (Hirst 1994). In addition, auditors do attempt to corroborate the explanations of potentially unreliable sources. Specifically, Glover *et al.* (2000) found that auditors increased the level of audit testing for an explanation from a potentially low integrity client when there was minimal (as opposed to extensive) corroboration for the auditee's explanation.

Further, the auditor's judgment during the investigation of significant differences has been found to be influenced by interactions between members of the audit team. Peecher (1996) examined whether the effect of the client's integrity on auditor judgment during AP depends on the preferences of the audit partner. He found that when auditors were advised to maximize audit efficiency, they weighted the explanations of high integrity clients more than those of low integrity clients. Interestingly, there was little evidence that the partner's preferences influenced the search for competing explanations, which indicated a potential disconnect between assessing auditee explanations and actually investigating differences. Moreover, interactions between auditors in the review process have been found to influence the judgments of the supervising auditor in addition to those of the subordinate. In a key study, Yip-Ow and Tan (2000) found that, when subordinates provide a one-sided justification for a non-misstatement explanation, reviewers were less able to develop alternative explanations and were more likely to believe the non-misstatement explanation.

Finally, the performance of APs may depend on how the procedure itself is performed. For instance, in practice auditors commonly confront the need to assess multiple competing explanations. However, there is evidence that auditors tend to assess and revise their beliefs about one explanation at a time, and fail to recognize the interdependencies between explanations (Asare and Wright 1997a, 1997b). Further, the opportunity to quantify an explanation could help auditors to assess its credibility, if they take advantage of this opportunity. However, there is evidence that auditors may not independently quantify the explanations of others, even when they have a chance to do so. Moreover, they are more likely to accept an incorrect explanation than they are to reject a correct explanation.

Unresolved issues

Based on this brief review of the academic literature and of recent observations by regulators, some practical issues remain unresolved. A general unresolved issue of great importance relates to enhancing auditors' formation of expectations. It is unknown how firms can prompt auditors to develop more independent expectations, and how auditors determine that the information on which they form expectations is sufficiently accurate and complete.

Also, because auditors frequently inherit explanations from auditees – frequently non-misstatement explanations – it would be beneficial to apply theory to understand the conditions under which client explanations are likely to hinder or possibly enhance the performance of APs. For instance, if one considers the interactions between auditor and auditee as a strategic game, then auditees are likely to try to conceal misstatements in accounts that they anticipate auditors will not test. Auditee explanations may actually improve auditors' performance by revealing information about auditee intentions or by revealing information about unobservable client attributes (e.g., integrity). It is also largely unknown to what extent training and decision aids to improve the use of auditee explanations – specifically, to avoid anchoring on client explanations – or identify personality traits (e.g., need for cognition, innate skepticism) may influence auditors' use of auditee explanations.

As discussed above, general improvements in organizations' internal controls have led to increased reliance on APs (Trompeter and Wright 2010). Because increasing the effectiveness of APs leads to lower risks that tests of details will fail to detect a misstatement, it is possible that auditors have substituted analytical procedures for tests of details. It is unknown to what extent audit efficiency gains are traded off against potential effectiveness.

Also, the broader availability of non-financial information represents an opportunity and a challenge for auditors. Neither research nor regulatory pronouncements have lent sufficient insight as to when auditors will use or should use non-financial information to form expectations, or into how auditors' understanding of this information can be improved. Auditors will also increasingly confront "big data" – data sources too large and complex for traditional database management – and third-party tools that purport to improve the use of big data. Big data may be particularly important in assessing the risk of and detecting fraud. However, it is unknown under what conditions auditors will or should develop trust in these sources and what training or tools could help auditors better access, analyze, and ultimately rely upon large volumes of information.

A further issue of importance is how APs are influenced and can be improved by audit firms' quality control mechanisms, such as consultation and brainstorming. By exposing auditors to alternative sources of information and points of view, consultation with superiors or peers has the potential to improve the formation of expectations, planning of procedures, generation and analysis of hypotheses, etc. It is unknown when (and whom) auditors consult during analytical procedures, how they use the advice of their peers, and the ultimate implications on APs performance. In addition, a good deal of interaction and consultation likely occurs outside of formal, documented channels, and it is unknown how these informal quality controls during APs may influence more formal quality control mechanisms such as the involvement of specialists, reviews, etc.

Finally, the bulk of research on analytical procedures has focused on planning stage procedures, while little research has examined APs during the review stage. For instance, it is largely unknown what factors affect auditors' determination that financial statements make sense as a whole and that sufficient evidence has been collected. Expectation formation is heavily emphasized at this stage of the audit (Hirst and Koonce 1996), and we know very little about how expectation formation for review compares to expectation formation for planning.

Conclusions

APs are, without doubt, relatively low cost procedures that have the potential to be powerful tools for directing auditors' attention to risk areas and for detecting financial misstatements (e.g., Wright and Ashton 1989). The question, for regulators, practitioners, users, and researchers, is delineating the conditions under which this potential is harnessed or undermined. Because APs are expectation-based, substantial regulatory scrutiny and research have focused on the precision of auditors' expectations. Of concern, some auditors do not develop expectations prior to using APs and their expectations, when they develop them, are influenced by the client's unaudited balances, are not disaggregated sufficiently, and do not sufficiently incorporate non-financial information. A recurring concern in the investigation phase is the effect of an explanation inherited from management. Yet, regulatory and research findings suggest that inheriting such an explanation impairs auditors' ability to effectively test the explanation.

In light of the numerous issues that remain unresolved in practice and research, substantial work remains before concrete and comprehensive prescriptions can be formed as to the appropriate performance of APs. In order to be successful, efforts to resolve longstanding and recently identified difficulties in the performance of APs will require extensive cooperation between researchers, practitioners, users, and standard setters. These efforts are likely to confront hurdles such as limited availability of data (both archival data and the availability of professional experimental participants) and rapidly changing environmental conditions, including new standards, technological developments, and theoretical frameworks.

Note

1 Due to the convergence efforts of the ASB and the IAASB, there is cross-jurisdiction consensus in the content and format of APs standards (AICPA 2012, AU-C 520 and IAASB 2009, ISA 520; AUASB 2009, ASA 520).

References

American Accounting Association (AAA). 1934. Editorial: "Capital surplus; Dated surplus; Scanning; Economists and costs; New definitions", *The Accounting Review* 9(3): 257–8.

American Institute of Certified Public Accountants (AICPA). 1972. *Codification of Auditing Standards and Procedures*. Statement on Auditing Standards No. 1. AICPA: New York.

American Institute of Certified Public Accountants (AICPA). 1978. *Analytical Review Procedures*. Statement on Auditing Standards No. 23. AICPA: New York.

American Institute of Certified Public Accountants (AICPA). 1988. *Analytical Procedures*. Statement on Auditing Standards No. 56. AU Section 329. AICPA: New York.

American Institute of Certified Public Accountants (AICPA). 2008. *Audit Guide: Analytical Procedures*. AICPA: New York.

American Institute of Certified Public Accountants (AICPA). 2012. *Analytical Procedures*. Statement on Auditing Standards No. 122. AU Section 520. AICPA: New York.

Asare, S. and A. Wright. 1997a. "Evaluation of Competing Hypotheses in Auditing", *Auditing: A Journal of Practice & Theory* 16(1): 1–13.

Asare, S. and A. Wright. 1997b. "Hypothesis Revision Strategies in Conducting Analytical Procedures", *Accounting, Organizations and Society* 22(8): 737–55.

Auditing and Assurance Standards Board (AUASB) 2009. *Analytical Procedures*. Auditing Standard No. 520. Available online at www.comlaw.gov.au/Details/F2009L04090 (accessed 9 May 2014).

Dick, M. 2002. "Remarks to the U.S. House of Representatives Committee on Financial Services on 8 July 2002." Available online at http://financialservices.house.gov/media/pdf/070802md.pdf (accessed 30 Dec 2012).

Glover, S., J. Jiambolvo and J. Kennedy. 2000. "Analytical Procedures and Audit-planning Decisions", *Auditing: A Journal of Practice & Theory* 19(2): 27–45.

Heintz, J., G. White and J. Bedard. 1999. "The Effect of Data Reliability on the Influence of Unaudited Values in Audit Analytical Procedures", *International Journal of Auditing* 3: 135–46.

Hirst, D.E. 1994. "Auditors' Sensitivity to Source Reliability", *Journal of Accounting Research* 32(1): 113–26.

Hirst, E. and L. Koonce. 1996. "Audit Analytical Procedures: A Field Investigation", *Contemporary Accounting Research* 13(2): 457–86.

International Auditing and Assurance Standards Board (IAASB). 2009. *Analytical Procedures*. International Standard on Auditing (ISA) 520. Available online at www.ifac.org/auditing-assurance (accessed 30 Dec 2012).

Knechel, W.R., S. Salterio and N. Kochetova-Kozloski. 2010. "The Effect of Benchmarked Performance Measures and Strategic Analysis on Auditors' Risk Assessments and Mental Models", *Accounting, Organizations and Society* 35: 316–33.

Koonce, L. 1993. "A Cognitive Characterization of Audit Analytical Review", *Auditing: A Journal of Practice & Theory* 12(Supplement): 57–76.

Libby, R. 1985. "Availability and the Generation of Hypotheses in Analytical Review", *Journal of Accounting Research* 23(2): 648–67.

Messier, W., C. Simon and J. Smith. 2013. "Two Decades of Behavioral Research on Analytical Procedures: What Have we Learned?", *Auditing: A Journal of Practice & Theory* 32(1): 139–81.

National Commission on Fraudulent Financial Reporting (NCFFR). 1987. *Report of the National Commission on Fraudulent Financial Reporting*. AICPA: New York.

O'Donnell, E. and J. Schultz. 2005. "The Halo Effect in Business Risk Audits: Can Strategic Risk Assessment Bias Auditor Judgment about Accounting Details?", *The Accounting Review* 80(3): 921–39.

Peecher, M.E. 1996. "The Influence of Auditors' Justification Processes on their Decisions: A Cognitive Model and Experimental Evidence", *Journal of Accounting Research* 34(1): 125–40.

Public Company Accounting Oversight Board (PCAOB). 2003. *Interim Auditing Standards*. Rule 3200T. Available online at http://pcaobus.org/Rules/PCAOBRules/Pages/Section_3.aspx#rule3200t (accessed 30 Dec 2012).

Public Company Accounting Oversight Board (PCAOB). 2007. *Observations on Auditors' Implementation of PCAOB Standards Relating to Auditors' Responsibilities with Respect to Fraud*. Available online at http://pcaobus.org/Inspections/Documents/2007_01–22_Release_2007–001.pdf (accessed 30 Dec 2012).

Public Company Accounting Oversight Board (PCAOB). 2008. *Report on the PCAOB's 2004, 2005, 2006, and 2007 Inspections of Domestic Annually Inspected Firms*. Available online at http://pcaobus.org/Inspections/Documents/2008_12–05_Release_2008–008.pdf (accessed 30 Dec 2012).

Public Company Accounting Oversight Board (PCAOB). 2010a. *Substantive Analytical Procedures*. AU Section 329. Available online at http://pcaobus.org/Standards/Auditing/Pages/AU329.aspx (accessed 30 Dec 2012).

Public Company Accounting Oversight Board (PCAOB). 2010b. *Identifying and Assessing Risks of Material Misstatement*. PCAOB Auditing Standard No. 12. Available onlione at http://pcaobus.org/Standards/Auditing/Pages/Auditing_Standard_12.aspx (accessed 30 Dec 2012).

Public Company Accounting Oversight Board (PCAOB). 2010c. *Evaluating Audit Results.* PCAOB Auditing Standard No. 14. Available online at http://pcaobus.org/Standards/Auditing/Pages/Auditing_Standard_14.aspx (accessed 30 Dec 2012).

Public Company Accounting Oversight Board (PCAOB). 2011. *PCAOB Release No. 104–2011-289: Report on 2010 Inspection of PricewaterhouseCoopers LLP.* Available online at http://pcaobus.org/Inspections/Reports/Documents/2011_PricewaterhouseCoopers_LLP.pdf (accessed 30 Dec 2012).

Public Company Accounting Oversight Board (PCAOB). 2012. *PCAOB Release No. 2012–006: Observations from 2010 Inspections of Domestic Annually Inspected Firms Regarding Deficiencies in Audits of Internal Control over Financial Reporting.* Available online at http://pcaobus.org/Inspections/Documents/12102012_Release_2012_06.pdf (accessed 30 Dec 2012).

Schuetze, W. 1998. "Enforcement Issues: Good News, Bad News, Brillo Pads, Miracle-Glo, and Roundup." Remarks delivered at Twenty-sixth Annual AICPA National Conference on SEC Developments, Washington, DC, 8 December. Available online at www.sec.gov/news/speech/speecharchive/1998/spch241.htm (accessed 30 December 2012).

8 December. Available online at www.sec.gov/news/speech/speecharchive/1998/spch241.htm (accessed 30 Dec 2012).

Securities and Exchange Commission (SEC). 2012. *Report Pursuant to Section 704 of the Sarbanes-Oxley Act of 2002.* Available online at www.sec.gov/news/studies/sox704report.pdf (accessed 30 Dec 2012).

Solomon, I., M. Shields and O.R. Whittington. 1999. "What do Industry-specialist Auditors Know?", *Journal of Accounting Research* 37(1): 191–208.

Trompeter, G. and A. Wright. 2010. "The World has Changed: Have Analytical Procedure Practices?", *Contemporary Accounting Research* 27: 669–700.

Wright, A. and R. Ashton. 1989. "Identifying Audit Adjustments with Attention-directing Procedures", *The Accounting Review* 64(4): 710–28.

Yip-Ow, J. and H.T. Tan. 2000. "Effects of the Preparer's Justification on the Reviewer's Hypothesis Generation and Judgment in Analytical Procedures", *Accounting, Organizations and Society* 25: 203–15.

18

Internal audit

Urton Anderson and Margaret Christ

Introduction

The Institute of Internal Auditors (IIA), the global professional association for the practice of internal auditing, defines the internal audit function (IAF) as an assurance and consulting activity implemented to evaluate and improve the effectiveness of the governance, risk management, and control (GRC) processes within the organization. In particular, the IAF's role is to provide objective assurance and insight regarding GRC processes to two different groups: (1) those charged with organizational governance (e.g., executive management and the board); and (2) those managing the organizational operations (e.g., operational managers, and staff functions). The IAF provides value to each of these groups differently, with the former group primarily seeking assurance, and the latter group looking for insight and recommendations. In this chapter, we examine the IAF's relationship to each group as a framework for our discussion of how these relationships have evolved over time, what researchers have learned regarding internal auditing, and what questions remain unanswered.

Governance, risk management and control

GRC processes are the activities that help an organization achieve its objectives. Organizational governance includes relationships among different stakeholders (e.g., investors, employees, customers, vendors) and representatives of the organization (e.g., the board, external auditors) which shape the direction and performance of the organization. Key aspects of governance include setting strategic direction and objectives, determining organizational boundaries, values and tolerance for risk, and establishing processes for monitoring, risk management, assurance, internal control, accountability, recognition of stakeholders' interests, and stewardship (Hermanson and Rittenberg 2003).

While the term corporate governance is often used synonymously with the term "governance," for the purpose of this discussion we distinguish between "corporate governance," which is specific to organizations in the corporate form (and in most academic research is even more restrictively applied to publicly traded corporations) and "organizational governance" which not only includes corporations, but government entities, colleges and universities, non-profit organizations, etc. In the corporate form, governance includes a governing board composed typically of directors independent of the day-to-day operations of the organization and senior management. In other organizational forms, this governing body may be a group of elected officials, an executive director, a committee of senior managers, a workers' council or others – whatever the structure, we will refer to this governing body as "those charged with governance." IAFs exist in all of these organizational forms and play a similar role in governance processes. Much of the prior research has examined the corporate form and has found that strong corporate governance is associated with positive accounting outcomes, such as less fraudulent financial reporting, fewer restatements, less earnings management, and greater accounting conservatism (see Carcello *et al.* 2011).

The IAF and those charged with governance

Those charged with governance, typically executive management and the board of directors (hereafter, the board), have two fundamental responsibilities: (1) setting the strategic direction of the organization; and (2) providing governance oversight. Following major corporate failures of the early 2000s a number of significant changes were made to organizational governance practices, particularly an increased emphasis on the oversight responsibilities. These oversight responsibilities primarily consist of two components: (1) management of risks that organizational objectives will not be achieved; and (2) obtaining assurance that the organization's risk management practices are effective. Today, the IAF has become one of the primary tools through which executive management and the board can fulfill their governance oversight responsibilities. The IAF provides valuable inputs and guidance to the board, management, and the external auditors, who help facilitate effective governance processes. IAF activities can vary widely among organizations, but typically include risk assessments, control evaluations, financial and operational audits, fraud investigations, external audit support, and consulting engagements.

The IAF and the board of directors

The relationship between the IAF and the board has evolved since 2001 when the business world was rocked by the scandals, frauds, and bankruptcies at companies like Enron and WorldCom, and the resultant closure of Arthur Andersen. These events precipitated the passage of the Sarbanes-Oxley Act of 2002 (SOX). Prior to the passage of SOX, the IAF often reported directly to the CFO or other operational managers, the same individuals whose operations the IAF was auditing. This created the potential for a conflict of interest and a lack of independence, or at least the perception of a lack of independence (regardless of the reality).

However, SOX required significant changes to corporate governance and financial reporting for public companies, including an increased focus on internal controls. While the role of the IAF is not delineated explicitly in SOX, many public companies changed their IAF processes and elevated the IAF's importance within the organization. One primary institutional change made by most organizations was to have the IAF report directly to the audit committee. As evidence, the IIA's Comprehensive Body of Knowledge (CBOK) study for the internal audit (IA) profession finds that 34 percent of chief audit executive (CAE) respondents report administratively to – versus just meeting with – the audit committee or board (Alkafaji *et al.* 2010). Other changes to the structure and activities of the IAF have also occurred, such as a shift in the focus of IAF activities toward more audits of financial reporting activities and SOX testing (at least temporarily), increased staffing and budgets, and improved relationships with the board and executive management. Indeed, Carcello *et al.* (2005b) survey 271 CAEs from US public companies and find that IA budgets and staffing levels increased by over 10 percent from 2001 to 2002. Further, IAF meetings with the audit committee increased in frequency and length by 25 percent.

Today, the IAF provides value to the board by assessing the organization's governance activities and making appropriate recommendations for improving those processes. In particular, the IAF considers whether the governance processes: (1) communicate risk and control information appropriately; (2) ensure effective organizational performance management and accountability; (3) coordinate activities and communication among the board, external and internal auditors, and management; and (4) promote ethics and values within the organization (IIA 2013: Std 2110). Professional guidance and standards encourage a quality relationship between the IAF and the board (or the audit committee). For example, IIA standards require the IAF to interact and communicate directly with the board. This interaction occurs not only during regularly scheduled meetings with the audit committee/board, but increasingly CAEs meet with the audit committee outside of regularly scheduled meetings. Indeed, 74 percent of CAEs report additional meetings with the audit committee, up from 63 percent in 2006 (Anderson and Svare 2011). Further, the IAF must communicate significant risk exposure, control issues, fraud risks, governance issues, and other information needed or requested by the board. A quality relationship between the IAF and the board is mutually beneficial – the board receives information and assurance and, in return, supports the IAF by providing sufficient organizational status so that the IAF can carry out its responsibilities effectively (Cohen *et al.* 2004).

Academic literature describing the relationship between the IAF and the board is somewhat limited, focusing primarily on associations between characteristics of the audit committee and its interactions with the IAF (see Gramling *et al.* 2004). Most prior research relies on surveys of internal auditors. For example, studies examine the extent and frequency of meetings between the IAF and the audit committee because meeting frequency is associated with corporate governance quality. This research concludes that higher quality audit committees (i.e., those composed of independent members with a financial expert) have longer and more frequent private meetings with the IAF and review the work of the IAF to a greater extent (Raghunandan *et al.* 2001). According to CBOK respondents, the IAF on average meets with the audit committee four times per year with a significant number meeting at least ten times per year (Alkafaji *et al.* 2010). Relatedly, Goodwin (2003) finds that it is necessary for the audit committee to possess sufficient financial knowledge to effectively oversee the work of the IAF.

Research has also examined the extent to which the audit committee is involved in decisions to hire or fire the CAE and its effects. The IIA standards state that independence can be achieved effectively if the board is responsible for "approving decisions regarding the appointment and removal of the chief audit executive" (IIA 2013: Std 1110). Anderson *et al.* (2010) survey 449 CAEs from public and private organizations and find that audit committees from approximately 40 percent of public and 60 percent of private companies are responsible for hiring and firing the CAE. Raghunandan and McHugh (1994) find that internal auditors believe that the IAF is more objective when the audit committee has hiring and firing authority. Little to no research has delved deeper into specific interactions between the IAF and the audit committee. Research examining the types of information discussed, and the manner and extent of reporting during meetings between the IAF and the audit committee, would be useful as it would shed light on how the IAF influences governance process. As described by Carcello *et al.* (2011) regulatory requirements are reducing the variation in the objective determinants of governance. As a result, researchers could explore the substance of governance activities to truly understand what factors improve governance and improve financial reporting quality.

An emerging stream of IA literature focuses on the scope of work of the IAF. The audit committee, in conjunction with the CAE, establishes the IA charter, which identifies the activities the IAF is expected to perform. Importantly, charters vary widely from organization to organization. For example, according to CBOK, most IAFs perform operational audits (89 percent), compliance audits (75 percent), audits of financial risks (71 percent), and fraud investigations (71 percent), while fewer perform audits of enterprise risk management processes (56 percent) and audits of specific large projects (55 percent) (Alkafaji *et al.* 2010). Activities such as security assessments, ethics audits, and executive compensation assessments were mentioned even less frequently. Similarly, Anderson *et al.* (2010) find that most organizations explicitly include auditing of operations, financial reporting, and IT. Approximately 40 percent (and 55 percent of public companies) also include external audit support. However, fewer than 25 percent of companies include auditing third parties, performing continuous control activities, or leadership development programs. Anderson *et al.* (2011) examine the size of IAFs and find an association between IAF size and the performance of IT audits, suggesting that it requires a larger IA staff with a diverse set of skills to audit IT. However, current research does not address the specific activities that the IAF performs and the effect of different mixes of activities on the quality of corporate governance and financial reporting, thus a gap remains in our knowledge about the scope of the work of IAFs.

Another emerging stream of literature sheds light on the effectiveness of the IAF's risk management and assurance activities by exploring the effect of the IAF on various financial reporting outcomes of the organization. Most of these studies use proprietary data from the IIA which includes information on IAF experience, training, and certification which (together) are used as a proxy for IAF quality. For example, Prawitt *et al.* (2009) examine associations between IAF quality and earnings management and find that higher quality IAFs are associated with less earnings management (measured as lower abnormal accruals[1] and a lower likelihood of barely beating analysts' earnings forecasts[2]). Prawitt *et al.* (2012) examine whether the manner in which the IAF is sourced (i.e., in-house versus outsourced) affects accounting risk. In their study, the authors measure accounting risk using a proprietary dataset that estimates the likelihood of misleading or fraudulent information in the financial reports. The authors find that accounting risk is lower when IA activities are performed by an in-house IA department, or by the organization's external auditor, as compared to when it is outsourced to another service provider.

This finding suggests that the organizational knowledge of an in-house IAF (or the external auditor) can improve financial reporting quality. Christ *et al.* (2012) similarly find that accounting risk is higher when the IAF is used as a management training ground such that internal auditors rotate out of the IAF into management positions in other parts of the organization. Finally, Ege (2012) examines the IAF quality of companies with observable instances of management misconduct, such as SEC (Securities Exchange Commission) enforcement actions or class-action lawsuits, and finds that IAF quality is negatively associated with management misconduct. He concludes that high-quality IAFs are effective at deterring both accounting and non-accounting types of misconduct. Further, he finds that companies with evidence of management misconduct have higher quality IAFs in the years that follow the misconduct than in the years preceding it. In sum, this growing line of research suggests that a high-quality IAF can improve financial reporting quality and overall organizational governance.

The IAF and external auditors

Because of the IAF's governance responsibilities and detailed organizational knowledge, external auditors often rely upon its work during the external audit of internal control and financial statements. Auditing standards encourage external auditors to rely on the IAF to improve the efficiency and effectiveness of audits, and external auditors can rely either on work previously performed by the IAF (e.g., existing IAF reports) or engage internal auditors to assist during the course of the audit (e.g., perform detailed testing). The most mature stream of academic literature on the IAF relates to how and why various stakeholders and organization representatives, such as external auditors, rely on the IAF and the factors that increase reliance.

The prior literature and auditing standards recommend that external auditors evaluate the objectivity, competence, and work performed by the internal auditor when determining their reliance.[3] As described by Gramling *et al.* (2004) and Bame-Aldred *et al.* (2013), extant literature suggests that these three factors interact with each other and various other factors when external auditors make decisions about relying on the IAF. Factors such as IAF availability, coordination between the IAF and the external auditor, client risk, and the nature of audit evidence (subjective versus objective) are also considered. Other literature on the external auditors' reliance on the IAF indicates that external auditors believe that the quality of the audit committee is positively related to the quality of the IAF. Further, other indicators of quality corporate governance, such as accounting expertise on the audit committee, and audit committee independence, are associated with external auditors' evaluations of IAF quality.

The external audit reliance literature also explores differences in external auditors' perceptions of IAF quality when the IAF is outsourced versus performed in-house. CBOK reports that outsourcing the IAF has declined since its peak in the late 1990s, such that only about 43 percent of respondents report using some outsourcing arrangement as part of their IAF (Alkafaji *et al.* 2010). There has been much debate among practitioners regarding the pros and cons of outsourcing the IAF rather than keeping it in house. Advocates of outsourcing proclaim that outsourced IAFs can be more objective, are likely to have more expertise (especially in technical areas), and have the benefit of auditing a variety of clients so as to increase their knowledge of industry best practices and norms. On the other hand, those preferring in-house IAFs suggest that valuable organizational knowledge is lost when the IAF is outsourced. The extant accounting literature finds that external auditors are more likely to rely on an outsourced IAF when inherent risk is high because they believe an outsourced IAF to be more objective than an in-house IAF (Glover *et al.* 2008). Archival literature supports this and finds that outsourced IAFs are associated with lower external audit fees, although this benefit is reduced when the IAF budget and reporting lines are also considered, again suggesting that the primary benefit of outsourcing is increased objectivity.

The IAF and those managing the operations of the organization

Within the organization, internal auditors are viewed as risk and control experts. Thus, operational management often relies on the IAF to act in a consulting capacity to identify emerging risks, develop risk management strategies, and provide insights for improving controls, processes, and procedures with an eye to also increasing profits. Further, because of its assurance responsibilities, which require the IAF to audit all aspects of the organization, the IAF has a broad view of the organization and can add value by conducting consulting engagements throughout the organization.

Consulting engagements can vary widely in scope. Often, the IAF is asked to provide insights for increasing the efficiency or effectiveness of a particular business process, improving control design, or developing policies and procedures. The IAF can also provide training on risk management and internal control, or facilitate processes, such as the risk assessment process. For example, as described by Cohen *et al.* (2004), prior research indicates that the IAF is often involved in strategic management initiatives – including implementation of a Balanced Scorecard – and provides assurance on the quality of related financial and non-financial performance measures.

A recent study commissioned by the IIA exploring the IAF's ability to provide insights for practice improvements to various stakeholders identifies factors that can improve the value gained from the IAF. When asked which factors are necessary to enable the IAF to deliver value to stakeholders, over 50 percent of CAE survey respondents indicated that the following are all necessary: (1) a reporting relationship that supports the independence of the IAF; (2) a board and operational management who expect value-added insights from the IAF; (3) a strong control environment within the organization; and (4) a highly competent CAE. Responses to the same question provided by other stakeholders (e.g., board members and executive management) are similar; however both stakeholder groups also indicated that having IA personnel with significant industry and organizational knowledge is one of the four most important characteristics to enable value-added consulting from the IAF (Miller and Smith 2011).

This recent IIA study investigates the perceptions of the IAF and various stakeholders regarding the IAF's ability to deliver value-added insights and recommendations to help improve organizational performance and therefore provides a starting point for future research into this important IAF responsibility. Importantly, however, more is left to learn about how specific characteristics of the IAF, as well as the organization's control environment, affect the IAF's ability to deliver value-added insights, as well as their effects on organizational performance.

Some recent accounting literature on the IAF has explored the effect of the IAF on organizational performance and activities. Arena and Azzone (2009) survey CAEs from Italian companies to examine factors associated with IAF effectiveness, defined as the percentage of recommendations from the IAF actually implemented. The authors find that the percentage of IAF recommendations implemented increases when: (1) the ratio between the number of internal auditors and employees is higher; (2) the CAE is affiliated with the IIA (a proxy for an IAF focused on training and competency); (3) the company adopts control risk self-assessment; and (4) the audit committee is involved in the activities of the internal auditors (e.g., monitors and controls IAF activities, reviews IAF reports). The dependent measure used in this study, IAF effectiveness, is somewhat novel and captures not only the quality of the IAF and its recommendations, but also the extent to which the IAF is supported and respected by the organization. Further insight could be obtained in the future by examining the association between IAF effectiveness and organizational outcomes. Research along these lines examining associations between organizational outcomes and the specific types of recommendations made by the IAF (not just the percentage of implemented recommendations) would be particularly interesting; however, obtaining data on specific recommendations may be difficult.

Gaps in current knowledge about the IAF

In 2003, in the wake of the major accounting, governance, and control failures of Enron, WorldCom, Vivendi, SK Group, and Nortel, the IIA published *Research Opportunities in Internal Auditing* which presented a comprehensive discussion of research questions surrounding internal auditing and its evolution in a rapidly changing environment (Bailey *et al.* 2003). Despite the major changes in corporate governance that have occurred in the years since, there continues to be an urgent need for stronger, more effective governance. Indeed, poor governance by the board, inadequate risk management, and ineffective monitoring have all been cited as causes for the global financial crises beginning around 2008 (Sarens *et al.* 2012). Thus, we can expect future improvements and innovations in corporate governance to continue to shape the roles and responsibilities of the IAF. The questions presented a decade ago in *Research Opportunities in Internal Auditing* remain relevant and, unfortunately, for the most part, unaddressed. However, as the IAF's role in organizational governance continues to grow and evolve, five areas in particular emerge for additional inquiry to improve IA practice and enhance our understanding of organizational governance. These areas are: (1) risk management; (2) compliance and ethics; (3) combined assurance; (4) resource allocation; and (5) disclosure of IAF related information to external stakeholders.

First, as organizations embrace risk management (including enterprise risk management [ERM]), it is necessary to increase our understanding of the role of the IAF in ERM processes. In some organizations, the IAF may be the owner of ERM processes, while in others there may be a separate risk officer overseeing a risk management division. It is important that we consider the relationship between IAF quality and the quality of the organization's ERM process, including the strength of the control environment, identification of the organization's objectives, risk identification and assessment, implementation of control practices, monitoring practices, and communication throughout the organization.

A second area that has emerged is the IAF's role in ethics and compliance programs. Complex compliance systems have arisen to meet the demand for increased organizational accountability for the legal and ethical behavior of organizations and their employees. As with ERM, there is considerable variance across organizations regarding the relationship between these compliance programs and the IAF – in certain industries such as health care and higher education the functions are frequently combined so that the CAE is also the chief compliance officer; in others they operate independently from one another. Further, often, organizations have a number of siloed compliance functions such as privacy, environmental, etc. each with their own responsibilities, reporting structure, and assurance process. Regardless of how these programs are structured, the board must understand the compliance risks and implement programs to effectively manage these compliance risks. Both the board and executive management thus need assurances that their programs are effective. Providing this assurance over compliance programs is in the early stages of maturity for many IAFs as little is known about what organizational structures and practices are effective.

Third, a recent and innovative approach to the problems of assurance over organizational compliance and risk was initiated in the new South African corporate governance code, King III, and is known as combined assurance (Sarens *et al.* 2012). In particular, organizations have many different assurance functions operating from inside and out. For example, organizations may have an IAF, a quality control division, a compliance department, and environmental health and safety personnel, and various regulators and external auditors may perform assurance services from outside of the organization. A 2010 survey by Ernst & Young reports that 73 percent of organizations have at least seven assurance-type functions. More importantly, 67 percent report that some of these assurance functions have overlapping risk coverage and 50 percent report that they still have gaps in risk management (Ernst & Young 2010). The notion that risk management can be an isolated activity or that risks within a single department remain the sole responsibility of that department is antiquated. To adequately incorporate effective organizational risk management into corporate governance, executive management and the board require a holistic view of the organization's risk management activities. Given the many sources of assurance within one organization, it is necessary to ensure proper coordination of activities and prompt communication of findings and recommendations. Further, it can be difficult to determine whether each assurance activity is performed effectively, if all risks are addressed, and if recommendations for improvement by one assurance function could result in new risks emerging somewhere else within the organization. In some organizations, the IAF may facilitate the coordination of and communication between the various assurance providers, with all assurance activities managed by and reported to the IAF. However, in other organizations each assurance function may operate separately, with no central coordination. A deeper understanding of the IAF's role in the coordination of assurance activities would be valuable to academics, practitioners, and standard setters.

Fourth, more research is needed on how resources are allocated within the IAF and the effects of that allocation. Prior research has examined factors associated with IAF size in terms of IAF budget (e.g., Carcello *et al.* 2005a; Barua *et al.* 2010) and full-time employees (e.g., Anderson *et al.* 2010, 2011). These studies show that IAF budgets are positively related to company size, leverage, relative inventory levels, operating cash flows, audit committee review of the IAF budget, and membership in financial, service, or utility industries (Carcello *et al.* 2005a) and the number of audit committee meetings (Barua *et al.* 2010). IAF budgets are negatively associated with the percentage of IAF that is outsourced (Carcello *et al.* 2005a) and the presence of auditing experts on the audit committee, and the average tenure of audit committee members (Barua *et al.* 2010).

Carcello *et al.* (2005b) also examined changes to the IAF during the accounting scandals of the early 2000s and find that IAF budgets, staffing levels, and frequency and length of meetings between the IAF and the audit committee increased during this period (Carcello *et al.* 2005b). Anderson *et al.* (2010, 2011) find that IAF size (in terms of employees) is positively associated with: (1) stronger audit committee governance; (2) CAEs with greater organizational experience; (3) IAF missions including IT auditing; (4) the use of sophisticated audit technologies; (5) the use of the IAF as a management training ground; (6) organization size; and (7) the number of foreign subsidiaries. IAF size is inversely associated with: (1) the percentage of IA employees that are Certified Internal Auditors; and (2) the extent of IA outsourcing. While these papers provide important initial insights into the factors related to resources allocated to the IAF, a deeper understanding is needed regarding resource allocation within the IAF. For example, it would be important to learn how IAFs determine the activities they will perform (e.g., IT audits, financial audit support, consulting engagements) and how they will allocate staff to specific activities.

A final issue involves the disclosure of information regarding the IAF to external stakeholders. Archambeault *et al.* (2008) make the argument that because the IAF is a critical part of the governance process, increased disclosure regarding the IAF could complement current governance disclosures and increase stakeholders' confidence in governance quality. They propose that companies disclose the IAF's composition, responsibilities, accountability, activities, and resources. They find support for such disclosure in a series of structured interviews with internal auditors, audit committee members, analysts, and regulators. Holt and DeZoort (2009) use an experimental setting to demonstrate that such information significantly affects investors' perception of corporate oversight effectiveness and confidence in financial reporting reliability. Additional investigations are needed to determine what information about the IAF is useful to investors and to demonstrate that the information has value in actual market settings. With the IAF increasingly used to provide assurance to parties outside the organization such as regulators, strategic partners, rating agencies, and citizens, the demand for information about the IAF, particularly its quality, will rise.[4]

Conclusion

This chapter describes the extant research on the IAF's role in GRC. The majority of existing research addresses how the IAF provides assurance to the board, executive management, and external auditors regarding the organization's GRC practices. Many of these studies focus on the effects of IAF quality on various financial reporting outcomes and on users' reliance on the IAF. Additional research focuses on the IAF's role in providing guidance on risk, control, and process improvements to operational management. Given the rapidly evolving and expanding role of the IAF, there are many fruitful areas for future investigation. Areas where the profession can benefit from increased insight and understanding include the IAF's role in ERM, compliance, and combined assurance, as well as resource allocation within the IAF and the disclosure of IAF information to external stakeholders. Future research in these areas would not only advance academic literature and our understanding of the GRC processes within organizations, but it would inform practitioners and standard setters on ways to improve organizational governance.

Notes

1 Abnormal (or unexpected) accruals are used to proxy for earnings management because they measure managers' use of accounting discretion. To estimate abnormal accruals, researchers begin with total accruals (i.e., the difference between reported net income and cash flows from operations) and account for the normal accruals (e.g., revenues, working capital, fixed assets). The difference is the unexplained accruals that could be the result of earnings management. (Healy and Whalen 1999).

2 Barely beating analysts' forecasts is also commonly used to identify earnings management because prior research finds that the market reacts positively when companies' earnings numbers meet or beat analysts' earnings forecasts and negatively when actual earnings are below the forecasts (Kasznik and McNichols 2002). Therefore, companies have an incentive to manage earnings up (or forecasts down) so that actual earnings meet or beat the forecasts. Burgstahler and Eames (2006) provide evidence that there is an unusually high frequency of zero or small positive differences between actual earnings and analyst forecasts and an unusually low frequency of small negative differences (i.e., barely missing the forecast).

3 Bame-Aldred, *et al.* (2013) provide a detailed review of the external auditor reliance literature published in the post-SOX era. See Gramling *et al.* (2004) for a review of the literature before SOX.

4 For example, for merchant and financial institutions, IAFs can provide assurance on Payment Card Industry compliance to card vendors.

References

Alkafaji, Y., Hussain, S., Khallaf, A., and Majdalawieh, M. 2010, *Characteristics of an Internal Audit Activity.* Institute of Internal Auditors Research Foundation, Altamonte Springs, FL.

Anderson, R. and Svare, J. 2011, *Imperatives for Change: The IIA's Global Internal Audit Survey in Action.* Institute of Internal Auditors Research Foundation, Altamonte Springs, FL.

Anderson, U., Christ, M., Johnstone, K., and Rittenberg, L. 2010, *Effective Sizing of Internal Audit Departments.* Institute of Internal Auditors Research Foundation, Altamonte Springs, FL.

Anderson, U., Christ, M., Johnstone, K., and Rittenberg, L. 2011, "A Post-Sox Examination of Factors Associated with the Size of Internal Audit Functions", *Accounting Horizons* 26(2): 167–91.

Archambeault, D., DeZoort, T., and Holt, T. 2008, "The Need for an Internal Auditor Report to External Stakeholders to Improve Governance Transparency", *Accounting Horizons* 22(4): 375–88.

Arena, M. and Azzone, G. 2009, "Identifying Organizational Drivers of Internal Audit Effectiveness", *International Journal of Auditing* 13: 43–60.

Bailey, A., Gramling, A., and Ramamoorti, S. 2003, *Research Opportunities in Internal Auditing.* Institute of Internal Auditors Research Foundation, Altamonte Springs, FL.

Bame-Aldred, C., Brandon, D., Messier, B., Rittenberg, L., and Stefaniak, C. 2013, "A Summary of Research on External Auditor Reliance on the Internal Audit Function", *Auditing: A Journal of Practice and Theory* 32(Supp. 1): 251–86.

Barua, A., Rama, V., and Sharma, V. 2010, "Audit Committee Characteristics and Investment in Internal Auditing", *Journal of Accounting and Public Policy* 29: 503–13.

Burgstahler, D. and Eames, M. 2006, "Management of Earnings and Analysts' Forecasts to Achieve Zero and Small Positive Earnings Surprises", *Journal of Business Finance and Accounting* 23(5–6): 633–52.

Carcello, J., Hermanson, D., and Raghunandan, K. 2005a, "Factors Associated with US Public Companies' Investment in Internal Auditing", *Accounting Horizons* 19: 69–84.

Carcello, J., Hermanson, D., and Raghunandan, K. 2005b, "Changes in Internal Auditing during the Time of the Major US Accounting Scandals", *International Journal of Auditing* 9: 117–127.

Carcello, J., Hermanson, D., and Ye, Z. 2011, "Corporate Governance Research in Accounting and Auditing: Insights, Practice Implications, and Future Directions", *Accounting Horizons* 30(3): 1–31.

Christ, M., Masli, A., Sharp, N., and Wood, D. 2012, "Using the Internal Audit Function as a Management Training Ground: Is Monitoring Effectiveness Compromised?", working paper. University of Georgia, GA, Department of Accounting.

Cohen, J., Krishnamoorthy, G., and Wright, A. 2004, "The Corporate Governance Mosaic and Financial Reporting Quality", *Journal of Accounting Literature* 23: 87–152.

Ege, M. 2012, "Does Internal Audit Function Quality Deter Management Misconduct?", working paper. University of Texas at Austin, TX, Department of Accounting.

Ernst & Young 2010, *IT Governance, Risk and Compliance: Implementing Effective Governance, Risk, and Compliance Measures*. Ernst & Young Economist Intelligence Unit Survey.

Glover, S., Prawitt, D., and Wood, D. 2008, "Internal Audit Sourcing Arrangement and the External Auditor's Reliance Decision", *Contemporary Accounting Research* 25(1): 193–213.

Goodwin, J. 2003, "The Relationship between the Audit Committee and the Internal Audit Function: Evidence from Australia and New Zealand", *International Journal of Auditing* 7(3): 263–76.

Gramling, A., Maletta, M., Schneider, A., and Church, B. 2004, "Role of the Internal Audit Function in Corporate Governance: A Synthesis of the Extant Internal Auditing Literature and Direction for Future Research", *Journal of Accounting Literature* 23: 194–244.

Healy, P. and Wahlen, J. 1999, "A Review of the Earnings Managmenet Literature and its Implications for Standard Setting", *Accounting Horizons* 14(3): 365–83.

Hermanson, D. and Rittenberg, L. 2003, "Internal Audit and Organizational Governance", *Research Opportunities in Internal Auditing* 1: 25–71.

Holt, T. and DeZoort, T. 2009, "The Effects of Internal Audit Report Disclosure on Investor Confidence and Investment Decisions", *International Journal of Auditing* 13: 61–77.

Institute of Internal Auditors (IIA) 2013, *International Standards for the Professional Practice of Internal Auditing (Standards)*, Institute of Internal Auditors, Altamonte Springs, FL.

Kasznick, R. and McNichols, M. 2002, "Does Meeting Expectations Matter? Evidence from Analyst Forecast Revisions and Share Prices", *Journal of Accounting Research* 40(3): 727–59.

Miller, P. and Smith, T. 2011, *Insight: Delivering Value to Stakeholders*. Institute of Internal Auditors Research Foundation, Altamonte Springs, FL.

Prawitt, D., Smith, J., and Wood, D. 2009, "Internal Audit Quality and Earnings Management", *The Accounting Review* 84(4): 1255–80.

Prawitt, D., Sharp, N., and Wood, D. 2012, "Internal Audit Outsourcing and the Risk of Misleading or Fraudulent Financial Reporting: Did Sarbanes-Oxley get it Wrong?", *Contemporary Accounting Research* 29(4): 1109–36.

Raghunandan, K. and McHugh, J. 1994, "Internal Auditors' Independence and Interactions with Audit Committees: Challenges of Form and Substance", *Advances in Accounting* 12(1): 313–33.

Raghunandan, K., Read, W., and Rama, D. 2001, "Audit Committee Composition, 'Gray Directors,' and Interaction with Internal Auditing", *Accounting Horizons* 15(2): 105–18.

Sarens, G., Decaux, L., and Lenz, R. 2012. *Combined Assurance: Case Studies on a Holistic Approach to Organizational Governance*. Institute of Internal Auditors Research Foundation, Altamonte Springs, FL.

19

Audit approaches and business risk auditing

Emer Curtis and Stuart Turley

This chapter examines the development of approaches to the conduct of the audit which place emphasis on evaluating the business risk of the entity being audited as a means of directing the collection of audit evidence to support the audit opinion.[1] Although the importance of understanding the business of an audited entity and the associated risks have long been recognized in audit methodologies, more specific business risk audit (BRA) approaches emerged during the 1990s. These were influential in the subsequent revision of standards for audit practice, including International Standards on Auditing (ISAs), and thus have had an impact for auditors worldwide. This chapter discusses the emergence of BRA, what research has revealed about its impact on the content and outcomes of financial statement audits, how the approach has been accommodated in auditing standards and the current status of business risk-based auditing as an influence on audit practice.

The term BRA is used here as a generic name for similar developments in audit methodology that emerged in the 1990s within several of the then Big 5 audit firms. There were, however, differences between firms' approaches; the concept of a BRA developed over time, and it was reshaped both by its implementation in practice and through the process of assimilation into auditing standards. The perspective taken in this chapter is that BRA can be seen as an example of a significant innovation in auditing, in terms of both the fundamental approach auditors take to providing assurance on financial statements and the evidence process undertaken to support that assurance. As such it is relevant to evaluate its progress and its impact on audit practice and audit standards.

The next section, 'Audit methodology and business risk auditing', places BRA in the context of longer term developments in audit methodology and outlines the debates over the reasons for its emergence. This is followed by a discussion of what we know about the adoption, implementation and impact of BRA, based on research relating to its key features and their operationalization. Current issues concerning business risk auditing are then discussed before a final section summarizes and draws conclusions.

Audit methodology and business risk auditing

Methods used by auditors have evolved and developed significantly over the last century and it is important to place the development of BRA as a distinct type of audit approach in the context of that broader evolution. It is possible to identify a number of overlapping stages of significant change, or generations of methodology (Davis, 1996; Higson, 1997), which, although not clearly separate or discrete periods, provide a convenient structure to describe major stages in the evolution of audit approaches.

The early audit approach, which was prevalent up to the late 1960s, was composed primarily of testing and checking large volumes of transactions and based on a principle of substantive verification. The 1960s and 1970s heralded the second generation, an era when so-called 'Systems Auditing' dominated (Felix and Kinney, 1982; Turley and Cooper, 1991). These approaches involved assessing the client's accounting system and testing the controls in that system (compliance testing) in order to obtain assurance about the ability of the system to produce reliable financial information as the basis for financial statements. Reliance on the internal control system reduced the need to conduct extensive substantive tests. This period also saw considerable interest in the application of statistical sampling techniques in auditing (Power, 1992; Carpenter and Dirsmith, 1993), which held the promise of providing defensible conclusions about the reliability of internal controls, thus helping to resolve problems associated with determining the extent of testing.

The development of the audit risk model (ARM) in the 1980s signalled the third significant stage in the evolution of audit methods. This model seeks to express the relationship between the overall level of audit risk, and the levels of inherent, control and detection risk.[2] It provides a conceptual basis for recognizing the balance of audit evidence collected from compliance and substantive testing and so is consistent with the rationale underlying systems based auditing (Cushing and Loebbecke, 1983, 1986).

More recently, the BRA was an important innovation in audit approach which emerged in the mid-1990s from the major audit firms. The significant aspect of this development was the shift in emphasis from audit risk, essentially the risk that material misstatement remains in audited financial statements, to business risk, the risk that the audited entity fails to meet its objectives. This fundamental re-conceptualization of how an audit should be planned and approached rests on the logic that underlying problems in a business will ultimately have a significant impact on the financial statements and are the primary threat to the quality of those statements. Consequently auditor effort will be most effective when it addresses the nature of the business and not just the system of financial records.

Understanding the development of business risk auditing

The introduction of BRA approaches has been reported as a major innovation in audit methodology (Higson, 1997; Lemon *et al.*, 2000; Eilifsen *et al.*, 2001), and was heralded by major audit firms, particularly Arthur Andersen and KMPG, with considerable fanfare (Jeppesen, 1998).[3] The merits of the approach were expressed in terms of providing both a more effective audit and a more valuable service to the client. As Lemon *et al.* (2000) explain

> ... firms had concluded that perceived audit failures result not from the ineffectiveness of procedures in detecting misstatements but because of difficulties, for example in recognizing going concern problems or identifying fraud, arising from other aspects of the business context.
>
> *(Lemon* et al., *2000: 12)*

As technology has improved the accuracy of accounting systems, extensive testing of transactions was seen to provide little by way of valuable audit evidence. Audit risk was considered to stem primarily from the impact of broader business risks on judgements and decisions reflected in the financial statements. Thus identifying indicators of business risk and assessing the client's risk management systems were viewed as of paramount importance to an effective audit. The suggestion, therefore, was that BRA developed as a better way to carry out auditing given the complexity of the modern business environment (Bell *et al.*, 1997; Eilifsen *et al.*, 2001).

A second aspect of the emphasis on business risk was the potential that obtaining insight into the business and its risks gave for offering 'added-value' advice to the audited entity. The potential for such a contribution arose from the intended change in the nature of the audit work. An assessment of business risks and related controls which would be of greater relevance to management than repetitive tests of low-level controls and substantive tests of details could reveal opportunities for audit firms to offer services to assist clients to rectify deficiencies. This emphasis was evident in the views of practitioners within firms (Higson, 1997) and, around the time of implementation of the BRA, in the many references on major firms' websites to adding value (Jeppesen, 1998). Thus it has been argued that the BRA was motivated by an attempt to improve both audit effectiveness and the value of the audit to audit clients.

The attraction of the new approach can also be seen as a response to competitiveness in the auditing profession during the 1980s and early 1990s which had resulted in pressure on audit fees and audit margins (Matthews, 2006: 159), diversification into non-audit services and 'low-balling' fees in order to acquire or retain clients (Knechel, 2007). In this context, some authors have questioned whether the BRA was an attempt to reverse the commoditization of the audit, increase profitability and improve auditors' status within their organizations (Jeppesen, 1998; Robson *et al.*, 2007).

Additionally, some firms believed that the BRA would enhance their own management of engagement risk (Lemon *et al.*, 2000). Management fraud and going-concern problems are the primary issues associated with auditor litigation. Assuming that the BRA could appropriately identify these risks, anticipated reductions in substantive procedures were unlikely to result in increased exposure to litigation. Given that the BRA was to be underpinned by stringent engagement risk management procedures within audit firms (Higson, 1997; Lemon *et al.*, 2000), clients with high levels of business risk and poor control environments, which might be unsuitable for this audit approach, would also be excluded from the client base.

The development of BRA approaches can therefore be seen as having both a technical dimension and an economic one. It was argued that BRA could provide a better way of addressing the risk of material misstatement in financial statements but also one that would be more valued by clients, enhance the status of auditing as an analytical activity and have the potential to affect the economics of auditing through an impact on costs, the generation of additional revenue and by reducing the likelihood of failure.

Issues arising from the emergence of business risk audit

In order to evaluate the contribution of a business risk perspective as a basis for the approach to the conduct of an audit, a number of important issues can be considered, regarding the significance and impact of this development in methodology and related standards for auditing practice.

1 There are questions regarding exactly how different the BRA approaches were from what went before. The importance of an understanding of the business of an audited entity and the associated risks has long been recognized in audit practice, and (as will be argued later) ultimately auditing standards were adapted to respond to BRA rather than completely reformulated. Consequently some commentators were sceptical about the level of true innovation in the new approach (Flint *et al.*, 2008).

2 Taking the BRA as a novel way of approaching the audit, there are inevitable issues concerning the manner in which firms implemented their new methodology, what difficulties were encountered in implementation and how the perspective was received by auditors trained in pre-existing methods.
3 The reasons advanced for the development of business risk approaches include the need for more effective means of addressing the causes of problems that can undermine the integrity of the financial statements in a business. An important aspect to consider is therefore what impact adoption of a business risk perspective has on specific audit procedures, steps and outcomes, that is, what do auditors do differently as a result of focusing on business risk?
4 Any major innovation in practice has the potential to affect the economics of auditing as a professional service and it is relevant to consider what impact adoption of BRA approaches has on the way audit firms do business. The change could be expected to affect staffing on audits, costs incurred and even the portfolio of clients accepted by a firm.
5 The BRA methodologies attracted the attention of auditing regulators and ultimately resulted in the issue of three new auditing standards, approved by the International Auditing and Assurance Standards Board (IAASB) in October 2003. These lengthy standards, often referred to as 'the audit risk standards', increased the requirements of the auditor in the areas of understanding the business, assessing risk and linking risks to testing procedures. It is therefore of interest to look at the process of assimilation of BRA into standard practice.

Research evidence

This section discusses the results of research that has considered the impact and significance of the role of business risk in audit methodology, organized around each of the five issues introduced in the preceding subsection, 'Issues arising from the emergence of business risk audit'. The key distinctive features of the BRA are discussed, followed by evidence about its implementation, the impact of business risk on audit practice, and the effect on the economics of auditing; finally the influence of BRA on audit standards is explained.

What is distinctive about a business risk based audit?

A number of authors have provided descriptions of the business risk approaches. Lemon *et al.* (2000) conducted the first international study of the BRA and outlined the significant features of the new approach. The large audit firms themselves have contributed to the literature. KPMG distributed booklets (Bell *et al.*, 1997) explaining the theory and structure underpinning its methodology; and Winograd *et al.* (2000) reported a description of the Pricewaterhouse-Coopers methodology. Although it should be recognized that there were differences between firms in the construction of detailed audit methodology, the key novel features of the BRA audit were the wider scope of risk assessment and a change in the nature of evidence used to support the audit opinion. These features are elaborated below. The BRA was intended to widen the auditor's focus from audit risk to business risk, defined as the risk that an entity will fail to meet its objectives (Higson, 1997; Lemon *et al.*, 2000; Eilifsen *et al.*, 2001).

> A common theme of these changes is that audit risk is inextricably entwined with client business risk. Risks that threaten an organization are also the source of risks that will affect an audit. Consequently, an effective audit requires an in-depth understanding of the client's

> industry, strategic goals and plans, source of competitive advantage, critical internal processes and residual risks most likely to threaten its success. This perspective is much broader than the risk perspective underlying the traditional audit risk model with its focus on financial statement results and related assertions.
>
> *(Knechel, 2001: vi)*

Knechel (2001) published the first textbook to include a detailed description of the BRA, and documents the stages involved in this wider scope audit as comprising: strategic analysis of the external threats in the organization's environment; analysis of the strategic risk management processes to ascertain how internal control reduces the risk from external threats; identification and mapping of critical business processes, to provide a framework for assessing the impact of process risks on the organization; and consideration of control activities which mitigate the risks in order to identify significant residual risks, that is, those that are not reduced to an acceptable level through the operation of controls. Those residual risks must then be linked to financial statement assertions, and substantive procedures are only performed to address assertions that are considered to have residual risk.

The analysis of business risk requires a comprehensive analytical review of financial information, key performance indicators (KPIs) and controls used by management to manage key risks. Knowledge and understanding of the auditee's business is recognized as evidence in its own right, whereas traditional approaches viewed such knowledge as a prerequisite to planning the audit evidence required. Since audit risk is assumed to derive from business risk, the audit approach is controls based (Lemon *et al.*, 2000; Winograd *et al.*, 2000). Logically, a risk cannot be substantively tested like a financial statement balance; the auditor can only audit the controls in place to mitigate a risk. A critical element of the approach is the importance placed on the role of high-level monitoring controls for mitigating the risk arising from external threats. According to the logic of this approach, if the auditor can identify the sources of business risk and ensure that the client has appropriate systems to monitor and manage that risk, there is little value in extensive substantive testing. Detailed substantive testing is only performed where, in the auditor's judgement, risks are not sufficiently mitigated by controls.

How were BRA methodologies implemented in audit firms?

This section considers evidence on the implementation of the BRA. In addition to a number of illustrative teaching case studies produced by KPMG in association with the firms' publication of its methodology (Bell and Solomon, 2002), two major studies have employed a case study methodology to examine the overall implementation of BRA on actual audit engagements.

In 1997, Eilifsen *et al.* (2001) studied the impact of implementing KPMG's methodology on the audit of a Czech Bank. This study found that the audit team obtained a better understanding of the client's business, which led the team to revise the set of specific risks deemed significant to the audit. They also found a significant shift from substantive evidence to evidence concerning risks and controls. In particular, the study found reliance on higher level controls with the audit team using evidence from interviews with multiple participants, available performance measures and management's handling of exceptions, rather than testing individual transactions. The audit team justified reducing or eliminating substantive testing in areas judged to have little or no residual risk.

Implementation of the BRA was not without its problems, however, and in a study of the audit of a single audit client over a five-year period from 1996 to 2000, Curtis and Turley (2007) reported significant challenges faced by auditors implementing the BRA in practice. This study found that audit seniors struggled with the identification of business risk from an unlimited 'universe of business risk' (Curtis and Turley, 2007: 449) compared with identifying risks associated with a finite number of financial statement captions. The identification of business risks unrelated to financial statement captions raised a problem of 'linkage' as auditors struggled to assess the potential impact of some business risks on the financial statements and thus found it difficult both to judge the appropriate extent of controls testing and to evaluate residual risk. The audit team struggled to find convincing evidence of the operation of high-level controls, given that many of these controls consisted of management review. They also questioned the sensitivity of those types of controls to identify and correct misstatements, particularly in the case of judgements and estimates (Curtis and Turley, 2007: 454).

Does the use of procedures linked to business risk have an impact on auditors' assessments and choices?

A considerable body of research has investigated the impact of risk assessment on auditor decisions, looking at factors such as fraud risk and the components of the ARM (see for example Mock and Wright (1999); also see Allen *et al.* (2006) for a review of this literature); but only a small, developing body of research has examined what changes when auditors adopt the broader and more holistic view of business risk.

A number of judgement and decision making (JDM) experiments have attempted to evaluate whether auditors' use of strategic analysis affects the identification of risks and auditors' planned audit procedures. Schultz *et al.* (2010) compare strategic systems- and transactions-based audit approaches. They find that if auditors are trained in the strategic approach and information is presented in a manner consistent with that approach, they are more likely to integrate their business risk assessment into their assessment of the risk of misstatement in the financial statements.

Other studies have found that the use of performance metrics and strategic analysis leads to more balanced assessments of risk in audit planning (Knechel *et al.*, 2010) and that broad client risks have an impact on the allocation of resources in the audit process (Fukukawa *et al.*, 2011). Strategic analysis has also been shown to influence judgements about the risk of material misstatement in the overall financial statements, which is relevant to the important issue of the linkage between business risk analysis and financial statement misstatement (Kochetova-Kosloski and Messier, 2011). Knechel *et al.* (2010) comment that strategic assessment aids the auditor to develop a more complete 'mental model' of the client. However, O'Donnell and Schultz (2005) have expressed concern that strategic assessment can 'impair auditor judgment', reporting a 'halo effect', whereby the broad strategic risk assessments could lead auditors to give less attention to potential risks at the account level.

Another small group of research studies has examined more specific procedural activities that could be associated with BRA approaches. Audit support software organized around the value chain in the business rather than transaction or account class has been found to lead to better identification of risk factors (O'Donnell and Schultz, 2003). Organizing internal control information with reference to business process rather than control objectives has been found to improve trainees' effectiveness in identifying control weaknesses (Kopp and O'Donnell, 2005).

While the above JDM studies provide some evidence about the potential of strategic analysis to enhance auditor risk assessment, there is much less evidence available about the change in the nature of audit evidence gathered. The potential for such studies is hampered by limited access to actual audit files which contain the choices made by audit staff subject to the practical complexities and pressures which are typically absent in experiments.

Finally, the key question of whether employing a BRA approach results in different audit conclusions has been subject to very limited research enquiry, although one study has examined reporting decisions on financially distressed companies and found that auditors using a business risk approach were in fact less likely to issue a going concern modified audit opinion if the client was undertaking operating initiatives to mitigate the distress (Bruynseels *et al.*, 2011).

What impact does a business risk approach have on the economics of auditing?

The changes associated with adopting a BRA perspective have implications for the nature and extent of work done by auditors and can therefore have consequences for the economics of auditing as a professional service. A small number of studies have investigated the relationship between BRA and factors such as audit costs, audit prices, client acceptance and the management of litigation risk.

In an examination of the impact of BRA on the profile and amount of staff time devoted to an audit, Bell *et al.* (2008) report evidence from one firm that implementation of BRA led to the use of a greater proportion of higher ranked staff. They also find that higher assessed risk was associated with greater volume of staff use and greater use of high ranked staff. Where higher assessed business risk results in a more costly audit, firms may find it difficult to pass on those costs to their clients because of market conditions or because of the difficulty of including risk explicitly in fee negotiations. Some evidence on this point has been documented by Bell *et al.* (2001) who, based on confidential data from 422 audits, found that higher perceived risk was associated with increases in staff hours but not the hourly fee rate. This suggests that auditors may manage business risk by doing more work rather than by charging more.

Rather than adjusting prices at the level of the individual audit, firms may also seek to manage the potential negative consequences that can result from high levels of client business risk, such as business failure and litigation, through the overall portfolio of clients audited. Some evidence has been reported that there is a link between business risk and the likelihood of a client being accepted by a firm. Studies using both an experimental task (Johnstone, 2000) and archival data from one audit firm (Johnstone and Bedard, 2004) have suggested that auditors are more likely to respond to higher business risk with a strategy of risk avoidance than to manage client business risk in other ways, such as higher pricing and making greater use of specialist staff.

Two major limitations of the existing studies on the link between BRA and the economics of auditing are, first, that they rely on either proprietary data from a single firm or stylized experimental tasks which make it difficult to judge whether findings can be generalized to widespread real settings, and second, while studies have looked for an association between measures of *business risk* and audit variables, this does not mean that the adoption of a *business risk audit methodology* per se affects those variables. Nonetheless, there is evidence to suggest that auditors are conscious of business risk in making decisions about acceptance and pricing of and staffing on audit engagements (Houston *et al.* 2002). What remains open to investigation is the extent to which a BRA methodology makes an incremental difference to auditor decisions on these matters.

How has the BRA influenced auditing standards?

The innovation of the BRA attracted the attention of three auditing standard setters in the UK, US and Canada. A joint working group was established in 1998 and its report, setting out the key features of the BRA, possible advantages and disadvantages of the approach and recommendations for standard setters, was submitted to the body setting international standards for auditors (then known as the International Auditing Practices Committee but now the IAASB) in May 2000. Around the same period, the publicity surrounding BRA and a worrying increase in the number of restatements of public company accounts led the Securities Exchange Commission (SEC) to establish the Panel on Audit Effectiveness (the Panel) in 1998 to investigate the quality and effectiveness of the external audit. These concerns were reinforced by high profile corporate failures in the early 2000s.[4] The joint working group and the Panel reports formed two key inputs for a joint task force of the IAASB and its US counterpart, the Auditing Standards Board. The task force had responsibility for the development of three standards collectively known as the Audit Risk Standards (ISA 315, ISA 330 and ISA 500) which were approved for issue by the IAASB in October 2003.

At first sight, therefore, it might appear that the BRA approaches had a significant influence on the development of new international standards, but in fact in the standards the more radical elements of the BRA were embraced only to a limited extent. The audit risk standards do reflect some of the logic underlying the BRA and include new requirements for risk assessment and consideration of the impact of risks on financial statement assertions. However, the approach adopted by the new standards differed from the BRA in a number of important ways.

First, the approach adopted by the standards differs in terms of the *objective*, and hence the *scope* of the required understanding of the business. Under the BRA, the objective is to identify and assess a broad range of business risks, from external strategic risks to internal process risks. The objective of the standards is limited to assessing the risks of material misstatement in the financial statements (IAASB, 2010a: para. 3).

Second, given that the standards limit the requirement to assessing risk of material misstatement, the issue of linkage between business risks and the financial statements is not problematic in the same way as in the BRA. The requirement in the standards for risks to be linked to the financial statements assertions is explicit and specific (IAASB, 2010a: para. 25). This represents a significant difference in approach from BRA, because the emphasis of the auditor's procedures is inevitably shifted away from wider business risk to focus on the financial statements.

Third, the focus on linkage at the assertions level directs attention towards testing of low-level transaction controls that typically relate to specific assertions and detailed substantive testing at the assertions level. This is in direct contrast to the BRA, which envisaged an audit primarily based on testing of high-level controls over business risks, supported by sophisticated analytical procedures. The standards make no attempt to give preference to testing of high-level controls, and specifically suggest that the auditor obtain evidence about both specific and monitoring controls.

Fourth, there are important differences between the BRA and the ISAs in terms of the approach to the evaluation and testing of controls. While the BRA emphasized understanding of *controls over business risks*, the standards require an understanding of *controls relevant to the audit* (IAASB, 2010a: para. 20). This different focus for controls testing follows logically from the narrower scope of risk assessment adopted in the standards.

Finally, unlike the BRA methodologies, the standards do not logically require a controls-based approach to the audit, as risks are linked to assertions. Financial statement assertions can be subject to either controls or substantive testing and thus the auditor may choose to adopt a substantive approach to audit testing on the grounds of efficiency (IAASB, 2010b: para. A4[b]) in a similar manner to the ARM. Rather than adopting the BRA approach of limiting substantive testing to areas where controls are not operating effectively, the new standards mandate substantive procedures in respect of each material class of transactions, account balance and disclosure, and significant risks (IAASB 2010b: paras 18–21). This represents more extensive and specific substantive testing requirements than were required by previous standards *and* the BRA.

Although a number of research papers have been written about the BRA since the issue of these standards, there has been relatively little acknowledgement of the extent to which the innovative aspects of the approach were not adopted in the audit risk standards. A combination of factors may have been influential in this outcome, notably a lack of consensus over key features of the BRA among the top tier firms, practical problems with implementation and pressure from the Panel report to 'raise the bar' in auditing, particularly in relation to minimum levels of substantive testing and documentation. Finally, the IAASB's desire to establish its legitimacy as the global regulator for auditors, may have been influential in swaying the agenda away from innovative approaches in favour of more a conservative approach with detailed, specific testing requirements.

Issues for continued research

In considering valuable issues for further research investigation, it is perhaps appropriate to draw a distinction between the BRA as a specific set of methodologies developed and introduced in the late 1990s, and the more general question of the continuing relevance of the auditor's consideration of business risk and related audit procedures.

Turning first to the overall influence of the BRA and audit methodology, the fact that we do not see the BRA methodologies widely employed in practice as originally developed but that we do have business risk influenced auditing is itself an important topic for further research enquiry. Understanding if and how the concepts and reasoning of BRA have been internalized by firms and individual auditors is relevant for an appreciation not just of the long-term significance of this stage of methodological development but of the nature of audit practice more generally. For example, it seems likely that the injunction to consider and evaluate business risk but without the detailed framework of the BRA may mean that auditors apply relatively subjective interpretations to what business risk auditing means. It is still relevant to ask how different auditors conceptualize business risk and how those concepts influence audit practice. There may be significant differences in the approach in, say, smaller audit practices compared to the large international firms. Another important topic on which relatively limited research has been undertaken concerns the role, if any, of the ideas of business risk methodology in relation to the way in which auditors approached clients in the financial sector and whether auditors could have acted differently in relation to organizations that have suffered during the continuing global financial crisis.

There is scope for further work to examine how the ideas of BRA still play a part in the culture of the firms where new ideas were developed. While some sceptics may see the BRA as an innovation that did not catch on, this is unlikely to be the whole story. Many aspects of the BRA will continue to play a role in the training of staff, the design of audit plans and the management of the relationship with the audit client. Again, the history of the development of audit methodology tends to suggest that, while the language and rhetoric may change, many ideas come round again and it seems likely that auditors will have cause to give renewed attention to the principles of BRA in the future.

It is clear from research over a significant period that risk considerations can have an impact on decisions and choices made in the conduct of an audit (although not always to the extent that might have been expected). However, only a relatively small number of studies have looked at procedures and assessments specifically linked to business risk. The research reported earlier, for example looking at the use of strategic analysis and audit software tools designed around business systems, could be significantly extended. There is a need to understand better the 'quality' of business risk assessments by auditors and how this is influenced by the use of particular tools. More evidence is needed about how good auditors are at approaching risk assessment in practice, and whether they possess the broad-based and flexible skills that may be necessary to address the complexities of business risk in the real world.

Very little is known about whether the BRA induced any lasting change to the nature and extent of audit evidence supporting the audit opinion. Clearly the audit risk standards have influenced this by mandating minimum levels of substantive testing and requiring controls testing in certain circumstances. However, it is not clear if the BRA has resulted in lasting moves towards more controls based audit evidence, or greater reliance on high-level controls. In addition, more needs to be known about how procedures are validated and developed within the audit firms. Last, given the possibility that by following specific audit steps and procedures in a relatively discreet manner the auditor might miss some important issues in the client's bigger picture, research could usefully examine how different steps and procedures are integrated together in response to risk assessments concluded in actual audit settings. As with a number of areas of audit practice research, this kind of enquiry would benefit significantly from greater access to actual audit records within firms.

Conclusion

Discussion in this chapter has referred to a varied set of sources, including not only experimental and archival research on the relevance of business risk to decisions made in the conduct of an audit, but also case studies and documentary analysis of the implementation of BRA in practice and the policy process associated with the development of auditing standards which now have widespread application internationally. A variety of interpretations are available for making sense of the specific development generally referred to as BRA in the larger audit firms as an episode in the evolution of audit methodology (Knechel, 2007). Some have argued that, as auditors could already be seen to be giving consideration to client business risk even before the BRA development, it was not really a revolutionary change and its significance should not be overemphasized (Flint *et al.*, 2008). A positive perspective on the development is that it was a major and reasoned attempt genuinely to improve audit quality (Peecher *et al.*, 2007). Others have interpreted it as a response to the competitive pressures faced by audit firms in the 1990s and an attempt to develop auditing with a more commercial logic, aligning the audit with managerial interests and taking it away from a public interest professional service that was overturned by the actions of regulators and standard setters in response to concerns about major corporate failures and the limited contribution of auditing in relation to those failures (Fogarty and Rigsby, 2010).

It is dangerous, however, both to underestimate the significance of the BRA and how different was the view of auditing it offered, and to dismiss it as an attempted development which did not mature to have the radical influence on audit practice that its developers and proponents envisaged. It was never likely to be the case that a new methodological approach would be easily adopted and implemented universally more or less overnight. The history of the development of audit methodology suggests that change happens in an evolutionary way, with remnants of old rationales being combined with new ideas so that the resulting approach has a heritage in all the preceding generations of methodology. This has perhaps also proved to be the case with BRA. There was evolution within firms as they gained experience of the operation of the new approach. The ideas were also adapted as the broader professional groups and standard setters sought to consider the need for change in official requirements and guidance for auditors in response to the BRA. The outcome has been that auditors now have a set of standards which do not directly mirror the BRA as originally envisaged but have been influenced to require auditors to pay greater attention to business risks in their audit clients.

'Business risk' has become a more prominent and significant term in the auditors' vocabulary than it was in the mid-1990s. The more radical ideas that involved rethinking the underlying objective of the audit and a fundamental change in the approach to the design of evidence collection have not been reflected in standards, which have retained the need to ensure linkage to the financial statements, but the BRA has nonetheless been a significant influence on how auditing is carried out. As the, often critical, questioning of the role of auditing continues following the financial crises of recent years and auditors seek a convincing rationale for their contribution to corporate reporting and governance, the BRA may yet prove an appealing framework for future developments in the role of auditing and the methodologies developed to execute that role.

Notes

1 The term 'business risk' has also sometimes been used to refer to the risks, including litigation risk, faced by the audit firm itself in undertaking the business of auditing. This aspect of risk is outside consideration here; the term 'business risk' is restricted to risk in the audited entity.
2 For definitions of these terms see the Glossary of Terms published in association with International Standards on Auditing (IAASB, 2013: 11–13).
3 For example, KPMG sought to publicize their new approach to academics and regulators by distributing a booklet, 'Auditing Organizations through a Strategic-systems Lens' (Bell *et al.*, 1997), to all members of the American Accounting Association.
4 For example, a Wall Street Journal on-line article on 9 August 2002 under the headline 'Drive-By Audits Have Become Too Common and Too Dangerous', illustrates concerns about the extent of evidence collection undertaken by auditors.

References

Allen, R.D., Hermanson, D.R., Kozloski, T.M. and Ramsay, R.J. (2006). 'Auditor Risk Assessment: Insights from the Academic Literature', *Accounting Horizons* 20: 157–77.

Bell, T. and Solomon, I. (eds) (2002). *Cases in Strategic-systems Auditing*. Champaign, IL: KPMG and University of Illinois at Urbana-Champaign.

Bell, T., Marrs, F., Solomon, I. and Thomas, H. (1997). *Auditing Organizations through a Strategic-systems Lens*. Montvale, NJ: KPMG LLP.

Bell, T., Landsman, W. and Shackelford, D. (2001). 'Auditors' Perceived Business Risk and Audit Fees: Analysis and Evidence', *Journal of Accounting Research* 39: 35–43.

Bell, T., Doogar, R. and Solomon, I. (2008). 'Audit Labor Usage and Fees under Business Risk Auditing', *Journal of Accounting Research* 46: 729–60.

Bruynseels, L., Knechel, R. and Willekens, M. (2011). 'Auditor Differentiation, Mitigating Management Actions and Audit-reporting Accuracy for Distressed Firms', *Auditing: A Journal of Practice & Theory* 30: 1–20.

Carpenter, B. and Dirsmith, M. (1993). 'Sampling and the Abstraction of Knowledge in the Auditing Profession: An Extended Institutional Theory Perspective', *Accounting, Organizations and Society* 18: 41–63.

Curtis, E. and Turley, S. (2007). 'The Business Risk Audit: A Longitudinal Case Study of an Audit Engagement', *Accounting, Organizations & Society* 32: 439–61.

Cushing, B. and Loebbecke, J.K. (1983). 'Analytical Approaches to Audit Risk: A Survey and Analysis', *Auditing: A Journal of Practice & Theory* 3: 23–41.

Cushing, B. and Loebbecke, J. (1986). *Comparison of Audit Methodologies of Large Accounting Firms*. Sarasota, FL: American Accounting Association.

Davis, R. (1996). 'Serving the Public Interest', *True & Fair,* December 1995/January 1996, p. 6.

Eilifsen, A., Knechel, R. and Wallage, P. (2001). 'Application of the Business Risk Audit Model: A Field Study', *Accounting Horizons* 15: 193–207.

Felix, J.W.L. and Kinney, J.W.R. (1982). 'Research in the Auditor's Opinion Formulation Process: State of the Art', *The Accounting Review* 57: 245.

Flint, C., Fraser, I.A.M. and Hatherly, D. (2008). 'Business Risk Auditing: A Regressive Evolution? – A Research Note', *Accounting Forum* 32: 143–7.

Fogarty, T. and Rigsby, J. (2010). 'A Reflective Analysis of the "New Audit" and the Public Interest: The Revolutionary Innovation that Never Came', *Journal of Accounting & Organizational Change* 6: 300–29.

Fukukawa, H., Mock, T. and Wright, A. (2011). 'Client Risk Factors and Audit Resource Allocation Decisions', *Abacus* 47: 85–108.

Higson, A.W. (1997). 'Developments in Audit Approaches: From Audit Efficiency to Audit Effectiveness', in M. Sherer and S. Turley (eds) *Current Issues in Auditing*, pp. 198–215. London: Paul Chapman.

Houston, R.W., Peters, M.F. and Pratt, J.H. (2002). 'The Audit Risk Model, Business Risk and Audit-Planning Decisions', *The Accounting Review* 74: 281–98.

International Auditing and Assurance Standards Board (IAASB). (2010a). ISA 315. *Identifying and Assessing the Risks of Material Misstatement through Understanding the Entity and its Environment.* IAASB.

International Auditing and Assurance Standards Board (IAASB). (2010b). ISA 330. *The Auditor's Responses to Assessed Risks.* IAASB.

International Auditing and Assurance Standards Board (IAASB). (2013). *Handbook of International Quality Control, Auditing, Review, Other Assurance and Related Services Pronouncements.* IAASB.

Jeppesen, K.K. (1998). 'Reinventing Auditing, Redefining Consulting and Independence', *European Accounting Review* 7: 517–39.

Johnstone, K.M. (2000). 'Client-acceptance Decisions: Simultaneous Effects of Client Business Risk, Audit Risk, Auditor Business Risk, and Risk Adaptation', *Auditing: A Journal of Practice & Theory* 19: 1–25.

Johnstone, K.M. and Bedard, J.C. (2004). 'Audit Firm Portfolio Management Decisions', *Journal of Accounting Research* 42: 659–90.

Knechel, R. (2001). *Auditing, Assurance & Risk.* Cincinnati, OH: South-Western College Publishing.

Knechel, R. (2007). 'The Business Risk Audit: Origins and Obstacles and Opportunities?', *Accounting Organizations & Society,* 32: 379–82.

Knechel, R., Salterio, S. and Kochetova-Kosloski, N. (2010). 'The Effect of Benchmarked Performance Measures and Strategic Analysis on Auditors' Risk Assessments and Mental Models', *Accounting Organizations & Society* 35: 316–33.

Kochetova-Kosloski, N. and Messier, W. (2011). 'Strategic Analysis and Auditor Risk Assessments', *Auditing: A Journal of Practice and Theory* 30: 149–71.

Kopp, L.S. and O'Donnell, E. (2005). 'The Influence of a Business-process Focus on Category Knowledge and Internal Control Evaluation', *Accounting, Organizations and Society* 30: 423–34.

Lemon, M., Tatum, K. and Turley, S. (2000). *Developments in the Audit Methodologies of Large Accounting Firms.* London: ABG Publications.

Matthews, D. (2006). *A History of Auditing: The Changing Audit Process in Britain from the Nineteenth Century to the Present Day.* Abingdon: Routledge.

Mock, T. and Wright, A. (1999). 'Are Audit Program Plans Risk Adjusted?', *Auditing: A Journal of Practice & Theory* 18: 55–74.

O'Donnell, E. and Schultz, J.J. Jr (2003). 'The Influence of Business-process-focused Audit Support Software on Analytical Procedures Judgments', *Auditing: A Journal of Practice & Theory* 22: 265–79.

O'Donnell, E. and Schultz, J.J. Jr (2005). 'The Halo Effect in Business Risk Audits: Can Strategic Risk Assessment Bias Auditor Judgment about Accounting Details?', *The Accounting Review* 80: 921–39.

Peecher, M.E., Schwartz, R. and Solomon, I. (2007). 'It's All about Audit Quality: Perspectives on Strategic-systems Auditing', *Accounting, Organizations & Society* 32: 463–85.

Power, M.K. (1992). 'From Common Sense to Expertise: Reflections on the Prehistory of Audit Sampling', *Accounting, Organizations and Society* 17: 37–62.

Robson, K., Humphrey, C., Khalifa, R. and Jones, J. (2007). 'Transforming Audit Technologies: Business Risk Audit Methodologies and the Audit Field', *Accounting, Organizations & Society* 32: 409–38.

Schultz, J.J. Jr, Bierstaker, J. and O'Donnell, E. (2010). 'Integrating Business Risk into Auditor Judgment about the Risk of Material Misstatement: The Influence of a Strategic-systems-audit Approach', *Accounting, Organizations & Society* 35: 238–51.

Turley, S. and Cooper, M. (1991). *Auditing in the United Kingdom*. Hemel Hempstead: Prentice Hall, published in association with the Institute of Chartered Accountants in England and Wales.

Winograd, B., Gerson, J. and Berlin, B. (2000). 'Audit Practices at PricewaterhouseCoopers', *Auditing: A Journal of Practice & Theory* 19: 175–82.

20

The external auditor and the audit committee

Jean Bédard and Tiphaine Compernolle

Overview of the topic and its importance

Corporate governance is the system of rules, laws and factors that control operations in a company (Gillan 2006). These mechanisms can be either internal (e.g., boards of directors, charter provisions) or external (e.g., legal and regulatory rules, investor monitoring, external auditors). As a board committee, an audit committee (AC) is an internal governance mechanism responsible for overseeing a company's financial reporting process. It plays an important governance role in contemporary companies. Following the accounting scandals of the early 2000s, regulators around the world have imposed the establishment of audit committees, regulated their structure (independence, competency) and stipulated oversight responsibilities regarding financial statements, audits, and internal financial controls.

Regarding the external audit, the audit committee's role is to reinforce external auditors' independence vis-à-vis management and ensure audit quality. The committee is therefore responsible for the appointment of external auditors, the provision of non-audit services (NAS) by the audit firm, and audit work, including the solving of disagreements between management and auditor regarding financial reporting. By overseeing the company's relations with the external auditor, the audit committee also bolsters confidence in the auditor's report.

Since the financial crisis of 2007–9, external auditors have been criticized for failing to issue warnings of imminent financial collapse, for being too close to the companies they audit and for operating in a non-competitive market. Given that audit committees are the governance body responsible for overseeing the auditor, it is important to determine how well these committees assume their responsibilities. This is particularly important given that some remedies proposed by regulators to improve audit quality assume that audit committees are effective by increasing their responsibilities (e.g. regular public tendering of audit contracts).

This chapter provides an overview of the state of knowledge on audit committees. Given the recent extensive literature reviews carried out on the topic, we focus on current issues and review relevant contemporary research. Our goals are twofold: first, to help standard setters and regulators develop and evaluate their current and future regulations regarding audit committees; and second to identify areas where research is needed.

The rest of the chapter is organized as follows. The next section, "Current issues in this area", provides an overview of past research results and introduces four contemporary issues in the area. The following section, "Summary of current state of research findings", reviews the current research findings on the four issues identified in the previous section. The next section, "Unresolved issues", discusses issues for which future research is required, and the last section presents the conclusion.

Current issues in this area

While audit committees have existed in many countries for decades, it was the accounting scandals from the beginning of the century that brought audit committees to the top of the international business and political agenda. This has led to regulations that gave audit committees responsibilities for audit quality, including the selection, compensation, work, and independence of the external auditor. These regulations also imposed requirements regarding their composition (minimum size, independence, expertise, etc.).

Less than a decade after these new requirements, issues and challenges remain regarding the audit committees' oversight of audit quality. Based on recent regulatory proposals and reviews of past research studies, we have identified four contemporary issues regarding audit committees. We introduce these issues below and summarize the research findings related to these issues in the next section.

Appointment and removal of auditors

Even if a company's shareholders are the main recipients of auditing services, the company remains the leading actor in decisions regarding external auditors' appointment and fees. To control this inherent threat to independence, regulators have given audit committees responsibilities regarding the appointment, reappointment and removal of external auditors. Depending on jurisdiction, the audit committee may recommend the auditor to the board/supervisory body, which in turn will submit it to shareholders for ratification (e.g. European Union, Canada). In some jurisdictions it also appoints the auditor (USA).

Recent reports question the audit committee's auditor selection process. The contemporary occurrence of decades-long audit engagements, "where the partner of a firm's long standing (sometimes over a hundred years) audit client naturally remains under pressure not to lose the client," is seen by the European Commission (EC) as an indication that audit committees have little impact on the elimination of the "familiarity threat" (EC 2011: 37). To reduce this independence risk and facilitate the entry of new audit providers into the market, regulators are considering mandatory audit firm rotation (Public Company Accounting Oversight Board (PCAOB) 2011; EC 2012); mandatory tendering of audits (Financial Reporting Council (FRC) 2012); or comprehensive audit firm review (e.g., Independence Working Group (IWG) 2012). These different regulatory options continue to be the object of discussion and controversy, even between the regulators of the same country or region.[1] All of these options imply greater audit committee involvement in the appointment/removal decision.

Oversight of non-audit services

While the issue of independence associated with the provision of NAS to audit clients has been present for years, the events at Enron and other important US companies, along with the growth in the provision of these services in the 1990s, have prompted regulators to intervene.[2] Among the measures adopted is the prohibition of certain NAS, the disclosure of fees for NAS and increased oversight responsibilities for audit committees regarding these services.[3] These regulations effectively made the audit committees the "gatekeepers" of auditor independence.

The capacity of audit committees to play this role has been questioned. For example, in the UK, following a consultation on the provision of NAS, the Auditing Practices Board (APB) (2010) concluded that audit committees should exercise greater oversight over NAS. It is also the position of the EC, which emphasized that audit committees should improve their oversight (EC 2011: 136, 165).

Interactions between external auditors and audit committees

According to the International Auditing and Assurance Standards Board (IAASB)'s Audit Quality Framework (2013), good two-way communication between the auditor and audit committee, including formal and informal communication, can influence the behaviors and views of both parties and contribute to improvement in audit quality. The importance of these communications is recognized by regulators, who have recently updated their standards of communications with audit committees to take into account the information needed relating to the "new" responsibilities of the audit committees and to encourage effective two-way communication between the two actors (e.g., IAASB 2012: ISA 260; PCAOB 2012: AS 16). Even if these new standards stipulate requirements, they leave considerable room for auditors' judgment on the issues, form and timing of communication.

Audit committees' role in external auditor/management disagreements

An important role for the audit committee is to preserve external auditor independence in disagreement situations. Thus, auditing standards require auditors to inform the audit committee of any disagreements with management about significant matters (e.g., IAASB 2012: ISA 260; PCAOB 2012: AS 16). This responsibility is explicitly recognized by regulators in some countries (US, Canada).

Summary of current state of research findings

Over the years, researchers have examined whether audit committees are effective in terms of strengthening the financial reporting process and improving audit quality. Most of these studies consider various audit committee characteristics such as members' independence, financial expertise, committee size and number of meetings, which can explain effective oversight. A recent review of 103 audit committee studies published between 1994 and 2008 in 18 journals (Bédard and Gendron 2010) suggests that two characteristics of audit committees (independence and members' competencies) are generally positively associated with effectiveness in its multiple dimensions.[4] In particular, independence and competence enable audit committees to oversee in an effective way, i.e. reinforce auditors' independence (different proxies were used such as avoiding the auditor's dismissal after a going concern opinion, supporting the auditor in a disagreement with management, or approving a lower level of NAS) and audit quality (different proxies were used such as selecting a Big 4 or an industry-specialized auditor, or sustaining a greater level of auditor work).

Current research continues to take an interest in audit committees' impact on audit quality. Researchers are also beginning to study how audit committees play their role by examining processes and the relationship between the audit committee, the auditor and management. We present the results of selected contemporary studies for each of the four issues already identified, along with a short summary of the relevant results compiled from previous literature reviews.

Audit committee involvement in the process of external auditor appointment/removal

Results from pre-2002 empirical studies reviewed by Bédard and Gendron (2010) suggest that "strong" (i.e. independent and financially competent) audit committees are more likely to select audit firms that specialize in the client's industry and to select a successor of higher quality (Big 4). While these papers indicate an association of independence and financial competence of audit committee members with audit firm quality proxies, they do not provide insight into how audit committees play their role in this selection process. Two recently published papers draw on interviews and case studies to answer this question.

Based on interviews with 30 audit partners and managers from Big 4 firms in the USA, Cohen *et al.* (2010) report that while the corporate governance environment has improved considerably in the post-SOX era, management continues to be seen as a major actor and often as the driving force behind auditor appointments and removals. Thus, when asked who has the most influence in the appointment and dismissal of auditors in a public company, both management (CEO, CFO) and audit committee were identified by more than 90 percent of the auditors. However, interviewees also stated that management is the group that has the most influence.[5] Cohen *et al.* (2013) replicated this study with 22 directors and found similar results: management still plays an important role.

Fiolleau *et al.*'s (2013) field study of the auditor tendering process at a Canadian company in 2008 sheds light on the auditor appointment and removal process. They find that management was in charge of the process and that the audit committee oversaw the process. First, the decision to put the audit contract out to tender was sparked by management dissatisfaction with the new engagement partner following partner rotation.[6] Management wrote the request for proposals, evaluated and summarized the audit firms' written proposals and provided a recommendation to the audit committee. The latter accepted the recommendation and brought it before the board. The auditors, perceiving who was in charge, tailored their service proposal to management's needs and desires.

These findings are corroborated by Dhaliwal *et al.* (2013). Using a sample of auditor changes in the US from 1995 to 2009, they study the influence of management on auditor selection using management's prior employment relationship with the incoming audit firm as a measure of influence. They find a significant association of management affiliation with the incoming audit firm in both the pre- and post-SOX periods, although smaller in the latter period.[7] This suggests that management influences the auditor appointment decision. They also find that hiring affiliate auditors reduces auditor independence as measured by the likelihood of providing going concern opinions.

Overall, these results suggest that the audit committee plays a role in the selection and termination process, but this role centers more on monitoring than on decision making. Management plays the dominant role and auditors know it.

These results from countries where regulation confers an auditor selection role on audit committees have implications for current regulatory proposals aimed at reducing the independence risk associated with long tenure periods with firms. Simply making the audit committee responsible for nomination might not be sufficient. Other measures such as guidance on the expected role and greater accountability through public reporting might be necessary to achieve the regulatory objective.

Audit committee oversight of non-audit services

In their review of the literature, Bédard and Gendron (2010) identified only three studies that examine the role of the audit committee in overseeing NAS. These studies show that, in the pre-SOX period, audit committees' strength (i.e. independence and vigilance) is negatively associated with the provision of NAS, suggesting that these committees are playing their oversight role. Recent studies support this conclusion.

Zaman *et al.* (2011) studied the relationship between audit committees' characteristics and the level of NAS using 540 company-year observations from the UK FTSE-350 companies for the 2001–4 period. They find that the level of NAS is negatively associated with committee members' financial expertise and independence.

Recognizing the prominence of tax services in NAS provided by auditors in the post-SOX US environment, Bédard and Paquette (2010) examined the association between the audit committee and tax NAS using a sample of 9,008 firm-year observations from the US for the 2004–7 period. They use three measures of purchases: the decision to purchase tax NAS or not, the amount of tax fees relative to audit fees (tax fee ratio), and the amount of tax fees purchased. They examine two audit committee characteristics: financial expertise and multiple directorships. They find a negative and significant association between the three measures of tax NAS and the presence of accounting financial expertise on the audit committee. They also find a negative and significant association between the tax fee ratio and the average number of boards on which audit committee members serve, suggesting that these members are sensitive to the potential negative effects of the high ratio of tax non-audit service fees to audit fees on their reputational capital.

Regulators are using a mix of fee disclosure and audit committee oversight to control NAS. Disclosure not only enables investors to decide for themselves whether the auditor's objectivity and independence may have been adversely affected, but it also affects audit committee members' judgment. In particular, in an experiment with 100 US directors made in 2003, Gaynor *et al.* (2006) examine whether mandated disclosures affect audit committees' pre-approval decisions. While audit committee members are more likely to approve joint audit services provision when audit quality improves, it is no more the case if public disclosures are required. In this case, audit committee members are less likely to approve these services even at the expense of audit quality, suggesting that greater accountability affects the weight members give to the costs and benefits of purchasing NAS. These experimental results are corroborated in an archival setting by Abbott *et al.* (2011). The authors compare the level of non-audit service purchases before and after the introduction of mandated disclosure of fees for the 338 US firms for both 2000 (pre-disclosure) and 2001 (post-disclosure). They test whether the relation between audit committees' characteristics and level of non-audit service purchases varies between the two periods. They find that the magnitude of the negative relationship is twice as large in the post-disclosure period, suggesting that "strong" (i.e. independent and vigilant) audit committees are more sensitive to market pressures.

These results indicate that "strong" audit committees actively control the risk associated with NAS. They also show that greater accountability (e.g. the disclosure of NAS fees) makes audit committee members more sensitive to investor perceptions in their pre-approval process.

Communications between the external auditor and the audit committee

Researchers are starting to examine the two-way relation between external auditor and audit committee, and how each party can influence the other's behavior. Recent studies have investigated these questions using experiments and interviews.

Pomeroy (2010) explores how auditor communication of a disagreement with management affects audit committee members' investigation of the disagreement issue. His results indicate that being informed of such disagreements increases the level of audit committee members' discomfort. He also shows that for accounting decisions with an outcome perceived as aggressive, audit committee members investigate more thoroughly, and that members with greater accounting experience ask more probing questions.

Fiolleau *et al.* (2013) approach communication between the external auditor and the audit committee from another angle. They examine the audit committee's influence on the level of auditor communication. Their experiment on an auditor/management disagreement demonstrates that the auditor does not always communicate the same level of written information to the audit committee, depending on its oversight approach. When the audit committee is involved in the conflict resolution process, there are no significant differences in the auditor's written communication to a proactive audit committee (which asks numerous probing questions on accounting decisions even when the auditor does not raise concerns) and a reactive one (which asks questions only when the auditor raises concerns). When the audit committee is less involved in the conflict resolution process, the auditor communicates significantly more information to a proactive audit committee than to a reactive one. Thus, a proactive audit committee appears to exert stronger accountability pressure on the auditor. Faced with a reactive audit committee, the external auditor tends to communicate less in order to avoid scrutiny.

The oversight approach of an audit committee influences external auditor communications. These communications can influence audit committee scrutiny. The two-way relation between auditor and audit committee is thus dynamic and complex, especially because it takes place within a tripartite relationship with management. A study based on interviews with attendees of audit committee meetings in French companies (Compernolle 2012) shows that the preparation of the auditor's communications to the audit committee is a long process during which there are numerous discussions and negotiations with management on what specific accounting decisions will be disclosed.

Thus, the auditor reviews management's slides and may invite management to change its presentation to the audit committee. In the same way, management may ask the auditor to remove some issues from his/her presentation, arguing that the disagreement has been resolved. The audit committee is rarely aware of these negotiations regarding which issues have to be disclosed or not during the audit committee meetings. On the contrary, Beattie *et al.*'s (2011) study shows that the UK audit committee chair is more involved in such discussions. The chair acts as a gatekeeper in deciding with the CFO which issues will be presented to the whole audit committee. The authors associated this result with the fact that UK audit committee meetings are attended by many other actors, such as the CEO, the company chair and directors who are not audit committee members. This situation increases the formality of audit committee meetings and the need for the meeting to run smoothly.

External auditor communications to audit committees are affected not only by the audit committee and other corporate governance actors but also by management, suggesting that two-way communication between the external auditor and the audit committee is a complex relational phenomenon.

Audit committee's role in external auditor/management disagreements

Previous studies reviewed by Bédard and Gendron (2010) find that audit committee characteristics can influence the audit committee's support for the external auditor in disagreements with management. While these studies indicate an association between the audit committee's characteristics and its involvement in disagreement processes, they do not specify the nature of the audit committee's concrete role in such processes. Recent research addresses this issue, with contradictory results.

After conducting 30 interviews with external auditors, Cohen *et al.* (2010) conclude that slightly more than half of their participants consider that discussions with the audit committee help them to resolve disagreements with management. Some interviewees indicate that the audit committee prefers that auditor and management resolve the issue before reporting to the audit committee.

Fearnley *et al.* (2011) find similar results in their case study of nine British audit committees. They report more than 40 accounting issues discussed extensively between management and the external auditor for all nine companies studied; the audit committee was effectively informed of about only two-thirds of these discussions. Only two of the nine audit committee chairs had been actively involved in the resolution process. The authors underline audit committee chairs' reluctance to engage in such a process.

These two studies show that whereas the audit committee wants to be informed about external auditor/management disagreements, it does not want to participate in the decision-making process, preferring to assume its oversight role at a distance.

Based on a qualitative study of seven Malaysian listed companies, Salleh and Stewart (2012) come to the opposite conclusion: the audit committee is actively involved in resolving external auditor/management conflicts. Specifying that the Malaysian culture is different from the North American one, they show that the audit committee plays the role of mediator. Rarely taking sides, the audit committee helps the auditor and management jointly find a compromise solution. Thus, the audit committee becomes "a forum of deciding"; it assumes a role beyond that of traditional oversight by making recommendations. Beyond cultural differences, Salleh and Stewart (2012) suggest an explanation for this divergence of results: they study only significant disagreements while Cohen *et al.* (2010) and Fearnley *et al.* (2011) investigate diverse negotiations. They observe that the audit committee is actively involved in serious external auditor/management disagreements exclusively. Interviewing directors in post-SOX area, Cohen *et al.* (2013) also find divergence in the interviewees' accounts regarding the extent and nature of the role played by audit committees to resolve auditor/management disagreements. The authors associate this situation to the fact that regulation does not give directions to audit committee members on how to fulfill their oversight role.

Brown-Liburd and Wright's (2011) experimental study shows that external auditors take into consideration audit committee willingness to get involved in auditor/management disagreements when they define their pre-strategy for upcoming negotiations. When the audit committee is perceived unwilling to be involved in these discussions, external auditors define the same pre-strategy, whatever the nature of their past relationships with management, contentious or compromising. On the other hand, when the audit committee is perceived willing to be involved, external auditors adapt their pre-strategy, depending on the nature of past relationships with management. They are more aggressive in the case of contentious past relationships since they consider that they have more chance of receiving support from the audit committee, and accordingly will have more bargaining power.

These studies highlight audit committees' reluctance to be actively involved in external auditor/management disagreements, depending on the country and on the company. Nevertheless, the possibility of audit committee involvement influences the auditor's perceived power in negotiations with management. Moreover, simply permitting the auditors to inform the audit committee could increase their power during such negotiations (Compernolle 2009). Despite audit committees' reluctance to be directly involved in auditor/management disagreements, their anticipated, possible or real involvement seems to have important effects on external auditors' power vis-à-vis management. In light of these results, it could be beneficial that regulators reaffirm, and specify the extent of, the role of the audit committee regarding auditor/management disagreements.

Unresolved issues warranting future research

Current research findings shed light on audit committees' functioning and on their effect on audit quality with regard to the four current issues; many unresolved matters related to these issues warrant further research. In this section we discuss potential research avenues.

Giving responsibilities to audit committees regarding NAS, resolving external auditor/management disagreements, and the appointment, reappointment and removal of the auditor are among the mechanisms that can be used to protect auditor independence. Other mechanisms include the disclosure of information related to the auditor (e.g. NAS, length of the relationship); the audit committee (e.g. disclose the justification and the audit committee's decision-making process regarding the retention or replacement of the auditor and NAS); and other governance factors (e.g., law and regulations, enforcement, investor monitoring).

Research on audit committee oversight of NAS has shown that fee disclosure increases audit committee members' sensitivity to investors' perceptions. Future research could examine the interaction between audit committee oversight and other mechanisms. For example, in the UK the new Guidance on Audit Committees (FRC 2012) requires the audit committee to report information on its work related to the assessment of the effectiveness of the audit process, the appointment or reappointment of the external auditor, the length of tenure of the current audit firm and when a tender was last conducted. Multi-country research might examine the interaction between audit committee effectiveness and certain characteristics of corporate governance systems (e.g. strength of the legal systems, regulation regarding audit committees or NAS).

Whereas previous research has shown that "strong" audit committees influence the level of NAS, little is known about how audit committees oversee these services in practice. Field studies on the processes involved, information exchanges and factors considered by audit committee members could be useful here. Moreover, following the study of Dhaliwal *et al.* (2013) on the influence of management affiliation with an audit firm on the auditor appointment decision, future research could be interested in the effect of social ties of audit committee members and external auditors on audit quality. This question could be explored through archival studies and field studies.

The level of audit committee involvement in external auditor/management disagreements seems to vary depending on the country, and perhaps depending on the company. Differences in terms of culture (both national and corporate) could account for this variation, as could the importance of the auditor/management conflict. It could also be interesting to investigate other factors that could explain this variation in audit committee involvement. As Fearnley *et al.* (2011) highlight, the audit committee chair is an important actor inside the audit committee. It could be interesting to further investigate his/her specific role in external auditor/management disagreements and other aspects of audit committee oversight duties. For example, does the chair play a specific role in establishing the audit committee's (reputation of) strength, in maintaining the two-way relation between the audit committee and the external auditor? The company culture and management willingness also deserves closer attention. Presently, we know that external auditors' communication is influenced by the audit committee's oversight approach and is negotiated with management. Also, the auditor has several ways of communicating with the audit committee: formal communication (written or oral) during the audit committee meeting, and informal communication with the audit committee chair outside formal meetings. It could be interesting to explore how the external auditors use these different communication channels, and if so, their rationale.

Conclusion

Over the last decade, audit committees have been asked to play a greater role in ensuring the quality of the financial audit and reassuring users of financial statements about their quality. New regulations (e.g., FRC 2012) and proposals (e.g., PCAOB 2011; EC 2012) indicate that this trend is continuing. Their responsibilities regarding auditor (re)appointment and removal, NAS and audit work are expected to increase.

This chapter presents the state of knowledge of audit committees relative to four contemporary issues: appointment and removal of auditors, provision of NAS, communication between the external auditor and the audit committee, and auditors' disagreements with management. Overall, the results of the studies reviewed suggest that "strong" audit committees affect audit quality. They also show that there is room for improvement. Audit committees are not the external auditor's "boss." For example, management may still play a predominant role in the selection process of an external auditor. These studies also highlight the important influence of the processes, relationships and communications among the audit committee, the auditor and management on the audit committee's oversight of the external audit. Further research is required to better understand how the audit committee plays its oversight role in practice.

Whether audit committees will be able to respond to regulators' and the public's expectations is an empirical question. However, Cohen *et al.* (2004) indicate that audit committees are only one piece in the corporate governance mosaic, and that it is the interaction among the various pieces that is most important.

Notes

1 In the US, the Hurt Bill, which would prohibit the PCAOB from adopting audit firm rotation, was passed by the House Financial Services Committee on June 19, 2013. In the UK, even though the FRC was supporting the mandatory tendering of audits option, in July 2013 the Competition Commission proposed to make audit firm rotation compulsory (UK Competition Commission, 2013). Similarly, after a controversy, the European Parliament Legal Affairs Committee in April 2013 approved audit firm rotation every 25 years (European Parliament 2013).

2 While regulators seem to assume that non-audit services (NAS) are "bad", research results show that provision of NAS rarely results in independence but in fact concerns and may even improve the audit quality (e.g. Gramling *et al.* 2010, Kinney *et al.* 2004). However, NAS appear to negatively influence perceptions of auditor independence (Gramling *et al.* 2010).

3 Similar measures have been proposed by the European Commission. Thus the commission is proposing a list of prohibited non-audit services (EC 2012: art. 10) and that the audit committee approve non-prohibited non-audit services (EC 2012: art. 38a).

4 As in Bédard and Gendron (2010), we define effectiveness as producing the desired effects or goals, which for an audit committee consists of providing quality financial reporting and strengthening investor confidence in the quality of financial reporting and financial markets. Audit committees can improve the quality of information by overseeing the financial reporting process, external auditing and internal controls.

5 When asked to specify the percentage of influence that they believe various stakeholders have on this decision, 53 percent was assigned to management and 41 percent to the audit committee.

6 Some audit committees may more actively select the new engagement partner when a partner rotates off the engagement. For example Beasley *et al.*'s (2009) interviewees indicate that some audit committees specified the audit firm criteria that they sought in the new partner and interviewed the candidate.

7 In Fiolleau *et al.*'s (2013) case study, the selected audit firm came from the CFO's former employer.

References

Abbott, L. J., S. Parker, and G. F. Peters. 2011. "Does Mandated Disclosure Induce a Structural Change in the Determinants of Nonaudit Service Purchases?", *Auditing: A Journal of Practice & Theory* 30(2): 51–76.

Auditing Practices Board (APB). 2010. *The Provision of Non-Audit Services by Auditors – Feedback on Previous Consultations and Consultation Paper on Revised Draft Ethical Standards for Auditors*. London: FRC 183.

Beasley, M. S., J. V. Carcello, D. R. Hermanson, and T. L. Neal. 2009. "The Audit Committee Oversight Process", *Contemporary Accounting Research* 26(1): 65–122.

Beattie, V., S. Fearnley, and T. Hines. 2011. *Reaching Key Financial Reporting Decisions: How Directors and Auditors Interact*. Chichester: John Wiley & Sons.

Bédard, J. and Y. Gendron. 2010. "Strengthening the Financial Reporting System: Can Audit Committee Deliver?", *International Journal of Auditing* 14(2): 174–210.

Bédard, J. and S. Paquette. 2010. *Perception of Auditor Independence, Audit Committee Characteristics, and Auditor Provision of Tax Services*. Available online at http://ssrn.com/abstract=1084099 (accessed 5 May 2014).

Brown-Liburd, H. L. and A. M. Wright. 2011. "The Effect of Past Client Relationship and Strength of the Audit Committee on Auditor Negotiations", *Auditing* 30(4): 51–69.

Cohen J., G. Krishnamoorthy, and A. Wright. 2004. "The Corporate Governance Mosaic and Financial Reporting Quality", *Journal of Accounting Literature*: 23: 87–152.

Cohen, J., G. Krishnamoorthy, and A. Wright. 2010. "Corporate Governance in the Post-Sarbanes-Oxley Era: Auditors' Experiences", *Contemporary Accounting Research* 27(3): 751–86.

Cohen, J. R., C. Hayes, G. Krishnamoorthy, G. S. Monroe, and A. M. Wright. 2013. "The Effectiveness of SOX Regulation: An Interview Study of Corporate Directors", *Behavioral Research in Accounting*: 25(1): 61–87.

Compernolle, T. 2009. "La construction collective de l'indépendance du commissaire aux comptes: La place du comité d'audit" ["The collective construction of external auditor independence: The role of the audit committee"], *Comptabilité contrôle audit* 15(December): 91–116.

Compernolle, T. 2012. *Accountability to the Audit Committee: Running Risks and Managing Impressions*, paper presented to the Interdisciplinary Perspectives on Accounting Conference, Cardiff, July.

Dhaliwal, D. S., P. T. Lamoreaux, C. S. Lennox, and L. M. Mauler. 2013. "Post-SOX Management Influence on Auditor Selection and Subsequent Impairments of Auditor Independence during the Post-SOX Period. Available online at http://papers.ssrn.com/sol3/papers.cfm?abstract_id=2018702 (accessed 5 May 2014).

European Commission (EC). 2011. "Commission Staff Working Paper Impact Assessment Accompanying the Document Proposal for a Directive of the European Parliament and of the Council Amending Directive 2006/43/EC on statutory audits of annual accounts and consolidated accounts." Brussels: EC, 279.

European Commission (EC). 2012. *Draft Report on the Proposal for a Regulation of the European Parliament and of the Council on Specific Requirements Regarding Statutory Audit of Public-interest Entities 2011/0359(COD)*. Brussels: EC, 98.

European Parliament (EP). 2013. *Committee on Legal Affairs, Minutes from the Meeting of 24 April 2013, JURI_PV(2013)0424*. Brussels: EP.

Financial Reporting Council (FRC). 2012. *Guidance on Audit Committees*. London: FRC.

Fiolleau, K., K. J. Hoang, and B. Pomeroy. 2013. "Auditors' Communications with Audit Committees: The Influence of the Audit Committee's Oversight Approach. Available online at http://papers.ssrn.com/sol3/papers.cfm?abstract_id=1963950 (accessed 5 May 2014).

Fiolleau, K., K. Hoang, K. Jamal, and S. Sunder. 2013. "How Do Regulatory Reforms to Enhance Auditor Independence Work in Practice?", *Contemporary Accounting Research* 30(3): 864–90.

Gaynor, L. M., L. S. McDaniel, and T. L. Neal. 2006. "The Effects of Joint Provision and Disclosure of Nonaudit Services on Audit Committee Members' Decisions and Investors' Preferences", *Accounting Review* 81(4): 873–96.

Gillan, S. L. 2006. "Recent Developments in Corporate Governance: An Overview", *Journal of Corporate Finance* 12(3): 381–402.

Gramling, A. A., J. G. Jenkins, and M. H. Taylor. 2010. "Policy and Research Implications of Evolving Independence Rules for Public Company Auditors", *Accounting Horizons* 24(4): 547–66.

Independence Working Group (IWG). 2012. *Enhancing Audit Quality: Canadian Perspectives – Auditor Independence*. Toronto: The Canadian Institute of Chartered Accountants and Canadian Public Accountability Board, 31.

International Auditing and Assurance Standards Board (IAASB). 2012. "ISA 260, Communication with Those Charged with Governance," in *Handbook of International Quality Control, Auditing, Review, Other Assurance, and Related Services Pronouncements: Part I*, pp. 214–38. International Federation of Accountants (IFAC).

International Auditing and Assurance Standards Board (IAASB). 2013. *A Framework for Audit Quality*, consultation paper: International Federation of Accountants (IFAC).

Kinney, W. R., Z.-V. Palmrose, and S. Scholz. 2004. "Auditor Independence, Non-Audit Services, and Restatements: Was the US Government Right?", *Journal of Accounting Research* 42(3): 561–88.

Pomeroy, B. 2010. "Audit Committee Member Investigation of Significant Accounting Decisions", *Auditing: A Journal of Practice & Theory* 29(1): 173–205.

Public Company Accounting Oversight Board (PCAOB). 2011. *Concept Release on Auditor Independence and Audit Firm Rotation,* No. 2011–006. Washington, DC: PCAOB.

Public Company Accounting Oversight Board (PCAOB). 2012. *Auditing Standard No. 16: Communications with Audit Committees*. Washington, DC: PCAOB.

Salleh, Z. and J. Stewart. 2012. "The Role of the Audit Committee in Resolving Auditor-Client Disagreements: A Malaysian Study", *Accounting, Auditing & Accountability Journal* 25(8): 1340–72.

UK Competition Commission. 2013. *Statutory Audit Services Market Investigation: Provisional Decision on Remedies,* Notified: 22 July 2013. London: Competition Commission.

Zaman, M., M. Hudaib, and R. Haniffa. 2011. "Corporate Governance Quality, Audit Fees and Non-Audit Services Fees", *Journal of Business Finance & Accounting* 38(1–2): 165–97.

21

Auditing ethics

Michael K. Shaub and Robert L. Braun

Overview

The purpose of this chapter is to provide a framework for understanding why ethics is such an important part of auditing and why auditors are continually confronted by ethical choices. We also seek to provide readers with an understanding of why some issues seem self-evident, while others are controversial and seem largely intractable. A number of issues of real ethical concern have gone largely unaddressed by the accounting profession, even in the presence of an increasingly invasive regulatory environment. We provide insight as to why this might be so.

Auditing issues have moral content because they involve volitional choices that affect others (Rachels 1986; Jones 1991; Coram *et al.* 2008). Auditors' decisions often have broad impact on investors and other interested users of financial information. So it is important for auditors to consider the ethical implications of their choices. Auditing is unique among professions because the audit is a three-party contract with only two signatories. The third party, the user of financial statements, relies on the auditor's ethics in order to gain representation. Arguably, ethics is at the very heart of the demand for auditing. Auditing is as much an ethical discipline as it is a technical discipline (Waddock 2005).

What the auditing ethics literature shows us is that auditors are ethically conflicted. While they are largely aware of their duties, narrowly defined, they are unschooled in virtue and preoccupied with consequence evaluation. This is consistent with changes in business schools over time (Ghoshal 2005), with emphasis on virtue and duty receding against the forces of rational decision-making in agency relationships. And research indicates that training, in Jensen and Meckling's (1976) presumption that all agents are driven strictly by self-interest, makes people more self-interested (Frank *et al.* 1993; Ferraro *et al.* 2005).

The recession of virtue and duty means that current issues in ethics, which are covered in the next section, are largely unchanged from what they were prior to the Sarbanes-Oxley Act (SOX), or even what they were in the 1980s. That is, absent a strong message regarding categorical duties of auditors, problems tend to be addressed on an *ad hoc* basis with consequences and probabilities of various outcomes driving decisions. As a result, resolution is contingent upon circumstances. Rather than having a clear statement of the values and duties that can be universally applied we have, at best, a precedent that fits a particular set of circumstances. As a result, audit firms and auditors do not tend to solve ethical problems in any long-term sense. This has resulted in increased regulation and more aggressive government enforcement of laws and regulations.

The following section, "Summary of research findings", summarizes some of the important research findings that provide a basis for understanding the current ethical temperature of auditors. Unlike many areas of audit research, auditing ethics research has moved in fits and starts, with few systematic streams of research that allow us progressive revelation and discovery. However, sufficient work has been done to address some of the larger ethical questions that confront the profession.

Because of the reduced emphasis on virtue and duty in the business school and in audit firms, auditors are often unaware of the ethical implications of the decisions they make daily. In the section "Unresolved issues needing future research", we demonstrate from one issue of a leading research journal that every major auditor choice issue being studied has an ethical component that is largely ignored in the way that the study is framed. We see this as an opportunity. Giving attention to this underlying ethical component has the potential to enrich our understanding of the audit process. After suggesting issues that remain to be addressed, we offer conclusions about what lies ahead for ethical decision-making in auditing.

Current issues in ethics

The realm of auditing ethics is a battle between the external and the internal, between rules and principles. Rules are driven by external, observable impacts of auditors' behavior, while principles direct the more subtle, day-to-day ethical decision-making of the auditor. Because auditors operate under codes of conduct, one helpful way to dichotomize the issues in auditing ethics is to divide them into those pertaining to a code of conduct, and those relating to duty, virtue, and justice.

Code of conduct issues are those with outward manifestations such as independence violations or engaging in acts discreditable to the accounting profession. They are often issues about which there is significant consensus, and they tend to be largely non-controversial. The issues related to morality and justice often deal in nuances. What is a "material" misstatement? Who has a right to know this information? Must an auditor always tell the truth, and the whole truth? How does the auditor balance the right to know with the potential for the "self-fulfilling prophecy" that may result from releasing information?

Current issues in ethics largely mirror those of the last 30 years. In some places, the ethics education bar has been set higher, both in the college classroom and in continuing professional education (Rockness and Rockness 2010). For example, the state of Texas moved from no ethics being a continuing professional education requirement, to a two-hour course every three years, to a four-hour course every other year. Texas also requires a three-semester-hour college course in accounting ethics, a standard that California has far surpassed with a mandatory ten-semester-hour standard. These requirements are just a part of the overall regulatory strategy to control auditors' behavior.

But today's auditor operates in an atmosphere eerily similar to the 1990s, prior to SOX, in its competition, profit fixation, and partner compensation emphases. And there is no powerful voice for ethics, either at the regulator level or at the Big 4 firm level. There is little actual ethics training beyond the courses that might be required by state boards of accountancy, which are mostly ordered around compliance with state rules, and almost no training in professional skepticism. And while research has indicated that professional skepticism is both a trait (Hurtt 2010) and a state of mind (Shaub and Lawrence 1996), there is much to be done to understand how it is activated, particularly in light of the Public Company Accounting Oversight Board (PCAOB)'s increasing emphasis on its importance.

What, in fairness, should we expect of auditors ethically? Frankel (1989) describes the tension between the profession's pursuit of autonomy and the public's demand for accountability. What are auditors responsible to provide in exchange for the monopoly protections of licensing? We would suggest the following: bringing moral persuasion to bear on clients by leveraging the opinion, not buckling to client pressure, staffing audits to match client size and complexity with people of appropriate competence and professional skepticism, and a firm-level layer of objectivity that prevents big mistakes.

Moral persuasion is necessary to ensure accurate accounting entries, full disclosure, and compliance with laws such as the Foreign Corrupt Practices Act. This requires internal moral strength on the part of individual auditors, supported by structures within the firm that allow these morally engaged auditors to follow through on decisions. It is very difficult to legislate this influence or write codes of conduct that are specific enough to significantly influence the level of moral persuasion that auditors exercise on their clients.

Not buckling to client pressure has historically been a complex and difficult issue for the auditing profession, and its presence in the current auditing environment is not distinctly different from what it was in the 1990s before SOX. The voluntary client turnover by accounting firms that took place in the first several years after the Act's passage has largely ended. With audit partner rotation on public clients, accounting firms have to be strategic to maintain client relationships.

Staffing audits to match client size and complexity with people of appropriate competence and professional skepticism is designed not just to detect fraud, but to help the client establish and enforce an accounting and reporting environment that helps to prevent fraud in the first place.

Accounting firms need a national office-level layer of objectivity that prevents big mistakes: Amoruso *et al.* (2013) present evidence of the decline of this protective layer contributing to the downfall of Andersen. Whereas historically practice group partners had a *de facto* veto power over engagement partners when it came to controversial accounting and reporting issues, this environment changed in the 1980s and 1990s, particularly with the rise of Andersen Consulting. Prior to spinning off Andersen Consulting, audit partners were pressured because of their declining contribution to firm profits, and they were seen as riding on consulting partners' coattails. After the spinoff, audit partners were pressured to expand non-audit services because of their higher profit margins. Evidence from Amoruso *et al.* (2013) indicates that, in general, audit partners were supposed to deliver two dollars in consulting services for every dollar in audit fees.

As documented by Amoruso *et al.* (2013), this created incentives to comply with clients' wishes, threatening auditor independence. Had Andersen given the needed attention to this issue, they would have strengthened control over the review process to offset this incentive. Instead, practice group partners who had historically controlled contentious client decisions found themselves reporting to regional practice partners with specific profitability goals. This undermined the historical protections that came from a detached review of challenging client issues. Enron was simply the ultimate example of the failures that arose from the removal of these protections.

Summary of research findings

Auditing ethics research is largely a product of the last 25 years, so most of the research findings continue to be relevant today. Early work in moral reasoning sought to understand individual auditors' ethical decision-making using a linear decision model proposed by Kohlberg (1969) and Rest (1986), with the focus on a measure of cognitive moral development. Beginning with Armstrong (1987) and pushed forward by the work of Ponemon (1992a, 1993), researchers have shown that auditors are only sensitive to certain ethical issues (Shaub *et al.* 1993) and tend to be conventional moral reasoners who are rule followers. Indeed, Ponemon (1992b) provides evidence to indicate that the selection–socialization process in public accounting firms may reinforce these tendencies.

Jones (1991) shifted the focus to the nature of the moral decision rather than the decision-maker. Moral intensity is a construct developed by Jones (1991) to describe the factors that impact an ethical decision. The six defining characteristics of an ethical issue are magnitude of consequences, social consensus, probability of effect, temporal immediacy, proximity, and concentration of effect. Cohen and Martinov-Bennie (2006), in a study using multiple scenarios with audit managers and partners, find that the most important moral intensity factors across the stages of the ethical decision-making process are the first three: magnitude of consequences, social consensus, and probability of effect.

This finding makes sense, because these characteristics make up two of the primary forces in ethical decision-making. Social consensus generally aligns with the first force, the *duties* to which auditors are held. These include protecting the public, disclosing things that users have a right to know, telling the truth, and performing audits in accordance with professional standards. Where social consensus exists, and the "ought" is greater than what is actually done, sanctions typically result. This is true in instances of independence violations and of auditor complicity with client fraud. As Jones (1991: 475) suggests, laws and rules reduce moral ambiguity. Social consensus may also be determined through reference to authority figures and peers (Singhapakdi *et al.* 1996).

Another important influence on ethical decision-making is *consequentialist calculation*, which combines the other two primary characteristics of moral intensity, magnitude of consequences and probability of effect. Where there is not a strong social consensus, there is a tendency to fall back on competence evaluations, measuring auditors' performance against technical auditing standards rather than evaluations of integrity. Materiality decisions and assessments of audit risk fall into this category, and the auditing literature tends to describe both of these audit judgments in mathematical terms that involve magnitude and probability (Shaub 2005).

However, Coram *et al.* (2008) studied the moral intensity of reduced audit quality acts such as inappropriate signoff and accepting weak client explanations, and found little variance in social consensus; their auditors judged reduced audit quality acts as uniformly wrong. However, the auditors varied on the perceived probability and magnitude of consequences of the acts, indicating that consequence calculation has a disproportionately large impact on ethical decisions.

This dichotomy based on moral intensity aligns with the earlier dichotomy based on a code of conduct versus morality and justice. Where there is consensus, then we would expect inclusion in a code of conduct. Where issues are more complex as to how to bring about a just outcome, those judgments are largely outside the code and guided, if anything, by broader principles. But those principles may be trumped by auditors' consequentialist calculations.

Moral intensity affects ethical sensitivity for both auditors (Karcher 1996) and accounting students (Wright *et al.* 1998). Brandon *et al.* (2007) found that those with higher moral development were less willing to accept earnings management and found it less ethical. Shafer *et al.* (1999) showed that moral intensity influences ethical intentions and behavior, and Shafer *et al.* (2001) showed that that effect may even swamp personal characteristics such as moral development. Brandon *et al.* (2007) reinforce this idea by finding that accounting students' attitudes toward earnings management are only impacted by moral reasoning when moral intensity is high.

The practitioner literature provides only limited insight into auditing ethics issues, since accounting practice is preoccupied with those few evident duties of the auditor for several reasons. First, the consensus that surrounds duties such as independence and objectivity in the auditor provides a level of certainty, a baseline accountability, which allows for the profession to retain its status without unduly extending its responsibilities.

The ethical component of auditing is arguably more important than it is in some other professions, because auditors are required to go against a natural tendency to be responsive to client interests. While doctors would naturally seek to bring healing to their patients, and attorney–client privilege is recognized under the law, auditors are required to be objective and independent in order to act with integrity. They are not *allowed* to be advocates, and even their attempts to bring "healing" to their clients through counsel to management are often considered a threat to their independence.

Auditing by its nature has responsibilities beyond many professions, because auditors are required to remain objective about a party that, at least under the US model, is compensating them. This is a far more severe requirement than that imposed on doctors, lawyers, or even tax accountants who act as advocates for their clients. Auditors are not anxious to extend their moral obligations further than necessary, as they already perceive their moral responsibilities as significant. Thus, the ability to identify with a high degree of certainty what is expected of the auditor is highly valued. The auditing professional literature is not known for articles advocating extending those requirements.

The second reason that auditors would prefer to constrain their ethical responsibilities is the significant legal exposure that accompanies their duties. The largest judgments against accounting firms have disproportionately been in the area of auditing rather than tax or consulting.[1] It is perhaps asking too much to expect auditing practitioners to look to broaden their duties because of the potential costs they incur once they acknowledge them.

Unresolved issues requiring future research

As noted in the section "Overview", few auditing ethics issues have been resolved by the firms, though some are more closely regulated than before. There is general consensus in the profession that egregious behavior such as that of the Grant Thornton partner who stole client fees (Raymond and Aubin 2013) or the KPMG partner who engaged in insider trading (Eaglesham *et al.* 2013) is morally wrong. Firms that experience this type of behavior generally act quickly to condemn it (Rapoport 2013) and to punish those involved through termination and lawsuits. But these still represent risk-taking behaviors by those at the partner level that threaten entire practices and, potentially, accounting firms. What incentives drive these behaviors, and what can accounting firms reasonably do to prevent them?

Indeed, numerous long-standing issues remain to be understood and addressed. Firms want a clear understanding of what they are required to do, and seek to comply with the letter of the law. Yet the entrepreneurial nature of the accounting firm business means that firms will sell business up to the edge of the law. Consulting practices have largely bounced back in the past decade since SOX, and the lines have become blurred about what consulting should be acceptable. Audit quality may be enhanced from the knowledge gained, but what can accounting firms do to maintain objectivity?

The deeper ethical questions of a partner's or firm's ability to maintain real objectivity are ignored. KPMG partner Scott London's insider trading brought to light the fact that he remained a relationship partner on Skechers when he rotated off as audit engagement partner, then returned as the engagement partner after the five years out of that role, mandated by SOX. Audit firms have been effective in opposing PCAOB proposals to rotate audit firms (Jamal *et al.* 2011), using evidence that a large number of failures occur in the first year or two of a new audit engagement. So, if an accounting firm is allowed to keep an audit client forever, how can they ensure objectivity in the audit?

This inability as a profession to address the deeper ethical issues has led to increasing regulation, which in turn is causing "regulation fatigue" in firms. The PCAOB has struggled to move proposals forward on auditor rotation, additional disclosure in the audit report (PCAOB 2011a), and identifying partners on engagements (PCAOB 2011b). There are even signs of firms refusing to act on regulators' demands in a timely manner, such as the recent release of Part II of back-to-back years' PCAOB inspections for PricewaterhouseCoopers (PCAOB 2013a). Does this impact the views of regulators held by those who are being recruited to public accounting firms? Does it impact promotion and success within the firms themselves? Perhaps we need to revisit the selection–socialization findings of Ponemon (1992b: 239) implying "that the ethical culture of the accounting firm stymies an individual's development to higher levels of ethical reasoning."

Another important profession-wide question with ethical implications that would benefit from further research is whether the Big 4 accounting firms are "too big to fail," or perhaps "too few to fail" (Cunningham 2006). The structural limits from SOX on consulting require a minimum number of accounting firms to provide the services auditors are restricted from providing, especially complex services for multinational corporations. This provides a protection that may make accounting firms unwilling to comply with regulators' wishes. The latest evidence is the PCAOB's announcement that it will reward those firms that actively cooperate in the case of audit failures (PCAOB 2013b). This action by the PCAOB serves as an implicit recognition of what the research shows – auditors are driven by consequence calculations in their ethical decision-making, at least at the firm level, and relying on duty or virtue is unlikely to be a successful strategy for regulators. This approach is similar to that taken by the Securities and Exchange Commission (SEC) and the Department of Justice to elicit cooperation (Files *et al.* 2013).

Besides pursuing these issues, perhaps it is time to recognize that all audit research is ethics research. The audit is a product with no value apart from the ethics, or at least the perception of ethics, of the auditor. As such, all of the research described in this volume, not just this chapter, is ethics research. This is not to say that all audit research is situated in a moral context, however.

Morality is concerned with issues of right and wrong and distinguishing between good and bad. Ethics is the philosophy of morality. While all audit research is ethics research in that it informs readers on what is, at its heart, an ethical discipline, much of the research is presented in an amoral context. Much of the research describes auditing without helping us to understand the moral motivation of auditors.[2] As a result, the discussion of what is right, and just, and fair is often deferred in favor of a discussion of costs and benefits of outcomes. Conclusions are framed in the analysis of consequences rather than duties and virtues.

Chapter 1 of this volume poses the existential question, "Why is there auditing?" It is a question also addressed in the first chapter of most auditing textbooks. The discussion in textbooks tends to follow the lines of agency theory, defining auditing as an agency cost born of differing goals of principal and agent and the information asymmetries that exist between the two parties. As a corollary to agency theory, the discussion may cast the demand for auditing in terms of information risk reduction and explain that information risk results from voluminous data, complexity of exchange transactions, remoteness of users of financial information, and biases and motives of the provider of financial statement information (Arens *et al.* 2012). These are reasonable explanations that provide tidy analyses within the amoral economic parlance of the profession.

Such discussions situate auditors as market players governed by market forces. What we are left with is a regulatory cat and mouse game with auditors acting as rational economic utility maximizing beings and regulators chasing after them with ever more complex regulations. Meanwhile, we rely on market forces to adjust for the information risk we identify through academic research about auditing outcomes. This research assists regulators so that they may effectively regulate auditors who, according to the theory, cannot or are unwilling to regulate themselves. It also informs investors and creditors of sources of information risk so that they may tweak their models. Largely absent from the research is a discussion of the moral sensitivity, reasoning, decision-making, and courage of the auditors whose outcomes are being studied. Such discussions would situate auditors within a rich context involving judgment of right and wrong within the values and principles of the profession.

In testimony before the United States Treasury Department, Kinney (2008: 3) laments that while research "about" auditing thrives, research "in" auditing is scarce. "These research results about audits are available because archival data are available – but these studies are largely devoid of any knowledge or consideration of audit process!" Taken further, how can we begin to understand the *ethical* processes involved in auditing when we cannot even gain access to assess the behavioral factors involved in audit processes? So, while all audit research is ethics research in that it is *about* a profession inextricably linked to its public interest mission, it falls short of lending insight into how ethics is done in auditing.

The auditing articles appearing in a recent edition of *The Accounting Review* illustrate the points raised in this section. Each article reports findings that have strong ethical implications. That said, none of the articles would normally be considered "ethics research" because they do not purport to provide insight into the moral issues that underlie the results. Appendix A provides a brief analysis of the ethical implications (and non-implications) of the articles.

The articles profiled in the appendix were not "cherry-picked."[3] They employ a variety of methods (two market studies, one behavioral experiment, and one analytical model). By focusing on technical aspects of auditing or by highlighting associations between audit events and market reactions they are not "ethics articles" *per se*. People who believe that auditing is simply a technical discipline in which auditors follow prescriptive standards in executing a certification process are likely to be dismissive of the foregoing discussion suggesting that the profiled articles are ethics articles. Those who recognize that auditing is at once a technical *and ethical* discipline where judgment[4] plays a role within a social and moral context, would consider how the research discussed in this volume and in accounting and auditing journals generally is, indeed, ethics research. It is impossible to do auditing in a vacuum, apart from the values, duties, and consequences that accompany the profession's social contract. The prescription for regulators and for researchers is to use what we know about auditing to ask questions about the moral sensitivity, reasoning, decision-making, and action of auditors, or to ask questions of how auditors fulfill their roles in the social contract. While other sections of this chapter describe research that has taken this step, this section asserts that all audit research is ethics research.

Conclusion

Nearly two decades ago, Francis (1994) lamented the movement of auditing from a hermeneutic (interpretive) approach to a mechanistic scientism that left little room for judgment.

Developments in expert systems and data analysis techniques, along with structured audit approaches, threatened to turn the audit process into little more than a "fill in the blanks" exercise. Francis warned of the dangers of deterioration in expertise, as those relying on expert systems and automatic approaches would not develop the creativity to become experts themselves. And with no need to exercise judgment, virtue in the profession (MacIntyre 1984) would be short-circuited. To quote Francis (1994: 263), "MacIntyre (1984) argues persuasively that merely following rules (such as structured audits) is not inherently virtuous because it does not involve reflection on and choice over one's actions."

Today, the profession finds itself face-to-face with numerous challenging judgments, particularly on public company audits. The financial crisis at the end of the last decade led to accusations that auditors were insufficiently skilled to challenge valuations of mortgage-backed securities and other derivative instruments. The general trend toward convergence of US GAAP (generally accepted accounting principles) with international financial reporting standards promises increased emphasis on fair value throughout the financial statements, requiring *phronesis* or practical reasoning (Francis 1994), a component of wisdom. This is accentuated by the current regulatory regime, particularly in the US through the PCAOB. In Francis's terms, standards like the PCAOB's Auditing Standard 3 (AS 3), "Audit Documentation," have reinforced what he saw two decades ago, when he said that

> … auditing practice is shifting away from a grounding in the auditor doing auditing (producing an audit), and toward the production instead of working papers, or what might be termed a discourse *about* the audit.
>
> *(Francis, 1994: 281)*

Accounting firms have been regularly criticized by the PCAOB for failing to meet the documentation standards of AS 3, even more than for their judgments.

In fact, recent PCAOB standards have largely moved away from using the word "judgment" (Palmrose 2013). While it may be true that eliminating the opportunity to exercise judgment reduces opportunism, it also eliminates the opportunity to make moral judgments involving choice, and it eliminates the opportunity to demonstrate virtue as a professional. In that environment, it is hard to make moral arguments about duties apart from legal duties, and we would expect to see auditors defaulting largely to consequentialist calculations.

And, if the research is any indication, that is exactly what we see.

Appendix A

Exploring ethics aspects of audit research: Analysis of audit articles in a recent issue of The Accounting Review

"Insider Trading, Litigation Concerns, and Auditor Going-concern Opinions" (Chen *et al.* 2013)

The authors find that the probability of receiving a going-concern opinion is negatively associated with the level of insider selling and that the effect is more pronounced when the client is economically significant to the auditor (but moderated by litigation risk and independence of audit committees). The results show an *association*, but the authors are careful to issue the caveat, "we offer no direct evidence that managers pressure their auditors when engaged in insider sales." (Chan *et al.* 2013: 367). They point out that alternative explanations could be responsible for the association. Even though the authors do not attempt to explain the moral reasoning or decision-making involved, there exist strong moral implications in their claim "that insiders have incentives to discourage auditors from issuing going-concern opinions after abnormal insider sales because the bad news from a first-time going-concern opinion is likely to attract regulators' scrutiny and class action lawsuits against insider trading from investors" (Chan *et al.* 2013: 387). While most reviews of audit ethics research would not identify a market study such as this as an ethics paper, it does raise issues that could impact our understanding of the moral choices involved in auditing.

"Financial Statement Disaggregation Decisions and Auditors' Tolerance for Misstatement" (Libby and Brown 2013)

The primary findings in this behavioral experiment are that auditors require correction of smaller errors in disaggregated numbers and that the effect is reduced when the disaggregated numbers are in the notes to the financial statements. The authors discuss the significant policy implications of these results. The study also reports results of an open-ended question about why auditors believe what they believe about materiality benchmarks. It is a question that verges on insight into moral reasoning processes, but instead focuses on a technical reasoning. It is notable, however, that the authors do not provide evidence of or speculate on what drives management's disaggregation decisions. They call for future research on strategies and auditor monitoring of strategic decisions – topics that would have a more direct connection to ethics.

"The Contagion Effects of Low-quality Audits" (Francis and Michas 2013)

This research demonstrates that offices with one audit failure are more likely to experience another audit failure within the subsequent five years. They also find that concurrent clients of offices experiencing a failure tend to have higher levels of abnormal accruals than clients of offices that have not experienced an audit failure. A contagion of this sort could be symptomatic of either technical or moral failure, although the article does not attempt to make that distinction. As such, it does not provide any insight into the moral sensitivity, reasoning, and decision-making associated with the contagion. By providing evidence of the effect, however, it raises questions with significant ethical implications.

"Group Audits, Group-level Controls, and Component Materiality: How Much Auditing is Enough?" (Stewart and Kinney 2013)

The last of the articles we profile here uses Bayesian probability theory to advance a "general unified audit materiality" model to guide auditors in optimizing the relationship between the level of assurance provided and the cost of providing that assurance. The article is motivated by inconsistencies in the current approach to determining materiality for individual components of a group audit (e.g., segments of a single company or consolidated subsidiaries of a complex corporation). While apparently a highly technical article representing priors, posteriors, and likelihoods using gamma probability distributions, the knowledge created here contributes not only to materiality decisions, but also to our understanding of the social contract under which auditors operate. By increasing auditors' ability to identify and control information risk and audit cost, the article can help improve audit quality and inform the discussion of distributive justice associated with the audit contract.

Notes

1 A significant exception is the $456 million judgment against KPMG for marketing abusive tax shelters. However, that judgment was primarily aimed at what was considered personal behavior of the partners involved.

2 This is not necessarily a problem for the profession or for audit research. As a social science, audit research invokes scientific methods. There is considerable debate as to whether science ought to weigh in on moral issues. Some hold that science is about the discovery of facts through empirical methods, and that science need not weigh in on matters of morality. The phrase, "you cannot derive an 'is' from an 'ought'" applies here. Others hold that we should look to scientific inquiry to measure the antecedents of human flourishing, thereby allowing us to derive our understanding of what "ought to be" from our knowledge of "what is." Most audit research examines issues that inform our understanding of auditing without engaging in a discussion of the morality of the auditor's reasoning, decision-making, or actions.

3 That is, they were not cherry-picked outside of the fact that they appear in a top-tier journal and were subjected to the highest standards of peer review. The issue selected was the most recently published issue at the time of writing this chapter. These were the four most auditing-specific articles appearing in the issue. We assert that analysis of most of the auditing research in well-regarded publications would reach similar conclusions.

4 Curiously, however, the Public Company Accounting Oversight Board (PCAOB) seems to be sending a mixed message on the role of judgment in auditing. Auditing Standards 8–15 collectively use the word "judgment" in reference to auditor judgment only three times, although they do seem to emphasize the importance of professional skepticism (Palmrose 2013).

References

Amoruso, A., Roberts, R., and Trompeter, G. 2013. "The misalignment of control and compensation in professional service firms: The case of Arthur Andersen", unpublished working paper. Elon, NC: Elon University and Orlando, FL: University of Central Florida.

Arens, A., Elder, R., and Beasley, M. 2012. *Auditing and Assurance Services*. 14th ed. New York: PrenticeHall.

Armstrong, M. B. 1987. "Moral Development and Accounting Education", *Journal of Accounting Education* 5: 27–34.

Brandon, D., Kerler, W. III, Killough, L., and Mueller, J. 2007. "The Joint Influence of Client Attributes and Cognitive Moral Development on Students' Ethical Judgments", *Journal of Accounting Education* 25: 59–73.

Chen, C., Martin, X., and Wang, X. 2013. "Insider Trading, Litigation Concerns, and Auditor Going-concern Opinions", *The Accounting Review* 88(2): 365–93.

Cohen, J. and Martinov-Bennie, N. 2006. "The Applicability of a Contingent Factors Model to Accounting Ethics Research", *Journal of Business Ethics* 68: 1–18.

Coram, P., Glavovic, A., Ng, J., and Woodliff, D. 2008. "The Moral Intensity of Reduced Audit Quality Acts", *Auditing: A Journal of Practice and Theory* 27(1): 127–49.

Cunningham, L. 2006. "Too Big to Fail: Moral Hazard in Auditing and the Need to Restructure the Industry before it Unravels", *Columbia Law Review* 106: 1698–748.

Eaglesham, J., Albergotti, R., and Karp, H. 2013. "Secret Recordings, Cash in Insider Sting", *The Wall Street Journal* (April 12), p. A1.

Ferraro, F., Pfeffer, J., and Sutton, R. 2005. "Economics Language and Assumptions: How Theories can become Self-fulfilling", *Academy of Management Review* 30(1): 8–24.

Files, R., Martin, G., and Rasmussen, S. 2013. "The monetary benefit of cooperation in regulatory enforcement actions", unpublished working paper. Dallas, TX: University of Texas at Dallas.

Francis, J. 1994. "Auditing, Hermeneutics, and Subjectivity", *Accounting, Organizations and Society* 19(3): 235–69.

Francis, J. and Michas, P. 2013. "The Contagion Effects of Low-quality Audits", *The Accounting Review* 88(2): 521–52.

Frank, R., Gilovich, T., and Regan, D. 1993. "Does Studying Economics Inhibit Cooperation?", *Journal of Economic Perspectives* 7(Spring): 159–71.

Frankel, M. 1989. "Professional Codes: Why, How, and with What Impact?", *Journal of Business Ethics* 8: 109–15.

Ghoshal, S. 2005. "Bad Management Theories are Destroying Good Management Practices," *Academy of Management Learning & Education* 4(1): 75–91.

Hurtt, K. 2010. "Development of a Scale to Measure Professional Skepticism", *Auditing: A Journal of Practice and Theory* 29(1): 149–71.

Jamal, K., Ball, T., Kassam, R., Glover, J., Kouri, K., Paterson, D., Radhakrishnan, S., and Sunder, S. 2011. "Comment Letter to Public Company Accounting Oversight Board Regarding Audit Firm Rotation" (December 30). Available online at http://faculty.som.yale.edu/shyamsunder/Research/Accounting%20and%20Control/Presentations%20and%20Working%20Papers/AuditFirmRotation/Audit_Firm_Rotation_%20Dec30_Jamal.pdf (accessed 4 May 2013).

Jensen, M. and Meckling, W. 1976. "Theory of the Firm: Managerial Behavior, Agency Costs, and Ownership Structure", *Journal of Financial Economics* 3(October): 305–60.

Jones, T. 1991. "Ethical Decision Making by Individuals in Organizations: An Issue-contingent Model", *Academy of Management Review* 16: 366–95.

Karcher, J. 1996. "Accountants' Ability to Discern the Presence of Ethical Problems", *Journal of Business Ethics* 15: 1033–50.

Kinney, W. R. 2008. *The Human Capital Role of Independent Scholarship in Auditing. Prepared Remarks for Testimony before the U. S. Department of the Treasury*. Washington, DC: Government Printing Office.

Kohlberg, L. 1969. "Moral Stages and Moralization: The Cognitive-developmental Approach to Socialization", in D. Goskin (ed.) *Handbook of Socialization Theory and Research*, pp. 347–480. Chicago, IL: Rand McNally.

Libby, R. and Brown, T. 2013. "Financial Statement Disaggregation Decisions and Auditors' Tolerance for Misstatement", *The Accounting Review* 88(2): 641–65.

MacIntyre, A. 1984. *After Virtue*. 2nd ed. Notre Dame, IN: University of Notre Dame Press.

Palmrose, Z. V. 2013. "PCAOB audit regulation a decade after SOX: Where it stands and what the future holds", unpublished working paper. Seattle, WA: University of Washington.

Ponemon, L. 1992a. "Auditor Underreporting of Time and Moral Reasoning: An Experiment Lab Study", *Contemporary Accounting Research* 7(1): 227–51.

Ponemon, L. 1992b. "Ethical Reasoning and Selection-socialization in Accounting", *Accounting, Organizations and Society* 17: 239–58.

Ponemon, L. 1993. "The Influence of Ethical Reasoning on Auditors' Perceptions of Management Competence and Integrity", *Advances in Accounting* 11: 1–29.

Public Company Accounting Oversight Board (PCAOB). 2011a. *Concept Release on Possible Revisions to PCAOB Standards Related to Reports on Audited Financial Statements*. PCAOB Release No. 2011–003 (June 21). Available online at http://pcaobus.org/Rules/Rulemaking/Docket034/Concept_Release.pdf (accessed 10 May 2014).

Public Company Accounting Oversight Board (PCAOB). 2011b. *Improving the Transparency of Audits: Proposed Amendments to PCAOB Auditing Standards and Form 2*. PCAOB Release No. 2011–007 (October 11). Available on line at http://pcaobus.org/Rules/Rulemaking/Docket029/PCAOB_Release_2011–007.pdf (accessed 10 May 2014).

Public Company Accounting Oversight Board (PCAOB). 2013a. *In the Matter of PricewaterhouseCoopers LLP's Quality Control Remediation Submissions*. PCAOB Release No. 104-2013-054 (March 7). Available online at http://pcaobus.org/Inspections/Documents/03072013_PwCReportStatement.pdf (accessed 10 May 2014).

Public Company Accounting Oversight Board (PCAOB). 2013b. *Policy Statement Regarding Credit for Extraordinary Cooperation in Connection with Board Investigations*. PCAOB Release No. 2013–003 (April 24). Available online at http://pcaobus.org/Enforcement/Documents/Release_2013_003.pdf (accessed 10 May 2014).

Rachels, J. 1986. *The Elements of Moral Philosophy*. New York: Random House.

Rapoport, M. 2013. "KPMG says it Plans Legal Action", *Wall Street Journal Online*. Available online at http://online.wsj.com/article/SB10001424127887324240804578417402301642528.html?KEYWORDS=KPMG (accessed 29 April 2013).

Raymond, N. and Aubin, D. 2013. "*Reuters*.com. Ex-Grant Thornton Partner Charged with Stealing $4 million". Available online at www.reuters.com/article/2013/02/06/us-grantthornton-theft-idUSBRE91513H20130206 (accessed 29 April 2013).

Rest, J. 1986. *Moral Development: Advances in Research and Theory*. New York: Praeger Press.

Rockness, H. and Rockness, J. 2010. "Navigating the Complex Maze of Ethics CPE," *Accounting and the Public Interest* 10(1): 88–104.
Shafer, W., Morris, R., and Ketchand, A. 1999. "The Effects of Formal Sanctions on Accountant Independence", *Auditing: A Journal of Practice and Theory* 18 (Supplement): 85–101.
Shafer, W., Morris, R., and Ketchand, A. 2001. "Effects of Personal Values on Auditors' Ethical Decisions", *Accounting, Auditing and Accountability Journal* 14(3): 254–77.
Shaub, M. 2005. "Materialism and Materiality", *International Journal of Accounting, Auditing and Performance Evaluation* 2(4): 347–55.
Shaub, M. and Lawrence, J. 1996. "Ethics, Experience and Professional Skepticism: A Situational Analysis", *Behavioral Research in Accounting* 8(Supplement): 124–57.
Shaub, M., Finn, D., and Munter, P. 1993. "The Effects of Accountants' Ethical Orientation on Commitment and Ethical Sensitivity", *Behavioral Research in Accounting* 5: 145–69.
Singhapakdi, A., Vitell, S., and Kraft, K. 1996. "Moral Intensity and Ethical Decision-making of Marketing Professionals", *Journal of Business Research* 36: 245–55.
Stewart, T. and Kinney, W. 2013. "Group Audits, Group-level Controls, and Component Materiality: How Much Auditing is Enough?", *The Accounting Review* 88(2): 707–37.
Waddock, S. 2005. "Hollow Men and Women at the Helm ... Hollow Accounting Ethics?", *Issues in Accounting Education* 20(2): 145–50.
Wright, G., Cullinan, C., and Bline, D. 1998. "Recognizing Ethical Issues: The Joint Influence of Ethical Sensitivity and Moral Intensity", *Research on Accounting Ethics* 4: 29–52.

22

Estimating audit fees and production models

Henri Akono and Mike Stein

An audit research tale

The current archival literature on audit fees and production can be traced to the late 1970s and the seminal University of Chicago dissertation by Dan A. Simunic published, in part, as Simunic 1980. The paper remains relevant to contemporary auditing researchers for its in-depth consideration of both the empirical challenges faced by investigators and the strategies used to address these problems. Consequently, even as interest in his specific research question has ebbed and flowed over time, it is instructive to review this study in detail as a device for gaining insight into the nature of this line of inquiry.

Using survey data drawn from US audit clients, Simunic addressed the competitiveness of audit markets – which at the time were dominated by eight national suppliers (popularly known as the Big 8). His analysis was influenced by the prevalent Structure–Conduct–Performance Paradigm[1] popular with both antitrust regulators and industrial organization scholars. Within this framework, the market share concentration levels he observed in audit markets raised questions of price competitiveness and the concomitant policy concerns of monopoly behavior by audit suppliers. While it was commonly believed that Big 8 auditors collected a premium in their fees relative to non-Big 8 auditors, it was unresolved whether any pricing differential was attributable to quality differentiation or to market power. Since either hypothesis was consistent with a fee premium, Simunic designed his study to distinguish between these two possibilities.

In an ideal test of his hypotheses, economic theory implied that Simunic should have started with a client-specific Lerner index defined as ([Price – Marginal Cost] / Price) created from observations of both fees and production costs. This index would then be analyzed relative to measures of market competitiveness and concentration (e.g., an 8-firm concentration ratio or Herfindahl index) and audit quality (e.g., the level of assurance in the engagement) using a regression model. Not surprisingly, appropriate data measuring both market competitiveness and audit quality (we will set aside the discussion of audit cost data for the moment) were not available. This required reliance upon several assumptions in order to formulate an interpretable empirical specification.

First, he observed that audit quality was an experience good. In economics, an experience good is one where the quality can only be observed after it has been purchased and consumed (e.g., a restaurant meal). That is, the client could only know the *expected* quality of the audit at the time of purchase (A1). In practice, this equates quality with the auditor's brand name, since quality-differentiating characteristics are expected to be uniform across each auditor's portfolio of clients. In effect, suppliers are limited to selling a single level of quality and, in turn, a direct but unobserved audit-by-audit quality measure is replaced (in the model) with a readily observed indication of brand name. Second, he asserted that audits performed by non-Big 8 audit firms were undifferentiated from each other in terms of quality (A2). This condition implies non-Big 8 audits are competitively priced with the further implication that only Big 8 fees have the potential to earn premium fees.[2] Finally, he assumed that audit markets are bifurcated by client size and that the market for audits of small clients has a different competitive structure than the market for large clients because small accounting firms cannot effectively audit large clients (A3). Upon this theoretical scaffolding, Simunic implemented a carefully designed test permitting the estimation of audit fees as a function of whether or not an auditor was a Big 8 firm.

Given the critical importance of his identification strategy to the success of the research we now turn to a detailed discussion of his design. Consider a pair of audit fee estimation models with a Big 8 auditor indicator included:

E1) $\textit{Audit Fees}_i = \text{constant} + \mathbf{b}_{\mathbf{kA}} \bullet \boldsymbol{\textit{control variables}}_i + b_{B8A} \bullet \textit{Big 8}_i + e_i$

E2) $\textit{Audit Fees}_j = \text{constant} + \mathbf{b}_{\mathbf{kB}} \bullet \boldsymbol{\textit{control variables}}_j + b_{B8B} \bullet \textit{Big 8}_j + e_j$

Where E1 is estimated audit fees for all clients (sample **A**) while E2 estimates audit fees only for clients that are small enough to be audited by a non-Big 8 firm (sample **B**, i.e., the small client sample).

The relationship of the estimated coefficients b_{B8A} and b_{B8B} (for the Big 8 indicator variable) can then be interpreted as follows:

R1) $b_{B8A} = 0$ and $b_{B8B} = 0$, implies the Big 8 audits are not priced differently from non-Big 8 audits, i.e., there is no fee premium in the market.

R2) $b_{B8A} > 0$ and $b_{B8B} > 0$, implies the Big 8 receive fee premia because they conduct superior audits, i.e., there is product differentiation in the market.

R3) $b_{B8A} > 0$ and $b_{B8B} = 0$, implies the Big 8 receive fee premia because of potential monopolistic pricing (earning economic rents), which disappears in the small client market, i.e., when audits are competitively priced.

By assumption A1, if $b_{B8A} > 0$ holds in E1, then this is evidence consistent with product differentiation. However, since Big 8 auditors hold a large share of the audit market, economic theory suggests that this result could also be due to monopolistic pricing. To disentangle the two possibilities, E2 is used to reflect assumption A3. Unlike the pooled sample (**A**), *all* the clients in **B** are auditable by either Big 8 or non-Big 8 auditors. The combination of a small client sample with A2 (i.e., non-Big 8 auditors priced competitively) assures that Big 8 auditors operating in the small client market (**B**) cannot charge monopoly prices because a client will simply hire a small audit firm and receive the same quality audit.

If R1 obtained, no Big 8 premium is detected and the literature would at that point have died (or gone into hibernation). Under R2, the evidence points toward the market differentiation hypothesis. The key is $b_{B8B} > 0$, in the small client sample. As noted above, Simunic argued this segment is competitive and, therefore, price premia can occur when a product is differentiated. If R3 occurred, the evidence swings toward the monopoly pricing hypothesis.

This follows since price premia only occur for the large client market (i.e., those clients in sample **A** but not **B**). Or, more succinctly, if the small clients of Big 8 auditors do not pay price premia but the large clients do, then it is not clear that audits are differentiated across the two groups of firms, otherwise the Big 8 should earn fee premia in both markets. This framework allows us to paraphrase the prolific nineteenth-century auditing researcher, S. Holmes: "Having eliminated the differentiation hypothesis, what remains must be a rent."

From the forest and into the weeds

Researchers have found audit fee models to be a useful tool for addressing a multitude of issues beyond the competitiveness of audit markets. Not surprisingly, a common economic structure underpins most of these studies and, as is evidenced by the empirical models E1 and E2 above, this structure can be opaque to the casual observer. It is not too difficult to get a sense of the unifying structure by tracing the "evolution" of the model from concept to empirical specification. Our version of these steps, with commentary, follows below.

M1a) Audit Fee = Audit Cost + Margin

Once again, Simunic 1980 did much of the heavy lifting. To ease the prior exposition we conveniently skated past how Simunic (and subsequent scholars) addressed the problems caused by the unobservability of audit costs. The initial step was to partition fees into audit costs and margin, as depicted in M1a. This partition was convenient for Simunic's research question since it adhered to the pertinent economic theory that implied competitive pricing could be tested against the profitability of audit suppliers. As fees are comprised of both costs and margin (or profits), he needed to control for costs in order to isolate the relationship between his experimental variable (a Big 8 indicator) and the cross-sectional variation in margins. Simply put, Simunic's empirical objective was to explain audit margins – but to do this he had to first model and then remove (control) the cost component from fees.

In principle, controlling for audit costs could be accomplished directly as shown in model M1b where, **w•h** denotes the inner product of the vector of wage rates (**w**) with the vector of audit hours by class of labor (**h**).

M1b) Audit Fee = **w•h** + Margin

This assumes fixed costs are of second order importance and, of course, requires **w** and **h** to be observable, an extravagantly rare luxury for an academic researcher. Without access to wages and hours a mapping from the observable data into unobserved costs must be conjured.

M2) Audit Fee = (Production Cost + Liability Cost) + Margin

A plausible mapping requires the researcher to specify both the functional form of the relationship and a candidate set of cost drivers. M2 can be thought of as a thought experiment in the quest of cost drivers. Here, audit costs are refined by the observation that audits are subject to an *ex post* settling up for negligent performance via litigation. With this in mind, Simunic reasoned that audit costs should be further partitioned into production costs and expected liability costs.

Comparing M1b and M2 we see that **w•h** corresponds to out-of-pocket production costs. Usefully, this highlights the fact that even if **w** and **h** were observable, a pure audit margin could not be calculated directly by (Fee – **w•h**). Nonetheless, the partitioning of audit costs into production costs and litigation costs proved fruitful in the literature as the auditing profession was in the throes of a long-lived obsession with legal liability. This was especially true in the US and spawned an academic research industry in its own right.

With a workable partition over fees in place, the hunt for potential cost drivers continues. Here M3, with its sudden hailstorm of notation, is of value. Formality aside, the intuition is that production costs, litigation costs, and margin (the unobserved constructs) can be expressed as functions of: client characteristics (**c**), the audit environment (**e**), the level of assurance or quality (q), and auditor technology (t).

M3) Audit Fee = k(**c**, q, t) + l(**c**, **e**, q, t) + m(**c**, **e**, q, t)

Referring to the roadmap, as the models evolve from abstract to specific the goal is for the researcher to obtain a set of relationships such as: k(**c**, q, t) ≈ **w•h** = production cost; l(**c**, **e**, q, t) ≈ liability cost; and m(**c**, **e**, q, t) ≈ margin. Importantly, **c**, **e**, q, t, represent observables that form the basis for estimating the unobserved constructs.

It is a fact of applied work that a complete specification of the model is beyond reach. Often elements of **e**, q, t, are left implicit in the model specification or handled through design or *ceteris paribus* assumptions rather than explicitly included in the model. IOHO, the desire to achieve "better" specifications can become something of a defensive fetish and many studies appear to compensate for deficiencies in the **e**, q, t, set with gluttonous servings from the **c** vector, leaving the resulting estimation snug to over-fit (see Babyak 2004 for a discussion of over-fitting problems in regression analysis) and, ironically, under-identified to boot – but we digress.

M4) Audit Fee = k(**c** = **{size**, **risk**, **complexity}**, q, t) + l(**c**{•}, **e**, q, t) + m(**c**{•}, **e**, q, t)

In M4 the helpful "size, risk, and complexity" meme is substituted for the vector, **c,** in M3. This substitution operationalizes guidance from professional audit practice that requires the scope of an audit program to fit the size, risk, and complexity of the client. From this perspective, observables such as the value of assets, degree of indebtedness, and the number of subsidiaries, among others, become the usual suspects to indenture in service of the estimation.

The development of M1a through M4 is an exercise in clarifying one's thinking. The overriding purpose is to solve the problem of unobserved audit costs by building a structure linking unobserved constructs to observable data. As always, it is important to be aware of the loose bolts in the scaffolding. In terms of econometric identification, it would be ideal if each of the observables could be uniquely linked to one of the partitions. For example, the level of client assets is usually assigned to production costs by the researcher and treated as a nuisance variable, even though it could be argued that client size contributes to all of the partitions, as denoted by the above notation. The concerns narrow upon the proper interpretation of the estimation results rather than model specification *per se*. To see this point, take the estimation of b_1 (the coefficient on client assets) in M5.

M5) $\ln(\textit{Audit Fees}_i) = b_0 + b_1 \ln(\textit{assets}_i) + \Sigma\, b_j\, \textit{controls}_{ji} + \Sigma\, b_k\, \textit{experimental}_{ki} + e_i$

If the researcher's purpose is to control for total audit costs, then the classification of client assets as a production cost rather than as a litigation cost is an error of the "no harm, no foul" variety. On the other hand, if the purpose of a study is to determine the impact of litigation risk in general on fees and that risk is measured by a specific experimental variable, then treating client assets as a control for audit costs may not be innocent. Suppose client size is a factor affecting litigation risk. This could happen if lawyers prefer to litigate when total losses are large. In this scenario, the relationship between fees and size is partly due to audit production and partly due to litigation risk. The net effect would be for the coefficient on the experimental variable to understate the cost of litigation risk on fees. It is doubtful whether empirical tests can be designed to avoid this type of problem altogether, but it is another reminder of why researchers should carefully run through their identification arguments as they construct their models.

The step from M4 to M5 is where, hopefully, the chrysalis becomes a butterfly and where many published papers appear to start the process. M5 is the standard formulation for audit fee or audit hour models. It is the log-linear form of the following natural units model:

$$\text{M6a)}\ \textit{Audit Fees}_i = e^{b_0 + \sum b_j \textit{controls}_{ji} + \sum b_k \textit{experimental}_{ki} + e_i}\, \textit{assets}_i^{\,b_1}$$

$$\text{M6b)}\ \textit{Audit Fees}_i = e^{b_0} e^{\sum b_j \textit{controls}_{ji}} e^{\sum b_k \textit{experimental}_{ki}} e^{e_i}\, \textit{assets}_i^{\,b_1}$$

While M5 is the most common formulation of the audit fee model used in estimation, the dependent variable is ln(*Audit Fees*). M6a or M6b is the equivalent model in terms of *Audit Fees*. It is helpful for researchers to refer to the natural unit model as a check on the sensibility of proposed innovations in the specification as well as in applications where it is important to assess economic along with statistical significance.

The real value of M6a or M6b is what is revealed about the functional relationships estimated by the M5 specification. First, the model is multiplicative in the explanatory variables. This implies that the marginal effect of any independent variable depends upon the level of the other independent variables in the model. This suggests that the slope parameters might be thought of as fee elasticities, but care is required as this interpretation is strictly true only if a full log-log model (e.g., log-linearized Cobb-Douglas) is estimated. To clarify these issues let us create a bare boned version of M5 and M6b where audit fees are a function of assets and another factor creatively labeled, *var*:

$$\text{M5}\star)\ \ln(\textit{Audit Fees}_i) = b_0 + b_1 \ln(\textit{assets}_i) + b_2\, \textit{var}_i$$

$$\text{M6b}\star)\ \textit{Audit Fees}_i = e^{b_0} e^{\,b_2\, \textit{var}_i}\, \textit{assets}_i^{\,b_1}$$

For M5⋆ the marginal effects are straightforward to calculate, but the derivatives are taken w.r.t. ln(*Audit Fees*) and not *Audit Fees*. We fix this by using M6b⋆; here the derivatives can be taken w.r.t. *Audit Fees* and are:

$$\partial \textit{Audit Fees}/\partial \textit{var} = b_2\, e^{b_0}\, e^{\,b_2\, \textit{var}}\, \textit{assets}^{b_1} = b_2\, \textit{AuditFees}$$

$$\partial \textit{Audit Fees}/\partial \textit{assets} = b_1\, \textit{assets}^{b_1 - 1} e^{b_0} e^{\,b_2\, \textit{var}} = b_1\, \textit{AuditFees}/\textit{assets}$$

As can be seen, the marginal effects w.r.t. *Audit Fees* are a bit complicated as the coefficients are multiplied by the level of the fee itself. As a practical matter we find it helpful to view the coefficient on *assets*, b_1 (typically found to be in the range [.25, .6]), as defining the curvature of the fundamental nonlinear relationship between fees and assets and the other coefficients as scaling factors. For instance, if in a simple M5 type estimation the coefficient on the Big 8 indicator variable were estimated as .10, then we could compare the expected fees when Big 8 = 1 with when Big 8 = 0 as:

$$AuditFees_{B8=1} = e^{b_0}\, e^{0.1\bullet 1} assets^{b_1} \text{ and } AuditFees_{B8=0} = e^{b_0}\, e^{0.1\bullet 0} assets^{b_1}$$

Now taking the ratio of these outcomes and simplifying we get:

$$AuditFees_{B8=1} \,/\, AuditFees_{B8=0} = e^{0.1} / e^{0}$$

or about 1.105, an increase of 10.5 percent. The point, of course, is that the marginal effect is multiplicative rather than additive and, as a result, the marginal effect scales with the size of the client.

Audit fees: Odds and ends

In applied work, estimation follows M5 and usually relies upon cross-sectional (one observation per client in a given calendar year) or, occasionally, panel data. If the latter then time-period fixed effects are included. Frequently, indicator variables are included in the model as either controls (e.g., client industry fixed effects) or experimental variables (e.g., Big 4 auditor, industry specialist, etc.). Natural indicator variables such as a Big 4 versus non-Big 4 auditor predictor pose no particular problem, though indicator variables derived by splitting continuous variables (such as an industry specialist dummy based on a continuous auditor market share measure) may be another story. Work by methodologists in psychology, for instance, suggests that the standard t-tests can reject the null too frequently for the stated level of Type I risk (see MacCallum *et al.* 2002). As far as we know this issue is yet to be addressed in the empirical accounting and auditing literature.

While the original Simunic study scaled fees by the square root of assets, it is standard practice to take the natural log of the continuous variables, *Audit Fees* and (client) *assets*. Other continuous variables are often used untransformed, but scaled continuous variables are sometimes winsorized by researchers, especially if they are based upon ratios or residuals from a first stage regression (e.g., discretionary accruals). Taking the logs of fees or hours and assets captures the nonlinearity between audit effort and client size inherent in the sampling nature of auditing. This data transformation also reduces, though does not eliminate, the heteroskedasticity found in the data and most researchers apply further techniques to correct the estimated standard errors. Estimated residuals from the model are often fat-tailed (platykurtic) relative to the assumed normal distribution, but this fact, when it occurs, is normally treated with a broom and floor covering.

Before leaving the topic of the nonlinearity of the audit fee model, it is sometimes useful to remember that researchers mostly assume that ln(*Audit Fees*) are normally distributed random variables, i.e., ln(*Audit Fees*) ~ N(μ, σ). This implies that *Audit Fees* ~ LogNormal(μ, σ) and, importantly,

$$E[AuditFees] = e^{\mu+\sigma/2} \text{ and } Var[AuditFees] = e^{2\mu+\sigma^2/2}(e^{\sigma^2}-1)$$

where, μ = E[ln(*Audit Fee$_i$*) | *assets$_i$*, ***controls$_{ji}$***, *experimental$_{ki}$*)] and σ is the standard error of the estimate from the regression. If the M5 results are transformed into *Audit Fees* it may be the case that the adjustment, $\sigma/2$, to expected ln(*Audit Fees*) is not large enough to be of economic significance. However, since the fundamental model of fees such as M6b is concave, Jensen's inequality holds and E[ln(*Audit Fees*)] $\leq$ ln(E[*Audit Fees*]). As a consequence, exponentiating the predicted ln(*Audit Fee*) from an M5 estimation results in a (usually slight) underestimate of the actual predicted fee.

In some situations the model may not fit very well and a good place to seek answers is the measurement of audit scale used in the sample. The intuition is simple; client size has been demonstrated to be by far and away the most important driver of audit production costs, so if the model is not performing well (low R^2) then it is likely the size measure is at fault. Several possibilities to investigate are: i) lack of variance, ii) poor choice of proxy, and iii) audit environment. The lack of variance problem occurs when a sample or subsample encompasses a limited range of assets, as for instance in a study of the clients of small audit firms. The econometric problem is that there is insufficient information to obtain a precise estimate for the coefficient on client assets. The poor choice of proxy concern is one of the reasons that many empirical fee studies exclude financial institutions from their sample. It is accepted that the audit requirements for, say, $1 billion in financial assets is quite different from the audit of an equal value of real assets. As a result, client assets are an inconsistent proxy for the scale of an audit in a pooled sample of financial and non-financial clients. Similarly, the market value of the client's equity can be a poor choice of proxy for scale since audits are not designed to verify market value *per se* – even though there is some support for the use of market volatility as a risk measure, it is a second order effect relative to scale. Audit environment considerations can occasionally play a role in the usefulness of client size as a scale measure. In low auditor business risk environments, auditors may have little incentive to provide more than a perfunctory audit, regardless of the client's size, risk, and complexity. In such environments client size tends to explain only a small proportion of the audit fee and this is reflected in the overall fit of the model.

Numerous studies address the impact of auditing on one set of clients versus another set, as chosen by the researcher. Such analyses often must cope with concerns of either selection or self-selection bias. To keep the discussion from becoming too abstract, suppose a study proposes to test whether the clients of specialist auditors pay a fee premium relative to non-specialist auditors. Further, allow that client inherent risks are not fully measured by the researcher. Econometrically, if the client risks across the two types of auditors are distinct, then estimation of the fee premium potentially suffers from selection bias (included among the rogues' gallery of regression problems caused when the error term is not conditionally independent). In the face of significant selection bias, it is unclear whether the estimated value of the specialist premium is due to a causal relationship with the included specialist measure or an artifact due to a correlation between the specialist measure and the unmeasured client risk.

Labor economists have proposed a number of techniques for coping with selection bias problems (instrumental variables, natural experiments, and Heckman's two-step model are the most prominent), and some of these have spilled over into the auditing literature. It turns out (spoiler alert), however, that applied audit researchers, like applied economists, struggle to find data that satisfy the conditions necessary for identification. In the above example, the Holy Grail would be an observable variable that strongly influences the choice of a specialist or non-specialist auditor, but has no direct impact on audit fees. Specifying such a set of valid exclusion restrictions has proven to be stubbornly resistant to researchers' efforts … none come to our minds either.

Many researchers (far more than are listed below) have contributed to the development of the audit fee model. The model was primarily formulated as reported in the study by Simunic 1980. Additional refinements within a variety of contexts were added by early contributors such as Francis 1984; Simon 1985; Francis and Stokes 1986; among others. Competition and product differentiation issues were looked at early on by Simunic and Stein 1987; Carcello *et al.* 1992; Pearson and Trompeter 1994. Among the limited number of audit hour studies are: Palmrose 1989; Davis *et al.* 1993; O'Keefe *et al.* 1994; Dopuch *et al.* 2003; Blokdijk *et al.* 2006; Bell *et al.* 2008. Craswell *et al.* 1995 let the genie out of the specialization bottle, and Ireland and Lennox 2002 comment upon selection bias issues. Hay *et al.* 2006 provide a meta-analysis of the literature and their study is a useful source of control and experimental variables.

A few words about audit production models

At the moment two branches of the fee literature focusing on archival audit production are ongoing. The older and more extensive branch is a continuation of the earlier models, but with the explicit goal of identifying new factors that influence audit fees and, presumably, audit costs. The smaller, second branch utilizes data on auditor hours to address either the estimation of audit production functions or comparative audit efficiency.

This first branch is characterized by research that rarely tests a tightly motivated economic theory, but rather seeks to identify additional variables, $newvar_{ki}$, associated with audit fees. Many of these studies are motivated by efforts to more effectively measure the risk or complexity faced by the auditor. Other studies in this vein focus on environmental factors that influence audit production, e.g., the existence of outside directors or changes in generally accepted auditing standards (GAAS). It is infrequently, if ever, argued that these new factors introduce cross-sectional variation in the profitability of audits. To connect this literature to our earlier models let us start with M1b and rewrite it in multiplicative form (markup as a percentage of direct cost) to arrive at M7, below. To keep things manageable we simplify the vector **h** to be a scalar, h (say, total audit hours), and then substitute M6b into M7. To link the literatures, we use the audit hours version of M6b rather than the audit fees version. Finally, after rearranging terms we get M8. A prime distinguishes coefficients estimated in the auditor hours model from those estimated in the audit fees model.

M1b) $\textit{Audit Fees} = \mathbf{w} \bullet \mathbf{h} + \text{Margin}$

M7) $\textit{Audit Fees} = \mathbf{w} \bullet \mathbf{h} \bullet (1 + \text{Margin\%}) = \text{M}(\mathbf{w} \bullet \mathbf{h})$

M8) $$\begin{aligned}\textit{Audit Fees} &= \text{M}(\text{w} \bullet \text{h}) = \text{M w} \bullet e^{b'_0} e^{\sum b'_j \, controls_j} e^{\sum b'_k \, newvar_k} \, assets^{b'_1} \\ &= \Omega \bullet e^{b'_0} e^{\sum b'_j \, controls_j} e^{\sum b'_k \, newvar_k} \, assets^{b'_1} \\ &= \Omega \bullet \text{h}(\textbf{\textit{controls}}, \textbf{\textit{newvars}}, \textit{assets})\end{aligned}$$

The algebraic calisthenics yield (i) a relationship between $newvars_k$ and *Audit Fees* and (ii) an interpretation of the model. As can be seen, M8 breaks into two multiplicative components: Ω, a constant "price" consisting of margin and the (average) wage rate; and a factor, h(•), representing the total hours required to produce the audit. If we specialize M8 to *Audit Fees* = f(*control, newvar, assets*) and take the derivative of *Audit Fees* w.r.t. *newvar*, then:

$$\partial \textit{Audit Fees}/\partial \textit{newvar} = b'_2 \bullet \Omega \bullet e^{b'_0} e^{b'_3 \, control} \, e^{b'_2 \, newvar} \, assets^{b'_1} = \Omega \bullet b'_2 \, \text{h}(\bullet)$$

where b'_2 is the estimated coefficient on the proposed factor, *newvar*. If there is a non-zero effect, then an interpretation is that the factor changes effort by b'_2 h(•). Multiplying by price, Ω, provides the effect upon fees.

In practice, studies in this branch of research usually start with the investigator asserting that a new factor or variable is important to audit production. Then, lacking access to audit hour data, the researcher designs a study to test whether the new factor is correlated with the audit fee charged by auditors. The study produces an estimate of the coefficient, b_2. Now by M8 the audit fee and audit hour equations differ by the multiplicative constant, Ω, therefore b_2 in the audit fee model provides an estimate of b'_2 in the audit hour model.

The second, and newest, branch of the audit production literature relies upon scarce audit hour data to directly measure audit production or production characteristics. A limited number of studies, e.g., Dopuch *et al.* 2003, have applied stochastic frontier analysis (SFE) or data envelope analysis (DEA) (Charnes *et al.* 1981) to calculate an efficiency score for each observation in a sample of audits. Stochastic frontier estimation is a variant of OLS (ordinary least squares) in which it is conjectured that the error consists of two components: a noise term and an asymmetric efficiency term. The efficiency component is asymmetric, since inefficient production can have only positive errors (too many hours). Using maximum likelihood the efficiency parameter is modeled and estimated. A practical difficulty encountered by researchers using SFE is that the method requires a relatively high signal to noise ratio to pick out inefficient production. If inefficiencies account for only a small amount of the residual variance in an hour model then the estimates of inefficiency are likely to be unreliable.

DEA models are based on linear programming techniques and are typically implemented within a deterministic framework. The DEA algorithm (of which there are many variants) uses input–output analysis to generate an efficient frontier (convex hull) for a given sample of audits. Observations that lie off the efficient frontier on all input–output dimensions are assigned a less than fully efficient rating. Unlike SFE, the DEA method does not normally include a provision for random error and so all variation from efficient production is allocated to inefficiency. Another difference between the two measures is that DEA can accommodate multiple outputs (dependent variables in regression models). This can be helpful in an auditing context where the input–output relationships may be specified as vectors of audited client characteristics (outputs) and vectors of auditor effort by type of labor (inputs). Since the DEA is not a causal model, the labeling of inputs and outputs is not as crucial as it is in most econometric approaches. Therefore, the input–output relationship can be determined by the researcher either to facilitate the research question or as a matter of convenience.

Regardless of technique, efficiency analysis has thus far been implemented in two steps. First, either DEA or SFE is applied to the sample in order to determine the technical audit efficiency parameter. In DEA this parameter is referred to as *theta*, and we will proceed from a DEA perspective to facilitate discussion, though one could easily adopt the SFE language. In the plain vanilla version of DEA, *theta* falls in the range [0, 1]. A fully efficient observation receives a 1 and *theta* < 1 indicates some level of inefficiency. *theta* can be interpreted as the extent that inputs would have to be shrunk in order for the audit to lie on the efficient frontier, relative to the benchmark efficient audits. An audit with a *theta* score of 85% would meet the efficient frontier if inputs were reduced by (1 – .85 =) 15%.

In to date efficiency studies it is usually assumed that audit quality is constant within each sample. If audit quality varies within a sample then higher quality audits are likely to be less "efficient" than are lower quality audits, given a positive relationship between quality and audit effort. Once an efficiency measure is obtained, then it is added to an extended audit fee model in the second stage. One would expect audit fees to decrease in efficiency. That is, since efficient audits use fewer hours some level of costs savings is likely to be passed on to the client. The finding of lower fees associated with higher levels of efficiency has been taken to validate the efficiency measure. Of course, audit practitioners and, perhaps, regulators would be more interested in such questions as: Can the efficiency measure be used as an indicator of audit quality? Or is there an association between efficiency and alternative approaches to audit programs (e.g., tests of controls versus tests of details)? The answers await future research.

The future

All in all, at this point empirical audit fee modeling has the appearance of a mature technology. Future innovations are likely to be driven by the availability of new data sets and by changes to the relevant institutional setting. For example, the arrival of combined cross-section and time-series data sets of audit fees offers the potential to explore questions not convincingly addressed in cross-section alone. Also, the continuous evolution of auditing regulation and the competitive environment of auditing markets constantly provide motivation for new studies that quantify the impact of these changes. In terms of the technology used to implement fee and production research, open questions remain regarding the identification of proxy variables, the adequacy of methods used to address selection (and self-selection) bias, and the homogeneity of these models across time, markets, and audit provider.

Notes

1 See http://en.wikipedia.org/wiki/Industrial_organization#Structure.2C_conduct.2C_performance (accessed 5 May 2014).

2 Premium fees represent an economic rent in this context. For the definition of an economic rent see http://en.wikipedia.org/wiki/Economic_rents (accessed 5 May 2014).

References

Babyak, M. A. 2004. "What You See May Not Be What You Get: A Brief, Nontechnical Introduction to Overfitting in Regression-type Models", *Psychosomatic Medicine* 66(3): 411–21.

Bell, T. B., R. Doogar and I. Solomon. 2008. "Audit Labor Usage and Fees under Business Risk Auditing", *Journal of Accounting Research* 46(4): 729–60.

Blokdijk, H., F. Drieenhuizen, D. A. Simunic and M. T. Stein. 2006. "An Analysis of Cross-sectional in Big and Non-Big Public Accounting Firms' Programs", *Auditing: A Journal of Practice and Theory* 25(1): 27–48.

Carcello, J. V., R. H. Hermanson and N. T. McGrath. 1992. "Audit Quality Attributes: The Perceptions of Audit Partners, Preparers, and Financial Statement Users", *Auditing: A Journal of Practice and Theory* 11(1): 1–15.

Charnes, A., W. W. Cooper and E. Rhodes. 1981. "Evaluating Program and Managerial Efficiency: An Application of Data Envelopment Analysis to Program Follow through", *Management Science* 27(6): 668–97.

Craswell, A., J. Francis and S. Taylor. 1995. "Auditor Brand Name Reputation and Industry Specialization", *Journal of Accounting and Economics* 20(3): 297–322.

Davis, L. R., D. N. Ricchiute and G. Trompeter. 1993. "Audit Effort, Audit Fees, and the Provision of Nonaudit Services to Audit Clients", *The Accounting Review* 68(1): 135–50.

Dopuch, N., M. Gupta, D. A. Simunic and M. T. Stein. 2003. "Production Efficiency and the Pricing of Audit Services", *Contemporary Accounting Research* 20(1): 47–77.

Francis, J. R. 1984. "The Effect of Audit Firm Size on Audit Prices: A Study of the Australian Market", *Journal of Accounting and Economics* 6(2): 133–51.

Francis, J. R. and D. Stokes. 1986. "Audit Prices, Product Differentiation, and Scale Economies: Further Evidence from the Australian Market", *Journal of Accounting Research* 24(2): 383–93.

Hay, D., W. R. Knechel and N. Wong. 2006. "Audit Fees: A Meta-analysis of the Effect of Supply and Demand Attributes", *Contemporary Accounting Research* 23(1): 141–92.

Ireland, J. C. and C. S. Lennox. 2002. "The Large Audit Fee Premium: A Case of Selectivity Bias?", *Journal of Accounting, Auditing and Finance* 17(1): 73–91.

MacCallum, R. C., S. Zhang, K. J. Preacher and D. D. Rucker. 2002. "On the Practice of Dichotomization of Quantitative Variables", *Psychological Methods* 7(1): 19.

O'Keefe, T. B., D. A. Simunic and M. T. Stein. 1994. "The Production of Audit Services: Evidence from a Major Public Accounting Firm", *Journal of Accounting Research* 32(2): 241–61.

Palmrose, Z. 1989. "The Relation of Audit Contract Type to Audit Fees and Hours", *The Accounting Review* 64(3): 488–99.

Pearson, T. and G. Trompeter. 1994. "Competition in the Market for Audit Services: The Effect of Supplier Concentration on Audit Fees", *Contemporary Accounting Research* 11(1): 91–114.

Simon, D. T. 1985. "The Audit Services Market: Additional Empirical Evidence", *Auditing: A Journal of Practice and Theory* 5(1): 71–8.

Simunic, D. A. 1980. "The Pricing of Audit Services: Theory and Evidence", *Journal of Accounting Research* 22(3): 161–90.

Simunic, D. and M. Stein. 1987. *Product Differentiation in Auditing: Auditor Choice in the Market for Unseasoned New Issues*. Vancouver, BC: Canadian Certified General Accountants Research Foundation.

Part IV

Issues concerned with audit reporting

23
Audit reports

Paul Coram

Overview of the topic and its importance

For the vast majority of financial statements users, the auditor's report is *the only tangible evidence of the audit process*. As such, it should provide valuable information to them on what the auditor has done and how this assurance enhances the reliability of the associated financial reports. The audit process is briefly presented in Figure 23.1.

The auditor's report is a fairly standard document to report to users on the outcome of the audit process. Although there have been changes over the years the basic structure of the auditor's report is fairly consistent, as follows:

- Title. States that the work was done by an independent auditor and is usually addressed to shareholders of the company.
- Scope. In this part of the auditor's report what was done is described as well as clarification of management and auditor's responsibilities. Included here will be the statement that "sufficient appropriate audit evidence" has been obtained to form the audit opinion.
- Opinion. The auditor gives an opinion on whether the financial report presents fairly in all material respects in accordance with the financial-reporting framework. (Note: In some jurisdictions such as the UK and Australia the term "true and fair view" is used for public companies.)[1]

The audit opinion is modified when the auditor concludes that the financial statements are not free from material misstatement based on the evidence obtained, or that sufficient appropriate audit evidence cannot be obtained. In either of these two circumstances where the misstatements or possible misstatements are material the auditor issues a qualified opinion. However, if the matter is material and *pervasive* to the financial statements the auditor issues an adverse opinion (when evidence is available) or disclaimer of opinion (when the evidence is not available).[2] If there are particular issues that are important to users' understanding of the financial statements or the auditor's report, the auditor includes an "emphasis of matter" paragraph in the auditor's report. This paragraph is not part of the audit opinion.[3] Although jurisdictions may differ

Management is responsible for the fair presentation of the financial statements. This implicitly involves making a number of assertions about the transactions and balances in the accounts, for example: whether they occurred and exist; whether they are complete; and whether they are appropriately calculated and valued.

↓

The audit process is to obtain sufficient appropriate audit evidence to validate the assertions made by management implicit in their statement on the fair presentation of the financial statements.

↓

The auditor's report provides an opinion on whether the financial statements present fairly, in all material respects, in accordance with the applicable financial reporting framework.

↓

Those for whom the auditor's report is prepared (usually the shareholders) can use the financial statement information with reasonable assurance that it is free of material misstatement.

Figure 23.1 The audit process

slightly, the above description of the auditor's report is consistent for most countries using International Standards on Auditing (ISA) and for the US.

There is a significant amount of evidence that shows the auditor's report is an important signal to users of financial statements. Archival research has also shown that users evaluate the quality of auditing by using surrogates such as auditor size, brand, or reputation. An overall evaluation of this research concludes the quality of auditing is high.[4] In relation to whether users determine the quality of the auditor's report through actually reading the auditor's report – it does not seem this is commonly done. Most people (including sophisticated financial statement users) have only a limited knowledge of what an auditor does and do not appear to focus much attention on the actual content of the auditor's report. Behavioral research in evaluating why this is the case has found that the "boilerplate"[5] structure of the auditor's report is the main reason why it does not provide much communicative value.

The importance of the audit function and an appropriate auditor's report to communicate the audit work should not be understated. The audit profession provides an important societal role and the communicative problems that contribute to the audit expectations gap undermine this role. Accounting regulators and professional bodies have come to a broad consensus that significant improvements to the auditor's report are necessary to deal with this issue.

Current issues in this topic area

Since the global financial crisis of 2008, there has been renewed attention on the value of the audit and also on how the auditor's report might be improved. Historically, the common way in which the accounting profession has attempted to deal with this problem has been to provide more description in the auditor's report of what an audit is, in an attempt to improve users' understanding and therefore reduce the expectations gap. The problem is that these efforts have been for the most part unsuccessful in improving the communicative value of the auditor's report.

Recent proposed changes have taken a more radical approach to improving the auditor's report so that it more clearly explains what is provided to users by an audit, and also provides information that users will perceive as having value in their evaluation of financial statements. Internationally, there have been a number of different proposals and reports to address this issue. In response to perceived deficiencies in the auditor's report, the Technical Committee of the International Organization of Securities Commissions (IOSCO) prepared a report that evaluated these perceived deficiencies and considered possible solutions, as well as advantages and disadvantages of the various alternatives for comment and discussion (IOSCO 2009). The Public Company Accounting Oversight Board (PCAOB) started a process in 2010 to consider improvements to the audit reporting model. In 2011 they issued a concept release to seek public comment on proposed changes to the auditor's reporting model (PCAOB 2011). They received a significant response to this release, which represented a diverse range of views and in 2013 they were still in the process of considering the development of a proposal for public comment. In 2011 the European Commission (EC 2011) proposed wide ranging changes to the auditor's reporting model through legislation. However, in September 2012 a counterproposal to limit these changes was put forward.

The International Auditing and Assurance Standards Board (IAASB) issued an Invitation to Comment in June 2012 on suggested changes to the auditor's report, significant changes were proposed in July 2013 when the IAASB issued an Exposure Draft titled *Reporting on Audited Financial Statements: Proposed New and Revised International Standards on Auditing (ISAs).* One of the main proposals in this Exposure Draft is for the auditor to report on key audit matters in the auditor's report. Key audit matters are those which in the auditor's professional judgment are most significant in the audit of the financial statements for the current period. They will be selected from the matters communicated by the auditor to those charged with governance and the auditor should consider: matters that are identified as significant risks; areas where the auditor had significant difficulties; or circumstances which required a change in approach, e.g., significant deficiency in internal control. The auditor should also provide insight as to why the issue was selected as a key audit matter.

Another significant change is that the auditor will be required to report on going concern. In a separate paragraph of the auditor's report, a statement will be required that includes a conclusion on which as part of the audit management's use of the going concern basis of accounting is appropriate. The main final proposed changes are that the auditor will need to include an explicit statement of auditor independence, the source of relevant ethical requirements, and disclosure of the name of the audit partner.[6]

In summary, the auditor's reporting model is currently the subject of significant re-evaluation by the profession and regulators. This provides a great opportunity for research to help inform deliberations and assist with the ongoing development of the auditor's reporting model.

Historical development

Auditing, and consequently audit reporting, has a long history. For over a thousand years there is evidence of auditing emerging where ownership is separated from control of organizations (Watts and Zimmerman 1983). Wherever auditing has occurred there is of course a need for a report to relevant parties and historically this was some type of certification to the owners or shareholders. There was however quite a length of time between the first regulation of audits in the English Joint Stock Companies Act of 1844 and the first regulation to specify what was to be contained in an auditor's report.

The first attempt to standardize the auditor's report occurred in 1917 in the United States, with a bulletin from the Federal Reserve which was not widely followed. However, the first regulated auditor's reports in a form that would be recognizable today emerged in 1934 from the American Institute of Accountants and the New York Stock Exchange. This report was similar to the *Statement on Auditing Procedure No. 24: Revision in Short-Form Accountant's Report of Certificate* issued in 1948. This report consisted of a scope paragraph and an opinion paragraph. Both paragraphs referred to GAAP (generally accepted accounting principles) and the first scope paragraph included the fairly general comment that such tests as were considered necessary should be performed. The auditor's report as developed about this time remained fairly similar for many years, and similar formats were developed and used in many other countries around the world.

It was not until the 1980s that there was a concerted effort to change the auditor's report. This was due partially to the greater prominence of the audit "expectations gap" at the time, as well as a response to the findings of the 1978 Cohen Commission, which recommended several areas where communication from the auditor to the user could be improved.[7] Although not following all of the recommendations of the Cohen Commission, this process resulted in an auditor's report (Statement on Auditing Standards (SAS) 58 *Reports on Audited Financial Statements* (AICPA 1988)) which included the following enhancements:

- description of core audit concepts
- explanation of the different roles of management and auditors.

Following this, the International Auditing Practices Committee (forerunner to the IAASB) issued ISA 700 in 1993 which was based on SAS 58 with only a few minor differences.

In 2005 international standard setters led the next major change to the auditor's report with the new ISA 700: *The Independent Auditor's Report on a Complete Set of General Purpose Financial Statements.* This has been described as an "expanded audit report" and included a number of new improvements to "enhance understanding of the auditor's role and auditor's report", including:

- a greater discussion of auditors' responsibilities
- a note that ethical requirements have been complied with
- a note that the audit evidence obtained is "sufficient and appropriate" to provide a basis for the audit opinion
- an explanation as to why the auditor evaluates internal control.

Again, these changes did not add anything to the auditor's responsibilities, as they were more associated with further explanation of the audit process and they remained standard wordings. The fact that this might be an issue in improving the communicative value of auditor's reports had been identified back in 1978 by the Cohen Commission Report where it was stated:

> One effect of using a standard report is that as a person becomes familiar with its words, he tends to stop reading it each time he sees it. … The entire report comes to be interpreted as a single, although complex, symbol that is no longer read.
>
> *(Cohen Commission 1978: 73)*

As outlined in the previous section of this chapter, "Current issues in this topic area", there has been a recent worldwide push by regulators and standard setters for a new approach to the auditor's report. Two of the main reasons are: (1) it has been quite apparent that previous attempts to improve the auditor's report have not been particularly successful; (2) the global financial crisis again increased the focus on auditing which has also made it important for changes to be brought in to improve the communicative value of the auditor's report. A consistent theme is that the various proposed changes are a significant rethink on what should be in an auditor's report, and these changes are consistent with the findings of the research that suggests that more information about the audit that was conducted would be of value to financial statement users.

Summary of current state of research findings

The research can be categorized as follows: the value of auditor's reports; users' evaluation of existing auditor's reports; and users' evaluation of possible new auditor's report disclosures.

The value of auditor's reports

The value of auditor's reports is difficult to disentangle from the value of having an audit *per se*. Watts and Zimmerman (1983) took a historical perspective to look back to before audits were mandated, and found that they occurred naturally in circumstances where there was a separation of ownership and control, providing evidence that audit reports have value. A study by Blackwell *et al.* (1998) examined a situation where auditing was voluntary for private companies and found that debt pricing was cheaper for those companies who chose to be audited, again showing the value of auditing. Another way of looking at the value of auditing is to look at audit quality. A review by Francis (2004) provides evidence, through a low level of audit failures (less than 1 percent) and through a variety of other metrics, that the audit process on balance is of high quality. In summary, archival literature provides some evidence of the value of having an audit, however, there is little in this research to inform us about the use of the content of auditor's reports.

One way in which the actual value of the content of an auditor's report can be disentangled by archival research is when the auditor's report is *different* – under these circumstances researchers can evaluate the differences and therefore assess the value of such reports. The main circumstances where this can occur relate to auditors issuing an auditor's report modified for going concern reasons; and the research findings in this area have been quite mixed (see literature synthesis by Carson *et al.* 2013). One possible reason for these mixed findings is because there is little value to the market in the going concern modified auditor's report once this underlying information is disclosed in the financial statements or through other sources. However, Carson *et al.* (2013) note that studies that examine "unexpected" going concern reports do find significant negative reactions; but this research does not help with examining the incremental value of the content of unmodified auditor's reports.

Users' evaluation of existing auditor's reports

Research on the actual evaluation of unmodified auditor's reports is mainly through behavioral research methods. As well as the difficulty noted in the previous subsection of this chapter, "The value of auditor's reports", regarding disentangling the value of the auditor's report from having an audit *per se*, there is also a problem in that users' perceptions are difficult to measure through market level studies.

A recent focus group study by Gray *et al.* (2011) comprised a variety of user groups. They found that: (1) the intended communications from an unqualified auditor's report[8] are not particularly clear to preparers, users, and auditors; (2) users have difficulty understanding key concepts in the auditor's report; and (3) users do not read the auditor's report, instead they merely check it to ascertain whether or not it is unqualified. They also noted that another issue that is usually evaluated by users is whether or not the audit was performed by a Big 4 auditor; this has been extensively studied in the archival literature as an important signal of quality (Francis 2004).

Experimental research has tried to evaluate how successful have been some of the changes to the auditor's report in improving its communicative value and potentially reducing the expectations gap. The first main research on the evaluation of existing auditors' reports emerged from changes in the US that arrived through SAS 58 in 1988. Derivatives of this report were implemented in other jurisdictions (including ISA 700 in 1993) so that a significant amount of research internationally examined these changes. In the US, Kelly and Mohrweis (1989) examined bankers' and investors' perceptions of the old and "new" auditors' reports and found that understandability about the purposes of the audit was increased. However, bankers actually perceived auditors to have less responsibility due to the expanded disclosures. Miller *et al.* (1993) performed an experiment with bank loan officers and found that the new disclosures on auditors' and managers' roles were better identified by these users. However, users' misperceptions on fraud and the scope of the audit remained unchanged.

In the UK, Hatherly *et al.* (1991) examined through an experiment with MBA students whether the new auditor's report reduced the expectations gap. They found the expanded auditor's report had an effect on perceptions in most of the areas that it directly addressed. However, they also found the expanded auditor's report increased perceptions that: the auditor is satisfied with the financial statements; the company is free of fraud; and the audit adds credibility to the financial statements. These issues were not addressed in the expanded auditor's report and they describe this finding as a "halo effect".[9] In Australia, Monroe and Woodliff (1994) compared the old to the new auditor's report across a number of different user groups and also included auditors. They found that the expectations gap did decrease in some of the areas addressed by the wording changes, such as on auditors' and managers' roles. However, consistent with the idea of a "halo effect", the gap actually increased because of the new auditor's report on some of the areas which are not the responsibility of auditors, such as whether the auditor should prevent fraud and evaluate the future prospects of the company. The research evidence showed that these changes to the auditor's report had a mixed effect on users' perceptions.

Changes to the auditor's report through further expansion of the wording were again made internationally with the issuance of ISA 700 (IAASB 2005). In Australia, Chong and Pflugrath (2008) experimentally evaluated whether the changes reduced the expectations gap or not by examining perceptions of shareholders and auditors. Consistent with previous research the changes did not reduce the expectations gap and in actual fact there were more perception differences with the longer form report. In Germany, Gold *et al.* (2012) conducted an experiment of users and auditors to assess the changes from the expanded disclosures in ISA 700. They also found a persistent expectations gap with regards to the auditor's responsibilities despite the changes.

In summary, from these representative studies into auditor's report changes across different time periods and across different countries, it is clear that increasing explanations in the auditor's report is not the solution if the objective is to reduce the expectations gap.

Users' evaluation of possible new auditor's report disclosures

One way of eliciting perceptions on possible new disclosures is through surveying users and this has been mainly achieved through professional organizations. A report by the Audit Quality Forum (2007) surveyed investors and noted some of the following ideas where more information would be useful: material issues encountered during the audit; tailored rather than standard auditor's reports; and more information on material area of judgment, and difficult or sensitive areas. More recently, a survey of members of the CFA Institute (2010) found 60 percent of users want more information about the audit process and 57 percent want more information about the audited entity. These viewpoints from investors are consistent with investors' comments issued by the PCAOB in 2011 on the concept release to change the auditor's report, where it was noted that they strongly supported the proposed changes to the report.

Other ways to evaluate changes are to look at jurisdictions where changes have occurred and then evaluate their effectiveness. In the US there have been changes relating to the provision of internal control opinions by auditors under Section 404 of the Sarbanes-Oxley Act (SOX). Research has found SOX internal control reporting decreases in the information risk to investors (Ashbaugh-Skaife *et al.* 2009). This is consistent with findings of the focus group paper by Gray *et al.* (2011) where it was noted that for users of auditor's reports there is a perception of PCAOB audits being superior – and this is mainly driven by the fact there is an internal control opinion provided.

France provides a case study on enhanced disclosure of auditor's reports; there, enhanced disclosure of information about the audit has been required since 2003. Auditors must make "justifications of assessments" that relate to four categories of items, relating to: accounting policy choice; significant accounting estimates; overall presentation of the financial statements; and internal control procedures (for more discussion see Mock *et al.* 2013). A report as to whether this was seen as useful to users was prepared (Footprint Consultants 2011). It was noted that such audit reports provide some benefits to users; but when the justification was merely describing audit procedures it was not very useful. The report also noted that auditors had begun to standardize these justifications rather than tailor them to each client.[10] The French experience suggests that developing a more informative auditor's report will not be a straightforward task.

Research summary

This section offers a brief summary of the literature on auditor reports, focusing on several key papers addressing important representative issues. In summary, the auditor's report is generally seen to have value but the audit expectations gap is persistent. The research suggests this is partially due to the auditor's report not generally being read or sufficiently understood. Users want more information about the work performed and on the auditor's findings from the actual audit.

Further details of literature in this area can be obtained from two recent academic literature reviews. The first, by Church *et al.* (2008) evaluated research into the auditor's reporting decision and the content of the auditor's report, and raised many suggestions for future research. An important finding from their review is that they conclude that the auditor's report "has symbolic value, but conveys little communicative value" (Church *et al.* 2008: 85). They suggest that additional disclosures may improve the auditor's report but issue a challenge for researchers and regulators on how to improve the communicative value of the report, without creating confusion for users.

Subsequent to this synthesis, a review by Mock *et al.* (2013) was conducted, which was concerned mainly with the literature post-2007, but which also focused more on users' evaluations of the auditor's report. They find that users consider the auditor's report important, but that "they desire more information about the entity and the audit" (Mock *et al.* 2013: 344). They note some key areas where users want more information, including: accounting policies and risk related information; audit judgments; auditor independence; audit process; materiality; and level of assurance provided by the auditor.

Both of these are useful resources for more information about research on auditor's reports.

Unresolved issues requiring future research

The most significant unresolved research issue for auditor reports relates to improving their communicative value. Archival literature on this topic has shown that auditor's reports *per se* have value. However, attempts to improve the communicative value of reports means that alternative types of auditor's reports should be considered. In attempting to address questions of this type, behavioral research methods would seem to be most appropriate because they can evaluate options that do not exist in practice. Researchers should also draw from theories on communication (see Fiske 2011) to better understand the communication process in evaluating new types of auditor reports.

There is already much research on the type of information that users want in auditor's reports and what they think the auditor provides. Future research should utilize experimental work to more specifically evaluate the effect of differing report types on whether they reduce the expectations gap. Types of additional disclosures that could be experimentally examined are noted below. They are split into two categories:

(a) disclosures that report on matters already considered by auditors but not reported. These types of disclosures were considered by Turner *et al.* (2010). They noted that recent SASs issued in the US expanded communications requirements to their clients. These additional disclosures relate to: the audit; the quality of the financial statements; the quality of the financial reporting system; and the sustainability of the business. As these disclosures are already required to be reported to management, one would assume it would not be a significant cost to also report them to users, although there may be resistance from auditors.

(b) disclosures that require additional work by auditors. These disclosures have been previously highlighted as being part of the audit expectations gap. Some prominent examples here are reporting on internal control (although it is now done in the US under SOX Section 404); reporting on going concern; and greater responsibility for fraud.

As well as researching how these additional disclosures potentially add value to users, it is important for researchers to try and address the issue of cost. These costs may relate to doing more work to satisfy the new disclosure requirements or from costs associated with the litigation risk from disclosing more of this type of information to auditor's report users.

The changes being proposed by the IAASB in the 2013 Exposure Draft (discussed in the section "Current issues in this topic area" of this chapter) relate to some of the above and will provide opportunities in the future for archival research. Research can examine the effect of the changes in the jurisdictions which are first to implement these changes.[11] This type of research can also evaluate the benefits and costs in the market to provide information on the value of the changes.

Conclusion

The role of the auditor's report has been a valuable one to the market and society in general for as long as financial reporting has existed. For most companies, the auditor's report continues to be of value to users of financial statements to highlight that the financial statements "present fairly" the operations of the company. However, when there are crises in financial reporting the focus usually turns also to the auditor and these are times when the misperceptions of users that create the audit expectations gap are highlighted. A historical approach to these issues has been to change the auditor's report to clarify these "misperceptions" to users and to educate users about what an auditor's report means.

The persistent nature of the auditor expectations gap despite these changes means that a rethink is needed in how to address the issue of auditor reporting. Communication theory suggests that to determine the meaning of a message the various interrelationships between parties needs to be considered. The evidence suggests that users are interested in information that is not currently being provided in the auditor's report. More "boilerplate" explanations about what an audit is are not required, but more information about the audit that was conducted is needed. The importance of this has recently been highlighted by the global financial crisis but is also part of a wider trend for more transparency in the marketplace. Standard setters and regulators are pushing for substantive changes to the auditor's report to address these concerns and it is also in the interests of professional auditors to embrace these changes to maintain their relevancy as the main providers of financial assurance services. Obviously changes such as these have cost implications and the users who are demanding these extra disclosures should be prepared to pay for them.[12]

Irrespective of the current changes to the auditor's report that are being suggested – the auditor's report will always be changing. As noted by the chairman of the IAASB, Arnold Schilder, "More than ever before, however, users of audited financial statements are calling for more pertinent information for their decision-making in today's global business environment with increasingly complex financial reporting requirements" (IAASB 2012: 1). To be relevant in a changing business environment, change in the type and nature of disclosure is as much a constant for auditors as it is for financial accountants. Research provides insight into pathways that might be successful for current changes being considered, and will continue to be a way in future to assist in determining the appropriate nature of changes.

The audit process and the communication of this process through the auditor's report has been an invaluable part of the financial reporting system for over a hundred years. Ensuring it appropriately adapts will guarantee the reliability and integrity that audits bring to financial reporting will continue to be a valued and integral part of our financial reporting environment.

Notes

1 Details on the required contents of an auditor's report are in ISA 700 *Forming an Opinion and Reporting on Financial Statements* (IAASB 2009).

2 Details are in ISA 705 *Modifications to the Opinion in the Independent Auditor's Report*.

3 Details are in ISA 706 *Emphasis of Matter Paragraphs and Other Matter Paragraphs in the Independent Auditor's Report*. Examples of emphasis of matter paragraphs are: uncertainty related to future outcomes of exceptional legal or regulatory action; early application of a new accounting standard; or a major catastrophe.

4 Francis (2004) provides a comprehensive summary of this research.

5 "Boilerplate" in the context of text or contracts relates to something that is reused in a standard format. It is a term that has been used to describe the auditor's report in academic and professional literature (e.g. Church *et al.* 2008; IOSCO 2009).

6 Other proposed changes include: more transparency about the audit performed; and further clarification of the respective responsibilities of the auditor, management, and those charged with governance (IAASB 2013).

7 For a comprehensive historical background of auditor reports (with a US focus) see King and Case (2003).
8 This was the accepted terminology at the time. The appropriate description for this type of audit report according to ISA 700 is "unmodified" audit opinions.
9 In psychology, the "halo effect" relates to a judgement of a particular person being overly influenced by the impression of that person. In Hatherly *et al.* (1991) they describe the "halo effect" where "the expanded wording [of the auditor's report] seems to generate a feeling of well-being which spills over to provide significant changes for certain other dimensions not directly addressed by the expanded wording of the report." (Hatherly *et al.* 1991: 315).
10 Which is of course heading back to one of the key "problems" of the current auditor's report in other jurisdictions, as discussed in the section, "Historical development", in this chapter.
11 The research on changes to internal control reporting under the Sarbanes-Oxley Act (SOX) in the US provides a good example of this.
12 As a side effect, it is not unreasonable to think that an auditor's report that is read by and has more communicative value to users would also make it easier for auditors to justify their fees for these services.

References

American Institute of Certified Public Accountants (AICPA). 1988. "Statement on Auditing Standards (SAS) No. 58", *Reports on Audited Financial Statements*. New York: American Institute of Certified Public Accountants.

Ashbaugh-Skaife, H., D. Collins, W. Kinney Jr., and R. LaFond. 2009. "The Effect of SOX Internal Control Deficiencies on Firm Risk and Cost of Equity", *Journal of Accounting Research* 47(1): 1–43.

Audit Quality Forum. 2007. *Audit Quality Fundamentals: Auditor Reporting*. Milton Keynes: Institute of Chartered Accountants in England and Wales (ICAEW), February.

Blackwell, D., T. Noland, and D. Winters. 1998. "The Value of Auditor Assurance: Evidence from Loan Pricing", *Journal of Accounting Research* 36(1): 57–70.

Carson, E., N. Fargher, M. Geiger, C. Lennox, K. Ragunandan, and M. Willekens. 2013. "Audit Reporting for Going Concern Uncertainty: A Research Synthesis", *Auditing: A Journal of Practice and Theory* 32(Supplement 1): 353–84.

Chartered Financial Analyst (CFA) Institute. 2010. *Independent Auditor's Report Survey Results*. Charlottesville, VA: CFA Institute.

Chong, K. and G. Pflugrath. 2008. "Do Different Audit Report Formats Affect Shareholders' and Auditors' Perceptions?", *International Journal of Auditing* 12(3): 221–41.

Church, B., S. Davis, and S. McCracken. 2008. "The Auditor's Reporting Model: A Literature Overview and Research Synthesis", *Accounting Horizons* 22(1): 69–90.

Cohen Commission. 1978. *The Commission on Auditors' Responsibilities: Report, Conclusions and Recommendations*. Manuel F. Cohen, Chairman. New York: AICPA.

European Commission (EC). 2011. *Proposal for a Regulation of the European Parliament and of the Council on Specific Requirements Regarding Statutory Audit of Public-interest Entities*. Brussels: EC November 30.

Fiske, J. 2011. *Introduction to Communication Studies*. London: Taylor and Francis.

Footprint Consultants. 2011. "Study of the Perception of Statutory Auditors' 'Justification of Assessments'". February. Available online at www.cncc.fr/download/footprintconsultant_reportstudy_va_cncc_fev2011.pdf (accessed 6 May 2014).

Francis, J. 2004. "What do we Know about Audit Quality?", *British Accounting Review* 36: 345–68.

Gold, A., U. Gronewold, and C. Pott. 2012. "The ISA 700 Auditor's Report and the Audit Expectation Gap – Do Explanations Matter?", *International Journal of Auditing* 16(3): 286–307.

Gray, G., J. Turner, P. Coram, and T. Mock. 2011. "Perceptions and Misperceptions Regarding the Unqualified Auditor's Report by Financial Statement Preparers, Users, and Auditors", *Accounting Horizons* 25(4): 659–84.

Hatherly, D., J. Innes, and T. Brown. 1991. "The Expanded Audit Report: An Empirical Investigation", *Accounting and Business Research* 21(84): 311–19.

International Auditing and Assurance Standards Board (IAASB). 2005. "International Standard on Auditing (ISA) 700", *The Independent Auditor's Report on a Complete Set of General Purpose Financial Statements*. New York: International Federation of Accountants (IFA).

International Auditing and Assurance Standards Board (IAASB). 2009. "International Standard on Auditing (ISA) 700", *Forming an Opinion and Reporting on Financial Statements*. New York: International Federation of Accountants (IFA).

International Auditing and Assurance Standards Board (IAASB). 2012. *Invitation to Comment: Improving the Auditor's Report*. New York: International Federation of Accountants (IFA), June.

International Auditing and Assurance Standards Board (IAASB). 2013. *Reporting on Audited Financial Statements: Proposed New and Revised International Standards on Auditing*. New York: International Federation of Accountants (IFA), July.

International Organization of Securities Commissions (IOSCO). 2009. *Auditor Communications Consultation Report*. Madrid: IOSCO, September.

Kelly, A. and L. Mohrweis. 1989. "Bankers' and Investors' Perceptions of the Auditor's Role in Financial Statement Reporting: The Impact of SAS No. 58", *Auditing: A Journal of Practice and Theory* 9(1): 87–97.

King, D. and C. Case. 2003. "The Evolution of the United States Audit Report", *Academy of Accounting and Financial Studies Journal* 7(1): 1–16.

Miller, J., S. Reed, and R. Strawser. 1993. "Bank Loan Officers' Perceptions of the New Audit Report", *Accounting Horizons* 7(1): 39–52.

Mock, T., J. Bedard, P. Coram, S. Davis, R. Espahbodi, and R. Warne. 2013. "The Audit Reporting Model: Current Research Synthesis and Implications", *Auditing: A Journal of Practice and Theory* 32(Supplement 1): 323–52.

Monroe, G. and D. Woodliff. 1994. "An Empirical Investigation of the Audit Expectation Gap: Australian Evidence", *Accounting and Finance* 34(1): 47–74.

Public Company Accounting Oversight Board (PCAOB). 2011. *Concept Release on Possible Revisions to PCAOB Standards Related to Reports on Audited Financial Statements. No. 2011–003*, June. Available online at http://pcaobus.org/Rules/Rulemaking/Docket034/Concept_Release.pdf (accessed 6 May 2014).

Turner, J., T. Mock, P. Coram, and G. Gray. 2010. "Improving Transparency and Relevance of Auditor Communications with Financial Statement Users", *Current Issues in Auditing* 4(1): A1–A8.

Watts, R. and J. Zimmerman. 1983. "Agency Problems, Auditing and the Theory of the Firm: Some Evidence", *Journal of Law and Economics* 26(3): 613–33.

24
Going concern

Marshall Geiger

Overview

Auditor reporting on the ability of their client to remain a going concern (i.e., continue in business) has had a long history of legislative and research interest around the globe. Auditor reporting on going concern uncertainty is of interest to standard setters, practitioners, academics, investors, and the business press because it represents the only allowable communication from the auditor (a knowledgeable "insider") regarding their professional assessment of the continued viability of the company under audit. While professional standards from all jurisdictions would stress that it is not a prediction of future viability, audit reports modified for going concern uncertainty are viewed with great importance and are often treated as such. So whenever a business fails it is commonplace for regulators, investors, the business press, and interested parties to ask "where were the auditors?" and "what did their audit report say?" And in that context many believe that lately auditors have not been providing the investing public with enough forewarning of impending business failures through their reports. In fact, as of the writing of this chapter, standard setters in the European Union, the United Kingdom (UK), and the United States (US), at a minimum, are simultaneously considering changes in auditor reporting responsibilities with respect to going concern uncertainties in order to enhance communication of this information to readers of the financial statements.

The purpose of this chapter is to discuss the current issues regarding audit opinions modified for going concern uncertainty (hereafter GCO) and to present a high-level review of the research in this area in order to provide background as well as direction for future research.

Current issues

As noted in the Overview above, several auditing standard setters from around the world are currently considering modifications to their standards for auditor responsibility with respect to reporting on GCOs. A considerable proportion of this universal push to re-evaluate auditor responsibility in this area has its genesis in the recent global financial crisis that peaked during 2008, along with the commensurate volume of business failures that coincided with this challenging economic environment. In that context, many believed that GCOs should have been issued more often and they have called into question the culpability of auditors during this time period including their role in providing the requisite warning about impending business failures.[1] These and similar issues have sparked a series of high-level inquiries into the role and effectiveness of independent auditing and the usefulness of auditor reports (e.g., EC 2010; PCAOB 2011, 2013; Sharman Inquiry 2011; IAASB 2012, 2013; EP 2013), with particular interest directed at the auditor's assessment and reporting on a company's ability to continue as a going concern.

To date, the approach to addressing the issue of providing heightened information regarding GCO by most standard setters has been through the auditing standards, and more specifically by improving the auditor's reporting obligation with respect to calling attention to their concerns regarding the continued viability of their client. In fact, the current proposal of the International Auditing and Assurance Standards Board (IAASB) would require a separate section in the auditor's report to specifically address the assessment of GCOs (IAASB 2013).

However, the Financial Accounting Standards Board (FASB) in the US has recently questioned this "auditor-driven disclosure" model and has proposed that *management* be required to assess and report on their company's ability to continue as a going concern at each reporting period, and not wait for the auditor to raise the issue in their report (FASB 2013). Under FASB's "management-driven disclosure" approach, management would be responsible for disclosing information concerning their going concern assessment in the notes to the financial statements. Auditors would then be responsible for auditing those disclosures, similar to their responsibility for auditing all financial statement disclosures.

In addition to this reoriented reporting responsibility is the notion that readers of the financial statements should be provided with some sort of additional early warning about the company's financial condition so they would not have to wait until the company is already at a high risk of not continuing as a going concern. Accordingly, the FASB's current proposal requires additional disclosures if management believes that it is more likely than not that the business cannot continue in its normal course without additional measures to address their financial stress. While this is currently a proposal, and discussions are ongoing as to when and in what form management's early disclosures might take, any additional formalized early warning regarding going concern uncertainties from management prior to the auditor rendering a GCO is a substantial departure from current practice, not only in the US but around the world.

Irrespective of the final outcome of the various deliberations across multiple jurisdictions, what have surfaced thus far are proposed changes that, if adopted, would result in substantial departures from current reporting and disclosure standards. Many of the contemplated changes may have a profound impact on current practice with respect to the auditor's going concern opinion decisions. The resolution of these proposals is certain to result in numerous opportunities for future research with respect to auditor (and possibly management) reporting on going concern uncertainties.

Summary of research findings

This section relies on the research framework presented in Carson *et al.* (2013), and reproduced in Figure 24.1, to provide a high-level overview of the extant research from around the world on GCOs.[2]

Determinants of going concern uncertainties

Current auditor GCO reporting frameworks generally commence with the auditor's assessment of an underlying uncertainty regarding the ability of the company to continue as a going

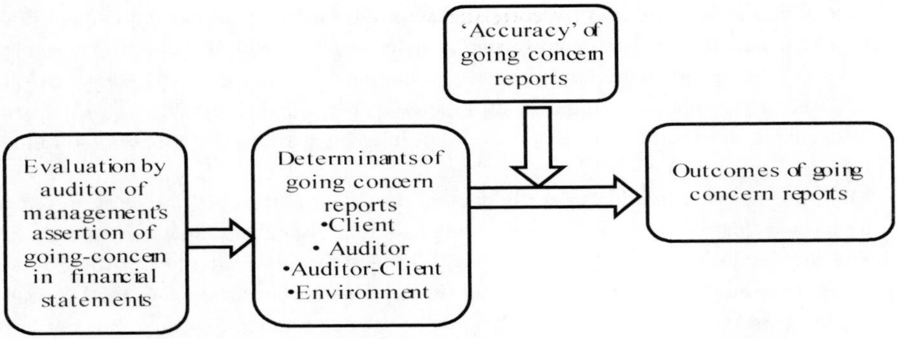

Figure 24.1 Audit reporting of going-concern uncertainty research framework

concern and then moves to the auditor assessing factors that either contribute to or mitigate their "significant doubt" (internationally) or "substantial doubt" (in the US) with respect to the going concern uncertainty. This assessment then leads to the auditor's decision to issue or not issue a GCO to the financially troubled client. Accordingly, a large body of extant research has attempted to identify which characteristics or circumstances are associated with auditors rendering GCOs.

Client factors

The literature documents a broad variety of client characteristics associated with the issuance of GCOs. A major insight from this research is that publicly available information is often associated with the GCO decision. Studies generally find that auditors are more likely to issue GCOs when companies are less profitable, have higher leverage, lower liquidity, are smaller, and are in default on debt obligations. In addition, Mutchler (1984) and LaSalle and Anandarajan (1996) provide survey evidence from auditors about the relative importance of different financial ratios to their GCO decisions.

Several studies find significant associations between accounting accruals (a proxy for low financial reporting quality) and the auditor's issuance of modified audit reports. The central premise of these studies is that low financial reporting quality prompts auditors to issue a GCO. However, others argue that auditors issue GCOs when a company has going concern uncertainties, not when they have poor financial reporting quality, and have found that the relation between accounting accruals and GCOs is driven by companies that have large *negative* accruals which seem to reflect poor financial condition rather than earnings management. Kausar and Lennox (2011) argue that one purpose of the GCO is to warn lenders about potential differences in book values and eventual liquidation values, and consistent with this argument they find that companies receiving a GCO prior to bankruptcy have greater differences between the book values and the eventual liquidation values of net assets settled in bankruptcy.

Non-financial statement related variables including stock returns and price volatility, management's strategic initiatives, and governance characteristics have been shown to be important. Market variables, such as low industry-adjusted returns and high return volatility have also been found to be related to GCOs. However, extant research has not specifically addressed whether auditors use these market measures in making their GCO determinations or whether they are simply a different reflection of distressed companies that receive a GCO from their auditor. More recent research across several countries has found that management plans to raise cash by issuing equity and debt are negatively correlated with GCOs while operating initiatives such as cost-cutting strategies are positively correlated with GCOs (Behn *et al.* 2001; Bruynseels *et al.* 2011; Bruynseels and Willekens 2012). US studies have also found that auditors are more likely to issue GCOs to companies that have stronger, more experienced and independent audit committees (Carcello and Neal 2000).

Auditor factors

Auditor GCO decisions are an area where experimental research designs can provide needed insight, particularly with respect to auditor factors that impact the decision. For example, Kida (1980) provides a comparison of the beliefs and evaluations of auditors who qualified their opinions most and those who qualified least. Auditors who qualified least had slightly stronger beliefs that: (1) they would lose the client; (2) the client would sue; and (3) the accounting firm's reputation would be negatively affected. Auditors who qualified most tended to have stronger beliefs regarding the importance of the audit firm's reputation. His findings are supported by more recent research finding that auditors with a strong belief that a GCO would precipitate the bankruptcy of a troubled company (i.e., the "self-fulfilling prophecy" effect) give more weight to mitigating information and less weight to contrary information. Hence, taking into account differences in personal characteristics and traits is an important, but under-researched area regarding GCO decisions.

With respect to the influence of larger, more "important" clients on GCO decisions, international evidence generally fails to find an association between larger, more important clients and GCO decisions. In contrast, Ettredge *et al.* (2011) find that in 2008 auditors were less likely to issue first-time GCOs to large clients of local audit firm offices (mid-financial crisis) compared with 2006 (pre-financial crisis).

In addition, several studies have investigated the association between audit firm size and GCOs, but the results are rather mixed. Studies using more recent years, however, find that Big 4 auditors are less likely to issue GCOs, which has been attributed to the fact that Big 4 auditors are more reluctant to retain financially distressed clients and are therefore less likely to have clients requiring GCOs than non-Big 4 auditor firms (Kaplan and Williams 2012). However, Australian research finds that Big 4 auditors responded earlier to the global financial crisis by issuing GCOs earlier than did non-Big 4 auditors (Xu *et al.* 2012). It has also been argued that industry specialist auditors supply higher quality audits. However, research results are generally mixed with respect to an association between specialist auditors and GCOs.

Auditor–client relationship

A significant issue of debate has been the "client pay model" where auditors receive their compensation directly from their audit clients, leading to potential independence problems because of the direct economic tie between the auditor and client. While most studies find that GCOs are associated with higher audit fees, the association of GCOs and non-audit services (NAS) fees is less clear. Early large sample studies in the UK and Australia, along with US evidence from around 2000 (the first year fee data was available) generally find no association between NAS fees and GCOs; whereas more recent research in the US, UK, and Australia have generally found a negative association between NAS fees and GCO decisions. In addition, Blay and Geiger (2013) document that the different US results across time periods is not due to methodological choices. They also report a negative relation between current GCO decisions and future total fee receipts from incumbent audit clients. Accordingly, these more recent studies suggest that auditors across several jurisdictions might be adversely affected by clients that pay higher NAS fees and future total fees. Yet recent findings of Vandenbogaerde *et al.* (2011) examining private companies from Norway and Belgium do not find an association between fees and GCO decisions. Whether these different findings are the result of public versus private company reporting differences or cross-country differences has yet to be examined.

With respect to personnel affiliations, Lennox (2005) examines whether auditors report differently on clients that employ former audit partners from their firm ("affiliated" partners) and finds that auditors issue GCOs less frequently to clients that have affiliated partners, suggesting that personnel relationships can significantly affect auditor reporting decisions. Another area of recent debate concerns the length of the auditor–client relationship. In this context, Geiger and Raghunandan (2002) find in the US a positive association between audit firm tenure and the propensity to issue a GCO prior to bankruptcy. Their results support the argument that longer tenures enable auditors to gain additional insights, leading to more accurate GCOs. In Australia, where partners sign their names to opinions, prior studies have found that long *partner* tenures are associated with fewer GCOs (Carey and Simnett 2006); yet when examining private companies in Belgium or public companies in Spain research finds no association between audit partner tenure and GCOs (Ruiz-Barbadillo *et al.* 2004; Knechel and Vanstraelen 2007). Studies using more recent data are needed to determine if these relationships still hold in the current auditing environment and what, if any, differences are driven by country specific factors and whether reporting decisions differ between public and private companies.

Related to the issue of tenure and GCOs, studies from numerous countries have generally found that auditors are more likely to be dismissed after they issue GCOs, providing strong empirical support for the argument that auditor dismissal represents a realistic economic threat to auditors contemplating a GCO. Another related question is whether such switching behavior is successful in terms of removing the GCO (i.e., "opinion shopping"). Early research in the US generally finds no association between auditor switching and subsequent GCO removal. However, Lennox (2000) compares observed UK pre- and post-switch audit reports to predicted reports assuming opposite switch decisions and concludes that companies received more favorable opinions by switching. Research has also shown that opinion shopping is more likely to be successful when companies have a higher percentage of affiliated directors (i.e. former partners) on the audit committee, and that there are fewer overall dismissals following GCOs during the post- Sarbanes-Oxley Act (SOX) era, suggesting that this threat may have been reduced. There is considerable room for further examination of these auditor and client behaviors in the post-SOX environment.

Effects of reporting environment

Prior research has shown that the probability of issuing a GCO is affected by the regulatory environment. For example, the enactment of the Private Securities Litigation Reform Act is associated with a significant reduction in GCOs, while the adoption of SOX is associated with significant increases in GCO rates during the early post-SOX period with rates reverting back to their pre-SOX levels by 2006–7. Further, research examining the regulatory oversight provided by PCAOB inspections on non-Big 4 firms finds that auditors are more likely to issue GCOs after they receive unfavorable inspection reports, consistent with regulatory oversight having an impact on the auditor's decision to issue GCOs (Gramling *et al.* 2011). In addition, research has found that subsequent to SOX there was a reduction in the number of small audit firms in the US which in turn led to more accurate GCO decisions by successor auditors (DeFond and Lennox 2011).

"Accuracy" of going concern uncertainties

Many studies examine the proportion of firms with GCOs that do not subsequently fail (type I misclassifications), or the proportion of firms entering bankruptcy without a prior GCO (type II misclassifications).[3] While the term "misclassification" or "error" is often applied in these instances, as noted previously, GCOs are not intended to be predictive of business failure; therefore such labels should be interpreted with caution.

In general, research has consistently found that since the adoption of the Statement on Auditing Standards (SAS) No. 59, between 40 and 50 percent of companies going bankrupt in the US do not receive a GCO immediately prior to bankruptcy. Research has suggested that the variation over time in type II misclassifications has closely reflected auditing's economic and regulatory environment, noted in the previous section, "Effects of reporting environment". Another possible explanation for the high misclassification rate is that auditors are not adequately trained in failure prediction and they simply lack the expertise to accurately predict future bankruptcies, leading to large type II "error" rates.

In contrast, there have been comparatively fewer studies examining type I misclassifications, partly because of the difficulty in obtaining accurate subsequent viability data. Nonetheless, prior studies from around the globe have generally found that around 80–90 percent of companies receiving a GCO do not fail in the subsequent year, where failure is generally defined in terms of bankruptcy filing. These percentages are fairly consistent based on single period studies, longitudinal studies, and across multiple countries – especially Australia, Belgium, the UK, and the US.

Using a different approach, Nogler (1995) tracked US firms that received GCOs to the final resolution of their going concern uncertainty and finds that approximately 33 percent eventually filed for bankruptcy, 18 percent were acquired or merged with other firms, ten percent no longer filed public reports or were taken private, three percent were voluntarily liquidated, and 36 percent remained viable and received an unmodified opinion in subsequent years. Thus, Nogler's (1995) study suggests that the proportion of firms that do not fail after receiving a GCO is considerably lower than in studies examining bankruptcy outcomes over horizons of just one or two years.

Explaining the variation in going concern opinion "accuracy" across auditors

Research has attempted to improve our understanding of how reporting accuracy varies across auditors. Several studies in Australia, the US, and UK have examined large samples of companies over extended periods, or in varying reporting contexts (i.e., initial public offering (IPO) markets) and generally find that misclassifications are significantly lower for the Big N auditors compared to the non-Big N auditors for both types of misclassifications; and that larger national firms have lower misclassifications than smaller regional firms.

Consequences of going concern uncertainties

To the extent that GCOs reflect an auditor's private information (i.e., information not available to those outside the company), it is expected that the issuance of a GCO would affect the company's stock market valuation. The majority of early studies that examines the market reaction to GCOs found large negative abnormal returns in the weeks preceding the issuance of the GCO, but no response to the issuance of the GCO itself. However, subsequent research finds negative price (and increased trading volume) reactions to the media announcement of a GCO, particularly if the GCO was unexpected by the market. Several studies have examined whether the market responds fully to the news of a GCO or whether there is a further downward drift in abnormal returns in the weeks after the opinion's release, producing rather mixed results regarding any market anomaly surrounding announcements of GCOs. However, Blay *et al.* (2011) find that GCOs are associated with a shift in the market's valuation of a firm away from a dominant focus on net income toward a valuation that is based primarily on the balance sheet.

A GCO also has potential consequences for both the audited company and their lenders because it can result in the accelerated financial demise of a company that might have survived if it had not received a GCO – i.e., the "self-fulfilling prophecy" phenomenon. Research on the relation between GCOs and subsequent failures in the US has largely substantiated this concern, finding that firms receiving GCOs are significantly more likely to file for bankruptcy than similarly stressed non-GCO firms. In contrast, non-US studies have yielded mixed results on this issue. Studies examining Australian and UK companies generally do not support a self-fulfilling prophesy effect, yet an examination of private companies in Belgium does support the effect. The vast majority of these studies use data from much earlier time periods, highlighting the need for examination of more recent periods in order to determine if these relationships still hold in the current audit environments in the countries examined. Future research should also attempt to explain the disparate results between studies from different countries. One potential avenue for future research in the context of the "self-fulfilling prophecy" would be to examine the legal and institutional structures in the various countries in an attempt to reconcile these disparate country results.

Issues in need of future research

While areas of research need have been identified in conjunction with the overview of the literature, this section will highlight some of the more salient areas in need of further examination. Although the research on determinants of GCOs is rather voluminous, the examination of how factors such as management's plans and strategic and operating initiatives, contrary and mitigating factors, and other non-financial information impact GCO decisions deserves additional research attention. Some aspects of managements' plans have been identified as being associated with GCOs, however there exists a considerable amount of GCO decision variability that remains unexplained. Systemic identification of additional specific factors or conditions leading to GCO decisions would be a considerable advancement in the extant literature.

Similarly, field studies and experimental investigations regarding what auditors are currently evaluating and weighing in the process of making "significant/substantial doubt" and final GCO assessments would be informative to the current debate and would contribute substantially to the extant literature. In fact, other than Mutchler (1984) and LaSalle and Anandarajan (1996), studies have rarely used detailed interviews with audit partners and managers for insights about the GCO decision-making process. For example, research examining how auditors interpret and apply the phrase "significant/substantial doubt" and what level of doubt is necessary to trigger a GCO by practicing auditors would be a considerable enhancement to our present knowledge.

Further research on auditor–client interactions and the related issues of audit quality and independence is also warranted, and the need for better measures of auditor–client ties, audit quality and interactions remain a challenge. In addition, a substantial number of studies use data from earlier pre-SOX periods, creating opportunities, where warranted, to update our prior findings with respect to current auditing environments around the world.

I would expect that there will be continuing interest from market participants, regulators, and standard setters in research that examines the accuracy of GCOs, particularly the incidence of type II misclassifications. There is also ongoing interest with respect to reporting accuracy, including type I misclassifications, and the factors associated with accuracy and changes in reporting accuracy over time. Included in these assessments is both the issue of the time horizon for evaluation (currently 12 months in most jurisdictions) as well as what violates "going concern" (e.g., bankruptcy, business interruptions, defaulting on debt, etc.). Future research should extend prior research by examining the time frame actually used by auditors in their GCO decisions, along with expanded examinations beyond bankruptcy filings as to what constitutes a "non-going concern." Such research can inform the ongoing policy debate as well as provide more robust examinations of GCO decisions and outcomes, leading to better assessments of GCO report "misclassifications."

As noted at the outset, a considerable amount of the current push to re-evaluate auditor responsibility with respect to GCOs has its genesis in the recent global financial crisis that systemically involved banks and financial institutions around the world. Prior research on GCOs typically excludes financial institutions from analysis; yet research on financial institutions, including auditor GCO reporting decisions, is urgently needed. Accordingly, GCO decisions on financial institutions represent an area in need of critical examination. Likewise, the municipal, non-profit, and private company sectors constitute large and relevant portions of our economies that remain under-researched with respect to going concern issues and auditor reporting. Some of the lack of research attention has been due to lack of data availability; however, as databases expand to include these sectors, researchers are presented with additional opportunities to explore GCO reporting decisions in these contexts.

In addition to the above research needs, if the going concern reporting model changes in the international auditing standards to require a separate paragraph regarding going concern assessments in each audit; or if the US changes from a model of "auditor-driven disclosures" to "management-driven disclosures," research on the impact of these changes would certainly be needed. Depending on the requirements of the potential new standards (both financial reporting and auditing), research should address the new reporting requirements and disclosures. For example, do auditors report going concern uncertainties more or less frequently under the potential new international reporting standards? Do companies disclose different types of information under the new standards compared to current disclosures; are disclosures of financial stress more salient and/or more consistent in the financial statements and notes under the new standards, particularly in the US; and do they lead to more or fewer GCOs? What is the amount of redundancy between the required note disclosures that are audited and the unaudited management discussion and analysis (MD&A) discussions included in US public company Securities and Exchange Commission (SEC) filings? In addition, future research should examine how such disclosures by management versus those made by auditors might be used and interpreted differently by investors, lenders, analysts, and other financial statement users.

Importantly for this review, research would be needed to examine whether any new auditing standards significantly impacted auditor GCO decision-making or any of the associations noted in the prior literature. For example, have thresholds for issuing GCOs changed under the new standards? (For example, US standard setters currently intend for any new standards to reflect practice and not to have a significant impact on final GCO decisions); are type I and type II misclassification rates similar under the new standards and if not, what are the causes for the differences? – comparing both pre- and post-new standards, as well as partitioned examinations under the new standards (e.g., Big N versus non-Big N firms; experts versus non-experts; possible differences in NAS fee or firm affiliation impacts, etc.); do auditors evaluate and weight the same types of information in arriving at GCOs under the new standards? Do the markets react similarly to the new GCOs? These and other research questions based on any new standards would be fertile ground for future research.

Conclusion

The global financial crisis has provided the catalyst for renewed interest from regulators, standard setters, academics, and investors regarding the auditor's assessment and reporting on a company's ability to continue as a going concern. The purpose of this chapter has been to discuss the current issues regarding audit opinions modified for GCOs and to present a high-level overview of the research in this area in order to provide background and direction for future research.

As noted throughout the chapter, there remain several significant issues in need of additional research with respect to the auditor's GCO reporting decision. In addition, the chapter identifies several issues with respect to GCOs currently on the agendas of several standard setters from around the world. However, as of the writing of this chapter it is too early to tell whether or not any of these standard setters will modify or radically alter the current GCO reporting standards, or the entire current GCO reporting model – characterized as an "auditor-led disclosure" model. Nonetheless, and irrespective of any current standard-setting outcomes, there remain numerous areas that would benefit from additional inquiry in our pursuit of knowledge regarding the important multidimensional subject of the auditor's GCO decision.

Notes

1 In contrast to this perception, Geiger *et al.* (2014) find that GCOs were issued no less frequently to bankrupt US companies during the global financial crisis than for the immediately preceding period.
2 This overview of the literature relies heavily on Carson *et al.* (2012, 2013). See these two works for a more detailed discussion of the literature on auditor's reporting on going concern uncertainties.
3 As noted in the literature, bankruptcy is only one of the possible outcomes for a firm receiving a going concern modified opinion. Other possible outcomes include reorganization, takeover, merger, voluntary delisting, entering receivership, etc.

References

Behn, B. K., S. E. Kaplan, and K. R. Krumwiede. 2001. "Further Evidence on the Auditor's Going-concern Report: The Influence of Management Plans", *Auditing: A Journal of Practice and Theory* 20(1): 13–28.

Blay, A. D. and M. A. Geiger. 2013. "Auditor Fees and Auditor Independence: Evidence from Going-concern Opinions", *Contemporary Accounting Research* 30(2): 579–606.

Blay, A. D., M. A. Geiger, and D. North. 2011. "The Auditor's Going-concern Opinion as a Communication of Risk", *Auditing: A Journal of Practice and Theory* 30(2): 77–102.

Bruynseels, L. and M. Willekens. 2012. "The Effect of Strategic and Operating Turnaround Initiatives on Audit Reporting for Distressed Companies", *Accounting, Organizations and Society* 37(4): 223–41.

Bruynseels, L., W. R. Knechel, and M. Willekens. 2011. "Auditor Differentiation, Mitigating Management Actions, and Audit-reporting Accuracy for Distressed Firms", *Auditing: A Journal of Practice Theory* 30(1): 1–20.

Carcello, J. V. and T. L. Neal. 2000. "Audit Committee Composition and Auditor Reporting", *The Accounting Review* 75(4): 453–67.

Carey, P. and R. Simnett. 2006. "Audit Partner Tenure and Audit Quality", *The Accounting Review* 81(3): 653–76.

Carson, E., N. L. Fargher, M. A. Geiger, C. Lennox, K. Raghunandan, and M. Willekens. 2012. *Auditor Reporting on Going-concern Uncertainty: A Research Synthesis.* Report presented to the Public Company Accounting Oversight Board, January 30. Available online at SSRN: http://ssrn.com/abstract=2000496 (accessed 10 October 2013).

Carson, E., N. L. Fargher, M. A. Geiger, C. Lennox, K. Raghunandan, and M. Willekens. 2013. "Auditor Reporting on Going-concern Uncertainty: A Research Synthesis", *Auditing: A Journal of Practice and Theory* 32(Supplement): 353–84.

DeFond, M. L. and C. Lennox. 2011. "The Effect of SOX on Small Auditor Exits and Audit Quality", *Journal of Accounting and Economics* 52(1): 21–40.

Ettredge, M., C. Li, and E. Emeigh. 2011. *Auditor Independence during the "Great Recession" of 2007–2009*, working paper. Lawrence, KS: University of Kansas; Pittsburgh, PA: University of Pittsburgh; Lawrence, KS: University of Kansas.

European Commission (EC). 2010. *Green Paper, Audit Policy: Lessons from the Crisis*. Brussels: EC.

European Parliament (EP). 2013. *Report on the proposal for a directive of the European Parliament and of the Council amending Directive 2006/43/EC on statutory audits of annual accounts and consolidated accounts*. Plenary sitting, May 13. Brussels: EP.

Financial Accounting Standards Board (FASB). 2013. *Proposed Accounting Standards Update. Presentation of Financial Statements (Topic 205). Disclosure of Uncertainties about an Entity's Going Concern Presumption* (June 26). Norwalk, CT: FASB.

Geiger, M. A. and K. Raghunandan. 2002. "Auditor Tenure and Audit Reporting Failures", *Auditing: A Journal of Practice and Theory* 21(1): 67–78.

Geiger, M. A., K. Raghunandan, and W. Riccardi. 2014. "The Global Financial Crisis: US Bankruptcies and Going-concern Audit Opinions", *Accounting Horizons* 28(1): 59–75.

Gramling, A. A., J. Krishnan, and Y. Zhang. 2011. "Are PCAOB Identified Audit Deficiencies Associated with a Change in Reporting Decisions of Triennially Inspected Audit Firms?", *Auditing: A Journal of Practice and Theory* 30(3) 59–79.

International Auditing and Assurance Standards Board (IAASB). 2012. "Improving the Auditor's Report. Invitation to Comment." New York: IFAC.

International Auditing and Assurance Standards Board (IAASB). 2013. "Reporting on Audited Financial Statements: Proposed New and Revised International Standards on Auditing", Exposure Draft, July 25. New York: IFAC.

Kaplan, S. and D. Williams. 2012. "The Changing Relationship between Audit Firm Size and Going Concern Reporting", *Accounting, Organizations and Society* 37(3): 322–41.

Kausar, A. and C. Lennox. 2011. *Going Concern Opinions and Asset Values*, working paper. Singapore: Nanyang Technological University.

Kida, T. 1980. "An Investigation into Auditors' Continuity and Related Qualification Judgments", *Journal of Accounting Research* 18(2): 506–23.

Knechel, W. R. and A. Vanstraelen. 2007. "The Relationship between Auditor Tenure and Audit Quality Implied by Going Concern Opinions", *Auditing: A Journal of Practice and Theory* 26(1): 113–31.

LaSalle, R. and A. Anandarajan. 1996. "Auditors' Views on the Type of Audit Report Issued to Entities with Going Concern Uncertainties", *Accounting Horizons* 10(2): 51–72.

Lennox, C. 2000. "Do Companies Successfully Engage in Opinion-shopping? Evidence from the UK", *Journal of Accounting and Economics* 29(3): 321–37.

Lennox, C. 2005. "Audit Quality and Executive Officers' Affiliations with CPA Firms", *Journal of Accounting and Economics* 37(2): 201–31.

Mutchler, J. F. 1984. "Auditors' Perceptions of the Going-concern Opinion Decision", *Auditing: A Journal of Practice and Theory* 3(Spring): 17–29.

Nogler, G. E. 1995. "The Resolution of Auditor Going Concern Opinions", *Auditing: A Journal of Practice and Theory* 14(2): 54–73.

Public Company Accounting Oversight Board (PCAOB). 2011. *Docket No. 34: Concept Release on Possible Revisions to PCAOB Standards Related to Reports on Audited Financial Statements*, June 21. Washington, DC: PCAOB.

Public Company Accounting Oversight Board (PCAOB). 2013. *Docket No. 34: Proposed Auditing Standards – The Auditor's Report on An Audit of Financial Statements when the Auditor Expresses an Unqualified Opinion; The Auditor's Responsibilities Regarding Other Information in Certain Documents Containing Audited Financial Statements and the Related Auditor's Report; and Related Amendments to PCAOB Standards*, PCAOB Release No. 2013–005, August 13. Washington, DC: PCAOB.

Ruiz-Barbadillo, E., N. Gomez-Aguilar, C. D. Fuentes-Barbera, and M. A Garcia-Benau. 2004. "Audit Quality and the Going-concern Decision-making Process: Spanish Evidence", *European Accounting Review* 13(4): 597–620.

Sharman Inquiry. 2011. *Going Concern and Liquidity Risks: Lessons for Companies and Auditors.* Preliminary Report and Recommendations of the Panel of Inquiry. London: Financial Reporting Council (FRC).

Vandenbogaerde, S., A. Renders, and M. Willekens. 2011. "Expected client loss and auditor independence: a partner-level analysis in a low litigious setting", working paper. Katholieke Universiteit Leuven.

Xu, Y., E. Carson, N. Fargher, and L. Jiang. 2012. "Responses by Australian auditors to the global financial crisis", *Accounting and Finance* (forthcoming).

25
Reporting on internal control

Jean C. Bedard and Lynford Graham

Overview of the topic and its importance

For over 50 years, management and the auditing profession have been challenged to come to grips with the importance of companies instituting effective internal controls as a deterrent to fraud and as a means to publish reliable financial information for users of financial reports. In every major study of misstated financial statements, whether due to fraud or error, weaknesses in internal controls have been cited as a root condition contributing to or failing to prevent fraud or error. This background is discussed further in the section "Historical development".

COSO[1] and AICPA auditing standards have defined internal control as

> A process effected by those charged with governance, management, and other personnel that is designed to provide reasonable assurance about the achievement of the entity's objectives with regard to the reliability of financial reporting, effectiveness and efficiency of operations, and compliance with applicable laws and regulations.
>
> *(AICPA 2012: AU-C 315, para 4)*[2]

Currently, the Committee of Sponsoring Organizations (COSO) Framework (COSO 1992, 2013) is the benchmark from which companies measure the effectiveness of internal controls. While historical texts recognize the existence and importance of internal controls, in recent years public attention has been drawn to the need to more formally address the issue in corporate management, auditing, and public reporting. In the US, public company requirements of the Securities and Exchange Commission (SEC) now state that management will annually test and report on the effectiveness of their internal controls over financial reporting (ICFR). Auditors of accelerated filers[3] are also required to test ICFR, and to issue a separate report on their effectiveness (PCAOB 2007). Additionally, SOX Section 302 requires senior executives (e.g., CFOs and CEOs) to attest quarterly on their financial reporting and disclosures, and any major changes in internal controls or material weakness that are known to exist.

External auditors of private companies, non-profits, and state and local governments must also, at a minimum, evaluate the design of their internal controls (all five COSO components) and seek evidence that the controls described are actually in place (AICPA 2012). However, to rely on internal control effectiveness in planning the audit engagement, auditors should test those controls on which they place reliance. Non-public US entities are not yet required to report on the effectiveness of controls to financial statement users, but control weaknesses and significant deficiencies are required to be reported, in writing, to management and governance groups.

Some countries outside of the US also require internal control reporting. For example, Japan's system is much like the US, in that management is required to evaluate ICFR, and the auditor presents an independent opinion on control effectiveness. And in Canada, companies are required to disclose weaknesses in the design of ICFR in Management's Discussion and Analysis (MD&a), but these disclosures are not certified by management or tested by auditors. A broadly similar, but less stringent requirement, applies in some other jurisdictions. For example, the European Union applies a comply-or-explain principle (e.g., EU 2006), in which companies may deviate from their national corporate governance code, but if so must disclose in the annual report how and why they do not apply certain provisions of the code.

Current issues in this topic area

Despite the agreed importance of internal controls, some vocal public companies continue to debate the cost-effectiveness of requiring management and (for the larger public companies) the auditor to publicly report on the effectiveness of ICFR as required by the Sarbanes-Oxley Act (SOX) (U.S. Congress 2002).[4] However, current surveys reveal continuing declining costs and some support for the benefits of the focus on internal controls. Results of a 2012 Survey by Protiviti (2012) show that about half of respondents felt that the benefits from SOX exceeded its costs. While the survey reports that smaller public companies believe they should be exempted from separate auditor attestation on internal controls (404b), current accelerated filers (53 percent) feel that 404b should be required for all public companies. The latter view is supported by research by Bedard and Graham (2011), which shows that over 70 percent of identified deficiencies were discovered by the auditor, and not the company procedures that preceded auditor involvement. This finding demonstrates the ineffectiveness of many company self-assessments, although Bedard and Graham (2011) do identify some company processes that enhance ICD detection. The Protiviti (2012) survey results additionally support the assertion that controls have at least moderately improved after SOX (69 percent of respondents). It also notes the importance of automated control procedures in achieving efficiencies. While initiating automated controls is expensive, in general the costs of annual compliance have generally decreased for most companies in recent years. Other surveys by the Financial Executives Institute and firms such as Ernst & Young make similar observations.

From a research perspective, additional evidence is needed as to the value, importance, and efficacy of the increased attention given to internal control. Annual surveys of fraudulent activity by the Association of Certified Fraud Examiners (e.g., ACFE 2012) note a decline in the median value of corporate business frauds compared to the pre-SOX era. However, the most recent 2014 survey showed a slight uptick in the median public company fraud loss over the 2012 survey, but some improvement trend for private companies. The ACFE has also consistently noted in recent years that global revenue losses due to fraud could still amount to five percent of total revenues. Also noteworthy is the effectiveness in reducing the severity of loss (if not the incidence of fraud) when anti-fraud measures are incorporated into the business environment. For example, instituting an anonymous hotline, surprise audits, mandatory vacations, and providing incentives to whistleblowers have been shown to reduce the duration of the fraud by half and its severity of any losses by more than a third (ACFE 2012: 37). The most recent survey continues to show the value of hotlines and previous measures, but also the value of data monitoring by the entity (ACFE 2014: 38).

In addition to fraud, companies are increasingly exposed to issues of corruption as business expands into the worldwide environment. Whether directed by management or initiated solely by employees, companies face increasing risks and fines when violating restrictions on corruption or even purchasing from rogue sources. New laws are developed continuously and older laws may be selectively enforced with renewed vigor. For example, the 2012 "conflict minerals" regulations coming from the 2010 Dodd-Frank Financial Reform and Consumer Protection Act (U.S. Congress 2010) cover the disclosure of any minerals originating in countries such as the Democratic Republic of Congo where mining proceeds are often used to finance wars on segments of the populace.[5] A current trend at the time of this writing is more enforcement actions under the 1977 Foreign Corrupt Practices Act.

Historical development

As already noted, internal controls failures are consistently identified as root causes in frauds and financial reporting misstatements. There is a long history of research and legislation focused on this topic. A summary of some important studies and legislation is presented in Table 25.1.

Table 25.1 Important professional studies and legislation in the US

Year	*Study or Legislation*	*Conclusions and Summary Implications*
1977	Foreign Corrupt Practices Act	The Act prohibited US companies from making payments to foreign officials that are of the nature of bribes or influence payments. It also requires public companies to keep and maintain adequate books and records; later amendments established criminal liability for failing to do so.
1978	Cohen Commission (Commission on Auditor's Responsibilities)	The commission made recommendations for narrowing the gap between user expectations and the perceived state of financial reporting. Specifically it addressed the auditor's role in detecting material fraud and violations of laws and recommending more disclosures of uncertainties to financial statement users. In addition it made a variety of recommendations to improve the quality of auditing firm practice.
1987	Treadway Commission (National Commission of Fraudulent Financial Reporting)	In its review of failed audits and instances of fraud, the commission report recommended stronger and more independent audit committees. In addition, its work identified the void of a framework for assessing internal control, which led to the 1992 COSO report.
1991	Federal Sentencing Guidelines	Established guidelines for sentencing organizations convicted of crimes or corruption by employees or agents. When companies demonstrate implementation of due diligence regarding internal controls and corruption, substantial fines may be reduced.
1992	Internal Control: Framework (Committee of Sponsoring Organizations; COSO)	In response to the Treadway Commission findings, COSO issued a framework document that defined internal control and its key component elements. While it was hoped that such a framework would result in better controls and voluntary public reporting on control effectiveness, auditors testing the reporting mechanism noted that investors and analysts did not seem to value the additional information in these reports. The COSO framework did work its way into the internal controls discussions of the auditing literature of the 1990s, but reporting on internal controls was never mandated.

Table 25.1 (continued)

Year	*Study or Legislation*	*Conclusions and Summary Implications*
		Refinements and more guidance followed the SOX mandates, and a specific report for smaller public companies followed in 2006; in 2009 a report better defining the concept of monitoring was published. In spring 2013 the COSO released a new version of the framework document, which subsumed and superseded the previous reports and guidance.
2002	Sarbanes-Oxley Act of 2002	Enacted by Congress in 2002, this followed a spate of frauds and audit failures in the recent period. The large firm of Arthur Andersen dissolved in response to pending litigation from undetected fraud and financial reporting mistakes such as ENRON, WorldCom, Global Crossings, and the Baptist Pension Funds. For the first time managements and auditors were required to explicitly report on the effectiveness of internal control over financial reporting. The Act created the Public Company Accounting Oversight Board (PCAOB) and that led to separate audit and quality inspection standards for audits of public companies. After company protests in 2004 and 2005 over the costs of implementing the rules, the PCAOB issued a revised Standard allowing more consideration of risk in performing these audits. In 2010, the Dodd-Frank Financial Reform and Consumer Protection Act permanently deferred the requirement for auditors of non-accelerated (smaller) public companies to separately report on internal controls.

* For further information on these reports and current developments, see www.COSO.org.

While historically internal controls were thought of as transactional controls and segregation of duties issues, current thinking assigns more importance to the control environment and other entity-level elements. The COSO Framework embodies this modern thinking and continues to be refined in light of increased attention and use and further thought. The COSO Framework is widely accepted in the US as well as worldwide. Broadly, the COSO Internal Control Framework recognizes five major components: control environment, risk assessment, control activities, information and communication, and monitoring. To have effective internal control, a "passing grade" must be attained in all five component areas. A helpful refinement introduced in 2006 was the identification of 20 principles associated with the five components. These principles help users identify and focus on the elements of the component for which evidence of effective design and implementation is sought. Assertions and control objectives can then be utilized for even more granularity in assessing effective design and operation of the underlying controls.

In 2009 COSO issued a document focused on monitoring (i.e., what it is and is not), to deter over-reliance on monitoring controls when the underlying detailed controls are not present or are present but not effective. In 2013 COSO released an updated version of its Internal Control Framework, which combines and replaces the prior publications. While retaining the five components, the number of principles has been reduced to 17 by combining some principles and articulating two new ones. The expanded guidance is accompanied by additional practice aids to assist implementation.[6] The five components and 17 principles comprising the basic structure of the guidance are provided in Table 25.2. Information technology is a concept that cuts across the components of internal control.[7]

There exist similar frameworks in other parts of the world, such as COCO (Canada), Turnbull (UK), and J-SOX (Japan); however, the concepts from the seminal contribution of COSO

Table 25.2 COSO components and principles

Control Environment	*Risk Assessment*	*Control Activities*	*Information and Communication*	*Monitoring*
1. Demonstrates commitment to integrity and ethical values 2. Exercises oversight responsibility 3. Establishes structure, authority, and responsibility 4. Demonstrates commitment to competence 5. Establishes accountability	6. Specifies relevant objectives 7. Identifies and assesses risk 8. Identifies and assesses significant change 9. Assesses fraud risk	10. Selects and develops control activities 11. Selects and develops general controls over technology 12. Deploys through policies and procedures	13. Generates relevant information 14. Communicates internally 15. Communicates externally	16. Conducts ongoing and separate evaluations 17. Evaluates and communicates deficiencies

are apparent in these systems and COSO remains the *de facto* "standard" for assessing ICFR. Nevertheless, the COSO Framework continues to evolve. It was not until the 1960s that the auditing profession introduced a more formal way to reflect effective internal controls in planning the nature, timing, and extent of various audit procedures. The audit risk model provided a conceptual framework from which to balance the various audit procedures to achieve the required level of professional assurance before issuing an audit opinion. While most auditors use judgment in achieving this goal, some have applied the risk model as a formula.[8]

Summary of current state of research findings

There is a considerable body of research addressing internal control reporting. Most of these studies use data from US SOX Section 404/302 reports and generally focus on the determinants of reported deficiencies in ICFR, the consequences of disclosures for stakeholders, and remediation of previously disclosed deficiencies.[9]

Determinants

Regarding determinants of deficiencies reported under Section 404/302, research commonly finds that disclosures of ineffective controls are greater for companies with higher financial risk, faster growth, and smaller size (e.g., Ge and McVay 2005). Such companies likely do not have the resources available to design and/or maintain effective systems of control, including control processes at the account level, systems controls, and higher-level monitoring controls and control environments. In terms of company complexity (e.g., in terms of number of segments and foreign operations), Hoitash *et al.* (2009) are consistently shown to be positively associated with reports of ICFR deficiencies. In terms of corporate governance, Hoitash *et al.* (2009) show that the strength of the board of directors and the accounting expertise of audit committee activity are both associated with lower likelihood of ineffective ICFR. Ashbaugh-Skaife *et al.* (2007) show that companies with material weakness (MW) disclosures have more financial restatements.[10]

Research also examines the association of auditor affiliation and auditor change with reports of ineffective ICFR. Ashbaugh-Skaife *et al.* (2007) and Ge and McVay (2005) use a single variable representing the largest six (Big 6) audit firms. They find more reports of ineffective ICFR in clients of those firms, and conclude that audit quality is higher for those firms. However, Hoitash *et al.* (2009) separate the largest audit firms into the Big 4 and next-tier firms, finding more reports of ineffective controls only for the next tier. This implies that the clients of Big 4 firms were not more likely to disclose ineffective ICFR during the early years of Section 404. Likely, the larger clients of those firms had better controls (and thus fewer control flaws to find) while the next-tier firms were effective in reporting the control problems uncovered in their Section 404 activity.

Several studies also examine auditor change. Ettredge *et al.* (2011) find that companies receiving adverse ICFR opinions are more likely to subsequently dismiss their auditors. In addition, Ashbaugh-Skaife *et al.* (2007) and Hoitash *et al.* (2009) both find increased incidence of adverse ICFR opinions following auditor change. This suggests that the predecessor auditor may have resigned due to control problems that are then recognized by the successor auditor.[11]

The controls assessments themselves also appear to be influenced by the process followed and whether there is oversight or re-performance by the independent auditor. While public company assessments and testing of internal control are required to precede auditor assessment and testing for accelerated filers, Bedard and Graham (2011) show that company processes initially missed over 70 percent of the deficiencies eventually identified for that reporting period. Their research also shows that companies frequently under-assessed the severity of the MWs and significant deficiencies they initially discovered. While their study was conducted in the early years of SOX implementation on larger public companies, the implication is that the self-assessments required of today's non-accelerated filers (under Section 404(a), auditor assessments are not required) need to be of much higher quality than previously observed to be effective.

Consequences

An important line of research involves investigating whether internal control reporting provides valuable information to market participants. Several studies examine the link between ICFR problems and measures of financial reporting quality. For instance, studies find that internal control reporting is associated with financial reporting quality as measured by abnormal levels of accruals (e.g., Ashbaugh-Skaife *et al.* 2008a). Hammersley *et al.* (2008) show that the impact of internal control disclosure on the company's stock price depends on the nature of the weaknesses disclosed, including their severity. Ashbaugh-Skaife *et al.* (2008b) find that companies with internal control deficiencies have significantly higher risk, and higher cost of equity capital. Li *et al.* (2010) find that companies receiving an adverse SOX 404 opinion have less-qualified CFOs, and those companies experience more CFO turnover following disclosure. Many studies find that entity-level control deficiencies (e.g., problems in control environment, expertise/training, monitoring, and information technology) have more serious consequences.

Research on public/listed companies outside the US

While the greatest number of studies on internal control (IC) reporting examine data from US public companies, some research investigates reporting in jurisdictions outside the US. For instance, Lu *et al.* (2011) find a negative association between IC weaknesses and financial reporting quality, which they say "establishes the credibility of Canadian IC disclosures and replicates findings in the much costlier and more monitored US setting." Van de Poel and Vanstraelen (2011) find (in the Netherlands) that the description of the IC system (to which most EU countries have limited their IC regulations) does not provide information about the quality of financial reporting. While there is a negative association between a statement of effective ICs and financial reporting quality, very few companies provide this statement. They also conclude that in the Dutch "comply-or-explain" regime, the types of explanations given for noncompliance are unsatisfactory. In a study of IC disclosures in Japan, Yazawa (2010) finds that MW disclosures are associated with financial reporting quality, but this influence differs depending on the severity of, and reasons for, the material weakness. Particularly, he does not find a significant association between stock price and MW disclosure, while prior research in the US generally finds a significant price reaction.

Research on nonprofit entities

A few studies examine internal controls in nonprofit entities. The most recent is Petrovits *et al.* (2011), who find that entity characteristics influencing public disclosure of internal control problems in non-profits are similar to those in the public company sector: complexity, financial distress, smaller size, and rapid growth. Further, they find an impact of disclosure, as reportable conditions (i.e., material weaknesses) in financial reporting controls are negatively associated with future public support, federal program compliance, and subsequent government contributions. Recent examples reported in the business press include the United Way of the National Capital area (e.g., Jackson and Fogarty 2006) and the New York Chapter of the American Red Cross (Devaney *et al.* 2013), in which control weaknesses resulting in financial losses or alleged improprieties led to a period of diminished contributions.

Remediation

Under Section 404, companies must disclose any MWs that remain unremediated at year end. Corporate controls are improved when management remediates deficiencies that company personnel (or consultants engaged for the purpose, if applicable) or the external auditor have identified, prior to the balance sheet date.[12] Public reports of IC reveal (through the absence of a subsequent report) when companies remediate previously disclosed MW. Overall, rates of disclosure of ineffective ICFR under Section 404 have declined over time (e.g., Kinney and Shepardson 2011), suggesting that remediation of control flaws is improving ICFR.

Several studies examine factors associated with remediation of publicly reported Section 404 MW disclosures subsequent to initial disclosure. Some examine full remediation at the company level through a subsequent report of effective controls (e.g., Goh 2009), or remediation at the individual control level through the subsequent absence of a specific type of previously disclosed MW (e.g., Bedard *et al.* 2012b). In terms of company characteristics, these studies generally find that remediation is reduced by publicly observable characteristics that might affect incentives and ability to remediate, such as complexity, resource constraints, and corporate governance. In terms of characteristics of deficiencies, research consistently shows that entity-level control deficiencies are less likely to be remediated, as well as deficiencies in certain accounts such as revenues and taxes. Extending their results on CFO turnover mentioned under the subsection Consequences, Li *et al.* (2010) report that remediation of ICFR disclosures is only associated with remediation if the new CFO has better qualifications than those of the CFO that was replaced.

Unresolved issues demanding future research

The debate will continue regarding the value of required procedures on the part of management and auditors to implement and monitor the effectiveness of internal controls. To counter the arguments of increased costs, the benefits of addressing internal controls issues need to be identified and better articulated. Quantification of the benefits of more reliable financial reporting (e.g., fewer or less severe or more timely discovered restatements) would also assist in the dialogue.

Users, regulators, and those responsible for the integrity of our financial markets will continue to assess the progress made and the failures remaining to be addressed toward the ability of entities to implement cost-effective systems of internal controls to prevent and detect frauds and to produce more reliable financial reporting. Data and research assisting in benchmarking where we were, where we are, and the observable trends will prove valuable to the assessment.

Insights into how critical management and auditor judgments are made are helpful in refining the approaches of management and auditors to the assessment of controls. Additional insight into factors influencing management and auditor views about the quality of controls and the decisions surrounding the classification of the severity of control deficiencies will continue to be welcome.

Further, information is lacking on what lies below the publicly reported surface reports and disclosures, including advice auditors are giving to companies as they try to prevent adverse opinions on IC, and what companies are doing to remediate identified deficiencies. For instance:

- Surveys could investigate how companies have changed ICFR in response to public reporting.
- In-depth field studies could examine the cost/benefit of specific internal control changes. What are the deficiencies that lead to change, and what is the process by which companies made these changes?
- Cross-national comparisons on these issues would also be useful.

Conclusion

We are in a period of increased attention to the importance of internal controls in the effective governance of entities, and to their meeting of business objectives with corporate responsibility and ethics. The SOX mandate of reporting on the effectiveness of internal controls by public companies in the US was unwelcome, but the pressure had been building for decades to pay attention to IC, and repeatedly the issue had been pushed aside after the periodic storm of public criticism had passed. No longer is this the case. Not far behind is the potential requirement that governments publicly report on the effectiveness of their controls as a part of their stewardship of public monies. Foundations and non-profits are also contemplating controls reporting as a means to distinguish their entity in the increasing competition for funding and contributions.

We are still finding our way in this new era. The rigor implied in the first SEC regulations and PCAOB audit standard (PCAOB 2004: AS2) created a need for a "kinder and gentler" benchmark, that accepted more judgment based on risk assessment in deciding what to test and more flexibility to rely on the work of others when it was competently and objectively performed. Nevertheless, the intention was not to weaken the legislative mandate, but make it more efficient. Court and legislative challenges to SOX have eased the burden to smaller public companies in as much as now, only management's assessment requires disclosure in the 10-K; but some research questions the effectiveness of self-assessments in the absence of independent auditor oversight and testing. It remains to be seen if company self-assessment over time is sufficient to provide quality reporting.

There is much to learn about user needs and the value and importance various users attach to quality financial reporting. Research has provided a framework from which to discuss and debate some of the benefits of public reporting on internal controls. Based on research to date, effective control environments are associated with lower costs of capital. Not surprisingly, smaller entities, more complex entities, and entities in financial distress have more internal control issues. The association of the auditor and the quality of the company and auditor processes also appear to influence the quality of the reporting on ICs.

We have entered a new era of reporting on the effectiveness of ICFR. While some evidence suggests that increased attention to internal controls has resulted in improvements in financial reporting, research should continue to investigate this association over time. In the current circumstances, there are many differences between countries. The US has taken a strong position on introducing reporting on IC effectiveness. Some other countries have opted for less stringent requirements in this area, and others have chosen not to implement IC reporting at this time. Differences in regulations in different countries may provide insight as to the more optimal balance of benefits and costs of compliance.

Notes

1 COSO is the acronym for the Committee of Sponsoring Organizations, which developed the 1992 Internal Control – Integrated Framework and the subsequent updates providing additional guidance.
2 International Standards on Auditing also include this definition (IAASB, ISA 315, paragraph 4(c)).
3 Public float of over $75 million (among other criteria) defines the status of a company as an accelerated filer. The JOBS (Jumpstart our Business Start-Ups) Act of 2012 provides additional exemption from auditor reporting for new filers with less than $1billion in revenue.
4 For an historical commentary on developments leading to Section 404 of the Sarbanes-Oxley Act (SOX), see Gupta *et al.* (2013).
5 sec.gov/rules/final/2012/34–67716.pdf (accessed 9 May 2014).
6 The documents mentioned here can be obtained through the website, www.CPA2biz.com (accessed 9 May 2014). Links to this site are available through the COSO website or the websites of any of the sponsoring organizations (AICPA, AAA, IIA, IMA, FEI).
7 COBIT (Control Objective for Information Technology) is a set of objectives for effective information technology (computer systems) operations, available at www.isaca.org (accessed 9 May 2014). A set of tailored IT objectives specific to SOX applications is also available (Fox *et al.* 2006). Neither document is specifically endorsed by regulators, but they can be helpful to entities and auditors in addressing issues related to the IT environment, security and access, changes to systems, and effective operations of computer systems and applications.
8 For additional information regarding the development of the role of internal control in auditing, see Bell and Wright (1995: 23–8).
9 As this chapter focuses on internal control reporting, we consider research that examines the determinants and consequences of publicly available reports of controls made by auditors and/or entity management. However, there is also an active line of experimental research on auditors' assessments of their clients' internal control quality during the audit engagement. For a summary see Asare *et al.* (2013).
10 According to Audit Analytics (2011), the number and severity of financial restatements in the US has declined since a peak in the mid-2000s, which could be due in part to improved controls.
11 In addition, based on the experience of one of the authors, in the period of initial implementation, some audit firms resigned in advance of completing the audit when it became apparent that the client was unable or unwilling to complete their required assessments and testing on a timely basis, or were unlikely to be able to support an opinion that controls were effective.
12 Companies also have the opportunity to avoid disclosure by remediating the control deficiency after detection but prior to the balance sheet date. Graham and Bedard (2013) provide the only evidence on this level of disclosure, finding about 26 percent of deficiencies are remediated in this phase of the process.

References

American Institute of Certified Public Accountants (AICPA). 2012. AU-C 315 *Understanding the Entity and Its Environment and Assessing the Risks of Material Misstatement.* New York: AICPA.

Asare, S., B. C. Fitzgerald, L. Graham, J. Joe, and E. Negangard. 2013. "Auditors' Internal Control over Financial Reporting Decisions: Analysis, Synthesis, and Research Directions", *Auditing: A Journal of Practice & Theory* 32(Supp. 1): 131–66.

Ashbaugh-Skaife, H., D. W. Collins, and W. R. Kinney. 2007. "The Discovery and Reporting of Internal Control Deficiencies Prior to SOX-mandated Audits", *Journal of Accounting and Economics* 44(1–2): 166–92.

Ashbaugh-Skaife, H., D. Collins, W. Kinney, and R. LaFond. 2008a. "The Effect of SOX Internal Control Deficiencies and their Remediation on Accrual Quality", *The Accounting Review* (83): 217–50.

Ashbaugh-Skaife, H., D. W. Collins, W. R. Kinney, and R. Lafond. 2008b. "The Effect of SOX Internal Control Deficiencies on Firm Risk and Cost of Equity", *Journal of Accounting Research* 47(1): 1–43.

Association of Certified Fraud Examiners (ACFE). 2012, 2014. *Report to the Nation on Occupational Fraud and Abuse.* Austin, TX: ACFE.

Audit Analytics. 2011. *2011 Financial Restatements: An Eleven Year Comparison.* Sutton, MA: Audit Analytics.

Bedard, J. C. and L. Graham. 2011. "Detection and Severity Classifications of Sarbanes-Oxley Section 404 Internal Control Deficiencies", *The Accounting Review* 86(3): 825–55.

Bedard, J. R., R. Hoitash, U. Hoitash, and K. Westermann. 2012b. "Material Weakness Remediation and Earnings Quality: A Detailed Examination", *Auditing: A Journal of Practice & Theory* 31(1): 57–78.

Committee of Sponsoring Organizations (COSO). 1992. *Internal Controls: Integrated Framework.* [Subsequent to this seminal work, a supplement on External Reporting was issued in 1993 and further updates were published in 2006 (Smaller Public Companies); 2009 (Monitoring); and a general revision in 2013.]

Bell, T. B. and A. M. Wright. 1995. *Auditing Practice, Research and Education: A Productive Collaboration.* New York: American Institute of CPAs.

Devaney, W., D. Martin, N. Buell, and J. S. Tenenbaum. 2013. "Preventing Fraud and Embezzlement in your Nonprofit Organization", Venable LLP. Available at: www.mondaq.com/unitedstates/x/273810/Charities+Non-Profits/Preventing+Fraud+and+Embezzlement+in+Your+Nonprofit+Organization (accessed 24 June 2014).

Ettredge, M., J. Heintz, C. Li, and S. Scholz. 2011. "Auditor Realignments Accompanying SOX 404 ICFR Reporting Requirements", *Accounting Horizons* 25(1): 17–40.

European Union (EU). 2006. Directive 2006/46/Ec of the European Parliament and of the Council. Available online at http://eur-lex.europa.eu/LexUriServ/LexUriServ.do?uri=OJ:L:2006:224:0001:0007:EN:PDF (accessed 9 May 2014).

Fox, C., P. Zonneveld, and the IT Governance Institute. 2006. *IT Control Objectives for Sarbanes-Oxley: The Role of IT in the Design and Implementation of Internal Control over Financial Reporting,* 2nd ed. ISACA.

Ge, W. and S. McVay. 2005. "The Disclosure of Material Weaknesses in Internal Control after the Sarbanes-Oxley Act", *Accounting Horizons* 19(3): 137–58.

Graham, L. and J.C. Bedard. 2013. "Remediation of Section 404 Internal Control Deficiencies Prior to Year-end", *Auditing: A Journal of Practice & Theory* 32(4): 45–69.

Goh, B. W. 2009. "Audit Committees, Boards of Directors, and Remediation of Material Weaknesses in Internal Control", *Contemporary Accounting Research* 26(2): 549–79.

Gupta, P., T. Weirich, and L. E. Turner. 2013. "Sarbanes-Oxley and Public Reporting on Internal Control: Hasty Reaction or Delayed Action?", *Accounting Horizons* 27(2): 371–408.

Hammersley, J., L. Myers, and C. Shakespeare. 2008. "Market Reactions to the Disclosure of Internal Control Weaknesses and to the Characteristics of Those Weaknesses under Section 302 of the Sarbanes-Oxley Act of 2002", *Review of Accounting Studies* 13(1): 141–65.

Hoitash, U., R. Hoitash, and J. Bedard. 2009. "Corporate Governance and Internal Control Quality: A Comparison of Regulatory Regimes", *The Accounting Review* 84(3): 839–67.

Jackson, P. and T. Fogarty. 2006. *Sarbanes–Oxley and Nonprofit Management: Skills, Techniques, and Methods,* New York: John Wiley & Sons.

Kinney, W.R. and M. Shepardson. 2011. "Do Control Effectiveness Disclosures Require Internal Control Audits? A Natural Experiment with Small U.S. Public Companies", *Journal of Accounting Research* 49(2): 413–48.

Li, C., L. Sun, and M. Ettredge. 2010. "Financial Executive Qualifications, Financial Executive Turnover, and Adverse SOX 404 Opinions", *Journal of Accounting and Economics* 50(1): 93–110.

Lu, H., G. Richardson, and S. Salterio. 2011. "Direct and Indirect Effects of Internal Control Weaknesses on Accrual Quality: Evidence from a Unique Canadian Regulatory Setting", *Contemporary Accounting Research* 28(2): 675–707.

Petrovits, C., C. Shakespeare, and A. Shih. 2011. "The Causes and Consequences of Internal Control Problems in Nonprofit Organizations", *The Accounting Review* 86(1): 325–57.

Protiviti. 2012. *2012 Sarbanes-Oxley Compliance Survey: Where US-Listed Companies Stand: Reviewing Cost, Time, Effort and Processes.* Available online at www.protiviti.com/en-US/Documents/Surveys/2012-SOX-Compliance-Survey-Protiviti.pdf (accessed 9 May 2014).

Public Company Accounting Oversight Board (PCAOB). 2004. *An Audit of Internal Control over Financial Reporting Performed in Conjunction with an Audit of Financial Statements.* Auditing Standard No. 2. PCAOB Release No. 2004–001. March 9. Washington, DC: PCAOB.

Public Company Accounting Oversight Board (PCAOB). 2007. *An Audit of Internal Control over Financial Reporting that is Integrated with an Audit of Financial Statements.* Auditing Standard No. 5. PCAOB Release No. 2007–005A. June 12. Washington, DC: PCAOB.

U.S. Congress. 2002. *The Public Company Accounting Reform and Investor Protection Act of 2002 (The Sarbanes-Oxley Act).* Public Law No. 107–204, 116 Statute 745 July 30. Washington, DC: Government Printing Office.

U.S. Congress. 2010. *Dodd-Frank Wall Street Reform and Consumer Protection Act.* Public Law No. 111–203 July 21. Washington, DC: Government Printing Office.

Van de Poel, K. and A. Vanstraelen. 2011. "Management Reporting on Internal Control and Accruals Quality: Insights from a 'Comply-or-Explain' Internal Control Regime", *Auditing: A Journal of Practice & Theory* 30(3): 181–209.

Yazawa, Kenichi. 2010. "Why Don't Japanese Companies Disclose Internal Control Weaknesses? Evidence from J-SOX Mandated Audits." Available online at http://papers.ssrn.com/sol3/papers.cfm?abstract_id=1607709 (accessed 26 April 2014).

Part V
Alternative auditing services

26

Assurance of environmental, social and sustainability information

Roger Simnett

Overview of topic and its importance

This chapter outlines issues and identifies research opportunities for assurance of general purpose stand-alone reports whose subject matter covers environmental, social and sustainability issues. The focus of this chapter is assurance of general purpose reports because these reports are made available to shareholders (or more broadly stakeholders), rather than being available only for internal or specific regulatory purposes, and therefore assurance of these reports is a matter of broader public interest. Stand-alone reports are examined as they can give rise to assurance engagements separate from the audits of general purpose financial reports (GPFRs), even though GPFRs can sometimes include elements of nonfinancial performance.

Two main categories of stand-alone general purpose environmental, social and sustainability reports are identified which give rise to separate assurance engagements, have significantly increased in frequency internationally over the last ten years, and for which separate subject matter reports and assurance reports are observable. These are analyzed separately as they comprise separate markets, are subject to different regulatory and standard-setting initiatives and give rise to different research opportunities. The first of these are assurance on general purpose reports which are voluntarily prepared and involve the public dissemination of information about an organization's nonfinancial performance, including environmental, social and governance considerations, to produce what are commonly known as sustainability reports (a terminology used throughout this chapter).

The second type of assurance engagement is on a specific aspect of environmental reporting which has gained increased attention over the last ten years, assurance on greenhouse gas (GhG) emissions reports. Throughout the world, there have been many regulatory initiatives which have led to reporting regulations being implemented by specific countries or regions, and global initiatives on disclosure and assurance by international bodies such as the Carbon Disclosure Standards Board (CDSB). A need for credible emissions figures has created a strong demand for assurance of GhG emission reports and this is further evidenced by the recent release from the International Auditing and Assurance Standards Board (IAASB) of an assurance standard providing comprehensive guidance on GhG assurance engagements, ISAE 3410 "Assurance on a Greenhouse Gas Statement" (IAASB 2012).

At the same time that more organizations are publicly reporting these types of information, report users are demanding that the information reported be relevant and reliable. One of the main ways of demonstrating this is through having information independently assured. Providing assurance on environmental, social and sustainability reports is one way to mitigate the skepticism with which they are often received. Thus, around the world we have seen significant growth in the assurance of these stand-alone reports.

Research on these two types of assurance engagements has the ability to contribute significantly to, or challenge, current knowledge about the assurance function. While research on financial statement audits is a mature area, with the knowledge gained from research adding to what is an extensive existing body of knowledge, research on assurance of sustainability and GhG information is in its infancy and offers many opportunities and abilities to challenge or extend existing knowledge of the assurance function. For example, the nature of the assurance market is different from that of the financial statement audit market, as it is potentially more competitive in structure; assurance is not mandatory and is therefore subject to (and is capable of being shaped by) a market evaluation. Thus, if it is determined that the benefits of assurance exceed the costs, there is then a choice of type of assurance provider from either within or outside the accounting profession. Further, when researching at the engagement level, many of the concepts underpinning the financial statement audit methodology are challenged when it comes to assuring sustainability reports. As an example, the concept of materiality needs to be approached differently as not every risk of material misstatement is capable of being measured with a common unit of measurement. If working at the individual level or group decision-making level, there are significant differences in the types of engagements that will affect how decisions are made; for example, how engagement teams with diverse subject matter expertise can best be assembled, or how performance of multidisciplinary teams can be enhanced. Thus there are many challenges and interesting research questions that can be addressed, and with each of these assurance areas growing significantly in practice and being on the radar of the standard setters and regulators, the research has the potential to significantly inform theory, policy and practice.

The next section of this paper, "Growth in these types of assurance engagements", explores the growth in these types of assurance engagements, and outlines the current issues associated with it. The following section summarizes the current state of research findings and the next section identifies areas for further research. The next section identifies expected future trends which may significantly influence the market for environmental, social and sustainability assurance, and the final section outlines the major conclusions.

Growth in these types of assurance engagements and current regulatory and practice issues

Sustainability and GhG reporting are subject to concerns regarding the completeness and credibility of the information that is being provided, and obtaining independent third-party assurance is considered to be a valuable tool for addressing these concerns (Holder-Webb *et al.* 2009; Simnett *et al.* 2009b). One of the major difficulties in providing assurance services on sustainability and GhG reports has been concerns about the development of generally accepted suitable reporting criteria for such engagements. This section examines the development of suitable reporting criteria, and the growth in public reporting and assurance for each type of engagement.

Assurance of sustainability reports

The number of stand-alone sustainability reports has grown dramatically over the last ten years (Pflugrath *et al.* 2011). For example, data from Corporate Register (2012), a large international collection of publicly available sustainability reports, shows almost 6,000 companies publishing a sustainability report in 2011, compared to about 500 companies in 1998. KPMG also undertakes triennial reviews of the current practice in sustainability reporting and assurance. In the most recent of these, KPMG (2011) identified whether the largest companies in the world, the Global Fortune 250 (G250), together with the largest 100 companies in each of 34 countries (N100), are currently reporting and assuring these types of information. The report identified that 95 per cent of G250 companies now produce a sustainability report, up more than 14 per cent from the 2008 survey, leading KMPG to conclude that producing a sustainability report now seems to have become virtually mandatory for large international companies. Also, 64 per cent of N100 companies produce a sustainability report, up 11 percentage points from the 2008 survey. The report also outlined that the number assured is increasing, finding that 46 per cent of the G250 and 38 per cent of the N100 are currently assured. Of those that undertake assurance, more than 70 per cent of the G250 and close to 65 per cent of the N100 engage assurers from the major accounting firms. This shows that the accounting firms are increasing their market share for sustainability assurance engagements for large international companies, but that other assurance providers still maintain a significant market presence.

The major reporting framework currently in use is the one developed by the Global Reporting Initiative (GRI). GRI recognizes that the verification of sustainability reports is at an early stage in its evolution, and encourages the development and adoption of principles for verification, which are seen to enhance the quality, usefulness and credibility of information used within the reporting organization and the underlying management systems and processes.

With regard to assurance standards identified by the KPMG (2011) survey, the main assurance standard referred to in the assurance reports is the IAASB's (2005) ISAE 3000 "Assurance Engagements Other than Audits and Reviews of Historical Financial Information", or its national equivalent. This is used in nearly all instances where the assurer is from the accounting profession, and is also referred to by some assurers from outside the profession. AA1000AS, an assurance standard issued by the non-profit organization AccountAbility, is the standard referred to most frequently by assurance providers from outside the accounting profession.

Assurance of GhG reports

The reporting and assurance of GhG emission reports has received increasing international impetus in the last ten years due to the heightened awareness of global warming among investors, stakeholders and regulators. A growing number of countries have mandated the reporting of GhG emissions as the basis of government mandated Emissions Trading (or Taxation) Schemes (ETSs) which aim to enable reductions in GhG emissions in the future (e.g. the European ETS (EU 2005) and the Regional Greenhouse Gas Initiative (RGGI 2008) in the USA). In addition, many entities also report their emissions under voluntary emissions reporting schemes (ERSs) (e.g. The Carbon Disclosure Project (CDP 2012) and Japan's Voluntary ETS (Japan's Ministry of the Environment 2009)).

While national or regional regulations on GhG reporting would normally be considered as suitable criteria for reporting and assurance purposes, a general purpose reporting framework has also recently been developed by the Climate Disclosure Standards Board (CDSB 2012). Relatedly, an extensive international collection of stand-alone GhG reports and associated assurance services has been assembled by the CDP (CDP 2012). Since CDP sent out the first request for climate change information in 2003, it has gained widespread recognition as a leading repository of information on carbon reports. It currently has responses from nearly 2,000 unique companies from 55 countries. Different forms of GhG statements have been observed to occur in practice. These include disclosures required by regulation, disclosures related to emissions trading schemes and voluntary disclosures.

The importance of ensuring GhG emissions are measured and reported with rigor and credibility is evidenced by the fact that according to the World Bank (WB 2011) the global carbon market has grown rapidly from a total of $11 billion in 2005 to $142 billion in 2011. The need for credible emission figures has created a strong demand for the assurance on GhG emissions (Simnett *et al.* 2009a; Huggins *et al.* 2011) and is further evidenced by the recent release by the IAASB of ISAE 3410 (IAASB 2012). The assurance standard covers the assurer's responsibilities for identifying, assessing and responding to risks of material misstatement in GhG reports. The standard also recognizes that most engagements will be undertaken by a multidisciplinary team (including, for example, accountants, engineers or environmental scientists) and thus addresses the need to integrate such experts into the various stages of the engagement. Prior to the release of this standard the assurance standard mainly used by the accounting firms for such engagements was ISAE 3000.

Approximately 36 per cent of the 2007–11 GhG reports available from the CDP are assured. The market for assurance providers was found to be fairly evenly split between accounting firm providers and other providers (Zhou *et al.* 2012). When GhG reports are assured by practitioners external to the accounting profession, including engineers and environmental scientists, the ISO's (2006) ISO 14064–3 is the assurance standard that is most commonly used.

Current state of research findings

Paralleling (but trailing) the growth in the assurance services provided is research that has examined assurance of environmental, social and sustainability issues. In this section the research on assurance of sustainability information is covered, followed by research on the assurance of GhG reports. The concentration will be on empirical research, and will categorize the types of research undertaken by method under the headings archival, behavioral and other.

Research on assurance of sustainability reports

Most sustainability reports that gain public interest and research attention are usually presented as stand-alone reports, in a document distinct from the annual report (Simnett *et al.* 2009a, 2009b; Dhaliwal *et al.* 2011; KPMG 2011; Pflugrath *et al.* 2011). Researching assurance engagements on stand-alone sustainability reports allows the researcher to concentrate their attention on the specifics of these assurance engagements.

Archival research aimed at understanding the market and benefits of assurance

Initially, archival research was aimed at identifying factors associated with the decisions to assure stand-alone sustainability reports, and if assured, the choice of the assurance provider. Researchers have capitalized on the differences in the structure of the market, and used agency theory, stakeholder theory, legitimacy theory and signaling theory as the theoretical bases for their hypotheses. Focusing on international firms producing stand-alone sustainability reports,

Simnett *et al.* (2009b) examined the impact of both country-level and firm specific factors on the choice to have these reports assured. Simnett *et al.*'s (2009b) results indicate that companies seeking to enhance the credibility of their reports and build their corporate reputation are more likely to have their sustainability reports assured, although it does not matter whether the assurance provider comes from the auditing profession. They also found that companies operating in stakeholder orientated countries are more likely to choose the auditing profession as an assurer. When US observations were deleted from the sample (the US having a very low rate of assurance on sustainability reports), it was only firm size and industry affiliation (not stakeholder orientation) that continued to hold significance, leading Simnett *et al.* (2009b) to conclude that it is the need for enhanced credibility that drives demand for assurance. These findings were supported by Kolk and Perego (2010), in their examination of assurance reports for sustainability engagements by the G250. Focusing exclusively on the Fortune 500 companies from the United States, Cho *et al.* (2012) found that the US companies that obtain assurance on their stand-alone corporate social responsibility (CSR) reports tend to operate in environmentally sensitive industries or in the finance industry, supporting the view that the need for enhanced credibility of the CSR disclosures increases the likelihood of obtaining assurance.

More recent archival studies have moved from the market for assurance to examining its benefit, although this research is still in its infancy. Dhaliwal *et al.* (2011), examining the issuance of sustainability reports by US firms from 1993–2007, found that firms with a high cost of equity capital tend to initiate disclosure of sustainability activities and that initiating firms with superior social responsibility performance enjoy a subsequent reduction in the cost of equity capital. In additional analysis they found that, conditional on first-time CSR disclosure, external assurance further reduces the cost of equity capital. Dhaliwal *et al.* (2012) examined the relationship between the issuance of stand-alone sustainability reports and analyst forecast accuracy across 31 countries. They found that this issuance was associated with lower analyst forecast error (improved analyst forecast accuracy). In additional analysis they found that the assurance of sustainability reports is not significant in any of the three forecasting horizons examined.

Experimental research examining individual and team differences

Recent experimental research suggests that assurance of sustainability reports increases their perceived credibility. A number of experimental studies have examined the relative advantages that assurance providers from professional accounting firms have over alternative assurance providers (mainly, expert sustainability consultants). Professional accountants are commonly argued to be higher quality assurance providers, with significant reputational capital, access to global networks, with stringent organizational quality controls and an understanding of a well developed financial statement audit methodology that can be translated to other subject matter (Huggins *et al.* 2011; Pflugrath *et al.* 2011). Other assurers are commonly argued as having greater subject matter expertise, appropriate assurance expertise, charging less for the provision of their services, and are seen as having more of a focus on adding value to the organization (Simnett *et al.* 2009a; Huggins *et al.* 2011).

Coram *et al.* (2009) showed that the assurance of voluntary nonfinancial disclosures was able to positively affect stock price estimation by sophisticated users only if the nonfinancial performance was positive but not when performance was negative. Using an experimental design, Pflugrath *et al.* (2011) report that assurance on sustainability reports led to increased credibility for a sample of financial analysts from Australia, the United States and the United Kingdom. However, they also found that impacts on credibility are higher when reporting companies are from industries where assurance is more common, and that, for the US, assurance by a professional accountant leads to more credibility in the reporting than when assurance is from a sustainability consultant. Both Pflugrath *et al.* (2011) and Coram *et al.* (2009) therefore provide evidence that contextual variables play an important role in the way individuals interpret the voluntarily disclosed information, as well as the value of independent assurance. As can be seen from this review, there is very little experimental research that has used assurers as subjects and examined assurance quality, however, this is likely to be an evolving field in the coming years.

Other empirical research

Some early research on the assurance of sustainability reports used surveys to identify antecedents of choice of assurance provider. Knechel *et al.* (2006), in a survey of 42 senior Dutch accounting and financial officers, found that overall expertise and objectivity are important attributes when selecting an assurance service provider, while cost was the least important attribute of those surveyed. Assurers from the accounting profession were more likely to be the preferred type of assurance provider when professional integrity and reputation were perceived as important. Other research documents qualitative differences among assurance reports issued by the various types of assurance providers (O'Dwyer and Owen 2005; Deegan *et al.* 2006; Mock *et al.* 2007; Perego and Kolk 2012). In general, professional accounting firms tend to provide more detailed and consistent reports, but limit the extent of assurance to that of limited (negative) assurance. In contrast, consultants and other third-party providers tend to provide reasonable (positive) assurance with more of a focus on adding value to the organization. Attempting to explain these differences, Perego and Kolk (2012) argue that the above differences are likely due to the conservative and cautious approaches taken by professional accountants when assessing the extent of assurance that can be provided in the face of the disparate and voluntary reporting standards that companies follow when issuing sustainability reports.

O'Dwyer (2011), using a longitudinal case study approach and interview data from 36 Big 4 practitioners, examined how assurance practitioners construct the practice of assurance of sustainability reports, and whether these efforts have rendered sustainability reports auditable. Practitioners' tacit knowledge and gut feel were identified as being important in making assurance possible in the face of vague guidance from global assurance standards. Differences between trained financial auditors and non-accountant practitioners were observed in the approaches to gathering and assessing evidence. Further, O'Dwyer *et al.* (2011) examined the sustainability assurance practice process to identify how a more refined conception of legitimation processes adopted by sustainability assurance practitioners have co-evolved and impacted the development of assurance reports.

Research on assurance of GhG reports

While a number of studies have examined the drivers for and impact of GhG emissions disclosures, only a few studies have examined the GhG assurance market. This market is distinguished from the sustainability assurance market, although it is possible that GhG disclosures may comprise part of broader sustainability disclosures. The subject matter has similarities to financial statement audits, as all GhGs are measured in a common unit, CO_2 equivalents, and the assurance methodology contained in the recently approved ISAE 3410 is risk and assertion-based, similar to that contained in the International Auditing Standards. However the subject matter requires very different expertise and the reporting does not have the double-entry controls inherent in financial accounting.

Archival research aimed at understanding the market for and benefits of assurance

A key finding from early archival research is that the GhG assurance market is characterized by a dichotomous market, including assurance providers from both accounting firms and non-accounting firms (Simnett *et al.* 2009a; Huggins *et al.* 2011). Darnall *et al.* (2009) examined companies' choice of internal and/or external auditors for environmental audits (potentially broader than GhG assurance). Analyzing survey data collected across France, Germany, Hungary, Japan, Norway and USA, they identified 670 instances of no assurance, 406 of internal assurance only, 150 of external assurance only, and 1,023 of both external and internal assurance. They further show that internal assurance is more common when perceived influence from internal stakeholders is higher (e.g. management, employees and members of the board), while external assurance is more common when perceived influence from external stakeholders (regulators, interest groups, suppliers, and customers) is higher.

Zhou *et al.* (2012) examined the drivers for GhG emissions assurance and GhG assurer choice for an international sample of companies. Information on GhG emissions assurance for a sample of 4,755 companies from 55 countries responding to the CDP's questionnaires during 2008 to 2011 was analyzed. Their results support the view that companies use assurance from a third party as a signal to address the asymmetry concern on the information quality of their GhG emissions disclosures. This is supported by the finding that the demand for assurance is higher when companies disclose GhG related information in general purpose reports. Further, companies adjust the level of signal by being more likely to choose assurance providers from outside the accounting profession for special purpose reporting to regulators and from inside the accounting profession for providing assurance on general purpose GhG reports.

Experimental research examining individual and team differences

Using an experimental survey, Green and Li (2012) identified differences between three stakeholder groups (GhG report preparers, assurers and shareholders) in relation to the perceived responsibilities of the assurer and management, as well as the reliability and decision usefulness of emissions statements. This suggests that an expectation gap exists for this type of assurance engagement and that care needs to be exercised by both the assurance profession and standard setters when developing standards and providing assurance.

However, while there are unique elements of GhG assurance engagements which could be the subject of experimental research, such as assurance team composition requiring both subject matter and assurance expertise, little published research of this nature was identified. Research opportunities in this area will be explored in the next section, "Further research opportunities".

Other empirical research

Earlier research documents the provision of assurance on GhG reports by various types of assurance providers (Nugent and Simnett 2007). For example, in Australia most early carbon emissions disclosures were contained in sustainability reports rather than stand-alone GhG reports (Nugent and Simnett 2007). While assurance engagements were found to not necessarily cover all aspects of the sustainability report, they generally covered the carbon emissions information, and the accounting profession was the assurer for about 50 per cent of these engagements. Simnett *et al.* (2009a) examined issues associated with the development of the international assurance standard ISAE 3410. These included the different measurement bases for GhGs, including direct measurement and estimation techniques used in practice, and how assurance procedures will need to adjust to these different techniques. They also discussed a number of technical issues and how they were dealt with in the early stages of ISAE 3410 development, including scoping out of offsets, suitability of criteria, level of assurance, evidence gathering procedures, using the work of experts, and the form and content of the assurance report.

Further research opportunities

In this section, research opportunities that relate to both assurance on sustainability reports and assurance on GhG reports are reviewed. The discussion will begin with the assurance market, using mainly archival research techniques, followed by behavioral research opportunities related to individual and group performance for these types of engagements. Finally, other research opportunities will be covered.

Archival research opportunities aimed at understanding the market and benefits of assurance

At the market level, using mainly archival research techniques, the research undertaken to date has mainly related to understanding the market (e.g. Simnett *et al.* 2009b; Cho *et al.* 2012; Zhou *et al.* 2012). At the same time research has also examined, for those organizations that have chosen to assure, the choice between accounting firms and other assurance providers. This setting has provided a better platform for investigating the benefits of assurance, and the signaling effects of the type of assurance provider. As external assurance is voluntary, this research could be further extended to consider choices between internal and external assurance. While other research is able to capitalize on the databases that have been developed, such as Corporate Register and GRI for sustainability assurance, and CDP for GhG assurance, choice between internal and external assurance provider, or other means of obtaining assurance would need to be sourced from research techniques such as surveys, as reports by internal auditors are not generally observable from archival sources.

While we need to understand the evolution of the markets for sustainability and GhG assurance, there is a limit to what we learn from these types of studies. The next logical research frontier is an evaluation of whether there is economic benefit arising from assurance of organizations' sustainability or GhG reports. For example, Dhaliwal *et al.* (2011) in supplementary analysis shows that US organizations with a high cost of equity capital in previous years are more likely to initiate and assure stand-alone sustainability disclosures, and receive a cost of equity capital advantage. This thinking could easily be extended to other performance measures, such as changes in share price or types of investors on share registers, in response to assured sustainability reports compared with non-assured sustainability reports, or the impact on accuracy (dispersion) of analysts' forecasts (e.g. Dhaliwal *et al.* 2012).

Experimental research opportunities examining individual and team differences

There are numerous experimental research opportunities for understanding and examining the risk identification and evidence evaluation stages of the assurance process, as well as how intended users react to assurance and its description. At the individual or engagement level, there are a number of concepts that differ between financial statement audits and assurance of sustainability information. For example, in a broad sustainability report, does risk identification work in the same way as it does for the financial statement audit? How is the process for determining material items changed when considering a variety of subject matter where many significant issues are not capable of being monetized? How does the consideration of the reporting entity concept change when you are looking at carbon emissions? For example, how are the concepts of control and significant influence over emissions attested to by the assurer?

In examining teams or group experimental research, it is recognized that members of a sustainability assurance team will have to grapple with significantly different subject matter (including environmental, social, labor practices and human rights, among others). The concept of a multidisciplinary team is therefore more pronounced for these types of engagements. It may be that different types of experts are involved in the engagement, and research could examine how these teams perform, make decisions and the factors and techniques, such as familiarization techniques or brainstorming, that drive team performance.

Other empirical research opportunities

There are also research opportunities in the communication of assurance. Just as the financial statement audit profession is currently examining ways of improving communication to intended users (IFAC 2012), there are significant questions as to how best to communicate the level of assurance for sustainability engagements. For example, perhaps there is scope for some information in a sustainability report to be assured to a reasonable assurance level, with limited assurance being provided on other information. The research question is then, how is this determined and best communicated?

There are also research questions about the relationship between corporate governance mechanisms and the provision and level of assurance. For example, are corporate governance mechanisms, such as risk committees of the board, complementary or substitutes to assurance? Does the quality of the corporate governance mechanisms, such as the person or committee within the company taking responsibility for the subject matter information, impact on the level of assurance? Also, what is the role of the audit committee regarding assurance on sustainability or GhG information?

There is the opportunity for such research to directly inform the standard-setting process. While we have seen assurance of stand-alone sustainability reports grow dramatically over the last few years, there has been no specific assurance standard developed for assuring sustainability reports. Part of the reason that there was no assurance standard developed is that, conceptually, this is a difficult standard to develop. Given their current work schedule, it is unlikely that the IAASB will undertake the development of a subject matter specific assurance standard on the issue of assurance of sustainability reports, and these engagements will continue to be undertaken under the umbrella assurance standard ISAE 3000. While ISAE 3000 and ISAE 3410 are conceptually informed by the more developed International Standards for Audit (ISAs), it is recognized that in some areas there is further work required. These include identifying the most appropriate and effective assurance techniques for assuring nonfinancial information. What are the assurance techniques that can be used for providing assurance on information which in many circumstances is not monetized, but is non-quantitative (qualitative) in nature? Also, there is more pressure on the report providers to supply more forward-looking information, and the assurance techniques are less well developed for this type of subject matter.

Expected future trends

This section examines two major expected future trends regarding the assurance of environmental, social and sustainability information. These are the integrated reporting (IR) initiative which aims to integrate financial accounting information with other information to tell a comprehensive and coordinated story as to how an organization creates value, and the impact of technology on assurance of environmental, social and sustainability information.

Integrated reporting

IR reflects the growing realization that a wider range of factors than is currently reflected in current reporting practices determines the value of an organization. It is becoming apparent that financial statement users are currently demanding to know more about an organization than the accounting profit it has made (the current emphasis of financial accounting), including ways they create value such as adding to intellectual knowledge, and the impact the organization has on the environment (Eccles and Krzus 2010; Adams *et al.* 2011; Cohen *et al.* 2012; IIRC 2012). While companies have supplemented financial information with reports such as sustainability or GhG reports, such reports are not commonly integrated with the annual report in order to tell a coherent or consistent story of the position and performance of the organization. The IR initiative aims to provide a framework that enables an organization to communicate in a clear, articulate way how it is drawing on all the resources and relationships it utilizes to create and preserve value in the short, medium and long term, helping investors to manage risks and allocate resources most efficiently.

IR has already been introduced in certain countries such as South Africa, and the initiative has also been supported by many leading companies around the world, including Microsoft, Coca Cola and HSBC. There are other companies that are on the journey towards IR. As this reporting approach continues to gather momentum, it will mean that reporting beyond financial statements will become more mainstream, assurance on environmental, social and sustainability information more likely to become the domain of the accounting profession, and the issues outlined in this paper will become more pertinent.

Emerging technologies and related assurance

Sustainability and GhG reporting is expected to take advantage of emerging technology in providing information and targeting it to specific stakeholders. Many of the existing approaches endorse the use of Extensible Business Reporting Language (XBRL 2012), and this technology is likely to remain an important instrument for generating reports. Through XBRL, each piece of company data is stored and communicated as a unique item that can be integrated with a variety of communication, presentation and analysis tools. The XBRL format is flexible and can be adapted to meet different requirements and uses, and its extensible nature offers many opportunities for sustainability reporting approaches. XBRL is particularly useful in communicating the parameters and calculation of each piece of data, as well as indicating how it is linked to other pieces of information. XBRL can play an important role in the transparency, comparability and reducing the complexity of reporting models.

There are many unexplored opportunities associated with the internet's capacity to communicate and disseminate data, which allows companies to remain in charge of the information they choose to provide, while at the same time empowering stakeholders to further engage with a company. This signals the need for technological development for both financial statement auditors and sustainability and GhG assurance providers in familiarizing themselves with the new technologies that will accompany extended data collection and reporting (Armbrester 2010).

Conclusion

While audit processes over financial information are well established, assurance processes of the less familiar environmental, social and sustainability information will require adaptation. While the risk- and assertion-based methodology developed for financial statements has been heavily drawn upon in developing assurance methodologies for sustainability and GhG information, there are many differences in the nature of the underlying subject matter information and the expertise required that suggest other appropriate verification techniques that may be beneficial, or that this methodology at least needs to be adapted to best suit these types of assurance engagements. In the short term, there is also a need for assurers of environmental, social and sustainability reports to clearly specify the scope of their assurance.

These differences in the nature of the underlying subject matter information and the expertise required to undertake an assurance engagement provide a research environment that is rich in opportunities. In comparison to research on financial statement audits, research on assurance of sustainability and GhG information is fairly embryonic and offers many opportunities to challenge or extend existing thinking about the assurance function. This chapter identifies the major empirical research on sustainability and GhG assurance that has been undertaken, as well as a number of potential future research opportunities.

Acknowledgements

The comments from Julie Cogin, Hien Hoang and Anna Huggins are much appreciated and the financial support from the Australian Research Council, CPA Australia and the Institute of Chartered Accountants in Australia is acknowledged.

References

Adams, S., J. Fries, and R. Simnett. 2011. "The Journey toward Integrated Reporting", *Accountant's Digest* May(558): 1–45.

Armbrester, K. 2010. "Leveraging the Internet for Integrated Reporting", in R. Eccles, B. Cheng and D. Saltzman (eds) *The Landscape of Integrated Reporting Reflections and Next Steps*, pp. 174–6. Boston, MA: Harvard Business School.

Carbon Disclosure Project (CDP). 2012. *Carbon Disclosure Project*. Available online at www.cdproject.net/en-US/Pages/About-Us.aspx (accessed 31 December 2012).

Carbon Disclosure Standards Board (CDSB). 2012. *About CDSB*. Available online at www.cdsb.net/about/ (accessed 31 December 2012).

Cho, C., G. Michelon, D. Patten, and R. Roberts. 2012. "CSR Report Assurance in the United States: An Empirical Investigation of Demand and Stakeholder Benefits", working paper. Cergy-Pontoise: ESSEC Business School.

Cohen, J. R., L. Holder-Webb, D. Wood, and L. Nath. 2012. "Corporate Reporting of Nonfinancial Leading Indicators of Economic Performance and Sustainability", *Accounting Horizons* 26(1): 65–90.

Coram, P. J., G. S. Monroe, and D. R. Woodliff. 2009. "The Value of Assurance on Voluntary Nonfinancial Disclosures: An Experimental Evaluation", *Auditing: A Journal of Practice and Theory* (March): 137–51.

Corporate Register. 2012. *The CR Reporting Awards: Global Winners and Reporting Trends*. Available online at www.CorporateRegister.com (accessed 31 December 2012).

Darnall, N., I. Seol, and J. Sarkis. 2009. "Perceived Stakeholder Influences and Organizations' use of Environmental Audits", *Accounting, Organizations and Society* 34(2): 170–87.

Deegan, C., B. Cooper, and M. Shelly. 2006. "An Investigation of TBL Report Assurance Statements: Australian Evidence", *Australian Accounting Review* 16(2): 2–18.

Dhaliwal, D. S., O. Z. Li, A. Tsang, and Y. G. Yang. 2011. "Voluntary Nonfinancial Disclosure and the Cost of Equity Capital: The Initiation of Corporate Social Responsibility Reporting", *The Accounting Review* 86(1): 59–100.

Dhaliwal, D. S., S. Radhakrishnan, A. Tsang, and Y.G. Yang. 2012. "Nonfinancial Disclosure and Analyst Forecast Accuracy: International Evidence on Corporate Social Responsibility Disclosure", *The Accounting Review* 87(3): 723–59.

Eccles, R. and Krzus, M. 2010. *One Report: Integrated Reporting for a Sustainable Strategy*. Hoboken, NJ: John Wiley & Sons.

European Union (EU). 2005. *European Union Emissions Trading Scheme*. Available online at http://ec.europa.eu/environment/climat/emission.htm (accessed 31 December 2012).

Extensible Business Reporting Language International (XBRL). 2012. *XBRL International*. Available online at www.xbrl.org (accessed 31 December 2012).

Green, W. and Q. Li. 2012. "Evidence of an Expectation Gap for Greenhouse Gas Emissions Assurance", *Accounting, Auditing and Accountability Journal* 25(1): 146–73.

Holder-Webb, L., J. Cohen, L. Nath, and D. Wood. 2009. "The Supply of Corporate Social Responsibility Disclosures among US Firms", *Journal of Business Ethics* 84(4): 487–527.

Huggins, A., W. Green, and R. Simnett. 2011. "The Competitive Market for Assurance Engagements on Greenhouse Gas Statements: Is There a Role for Assurers from the Accounting Profession?", *Current Issues in Auditing* 5(2): A1–A12.

International Auditing and Assurance Standards Board (IAASB). 2005. "International Standard on Assurance Engagements (ISAE) 3000": *Assurance Engagements other than Audits or Reviews of Historical Financial Information*. Available online at www.ifac.org/publications-resources/2012-handbook-international-quality-control-auditing-review-other-assurance-a (accessed 31 December 2012).

International Auditing and Assurance Standards Board (IAASB). 2012. International Standard on Assurance Engagements (ISAE) 3410: *Assurance Engagements on Greenhouse Gas Statements*. Online. Available online at www.ifac.org/publications-resources/2012-handbook-international-quality-control-auditing-review-other-assurance-a (accessed 31 December 2012).

International Federation of Accountants (IFAC). 2012. *Improving the Auditor's Report*. Available online at www.ifac.org/sites/default/files/publications/files/Auditor_Reporting_Invitation_to_Comment-final_0.pdf (accessed 31 December 2012).

International Integrated Reporting Committee (IIRC). 2012. *Integrated Reporting < IR >*. Available online at http://theiirc.org/ (accessed 31 December 2012).

International Organization for Standardization (ISO). 2006. *ISO 14064:3: Specification with Guidance for the Validation and Verification of Greenhouse Gas Assertions*. Geneva: ISO.

Japan's Ministry of the Environment. 2009. "Japan's Voluntary Emissions Trading Scheme (JVETS)". Available online at www.env.go.jp/en/earth/ets/jvets090319.pdf (accessed 31 December 2012).

Knechel, W. R., P. Wallage, A. Eilifsen, and B. Van Praag. 2006. "The Demand Attributes of Assurance Services Providers and the Role of Independent Accountants", *International Journal of Auditing* 10(2): 143–62.

Kolk, A. and P. Perego. 2010. "Determinants of the Adoption of Sustainability Assurance Statements: An International Investigation", *Business Strategy and the Environment* 19(3): 182–98.

KPMG. 2011. *KPMG International Survey of Corporate Responsibility Reporting 2011*. Available online at www.kpmg.com/au/en/issuesandinsights/articlespublications/pages/kpmg-international-surveycorporate-responsibility-reporting-2011.aspx (accessed 31 December 2012).

Mock, T., C. Strohm, and K. Swartz. 2007. "An Examination of Worldwide Assured Sustainability Reporting", *Australian Accounting Review* 17(1): 67–77.

Nugent, M. and R. Simnett. 2007. "Developing an Assurance Standard for Carbon Emissions Disclosures", *Australian Accounting Review* 17(2): 37–47.

O'Dwyer, B. 2011. "The Case of Sustainability Assurance: Constructing a New Assurance Service", *Contemporary Accounting Research* 28(4): 1230–66.

O'Dwyer, B. and D. Owen. 2005. "Assurance Statement Quality in Environmental, Social and Sustainability Reporting: A Critical Evaluation of Leading Edge Practice", *British Accounting Review* 37(2): 205–29.

O'Dwyer, B., D. L. Owen, and J. Unerman. 2011. "Seeking Legitimacy for New Assurance Forms: The Case of Sustainability Assurance", *Accounting, Organizations and Society* 36(1): 31–52.

Perego, P. and A. Kolk. 2012. "Multinationals' Accountability on Sustainability: The Evolution of Third Party Assurance of Sustainability Reports", *Journal of Business Ethics* 110: 173–90.

Pflugrath, G., P. Roebuck, and R. Simnett. 2011. "Impact of Assurance and Assurer's Professional Affiliation on Financial Analysts' Assessment of Credibility of Corporate Social Responsibility Information", *Auditing: A Journal of Practice & Theory* 30(3): 239–54.

Regional Greenhouse Gas Initiative (RGGI). 2008. *Regional Greenhouse Gas Initiative Model Rule*. Available online at www.rggi.org/ (accessed 31 December 2012).

Simnett, R., M. Nugent, and A. Huggins. 2009a. "Developing an International Assurance Standard on Greenhouse Gas Statements", *Accounting Horizons* 23(4): 347–64.

Simnett, R., A. Vanstraelen, and W. F. Chua. 2009b. "Assurance on Sustainability Reports: An International Comparison", *The Accounting Review* 84(3): 937–67.

World Bank (WB). 2011. "State and Trends of the Carbon Market 2011". Available online at http://siteresources.worldbank.org/INTCARBONFINANCE/Resources/State_and_Trends_Updated_June_2011.pdf (accessed 31 December 2012).

Zhou, S., W. Green, and R. Simnett. 2012. "The Decision to Assure and Assurance Provider Choice: Evidence from the GHG Assurance Market", *UNSW Australian School of Business Research Paper* No. 2012 ACCT 10. Available online at http://ssrn.com/abstract=2147359 or http://dx.doi.org/10.2139/ssrn.2147359 (accessed 31 December 2012).

27

Continuous auditing

D. Kip Holderness Jr

Overview of continuous auditing

Over the past several decades, information and communication technologies (ICT) have dramatically increased the speed of business. For example, the rise of enterprise resource planning (ERP) systems, proprietary corporate networks, digital supply chains, and the internet have contributed immensely to the compression of business cycle times, such as the sales-to-collection and purchase-to-pay cycles. The proliferation and sophistication of ICT provides companies with the ability to efficiently synchronize business processes, rapidly analyze performance metrics, and quickly adapt to changing global conditions. While such changes are undoubtedly good for commerce, auditors need to be cognizant of associated internal control risks.

From an audit perspective, faster business cycle times require commensurately rapid observation cycle times to ensure, on a (near) real-time basis, that internal controls are effective. Should auditors' observation processes lag considerably behind business cycles, the volume and magnitude of errors and/or irregularities that might go unnoticed during the interim could exceed materiality thresholds. In addition, it may be difficult if not impossible for a company to recover from espionage intrusions and financial damages should too much time pass before irregularities are detected, particularly those caused by fraud.

The notion of (near) real-time observation cycle times, termed *continuous monitoring* and *continuous auditing*, is defined by Kuhn and Sutton (2010: 93) as "the analysis of data on a real- or near real-time basis against a set of predetermined rule sets." While the terms continuous monitoring and continuous auditing are often used interchangeably, there is an important distinction between them. Continuous monitoring deals with (near) real-time tracking of a company's financial and nonfinancial transactions, mainly for the purpose of internal control oversight. The notion of continuous monitoring is typically viewed as the responsibility of management and internal auditors. Continuous auditing focuses on assuring the reliability of financial transactions underlying a company's financial statements. The concept of continuous auditing is primarily associated with external auditors, although internal auditors also can be involved in continuous auditing when their objective is to provide assurance over financial transactions.

The application of continuous monitoring is gaining popularity among internal auditors. Using a survey of 2,700 members of the Institute of Internal Auditors, Glover *et al.* (2000)

report that nearly half of the respondents used some type of continuous monitoring software, which is approximately double the proportion that reported using such software in a similar survey conducted in 1998. External auditors, on the other hand, have been far less eager to embrace continuous auditing.

Current issues in continuous auditing

Current research in the field of continuous auditing is centered on two broad themes. First, how should continuous auditing systems be designed? Second, how should companies and audit firms actually use such systems?

Beginning with Groomer and Murthy (1989) and Vasarhelyi and Halper (1991), researchers began discussing various modes of gathering audit information from computer-based accounting systems (for a review, see Kuhn and Sutton 2010). Because the integration of complex ICT systems in business organizations was still maturing in the late 1980s and early 1990s, early continuous auditing research tended to be theoretical in nature. By the late 1990s, the vast majority of large organizations had adopted database-centric ERP systems; and the internet had matured to the point where web-based applications offered portals through which customers and vendors could transact business, thus allowing for the creation of e-commerce. This led researchers to begin to investigate whether and how auditors could keep pace with the rapidly evolving digitization of business.

By the early 2000s, advances in ICT had made the practical use of continuous auditing software technically feasible. However, research revealed an unintended consequence of continuous auditing implementation; that is, when continuous auditing systems are running simultaneously with "live" business systems, the auditing software can dramatically slow down system performance, particularly in ERP (Kuhn and Sutton 2010) and e-commerce (Murthy 2004) environments. Researchers are currently examining ways to improve the integration of continuous auditing into live environments either through alternative design architectures or by including continuous auditing programs as a native component of enterprise-wide systems (Kuhn and Sutton 2010).

Many internal auditors nevertheless pushed forward with the integration of continuous auditing software into business systems during the 2000s, as they believed that the benefit of (near) real-time monitoring of internal controls and financial transactions outweighed the cost of degrading overall system performance. The steadfast progress of internal auditors in this area appears to have been a wise strategy, as the speed and power of ICT have accelerated considerably in recent years, largely offsetting the aforementioned system degradation effect. At the same time, the cost of purchasing advanced ICT has dropped dramatically to the point that widespread adoption of continuous auditing appears to be technically and economically feasible.

The use of continuous auditing by external auditors, though, has not kept pace with that of internal auditors. There are valid regulatory and legal reasons for their deliberate and measured response, particularly independence and objectivity concerns. While these thorny issues are being contemplated by practitioners, research on continuous auditing is pressing onward. For instance, Vasarhelyi *et al.* (2004) developed a theoretical framework for continuous auditing in which they proposed automating routine audit processes, thereby allowing auditors to focus more time on increasingly complex judgment-oriented audit objectives. Recently, Chan and Vasarhelyi (2011) described innovations to traditional audit practice that could enhance and improve the audit. Indeed, the use of continuous auditing by external auditors likely will become standard practice in due time; however, their cautious approach toward this end is understandable, as they face myriad limitations and constraints beyond technical and economic feasibility.

Historical development of continuous auditing

Continuous auditing research is a relatively new field of study – one that has its roots in the computerization of accounting systems. The advent of computerized accounting operations spurred the creation of electronic data processing (EDP) auditing as a new field (Cash Jr *et al.* 1977). As companies developed increasingly sophisticated computer-based accounting systems, accounting researchers began to address how these systems could be used to facilitate the audit process. This line of research started with Groomer and Murthy (1989), who proposed the use of a system that would continuously audit database applications. Their proposed system made use of embedded audit modules (EAMs), which could be built into clients' application programs to capture information of audit significance on a continuous basis. Such information could then be used to supplement and enhance the audit. Building upon their work, Vasarhelyi and Halper (1991) developed the continuous process audit methodology (CPAM), explained how EAMs could be used to audit large paperless database systems, and discussed the implementation of a CPAM at AT&T.

Shortly after the early works of Groomer and Murthy (1989) and Vasarhelyi and Halper (1991), the accounting profession, represented by the American Institute of Certified Public Accountants (AICPA) and the Canadian Institute of Chartered Accountants (CICA), began to realize that the evolving economic and technological environment required commensurate changes in the auditing profession. The AICPA's Special Committee on Assurance Services (the Elliott Committee, *circa* 1998–9) addressed some of these issues in detail, and recommended that auditors expand their role beyond the assurance of annual financial reports. Expanded assurance services would incorporate the use of client systems, databases, and the internet, enabling auditors to provide assurance on a frequent or even continuous basis. Recommendations from the Elliott Committee had a powerful impact on the audit profession and later led to formalized assurance services related to client system reliability (e.g., WebTrust and SysTrust). Currently, the notion of having Certified Public Accountants (CPAs) offer unique and diverse assurances services has fallen out of favor. However, discussions surrounding continuous auditing persist.

In 1999, the CICA and the AICPA issued a joint report on the nature, purpose, scope, and fundamentals of continuous auditing (CICA/AICPA 1999). The report spurred a stream of academic research on the subject. Despite improvements in technology that make continuous auditing more affordable, the use of continuous auditing in practice has been limited. Alles *et al.* (2002) indicated that continuous auditing is not an inevitable outcome of technology, but instead must be driven by business necessity. Rezaee *et al.* (2002) suggested that real-time financial reports likely would be the driving force behind the demand for continuous auditing. However, it appears that consumer demand for more frequent financial reporting has not been sufficiently strong, at this point, to merit the acceptance of continuous auditing.

The implementation of continuous auditing received an unexpected boost from internal auditors after the passage of the Sarbanes-Oxley Act (SOX) (US Congress 2002). Internal auditors saw continuous auditing as an opportunity to improve the efficiency and effectiveness of SOX 404 control testing, and consequently internal auditors have become champions of continuous auditing (Vasarhelyi *et al.* 2010). While the increased use of continuous auditing by internal auditors would seem to facilitate its acceptance by external auditors, the extent to which audit firms utilize continuous auditing is far below its full potential.

Continuous auditing research

The field of continuous auditing has greatly expanded in the past 30 years. For the sake of parsimony, I divide continuous auditing research into two main streams: 1) the design of continuous auditing systems; and 2) the use of continuous auditing systems.

The design of continuous auditing systems

The first stream of continuous auditing research is primarily concerned with the design and architecture of the systems that make real-time monitoring and assurance possible. Early research on continuous auditing proposed how such systems might be designed long before their widespread adaptation was technically and economically feasible. Research on design issues has gradually led to multiple methodological approaches to continuous auditing in computerized environments. The two dominant continuous auditing architectures are EAMs and a monitoring control layer (MCL).

EAMs are software modules built directly into an organization's information system to monitor business processes. Groomer and Murthy (1989) and Vasarhelyi and Halper (1991) discuss and demonstrate how EAMs could be used to capture audit-related information on an ongoing basis. EAMs can also be used in many other ways, such as monitoring transaction flows, evaluating the effectiveness of internal controls, and automatically notifying specific individuals when certain parameters are violated. One of the primary concerns regarding the use of EAMs is that the modules are internal to a company's information systems, thus, independent monitoring may not be possible (Alles *et al.* 2002). The worry is that clients could possibly "hack" into the EAMs to gain intelligence on what the auditors are monitoring and possibly change programs in the EAMs to bypass certain monitoring routines. The possibility of client activity of this nature raises serious independence and objectivity issues for external auditors.

Vasarhelyi *et al.* (2004) introduce the concept of an MCL as an alternative continuous auditing methodology. An MCL provides the same basic functions as EAMs, in that the software monitors data and sends notifications when audit procedures are violated and predefined benchmarks are exceeded. Unlike EAMs, an MCL resides outside of the organization's information system and can be controlled by an independent third party (e.g., external auditors), thereby providing greater security, reliability, and integrity. The MCL receives client data on a periodic basis; thus, monitoring can occur relatively frequently but not necessarily in real time. Kuhn and Sutton (2006) believe that the MCL concept reflects a promising architecture for continuous auditing design and suggest that the WorldCom fraud could have been detected much earlier had an MCL been implemented. Indeed, the MCL approach appears to address external auditors' independence and objectivity concerns.

Vasarhelyi *et al.* (2004) theorize that the information flow occurring within an ERP environment is especially conducive to continuous auditing due to the database concept underlying ERP systems. Debreceny *et al.* (2005) examined the use of EAMs in ERP systems and suggested that continuous auditing is technically feasible in an ERP environment. However, the use of EAMs can dramatically decrease the processing speed of the ERP systems, primarily because EAMs are generally not included as a native component of systems (Kuhn and Sutton 2010). The use of an MCL to audit ERP systems is also feasible. However, such use likely would require warehousing or ghosting of the client's database, which would consume valuable processing power and involve some delay. Another emerging technology, eXtensible Business Reporting Language (XBRL) could have a profound influence on continuous auditing system design, particularly in web-based environments. As companies incorporate the use of XBRL for communicating financial information through the internet, reusable continuous audit modules can be built to compare financial data across companies (Brown *et al.* 2007).

It seems clear that more design-oriented research is needed in the area of continuous auditing. Design issues notwithstanding, there has been movement in the practitioner communities toward adopting some aspects of continuous auditing.

The use of continuous auditing systems

While advances in ICT have increased the feasibility of widespread implementation of continuous auditing, the adoption of continuous auditing in accounting practice has been somewhat limited. This begs the question – if continuous auditing is technically feasible, why does it appear to be underutilized? There are many potential explanations for the gap between the technological capability and the adoption of continuous auditing, such as unwillingness to change, unclear economic advantage, uncertain impact on auditor independence and objectivity, unsettling litigation concerns, and unintended consequences. These concerns are likely symptomatic of a larger issue – disagreement over the fundamental objectives of continuous auditing.

On a holistic scale, external auditors are wondering why they should transition from traditional auditing to continuous auditing when the current audit model appears to be working just fine; in other words, "If it ain't broke, don't fix it!" In a world where audit clients' business models are fairly stable, this mindset is understandable. However, this is not reflective of reality. Business models are rapidly changing. Due primarily to advances in ICT, many brick-and-mortar clients have a sizeable internet presence, and some clients are totally virtual. Furthermore, most clients operate on a global scale and nearly all clients offer a 24/7 presence.

As companies adopt increasingly sophisticated ERP systems and continuously improve their accounting systems, many have the ability to publish financial reports online on a frequent or perhaps even real-time basis. In this environment, are the goals of continuous auditing to provide assurance on real-time financial statements, assurance over the reporting processes, or assurance over the effectiveness of internal controls? Until design issues are resolved and audit objectives are clarified, the use of continuous auditing likely will continue to lag behind technological capability. In the following two subsections, "Continuous auditing", and "Continuous monitoring", I review prior research on the use of continuous auditing and monitoring systems in practice.

Continuous auditing

There are some who argue that the traditional audit paradigm is outdated in today's fast-paced business environment, and that audit practice can become more effective and efficient by using technology and automation (Vasarhelyi *et al.* 2010; Chan and Vasarhelyi 2011). Under a theoretical framework for continuous auditing developed by Vasarhelyi *et al.* (2004), audit objectives can be divided into four categories.

1 *Transactional evaluation*, in which auditors focus on the detection of irregularities in business transaction;
2 *Measurement rule assurance*, which is concerned with the substantiation that measurement rules (e.g. generally accepted accounting principles [GAAP]) have been properly applied;

3 *Estimate assurance and consistency of aggregate measures* (e.g. bad debt and warranty expense), which encompasses estimates that depend to some degree on judgments;
4 *Judgment assurance*, which relates to high-level judgments essential to the future of a client's organization.

According to the framework, less complex objectives, as reflected by the first two objectives, can be largely automated and should require auditor attention only when irregularities are detected by continuous auditing programs. Auditors should spend most of their time and effort on the latter two, more complex audit objectives that require judgment. Further, the use of automation can increase the effectiveness of the audit because it would enable all transactions to be tested, as opposed to samples of transactions. Continuous auditing has the potential to transform auditing into a proactive, rather than a reactive process, and facilitate continuous reporting (Chan and Vasarhelyi 2011).

While the principles of continuous auditing apply to both internal and external auditors, it would seem that external auditors must work through a number of distinct issues before continuous auditing becomes standard practice. First, the lack of consumer demand for real-time financial statements may not create enough financial incentive for auditors to undertake large-scale changes to their audit programs. In addition, Kuhn and Sutton (2010) point out several issues regarding external auditors' use of client information systems to implement continuous auditing programs. Clients may be unwilling to allow auditors to have unrestricted access to their systems, and audit firms may have difficulty finding auditors with the required technical expertise to implement EAMs or an MCL. Moreover, because continuous auditing software most likely would rely on client information systems, auditors run the risk that clients could become aware of audit procedures, which could impair audit effectiveness. Finally, audit firms may be concerned about the potential legal liability should their use of continuous auditing software damage clients' systems.

External auditors' hesitance to use continuous auditing may explain why prior studies on the topic have focused on the adoption of continuous auditing by internal auditors at various companies (e.g., AT&T, Siemens, IBM; see Chan and Vasarhelyi 2011). Even though external auditors underutilize continuous auditing techniques and methods, they may benefit from the decreased control risk associated with internal auditors' use of continuous auditing as it relates to financial reporting. At least for the time being, the external auditor's role may be more suited to performing high-level analytics, detecting of inconsistencies or fraud by management, and providing independent certification of the continuous auditing system used by internal auditors (Chan and Vasarhelyi 2011).

Continuous monitoring

Internal auditors have become an important source of demand for continuous auditing, particularly as it relates to the monitoring and testing of internal controls as required by SOX. However, the application of continuous auditing techniques within companies extends well beyond financial reporting. In a non-audit context, I refer to the computerized monitoring of transactions as continuous monitoring. Continuous monitoring is an important tool that provides management with greater oversight of an entity's internal control system (White 2005). Increased monitoring frequency is vitally important in today's enterprise-wide system environments, where voluminous intra-firm information exchanges take place in an instant. Furthermore, companies within supply chains often interlink their information systems, thereby increasing the need for companies to scrutinize the integrity of transactions (Vasarhelyi *et al.* 2004).

Previous research has shown several examples of how continuous monitoring can enhance internal controls and protect against unnecessary business loss. Coderre (2006) discusses the application of continuous monitoring by the Royal Canadian Mounted Police to process nearly 500,000 payments a year. The use of continuous monitoring improved the accounts payable operation, reduced financial errors, and decreased the potential for fraud, waste, and abuse. Boccasam and Kapoor (2003) use a case study to demonstrate how continuous monitoring can be used to detect and correct problems related to the improper segregation of duties. Murthy (2004) examines the effect of various monitoring controls in web-based e-commerce applications on system performance. Web-based controls are particularly important given the pervasiveness of online transactions, and Murthy provides insight to managers regarding capacity planning and capacity management.

While the use of continuous monitoring certainly has led to several benefits for companies, psychology-based accounting research has shown that extensive monitoring can beget unintended consequences. For instance, Hunton *et al.* (2008) suggest that continuous monitoring can trigger an interesting effect on managerial decision making. They find that while the use of a continuous monitoring system deters managers from maximizing short-term profits at the expense of long-term profits, continuous monitoring also increases risk aversion. Specifically, experimental participants were unwilling to invest in and continue with a viable but risky project in the presence of a continuous monitoring system due to the "invisible hand" of perceived justification pressure. Unintended consequences of this nature shed light on the reluctance of some companies to adopt continuous monitoring.

Unresolved issues in continuous auditing

Previous research has both supported and informed the beginning stages of continuous auditing adoption by companies and audit firms. However, there are several issues that should be further investigated if continuous auditing is to become a standard component of auditing.

More studies are needed that focus on the design of continuous audit systems; specifically, future design science research should examine alternative architectures aimed at improving security, gaining efficiency, and reducing computational demand. Kuhn and Sutton (2010) propose EAM ghosting as a possible solution to the drain of continuous auditing on companies' operation processing. Are there viable options beyond the established EAM and MCL architectures? Also, given the growing use of XML reporting, future research should examine how to incorporate continuous auditing in an environment using XML formats. Future research in this area may initiate the creation of novel technologies, processes, and procedures for designing and implementing continuous auditing systems.

Future research should also focus on the use of continuous auditing by companies and audit firms. Why has accounting practice failed to take advantage of the benefits afforded by continuous auditing? Audit firms may be hesitant to adopt continuous auditing for a variety of valid reasons. Is adoption economically feasible? Is there sufficient demand for more frequent (or real-time) audited financial statements that would compel audit firms to make extensive changes to the traditional audit processes? If so, how frequently should financial statements be issued and assured? Is the demand for frequent financial reports limited only to certain portions of the financial statements? Do the costs of real-time financial statements outweigh the benefits of more timely information?

Other issues facing external auditors regard concerns over independence, objectivity, and legal liability. Future research should identify the extent to which actual and perceived independence and objectivity is impaired when external auditors use EAMs, and investigate whether possible impairment can be avoided by alternative design architectures. With regard to legal liability, research should be conducted to understand how auditors' use of continuous auditing affects jurors' perceptions in cases of fraud or material misstatements.

Future research is also needed to bolster our understanding of continuous auditing use within companies. For instance, are continuous auditing techniques more amenable to certain industries? What are other possible determinants for the adoption of continuous auditing? What is the relationship between continuous audit risk and the strength of a company's control environment? More research is needed to determine how those who are audited are influenced by continuous auditing. Does continuous auditing deter unwanted behavior over a long-period of time or do audited individuals become acclimated to increased monitoring? Does continuous auditing really thwart undesirable behavior, or does it shift deviant behavior to areas that are not monitored?

Another interesting avenue for future research would be to examine the interaction between external and internal auditors in a continuous auditing context. How does continuous auditing affect external auditors' assessment of client risk? How is the reliance of external auditors on audit procedures performed by internal auditors affected by internal auditors' use of continuous auditing? The growing trend of continuous auditing techniques within companies will undoubtedly provide greater opportunities for research that can have a profound impact on accounting practice.

Conclusion

Accounting systems have changed dramatically in recent history in response to an increasingly fast-paced business environment. Sales, purchases, manufacturing, and other vital business processes have become largely automated through advanced ICT. The cycle-speed at which business operates is becoming exponentially faster over time. Such rapid changes in the velocity of business necessitate commensurate changes to the external audit; specifically, a transition from periodic auditing to continuous auditing. Yet a paradigm shift of this nature has yet to materialize.

Internal auditors have made significant strides in adopting continuous auditing. Most of the methods and techniques they use involve software applications designed to analyze business transactions after-the-fact, rather than in real time. While such applications allow internal auditors to increase the frequency, breadth, and depth of their analytics, real-time online auditing has yet to become a reality. Design issues appear to be the main reason, as the two dominant techniques of continuous auditing have drawbacks. The embedded audit module approach degrades overall system performance and the MCL concept involves a time lag. Practitioners and researchers should work cooperatively through these design issues. Overall, internal auditors are moving steadily forward in the area of continuous auditing.

The use of continuous auditing by external auditors lags behind that of internal auditors. On one hand, it is easy to understand external auditors' steadfast adherence to the traditional periodic audit, since companies continue to publish "official" financial statements on a quarterly basis. Although (near) real-time external reporting is now possible, most companies have not adopted such rapid dissemination of financial reports. Perhaps (near) real-time reporting will become the norm in the future, but for now mandatory quarterly reporting remains in force; hence, the historical periodic audit continues.

On the other hand, one would think that external auditors could gain efficiencies by performing significant portions of their audits throughout the year, rather than parachuting a strike team of auditors into the client's compound after the end of the fiscal year. Conducting audits, particularly transactional analytics, on a more frequent basis throughout the year is possible, but the concept is slow to take root in practice. Nevertheless, given the rapid adoption of advanced ICT in commerce and the associated radical redesign of business processes, there is little question that continuous auditing will eventually become a reality for external auditors – it is simply a matter of when and how.

Researchers have been giving the notion of continuous auditing much thought since the late 1980s. Most of the early continuous auditing research was theoretical in nature and oriented toward design issues. As continuous auditing became technically and economically feasible, research attention turned to practical concerns. Although plaguing design issues remain, the audit profession struggles with clarifying the objectives of continuous auditing. Toward this end, Vasarhelyi *et al.* (2004) recommends four major audit objective categories: transactional evaluation, measurement rule assurance, estimate assurance and consistency of aggregate measures, and judgment assurance. His advice is to automate, as much as possible, the more predictable and routine matters, as reflected by the first two categories, which will allow auditors time to focus on the latter two more complex objectives.

As indicated throughout this chapter, continuous auditing involves myriad conceptual, technical, economic, practical, professional, regulatory, and legal issues, most of which need further thought and development. One possible reaction to such complexity is to retreat, retrench, and remain with the traditional periodic audit. However, in light of inescapable exogenous forces, such as progressively advancing ICT, radically changing business models, exponentially increasing information demand, and steadily intruding regulatory oversight, it seems as though burying one's head in the sand is not a viable long-term strategy. Instead, researchers, practitioners, regulators, and auditors should work in unison to tackle the difficult issues and set a strategic course toward the eventual adoption of continuous auditing.

References

Alles, M., Kogan, A., and Vasarhelyi, M.A. 2002. "Feasibility and Economics of Continuous Assurance", *Auditing, A Journal of Practice & Theory* 21(1): 125–38.

Boccasam, P.V. and Kapoor, N. 2003. "Managing Separation of Duties Using Continuous Monitoring", *IT Audit* 6. Available online at www.theiia.org/ITAuditArchive/index.cfm?act=ITAudit.archive& fid=5433 (accessed 15 August 2012).

Brown, C.E., Wong, J.A. and Baldwin, A.A. 2007. "A Review and Analysis of the Existing Research Streams in Continuous Auditing", *Journal of Emerging Technologies in Accounting* 4: 1–28.

Canadian Institute of Chartered Accountants and American Institute of Certified Public Accountants (CICA/AICPA). 1999. *Continuous Auditing: Research Report*. Toronto, ON: CICA.

Cash, J.I. Jr, Bailey, A.D. Jr, and Whinston, A.B. 1977. "A Survey of Techniques for Auditing EDP-based Accounting Information Systems", *The Accounting Review* 52(4): 813–32.

Chan, D.Y. and Vasarhelyi, M.A. 2011. "Innovation and Practice of Continuous Auditing", *International Journal of Accounting Information Systems* 12: 152–60.

Coderre, D. 2006. "A Continuous View of Accounts", *Internal Auditor* 63(2): 25–31.

Debreceny, R.S., Gray, G.L., and Lee, K.S.-P. 2005. "Embedded Audit Modules in Enterprise Resource Planning Systems: Implementation and Functionality", *Journal of Information Systems* 19(2): 7–27.

Glover, S.M., Prawitt, D., and Romney, M.B. 2000. "The Software Scene", *Internal Auditor* August: 49–57.

Groomer, S.M. and Murthy, U.S. 1989. "Continuous Auditing of Database Applications: An Embedded Audit Module Approach", *Journal of Information Systems* 3(2): 53–69.

Hunton, J., Mauldin, E., and Wheeler, P. 2008. "Potential Functional and Dysfunctional Effects of Continuous Monitoring", *The Accounting Review* 83(6): 1551–69.

Kuhn, J.R. Jr and Sutton, S.G. 2006. "Learning from WorldCom: Implications for Fraud Detection through Continuous Assurance", *Journal of Emerging Technologies in Accounting* 3: 61–80.

Kuhn, J.R. Jr and Sutton, S.G. 2010. "Continuous Auditing in ERP System Environments: The Current State and Future Directions", *Journal of Information Systems* 24(1): 91–112.

Murthy, U.S. 2004. "An Analysis of the Effects of Continuous Monitoring Controls on E-commerce System Performance", *Journal of Information Systems* 18(2): 29–47.

Rezaee, Z., Sharbatoghlie, A., Elam, R., and McMickle, P.L. 2002. "Continuous Auditing: Building Automated Auditing Capability", *Auditing: A Journal of Practice & Theory* 21(1): 147–63.

US Congress. 2002. *The Public Company Accounting Reform and Investor Protection Act of 2002 (The Sarbanes-Oxley Act).* Pub. L. No. 107–204, 116 Stat. 745 (July 30). Washington, DC: US Government Printing Office.

Vasarhelyi, M.A. and Halper, F.B. 1991. "The Continuous Audit of Online Systems", *Auditing: A Journal of Practice & Theory* 10(1): 110–25.

Vasarhelyi, M.A., Alles, M., and Kogan, A. 2004. "Principles of Analytic Monitoring for Continuous Assurance", *Journal of Emerging Technologies in Accounting* 1(1): 1–21.

Vasarhelyi, M.A., Alles, M., and Williams, K. 2010. *Continuous Assurance for the Now Economy*. Sydney, NSW: The Institute of Chartered Accountants in Australia.

White, L. 2005. "Does Internal Control Enhance or Impede", *Strategic Finance* 86(8): 6–7.

Part VI
Conclusion

28
The future of auditing research

David Hay, W. Robert Knechel and Marleen Willekens

Auditing is a *professional*, *economic* and *regulated* activity executed by *individuals* with the help of *audit technology*. All these aspects of auditing are interrelated and jointly affect what will be the eventual quality of an audit. An audit is conducted by professionals who have acquired the specific skills and knowledge necessary to perform the audit, and who possess the appropriate licence to hold themselves up as professional. In the course of an audit, specialized technology is used to augment the professional expertise of individuals. Further, audits are economic goods in the sense that a market exists to match those who will supply an audit with those who would demand an audit. In that market, auditors compete with each other to obtain new clients. However, audits and the audit market are also very heavily regulated. Who needs an audit, who can supply an audit, and the conditions under which the two parties can contract for audit services are all subject to various forms of regulation. There is also a risk of litigation against the auditor in case of malpractice. In the past decade we have seen a large increase, globally, in regulation of auditing and auditors. Nevertheless, because the audit is a human activity conducted by individual auditors, the quality of a specific audit is conditional on individual auditor characteristics and the incentives that auditors face. Given all these aspects, auditing is a complex phenomenon to study and understand.

Over the past 30 years, audit research has grown exponentially and we have learned a tremendous amount about auditing, auditors and audit markets. This book was designed to present key research findings to a broad audience interested in the auditing profession. The various chapters report and summarize a number of significant audit research areas. In this closing chapter we will not repeat what we learn from the chapters. Instead we will reflect on what we believe are some key issues for future research.

Audit quality research

Audit quality has been a key concern for auditors, regulators and users of audited financial information. A large portion of previous audit research has examined the question of audit quality in one way or another. Yet we still have no clear understanding of what audit quality really means. Despite decades of research on audit quality, there is no consensus as to what constitutes audit quality (Knechel and Shefchik, Chapter 11). What constitutes audit quality for one stakeholder may not be so for another. Nevertheless, audit quality research remains a very useful and fertile research domain. Hence, an interesting topic for future research is to investigate what constitutes audit value and/or quality for different types of stakeholders or in different institutional settings. In this context, the role of auditing cannot be separated from the role of accounting information, and the role of accounting information is likely to vary across institutional settings, stakeholder categories and types of companies.

Various definitions of audit quality have been advanced, as discussed in Chapter 11, from the traditional DeAngelo approach based on the combination of auditor independence and competence, to audit quality defined as the amount of work performed by the auditor. Numerous empirical audit quality studies define audit quality in terms of a financial statement outcome, e.g. an auditor's ability to constrain earnings management (see Cahan, Chapter 10). Future research could address how the primary attributes of an audit affect different indicators of audit quality. Another useful area could be to study the links between the different indicators of audit quality. Furthermore, development of new metrics for measuring audit quality beyond those borrowed from financial accounting research seems necessary and warranted. However, such research is difficult unless auditors and regulators are willing to share important data with the research community. Audit quality remains an area where development of our understanding is continuing.

Independence research

Auditor independence has attracted and continues to attract significant global interest from various stakeholders, regulators, policy makers and the audit profession itself. In various countries, auditor independence rules have become stricter. However, generally there is a lack of causal evidence that certain auditor characteristics, such as long tenure and the provision of non-audit services (NAS), impair independence. Research that investigates auditor independence typically tests the association between an auditor characteristic (such as tenure or joint NAS supply) and a financial statement or auditor based dependent variable (such as earnings management or the likelihood of a going concern opinion). When (on rare occasions) a significant association is found, it is then attributed to the presence of an auditor independence problem. However, associations between auditor characteristics and quality measures could equally be attributable to competence issues. For example, when no significant association between tenure and earnings management is found, this could be due to the fact that independence and competence are not readily separable in such an analysis.

Research so far has only provided circumstantial evidence, as Sharma points out in Chapter 7, and causal links between specific auditor/auditee attributes and audit quality are difficult to prove. Clever research designs that enable demonstration of a causal relationship between certain auditor attributes and audit quality would be a welcome addition to auditing research. Regarding a link between auditor rotation, Lennox (in Chapter 8) argues that the literature has not yet answered the question as to whether rotation is desirable and offers an interesting suggestion to regulators, namely if mandatory rotation is to be introduced then it should be done on a partial basis so that the experience of one group can be compared to another. Such an approach would be informative for policymakers and regulators.

Regulation research

As indicated above, auditing is a highly regulated activity and much new regulation has arisen during the last decade. As auditing has become a global activity, regulatory concerns also have expanded (see Carson, Chapter 3). The recent financial crisis and its impact throughout the rest of the world demonstrated the interconnectedness of the global economy, particularly in relation to the tightness of credit markets. However, there is little global regulatory oversight of the activities of global firm networks despite the existence of international auditing standards. Future research could address the question as to whether audit quality differs across countries and regulatory settings, and if so, why. Another area of potential research relates to the audit of multinationals and of cross-border transactions.

An area of major change in regulation is oversight and inspection (see Offermanns and Vanstraelen, Chapter 14). So far research on the effects of oversight and inspection mainly stems from US experiences. With the introduction of various forms of inspection around the world, future research should examine the differential effects experienced in non-US settings. In addition we know very little about the efficiency and effectiveness of different forms of public oversight, and hence more research into that area would be valuable. Another interesting but unaddressed question is to examine differences between inspection regimes that disclose or do not disclose outcomes to the public. Finally, it would be interesting to learn more about the implications of changes in the audit process brought about by inspections. To what extent do audit firms learn about inspection attitudes and likely inspection targets?

Recently there has been a lengthy debate about whether auditor reporting is being appropriate and sufficient. Many believe that auditors do not provide the investing public with enough of an insight into the quality of a company's financial reporting, and, particularly, have not provided adequate warning of impending business failures. Standard setters are currently considering changes in the auditor's reporting responsibilities, including reconsideration of how an auditor should address issues related to a client who may have significant going concern uncertainties (see Chapters 24 and 23). A new issue in the discussion of standards is whether auditors should disclose key audit issues in their report, an area where there is virtually no research. Future research could address the question of whether the changes in auditor reporting do indeed affect stakeholder decisions.

Audit markets research

As indicated earlier, auditing is an economic activity that takes place in a market. Cahan *et al.* (2011) argue that the audit market is characterized by a type of segmentation in which some specialists pursue a product differentiation strategy, focusing more extensively on the acquisition of requisite skills and expertise, while other specialists pursue a cost minimization strategy, producing lower cost, lower quality audits. Though this seems a very plausible conjecture, very little is known so far about audit market segmentation and the way auditors compete in the audit market. Research about the cost minimization strategies of auditors is virtually non-existent due to lack of auditor cost data. However, such studies could add tremendously to our understanding of the drivers of audit quality. Various studies have investigated the effects of industry specialization on audit pricing and quality. However, an auditor differentiation strategy can be defined in many ways. As Jeter states in Chapter 15, specialization could be defined in a variety of ways, such as specialization in particular income statement or balance sheet accounts (e.g. valuation of intangibles) or in specific aspects of the audit engagement (e.g. accounting for mergers). Furthermore, the way industry specialization is measured in prior research is subject to limitations, as most studies use proxies based on market share, which may actually capture the market power an auditor has in the market segment rather than the firm's level of expertise. Hence, future research that addresses the effects on quality, pricing and competition of auditor differentiation beyond industry specialization would be very valuable.

The structure of the global audit market has changed significantly as a result of mergers and by the collapse of one global firm. As product markets and financial markets become more widespread, the demand for related professional services on a global scale has also risen which has accelerated the globalization of the audit industry (see Carson, Chapter 3). An interesting unresolved research question is the nature of auditor competition at the local, national and global levels, and how that competition manifests in terms of fees, audit quality and market reaction to an auditor's reports. For example, while signing off an audit report with the name of an individual partner of a firm – a regulation that exists in many countries and is currently under discussion in the US – may be relevant in a local market, it is not clear that it matters at all at a global level.

Auditing and governance research

An external audit can be seen as one aspect within a broader set of governance tools that a company has established to assure truthful financial reporting. Other important governance mechanisms in this setting are internal control over financial reporting, internal auditing and the board of directors, especially the audit committee. Ineffective internal control systems have been recognized as a major factor in facilitating large-scale frauds and erroneous financial reporting, and during the past decade major regulatory changes have been imposed with respect to internal control reporting both by directors and auditors. A key issue in this respect is attaining the right balance of benefits versus costs of internal controls through legislation and regulation. As Bédard and Graham state in Chapter 25 the research community is still finding its way in this new era and while some evidence suggests that increased attention to internal controls has resulted in improvements in financial reporting, research should continue to investigate the association over time. In addition, studies that address the effects of the variation in regulations across countries may provide insight as to the more optimal balance of benefits and costs of compliance. A major challenge in this respect, however, will be to define a proper research design that controls for related differences in other institutional factors.

Internal auditing is also an important monitoring mechanism in many companies and the audit profession could benefit from insights with respect to the internal audit function's role in enterprise risk management (ERM), compliance and combined assurance, as well as for external audit resource allocation and planning. This could also inform practitioners and standard setters on ways to improve organizational governance (see Anderson and Christ, Chapter 18).

Finally, the audit committee is specifically assigned the task of overseeing the company's relations with the external auditor and to safeguard auditor independence. As such, it contributes to ensuring the quality of the external audit and reinforces confidence in the auditor's report. As Bédard and Compernolle state in Chapter 20, future research could address how well audit committees assume their roles, as regulators seem to rely on the audit committee by increasing their responsibilities. Prior studies have highlighted the important influence of the processes, relationships and communications among the audit committee, the auditor and management on the audit committee's oversight of the external audit. Further research is required to better understand how the audit committee plays its oversight role in practice. Whether audit committees are able to respond to regulators' and the public's expectations is an unanswered empirical question. As audit committees are only one piece in the corporate governance mosaic, future research on the interaction among the various pieces of governance would also be worthwhile.

Research on auditing in private companies

In many countries, auditing is not only mandatory for publicly listed companies due to securities laws (as in the US and Australia), it is also mandatory for many private companies due to an audit requirement in company laws (as in Europe). Research on auditing in private companies has so far mostly chosen topics that have previously been analyzed for public companies. However, as Langli and Svanström in Chapter 12 point out, it is possible to further advance the literature by asking questions that are more relevant for private companies and also to conduct tests that are not feasible in a public company setting. An example of the first is to examine how the value of auditing differs for private companies as compared to our knowledge in public company settings. An example of the latter is related to the presence of audit partner data in several European countries, which enables researchers to address the effects of individual partner characteristics on audit decision making, pricing, quality and other. This offers tremendous research potential for the future.

Under-researched auditing research areas

Auditing ethics

Although ethics are at the heart of the demand for auditing, it remains an under-researched area in auditing. As Shaub and Braun state in Chapter 21, the current issues in ethics are largely unchanged from what they were prior to SOX (the Sarbanes-Oxley Act of 2002) or even what they were in the 1980s. This offers much research potential for the future, especially in investigating the link between individual auditor ethics characteristics and audit quality issues.

Expectations gap

Although the expectations gap is a widely recognized and experienced phenomenon, research in this area is mainly limited to two countries, namely New Zealand and the UK (see Chapter 5). Research about the link between the size and composition of the expectations gap and the institutional setting of where it is observed seem worthwhile topics for future research. Other research in this area could relate to the consequences of variation in the expectation gap across countries.

New forms of assurance

Assurance has gone through significant changes over the past two decades, mainly with respect to two dimensions. First, assurance has moved beyond financial statement assurance alone. Second, an evolution has taken place with regard to techniques of assurance. In Chapter 26, Simnett discusses research with respect to assurance of publicly available environmental, social and sustainability reports. Research on assurance in these areas is still in its infancy, which offers tremendous potential for valuable future research. For example future research could investigate competition in this segment of the assurance market which is mostly unregulated, and the effect of these new assurance services on competition, pricing and quality in the financial statement assurance market. With respect to new techniques in assurance, continuous auditing can also be seen as a new form of assurance.

Holderness in Chapter 27 notes that the rate of adoption of continuous auditing lags considerably behind the technological capabilities. However, rapid changes in the velocity of business necessitates commensurate changes to the external audit. For a paradigm shift to materialize, an interesting domain for research would be to study the reasons for such a lag. As the use of continuous auditing by external auditors lags behind that of internal auditors, studying continuous auditing in internal auditing settings may be a worthwhile avenue for future research from which the external audit profession could learn. Another interesting approach could be to examine the circumstances under which the reliance on transactional analysis (which is typically done in continuous auditing) on a more frequent basis throughout the year leads to an improvement in overall audit quality.

Fraud research

Carpenter and Austin in Chapter 9 argue that the public does not fully understand the auditor's responsibility for fraud or the rarity of its occurrence, creating an expectations gap between the audit profession and the public. Improving auditors' fraud detection skills is a significant challenge for the accounting profession, and the audit research community could help by studying fraud situations and contexts. However, just as fraud detection is challenging for auditors, so is fraud research for researchers. One major reason is lack of sufficient data. Carpenter and Austin suggest that researchers, policymakers and auditors should work together to study this important topic and disentangle risky fraud situations and incentives to develop effective measures against fraud. One important question to answer is whether the systematic use of forensic specialists is cost effective given the relatively low base rate of actual fraud. They further suggest that those interested in fraud detection research should consider work in related disciplines such as criminal justice, psychology and organizational behavior.

Judgment research

A final area for future research that we address in this chapter is judgment research. As Trotman points out in Chapter 16, the entire process of auditing is permeated by professional judgment. Today more than ever the profession finds itself face-to-face with numerous challenging and complex judgments. Hence, judgment research is and will continue to be a crucial and fertile research domain that will contribute to our understanding of the determinants of audit quality. Examples of auditor related judgments that require deeper investigation include evaluating fair value and other estimates, professional skepticism, the use of analytical procedures, audit sampling, the effect of clients' use of service organizations, the degree of reliance on the internal audit function, and the audit report decision. Interestingly, the judgment side of auditing also has an ethical dimension and this in itself opens up a large avenue for future research. As Shaub and Braun illustrate in Chapter 21, every major auditor choice issue being studied has an ethical component that is largely ignored. Recognizing and dealing with this flaw in our research designs may tremendously advance our knowledge about auditor decision making.

Conclusion

Auditing is a *professional*, *economic* and *regulated* activity executed by *individuals* with the help of *audit technology* and all these aspects of auditing jointly affect what will be the eventual quality of an audit. This book has tried to provide an overview of major research findings with the hope that stakeholders in the audit process will learn about what we know about auditing, and what is possible from active research. For academics, we hope to instigate much more valuable research in the future. Auditing offers more than ever a challenging and vibrant domain for research. While large breakthroughs in audit research are rare, as noted by Trotman (Chapter 16),

> our contribution to knowledge and practice can be enhanced by a concentration on some central themes and incrementally building on previous research. I believe the discipline may benefit more from theory refinement rather than individual papers all looking to be the first in some way!

In short, a steady accumulation of insightful research will facilitate the understanding of audits, auditors and audit markets as seen from the perspective of professionals, regulators, investors and the academy.

Auditing is going through a period of continuing change – there have been recent reforms, and more changes will continue. The changes that have taken place are generally attempts to resolve known problems in auditing. These reforms are often not based on what is known from research – perhaps because there is not enough relevant research, and also perhaps because research findings are not widely known. This book is intended to help to resolve both of these issues, by proposing directions for future research and by disseminating the results of existing research.

Reference

Cahan, S.F., D. Jeter and V. Naiker. 2011. "Are All Industry Specialist Auditors the Same?", *Auditing: A Journal of Practice & Theory* 30(4, November): 191–222.

Index

Figures are shown by a page reference in *italics* and tables are indicated by a reference in **bold**.